Pro LINQ

Language Integrated Query in VB 2008

■ ■ ■

Joseph C. Rattz, Jr. and Dennis Hayes

Apress®

Pro LINQ: Language Integrated Query in VB 2008

Copyright © 2009 by Joseph C. Rattz, Jr. and Dennis Hayes

ISBN-13 (pbk): 978-1-4302-1644-5

ISBN-13 (electronic): 978-1-4302-1645-2

Printed and bound in the United States of America 9 8 7 6 5 4 3 2 1

Lead Editor: Ewan Buckingham
Technical Editor: Joseph C. Rattz, Jr.
Technical Reviewers: Joseph C. Rattz, Jr., Fabio Ferracchiati
Editorial Board: Clay Andres, Steve Anglin, Mark Beckner, Ewan Buckingham, Tony Campbell,
    Gary Cornell, Jonathan Gennick, Michelle Lowman, Matthew Moodie, Jeffrey Pepper,
    Frank Pohlmann, Ben Renow-Clarke, Dominic Shakeshaft, Matt Wade, Tom Welsh
Project Manager: Richard Dal Porto
Copy Editor: Heather Lang
Associate Production Director: Kari Brooks-Copony
Production Editor: Kelly Winquist
Compositors: Dina Quan, Patrick Cunningham
Proofreader: April Eddy
Indexer: Carol Burbo
Artist: April Milne
Cover Designer: Kurt Krames
Manufacturing Director: Tom Debolski

Distributed to the book trade worldwide by Springer-Verlag New York, Inc., 233 Spring Street, 6th Floor, New York, NY 10013. Phone 1-800-SPRINGER, fax 201-348-4505, e-mail orders-ny@springer-sbm.com, or visit http://www.springeronline.com.

For information on translations, please contact Apress directly at 2855 Telegraph Avenue, Suite 600, Berkeley, CA 94705. Phone 510-549-5930, fax 510-549-5939, e-mail info@apress.com, or visit http://www.apress.com.

Apress and friends of ED books may be purchased in bulk for academic, corporate, or promotional use. eBook versions and licenses are also available for most titles. For more information, reference our Special Bulk Sales–eBook Licensing web page at http://www.apress.com/info/bulksales.

The source code for this book is available to readers at http://www.apress.com. You may need to answer questions pertaining to this book in order to successfully download the code.

To my father-in-law, Samuel Arthur Sanders, I dedicate this book. Art Sanders was my most supportive cheerleader while I was working on Pro LINQ: Language Integrated Query in C# 2008. *Unfortunately, Art's health began to fail toward the end of that book, and for a while, it seemed doubtful he would live to see it completed. Not one to give up, Art overcame numerous hospitalizations and did indeed receive his personally signed copy. Sadly, Art will never see this book because he passed away on February 25, 2009, at the age of 80. Rest in peace, Art.*

Contents at a Glance

PART 1 ▪▪▪ Pro LINQ: Language Integrated Query in VB.NET 2008

PART 2 ▪▪▪ LINQ to Objects

PART 3 ▪▪▪ LINQ to XML

Part 4 ▪▪▪ LINQ to DataSet

Part 5 ▪▪▪ LINQ to SQL

Contents

PART 1 ■■■ Pro LINQ: Language Integrated Query in VB.NET 2008

PART 2 ■■■ LINQ to Objects

PART 3 ■■■ LINQ to XML

PART 4 ■■■ **LINQ to DataSet**

PART 5 ■ ■ ■ LINQ to SQL

About the Author

JOSEPH C. RATTZ, JR. unknowingly began his career in software development in 1990 when a friend asked him for assistance writing an ANSI text editor named ANSI Master for the Commodore Amiga. A hangman game (The Gallows) soon followed. From these compiled Basic programs, he moved on to programming in C for more speed and power. Joe then developed applications that were sold to *JumpDisk*, an Amiga disk magazine, as well as *Amiga World* magazine. Due to developing in a small town on a fairly isolated platform, Joe learned all the wrong ways to write code. It was while trying to upgrade his poorly written applications that he gained respect for the importance of easily maintainable code. It was love at first sight when Joe spotted a source-level debugger in use for the first time.

Two years later, Joe obtained his first software development opportunity at Policy Management Systems Corporation as an entry-level programmer developing a client/server insurance application for OS/2 and Presentation Manager. Through the years, he added C++, Unix, Java, ASP, ASP.NET, C#, HTML, DHTML, and XML to his skill set while developing applications for SCT, DocuCorp, IBM and the Atlanta Committee for the Olympic Games, CheckFree, NCR, EDS, Delta Technology, Radiant Systems, and the Genuine Parts Company. Joe enjoys the creative aspects of user interface design, and he appreciates the discipline necessary for server-side development. But, given his druthers, his favorite development pastime is debugging code.

Joe can be found working for the Genuine Parts Company—the parent company of NAPA—in the Automotive Parts Group Information Systems department, where he works on his baby, the Storefront web site. This site for NAPA stores provides a view into their accounts and data on a network of AS/400s.

Joe's first book, *Pro LINQ: Language Integrated Query in C# 2008*, was published on November 19, 2007, which is the exact same date that Visual Studio 2008 was released to manufacturing. One final LINQ coincidence is that Visual Studio 2008 was officially launched on February 27, 2008, which just happens to be Joe's birthday.

Joe can be reached at his web site, www.linqdev.com.

About the Technical Reviewer

FABIO CLAUDIO FERRACCHIATI is a senior consultant and a senior analyst/developer using Microsoft technologies. He works for Brain Force (`www.brainforce.com`) in its Italian branch (`www.brainforce.it`). He is a Microsoft Certified Solution Developer for .NET, a Microsoft Certified Application Developer for .NET, a Microsoft Certified Professional, and a prolific author and technical reviewer. Over the past ten years, he's written articles for Italian and international magazines and coauthored more than ten books on a variety of computer topics. You can read his LINQ blog at `www.ferracchiati.com`.

Acknowledgments

Well, it appears that it is time to write the acknowledgments for another book. Readers of *Pro LINQ: Language Integrated Query in C# 2008* may recall the endless delays in publishing that book. A project that initially started as a 9-month project grew into a 17-month project. This book turned out to be no less challenging in terms of scheduling and delays. If you were one of those who patiently waited for this book to be published, I want to thank you for your patience. I hope you find it worth the wait.

When I wrote the acknowledgments for my C# LINQ book, I expected that to be my single opportunity to show my appreciation to all those people who made the book possible. I did not imagine that I would have another opportunity to write acknowledgments, so I spilled my guts on the first one. Obviously, most of the people who made the C# book possible also made this one possible. The beauty of writing this book's acknowledgments is that I have the luxury of getting to correct any errors of omission that occurred in the first book's Acknowledgments.

The first person that I want to thank is my wife, Vickey. I mentioned in the first book that she had to do many of my chores during the 17 months I worked on it. Then, a mere 7 months after it was published, I was engaged in yet another book—for a year. She has waited more than long enough for us to resume a normal life. I have promised her that I *will* straighten the basement before I begin any more books. So this may be my last.

I would like to thank Apress for another opportunity to write a book. Specifically, I want to thank Ewan Buckingham. I can't help but think I have taken years off his life. Richard Dal Porto performed project management duties for this book and with chapters flying about, it is amazing that he could keep it all straight. Heather Lang handled the role of copy editor. She also took over the reins as copy editor on my C# LINQ book, so I have been twice privileged to have her make my writing look coherent, well-formed, and written in a language consisting of characters other than commas. Sadly, I still haven't learned when to use commas. Kelly Winquist was the production editor for this book, and I certainly appreciate her and her team's effort, which is apparent when you get to see the finished product. I turn in Microsoft Word documents, and a book comes out on the other side. It is a fabulous machine! Thank you April Eddy for proofreading the book once I was finished with it. I know there are unnamed others who worked on this book, and while you don't get to see your name here, you get the more valuable benefit of probably never having had an interaction with me. Kudos to you too!

Next, I must extend my appreciation to Fabio Ferracchiati. Not only did he perform the technical reviewer duties, he filled in as stunt author. This book still might not be finished were it not for his assistance.

In the C# book's acknowledgments, I thanked Anders Hejlsberg for the vision from which LINQ grew. Since that time, I have come to realize that I significantly short-changed Erik Meijer. Erik, I apologize for that. From what I know now, it is quite clear that LINQ would not exist without him. If instead of naming the new technology LINQ, he had named it Enumerable Restricting Integrated Kwery, I would have known.

I want to thank the Microsoft VB language team for wonderful LINQ support being added to the language. Your VB.NET XML enhancements are enough to make this C# programmer envious. I hope the C# design team was paying attention.

Again, I must thank my parents: my dad for giving me the confidence to think I could actually write a book, and my mom for her constant input of ideas.

Last, I want to thank all the readers of the C# LINQ book who sent in comments, suggestions, and corrections. Specifically, I want to thank Jon Skeet and Judson White for their much-appreciated effort. Both of these fine developers took the time to send me detailed notes. This book is better because of their efforts.

Joseph C. Rattz, Jr.

PART 1

Pro LINQ: Language Integrated Query in VB.NET 2008

CHAPTER 1

∎∎∎

Hello LINQ

Listing 1-1. *Hello LINQ*

```vb
Option Explicit On
Option Infer On
Option Strict On

Imports System
Imports System.Linq

Module Module1
  Sub Main()
    Dim greetings() As String = {"hello world", "hello LINQ", "hello Apress"}

    Dim items = _
      From s In greetings _
      Where s.EndsWith("LINQ") _
      Select s

    For Each item In items
      Console.WriteLine(item)
    Next item
  End Sub
End Module
```

∎**Note** The code in Listing 1-1 is a complete console program created in Visual Studio 2008. In most places, I will leave out the `Module`, `Sub Main`, and common `Imports` statements, but I will include any unusual `Imports` that an example requires.

Running the previous code by pressing Ctrl+F5 outputs the following data to the console window:

hello LINQ

■**Note** Also note that, in most cases, you do not need to have the common `Imports` statements in your code, because VB.NET adds them behind the scenes at compile time. You can see (and modify) the list of namespaces added by looking in the project's Properties, on the Reference tab, in the "Imported namespaces" table.

A Paradigm Shift

Did you just feel *your* world shift? As a .NET developer, you should have. With the trivial programming example in Listing 1-1, you just ran what somewhat appears to be a Structured Query Language (SQL) query on an array of strings.[1] Check out that `where` clause. Did you notice that I used the `EndsWith` method of a `String` object? You may be wondering why, with `Option Strict On`, an error was not generated when I declared `items` without a type or when I used `item` as a variable in the `For Each` loop without giving it a type. To those used to programming in VB6 or VB.NET with `Option Explicit` and `Option Strict` set to `Off`, declaring a variable without giving it a type may not seem like a big deal. But with `Option Strict On`, it is. Explaining why we do not get a compilation error from this would be a distraction right now, but I will pick up this idea again at the start of Chapter 2. So, what features of VB.NET are allowing all of this? The answer is Microsoft's Language Integrated Query, otherwise known as LINQ.

Query XML

While the example in Listing 1-1 is trivial, the example in Listing 1-2 may begin to indicate the potential power that LINQ puts into the hands of the .NET developer. It displays the ease with which one can interact with and query Extensible Markup Language (XML) data utilizing the LINQ to XML API. You should pay particular attention to how I construct the XML data into an object named `books` that I can programmatically interact with.

Listing 1-2. *A Simple XML Query Using LINQ to XML*

```
Imports System
Imports System.Linq
Imports System.Xml.Linq

Dim books As XElement = _
<books>
```

---

1. Most noticeably, the order is inverted from typical SQL. Additionally, there is the added "s In" portion of the query that provides a reference to the set of elements contained in the source, which in this case is the array of strings "hello world", "hello LINQ", and "hello Apress".

```
<book>
  <title>Pro LINQ: Language Integrated Query in VB.NET 2008</title>
  <author>Dennis Hayes</author>
</book>
<book>
  <title>Pro WF: Windows Workflow in .NET 3.5</title>
  <author>Bruce Bukovics</author>
</book>
<book>
  <title>Pro C# 2008 and the .NET 3.5 Platform, Fourth Edition</title>
  <author>Andrew Troelsen</author>
</book>
</books>

'CStr cast not needed if Option Strict is off
Dim titles = _
  From book In books.Elements("book") _
  Where CStr(book.Element("author")) = "Dennis Hayes" _
  Select book.Element("title")

For Each title In titles
  Console.WriteLine(title.Value)
Next title
```

■**Note** The code in Listing 1-2 requires adding the `System.Xml.Linq.dll` assembly to the project refer-ences if it is not already added. Also notice that I added an `Imports` statement for the `System.Xml.Linq` namespace.

Running the previous code by pressing Ctrl+F5 outputs the following data to the console window:

```
Pro LINQ: Language Integrated Query in VB.NET 2008
```

Did you notice how I simply loaded the XML data into an object of type `XElement`? Among the new features in VB.NET 2008 are XML literals, where a block of XML can be assigned to an XML element. I will cover this in more detail in Chapter 2. Also, LINQ to XML expands the XML API with its richer API. While the W3C Document Object Model (DOM) XML API requires `XmlDocument`-centric development, LINQ to XML allows the developer to interact at the ele-ment level using the `XElement` class. The LINQ to XML API will be covered in Chapter 7.

■**Note** In addition to query features, LINQ to XML provides a more powerful and easier-to-use interface for working with XML data.

Again notice that I utilized the same SQL-like syntax to query the XML data, as though it were a database.

Query a SQL Server Database

My next example shows how to use LINQ to SQL to query database[2] tables. In Listing 1-3, I query the standard Microsoft Northwind sample database.

Listing 1-3. *A Simple Database Query Using LINQ to SQL*

```
Imports System
Imports System.Linq
Imports System.Data.Linq

Imports Chapter1.nwind

Dim db As New Northwind( _
  "Data Source=.\SQLEXPRESS;Initial Catalog=Northwind;Integrated Security=SSPI;")

Dim custs = _
  From c In db.Customers _
  Where c.City = "Rio de Janeiro" _
  Select c

For Each cust In custs
  Console.WriteLine("{0}", cust.CompanyName)
Next cust
```

■**Note** The code in Listing 1-3 requires adding the `System.Data.Linq.dll` assembly to the project references if it is not already added. Also notice that I added an `Imports` statement for the `System.Data.Linq`
namespace.

When working with the files generated by SqlMetal, you need to use namespaces and `Imports` statements that are appropriate for the way to set up your project. Depending on how you set up your project, you
may need to include the project's default namespace, such as `Imports Chapter1.nwind`, just the generated namespace, `Imports nwind`, or you may not need any `Imports` statement at all. I cover this in more
detail in Chapter 2.

You can see that I added an `Imports` statement for the `Chapter1.nwind` namespace. For this
example to work, you must use the SqlMetal command-line utility, or the Object Relational
Designer, to generate entity classes for the targeted database, which in this example is the
Microsoft Northwind sample database. See Chapter 12 to read how this is done with SqlMetal.

---

2.   At the present time, LINQ to SQL only supports SQL Server.

The generated entity classes are created in the nwind namespace, which I specify when generating them. I then add the SqlMetal generated source module to my project and add the Imports statement for the nwind namespace.

■ **Note** You may need to change the connection string that is passed to the Northwind constructor in Listing 1-3 for the connection to be properly made. Read the section on DataContext() and [Your]DataContext() in Chapter 16 to see different ways to connect to the database.

Running the previous code by pressing Ctrl+F5 outputs the following data to the console window:

```
Hanari Carnes
Que Delícia
Ricardo Adocicados
```

This simple example demonstrates querying the Customers table of the Northwind database for customers in Rio de Janeiro. While it may appear that there is nothing new or special going on here that I wouldn't already have with existing means, there are some significant differences. Most noticeably, this query is integrated into the language, and this means I get language-level support, which includes syntax checking and IntelliSense. Gone will be the days of writing a SQL query into a string and not detecting a syntax error until runtime. Want to make your where clause dependent on a field in the Customers table but you cannot remember the name of the field? IntelliSense will show the table's fields to you. Once you type **c.** in the previous example, IntelliSense will display all the fields of the Customers table to you.

All of the previous queries use the *query expression* syntax. You will learn in Chapter 2 that there are two syntaxes available for LINQ queries, of which the query expression syntax is one. Of course, you may always use the *standard dot notation* syntax that you are accustomed to seeing in .NET instead. This syntax is the normal object.method() invocation pattern you have always been using.

Introduction to LINQ

As the Microsoft .NET platform, and its supporting languages C# and VB.NET, have matured, it has become apparent that one of the more troublesome areas still remaining for developers is that of accessing data from different data sources. In particular, database access and XML manipulation are often cumbersome at best, and problematic in the worst cases.

The database problems are numerous. First, there is the issue that we cannot programmatically interact with a database at the native language level. This means syntax errors often go undetected until runtime. Incorrectly referenced database fields are not detected either. This can be disastrous, especially if this occurs during the execution of error-handling code. Nothing is more frustrating than having an entire error-handling mechanism fail because of syntactically invalid code that has never been tested. Sometimes this is unavoidable due to unanticipated error behavior. Having database code that is not validated at compile time can certainly lead to this problem.

A second problem is the nuisance caused by the differing data types utilized by a particular data domain, such as database or XML data types vs. the native language in which the program is written. In particular, dates and times can be quite a hassle.

XML parsing, iterating, and manipulation can be quite tedious. Often an XML fragment is all that is desired, but due to the W3C DOM XML API, an XmlDocument must be created just to perform various operations on the XML fragment.

Rather than just add more classes and methods to address these deficiencies in a piece-meal fashion, the development team at Microsoft decided to go one step further by abstracting the fundamentals of data query from these particular data domains. The result was LINQ. LINQ is Microsoft's technology to provide a language-level support mechanism for querying data of all types. These types include in-memory arrays and collections, databases, XML documents, and more.

LINQ Is About Data Queries

For the most part, LINQ is all about queries, whether they are queries returning a set of matching objects, a single object, or a subset of fields from an object or set of objects. In LINQ, this returned set of objects is called a *sequence*. Most LINQ sequences are of type IEnumerable(Of T), where T is the data type of the objects stored in the sequence. For example, if you have a sequence of integers, they would be stored in a variable of type IEnumerable(Of Integer). You will see that IEnumerable(Of T) runs rampant in LINQ. Many of the LINQ methods return an IEnumerable(Of T).

In the previous examples, all of the queries actually return an IEnumerable(Of T) or a type that inherits from IEnumerable(Of T). However, I declare the variables without types for the sake of simplicity at this point. This is unrelated to the old VB6 Variant or to how VB.NET has handled untyped variables prior to VB.NET 2008, because these variables are given a specific type by VB.NET. I will cover this in detail in Chapter 2, where you will see examples that begin demonstrating that sequences are truly stored in variables implementing the IEnumerable(Of T) interface.

Components

Because LINQ is so powerful, you should expect to see a lot of systems and products become LINQ compatible. Virtually any data store would make a good candidate for supporting LINQ queries. This includes databases, Microsoft's Active Directory, the registry, the file system, an Excel file, and so on.

Microsoft has already identified the components in this section as necessary for LINQ. There is no doubt that there will be more to come.

LINQ to Objects

LINQ to Objects is the name given to the IEnumerable(Of T) API for the Standard Query Operators. It is LINQ to Objects that allows you to perform queries against arrays and in-memory data collections. Standard Query Operators are the static methods of the static System.Linq. Enumerable class that you use to create LINQ to Objects queries.

LINQ to XML

LINQ to XML is the name given to the LINQ API dedicated to working with XML. This interface was known as *XLinq* in older prereleases of LINQ. Not only has Microsoft added the necessary XML libraries to work with LINQ, it has addressed other deficiencies in the standard XML DOM, thereby making it easier than ever to work with XML. Gone are the days of having to create an XmlDocument just to work with a small piece of XML. To take advantage of LINQ to XML, you must have a reference to the System.Xml.Linq.dll assembly in your project and have an Imports statement such as the following:

```
Imports System.Xml.Linq
```

LINQ to DataSet

LINQ to DataSet is the name given to the LINQ API for DataSets. Many developers have a lot of existing code relying on DataSets. Those who do will not be left behind, nor will they need to rewrite their code to take advantage of the power of LINQ.

LINQ to SQL

LINQ to SQL is the name given to the IQueryable(Of T) API that allows LINQ queries to work with Microsoft's SQL Server database. This interface was known as *DLinq* in older prereleases of LINQ. To take advantage of LINQ to SQL, you must have a reference to the System.Data.Linq.dll assembly in your project and have an Imports statement such as the following:

```
Imports System.Data.Linq
```

LINQ to Entities

LINQ to Entities is an alternative LINQ API that is used to interface with a database using the ADO.NET Entity Framework. It decouples the entity object model from the physical database by injecting a logical mapping between the two. With this decoupling comes increased power and flexibility, as well as complexity. Because LINQ to Entities appears to be outside the core LINQ framework, it is not covered in this book. However, if you find that you need more flexibility than LINQ to SQL permits, it would be worth considering as an alternative. Specifically, if you need looser coupling between your entity object model and database, entity objects composed of data coming from multiple tables, or more flexibility in modeling your entity objects, LINQ to Entities may be your answer.

How to Obtain LINQ

Technically, there is no LINQ product to obtain. LINQ is just the project code name for the query feature being added to VB.NET 2008 and the .NET Framework 3.5, which made their debut in Visual Studio 2008.

LINQ Is Not Just for Queries

Maybe by definition you could say LINQ is just for queries because it stands for *Language Integrated Query*. But please don't think of it only in that context. Its power transcends mere data queries. I prefer to think of LINQ as a data iteration engine, but perhaps Microsoft didn't want a technology named DIE.

Have you ever called a method and it returned data back in some data structure that you then needed to convert to yet another data structure before you could pass it to another method? Let's say for example you call method A, and method A returns an array of type String that contains numeric values stored as strings. You then need to call method B, but method B requires an array of integers. You normally end up writing a loop to iterate through the array of strings and populate a newly constructed array of integers. What a nuisance. Allow me to point out the power of Microsoft's LINQ.

Let's pretend I have an array of strings that I received from some method A, as shown in Listing 1-4.

Listing 1-4. *Converting an Array of Strings to Integers*

```
Dim numbers() As String = {"0042", "010", "9", "27"}
```

For this example, I'll just statically declare an array of strings. Now before I call method B, I need to convert the array of strings to an array of integers:

```
Dim nums() As Integer = numbers.Select(Function(s) Int32.Parse(s)).ToArray()
```

That's it. How much easier could it get? Even just saying "abracadabra" only saves you 65 characters. Here is some code to display the resulting array of integers:

```
For Each num As Integer In nums
  Console.WriteLine(num)
Next num
```

Here is the output showing the integers:

```
42
10
9
27
```

I know what you are thinking: maybe I just trimmed off the leading zeros. If I sort it, will you then be convinced? If they were still strings, 9 would be at the end, and 10 would be first. Listing 1-5 contains some code to do the conversion and sort the output.

Listing 1-5. *Converting an Array of Strings to Integers and Sorting It*

```
Dim numbers() As String = {"0042", "010", "9", "27"}

Dim nums() As Integer = _
  numbers.Select(Function(s) Int32.Parse(s)).OrderBy(Function(s) s).ToArray()
```

```
For Each num As Integer In nums
  Console.WriteLine(num)
Next num
```

Here are the results:

```
9
10
27
42
```

How slick is that? "OK," you say, "that is nice, but it sure is a simple example." Now, I'll give you a more complex example.

Let's say you have some common code that contains an Employee class. In that Employee class is a method to return all the employees. Also assume you have another code base of common code that contains a Contact class, and in that class is a method to publish contacts. Let's assume you have the assignment to publish all employees as contacts.

The task seems simple enough, but there is a catch. The common Employee method that retrieves the employees returns the employees in an ArrayList of Employee objects, and the Contact method that publishes contacts requires an array of type Contact. Here is that common code:

```
Namespace LINQDev.HR
  Public Class Employee
    Public id As Integer
    Public firstName As String
    Public lastName As String

    Public Shared Function GetEmployees() As ArrayList
      ' Of course the real code would probably be making a database query
      ' right about here.
      Dim al As New ArrayList()

      ' Man, do the new VB.NET object initialization features make this
      ' a snap.
      al.Add(New Employee With { _
        .id = 1, .firstName = "Dennis", .lastName = "Hayes"})
      al.Add(New Employee With { _
        .id = 2, .firstName = "William", .lastName = "Gates"})
      al.Add(New Employee With { _
        .id = 3, .firstName = "Anders", .lastName = "Hejlsberg"})

      Return al
    End Function
  End Class
End Namespace
```

```
Namespace LINQDev.Common
  Public Class Contact
    Public Id As Integer
    Public Name As String

    Public Shared Sub PublishContacts(ByVal contacts() As Contact)
      ' This publish method just writes them to the console window.
      For Each c As Contact In contacts
        Console.WriteLine("Contact Id: {0} Contact: {1}", c.Id, c.Name)
      Next c
    End Sub
  End Class
End Namespace
```

As you can see, the Employee class and GetEmployees method are in one namespace, LINQDev.HR, and the GetEmployees method returns an ArrayList. The PublishContacts method is in another namespace, LINQDev.Common, and requires an array of Contact objects to be passed.

Previously, this always meant iterating through the ArrayList returned by the GetEmployees method and creating a new array of type Contact to be passed to the PublishContacts method. LINQ makes it easy, as shown in Listing 1-6.

Listing 1-6. *Calling the Common Code*

```
Dim alEmployees As ArrayList = LINQDev.HR.Employee.GetEmployees()

Dim contacts() As LINQDev.Common.Contact = _
  alEmployees _
    .Cast(Of LINQDev.HR.Employee)() _
    .Select(Function(e) New LINQDev.Common.Contact _
      With { _
        .Id = e.id, _
        .Name = String.Format("{0} {1}", e.firstName, e.lastName) _}) _
    .ToArray()

LINQDev.Common.Contact.PublishContacts(contacts)
```

To convert the ArrayList of Employee objects to an array of Contact objects, I first cast the ArrayList of Employee objects to an IEnumerable(Of Employee) sequence using the Cast Standard Query Operator. This is necessary because the legacy ArrayList collection class was used. Syntactically speaking, objects of the System.Object class type are stored in an ArrayList, not objects of the Employee class type. So I must cast them to Employee objects. Had the GetEmployees method returned a generic List collection, this would not have been necessary. However, that collection type was not available when this legacy code was written.

Next, I call the Select operator on the returned sequence of Employee objects and in the *lambda expression*, the code passed inside the call to the Select method, I instantiate and initialize a Contact object using the new VB.NET 2008 object initialization features to assign the values from the input Employee element into a newly constructed output Contact element.

A lambda expression is a new VB.NET 2008 feature that allows new shorthand for specifying anonymous methods that I will explain in Chapter 2. Last, I convert the sequence of newly constructed `Contact` objects to an array of `Contact` objects using the `ToArray` operator because that is what the `PublishContacts` method requires. Isn't that slick? Here are the results:

```
Contact Id:  1  Contact:  Dennis Hayes
Contact Id:  2  Contact:  William Gates
Contact Id:  3  Contact:  Anders Hejlsberg
```

As you can see, LINQ can do a lot besides just querying data. As you read through the chapters of this book, try to think of additional uses for the features LINQ provides.

Tips to Get You Started

While working with LINQ to write this book, I often found myself confused, befuddled, and stuck. While there are many very useful resources available to the developer wanting to learn to use LINQ to its fullest potential, I want to offer a few tips to get you started. In some ways, these tips feel like they should come at the end of the book. After all, I haven't even explained what some of these concepts are at this point. But it would seem a bit sadistic to make you read the full text of the book first, only to offer the tips at the end. So with that said, this section contains some tips I think you might find useful, even if you do not fully understand them or the context.

Use Dim Without Specifying the Type When Confused

While it is necessary to use the `Dim` keyword without specifying a type when capturing a sequence of anonymous classes to a variable, sometimes it is a convenient way to get code to compile if you are confused. While I am very much in favor of developers knowing exactly what type of data is contained in a sequence—meaning that for `IEnumerable(Of T)` you should know what data type `T` is—sometimes, especially when just starting with LINQ, it can get confusing. If you find yourself stuck, where code will not compile because of some sort of data type mismatch, consider removing the data type from the `Dim` statement.

For example, let's say you have the following code:

```
'  This code will not compile.
Dim db As New Northwind("Data Source=.\SQLEXPRESS;Initial Catalog=Northwind")

Dim orders As IEnumerable(?) = db.Customers _
  .Where(Function(c) c.Country = "USA" AndAlso c.Region Is "WA") _
  .SelectMany(Function(c) c.Orders)
```

It may be a little unclear what data type you have an `IEnumerable` sequence of. You know it is an `IEnumerable` of some type `T`, but what is `T`? A handy trick is to assign the query results to a variable whose type is not specified, then to get the type of the current value of that variable so you know what type `T` is. Listing 1-7 shows what the code would look like.

Listing 1-7. *Code Sample Using the Dim Keyword Without Specifing the Type*

```
Dim db As New Northwind("Data Source=.\SQLEXPRESS;Initial Catalog=Northwind")

Dim orders = db.Customers _
  .Where(Function(c) c.Country = "USA" AndAlso c.Region Is "WA") _
  .SelectMany(Function(c) c.Orders)

Console.WriteLine(orders.GetType())
```

In this example, please notice that the orders variable type is now not specified. Running this code produces the following:

```
System.Data.Linq.DataQuery`1[Chapter1.nwind.Order]
```

There is a lot of compiler gobbledygook there, but the important part is the nwind.Order portion. You now know that the data type you are getting a sequence of is nwind.Order.

So you could rewrite the previous code, plus enumerate through the results, as shown in Listing 1-8.

Listing 1-8. *Sample Code from Listing 1-7 Except with Explicit Types*

```
Dim db As New Northwind( _
  "Data Source=.\SQLEXPRESS;Initial Catalog=Northwind;Integrated Security=SSPI;")

Dim orders As IEnumerable(Of Order) = db.Customers _
  .Where(Function(c) c.Country = "USA" AndAlso c.Region Is "WA") _
  .SelectMany(Function(c) c.Orders)

For Each item As Order In orders
  Console.WriteLine( _
    "{0} - {1} - {2}", _
    item.OrderDate, _
    item.OrderID, _
    item.ShipName)
Next item
```

■**Note** For the previous code to work, you will need to have an Imports statement for the System.
Collections.Generic namespace, in addition to the System.Linq namespace you should always expect to have when LINQ code is present.

This code would produce the following abbreviated results:

```
3/21/1997 12:00:00 AM - 10482 - Lazy K Kountry Store
5/22/1997 12:00:00 AM - 10545 - Lazy K Kountry Store
```

...
```
4/17/1998 12:00:00 AM - 11032 - White Clover Markets
5/1/1998 12:00:00 AM - 11066 - White Clover Markets
```

Use the Cast or OfType Operators for Legacy Collections

You will find that the majority of LINQ's Standard Query Operators can only be called on collections implementing the IEnumerable(Of T) interface. None of the legacy .NET collections—those in the System.Collection namespace—implement IEnumerable(Of T). So the question becomes, how do you use LINQ with legacy collections in your existing code base?

There are two Standard Query Operators specifically for this purpose, Cast and OfType. Both of these operators can be used to convert legacy collections to IEnumerable(Of T) sequences. Listing 1-9 shows an example.

Listing 1-9. *Converting a Legacy Collection to an IEnumerable(Of T) Using the Cast Operator*

```
'  I'll create a legacy collection.
Dim arrayList As ArrayList = _
  New ArrayList (New Object() { "Adams", "Arthur", "Buchanan" })

Dim names As IEnumerable(Of String) = _
  arrayList.Cast(Of String)().Where(Function(n) n.Length < 7)

For Each name As String In names
  Console.WriteLine(name)
Next name
```

Listing 1-10 shows the same example using the OfType operator.

Listing 1-10. *Using the OfType Operator*

```
'  I'll create a legacy collection.
Dim arrayList As ArrayList = _
  New ArrayList (New Object() { "Adams", "Arthur", "Buchanan" })

Dim names As IEnumerable(Of String) = _
  arrayList.OfType(Of String)().Where(Function(n) n.Length < 7)

For Each name As String In names
  Console.WriteLine(name)
Next name
```

Both examples provide the exact same results. Here they are:

```
Adams
Arthur
```

The difference between the two operators is that the Cast operator will attempt to cast every element in the collection to the specified type to be put into the output sequence. If there is a type in the collection that cannot be cast to the specified type, an exception will be thrown. This makes the Cast operator excellent for enforcing the data type of objects in a collection. The OfType operator will only attempt to put those elements that can be cast to the type specified into the output sequence. This makes the OfType operator excellent for filtering a collection by data type.

Prefer the OfType Operator to the Cast Operator

One of the most important reasons why generics were added to .NET was to give the language the ability to have data collections with static type checking. Prior to generics—barring creating your own specific collection type for every type of data for which you wanted a collection—there was no way to ensure that every element in a legacy collection, such as an ArrayList, a Hashtable, and so on, was of the same and correct type. Nothing in the language prevented code from adding a Textbox object to an ArrayList meant to contain only Label objects.

With the introduction of generics in .NET 2.0, .NET developers now have a way to explicitly state that a collection can only contain elements of a specified type. While either the OfType or Cast operator may work for a legacy collection, Cast requires that every object in the collection be of the correct type. When using the Cast operator, if any object is unable to be cast to the specified data type, an exception is thrown. If there is any legitimate possibility that objects of differing types exist in the collection, use the OfType operator. With it, only objects of the specified type will be stored in the output IEnumerable(Of T) sequence, and no exception will be thrown. The best-case scenario is that every object will be of the specified type and be in the output sequence. The worst case is that some elements will get skipped, but they would have thrown an exception had the Cast operator been used instead.

Don't Assume a Query Is Bug Free

In Chapter 3, I discuss that LINQ queries are often deferred and not actually executed when it appears you are calling them. For example, consider this code fragment from Listing 1-1:

```
Dim items = _
  From s In greetings _
  Where s.EndsWith("LINQ") _
  Select s

For Each item In items
  Console.WriteLine(item)
Next item
```

While it *appears* the query is occurring when the items variable is being initialized, that is not the case. Because the Where and Select operators are deferred, the query is not actually being performed at that point. The query is merely being called, declared, or defined, but not performed. The query will actually take place the first time a result from it is needed. This is typically when the query results variable is enumerated. In this example, a result from the query is not needed until the For Each statement is executed. That is the point in time that the query will be performed. In this way, we say that the query is *deferred*.

It is often easy to forget that many of the query operators are deferred and will not execute until a sequence is enumerated. This means you could have an improperly written query that will throw an exception when the resulting sequence is eventually enumerated. That enumeration could take place far enough downstream that it is easily forgotten that a query may be the culprit.

Let's examine the code in Listing 1-11.

Listing 1-11. *Query with Intentional Exception Deferred Until Enumeration*

```
Dim strings() As String = {"one", "two", Nothing, "three"}

Console.WriteLine("Before Where() is called.")
Dim ieStrings As IEnumerable(Of String) = strings.Where(Function(s) s.Length = 3)
Console.WriteLine("After Where() is called.")

For Each s As String In ieStrings
  Console.WriteLine("Processing " & s)
Next s
```

I know that the third element in the array of strings is Nothing, and I cannot call Nothing.Length without throwing an exception. The execution steps over the line of code calling the query just fine. It is not until I enumerate the sequence ieStrings, and specifically the third element, that the exception occurs. Here are the results of this code:

```
Before Where() is called.
After Where() is called.
Processing one
Processing two

Unhandled Exception: System.NullReferenceException: Object reference not set to an
instance of an object.
…
```

As you can see, I called the Where operator without exception. It's not until I try to enumerate the third element of the sequence that an exception is thrown. Now imagine if that sequence, ieStrings, is passed to a function that downstream enumerates the sequence, perhaps to populate a drop-down list or some other control. It would be easy to think the exception is caused by a fault in that function, not the LINQ query itself.

Take Advantage of Deferred Queries

In Chapter 3, I go into deferred queries in more depth. However, I want to point out that if a query is a deferred query that ultimately returns an IEnumerable(Of T), that IEnumerable(Of T) object can be enumerated over, time and time again, obtaining the latest data from the data source. You don't need to actually call or, as I earlier pointed out, declare the query again.

In most of the code samples in this book, you will see a query called and an IEnumerable(Of T) for some type T being returned and stored in a variable. Then, I typically call For Each on the IEnumerable(Of T) sequence. This is for demonstration purposes. If that code is executed multiple times, calling the actual query each time is needless work. It might make more sense to have a query initialization method that gets called once for the lifetime of the scope and to construct all the queries there. Then, you could enumerate over a particular sequence to get the latest version of the query results at will.

Use the DataContext Log

When working with LINQ to SQL, don't forget that the database class that is generated by SqlMetal inherits from System.Data.Linq.DataContext. This means that your generated DataContext class has some useful built-in functionality, such as a TextWriter property named Log.

One of the niceties of the Log object is that it will output the equivalent SQL statement of an IQueryable(Of T) query prior to the parameter substitution. Have you ever had code break in production that you think might be data related? Wouldn't it be nice if there was a way to get the query executed against the database, so that you could enter it in SQL Server Enterprise Manager or Query Analyzer and see the exact data coming back? The DataContext's Log object will output the SQL query for you. An example is shown in Listing 1-12.

Listing 1-12. *An Example Using the DataContext.Log Object*

```
Dim db As New Northwind( _
  "Data Source=.\SQLEXPRESS;Initial Catalog=Northwind;Integrated Security=SSPI;")

db.Log = Console.Out

Dim orders As IQueryable(Of Order) = _
  From c In db.Customers _
  From o In c.Orders _
  Where c.Country = "USA" AndAlso c.Region Is "WA" _
  Select o

For Each item As Order In orders
  Console.WriteLine ("{0} - {1} - {2}", item.OrderDate, item.OrderID, item.ShipName)
Next item
```

This code produces the following output:

```
SELECT [t1].[OrderID], [t1].[CustomerID], [t1].[EmployeeID], [t1].[OrderDate],
[t1].[RequiredDate], [t1].[ShippedDate],
[t1].[ShipVia], [t1].[Freight], [t1].[ShipName], [t1].[ShipAddress],
[t1].[ShipCity], [t1].[ShipRegion], [t1].[ShipPosta
lCode], [t1].[ShipCountry]
FROM [dbo].[Customers] AS [t0], [dbo].[Orders] AS [t1]
WHERE ([t0].[Country] = @p0) AND ([t0].[Region] = @p1) AND ([t1].[CustomerID] =
[t0].[CustomerID])
-- @p0: Input NVarChar (Size = 3; Prec = 0; Scale = 0) [USA]
-- @p1: Input NVarChar (Size = 2; Prec = 0; Scale = 0) [WA]
-- Context: SqlProvider(Sql2008) Model: AttributedMetaModel Build: 3.5.30729.1
```

```
3/21/1997 12:00:00 AM - 10482 - Lazy K Kountry Store
5/22/1997 12:00:00 AM - 10545 - Lazy K Kountry Store
6/19/1997 12:00:00 AM - 10574 - Trail's Head Gourmet Provisioners
6/23/1997 12:00:00 AM - 10577 - Trail's Head Gourmet Provisioners
1/8/1998 12:00:00 AM - 10822 - Trail's Head Gourmet Provisioners
7/31/1996 12:00:00 AM - 10269 - White Clover Markets
11/1/1996 12:00:00 AM - 10344 - White Clover Markets
3/10/1997 12:00:00 AM - 10469 - White Clover Markets
3/24/1997 12:00:00 AM - 10483 - White Clover Markets
4/11/1997 12:00:00 AM - 10504 - White Clover Markets
7/11/1997 12:00:00 AM - 10596 - White Clover Markets
10/6/1997 12:00:00 AM - 10693 - White Clover Markets
10/8/1997 12:00:00 AM - 10696 - White Clover Markets
10/30/1997 12:00:00 AM - 10723 - White Clover Markets
11/13/1997 12:00:00 AM - 10740 - White Clover Markets
1/30/1998 12:00:00 AM - 10861 - White Clover Markets
2/24/1998 12:00:00 AM - 10904 - White Clover Markets
4/17/1998 12:00:00 AM - 11032 - White Clover Markets
5/1/1998 12:00:00 AM - 11066 - White Clover Markets
```

Use the LINQ Forum

Despite providing the best tips I can think of, there will more than likely be times when you get stuck. Don't forget that there is a forum dedicated to LINQ at MSDN.com. You can find a link to it here: `http://www.linqdev.com`. This forum is monitored by Microsoft developers, and you will find a wealth of knowledgeable resources there.

Summary

I sense that by now you are chomping at the bit to move on to the next chapter, but before you do, I want to remind you of a few things.

First, LINQ *is* going to change the way .NET developers query data. Vendors will more than likely be lining up to add a "LINQ Compatible" sticker to their products, just like they currently do with XML.

Bear in mind that LINQ is not just a new library to be added to your project. It is a total approach to querying data that comprises several components depending on the data store being queried. At the present time, you can use LINQ to query the following data sources: in-memory data collections using LINQ to Objects, XML using LINQ to XML, DataSets using LINQ to DataSet, and SQL Server databases using LINQ to SQL.

Also, please remember what I said about LINQ being for more than just queries. In a sample project I have been working on using LINQ, I have found LINQ very useful not only for querying data but for getting data into the necessary format for presentation in a WinForm control.

Last but not least, I hope you didn't skip over the tips I provide in this chapter. If you don't understand some of them, that is no problem. They will make more sense as you progress through the book. Just keep them in mind if you find yourself stalled.

No doubt that after seeing some of the LINQ examples and tips in this chapter, you may find yourself puzzled by some of the syntax that makes this all possible. If so, don't worry because in the next chapter, I cover the enhancements Microsoft has made to VB.NET 2008 that make all of this possible.

■■■

CHAPTER 2

VB.NET 2008 Language Enhancements for LINQ

In the previous chapter, I introduced you to LINQ. I provided some examples to whet your appetite and shared some premature tips. You may be perplexed though by some of the syntax. If so, it is probably because the VB.NET you witnessed in that chapter is new and improved. The reason for the VB.NET language upgrade is that VB.NET 2005 just didn't have the muscle to pull off LINQ. In this chapter, I introduce you to the more powerful VB.NET 2008.

Please be aware that in this book, when I use the term *VB.NET 2008*, I am referring to VB.NET 9.0, which is shipped with Visual Studio 2008. So technically, the features I am covering in this chapter are in the VB.NET 9.0 language specification.

New VB.NET 2008 Language Additions

To make LINQ seamlessly integrate with VB.NET, significant enhancements were needed for the VB.NET language. Virtually every significant enhancement to the VB.NET language made in version 2008 was made specifically to support LINQ. While all of these features have merit on their own, it is really the sum of the parts contributing to LINQ that makes VB.NET 2008 so noteworthy.

To truly understand much of the syntax of LINQ, it is necessary for me to cover some of the new VB.NET 2008 language features before proceeding with the workings of the components of LINQ. This chapter will cover the following language additions:

- New options
- Lambda expressions
- Expression trees
- The new usage of the `Dim` keyword
- Object initialization and anonymous types
- Extension methods

- Partial methods

- Query expressions

- Nullable value types

- XML enhancements

In the examples in this chapter, I do not explicitly show which assemblies should be added and which namespaces you should specify in your Imports statements for the assemblies and namespaces I cover in Chapter 1. I do point out any new ones, but only in the first example introducing them.

New (and Not So New) Options

VB.NET 2008 supports the old VB6 Option Explicit and Option Compare, the not-so-old Option Strict from VB.NET 2003, and new for VB.NET 2008, Option Infer. Let's review these starting with the old VB6 options and moving forward.

■Note Don't forget that Visual Studio stores default values for these options in your project's properties. Select your project's Properties menu and examine the Compile tab. There you will see the project's default settings for each of these options. It is important to know how these are set before trying any of the code in this section.

Option Explicit

In VB6, by default, you did not have to declare a variable or give it a type before you used it. The following code was completely legal and would compile and run:

```
A = "hello world"
```

Because A has never been declared, VB6 would declare it on the fly. Because A was not given a type, it would be given the type of Variant, which can hold any type of variable. In the following example, it is set to a String, an Integer, and a Boolean:

```
A = "hello world"
A = 1
A = False
```

You could also declare a variable, but not give it a type, like in the following example:

```
A = "hello world"
Dim B
Dim S as String = "goodby world"
Dim I as Integer
B = A
B = S
B = I
B = B + 1
```

This had two effects. First, it made it easier to write programs. Second, it made it easier to make mistakes. I ran into a fine example of this when I recently converted a VB6 program to .NET. I was told the VB6 program worked well, except for a couple of glitches, including one function that, for reasons no one had been able to figure out, did not work at all. The programmer "always" declared his variables and gave them types but did not always set Option Explicit On on every form. When I tried to convert the program to VB.NET, I got a warning that sglCommand was undefined and would be upgraded as an object. Here was the VB6 code:

```
Dim sqlCommand As String
sqlCommand = "Select"
sqlCommand = sglCommand + Field1
```

I had to look at the code for several minutes before seeing what was wrong; someone had used a *g* instead of a *q*, setting the command section of the string to blank. Had Option Explicit been set to On, the compiler would have generated an undeclared variable error, and a problem that has lingered far too long would never have occurred. Option Explicit should always be set to On.

Option Compare

Another option available since VB6 is Option Compare, which can be set to Binary or Text; the default is Binary. For all the differences, check the MSDN documentation, but for applications using the Latin alphabet, the biggest difference is that Binary compare is case sensitive, and Text compare is not case sensitive.

Option Strict

VB.NET 2003 added another option, Option Strict. VB6 was nice about converting one type of variable to another type. Although convenient, it can lead to unexpected runtime errors. Here is an example:

```
Dim b As Byte
Dim i As Integer

i = 1
b = i  'OK

i = 300
b = i  'Compiles fine, but causes a runtime error
```

In the preceding code, the compiler allows assigning an Integer to a Byte. When the Integer is 255 or less, everything is fine, but if the Integer is 256 or larger, a runtime error will occur. Often, it is known that the conversion, in this case Integer to Byte, will always work, or the programmer can perform a runtime test to check the value, or even trap the error that is generated if the capacity of a Byte is exceeded. The problem, especially when a program grows in size, is that a programmer can write code which does a conversion without realizing the need to take precautions against runtime errors.

With Option Strict set to On, an Integer can still be assigned to a Byte, but it must be done explicitly, as in the following example:

```
b = Convert.ToByte(i)
```

If i is greater than 255, the conversion will still cause a runtime error, but any programmer working on the code will know immediately that an Integer is being assigned to a Byte and can take proper precautions. Interestingly, the following code

```
Dim b as Byte = 300
```

compiles without error (but generates an error at runtime) in VB6 but generates a compiler error in VB.NET, regardless of whether Option Strict is On or Off.

Option Infer

The Option Infer option was added to VB.NET 2008 to support the *implicit typing* of variables, which is required for some LINQ capabilities. Implicit typing allows a variable to be declared without a type being specified with the compiler determining the type at *compile* time, for example

```
Dim x As Integer = 1
```

and

```
Dim x = 1
```

Both of these statements generate the same code if Option Infer is On but different code if Option Infer is Off. This is best seen by using the debugger in Visual Studio. If you stop the debugger after the preceding statements have been executed and open a watch window, Dim x As Integer = 1, will give x a value of 1 and a type of Integer. No surprise there.

With Option Infer On, Dim x = 1 gives the same results: x has a value of 1 and a type of Integer. But with Option Infer Off, Dim x = 1 results in x having a value of 1{Integer} and a type of Object. The Object will contain a type of Integer with a value of 1.

What is happening here is that with the new Option Infer Off, VB.NET tries to emulate the old behavior of VB6, which would create the variable as a Variant in this situation. In VB.NET, the Variant type does not exist, so the best VB.NET can do is create the variable as an Object and set it to an Integer, otherwise known as boxing, with a value of 1.

With Option Infer On, VB.NET detects the 1 as an Integer and automatically types x as an Integer to match.

Note that with Option Infer Off and Option Strict On, Dim x = 1 gives the following compiler error:

```
Option Strict On requires all variable declarations to have an 'As' clause.
```

I will cover implicit typing in more detail later in this chapter in the section titled "Keyword Dim, Object Initialization, and Anonymous Types."

The defaults are Explicit On, Strict Off, Infer On (Off for upgraded projects), and Compare Binary.

Lambda Expressions

In VB.NET 2008, Microsoft has added *lambda expressions*. Lambda expressions have been used in computer languages as far back as LISP, and were conceptualized in 1936 by Alonzo Church, an American mathematician. These expressions provide shorthand syntax for specifying an algorithm.

But before jumping immediately into lambda expressions, let's take a look at the evolution of specifying an algorithm as an argument to a method, since that is the primary purpose of lambda expressions.

Using Named Methods

Prior to VB.NET 2008, when a method or variable was typed to require a `Delegate`, a developer would have to create a named method and pass the address of the method where the `Delegate` was required.

As an example, consider the following situation. Let's pretend we have two developers: one is a common-code developer, and the other is an application developer. It isn't necessary that there be two different developers, I just need labels to delineate the two different roles. The common-code developer wants to create general-purpose code that can be reused throughout the project. The application developer will consume that general-purpose code to create an application. In this example scenario, the common-code developer wants to create a generic method for filtering arrays of integers but with the ability to specify the algorithm used to filter the array. First, she must declare the `Delegate`. It will be declared to receive an `Integer` and return `True` if the `Integer` should be *included* in the filtered array.

So, she creates a utility class and adds the `Delegate` and filtering method. Here is the common code:

```
Imports System.Collections

Public Class Common
  Public Delegate Function IntFilter(ByVal i As Integer) As Boolean

  Public Shared Function FilterArrayOfInts _
    (ByVal ints() As Integer, ByVal filter As IntFilter) As Integer()

    Dim aList As New ArrayList()
    For Each i As Integer In ints
      If filter(i) Then
        aList.Add(i)
      End If
    Next i
  Return CType(aList.ToArray(GetType(Integer)), Integer())

  End Function
End Class
```

The common-code developer will put both the `Delegate` declaration and the `FilterArrayOfInts` into a common library assembly, a dynamic link library (DLL), so that it can be used in multiple applications.

The `FilterArrayOfInts` method listed previously allows the application developer to pass in an array of integers and a `Delegate` to his filter method and get back a filtered array.

Now, let's assume the application developer wants to filter (in) just the odd integers. Here is his filter method, which is declared in his application code.

The Application Developer's Filter Method

```
Public Class Application
  Public Shared Function IsOdd(ByVal i As Integer) As Boolean
    Return (i And 1) = 1
  End Function
End Class
```

Based on the code in the `FilterArrayOfInts` method, this method will get called for every `Integer` in the array that gets passed in. This filter will only return `True` if the `Integer` passed in is odd. Listing 2-1 shows an example using the `FilterArrayOfInts` method, followed by the results.

Listing 2-1. *Calling the Common Library Filter Method*

```
Dim nums() As Integer = {1, 2, 3, 4, 5, 6, 7, 8, 9, 10}

Dim oddNums() As Integer = _
  Common.FilterArrayOfInts(nums, AddressOf Application.IsOdd)

For Each i As Integer In oddNums
  Console.WriteLine(i)
Next i
```

Here are the results:

```
1
3
5
7
9
```

Notice that to pass the `Delegate` as the second parameter of `FilterArrayOfInts`, the application developer just passes the address of the method. By simply creating another filter, he can filter differently. He could have a filter for even numbers, prime numbers, whatever criteria he wants. Delegates lend themselves to highly reusable code.

Using Lambda Expressions

That's all well and good, but it can get tedious writing all these named filter methods and whatever other named methods you may need. Many of these methods will only get used in a single call, and it's a bother to create named methods for them all. What we need is a syntax that makes it simple to define a single-use `Delegate`. What we need is a lambda expression.

Lambda expressions are specified beginning with the `Function` statement followed by parentheses containing an optional comma-delimited list of parameters, followed by an expression. Therefore, a lambda expression in VB.NET looks like this:

```
Function(param1, param2, …paramN) expression
```

It is a requirement that the data type returned by the expression match the return type specified by the Delegate. In VB.NET, and unlike C#, a lambda expression must be a single line of code and return a value. In this way, lambda expressions are more limited in VB.NET than they are in C#. I mention this in case you need to convert C# 2008 code to VB.NET. You may find C# lambda expressions that you cannot convert to VB.NET lambda expressions. In these cases, you must create named methods for the lambda expressions.

■**Note** Lambda expressions will be getting a significant overhaul in the next version of VB.NET, VB.NET 2010. They will gain the ability to span multiple lines of code and the option of returning a value or not. By all accounts, they should be the equal of C# lambda expressions.

Here is an example lambda expression:

```
Function(x) x
```

This lambda expression could be read as "x goes to x," or perhaps "input x returns x." It means that for input variable x, return x. This expression merely returns what is passed in. It is important to know that it is the Delegate that is dictating what the type of x being input is and what type must be returned. For example, if the Delegate is defined as passing a String in but returning a Boolean, then Function (x) x could not be used: if x going in is a String, so x being returned would be a String as well, but the Delegate specified it must be Boolean. So with a Delegate defined like that, the lambda expression must evaluate to or return a Boolean, like this:

```
Function(x) x.Length > 0
```

This lambda expression could be read as "x goes to x.Length > 0," or perhaps "input x returns x.Length > 0." Since this expression does evaluate to a Boolean, the Delegate must specify that the method returns a Boolean; otherwise, a compiler error will result.

The following lambda expression will attempt to return the length of the input argument. So the Delegate must specify a return type of Integer:

```
Function(s) s.Length
```

If multiple parameters are passed into the lambda expression, separate them with commas like this:

```
Function(x, y) x = y
```

Your lambda expression may not have any parameters, and for that, just don't specify any inside the parentheses like this:

```
Function() DateTime.Today.Day And 1
```

What is important to remember is that the Delegate is defining what the input types are and what the return type must be. So make sure your lambda expression matches the Delegate definition.

■**Caution** Make sure your lambda expressions are written to accept the input types specified by the delegate definition and return the type the delegate defines to be returned.

To refresh your memory, here is the `Delegate` declaration that the common-code developer defined:

```
Public Delegate Function IntFilter(ByVal i As Integer) As Boolean
```

The application developer's lambda expression must support an `Integer` passed in and a `Boolean` being returned. This can be inferred from the method she is calling and the purpose of the filter method, but it is important to remember the `Delegate` is dictating this.

So the previous example—but using a lambda expression this time—would look like Listing 2-2.

Listing 2-2. *Calling the Filter Method with a Lambda Expression*

```
Dim nums() As Integer = {1, 2, 3, 4, 5, 6, 7, 8, 9, 10}

Dim oddNums() As Integer = _
  Common.FilterArrayOfInts(nums, Function(i) (i And 1) = 1)

For Each i As Integer In oddNums
  Console.WriteLine(i)
Next i
```

Wow, that's concise code. I know it may look a little funny because it is so new, but once you get used to it, it sure is readable and maintainable. As is required, the results are the same as with Listing 2-1:

```
1
3
5
7
9
```

For a recap, here are the significant lines from the sample code for each approach:

```
Dim oddNums() As Integer = _
  Common.FilterArrayOfInts(nums, AddressOf Application.IsOdd)

Dim oddNums() As Integer = _
  Common.FilterArrayOfInts(nums, Function(i) (i And 1) = 1)
```

Don't forget that there is a named method declared somewhere else defining what the `Application.IsOdd` method does too! Of course, if that filtering logic is going to be reused in several places, or perhaps if the algorithm is complex and should only be trusted to a specialized developer, it may make more sense to create a named method to be consumed by other developers. But in many cases, for a single-use delegate, lambda expressions are the way to go.

■**Tip** Complex or reused algorithms may be better served by named methods so they can be reused by any developer without that developer necessarily understanding the algorithm.

Whether named methods or lambda expressions are used is up to the developer. Use whatever makes the most sense for the situation at hand.

You will often take advantage of lambda expressions by passing them as arguments to your LINQ query operator calls. Since every LINQ query is likely to have unique or scarcely reused operator lambda expressions, this provides the flexibility of specifying your operator logic without having to create named methods for virtually every query.

Expression Trees

An *expression tree* is an efficient data representation, in tree form, of a query operator's lambda expression. These expression tree data representations can be evaluated, all simultaneously, so that a single query can be built and executed against a data source, such as a database.

In the majority of the examples I have discussed so far, the query's operators have been performed in a linear fashion. Let's examine the following code:

```
Dim nums() As Integer = { 6, 2, 7, 1, 9, 3 }
Dim numsLessThanFour As IEnumerable(Of Integer) = nums _
  .Where(Function(i) i < 4) _
  .OrderBy(Function(i) i)
```

This query contains two operators, Where and OrderBy, that are expecting delegates as their arguments. When this code is compiled, .NET intermediate language (IL) code is emitted for each of the query operator's lambda expressions.

When this query is executed, the Where operator is called first, followed by the OrderBy operator.

This linear execution of the operators seems reasonable for this example, but you should consider a query against a very large data source, such as a database. Would it make sense for a SQL query to first call the database with the Where statement, only to turn around and order it in a subsequent call? Of course, this just isn't feasible for database queries, as well as potentially other types of queries. This is where expression trees become necessary. Since an expression tree allows the simultaneous evaluation and execution of all operators in a query, a single query can be made instead of a separate query for each operator.

So there now are two different things the compiler can generate for an operator's lambda expression, IL code or an expression tree. What determines whether an operator's lambda expression gets compiled into IL code or an expression tree? The operator's declaration will define which of these actions the compiler will take. If the operator is declared to accept a Delegate, IL code will be emitted. If the operator is declared to accept an *expression* of a Delegate, an expression tree is emitted.

As an example, let's look at two different implementations of the Where operator. The first is the Standard Query Operator that exists in the LINQ to Objects API, which is defined in the System.Linq.Enumerable class:

```
<ExtensionAttribute> _
Public Shared Function Where(Of TSource) ( _
    source As IEnumerable(Of TSource), _
    predicate As Func(Of TSource, Boolean) _
) As IEnumerable(Of TSource)
```

The second Where operator implementation exists in the LINQ to SQL API and is defined in the System.Linq.Queryable class:

```
<ExtensionAttribute> _
Public Shared Function Where(Of TSource)( _
    source As IQueryable(Of TSource), _
    predicate As Expression(Of Func(Of TSource, Boolean)) _
) As IQueryable(Of TSource)
```

As you can see, the first Where operator is declared to accept a Delegate, as specified by the Func Delegate, and the compiler will generate IL code for this operator's lambda expression. I will cover the Func Delegate in Chapter 3. For now just be aware that it is defining the signature of the Delegate passed as the predicate argument. The second Where operator is declared to accept an expression tree (Expression), so the compiler will generate an expression tree data representation of the lambda expression.

The operators that accept an IEnumerable(Of T) sequence as their first argument are declared to accept a Delegate for their lambda expressions. The operators that accept an IQueryable(Of T) sequence as their first argument are declared to accept an expression tree.

Note   Extension methods on IEnumerable(Of T) sequences have IL code emitted by the compiler. Extension methods on IQueryable(Of T) sequences have expression trees emitted by the compiler.

Merely being a consumer of LINQ does not require the developer to be very cognizant of expression trees. It is the vendor's developer who adds LINQ capability to a data storage product who needs to fully understand expression trees. Because of this, I don't cover them in any detail in this book.

Keyword Dim, Object Initialization, and Anonymous Types

Be forewarned: it is nearly impossible to discuss the Dim keyword and implicit type inference without demonstrating object initialization or anonymous types. Likewise, it is nearly impossible to discuss object initialization or anonymous types without discussing the Dim keyword. All three of these VB.NET 2008 language enhancements are very tightly coupled.

Before describing each of these three new language features in detail—because each will describe itself in terms of the other—allow me to introduce all three simultaneously. Let's examine the following statement:

```
Dim¹ mySpouse = New With² {Key .FirstName = "Vickey"³, Key .LastName = "Rattz"³}
```

In this example, I declare a variable named mySpouse using the Dim keyword without defining the variable type. It is assigned the value of an anonymous type that is initialized using the new object initialization features. That one line of code is taking advantage of the Dim keyword, anonymous types, and object initialization.

Take a look at the first superscript; you can detect the line of code is using the Dim keyword because it is explicitly stated. At number 2, you are able to detect there is an anonymous type because I use the New With operator without specifying a named class. And, at number 3, you can see the anonymous object is being explicitly initialized using the new object initialization feature.

In a nutshell, the Dim keyword allows the data type of an object to be inferred based on the data type with which it has been initialized. However, for that data type to be inferred, Option Infer must be set to On; otherwise, late binding will occur if you have Option Strict set to On as was recommended in the previous section about the VB.NET options. Without Option Infer set to On, code utilizing the Dim keyword will not even compile.

■**Note** Make sure Option Infer is set to On either in your project's Compile Properties or specified at the top of your code module if you plan to take advantage of implicit type inference.

Anonymous types allow new class data types to be created on the fly at compile time. True to the word *anonymous*, these new data types have no name. You can't very well create an anonymous data type if you don't know what member variables it contains, and you can't know what members it contains unless you know what types those members are. Lastly, you won't know what data type those new members are unless they are initialized. The object initialization feature handles all that.

From that line of code, the compiler will create a new anonymous class type containing two public String members; the first being named FirstName and the second named LastName.

The Implicitly Typed Local Variable Keyword Dim (with Option Infer On/Option Strict On)

With the addition of anonymous types to VB.NET 2008, a new problem becomes apparent. If a variable is being instantiated that is an unnamed type, as in an anonymous type, of what type variable would you assign it to? Consider the following code as an example:

```
' This code will not compile.
Dim unnamedTypeVar as ??? = New With {.firstArg = 1, .secondArg = "Joe"}
```

What variable type would you declare unnamedTypeVar to be? This is a problem. The folks at Microsoft chose to remedy this by creating a new usage for the Dim keyword. This new usage of the Dim keyword informs the compiler that it should implicitly infer the variable type from the variable's initializer. This means that a variable declared with the new version of the Dim keyword *must* have an initializer.

If you leave off an initializer, you will get a compiler error (assuming Option Strict is set to On as recommended). Listing 2-3 shows some code that declares a variable with the new version of the Dim keyword but fails to initialize it.

Listing 2-3. *An Invalid Variable Declaration Using the Dim Keyword*

```
Dim name
```

And here is the compiler error it produces:

```
Option Strict On requires all variables to have an 'As' clause.
```

Because these variables are statically type checked at compile time, an initializer is required so the compiler can implicitly infer the type from it. Attempting to assign a value of a different data type elsewhere in the code will result in a compiler error. For example, let's examine the code in Listing 2-4.

Listing 2-4. *An Invalid Assignment to a Variable Declared Using the Dim Keyword*

```
Dim name = "Dennis"     ' So far so good.
name = 1                ' Uh oh. Will not work in VB.NET if Option Strict On
Console.WriteLine(name)
```

This code is going to fail to compile because the name variable is going to be implicitly inferred to be of type string; yet I attempt to assign an integer value of 1 to the variable. Here is the compiler error this code generates:

```
Option Strict On disallows implicit conversions from 'Integer' to 'String'.
```

As you can see, the compiler is enforcing the variable's type. Back to that original code example of an anonymous type assignment, using the Dim keyword, my code with an additional line to display the variable would look like Listing 2-5.

Listing 2-5. *An Anonymous Type Assigned to a Variable Declared with the Dim Keyword*

```
Dim unnamedTypeVar = New With {.firstArg = 1, .secondArg = "Joe" }
Console.WriteLine(unnamedTypeVar.firstArg & ". " & unnamedTypeVar.secondArg)
```

Here are the results of this code:

```
1. Joe
```

As you can see, using the Dim keyword, you get static type checking plus the flexibility to support anonymous types. This will become very important when I discuss projection type operators in the remainder of this book.

In these examples so far, usage of the Dim keyword has been mandatory because there is no alternative. If you are assigning an object of an anonymous class type to a variable, you have no choice but to assign it to a variable declared with the Dim keyword. However, it is possible to use Dim any time you declare a variable, as long as it is getting initialized properly. I recommend refraining from that indulgence though for the sake of maintainability. I feel like developers should always know the type of data they are working with, and while the actual data type may be known to you now, will it be when you revisit this code in six months? What about when another developer is responsible once you leave?

■**Tip** For the sake of maintainable code, refrain from using this new usage of the `Dim` keyword just because it is convenient. Use it when necessary, such as when assigning an object of anonymous type to a variable.

Object Initialization Expressions

Due to the need for the dynamic data types that anonymous types allow, there needed to be a change in the way objects could be initialized. Since expressions are provided in a lambda expression or an expression tree, object initialization was simplified for initialization on the fly.

Object Initialization

Object initialization allows you to specify the initialization values for publicly accessible fields and properties of a class during instantiation. As an example, consider this class:

```
Public Class Address
   Public address As String
   Public city As String
   Public state As String
   Public postalCode As String
End Class
```

Prior to the object initialization feature added to VB.NET 2008, without a specialized constructor, you would have to initialize an object of type `Address` as shown in Listing 2-6.

Listing 2-6. *Instantiating and Initializing the Class the Old Way*

```
Dim address As New Address()
address.address = "105 Elm Street"
address.city = "Atlanta"
address.state = "GA"
address.postalCode = "30339"
```

This will become very cumbersome in a lambda expression. Imagine you have queried the values from a data source and are projecting specific members into an `Address` object with the `Select` operator:

```
' This code will not compile.
Dim addresses As IEnumerable(Of Address) = somedatasource _
   .Where(Function(a) a.State = "GA")
   .Select(Function(a) New Address(???)????)
```

You just won't have a convenient way to get the members initialized in the newly constructed `Address` object. Have no fear: object initialization to the rescue. Now, you may be saying that you could create a constructor that would allow you to pass all those initialization values in when the object is instantiated. Yes, you could, some of the time. But what a hassle that would be, wouldn't it? And how are you going to do that with an anonymous type created on the fly? What if you don't own the source code for that class so that you can modify it to add a constructor? Wouldn't it be much easier to just instantiate the object as shown in Listing 2-7?

Listing 2-7. *Instantiating and Initializing the Class the New Fancy-Pants Way*

```
Dim address As Address = New Address With { _
    .address = "105 Elm Street", _
    .city = "Atlanta", _
    .state = "GA", _
    .postalCode = "30339"}
```

You *can* get away with that in a lambda expression. Also, remember these new object initialization capabilities can be used anywhere, not just with LINQ queries.

When using object initialization, the compiler instantiates the object using the class's parameterless constructor, then it initializes the named members with the specified values. Any members that are not specified will have the default value for their data type.

Anonymous Types

Creating a new language-level API for generic data queries is made more difficult by the VB.NET language's lack of ability to dynamically create new data types at compile time. If we want data queries to retrieve first-class language-level elements, the language must have the ability to create first-class language-level data elements, which for VB.NET are classes. So the VB.NET 9.0 language specification now includes the ability to dynamically create new unnamed classes and objects from those classes. This type of class is known as an *anonymous type.*

An anonymous type has no name and is generated by the compiler based on the initialization of the object being instantiated. Since the class has no type name, any variable assigned to an object of an anonymous type must have some way to declare it. This is the purpose of the new usage of the VB.NET 2008 Dim keyword.

The anonymous type is invaluable when projecting new data types using the Select or SelectMany operators. Without anonymous types, predefined named classes would always have to exist for the purpose of projecting data into the predefined named classes when calling the Select or SelectMany operators. It would be very inconvenient to have to create named classes for every query.

In the object initialization section of this chapter, I discussed the following object instantiation and initialization code:

```
Dim address As Address = New Address With _
    { _
    .address = "105 Elm Street", _
    .city = "Atlanta", _
    .state = "GA", _
    .postalCode = "30339" }
```

If instead of using the named Address class, I want to use an anonymous type, I would just omit the class name. However, you can't store the newly instantiated object in a variable of Address type, because it is no longer a variable of type Address. It now has a generated type name known only to the compiler. So I have to change the data type of the address variable too. This again is what the new usage of the Dim keyword is for, as demonstrated by Listing 2-8.

Listing 2-8. *Instantiating and Initializing an Anonymous Type Using Object Initialization*

```
Dim address = New With { _
  .address = "105 Elm Street", _
  .city = "Atlanta", _
  .state = "GA", _
  .postalCode = "30339"}

Console.WriteLine("address = {0} : city = {1} : state = {2} : zip = {3}", _
  address.address, address.city, address.state, address.postalCode)

Console.WriteLine("{0}", address.GetType().ToString())
```

■**Note** The anonymous type created in Listing 2-8 is flawed. Please make sure you continue and read "The Key Property" section next.

I added that last call to the Console.WriteLine method just so you can see the internal compiler-generated name for the anonymous class. Here are the results:

```
address = 105 Elm Street : city = Atlanta : state = GA : zip = 30339
VB$AnonymousType_1`4[System.String,System.String,System.String,System.String]
```

That anonymous class type certainly looks compiler-generated to me. Of course, your compiler-generated anonymous class name could be different.

The Key Property

There is a very important omission in the anonymous type that gets created in Listing 2-8. None of the anonymous type members have the Key property specified for them. This means that none of the members in the instances of those types are included in any object equality comparisons for any objects of that anonymous type. This can spell trouble. Let's take a look at the problems that can be caused by this in Listing 2-9.

Listing 2-9. *Comparing Two Anonymous Typed Objects Without the Key Property Specified*

```
Dim address1 = New With { _
  .address = "105 Elm Street", _
  .city = "Atlanta", _
  .state = "GA", _
  .postalCode = "30339"}

Dim address2 = New With { _
  .address = "105 Elm Street", _
  .city = "Atlanta", _
  .state = "GA", _
  .postalCode = "30339"}

Console.WriteLine(String.Format("{0}", address1.Equals(address2)))
```

If you examine address1 and address2, you can see that the instantiated objects are identical. But what happens when we run the code?

```
False
```

That's not at all the response I would have expected. So, what happened? Without specifying at least one member with the Key property, objects of an anonymous type cannot be successfully compared for equality.

Even more interestingly, only those members specified with the Key property will be included in the test for equality. Let's examine this in Listing 2-10.

Listing 2-10. *Comparing Two Anonymous Typed Unequal Objects With the Key Property Partially Specified*

```
Dim address1 = New With { _
  Key .address = "105 Elm Street", _
  Key .city = "Atlanta", _
  Key .state = "GA", _
      .postalCode = "30339"}

Dim address2 = New With { _
  Key .address = "105 Elm Street", _
  Key .city = "Atlanta", _
  Key .state = "GA", _
      .postalCode = "30340"}

Console.WriteLine(String.Format("{0}", address1.Equals(address2)))
```

I have made a few key (please pardon the pun) changes in that example. First, I have added the Key property to the first three members of each object. Second, I have intentionally omitted the Key property from the last member of each object. Last, I have changed the value of the last member of the second object, and this is the member without the Key property specified. Since only those members specified with the Key property are included in the test for equality, these two clearly unequal objects should test as equal in the code. Let's take a look at the results.

```
True
```

Fascinating! So the moral of this story is that if you want anonymously typed objects that behave as you would expect, make sure you specify the Key property for every member you want included in the equality comparison. That said, Listing 2-11 compares the same objects as Listing 2-10 except *every* member has the Key property specified.

Listing 2-11. *Properly Comparing Two Anonymous Typed Unequal Objects*

```vbnet
Dim address1 = New With { _
  Key .address = "105 Elm Street", _
  Key .city = "Atlanta", _
  Key .state = "GA", _
  Key .postalCode = "30339"}

Dim address2 = New With { _
  Key .address = "105 Elm Street", _
  Key .city = "Atlanta", _
  Key .state = "GA", _
  Key .postalCode = "30340"}

Console.WriteLine(String.Format("{0}", address1.Equals(address2)))
```

As you can see, this code is the same as that in Listing 2-10 except that I have specified the Key property for the postalCode member as well as all the others. Here are the results:

```
False
```

This is the result I expected, since the second object's postalCode is different than the first object's postalCode. Now, just to turn full circle, in Listing 2-12, I will modify the code so that the two anonymous objects are truly equal and should be properly compared for equality by specifying the Key property on every member.

Listing 2-12. *Properly Comparing Two Anonymous Typed Equal Objects*

```vbnet
Dim address1 = New With { _
  Key .address = "105 Elm Street", _
  Key .city = "Atlanta", _
  Key .state = "GA", _
  Key .postalCode = "30339"}
```

```
Dim address2 = New With { _
  Key .address = "105 Elm Street", _
  Key .city = "Atlanta", _
  Key .state = "GA", _
  Key .postalCode = "30339"}
```

```
Console.WriteLine(String.Format("{0}", address1.Equals(address2)))
```

Now, you should see in the results that these two identical objects are indeed equal.

True

Extension Methods

An *extension method* is a Shared method of a module that you can call as though it were an instance method of a different class. For example, you could create an extension method named ToDouble that is a Shared method in a module you create named StringConversions, but that is called as though it were a method of an object of type String.

Before I explain extension methods in detail, let's first review the problem that lead to their creation by discussing Shared (class) vs. instance (object) methods. Instance methods can only be called on *instances* of a class, otherwise known as *objects*. You cannot call an instance method on the class itself. Likewise, Shared methods should only be called on the class, as opposed to an instance of a class.

Instance (Object) vs. Shared (Class) Methods Recap

The String class ToUpper method is an example of an instance method. You cannot call ToUpper on the String class itself; you must call it on a String object.

In the code in Listing 2-13, I demonstrate this by calling the ToUpper method on the object named name.

Listing 2-13. *Calling an Instance Method on an Object*

```
'  This code will compile.
Dim name As String = "Joe"
Console.WriteLine(name.ToUpper())
```

The previous code compiles and, when run, produces the following output:

JOE

However, if I try to call the ToUpper method on the String class itself, I will get a compiler error because the ToUpper method is an instance method, and I am attempting to call it on the class, rather than the object. Listing 2-14 shows an example of an attempt to do this, and the compiler error generated by it.

Listing 2-14. *Trying to Call an Instance Method on a Class*

```
'  This code will not even compile.
String.ToUpper()
```

Just trying to compile this code produces the following compiler error:

```
Reference to a non-shared member requires an object reference.
```

This example seems a little hokey though, since it couldn't possibly work because I never gave it any string value to convert to uppercase. Any attempt to do so though would result in trying to call some variation of the ToUpper method that does not exist, because there is no prototype for the ToUpper method whose signature includes a String.

Contrast the ToUpper method with the String class Format method. This method is defined to be Shared. This means the Format method should be called on the String class itself, rather than on an object of type String. First, I will try to call it on an object with the code in Listing 2-15.

Listing 2-15. *Trying to Call a Class (Shared) Method on an Object*

```
Dim firstName As String = "Dennis"
Dim lastName As String = "Hayes"
Dim name As String = firstName.Format("{0} {1}", firstName, lastName)
Console.WriteLine(name)
```

This code produces the following compiler warning:

```
Access of shared member, constant member, enum member or nested type through an
instance; qualifying expression will not be evaluated.
```

■**Note** This will compile with only the preceding warning that anything is wrong. In most cases, this will give the results that you want and expect; but if there is a different Format function in scope, it will be called instead of the Shared Format function. This is an example of where treating warnings as errors may save some debugging time.

However, if instead I call the Format method on the String class itself, it compiles without warning and works properly as desired, as demonstrated in Listing 2-16.

Listing 2-16. *Calling a Class (Shared) Method on a Class*

```
Dim firstName As String = "Dennis"
Dim lastName As String = "Hayes"
Dim name As String = String.Format("{0} {1}", firstName, lastName)
Console.WriteLine(name)
```

The code produces the following results:

```
Dennis Hayes
```

It is sometimes obvious from parts of the signature other than the `Shared` keyword itself that the method must be an instance method. For example, consider the `ToUpper` method. It doesn't have any arguments other than one overloaded version taking a `CultureInfo` object reference. So if it isn't relying on a `String` instance's internal data, what string would it convert to uppercase?

The Problem Solved by Extension Methods

So what is the problem you ask? For this discussion, assume you are the developer responsible for designing a new way to query multitudes of objects. Let's say you decide to create a `Where` method to help with the `Where` clauses. How would you do it?

Would you make the `Where` operator an instance method? If so, to what class would you add that `Where` method? You want the `Where` method to work for querying any collection of objects. There just isn't a logical class to add the `Where` method to. Taking this approach, you would have to modify a zillion different classes if you want universal data querying capability.

So now that you realize the method must be `Shared`, what is the problem? Think of your typical (SQL) query and how many `Where` clauses you often have. Also consider the joins, grouping, and ordering.

Let's imagine that you have created the concept of a new data type, a sequence of generic data objects that we will call an `Enumerable`. It makes sense that the `Where` method would need to operate on an `Enumerable` (of data) and return another filtered `Enumerable`. In addition, the `Where` method will need to accept an argument allowing the developer to specify the exact logic used to filter data records from or into the `Enumerable`. This argument, that I will call the *predicate*, could be specified as a named method or a lambda expression.

■Caution The following three code examples in this section are hypothetical and will not compile.

Since the `Where` method requires an input `Enumerable` to filter, and the method is `Shared`, that input `Enumerable` must be specified as an argument to the `Where` method. It would appear something like the following:

```
Shared Function _
  Where(ByVal input As Enumerable, ByVal predicate As LambdaExpression) _
    As Enumerable Implements Enumerable.Where
...
End Function
```

Ignoring for the moment the semantics of a lambda expression, calling the Where method would look something like the following:

```
Dim enumerable As Enumerable = {"one", "two", "three"}
Dim filteredEnumerable As Enumerable = _
  Enumerable.Where(enumerable, lambdaExpression)
```

That doesn't look too ornery. But what happens when we need several Where clauses? Since the Enumerable that the Where method is operating on must be an argument to the method, the result is that chaining methods together requires embedding them inside each other. Three Where clauses suddenly change the code to the following:

```
Dim enumerable As Enumerable = {"one", "two", "three"}
Dim finalEnumerable As Enumerable = _
  Enumerable.Where(Enumerable.Where(Enumerable.Where(enumerable, lX1), lX2), lX3)
```

You have to read the statement from the inside out. That gets hard to read in a hurry. Can you imagine what a complex query would look like? If only there was a better way.

The Solution

A nice solution would be if you could call the Shared Where method on each Enumerable object itself, rather than on the class. Then it would no longer be necessary to pass each Enumerable into the Where method because the Enumerable object would have access to its own internal Enumerable. That would change the syntax of the query proposed previously to something more like this:

```
Dim enumerable As Enumerable = {"one", "two", "three"}
Dim finalEnumerable As Enumerable = enumerable.Where(lX1).Where(lX2).Where(lX3)
```

■**Caution** The previous code and the following code example are hypothetical and will not compile.

This could even be rewritten as the following:

```
Dim enumerable As Enumerable = {"one", "two", "three"}
Dim finalEnumerable As Enumerable = enumerable _
  .Where(lX1) _
  .Where(lX2) _
  .Where(lX3)
```

Wow, that's much easier to read. You can now read the statement from left to right, top to bottom. As you can see, this syntax is very easy to follow once you understand what it is doing. Because of this, you will often see LINQ queries written in this format in much of the LINQ documentation and in this book.

Ultimately, what you need is the ability to have a Shared method that you can call on a class instance. This is exactly what extension methods are and what they allow. They were added to .NET to provide a syntactically elegant way to call a Shared method without having to pass the method's first argument. This allows the extension method to be called as though it were a method of the first argument, which makes chaining extension method calls far more readable than if the first argument was passed. Extension methods assist LINQ by allowing the Standard Query Operators to be called on the IEnumerable(Of T) interface.

■**Note** Extension methods are methods that while Shared can be called on an instance (object) of a class rather than on the class itself.

Extension Method Declarations and Invocations

Adding the <System.Runtime.CompilerServices.Extension()> attribute to a method in a module will make that method an extension method. Unlike C#, you do not add Me (i.e., this) as the first parameter, VB.NET does this behind the scenes for you.

The extension method will appear as an instance method of any object with the same type as the extension method's first argument's data type. For example, if the extension method's first argument is of type String, the extension method will appear as a String instance method and can be called on any String object.

Also keep in mind that extension methods can only be declared in modules.

Here is an example containing a couple of extension methods:

```
Namespace Netsplore.Utilities
  Module StringConversions
    <System.Runtime.CompilerServices.Extension()> _
    Public Function ToDouble(ByVal s As String) As Double
      Return Double.Parse(s)
    End Function

    <System.Runtime.CompilerServices.Extension()> _
    Public Function ToBool(ByVal s As String) As Boolean
      Return Boolean.Parse(s)
    End Function
  End Module
End Namespace
```

■**Note** Because VB.NET requires extension methods to be defined in a module, the Shared keyword is unnecessary and not allowed in the extension method declaration.

To avoid conflicts with my project's root namespace, I have created another project for this module. Notice that the methods are defined at the module level and marked with the `<System.Runtime.CompilerServices.Extension()>` attribute. Because of these two things, `ToDouble` will be an extension method. Now, you can take advantage of those extension methods by calling the `Shared` methods on the object instances as shown in Listing 2-17.

Listing 2-17. *Calling an Extension Method*

```
Imports Netsplore.Utilities

Dim pi As Double = "3.1415926535".ToDouble()
Console.WriteLine(pi)
```

■**Note** Don't forget that I defined my `StringConversions` module and accompanying extension methods in a new project. If you put your module in your existing project, you will need to factor your project's root namespace into the `Imports` statement in Listing 2-17 like `Imports YourProjectRootNamesapce.Netsplore.Utilities`.

This produces the following results:

```
3.1415926535
```

It is important that you specify the `Imports` directive for the `Netsplore.Utilities` namespace (and don't forget to account for the project's root namespace). Otherwise, the compiler will not find the extension methods, and you will get compiler errors such as the following:

```
'ToDouble' is not a member of 'String'
```

Extension Method Precedence

Normal object instance methods take precedence over extension methods when their signature matches the calling signature.

Extension methods seem like a really useful concept, especially when you want to be able to extend a class you cannot, such as a sealed class or one for which you do not have source code. The previous extension method examples all effectively add methods to the `String` class. Without extension methods, you couldn't do that because the `String` class is sealed.

Partial Methods

Another new addition to VB.NET 2008, *partial methods*, adds a lightweight event-handling mechanism to VB.NET. Forget the conclusions you are more than likely drawing about partial methods based on their name. About the only thing partial methods have in common with partial classes is that a partial method can only exist in a partial class. In fact, that is rule one for partial methods.

Before I get to all of the rules concerning partial methods, let me tell you what they are. Partial methods are methods where the declaration of the method is specified in the declaration of a partial class, but an implementation for the method is not provided in that same declaration of the partial class. In fact, there may not be *any* implementation for the method in *any* declaration of that same partial class. And if there is no implementation of the method in any other declaration for the same partial class, no IL code is emitted by the compiler for the declaration of the method, the call to the method, or the evaluation of the arguments passed to the method. It's as if the method never existed.

Some people do not like the term "partial method," because it is somewhat of a misnomer due to their behavior when compared to that of a partial class. Perhaps the method modifier should have been Ghost instead of Partial.

A Partial Method Example

Let's take a look at a partial class containing the definition of a partial method in the following class file named MyWidget.vb:

The MyWidget Class File

```
Partial Public Class MyWidget
  Partial Private Sub MyWidgetStart(ByVal count As Integer)
  End Sub

  Partial Private Sub MyWidgetEnd(ByVal count As Integer)
  End Sub

  Public refCount As Integer

  Public Property ReferenceCount() As Integer
    Get
      refCount += 1
      Return refCount
    End Get
    Set(ByVal value As Integer)
      refCount = value
    End Set
  End Property

  Public Sub New()
    ReferenceCount = 0
    MyWidgetStart(ReferenceCount)
    Console.WriteLine("In the constructor of MyWidget.")
    MyWidgetEnd(ReferenceCount)
    Console.WriteLine("refCount = " & refCount)
  End Sub
End Class
```

In the `MyWidget` class declaration, I have a partial class named `MyWidget`. The first four lines of code are partial method declarations. I have declared two partial subroutines named `MyWidgetStart` and `MyWidgetEnd` that each accept an `Integer` input parameter. It is another rule that partial methods must be declared as subroutines using the `Sub` keyword, *not* as functions using the `Function` keyword.

Next in the `MyWidget` class is a member variable named `refCount` that I made `Public`. This class member is the backing data storage for the forthcoming `ReferenceCount` property. It is highly unusual for the backing data storage for a property to be `Public` and ill-advised under normal circumstances. Normally, you would want the property's backing storage member to be `Private` and only accessible through the `Public` property, but here, I have made it `Public`. This is intentional for instructional purposes. I need to demonstrate that the arguments for an unimplemented partial method do not even get evaluated. For this, I have created the `ReferenceCount` property, which will increment the backing data storage class member, `refCount`, just upon referencing it. However, at the end of the examples, I will want to access that backing data storage for the property to display its current value. To do so without using the `Public ReferenceCount` property, and thereby changing its value yet again, I must be able to access it directly. Therefore, I have made the backing data storage member `Public`.

The next piece of code in the `MyWidget` class is the constructor. As you can see, I initialize the `ReferenceCount` to 0. I then call the `MyWidgetStart` subroutine, passing it the `ReferenceCount` property, thereby incrementing it. Next, I write a message to the console. Then I call the `MyWidgetEnd` subroutine, again passing it the `ReferenceCount` property which increments it. Finally, I output the value of `refCount`, the property's backing data storage, to the console. Please realize that by passing the `ReferenceCount` property to the two partial methods, the property's `Get` accessor is called, and the backing data storage member is incremented. I am doing this to prove that if no implementation of a partial method exists, its arguments are not even evaluated.

In Listing 2-18 I instantiate a `MyWidget` object.

Listing 2-18. *Instantiating a MyWidget*

```
Dim myWidget As New MyWidget()
```

Let's take a look at the output of this example by pressing Ctrl+F5:

```
In the constructor of MyWidget.
refCount = 0
```

As you can see, even after the `MyWidget` constructor has referenced the `ReferenceCount` property twice, when it displays the value of `refCount` at the end of the constructor, it is still 0. This is because the code for the evaluation of the arguments to the unimplemented partial methods is never emitted by the compiler. No IL code was emitted for either of those two partial method calls.

Now, let's add an implementation for the two partial methods.

Another Declaration for MyWidget but Containing Implementations for the Partial Methods

```
Partial Public Class MyWidget
  Private Sub MyWidgetStart(ByVal count As Integer)
    Console.WriteLine("In MyWidgetStart(count is {0})", count)
  End Sub

  Private Sub MyWidgetEnd(ByVal count As Integer)
    Console.WriteLine("In MyWidgetEnd(count is {0})", count)
  End Sub
End Class
```

There is nothing complicated here. I have just added another declaration for the partial MyWidget class. However, please notice that I have omitted the Partial keyword from the partial method declarations. This is necessary for the implementation of partial methods. Now that I have added this declaration, run Listing 2-18 again, and look at the results:

```
In MyWidgetStart(count is 1)
In the constructor of MyWidget.
In MyWidgetEnd(count is 2)
refCount = 2
```

As you can see, not only are the partial method implementations getting called, the arguments passed are evaluated as well. You can see this because of the value of the refCount variable at the end of the output.

What Is the Point of Partial Methods?

So you may be wondering, "What is the point?" Others have said, "This is similar to using inheritance and virtual methods. Why corrupt the language with something similar?" Partial methods are more efficient if you plan on allowing many potentially unimplemented hooks in the code. They allow code to be written with the intention of someone else extending it via the partial class paradigm but without the degradation in performance if they choose not to.

The case in point for which partial methods were probably added is the code generated for LINQ to SQL entity classes by the entity class generator tools. To make the generated entity classes more usable, partial methods have been added to them. For example, each mapped property of a generated entity class has a partial method that is called before the property is changed and another partial method that is called after the property is changed. This allows you to add another module declaring the same entity class, implement these partial methods, and be notified every time a property is about to be changed and after it is changed. How cool is that? And if you don't do it, the code is no bigger and no slower. Who wouldn't want that? If you implement code generators, you should find partial methods quite an asset. You now have a manner to allow users of your generated code to receive method calls at no expense should they choose not to.

The Rules

It has been all fun and games up to here, but unfortunately, there are some rules that apply to partial methods. Here is a list:

- Partial methods must only be defined and implemented in partial classes.

- Partial methods must specify the `Partial` modifier in the class definition in which the partial methods are defined but must *not* specify the `Partial` modifier in the class definition in which they are implemented.

- Partial methods must be private, and the `Private` access modifier must be specified.

- Partial methods must be declared as subroutines using the `Sub` keyword and may not be declared as functions using the `Function` keyword.

- Partial methods may be unimplemented.

- Partial methods may be `Shared`.

- Partial methods may have arguments.

These rules are not too bad. For what we gain in terms of flexibility in the generated entity classes plus what we can do with them ourselves, I think VB.NET has gained a nice feature.

One other thing to keep in mind about partial methods is that the partial class definition containing the partial method implementations must be compiled into the same assembly as the partial class definition containing the partial method definitions. This means you can't create an assembly containing a partial class having partial methods and add it as a reference to another project and implement those partial methods. The partial method implementations must be compiled into the same assembly as their definitions.

Query Expressions

One of the conveniences that the VB.NET language provides is the For Each statement. When you use For Each, the compiler translates it into a loop with calls to methods such as GetEnumerator and MoveNext. The simplicity the For Each statement provides for enumerating through arrays and collections has made it very popular and often used.

One of the features of LINQ that seems to attract developers is the SQL-like syntax available for LINQ queries. The first few LINQ examples in the first chapter of this book use this syntax. This syntax is provided via the new VB.NET 2008 language enhancement known as *query expressions*. Query expressions allow LINQ queries to be expressed in nearly SQL form, with just a few minor deviations.

To perform a LINQ query, it is not required to use query expressions. The alternative is to use standard VB.NET dot notation, calling methods on objects and classes. In many cases, I find using the standard dot notation favorable for instructional purposes, because I feel it is more demonstrative of what is actually happening and when. There is no compiler translating what I write into the standard dot notation equivalent. Therefore, many examples in this book do not use query expression syntax and instead opt for the standard dot notation syntax. However, there is no disputing the allure of query expression syntax. The familiarity it provides in formulating your first queries can be very enticing indeed.

To get an idea of what the two different syntaxes look like, Listing 2-19 shows a query using the standard dot notation syntax.

Listing 2-19. *A Query Using the Standard Dot Notation Syntax*

```
Dim presidents() As String = _
{ _
  "Adams", "Arthur", "Buchanan", "Bush", "Carter", "Cleveland", _
  "Clinton", "Coolidge", "Eisenhower", "Fillmore", "Ford", "Garfield", _
  "Grant", "Harding", "Harrison", "Hayes", "Hoover", "Jackson", _
  "Jefferson", "Johnson", "Kennedy", "Lincoln", "Madison", "McKinley", _
  "Monroe", "Nixon", "Pierce", "Polk", "Reagan", "Roosevelt", "Taft", _
  "Taylor", "Truman", "Tyler", "Van Buren", "Washington", "Wilson" _
}

Dim sequence As IEnumerable(Of String) = _
  presidents _
    .Where(Function(n) n.Length < 6) _
    .Select(Function(n) n)

For Each name As String In sequence
  Console.WriteLine("{0}", name)
Next name
```

Listing 2-20 is the equivalent query using the query expression syntax.

Listing 2-20. *The Equivalent Query Using the Query Expression Syntax*

```
Dim presidents() As String = _
{ _
  "Adams", "Arthur", "Buchanan", "Bush", "Carter", "Cleveland", _
  "Clinton", "Coolidge", "Eisenhower", "Fillmore", "Ford", "Garfield", _
  "Grant", "Harding", "Harrison", "Hayes", "Hoover", "Jackson", _
  "Jefferson", "Johnson", "Kennedy", "Lincoln", "Madison", "McKinley", _
  "Monroe", "Nixon", "Pierce", "Polk", "Reagan", "Roosevelt", "Taft", _
  "Taylor", "Truman", "Tyler", "Van Buren", "Washington", "Wilson" _
}

Dim sequence As IEnumerable(Of String) = _
  From n In presidents _
  Where n.Length < 6 _
  Select n

For Each name As String In sequence
  Console.WriteLine("{0}", name)
Next name
```

The first thing you may notice about the query expression example is that unlike SQL, the From statement precedes the Select statement. One of the compelling reasons for this change is to narrow the scope for IntelliSense. Without this inversion of the statements, if in the Visual Studio 2008 text editor you typed **Select** followed by a space, IntelliSense will have no idea what variables to display in its drop-down list. The scope of possible variables at this point is not restricted in any way. By specifying where the data is coming from first, IntelliSense has the scope of what variables to offer you for selection. Both of these examples provide the same results:

```
Adams
Bush
Ford
Grant
Hayes
Nixon
Polk
Taft
Tyler
```

It is important to note that the query expression syntax only supports the most common query operators: Where, Select, SelectMany, Join, GroupJoin, GroupBy, OrderBy, ThenBy, OrderByDescending, ThenByDescending, Aggregate, Distinct, Skip, SkipWhile, Take, and TakeWhile.

Query Expression Grammar

Query expressions consist of several different types of clauses. These clauses must adhere to the query expression grammar. At compile-time, query expressions go through a translation process where each clause is attempted to be translated to VB.NET code, typically calling one of the supported Standard Query Operators. If every clause in the query expression is supported by query expression syntax and every clause's syntax is correct, the translation will be successful.

The following query expression grammar diagram comes from the Microsoft Visual Basic 9.0 language specification.

```
QueryExpression ::=
  FromOrAggregateQueryOperator   |
  QueryExpression QueryOperator

FromOrAggregateQueryOperator ::=   FromQueryOperator   |   AggregateQueryOperator

QueryOperator ::=
  FromQueryOperator   |
  AggregateQueryOperator   |
  SelectQueryOperator   |
```

```
      DistinctQueryOperator  |
      WhereQueryOperator  |
      OrderByQueryOperator  |
      PartitionQueryOperator  |
      LetQueryOperator  |
      GroupByQueryOperator  |
      JoinQueryOperator  |
      GroupJoinQueryOperator

CollectionRangeVariableDeclarationList ::=
    CollectionRangeVariableDeclaration  |
    CollectionRangeVariableDeclarationList  ,  CollectionRangeVariableDeclaration

CollectionRangeVariableDeclaration ::=
    Identifier [ As TypeName ] In  Expression

ExpressionRangeVariableDeclarationList ::=
    ExpressionRangeVariableDeclaration  |
    ExpressionRangeVariableDeclarationList  ,   ExpressionRangeVariableDeclaration

ExpressionRangeVariableDeclaration ::=
    Identifier [ As  TypeName ] =  Expression

FromQueryOperator ::=
    From  CollectionRangeVariableDeclarationList

JoinQueryOperator ::=
    Join  CollectionRangeVariableDeclaration [ JoinQueryOperator ]
    On  JoinConditionList

JoinConditionList ::=
    JoinCondition |
    JoinConditionList  And  JoinCondition

JoinCondition ::= Expression  Equals  Expression

LetQueryOperator ::=
    Let  ExpressionRangeVariableDeclarationList

SelectQueryOperator ::= Select  ExpressionRangeVariableDeclarationList
```

```
DistinctQueryOperator ::= Distinct

WhereQueryOperator ::= Where  BooleanExpression

PartitionQueryOperator ::=
  Take  Expression  |
  Take While  BooleanExpression  |
  Skip  Expression  |
  Skip While  BooleanExpression

OrderByQueryOperator ::= Order  By  OrderExpressionList

OrderExpressionList ::=
  OrderExpression  |
  OrderExpressionList  ,  OrderExpression

OrderExpression ::= Expression  [  Ordering  ]

Ordering ::= Ascending  |  Descending

GroupByQueryOperator ::=
  Group  ExpressionRangeVariableDeclarationList
  By  ExpressionRangeVariableDeclarationList
  Into  ExpressionRangeVariableDeclarationList

AggregateQueryOperator ::=
  Aggregate  CollectionRangeVariableDeclaration  [  QueryOperator+  ]
  Into  ExpressionRangeVariableDeclarationList

GroupJoinQueryOperator ::=
  Group  JoinQueryOperator
  Into  ExpressionRangeVariableDeclarationList
```

Query Expression Translation

Now, assuming you have created a syntactically correct query expression, the next issue becomes how the compiler translates the query expression into VB.NET code. It must translate your query expression into standard VB.NET dot notation. But how does it do this?

To translate a query expression, the compiler is looking for code patterns (the supported clauses) in the query expression that need to be translated. The compiler will translate each clause in the order it occurs in the query expression.

Translation Steps

Next, I discuss the translation steps. In doing so, I use the variable letters shown in Table 2-1 to represent specific portions of the query.

Table 2-1. *Translation Step Variables*

Variable	Description	Example
c	A **c**ompiler-generated temporary variable	N/A
e	An **e**numerator variable	From **e** In customers
f	Selected **f**ield element or new anonymous type	From e In customers Select **f**
g	A **g**rouped element	From e In s Group **g** By k
k	Grouped or joined **k**ey element	From e In s Group g By **k**
l	A variable introduced by **l**et	From e In s Let **l** = v
o	An **o**rdering element	From e In s Order By **o**
s	Input **s**equence	From e In **s**
v	A **v**alue assigned to a **l**et variable	From e In s Let l = **v**
w	A **w**here clause	From e In s Where **w**

Allow me to provide a word of warning. The soon-to-be-described translation steps are quite complicated. Do not allow this to discourage you. You no more need to fully understand the translation steps to write LINQ queries than you need to know how the compiler translates the For Each statement to use it. They are here to provide additional translation information should you need it, which should be rarely, if ever.

The translation steps are documented as code pattern > translation. Since query expressions must begin with either the From clause or the Aggregate clause, I will begin with them. Then, I will address the remaining clauses in alphabetical order.

From Clauses

If the query expression contains a single From clause, the following translation is made:

```
From e In s              > s
```

Here is an example:

```
From c In Customers
```

It is translated to:

```
Customers
```

Multiple From Clauses

If the query expression contains two From clauses followed by a Select clause, the following translation is made:

```
From e₁ In s₁ _                > s₁.SelectMany( _
From e₂ In s₂ _                      Function(e₁) s₂.Select( _
Select f                                  Function(e₂) New With {f}))
```

Here is an example:

```
From c In Customers _
From o In Orders _
Select c.Name, o.OrderID, o.OrderDate
```

It is translated to:

```
Customers.SelectMany( _
          Function(c) Orders.Select( _
             Function(o) New With {c.Name, o.OrderID, o.OrderDate}))
```

If the query expression contains two From clauses followed by something other than a Select clause, the following translation is made:

```
From e₁ In s₁ _                > s₁.SelectMany( _
From e₂ In s₂ _                      Function(e₁) s₂, _
...                                   Function(e₁, e₂) New With {e₁, e₂})...
```

Here is an example:

```
From c In Customers _
From o In Orders _
Order By o.OrderDate Descending _
Select c.Name, o.OrderID, o.OrderDate
```

It is translated to:

```
Customers.SelectMany( _
          Function(c) Orders, _
          Function(c, O) New With {c, o}) _
       .OrderByDescending(Function(co) co.o.OrderDate) _
       .Select(Function(co) New With {co.c.Name, co.o.OrderID, co.o.OrderDate})
```

Aggregate Clauses

If the query expression contains an Aggregate clause, the following translation is made:

```
Aggregate e In s _             > s.AnotherOperator( _
AnotherOperator expr _               Function(e) expr).AggregateOp()
Into AggregateOp
```

Here is an example:

```
Aggregate c In Customers _
Where c.Name.Length > 5 _
Into Count()
```

It is translated to:

```
Customers.Where(Function(c) c.Name.Length > 5).Count()
```

Distinct Clauses

If the query expression contains a Distinct clause, the following translation is made:

```
From e In s _                  > s.Distinct()
Distinct
```

Here is an example:

```
From o In Orders _
Select o.OrderDate _
Distinct
```

It is translated to:

```
Orders.Select(Function(o) New With {o.OrderDate}).Distinct()
```

Group By Clauses

If the query expression contains a Group By clause, and the grouped element g is the same identifier as the sequence enumerator e, the following translation is made:

```
From e In s _                  > s.GroupBy(Function(e) k)
Group g By k _
Into Group₁
```

where Group$_1$ is a keyword representing the logical group. Here is an example:

```
From c In Customers _
Group c By c.Country _
Into Group
```

It is translated to:

```
Customers.GroupBy(Function(c) c.Country)
```

If the grouped element g is *not* the same identifier as the sequence enumerator e, meaning you are grouping something other than the entire element stored in the sequence, the following translation takes place:

```
From e in s _                  > s.GroupBy(Function(e) k, Function(e) g)
Group g By k _
Into Group₁
```

Here is an example:

```
From c In Customers _
Group c.Country, c.Name By c.Country _
Into Group
```

It is translated to:

```
Customers.GroupBy(Function(c) c.Country, _
                  Function(c) New With {c.Country, c.Name})
```

You may also specify an aggregate operator instead of the $Group_1$ keyword like this:

```
From e in s _               > s.GroupBy(Function(e) k, _
Group g By k _                 Function(e) g, _
Into AggregateOp(OpArg)        Function(k, group) New With _
                                  {k,.AggregateOp = group.AggregateOp(OpArg)})
```

Here is an example:

```
From c In Customers _
Group c.Country, c.Name By c.Country _
Into Count()
```

It is translated to:

```
Customers.GroupBy(Function(c) c.Country, _
                  Function(c) New With {c.Country, c.Name}, _
                  Function(k, group) New With {k, .Count = group.Count()})
```

Group Join Clauses

If the query expression contains a Group Join clause, the following translation is made:

```
From e₁ In s₁ _             > s₁.GroupJoin(s₂, _
Group Join e₂ In s₂ _          Function(e₁) k_e₁, _
On k_e1 Equals k_e2 _          Function(e₂) k_e₂, _
Into Group₁                    Function(k_e₁, group) _
                                  New With {k_e₁, group})
```

where $Group_1$ is a keyword representing the logical group. Here is an example:

```
From c In Customers _
Group Join o In Orders _
On c.CustomerID Equals o.CustomerID _
Into Group
```

It is translated to:

```
Customers.GroupJoin(Orders, _
                    Function(c) c.CustomerID, _
                    Function(o) o.CustomerID, _
                    Function(c, group) New With {c.CustomerID, group})
```

Join Clauses

If the query expression contains a Join clause not being followed immediately by a Select clause, the following translation is made:

```
From e₁ In s₁ _          > s₁.Join(s₂, _
Join e₂ In s₂ _                   Function(e₁) k_{e1}, _
On k_{e1} Equals K_{e2}           Function(e₂) k_{e2}, _
                                  Function(e₁, e₂) New With {e₁, e₂})
```

Here is an example:

```
From c In Customers _
Join o In Orders _
On c.CustomerID Equals o.CustomerID
```

It is translated to:

```
Customers.Join(Orders, _
          Function(c) c.CustomerID, _
          Function(o) o.CustomerID, _
          Function(c, 0) New With {c, o})
```

If the query expression contains a Join clause followed immediately by a Select clause, the following translation is made:

```
From e₁ In s₁ _          > s₁.Join(s₂, _
Join e₂ In s₂ _                   Function(e₁) k_{e1}, _
On k_{e1} Equals K_{e2} _         Function(e₂) k_{e2}, _
Select f                          Function(e₁, e₂) New With {f})
```

Here is an example:

```
From c In Customers _
Join o In Orders _
On c.CustomerID Equals o.CustomerID _
Select c.Name, o.OrderDate, o.Total
```

It is translated to:

```
Customers.Join(Orders,
          Function(c) c.CustomerID,
          Function(o) o.CustomerID,
          Function(c, o) New With {c.Name, o.OrderDate, o.Total})
```

Let Clauses

If the query expression contains a From clause followed immediately by a Let clause, the following translation is made:

```
From e In s _            > s.Select(Function(e) New With {e, .l = v})
Let l = v
```

Here is an example:

```
From c In Customers _
Let cityStateZip = c.City & ", " & c.State & " " & c.Zip _
Select c.Name, cityStateZip
```

It is translated to:

```
Customers.Select(Function(c) New With { _
                c, .cityStateZip = c.City & ", " & c.State & " " & c.Zip}) _
        .Select(Function(t) New With {t.c.Name, t.cityStateZip})
```

Orderby Clauses

If the query expression contains an Order By clause and the direction of the ordering is Ascending, the following translation is made:

```
From e In s _                    > s.OrderBy(Function(e) o₁).ThenBy(Function(e) o₂)
Order By o₁, o₂
```

Here is an example:

```
From c In Customers _
Order By c.Country, c.Name _
Select c.Country, c.Name
```

It is translated to:

```
Customers.OrderBy(Function(c) c.Country) _
        .ThenBy(Function(c) c.Name) _
        .Select(Function(c) New With {c.Country, c.Name})
```

If the direction of any of the orderings is Descending, the translations will be to the OrderByDescending or ThenByDescending operators. Here is the same example as the previous, except this time the names are requested in Descending order:

```
From c In Customers _
Order By c.Country, c.Name Descending _
Select c.Country, c.Name
```

It is translated to:

```
Customers.OrderBy(Function(c) c.Country) _
        .ThenByDescending(Function(c) c.Name) _
        .Select(Function(c) New With {c.Country, c.Name})
```

Select Clauses

In the query expression, if the selected element f is the same identifier as the sequence enumerator variable e, meaning you are selecting the entire element that is stored in the sequence, the following translation is made:

```
From e In s _                  > s
Select f
```

Here is an example:

```
From c In Customers _
Select c
```

It is translated to:

```
Customers
```

If the selected element f is not the same identifier as the sequence enumerator variable e, meaning you are selecting something other than the entire element stored in the sequence such as a member of the element or an anonymous type constructed of several members of the element, the following translation is made:

```
From e In s _                  > s.Select(Function(e) f)
Select f
```

Here is an example:

```
From c In Customers _
Select c.Name
```

It is translated to:

```
Customers.Select(Function(c) c.Name)
```

Skip Clauses

If the query expression contains a Skip clause, the following translation is made:

```
From e In s _                  > s.Skip(N)
Skip N
```

Here is an example:

```
From c In Customers _
Skip 12
```

It is translated to:

```
Customers.Skip(12)
```

Skip While Clauses

If the query expression contains a Skip While clause, the following translation is made:

```
From e In s _                  > s.SkipWhile(BooleanExpression)
SkipWhile BooleanExpression
```

Here is an example:

```
From c In Customers _
SkipWhile c.Country = "USA"
```

It is translated to:

```
Customers.SkipWhile(Function(c) c.Country = "USA")
```

Take Clauses

If the query expression contains a Take clause, the following translation is made:

```
From e In s _                    > s.Take(N)
Take N
```

Here is an example:

```
From c In Customers _
Take 12
```

It is translated to:

```
Customers.Take(12)
```

Take While Clauses

If the query expression contains a Take While clause, the following translation is made:

```
From e In s _                    > s.TakeWhile(BooleanExpression)
TakeWhile BooleanExpression
```

Here is an example:

```
From c In Customers _
TakeWhile c.Country = "USA"
```

It is translated to:

```
Customers.TakeWhile(Function(c) c.Country = "USA")
```

Where Clauses

If the query expression contains a From clause followed immediately by a Where clause, the following translation is made:

```
From e In s _                > s.Where(Function(e) w)
Where w
```

Here is an example:

```
From c In Customers _
Where c.Country = "USA"
```

It is translated to:

```
Customers.Where(Function(c) c.Country = "USA")
```

Nullable Value Types

One of the challenges until now with the VB.NET language has been determining the difference between 0 (zero, or a value type's default value) and Nothing for value types. Let's take a look at Listing 2-21.

Listing 2-21. *Returning Nothing To an Integer*

```
Dim age As Integer = Nothing
Console.WriteLine("You are {0}.", age)
```

If we run that code, we get the following results:

```
You are 0.
```

Now, we know age isn't really 0, and there are times when we need to know the difference between 0 and Nothing. Had we written a LINQ query and it returned Nothing, we may want to know that and not mistakenly think that it returned 0.

To solve this problem, VB.NET 2008 has given us nullable value types. To declare a nullable value type, simply append the nullable type modifier ? to either the variable name or the value type it is declared as, *but not both*. Either of these two declarations is fine:

```
Dim age As Integer? = Nothing
Dim age? As Integer = Nothing
```

But the following declaration is not:

```
Dim age? As Integer? = Nothing
```

It causes the following compiler error.

```
Nullable modifier cannot be specified on both a variable and its type.
```

So in Listing 2-22, I will simply change the data type of age to a nullable Integer, Integer?, and the results will be different. I will also add code to detect if the value is Nothing and react accordingly.

Listing 2-22. *Returning Nothing To an Integer?*

```
Dim age As Integer? = Nothing
If (age.HasValue) Then
  Console.WriteLine("You are {0}.", age)
Else
  Console.WriteLine("There is no value for age.")
End If
```

Please notice that I used the nullable type's HasValue property to determine if the variable is set to Nothing. Listing 2-22 produces the following results:

```
There is no value for age.
```

Using nullable value types, we can now distinguish between 0 and Nothing.

XML Enhancements

You may already be aware that VB.NET 2008 received significant language enhancements for XML. You may also be wondering when I was going to cover them. Well, I have been saving the best—the XML enhancements—for last.

The LINQ to XML API that I cover later in this book already makes XML a pleasure to work with, but these VB-specific enhancements make it even better. Best of all, with Visual Studio 2008, these XML enhancements are exclusive to VB.NET. So your C# brethren can only look and be envious.

The XML enhancements for VB.NET 2008 follow:

- XML literals

- XML embedded expressions

- XML axis properties

- XML namespace imports

Please be aware that LINQ to XML includes an entirely new object model for XML that I will discuss in great detail in the LINQ to XML portion of this book. That new XML object model includes types XDocument and XElement as well as several others. While I will not explain them in this chapter because I think their meaning is fairly well understood from their names, I will be discussing them in this chapter. If you feel you need more understanding of each new class type, please consult Chapter 7. All of the VB.NET 2008 XML enhancements work in conjunction with the LINQ to XML API, so many of these enhancements covered in this section will make even more sense after you have read the LINQ to XML portion of this book.

XML Literals

One of VB.NET 2008's most touted new features is XML literals. XML literals allow XML documents and fragments to be specified directly in VB.NET source code, like the following.

A Sample XML Literal

```
Dim bookParticipants = _
  <BookParticipants>
    <BookParticipant type="Author">
      <FirstName>Joe</FirstName>
      <LastName>Rattz</LastName>
    </BookParticipant>
    <BookParticipant type="Editor">
      <FirstName>Ewan</FirstName>
      <LastName>Buckingham</LastName>
    </BookParticipant>
  </BookParticipants>
```

Please notice that I did *not* append the line-continuation character to the end of each line of the XML literal. The XML document or fragment is written directly in the code, thereby improving readability. The compiler will translate the XML literal into a constructor call to the appropriate System.Xml.Linq object type.

■**Note** XML literals must not have a line continuation character at the end of each line.

Creating an XElement with an XML Literal

Because the <?xml … ?> document prolog element was not provided in the sample XML literal previously, bookParticipants will be translated to type XElement. You can see this in Listing 2-23.

Listing 2-23. *Creating an XElement with an XML Literal*

```
Dim bookParticipants = _
  <BookParticipants>
    <BookParticipant type="Author">
      <FirstName>Joe</FirstName>
      <LastName>Rattz</LastName>
    </BookParticipant>
    <BookParticipant type="Editor">
      <FirstName>Ewan</FirstName>
      <LastName>Buckingham</LastName>
    </BookParticipant>
  </BookParticipants>
```

```
Console.WriteLine(bookParticipants.GetType())
```

Notice that I did not specify the <?xml … ?> document prolog element. Let's take a look at the results of Listing 2-23.

```
System.Xml.Linq.XElement
```

As you can see, the XML literal was indeed translated into an XElement.

Creating an XDocument with an XML Literal

To create an XDocument using an XML literal, simply add the <?xml … ?> document prolog element. Had the XML literal in Listing 2-23 included the <?xml … ?> document prolog element, the XML literal would have been translated to an XDocument and bookParticipants would be of type XDocument. You can see this in Listing 2-24.

Listing 2-24. *Creating an XDocument with an XML Literal*

```
Dim bookParticipants = _
  <?xml version="1.0" encoding="utf-8" standalone="yes"?>
  <BookParticipants>
    <BookParticipant type="Author">
      <FirstName>Joe</FirstName>
      <LastName>Rattz</LastName>
    </BookParticipant>
    <BookParticipant type="Editor">
      <FirstName>Ewan</FirstName>
      <LastName>Buckingham</LastName>
    </BookParticipant>
  </BookParticipants>

Console.WriteLine(bookParticipants.GetType())
```

Now that the <?xml … ?> document prolog element has been included, the XML literal will be translated to a type of XDocument, as demonstrated in the results.

```
System.Xml.Linq.XDocument
```

Creating Other XML Types with XML Literals

Of course, you can create many of the other LINQ to XML data types using XML literals. Listing 2-25 provides a simple example of this.

Listing 2-25. *Creating Other XML Types with XML Literals*

```
Dim pi = _
  <?BookCataloger out-of-print?>
Console.WriteLine("pi is type {0}.", pi.GetType())

Dim comment = _
  <!--This person is retired.-->
Console.WriteLine("comment is type {0}.", comment.GetType())
```

Let's take a look at the results of Listing 2-25.

```
pi is type System.Xml.Linq.XProcessingInstruction.
comment is type System.Xml.Linq.XComment.
```

As I previously mentioned, LINQ to XML makes working with XML a pleasure, but these VB.NET XML enhancements make it almost fun!

XML Embedded Expressions

In many of the XML examples in this book, and every XML example so far in this section, I use static XML documents or fragments to demonstrate the topic at hand. However, in your real code, you will rarely have a need to create static XML data. Instead, you will more than likely need to be able to create dynamic XML where nodes, elements, and values are created from data sources like variables, collections, and databases. What we need are *embedded expressions*, and VB.NET 2008 has got them!

Embedded expressions allow us to generate a dynamic XML document or fragment where its nodes are created at runtime and its values read from other variable's values or even from a LINQ query. XML literals without embedded expressions would be an incomplete feature because writing static XML in our code is not very useful in real-world scenarios. Using the embedded expression operator, <%= %>, you can specify either a variable or a LINQ query, and when your code is executed, the XML document will be generated substituting embedded expressions with their results. In Listing 2-26, you can see the first example using embedded expressions.

Listing 2-26. *Dynamically Generating XML Content Using Embedded Expressions*

```
Dim firstName As String = "Fabio"
Dim lastName As String = "Ferracchiati"
Dim type As String = "Technical Reviewer"

Dim bookParticipants = _
  <BookParticipants>
    <BookParticipant type=<%= type %>>
      <FirstName><%= firstName %></FirstName>
      <LastName><%= lastName %></LastName>
    </BookParticipant>
  </BookParticipants>

Console.WriteLine(bookParticipants)
```

Please notice that I have declared and initialized the firstName, lastName, and type variables before using them in the XML literal. In this example, I assigned static values to them, but they could be assigned using any technique such as calling a web service, querying a database, and so on. Also notice that for the type attribute's value, I didn't enclose the embedded expression within double quotes. When you run the code in Listing 2-26, the output will contain an XML document with the embedded expressions substituted with their results. Let's take a look at the results of Listing 2-26.

```
<BookParticipants>
  <BookParticipant type="Technical Reviewer">
    <FirstName>Fabio</FirstName>
    <LastName>Ferracchiati</LastName>
  </BookParticipant>
</BookParticipants>
```

This is interesting but far from truly useful to dynamically generate XML. We need to be able to generate XML from a data source such as a collection or database. So, in Listing 2-27, I will dynamically generate XML by embedding a LINQ query on the most LINQ-like of collections, the IEnumerable(Of T) interface of the generic List class. I will cover IEnumerable(Of T) in more detail in the next chapter. For this example, I will also use the Address class used in other examples earlier in this chapter. Let's examine the code in Listing 2-27.

Listing 2-27. *Embedded Expressions with LINQ Query*

```
Dim addresses As List(Of Address) = New List(Of Address)
Dim address As Address

address = New Address With { _
  .address = "1600 Pennsylvania Avenue NW", _
  .city = "Washington", _
  .state = "DC", _
  .postalCode = "20500"}
addresses.Add(address)

address = New Address With { _
  .address = "1 Grand Avenue", _
  .city = "Mackinac Island", _
  .state = "MI", _
  .postalCode = "49757"}
addresses.Add(address)

address = New Address With { _
  .address = "1 Approach Road", _
  .city = "Asheville", _
  .state = "NC", _
  .postalCode = "28803"}
addresses.Add(address)

Dim famousAddresses = _
  <FamousAddresses>
    <%= From a In addresses _
      Where a.postalCode.StartsWith("2") _
      Select _
      <FamousAddress>
        <Address><%= a.address %></Address>
        <City><%= a.city %></City>
        <State><%= a.state %></State>
        <PostalCode><%= a.postalCode %></PostalCode>
      </FamousAddress> %>
  </FamousAddresses>

Console.WriteLine(famousAddresses)
```

■**Note** Listing 2-27 requires that the `System.Collections.Generic` namespace be imported into your project either explicitly or by being selected on the References tab of your project's Properties.

This example starts out simple enough. I instantiate a generic `List(Of Address)` and three `Address` objects and add them to the `List`. Notice that I am taking advantage of the new object initialization feature here when creating my `Address` objects. I am merely creating a data source that I can query with LINQ. Once I have the `List`, I create an XML literal, and this is where all the magic happens.

The XML literal in this example is a bit more complex than it may first appear. Please allow me to explain what is happening in this XML literal. I start with an XML literal beginning with the `FamousAddresses` node. Since XML literals shouldn't use line-continuation characters, there isn't one at the end of that line. Notice that the content of the `FamousAddresses` node is not XML but is an embedded expression. Therefore, the code within that embedded expression will need line-continuation characters if the code exceeds a single line. In this case, the embedded expression contains a LINQ query using query expression syntax. Since that query is longer than a single line, it requires line-continuation characters, until it gets to the XML literal embedded within it, which again should not have line-continuation characters. That XML literal embedded within the LINQ query begins with the `FamousAddress` node. Then, within that XML literal, there are four embedded expressions, one for each member of the `Address` class, so that a node is produced in the XML.

To sum up, in Listing 2-27 I have an XML literal containing a single embedded expression consisting of a LINQ query that returns an XML literal that contains four embedded expressions. Wow, that's a lot going on! I feel so powerful, don't you? Let's take a look at the results of Listing 2-27.

```
<FamousAddresses>
  <FamousAddress>
    <Address>1600 Pennsylvania Avenue NW</Address>
    <City>Washington</City>
    <State>DC</State>
    <PostalCode>20500</PostalCode>
  </FamousAddress>
  <FamousAddress>
    <Address>1 Approach Road</Address>
    <City>Asheville</City>
    <State>NC</State>
    <PostalCode>28803</PostalCode>
  </FamousAddress>
</FamousAddresses>
```

As you can see, for every element in my `List` that matched the `Where` clause of my query expression, I got a `FamousAddress` node with all the relevant data. How cool is that? Now, you can see what all the fuss is about with VB.NET 2008 and the XML enhancements. But wait, there's more!

XML Axis Properties

So far, you have seen how to build XML documents using XML literals and embedded expressions but have not seen how to interact with XML. We could use the LINQ to XML API, and I will cover this quite thoroughly in the LINQ to XML portion of this book. However, VB.NET 2008 also provides a few *axis properties* that you will want to know about.

Axis properties are VB.NET extensions that make working with XML even easier than using their equivalent LINQ to XML (or even LINQ to Objects in some cases) API properties and methods. Using the axis properties, you can return all the descendants of an element matching a specified name, return only the children of an element matching a specified name, return the value of an attribute, return an element by index number from a collection of elements, and return the value of the first element from a collection of elements.

Let's take a look at the axis properties in Table 2-2.

Table 2-2. *XML Axis Properties*

Axis Property	Operator	Description
Child	.<>	This axis property returns all children matching the name within the angle brackets of the element, document, collection of elements, or collection of documents on which it is called. This axis property is translated to the LINQ to XML API Elements method.
Descendant	...<>	This axis property returns all descendants matching the name within the angle brackets of the element, document, collection of elements, or collection of documents on which it is called. This axis property is translated to the LINQ to XML API Descendants method.
Indexer	()	This axis property returns an element by index number from a collection of elements. This axis property is translated to the LINQ to Objects API ElementAtOrDefault method.
Value	.Value	This axis property returns a reference to the value of the first element from a collection of elements.
Attribute	.@<>	This axis property returns a reference to the value of the attribute whose name is specified within the angle brackets. It can be called on a single element or a collection of elements. If called on a collection of elements, it returns a reference to the attribute of the first element in the collection. The angle brackets are optional as long as the attribute name is a valid identifier in VB.NET. If it isn't, the angle brackets are required.

You should notice that in the description for the value and attribute axis property that I said they returned a reference. The significance of this is that they can be used to modify the value of what is returned. Let's examine the power of the child axis property in Listing 2-28.

Listing 2-28. *Using the Child Axis Property*

```
Dim bookParticipants = _
  <BookParticipants>
    <BookParticipant type="Author">
      <FirstName>Joe</FirstName>
      <LastName>Rattz</LastName>
    </BookParticipant>
```

```
    <BookParticipant type="Editor">
      <FirstName>Ewan</FirstName>
      <LastName>Buckingham</LastName>
    </BookParticipant>
  </BookParticipants>

Dim participants = bookParticipants.<BookParticipant>
For Each participant In participants
  Console.WriteLine(participant)
Next
```

In the preceding code, I create an XML fragment, technically an XElement, using an XML literal. I then use the child axis property to return a collection of all the BookParticipant child elements of the fragment's root element. Then I loop through the returned collection and display each element.

One thing I haven't mentioned, because it is covered in the LINQ to XML section, is that when you call the Console.WriteLine method on an element, because the WriteLine method doesn't have an overload for handling XElement objects, it calls the ToString method of the XElement, which causes the element's XML to be output. This is actually a convenience built into the LINQ to XML API that I will cover later. Let's take a look at the results of Listing 2-28.

```
<BookParticipant type="Author">
  <FirstName>Joe</FirstName>
  <LastName>Rattz</LastName>
</BookParticipant>
<BookParticipant type="Editor">
  <FirstName>Ewan</FirstName>
  <LastName>Buckingham</LastName>
</BookParticipant>
```

While you see more than just the two BookParticipant elements in the results, it is because the ToString method is outputting the XML for each BookParticipant element. This is why you also see the FirstName and LastName elements, as well as the XML itself. But rest assured that the two BookParticipant elements were returned.

Next, in Listing 2-29, I'll proceed to the indexer axis property.

Listing 2-29. *Using the Indexer Axis Property*

```
Dim bookParticipants = _
  <BookParticipants>
    <BookParticipant type="Author">
      <FirstName>Joe</FirstName>
      <LastName>Rattz</LastName>
    </BookParticipant>
```

```
    <BookParticipant type="Editor">
      <FirstName>Ewan</FirstName>
      <LastName>Buckingham</LastName>
    </BookParticipant>
  </BookParticipants>
```

```
Dim participant1 = bookParticipants.<BookParticipant>(1)
Console.WriteLine(participant1.Value)
```

In the preceding code, I have used the indexer axis property to return the second BookParticipant element, the one whose index is 1 because the index is zero based, from the collection of BookParticipant elements returned using the child axis property that I covered in Listing 2-28. So, Listing 2-29 used both the child axis property and the indexer axis property. Here are the results of Listing 2-29:

```
EwanBuckingham
```

Notice that, this time, I only retrieved the second BookParticipant element. Because I displayed the Value property of the element this time instead of the element itself, the output looks a little different. All of this will be explained in full detail in the LINQ to XML portion of this book.

Now, let's look at the descendant axis property in Listing 2-30.

Listing 2-30. *Using the Descendant Axis Property*

```
Dim bookParticipants = _
  <BookParticipants>
    <BookParticipant type="Author">
      <FirstName>Joe</FirstName>
      <LastName>Rattz</LastName>
    </BookParticipant>
    <BookParticipant type="Editor">
      <FirstName>Ewan</FirstName>
      <LastName>Buckingham</LastName>
    </BookParticipant>
  </BookParticipants>
```

```
Dim LastNames = bookParticipants...<LastName>
For Each lastName In LastNames
  Console.WriteLine(lastName.Value)
Next
```

In the preceding code, I use the descendant axis property to retrieve all descendant LastName elements and display their value. Let's look at the results of Listing 2-30.

```
Rattz
Buckingham
```

In Listing 2-31, I will use the value axis property to obtain a reference to the value of the first BookParticipant element from a collection of elements.

Listing 2-31. *Using the Value Axis Property*

```
Dim bookParticipants = _
  <BookParticipants>
    <BookParticipant type="Author">
      <FirstName>Joe</FirstName>
      <LastName>Rattz</LastName>
    </BookParticipant>
    <BookParticipant type="Editor">
      <FirstName>Ewan</FirstName>
      <LastName>Buckingham</LastName>
    </BookParticipant>
  </BookParticipants>

Dim participant2 = bookParticipants.<BookParticipant>.Value
Console.WriteLine(participant2)
```

It is important to remember that the value axis property used in Listing 2-31 retrieves a reference to the value of the *first* element in the collection. Also notice that this code listing is again using the child axis property to retrieve that collection. Let's look at the results of Listing 2-31.

```
JoeRattz
```

Now, let's look at using the attribute axis property in Listing 2-32.

Listing 2-32. *Using the Attribute Axis Property*

```
Dim bookParticipants = _
  <BookParticipants>
    <BookParticipant type="Author">
      <FirstName>Joe</FirstName>
      <LastName>Rattz</LastName>
    </BookParticipant>
    <BookParticipant type="Editor">
      <FirstName>Ewan</FirstName>
      <LastName>Buckingham</LastName>
    </BookParticipant>
  </BookParticipants>

Dim participants2 = bookParticipants.<BookParticipant>
For Each participant In participants2
  Console.WriteLine(participant.@type)
Next
```

In the preceding code, I use the attribute axis property to return a reference to the value of the type attribute of each BookParticipant element. Again, this example is using the child axis property. It is also important to realize that this returns a reference to the attribute's value and not the attribute itself. Let's look at the results of Listing 2-32.

```
Author
Editor
```

Now that I have covered the basics of each axis property, let's look at some of the more advanced uses of the axis properties. In Listing 2-32, I enumerated through each BookParticipant element in the collection and used the attribute axis property on each to obtain a reference to the value of the type attribute of each element. However, the attribute axis property can also be called on a collection of elements to return a reference to the value of the specified attribute on the *first* element in that collection, as is demonstrated in Listing 2-33.

Listing 2-33. *Using the Attribute Axis Property To Return the First Element's Specified Attribute*

```
Dim bookParticipants = _
  <BookParticipants>
    <BookParticipant type="Author">
      <FirstName>Joe</FirstName>
      <LastName>Rattz</LastName>
    </BookParticipant>
    <BookParticipant type="Editor">
      <FirstName>Ewan</FirstName>
      <LastName>Buckingham</LastName>
    </BookParticipant>
  </BookParticipants>

Dim type = bookParticipants...<BookParticipant>.@type
Console.WriteLine(type)
```

Please notice that in the preceding code, instead of using the attribute axis property on an individual element, I used it on the collection of BookParticipant elements to return a reference to the value of the type attribute of the first BookParticipant element in that collection. Here are the results of Listing 2-33:

```
Author
```

Notice that when discussing the attribute axis property I keep saying that it returns a reference to the value of the attribute. Since it returns a reference to the value, we can use the attribute axis property to set the attribute's value, as demonstrated in Listing 2-34.

Listing 2-34. *Using the Attribute Axis Property To Set The Attribute's Value*

```
Dim bookParticipants = _
  <BookParticipants>
    <BookParticipant type="Author">
      <FirstName>Joe</FirstName>
      <LastName>Rattz</LastName>
    </BookParticipant>
    <BookParticipant type="Editor">
      <FirstName>Ewan</FirstName>
      <LastName>Buckingham</LastName>
    </BookParticipant>
  </BookParticipants>
```

```
bookParticipants...<BookParticipant>(1).@type = "Lead Editor"
Console.WriteLine(bookParticipants)
```

As you can see, in the preceding code, I used the descendant and indexer axis properties to retrieve the second BookParticipant element, used the attribute axis property to obtain a reference to its type attribute's value, and then set the value to "Lead Editor" with that reference. Very cool! Here are the results of Listing 2-34:

```
<BookParticipants>
  <BookParticipant type="Author">
    <FirstName>Joe</FirstName>
    <LastName>Rattz</LastName>
  </BookParticipant>
  <BookParticipant type="Lead Editor">
    <FirstName>Ewan</FirstName>
    <LastName>Buckingham</LastName>
  </BookParticipant>
</BookParticipants>
```

Notice that the type attribute's value for the second BookParticipant element is now "Lead Editor". How sweet is that? Think it can't get any better? Guess again.

Listing 2-35. *Using the Attribute Axis Property To Create an Attribute*

```
Dim bookParticipants = _
  <BookParticipants>
    <BookParticipant type="Author">
      <FirstName>Joe</FirstName>
      <LastName>Rattz</LastName>
    </BookParticipant>
```

```
    <BookParticipant type="Editor">
      <FirstName>Ewan</FirstName>
      <LastName>Buckingham</LastName>
    </BookParticipant>
  </BookParticipants>
```

```
bookParticipants...<BookParticipant>(1).@country = "United Kingdom"
Console.WriteLine(bookParticipants)
```

Yes, you guessed it. The code in Listing 2-35 is using an attribute axis property to actually create an attribute and set its value. I know you want to see the results of that.

```
<BookParticipants>
  <BookParticipant type="Author">
    <FirstName>Joe</FirstName>
    <LastName>Rattz</LastName>
  </BookParticipant>
  <BookParticipant type="Editor" country="United Kingdom">
    <FirstName>Ewan</FirstName>
    <LastName>Buckingham</LastName>
  </BookParticipant>
</BookParticipants>
```

OK, now the VB.NET development team is just showing off! Also, the value axis property returns a reference and can also be used to set the value of an element, as I demonstrate in Listing 2-36.

Listing 2-36. *Using the Value Axis Property to Set an Element's Value*

```
Dim bookParticipants = _
  <BookParticipants>
    <BookParticipant type="Author">
      <FirstName>Joe</FirstName>
      <LastName>Rattz</LastName>
    </BookParticipant>
    <BookParticipant type="Editor">
      <FirstName>Ewan</FirstName>
      <LastName>Buckingham</LastName>
    </BookParticipant>
  </BookParticipants>
```

```
bookParticipants.<BookParticipant>(0).<FirstName>.Value = "Joseph"
Console.WriteLine(bookParticipants)
```

I am guessing you already know what the results of Listing 2-36 should look like.

```
<BookParticipants>
  <BookParticipant type="Author">
    <FirstName>Joseph</FirstName>
    <LastName>Rattz</LastName>
  </BookParticipant>
  <BookParticipant type="Editor">
    <FirstName>Ewan</FirstName>
    <LastName>Buckingham</LastName>
  </BookParticipant>
</BookParticipants>
```

As you can see, the value of the first BookParticipant element's FirstName element has been changed to "Joseph". Interestingly, the value axis property cannot be used to create an element in the same way that the attribute axis property can be used to create an attribute.

I hope you can see just how impressive the VB.NET 2008 XML axis properties are and how easy they can make your life. Many of the statements in Listings 2-28 through 2-36 used multiple axis properties to zero in on the specific element or attribute I wanted access to.

XML Namespace Imports

One of the most confusing aspects of working with XML is namespaces. It seems unfortunate that something as simple in concept as providing a means to prevent element name collisions comes at the price of such a high confusion. The last XML enhancement to cover is XML namespace imports. This nifty feature makes working with XML namespaces much less painful than normal.

To define a namespace simply use the Imports statement like this:

```
Imports <xmlns:prefix="http://PrefixedNamespace">
```

This syntax allows you to reference your XML elements using the specified prefix. If you omit the prefix, the namespace becomes the default namespace, and this means that if you omit a namespace from an XML element, the default namespace will be used. So this syntax would define a default namespace:

```
Imports <xmlns="http://DefaultNamespace">
```

So, in the final example for this chapter, Listing 2-37, I will import two namespaces, one of which will be the default and another for which I will specify a prefix. I will explain this listing one section at a time. First, take a look at the Imports statements and my XML in Listing 2-37.

Listing 2-37. *Using the XML Namespace Imports Statement*

```
Imports <xmlns="http://www.linqdev.com/schemas/ProLinq">
Imports <xmlns:cfg="http://schemas.microsoft.com/.NetConfiguration/v2.0">
```

```
Dim bookParticipants = _
  <BookParticipants>
    <BookParticipant type="Author">
      <FirstName>Joe</FirstName>
      <LastName>Rattz</LastName>
      <cfg:configuration>
        <cfg:configSections></cfg:configSections>
      </cfg:configuration>
    </BookParticipant>
    <BookParticipant type="Editor">
      <FirstName>Ewan</FirstName>
      <LastName>Buckingham</LastName>
    </BookParticipant>
  </BookParticipants>
```

```
Console.WriteLine(bookParticipants)
```

In the preceding code, I first import two namespaces using the XML namespace Imports statement. Notice that the first one does *not* specify a prefix, so it becomes the default namespace. This means that any element I reference without a prefix is defined to be in that namespace by default. The second namespace that is imported does specify a prefix of "cfg". This means that any element intended to be defined in the second namespace must specify the "cfg" prefix. This applies to both the XML literal creating the XML, and any calls I make trying to retrieve elements from the XML.

Next, I create an XML fragment using an XML literal. Please notice that I do not provide a namespace prefix for any element except for the configuration and configSections elements in the first BookParticipant element. This means that those two elements are defined to be in the http://schemas.microsoft.com/.NetConfiguration/v2.0 namespace, while all the other elements are in the default namespace, http://www.linqdev.com/schemas/ProLinq.

Then, I simply display the XML fragment to the screen. Here are the results of the code thus far:

```
<BookParticipants xmlns:cfg=http://schemas.microsoft.com/.NetConfiguration/v2.0
    xmlns="http://www.linqdev.com/schemas/ProLinq">
  <BookParticipant type="Author">
    <FirstName>Joe</FirstName>
    <LastName>Rattz</LastName>
    <cfg:configuration>
      <cfg:configSections></cfg:configSections>
    </cfg:configuration>
  </BookParticipant>
  <BookParticipant type="Editor">
    <FirstName>Ewan</FirstName>
    <LastName>Buckingham</LastName>
  </BookParticipant>
</BookParticipants>
```

There are no surprises yet, but notice that both namespaces are specified in the BookParticipants element. Now, I am ready to do some queries.

```
Dim bookParticipant = bookParticipants.<BookParticipant>(0)
Console.WriteLine("<BookParticipant>=")
Console.WriteLine(bookParticipant)


Console.WriteLine(vbCrLf)


bookParticipant = bookParticipants.<cfg:BookParticipant>(0)
Console.WriteLine("<cfg:BookParticipant>=")
Console.WriteLine(bookParticipant)
```

In that first block of code, I search for the BookParticipant element without specifying a prefix, which means I am looking for a BookParticipant element in the XML fragment belonging to the default namespace. Then, I display that element. Since the BookParticipant element is specified to be in the default namespace in the XML, I should see the element's data.

In the second block of code, I search for the BookParticipant element, and I specify the "cfg" prefix. Since the BookParticipant is not specified to be in the "cfg" prefixed namespace in the XML, I shouldn't get any data returned. Let's look at the results for this code segment.

```
<BookParticipant>=
<BookParticipant type="Author" xmlns="http://www.linqdev.com/schemas/ProLinq">
  <FirstName>Joe</FirstName>
  <LastName>Rattz</LastName>
  <cfg:configuration
      xmlns:cfg="http://schemas.microsoft.com/.NetConfiguration/v2.0">
    <cfg:configSections></cfg:configSections>
  </cfg:configuration>
</BookParticipant>


<cfg:BookParticipant>=
```

Exactly as I expected, the first query yielded results, but the second one did not. Let's take a look at the last block of code for this example.

```
Dim configuration = bookParticipants.<BookParticipant>(0).<configuration>(0)
Console.WriteLine("<configuration>=")
Console.WriteLine(configuration)


Console.WriteLine(vbCrLf)


configuration = bookParticipants.<BookParticipant>(0).<cfg:configuration>(0)
Console.WriteLine("<cfg:configuration>=")
Console.WriteLine(configuration)
```

In this block of code, I basically do the same thing that I did in the previous, except this time, I am querying for the `configuration` element. And, since the `configuration` element is defined to be in the `"cfg"`–prefixed namespace in the XML, the results should be reversed so that the first query retrieves no data, while the second query retrieves the `configuration` element. Let's verify the results.

```
<configuration>=
```

```
<cfg:configuration>=
<cfg:configuration xmlns:cfg="http://schemas.microsoft.com/.NetConfiguration/v2.0">
  <cfg:configSections></cfg:configSections>
</cfg:configuration>
```

While namespaces do add complexity to working with XML, I hope you now feel a little more comfortable dealing with them and see how XML namespace imports can help.

Summary

As you can see, Microsoft's VB.NET team has been busy adding enhancements to VB.NET. All of the VB.NET enhancements discussed in this chapter have been made specifically for LINQ. But even without LINQ, there is a lot to be gained from the new VB.NET features.

The new object initialization expressions are a godsend. Stubbing in static, sample, or test data is much easier than before, significantly reducing the lines of code needed to create the data. This feature combined with the new usage of the `Dim` keyword and anonymous types makes it much easier to create data and data types on the fly.

Extension methods now make it possible to add functionality to objects, such as sealed classes or perhaps classes for which you don't even have the source code, in an elegant way that just wasn't possible before. The syntax afforded by extension methods makes chaining calls to operators much cleaner than if you had to pass the previous call's results in as a parameter to the next operator, which would lead to many nested calls obfuscating what was being done.

Lambda expressions allow for concise specification of functionality. For those times when creating a named method is too much of a hassle, or just impractical, lambda expressions really shine. While you may initially be put off by them, I think with time and experience you will grow to appreciate them, too.

Expression trees provide third-party vendors wanting to make their proprietary data stores support LINQ with the ability to provide first-class performance.

Partial methods offer a very lightweight event-handling mechanism. Microsoft will leverage this in its LINQ to SQL entity class generation tools so that you can hook into the entity classes at key points in time.

Query expressions provide that warm fuzzy feeling when first seeing a LINQ query that makes you want to get on board with LINQ. Nothing makes a developer analyzing a new technology feel comfortable quicker than technology resembling a familiar and proven technology. By giving LINQ queries the ability to resemble SQL queries, Microsoft has made LINQ compelling to learn.

Last and by no means least, the XML enhancements make working with XML pleasurable. Coupled with the LINQ to XML API, XML will no longer be a painful chore. Grasp these enhancements well and your productivity with XML will skyrocket.

While all of these language enhancements by themselves are nice features, together they form the foundation for LINQ. I believe that LINQ will be the next SQL or object-oriented bandwagon, and most .NET developers will want LINQ on their résumé. I know it's going to be on mine.

Now that I have covered what LINQ is and what new VB.NET features and syntax it requires, it's time to get to the nitty-gritty. Please don't allow my technical jargon—*nitty-gritty*—to intimidate you. The next stop is learning about performing LINQ queries on in-memory data collections such as arrays, ArrayLists, and all of the new .NET 2005 generic collections. In Part 2, you will find a bevy of functions to supplement your queries. This portion of LINQ is known as LINQ to Objects.

PART 2

LINQ to Objects

CHAPTER 3

■ ■ ■

LINQ to Objects Introduction

Listing 3-1. *A Simple LINQ to Objects Query*

```
Dim presidents() As String = _
{ _
  "Adams", "Arthur", "Buchanan", "Bush", "Carter", "Cleveland", _
  "Clinton", "Coolidge", "Eisenhower", "Fillmore", "Ford", "Garfield", _
  "Grant", "Harding", "Harrison", "Hayes", "Hoover", "Jackson", _
  "Jefferson", "Johnson", "Kennedy", "Lincoln", "Madison", "McKinley", _
  "Monroe", "Nixon", "Pierce", "Polk", "Reagan", "Roosevelt", "Taft", _
  "Taylor", "Truman", "Tyler", "Van Buren", "Washington", "Wilson" _
}

Dim president As String = presidents.Where(Function(p) p.StartsWith("Lin")).First()

Console.WriteLine(president)
```

■Note This code has been added to a Visual Studio 2008 console application. See Listing 1-1 for details.

Listing 3-1 shows what LINQ to Objects is all about—performing SQL-like queries on in-memory data collections and arrays. I will run the example by pressing Ctrl+F5. Here are the results:

```
Lincoln
```

LINQ to Objects Overview

Part of what makes LINQ so cool and easy to use is the way it seamlessly integrates with the VB.NET 2008 language. Instead of having an entirely new cast of characters in the form of classes that must be used to get the benefits of LINQ, you can use all of the same collections[1]

---

1. A collection must implement IEnumerable(Of T) or IEnumerable to be queryable with LINQ to Objects.

and arrays that you are accustomed to with your preexisting classes. This means you can gain the advantages of LINQ queries with little or no modification to existing code. The functionality of LINQ to Objects is accomplished with the IEnumerable(Of T) interface, sequences, and the Standard Query Operators.

For example, if you have an array of integers and need it to be sorted, you can perform a LINQ query to order the results, much as if it were a SQL query. Maybe you have an ArrayList of Customer objects and need to find a specific Customer object. If so, LINQ to Objects is your answer.

I know there will be a tendency by many to use the LINQ to Objects chapters as a reference. While I have made significant effort to make them useful for this purpose, the developer will gain more by reading them from beginning to end. Many of the concepts that apply to one operator apply to another operator. While I have tried to make each operator's section independently stand on its own merit, there is a context created when reading from beginning to end that will be missed when just reading about a single operator or skipping around.

IEnumerable(Of T), Sequences, and the Standard Query Operators

IEnumerable(Of T), pronounced *I enumerable of T*, is an interface that all of the .NET generic collection classes implement, as do arrays. This interface permits the enumeration of a collection's elements.

A *sequence* is a logical term for a collection implementing the IEnumerable(Of T) interface. If you have a variable of type IEnumerable(Of T), then you might say you have a sequence of *T*s. For example, if you have an IEnumerable of String, written as IEnumerable(Of String) you could say you have a sequence of strings.

■**Note** Any variable declared as IEnumerable(Of T) for type T is considered a sequence of type T.

Most of the Standard Query Operators are extension methods in the System.Linq. Enumerable static class and are prototyped with an IEnumerable(Of T) as their first argument. Because they are extension methods, it is preferable to call them on a variable of type IEnumerable(Of T) as the extension method syntax permits instead of passing a variable of type IEnumerable(Of T) as the first argument.

The Standard Query Operator methods of the System.Linq.Enumerable class that are not extension methods are static methods and must be called on the System.Linq.Enumerable class. The combination of these Standard Query Operator methods gives you the ability to perform complex data queries on an IEnumerable(Of T) sequence.

The legacy collections, those nongeneric collections existing prior to .NET 2.0, support the IEnumerable interface, not the IEnumerable(Of T) interface. This means you cannot *directly* call those extension methods whose first argument is an IEnumerable(Of T) on a legacy collection. However, you can still perform LINQ queries on legacy collections by calling the Cast or OfType Standard Query Operator on the legacy collection to produce a sequence that implements IEnumerable(Of T), thereby allowing you access to the full arsenal of the Standard Query Operators.

■Note Use the Cast or OfType operators to perform LINQ queries on legacy, nongeneric .NET collections.

Returning IEnumerable(Of T) and Deferred Queries

It is important to remember that while many of the Standard Query Operators are prototyped to return an IEnumerable(Of T), and we think of IEnumerable(Of T) as a sequence, the operators are not actually returning the sequence at the time the operators are called. Instead, the operators return an object that, when enumerated, will return an element from the sequence. It is during enumeration of the returned object that the query is actually performed and an element returned to the output sequence. In this way, the query is deferred.

For example, examine the code in Listing 3-2.

Listing 3-2. *A Trivial Sample Query*

```
Dim presidents() As String = _
{ _
  "Adams", "Arthur", "Buchanan", "Bush", "Carter", "Cleveland", _
  "Clinton", "Coolidge", "Eisenhower", "Fillmore", "Ford", "Garfield", _
  "Grant", "Harding", "Harrison", "Hayes", "Hoover", "Jackson", _
  "Jefferson", "Johnson", "Kennedy", "Lincoln", "Madison", "McKinley", _
  "Monroe", "Nixon", "Pierce", "Polk", "Reagan", "Roosevelt", "Taft", _
  "Taylor", "Truman", "Tyler", "Van Buren", "Washington", "Wilson" _
}

Dim items As IEnumerable(Of String) = _
  presidents.Where(Function(p) p.StartsWith("A"))

For Each item As String In items
  Console.WriteLine(item)
Next item
```

The query using the Where operator is not actually performed when the line containing the query is executed. Instead, an object is returned. It is during the enumeration of the returned object that the Where query is actually performed. This means it is possible that an error that occurs in the query itself may not get detected until the time the enumeration takes place.

■Note Query errors may not be detected until the output sequence is enumerated.

The results of the previous query are the following:

```
Adams
Arthur
```

That query performed as expected. However, I'll intentionally introduce an error. The following code will attempt to index into the fifth character of each president's name. When the enumeration reaches an element whose length is less than five characters, an exception will occur. Remember though that the exception will not happen until the output sequence is enumerated. Listing 3-3 shows the sample code.

Listing 3-3. *A Trivial Sample Query with an Intentionally Introduced Exception*

```
Dim presidents() As String = _
{ _
  "Adams", "Arthur", "Buchanan", "Bush", "Carter", "Cleveland", _
  "Clinton", "Coolidge", "Eisenhower", "Fillmore", "Ford", "Garfield", _
  "Grant", "Harding", "Harrison", "Hayes", "Hoover", "Jackson", _
  "Jefferson", "Johnson", "Kennedy", "Lincoln", "Madison", "McKinley", _
  "Monroe", "Nixon", "Pierce", "Polk", "Reagan", "Roosevelt", "Taft", _
  "Taylor", "Truman", "Tyler", "Van Buren", "Washington", "Wilson" _
}

Dim items As IEnumerable(Of String) = _
  presidents.Where(Function(s) Char.IsLower(s(4)))

Console.WriteLine("After the query.")

For Each item As String In items
  Console.WriteLine(item)
Next item
```

This code compiles just fine, but when run, here are the results:

```
After the query.
Adams
Arthur
Buchanan

Unhandled Exception: System.IndexOutOfRangeException: Index was outside the bounds
of the array.
...
```

Notice the output of After the query. Not until the fourth element, Bush, was enumerated does the exception occur. The lesson to be learned is that just because a query compiles and seems to have no problem executing, don't assume the query is bug free.

Additionally, because queries returning IEnumerable(Of T) are deferred, you can call the code to define the query once but use it multiple times by enumerating it multiple times. If you do this, each time you enumerate the results, you will get different results if the data changes. Listing 3-4 shows an example of a deferred query where the query results are not cached and can change from one enumeration to the next.

Listing 3-4. *An Example Demonstrating the Query Results Changing Between Enumerations*

```
'  Create an array of ints.
Dim intArray() As Integer = { 1,2,3 }

Dim ints As IEnumerable(Of Integer) = intArray.Select(Function(i) i)

'  Display the results.
For Each i As Integer In ints
  Console.WriteLine(i)
Next i

' Change an element in the source data.
intArray(0) = 5

Console.WriteLine("---------")

' Display the results again.
For Each i As Integer In ints
  Console.WriteLine(i)
Next i
```

To hopefully make what is happening crystal clear, I will get more technical in my description. When I call the Select operator, an object is returned that is stored in the variable named ints of a type that implements IEnumerable(Of Integer). At this point, the query has not actually taken place yet, but the query is stored in the object named ints. Technically speaking, since the query has not been performed, a sequence of integers doesn't really exist yet, but the object named ints knows how to obtain the sequence by performing the query that was assigned to it, which in this case is the Select operator.

When I call the For Each statement on ints the first time, ints performs the query and obtains the sequence one element at a time.

Next, I change an element in the original array of integers. Then, I call the For Each statement again. This causes ints to perform the query again. Since I changed the element in the original array, and since the query is being performed again because ints is being enumerated again, the changed element is returned.

Technically speaking, the query I called returned an object that implemented IEnumerable(Of Integer). However, in most LINQ discussions in this book, as well as other discussions outside of this book, it would be said that the query returned a sequence of integers. Logically speaking, this is true and ultimately what we are after. But it is important for you to understand technically what is really happening.

Here are the results of this code:

```
1
2
3
---------
5
2
3
```

Notice that even though I only called the query once, the results of the enumeration are different for each of the enumerations. This is further evidence that the query is deferred. If it were not, the results of both enumerations would be the same. This could be a benefit or detriment. If you do not want this to happen, use one of the conversion operators that do not return an IEnumerable(Of T) so that the query is not deferred, such as ToArray, ToList, ToDictionary, or ToLookup, to create a different data structure with cached results that will not change if the data source changes.

Listing 3-5 is the same as the previous code example except instead of having the query return an IEnumerable(Of Integer>, it will return a List(Of Integer> by calling the ToList operator.

Listing 3-5. *Returning a List So the Query Is Executed Immediately and the Results Are Cached*

```vb
' Create an array of Integers.
Dim intArray() As Integer = { 1, 2, 3 }

Dim ints As List(Of Integer) = intArray.Select(Function(i) i).ToList()

' Display the results.
For Each i As Integer In ints
  Console.WriteLine(i)
Next i

' Change an element in the source data.
intArray(0) = 5

Console.WriteLine("---------")

' Display the results again.
For Each i As Integer In ints
  Console.WriteLine(i)
Next i
```

Here are the results:

```
1
2
3
```

```
---------
1
2
3
```

Notice the results do not change from one enumeration to the next. This is because the ToList method is not deferred, and the query is actually performed at the time the query is called.

To return to a technical discussion of what is different between this example and Listing 3-4, while the Select operator is still deferred in Listing 3-5, the ToList operator is not. When the ToList operator is called in the query statement, it enumerates the object returned from the Select operator immediately, making the entire query not deferred.

Func Delegates

Several of the Standard Query Operators are prototyped to take a Func delegate as an argument. This prevents you from having to explicitly declare delegate types. Here are the Func delegate declarations:

```
Public Delegate Function Func(Of TResult)() As TResult

Public Delegate Function Func(Of T1, TResult)(ByVal arg1 As T1) As TResult

Public Delegate Function Func(Of T1, T2, TResult) _
   (ByVal arg1 As T1, ByVal arg2 As T2) As TResult

Public Delegate Function Func(Of T1, T2, T3, TResult) _
   (ByVal arg1 As T1, ByVal arg2 As T2, ByVal arg3 As T3) As TResult

Public Delegate Function Func(Of T1, T2, T3, T4, TResult) _
   (ByVal arg1 As T1, ByVal arg2 As T2, ByVal arg3 As T3, _
   ByVal arg4 As T4) As TResult
```

In each declaration, TResult refers to the data type returned. Notice that the return type argument, TResult, is at the end of the parameter type template for every overload of the Func delegate. The other type parameters, T1, T2, T3, and T4, refer to the input parameters passed to the method. The multiple declarations exist because some Standard Query Operators have delegate arguments that require more parameters than others. By looking at the declarations, you can see that no Standard Query Operator has a delegate argument that will require more than four input parameters.

Let's take a look at one of the declarations of the Where operator:

```
<ExtensionAttribute> _
Public Shared Function Where(Of TSource) ( _
    source As IEnumerable(Of TSource), _
    predicate As Func(Of TSource, Boolean)) _
  As IEnumerable(Of TSource)
```

The predicate argument is specified as a Func(Of TSource, Boolean). From this, you can see the predicate method or lambda expression must accept a single argument, the TSource parameter, and return a Boolean. You know this because you know the return type is specified at the end of the parameter template list.

Of course, you can use the Func declaration, as shown in Listing 3-6.

Listing 3-6. *An Example Using One of the Func Delegate Declarations*

```
' Create an array of Integers.
Dim ints() As Integer = { 1,2,3,4,5,6 }

' Declare our delegate.
Dim GreaterThanTwo As Func(Of Integer, Boolean) = Function(i) i > 2

' Perform the query ... not really.  Don't forget about deferred queries!!!
Dim intsGreaterThanTwo As IEnumerable(Of Integer) = ints.Where(GreaterThanTwo)

' Display the results.
For Each i As Integer In intsGreaterThanTwo
  Console.WriteLine(i)
Next i
```

This code provides the following results:

```
3
4
5
6
```

The Standard Query Operators Alphabetical Cross-Reference

Table 3-1 shows the Standard Query Operators listed alphabetically. Since these operators will be separated into chapters based on whether they are deferred or not, this table will help you locate each operator in the remaining LINQ to Objects chapters. Note that Aggregate, Distinct, Skip, SkipWhile, Take, and TakeWhile have query expression support in VB.NET only, and not in C#.

Table 3-1. *Standard Query Operators Alphabetical Cross-Reference*

Operator	Purpose	Deferred?	Query Expression Support?
Aggregate	Aggregate		✔
All	Quantifiers		
Any	Quantifiers		

Operator	Purpose	Deferred?	Query Expression Support?
AsEnumerable	Conversion	✔	
Average	Aggregate		
Cast	Conversion	✔	
Concat	Concatenation	✔	
Contains	Quantifiers		
Count	Aggregate		
DefaultIfEmpty	Element	✔	
Distinct	Set	✔	✔
ElementAt	Element		
ElementAtOrDefault	Element		
Empty	Generation	✔	
Except	Set	✔	
First	Element		
FirstOrDefault	Element		
GroupBy	Grouping	✔	✔
GroupJoin	Join	✔	✔
Intersect	Set	✔	
Join	Join	✔	✔
Last	Element		
LastOrDefault	Element		
LongCount	Aggregate		
Max	Aggregate		
Min	Aggregate		
OfType	Conversion	✔	
OrderBy	Ordering	✔	✔
OrderByDescending	Ordering	✔	✔
Range	Generation	✔	
Repeat	Generation	✔	
Reverse	Ordering	✔	
Select	Projection	✔	✔
SelectMany	Projection	✔	✔
SequenceEqual	Equality		
Single	Element		
SingleOrDefault	Element		

Continued

Table 3-1. *Continued*

Operator	Purpose	Deferred?	Query Expression Support?
Skip	Partitioning	✔	✔
SkipWhile	Partitioning	✔	✔
Sum	Aggregate		
Take	Partitioning	✔	✔
TakeWhile	Partitioning	✔	✔
ThenBy	Ordering	✔	✔
ThenByDescending	Ordering	✔	✔
ToArray	Conversion		
ToDictionary	Conversion		
ToList	Conversion		
ToLookup	Conversion		
Union	Set	✔	
Where	Restriction	✔	✔

A Tale of Two Syntaxes

Since you may write LINQ queries using either query expression syntax or standard dot notation syntax, you may wonder which syntax you should use. In many cases, this is largely a
matter of preference as long as the standard query operators you are using in your query are
supported by query expression syntax. As you can see in the previous table, most of the operators are not supported by query expression syntax, so when using any of the unsupported
operators, you must defer to standard dot notation syntax.

However, you should be aware that you can use a mixture of both syntaxes by enclosing
a query expression inside parentheses and appending a call to an unsupported operator like
this:

```
Dim oddNumbers = (From n In nums _
                  Where n Mod 2 = 1 _
                  Select n) _
                 .Reverse()
```

Summary

In this chapter, I introduced you to the term *sequence*, and its technical data type,
IEnumerable(Of T). If you feel uncomfortable with some of this terminology, I am sure
that with time, it will become second nature for you. Just think of IEnumerable(Of T) as a
sequence of objects you are going to call methods on to do things with those objects.

However, if there is one thing I want you to take with you from this chapter, it is the importance of deferred query execution. It can work for you or against you. Understanding it is key, and being conscious of it is important. It is so important that I have divided the Standard Query Operators into separate chapters based on this characteristic. The deferred operators are covered in Chapter 4, and the nondeferred operators are covered in Chapter 5.

Since I have deferred queries in your thoughts right now, I will begin an in-depth examination of the deferred operators in the next chapter.

■ ■ ■

Deferred Operators

In the previous chapter, I covered what sequences are, the data type that represents them, and the impact of deferred query execution. Because of the importance of deferred query operator awareness, I have separated deferred and nondeferred operators into separate chapters to highlight whether a Standard Query Operator's action is deferred or not.

In this chapter, I will be covering the deferred query operators. A deferred operator is easy to spot because it has a return type of IEnumerable(Of T) or IOrderedEnumerable(Of T). Each of these deferred operators will be categorized by its purpose.

In order to code and execute the examples in this chapter, you will need to make sure you have Imports statements for all the necessary namespaces, references for all the necessary assemblies, and the common code that the examples will share.

Referenced Namespaces

The examples in this chapter will use the System.Linq, System.Collections, System. Collections.Generic, and System.Data.Linq namespaces. Therefore, you should add the following Imports directives to your code if they are not present, or included in your project settings:

```
Imports System.Linq
Imports System.Collections
Imports System.Collections.Generic
Imports System.Data.Linq
```

Referenced Assemblies

In addition to the typical assemblies, you will need references for the System.Data.Linq.dll assembly.

Query Expression Syntax vs. Standard Dot Notation Syntax

For most of the examples in this chapter, and indeed in this book, I use standard dot notation syntax for my queries. While any LINQ query can be written using standard dot notation syntax, just so you will have *some* examples using query expression syntax, I will use query expression syntax for a few examples in this chapter. In particular, I will be using query expression syntax in the examples of operators for which VB.NET supports query expression syntax but C# does not: Take (Listing 4-10), TakeWhile (Listing 4-12), Skip (Listing 4-14), SkipWhile (Listing 4-15), and Distinct (Listing 4-34). Be aware that all of these could have been done with standard dot notation syntax, and that some of the other examples could have been done with query expression syntax.

Common Classes

Several of the examples in this chapter will require classes to fully demonstrate an operator's behavior. The following is a list of classes that will be shared by more than one example. The Employee class is meant to represent an employee. For convenience, it contains shared methods to return an ArrayList or array of employees.

The Shared Employee Class

```
Public Class Employee
    Public id As Integer
    Public firstName As String
    Public lastName As String

    Public Shared Function GetEmployeesArrayList() As ArrayList
        Dim al As New ArrayList()

        al.Add(New Employee With _
            {.id = 1, .firstName = "Joe", .lastName = "Rattz"})
        al.Add(New Employee With _
            {.id = 2, .firstName = "William", .lastName = "Gates"})
        al.Add(New Employee With _
            {.id = 3, .firstName = "Anders", .lastName = "Hejlsberg"})
        al.Add(New Employee With _
            {.id = 4, .firstName = "David", .lastName = "Lightman"})
        al.Add(New Employee With _
            {.id = 101, .firstName = "Kevin", .lastName = "Flynn"})
        Return (al)
    End Function

    Public Shared Function GetEmployeesArray() As Employee()
        Return (GetEmployeesArrayList().ToArray(GetType(Employee)))
    End Function
End Class
```

The EmployeeOptionEntry class represents an award of stock options to a specific employee. For convenience, it contains a shared method to return an array of awarded option entries.

The Shared EmployeeOptionEntry Class

```
Public Class EmployeeOptionEntry
    Public id As Integer
    Public optionsCount As Long
    Public dateAwarded As DateTime

    Public Shared Function GetEmployeeOptionEntries() As EmployeeOptionEntry()
        Dim empOptions() As EmployeeOptionEntry = { _
            New EmployeeOptionEntry With { _
                .id = 1, _
                .optionsCount = 2, _
                .dateAwarded = DateTime.Parse("1999/12/31")}, _
            New EmployeeOptionEntry With { _
                .id = 2, _
                .optionsCount = 10000, _
                .dateAwarded = DateTime.Parse("1992/06/30")}, _
            New EmployeeOptionEntry With { _
                .id = 2, _
                .optionsCount = 10000, _
                .dateAwarded = DateTime.Parse("1994/01/01")}, _
            New EmployeeOptionEntry With { _
                .id = 3, _
                .optionsCount = 5000, _
                .dateAwarded = DateTime.Parse("1997/09/30")}, _
            New EmployeeOptionEntry With { _
                .id = 2, _
                .optionsCount = 10000, _
                .dateAwarded = DateTime.Parse("2003/04/01")}, _
            New EmployeeOptionEntry With { _
                .id = 3, _
                .optionsCount = 7500, _
                .dateAwarded = DateTime.Parse("1998/09/30")}, _
            New EmployeeOptionEntry With { _
                .id = 3, _
                .optionsCount = 7500, _
                .dateAwarded = DateTime.Parse("1998/09/30")}, _
            New EmployeeOptionEntry With { _
                .id = 4, _
                .optionsCount = 1500, _
                .dateAwarded = DateTime.Parse("1997/12/31")}, _
            New EmployeeOptionEntry With { _
                .id = 101, _
                .optionsCount = 2, _
```

```
                    .dateAwarded = DateTime.Parse("1998/12/31")} _
            }
        Return (empOptions)
    End Function
End Class
```

The Deferred Operators by Purpose

The deferred Standard Query Operators are organized by their purpose in this section.

Restriction

Restriction operators are used for including or excluding elements of an input sequence.

Where

The Where operator is used to filter elements *into* a sequence.

Declarations

The Where operator has two overloads.

■**Note** The first overload shows how the .NET Framework defines the Where operator. The <ExtensionAttribute> is used internally by the Microsoft .NET Framework and should not be used by any application code. It is not related to the <Extension()> attribute, which is meant to be used in applications. Also note that this is not a case of an evil Microsoft using secret functionality to gain an advantage over competitors. Frameworks typically need flags and functions for internal housekeeping, and this is just one of those occasions. Even though it is only meant for internal use, it is included in the .NET documentation.

The First Overload of the Where Operator

```
<ExtensionAttribute> _
Public Shared Function Where(Of TSource) ( _
    source As IEnumerable(Of TSource), _
    predicate As Func(Of TSource, Boolean) _
) As IEnumerable(Of TSource)
```

This overload of Where takes an input source sequence and a predicate delegate and returns an object that, when enumerated, enumerates through the input source sequence yielding elements for which the predicate delegate returns True.

Because this is an extension method, we do not actually pass the input sequence, as long as we call the Where operator using the instance method syntax.

■**Note** Thanks to extension methods, it is not necessary to pass the first argument to the Standard Query Operators that specify the `<ExtensionAttribute>` attribute, as long as we call the operator on an object of the same type as the first argument of the method.

When calling Where, you pass a delegate to a predicate method. Your predicate method must accept a type TSource as input, where TSoure is the type of elements contained in the input sequence, and return a Boolean. The Where operator will call your predicate method for each element in the input sequence and pass it the element. If your predicate method returns True, Where will yield that element into Where's output sequence. If your predicate method returns False, it will not.

The Second Overload of the Where Operator

```
<ExtensionAttribute> _
Public Shared Function Where(Of TSource) ( _
    source As IEnumerable(Of TSource), _
    predicate As Func(Of TSource, Integer, Boolean) _
) As IEnumerable(Of TSource)
```

The second Where overload is identical to the first one, except it specifies that your predicate delegate receives an additional integer input argument. That argument will be the index number for the element from the input sequence.

The index is zero based, so the index passed for the first element will be zero. The last element will be passed the total number of elements in the sequence minus one.

■**Note** Remember, the index that gets passed will be zero based.

Exceptions

ArgumentNullException is thrown if any of the arguments are Nothing.

Examples

Listing 4-1 is an example calling the first overload.

Listing 4-1. *An Example of the First Where Overload*

```
Dim presidents() As String = { _
    "Adams", "Arthur", "Buchanan", "Bush", "Carter", "Cleveland", _
    "Clinton", "Coolidge", "Eisenhower", "Fillmore", "Ford", "Garfield", _
    "Grant", "Harding", "Harrison", "Hayes", "Hoover", "Jackson", _
    "Jefferson", "Johnson", "Kennedy", "Lincoln", "Madison", "McKinley", _
```

```
      "Monroe", "Nixon", "Pierce", "Polk", "Reagan", "Roosevelt", "Taft", _
      "Taylor", "Truman", "Tyler", "Van Buren", "Washington", "Wilson"}

Dim sequence As IEnumerable(Of String) = _
  presidents.Where(Function(p) p.StartsWith("J"))

For Each s As String In sequence
  Console.WriteLine("{0}", s)
Next s
```

In the preceding example, restricting a sequence using the first overload of the Where operator is as simple as calling the Where method on the sequence and passing a lambda expression that returns a Boolean indicating whether an element should be included in the output sequence. In this example, I am only returning the elements that start with the String "J". This code will produce the following results when Ctrl+F5 is pressed:

```
Jackson
Jefferson
Johnson
```

Notice I am passing my predicate method using a lambda expression.

Listing 4-2 shows code calling the second overload of the Where operator. Notice that this version doesn't even use the actual element itself, p; it uses only the index, i. This code will cause every other element, the ones with an odd index number, to be yielded into the output sequence.

Listing 4-2. *An Example of the Second Where Overload*

```
Dim presidents() As String = { _
  "Adams", "Arthur", "Buchanan", "Bush", "Carter", "Cleveland", _
  "Clinton", "Coolidge", "Eisenhower", "Fillmore", "Ford", "Garfield", _
  "Grant", "Harding", "Harrison", "Hayes", "Hoover", "Jackson", _
  "Jefferson", "Johnson", "Kennedy", "Lincoln", "Madison", "McKinley", _
  "Monroe", "Nixon", "Pierce", "Polk", "Reagan", "Roosevelt", "Taft", _
  "Taylor", "Truman", "Tyler", "Van Buren", "Washington", "Wilson"}

Dim sequence As IEnumerable(Of String) = _
  presidents.Where(Function(p, i) (i And 1) = 1)

For Each s As String In sequence
  Console.WriteLine("{0}", s)
Next s
```

Pressing Ctrl+F5 produces the following results:

```
Arthur
Bush
Cleveland
```

```
Coolidge
Fillmore
Garfield
Harding
Hayes
Jackson
Johnson
Lincoln
McKinley
Nixon
Polk
Roosevelt
Taylor
Tyler
Washington
```

Projection

Projection operators return an output sequence of elements that are generated by selecting elements or instantiating altogether new elements containing portions of elements from an input sequence. The data type of elements in the output sequence may be different than the type of elements in the input sequence.

Select

The Select operator is used to create an output sequence of one type of element from an input sequence of another type of element. It is not necessary that the input element type and the output element type be the same.

Declarations

The Select operator has two overloads.

The First Overload of the Select Operator

```
<ExtensionAttribute> _
Public Shared Function Select(Of TSource, TResult) ( _
    source As IEnumerable(Of TSource), _
    selector As Func(Of TSource, TResult) _
) As IEnumerable(Of TResult)
```

This overload of Select takes an input source sequence and a selector delegate as input arguments, and it returns an object that, when enumerated, enumerates the input source sequence yielding a sequence of elements of type TResult. As mentioned before, TSource and TResult could be the same type or different types.

When calling Select, you pass a delegate to a selector method via the selector argument. Your selector method must accept a type TSource as input, where TSource is the type of elements contained in the input sequence, and it returns a type TResult element. Select will call your selector method for each element in the input sequence, passing it the element. Your selector method will select the portions of the input element it is interested in, creating a new, possibly different typed element, which may be of an anonymous type, and return it.

The Second Overload of the Select Operator

```
<ExtensionAttribute> _
Public Shared Function Select(Of TSource, TResult) ( _
    source As IEnumerable(Of TSource), _
    selector As Func(Of TSource, Integer, TResult) _
) As IEnumerable(Of TResult)
```

In this overload of the Select operator, an additional integer is passed to the selector delegate. This will be the zero-based index of the input element in the input sequence.

Exceptions

ArgumentNullException is thrown if any of the arguments are Nothing.

Examples

An example calling the first overload is shown in Listing 4-3.

Listing 4-3. *An Example of the First Select Overload*

```
Dim presidents() As String = { _
  "Adams", "Arthur", "Buchanan", "Bush", "Carter", "Cleveland", _
  "Clinton", "Coolidge", "Eisenhower", "Fillmore", "Ford", "Garfield", _
  "Grant", "Harding", "Harrison", "Hayes", "Hoover", "Jackson", _
  "Jefferson", "Johnson", "Kennedy", "Lincoln", "Madison", "McKinley", _
  "Monroe", "Nixon", "Pierce", "Polk", "Reagan", "Roosevelt", "Taft", _
  "Taylor", "Truman", "Tyler", "Van Buren", "Washington", "Wilson"}

Dim nameLengths As IEnumerable(Of Integer) = _
  presidents.Select(Function(p) p.Length)

For Each item As Integer In nameLengths
  Console.WriteLine(item)
Next item
```

Notice I am passing my selector method using a lambda expression. In this case, my lambda expression will return the length of each element in the input sequence. Also notice that while my input types are Strings, my output types are Integers.

This code will produce the following results when you press Ctrl+F5:

```
5
6
8
4
6
```

```
9
7
8
10
8
4
8
5
7
8
5
6
7
9
7
7
7
7
8
6
5
6
4
6
9
4
6
6
5
9
10
6
```

This is a simple example because I am not generating any objects. To provide an even better demonstration of the first overload, consider the code in Listing 4-4.

Listing 4-4. *Another Example of the First Select Overload*

```
Dim presidents() As String = { _
  "Adams", "Arthur", "Buchanan", "Bush", "Carter", "Cleveland", _
  "Clinton", "Coolidge", "Eisenhower", "Fillmore", "Ford", "Garfield", _
  "Grant", "Harding", "Harrison", "Hayes", "Hoover", "Jackson", _
  "Jefferson", "Johnson", "Kennedy", "Lincoln", "Madison", "McKinley", _
  "Monroe", "Nixon", "Pierce", "Polk", "Reagan", "Roosevelt", "Taft", _
  "Taylor", "Truman", "Tyler", "Van Buren", "Washington", "Wilson"}
```

```
Dim nameObjs = _
  presidents.Select(Function(p) New With {Key p, Key p.Length})

For Each item In nameObjs
  Console.WriteLine(item)
Next item
```

Notice that my lambda expression is instantiating a new, anonymous type. The compiler will dynamically generate an anonymous type for me at compile time that will contain a String p and an Integer Length, and my selector method will return that newly instantiated object. Because the type of the returned element is anonymous, I have no type name to reference it by. So, I cannot assign the output sequence from Select to an IEnumerable of some known type, as I did in the first example where I assigned a variable of type IEnumerable(Of Integer) to the output sequence. Therefore, I assign the output sequence to a variable specified with the Dim keyword; this is the VB.NET equivalent of the C# var keyword. This is different from the way Dim worked in VB6, because nameObjs is of type IEnumerable(Of <anonymous type>), and not a Variant, so the following code

```
Dim nameObjs = presidents.Select(Function(p) New With {Key p, Key p.Length})
nameObjs = 1
```

although valid in VB6, will generate the following error in VB.NET:

```
' Error Value of type 'Integer' cannot be converted to
'System.Collections.Generic.'IEnumerable(Of  <anonymous type>)'.
```

See Chapter 2 for more information on the difference between the VB6 Dim and the new implicitly typed VB.NET Dim.

■**Note** Projection operators whose selector methods instantiate anonymous types to return must have their output sequence assigned to a variable declared with the Dim keyword.

When run by pressing Ctrl+F5, the code in Listing 4-4 produces the following output:

```
{ p = Adams, Length = 5 }
{ p = Arthur, Length = 6 }
{ p = Buchanan, Length = 8 }
{ p = Bush, Length = 4 }
{ p = Carter, Length = 6 }
{ p = Cleveland, Length = 9 }
{ p = Clinton, Length = 7 }
{ p = Coolidge, Length = 8 }
{ p = Eisenhower, Length = 10 }
{ p = Fillmore, Length = 8 }
{ p = Ford, Length = 4 }
```

```
{ p = Garfield, Length = 8 }
{ p = Grant, Length = 5 }
{ p = Harding, Length = 7 }
{ p = Harrison, Length = 8 }
{ p = Hayes, Length = 5 }
{ p = Hoover, Length = 6 }
{ p = Jackson, Length = 7 }
{ p = Jefferson, Length = 9 }
{ p = Johnson, Length = 7 }
{ p = Kennedy, Length = 7 }
{ p = Lincoln, Length = 7 }
{ p = Madison, Length = 7 }
{ p = McKinley, Length = 8 }
{ p = Monroe, Length = 6 }
{ p = Nixon, Length = 5 }
{ p = Pierce, Length = 6 }
{ p = Polk, Length = 4 }
{ p = Reagan, Length = 6 }
{ p = Roosevelt, Length = 9 }
{ p = Taft, Length = 4 }
{ p = Taylor, Length = 6 }
{ p = Truman, Length = 6 }
{ p = Tyler, Length = 5 }
{ p = Van Buren, Length = 9 }
{ p = Washington, Length = 10 }
{ p = Wilson, Length = 6 }
```

There is one problem with this code as it is; I can't control the names of the members of the dynamically generated anonymous class. However, thanks to the new *anonymous type* and *object initialization* features of VB.NET 2008, I could write the lambda expression and specify the anonymous class member names as shown in Listing 4-5.

Listing 4-5. *A Third Example of the First Select Overload*

```
Dim presidents() As String = { _
  "Adams", "Arthur", "Buchanan", "Bush", "Carter", "Cleveland", _
  "Clinton", "Coolidge", "Eisenhower", "Fillmore", "Ford", "Garfield", _
  "Grant", "Harding", "Harrison", "Hayes", "Hoover", "Jackson", _
  "Jefferson", "Johnson", "Kennedy", "Lincoln", "Madison", "McKinley", _
  "Monroe", "Nixon", "Pierce", "Polk", "Reagan", "Roosevelt", "Taft", _
  "Taylor", "Truman", "Tyler", "Van Buren", "Washington", "Wilson"}

Dim nameObjs = presidents.Select( _
  Function(p) New With {Key .LastName = p, Key .Length = p.Length})

For Each item In nameObjs
  Console.WriteLine("{0} is {1} characters long.", item.LastName, item.Length)
Next item
```

Notice that I specified a name for each member in the lambda expression and then accessed each member by name in the `Console.WriteLine` method call. Here are the results of this code:

```
Adams is 5 characters long.
Arthur is 6 characters long.
Buchanan is 8 characters long.
Bush is 4 characters long.
Carter is 6 characters long.
Cleveland is 9 characters long.
Clinton is 7 characters long.
Coolidge is 8 characters long.
Eisenhower is 10 characters long.
Fillmore is 8 characters long.
Ford is 4 characters long.
Garfield is 8 characters long.
Grant is 5 characters long.
Harding is 7 characters long.
Harrison is 8 characters long.
Hayes is 5 characters long.
Hoover is 6 characters long.
Jackson is 7 characters long.
Jefferson is 9 characters long.
Johnson is 7 characters long.
Kennedy is 7 characters long.
Lincoln is 7 characters long.
Madison is 7 characters long.
McKinley is 8 characters long.
Monroe is 6 characters long.
Nixon is 5 characters long.
Pierce is 6 characters long.
Polk is 4 characters long.
Reagan is 6 characters long.
Roosevelt is 9 characters long.
Taft is 4 characters long.
Taylor is 6 characters long.
Truman is 6 characters long.
Tyler is 5 characters long.
Van Buren is 9 characters long.
Washington is 10 characters long.
Wilson is 6 characters long.
```

For the second `Select` overload's example, I will embed the index that is passed to my selector method into my output sequence's element type, as shown in Listing 4-6.

Listing 4-6. *An Example of the Second Select Overload*

```
Dim presidents() As String = { _
  "Adams", "Arthur", "Buchanan", "Bush", "Carter", "Cleveland", _
  "Clinton", "Coolidge", "Eisenhower", "Fillmore", "Ford", "Garfield", _
  "Grant", "Harding", "Harrison", "Hayes", "Hoover", "Jackson", _
  "Jefferson", "Johnson", "Kennedy", "Lincoln", "Madison", "McKinley", _
  "Monroe", "Nixon", "Pierce", "Polk", "Reagan", "Roosevelt", "Taft", _
  "Taylor", "Truman", "Tyler", "Van Buren", "Washington", "Wilson"}

Dim nameObjs = _
  presidents.Select(Function(p, i) New With {Key .Index = i, Key .LastName = p})

For Each item In nameObjs
  Console.WriteLine("{0}.  {1}", item.Index + 1, item.LastName)
Next item
```

This example will output the index number plus one, followed by the name. This code produces the following abbreviated results:

1. Adams
2. Arthur
3. Buchanan
4. Bush
5. Carter
...
34. Tyler
35. Van Buren
36. Washington
37. Wilson

SelectMany

The SelectMany operator is used to create a one-to-many output projection sequence over an input sequence. While the Select operator will return one output element for every input element, SelectMany will return zero or more output elements for every input element.

Declarations

The SelectMany operator has four overloads, two of which I will cover.

The First Overload of the SelectMany Operator

```
<ExtensionAttribute> _
Public Shared Function SelectMany(Of TSource, TResult) ( _
    source As IEnumerable(Of TSource), _
    selector As Func(Of TSource, IEnumerable(Of TResult)) _
) As IEnumerable(Of TResult)
```

This overload of the operator is passed an input source sequence of elements of type TSource and a selector delegate, and returns an object that, when enumerated, enumerates the input source sequence, passing each element individually from the input sequence to the selector method. The selector method then returns an object that, when enumerated, yields zero or more elements of type TResult in an intermediate output sequence. The SelectMany operator will return the concatenated output sequences from each call to your selector method.

The Second Overload of the SelectMany Operator

```
<ExtensionAttribute> _
Public Shared Function SelectMany(Of TSource, TResult) ( _
    source As IEnumerable(Of TSource), _
    selector As Func(Of TSource, Integer, IEnumerable(Of TResult)) _
) As IEnumerable(Of TResult)
```

This overload behaves just like the first overload, except a zero-based index of the element in the input sequence is passed to your selector method.

Exceptions

ArgumentNullException is thrown if any of the arguments are Nothing.

Examples

Listing 4-7 is an example calling the first overload.

Listing 4-7. *An Example of the First SelectMany Overload*

```
Dim presidents() As String = { _
    "Adams", "Arthur", "Buchanan", "Bush", "Carter", "Cleveland", _
    "Clinton", "Coolidge", "Eisenhower", "Fillmore", "Ford", "Garfield", _
    "Grant", "Harding", "Harrison", "Hayes", "Hoover", "Jackson", _
    "Jefferson", "Johnson", "Kennedy", "Lincoln", "Madison", "McKinley", _
    "Monroe", "Nixon", "Pierce", "Polk", "Reagan", "Roosevelt", "Taft", _
    "Taylor", "Truman", "Tyler", "Van Buren", "Washington", "Wilson"}

Dim chars As IEnumerable(Of Char) = presidents.SelectMany(Function(p) p.ToArray())

For Each ch As Char In chars
    Console.WriteLine(ch)
Next ch
```

In the preceding example, my selector method receives a string as input, and by calling the ToArray method on that String, it returns an array of Chars, which becomes an output sequence of type Char.

So, for a single input sequence element, which in this case is a String, my selector method returns a sequence of characters. For each input String, a sequence of characters is output. The SelectMany operator concatenates each of those character sequences into a single character sequence that is returned.

The output of the previous code is

```
A
d
a
m
s
A
r
t
h
u
r
B
u
c
h
a
n
a
n
B
u
s
h
...
W
a
s
h
i
n
g
t
o
n
W
i
l
s
o
n
```

That was a pretty simple query but not very demonstrative of a more typical usage. For the next example, I will use the `Employee` and `EmployeeOptionEntry` common classes.

I will call the `SelectMany` operator on the array of `Employee` elements, and for each `Employee` element in the array, my `selector` delegate will return zero or more elements

of the anonymous class I create containing the id and the optionsCount from the array of
EmployeeOptionEntry elements for that Employee object. Let's take a look at the code to accomplish this in Listing 4-8.

Listing 4-8. *A More Complex Example of the First SelectMany Overload*

```
Dim employees() As Employee = Employee.GetEmployeesArray()
Dim empOptions() As EmployeeOptionEntry = _
  EmployeeOptionEntry.GetEmployeeOptionEntries()

Dim employeeOptions = employees _
  .SelectMany(Function(e) empOptions _
                .Where(Function(eo) eo.id = e.id) _
                .Select(Function(eo) New With { _
                                    Key .id = eo.id, _
                                    Key .optionsCount = eo.optionsCount}))

For Each item In employeeOptions
  Console.WriteLine(item)
Next item
```

In this example, every employee in the Employee array is passed into the lambda expression that is passed into the SelectMany operator. That lambda expression will then retrieve
every EmployeeOptionEntry element whose id matches the id of the current employee passed
into it by using the Where operator. This is effectively joining the Employee array and the
EmployeeOptionEntry array on their id members. The lambda expression's Select operator
then creates an anonymous object containing the id and optionsCount members for each
matching record in the EmployeeOptionEntry array. This means a sequence of zero or more
anonymous objects for each passed employee is returned by the lambda expression. This
results in a sequence of sequences that the SelectMany operator then concatenates together.

The previous code produces the following output:

```
{ id = 1, optionsCount = 2 }
{ id = 2, optionsCount = 10000 }
{ id = 2, optionsCount = 10000 }
{ id = 2, optionsCount = 10000 }
{ id = 3, optionsCount = 5000 }
{ id = 3, optionsCount = 7500 }
{ id = 3, optionsCount = 7500 }
{ id = 4, optionsCount = 1500 }
{ id = 101, optionsCount = 2 }
```

While a bit contrived, the example in Listing 4-9 shows the second SelectMany overload
being called.

Listing 4-9. *An Example of the Second SelectMany Overload*

```
Dim presidents() As String = { _
  "Adams", "Arthur", "Buchanan", "Bush", "Carter", "Cleveland", _
  "Clinton", "Coolidge", "Eisenhower", "Fillmore", "Ford", "Garfield", _
  "Grant", "Harding", "Harrison", "Hayes", "Hoover", "Jackson", _
  "Jefferson", "Johnson", "Kennedy", "Lincoln", "Madison", "McKinley", _
  "Monroe", "Nixon", "Pierce", "Polk", "Reagan", "Roosevelt", "Taft", _
  "Taylor", "Truman", "Tyler", "Van Buren", "Washington", "Wilson"}

Dim chars As IEnumerable(Of Char) = _
  presidents.SelectMany(Function(p, i)If(i < 5, p.ToArray(), New Char(){}))

For Each ch As Char In chars
  Console.WriteLine(ch)
Next ch
```

The lambda expression I provided checks the incoming index and outputs the array of characters from the input `String` only if the index is less than five. This means I will only get the characters for the first five input strings, as evidenced by the output results:

```
A
d
a
m
s
A
r
t
h
u
r
B
u
c
h
a
n
a
n
B
u
s
h
C
```

a
r
t
e
r

Keep in mind that this lambda expression is not all that efficient, particularly if there are a lot of input elements. The lambda expression is getting called for *every* input element. I am merely returning an empty array after the first five input elements. For better performance, I prefer the Take operator that I cover in the next section for this purpose.

The SelectMany operator is also useful for concatenating multiple sequences together. Read the section on the Concat operator later in this chapter for an example.

Partitioning

The partitioning operators allow you to return an output sequence that is a subset of an input sequence.

Take

The Take operator returns a specified number of elements from the input sequence, starting from the beginning of the sequence.

Declarations

The Take operator has one overload.

The Only Overload of the Take Operator

```
<ExtensionAttribute> _
Public Shared Function Take(Of TSource) ( _
    source As IEnumerable(Of TSource), _
    count As Integer _
) As IEnumerable(Of TSource)
```

This overload specifies that Take will receive an input source sequence and an integer named count that specifies how many input elements to return, and it will return an object that, when enumerated, will yield the first count number of elements from the input sequence.

If the count value is greater than the number of elements in the input sequence, each element of the input sequence will be yielded into the output sequence.

Exceptions

ArgumentNullException is thrown if the input source sequence is Nothing.

Examples

Listing 4-10 is an example calling the Take operator using query expression syntax.

■**Note** In Listing 4-10, I am using query expression syntax instead of standard dot notation syntax. See the note at the start of this chapter for more information. Only in VB.NET, and not in C#, does query expression syntax support the Take operator.

Listing 4-10. *An Example of the Take Operator Using Query Expression Syntax*

```
Dim presidents() As String = { _
  "Adams", "Arthur", "Buchanan", "Bush", "Carter", "Cleveland", _
  "Clinton", "Coolidge", "Eisenhower", "Fillmore", "Ford", "Garfield", _
  "Grant", "Harding", "Harrison", "Hayes", "Hoover", "Jackson", _
  "Jefferson", "Johnson", "Kennedy", "Lincoln", "Madison", "McKinley", _
  "Monroe", "Nixon", "Pierce", "Polk", "Reagan", "Roosevelt", "Taft", _
  "Taylor", "Truman", "Tyler", "Van Buren", "Washington", "Wilson"}

Dim items As IEnumerable(Of String) = _
  From p In presidents _
  Take(5)

For Each item As String In items
  Console.WriteLine(item)
Next item
```

This code will return the first five input elements from the presidents array. The results are

```
Adams
Arthur
Buchanan
Bush
Carter
```

In Listing 4-9, I showed some code that I stated would be more efficient if the Take operator were used instead of relying on the index being passed into the lambda expression. Listing 4-11 provides the equivalent code using the Take operator. I will have the exact same results that I had with my code in Listing 4-9, but this code is much more efficient.

Listing 4-11. *Another Example of the Take Operator, This Time Using Standard Dot Notation*

```
Dim presidents() As String = { _
  "Adams", "Arthur", "Buchanan", "Bush", "Carter", "Cleveland", _
  "Clinton", "Coolidge", "Eisenhower", "Fillmore", "Ford", "Garfield", _
  "Grant", "Harding", "Harrison", "Hayes", "Hoover", "Jackson", _
  "Jefferson", "Johnson", "Kennedy", "Lincoln", "Madison", "McKinley", _
  "Monroe", "Nixon", "Pierce", "Polk", "Reagan", "Roosevelt", "Taft", _
  "Taylor", "Truman", "Tyler", "Van Buren", "Washington", "Wilson"}
```

```
Dim chars As IEnumerable(Of Char) = _
    presidents.Take(5).SelectMany(Function(s) s.ToArray())

For Each ch As Char In chars
    Console.WriteLine(ch)
Next ch
```

Just like in the SelectMany example using the second overload, Listing 4-9, the preceding code returns the following results:

```
A
d
a
m
s
A
r
t
h
u
r
B
u
c
h
a
n
a
n
B
u
s
h
C
a
r
t
e
r
```

The differences between this code example and Listing 4-9 are that this one takes only the first five elements from the input sequence and only they are passed as the input sequence into SelectMany. The other code example, Listing 4-9, passes all elements into SelectMany; it will just return an empty array for all except the first five.

TakeWhile

The TakeWhile operator yields elements from an input sequence while some condition is True, starting from the beginning of the sequence. The remaining input elements will be skipped.

Declarations

The TakeWhile operator has two overloads.

The First Overload of the TakeWhile Operator

```
<ExtensionAttribute> _
Public Shared Function TakeWhile(Of TSource) ( _
    source As IEnumerable(Of TSource), _
    predicate As Func(Of TSource, Boolean) _
) As IEnumerable(Of TSource)
```

The TakeWhile operator accepts an input source sequence and a predicate delegate and returns an object that, when enumerated, yields elements until the predicate method returns False. The predicate method receives one element at a time from the input sequence and returns whether the element should be included in the output sequence. If so, it continues processing input elements. Once the predicate method returns False, no other input elements will be processed.

The Second Overload of the TakeWhile Operator

```
<ExtensionAttribute> _
Public Shared Function TakeWhile(Of TSource) ( _
    source As IEnumerable(Of TSource), _
    predicate As Func(Of TSource, Integer, Boolean) _
) As IEnumerable(Of TSource)
```

This overload is just like the first except that the predicate method will also be passed a zero-based index of the element in the input source sequence.

Exceptions

ArgumentNullException is thrown if any arguments are Nothing.

Examples

Listing 4-12 shows an example calling the first overload of the TakeWhile operator.

■**Note** In Listing 4-12, I am using query expression syntax instead of standard dot notation syntax. See the note at the start of the chapter for more information. Only in VB.NET, and not in C#, does query expression syntax support the TakeWhile operator. Also, when using query expression syntax, Take While is written as two words, while in standard dot notation syntax, it is written as one word. Finally, keep in mind that only the first overload of the TakeWhile operator is supported by query expression syntax.

Listing 4-12. *An Example Calling the First TakeWhile Overload Using Query Expression Syntax*

```
Dim presidents() As String = { _
  "Adams", "Arthur", "Buchanan", "Bush", "Carter", "Cleveland", _
  "Clinton", "Coolidge", "Eisenhower", "Fillmore", "Ford", "Garfield", _
  "Grant", "Harding", "Harrison", "Hayes", "Hoover", "Jackson", _
  "Jefferson", "Johnson", "Kennedy", "Lincoln", "Madison", "McKinley", _
  "Monroe", "Nixon", "Pierce", "Polk", "Reagan", "Roosevelt", "Taft", _
  "Taylor", "Truman", "Tyler", "Van Buren", "Washington", "Wilson"}

Dim items As IEnumerable(Of String) = _
  From p In presidents _
  Take While p.Length < 10

For Each item As String In items
  Console.WriteLine(item)
Next item
```

In the preceding code, I wanted to retrieve input elements until I hit one ten or more characters long. Here are the results:

```
Adams
Arthur
Buchanan
Bush
Carter
Cleveland
Clinton
Coolidge
```

"Eisenhower" is the name that caused the TakeWhile operator to stop processing input elements. Now, I will provide an example of the second overload of the TakeWhile operator in Listing 4-13.

Listing 4-13. *Calling the Second TakeWhile Overload Using Standard Dot Notation Syntax*

```
Dim presidents() As String = { _
  "Adams", "Arthur", "Buchanan", "Bush", "Carter", "Cleveland", _
  "Clinton", "Coolidge", "Eisenhower", "Fillmore", "Ford", "Garfield", _
  "Grant", "Harding", "Harrison", "Hayes", "Hoover", "Jackson", _
  "Jefferson", "Johnson", "Kennedy", "Lincoln", "Madison", "McKinley", _
  "Monroe", "Nixon", "Pierce", "Polk", "Reagan", "Roosevelt", "Taft", _
  "Taylor", "Truman", "Tyler", "Van Buren", "Washington", "Wilson"}

Dim items As IEnumerable(Of String) = _
  presidents.TakeWhile( _
    Function(s, i) s.Length < 10 AndAlso i < 5)
```

```
For Each item As String In items
  Console.WriteLine(item)
Next item
```

This example will stop when an input element exceeds nine characters in length or when the sixth element is reached, whichever comes first. Here are the results:

```
Adams
Arthur
Buchanan
Bush
Carter
```

In this case, it stopped because the sixth element was reached.

Skip

The Skip operator skips a specified number of elements from the input sequence, starting from the beginning of the sequence, and yields the rest.

Declarations

The Skip operator has one overload.

The Only Overload of the Skip Operator

```
<ExtensionAttribute> _
Public Shared Function Skip(Of TSource) ( _
    source As IEnumerable(Of TSource), _
    count As Integer _
) As IEnumerable(Of TSource)
```

The Skip operator is passed an input source sequence and an integer named count that specifies how many input elements should be skipped and returns an object that, when enumerated, will skip the first count elements and yield all subsequent elements.

If the value of count is greater than the number of elements in the input sequence, the input sequence will not even be enumerated, and the output sequence will be empty.

Exceptions

ArgumentNullException is thrown if the input source sequence is Nothing.

Examples

Listing 4-14 shows a simple example calling the Skip operator.

■**Note** In Listing 4-14, I am using query expression syntax instead of standard dot notation syntax. See the note at the start of the chapter for more information. Only in VB.NET, and not in C#, does query expression syntax support the Skip operator.

Listing 4-14. *An Example of the Skip Opertor*

```
Dim presidents() As String = { _
  "Adams", "Arthur", "Buchanan", "Bush", "Carter", "Cleveland", _
  "Clinton", "Coolidge", "Eisenhower", "Fillmore", "Ford", "Garfield", _
  "Grant", "Harding", "Harrison", "Hayes", "Hoover", "Jackson", _
  "Jefferson", "Johnson", "Kennedy", "Lincoln", "Madison", "McKinley", _
  "Monroe", "Nixon", "Pierce", "Polk", "Reagan", "Roosevelt", "Taft", _
  "Taylor", "Truman", "Tyler", "Van Buren", "Washington", "Wilson"}

Dim items As IEnumerable(Of String) = _
  From p In presidents _
  Skip(1)

For Each item As String In items
  Console.WriteLine(item)
Next item
```

In this example, I wanted to skip the first element. Notice in the following output that I did indeed skip the first input element, "Adams":

```
Arthur
Buchanan
Bush
...
Van Buren
Washington
Wilson
```

SkipWhile

The SkipWhile operator will process an input sequence, skipping elements while a condition is True, and then yield the remaining elements into an output sequence.

Declarations

The SkipWhile operator has two overloads.

The First Overload of the SkipWhile Operator

```
<ExtensionAttribute> _
Public Shared Function SkipWhile(Of TSource) ( _
    source As IEnumerable(Of TSource), _
    predicate As Func(Of TSource, Boolean) _
) As IEnumerable(Of TSource)
```

The SkipWhile operator accepts an input source sequence and a predicate delegate and returns an object that, when enumerated, skips elements while the predicate method returns True. Once the predicate method returns False, the SkipWhile operator yields all subsequent elements. The predicate method receives one element at a time from the input sequence and returns whether the element should be skipped in the output sequence.

SkipWhile has a second overload, which follows.

The Second Overload of the SkipWhile Operator

```
<ExtensionAttribute> _
Public Shared Function SkipWhile(Of TSource) ( _
    source As IEnumerable(Of TSource), _
    predicate As Func(Of TSource, Integer, Boolean) _
) As IEnumerable(Of TSource)
```

This overload is just like the first except that our predicate method will also be passed a zero-based index of the element in the input source sequence.

Exceptions

ArgumentNullException is thrown if any arguments are Nothing.

Examples

Listing 4-15 shows an example calling the first SkipWhile overload.

■**Note** In Listing 4-15, I am using query expression syntax instead of standard dot notation syntax. See the note at the start of the chapter for more information. Only in VB.NET, and not in C#, does query expression syntax support the SkipWhile operator. Also, when using query expression syntax, Skip While is written as two words, while in standard dot notation syntax, it is written as one word. Finally, keep in mind that only the first overload of the SkipWhile operator is supported by query expression syntax.

Listing 4-15. *An Example of the First SkipWhile Overload*

```
Dim presidents() As String = { _
  "Adams", "Arthur", "Buchanan", "Bush", "Carter", "Cleveland", _
  "Clinton", "Coolidge", "Eisenhower", "Fillmore", "Ford", "Garfield", _
  "Grant", "Harding", "Harrison", "Hayes", "Hoover", "Jackson", _
  "Jefferson", "Johnson", "Kennedy", "Lincoln", "Madison", "McKinley", _
```

```
    "Monroe", "Nixon", "Pierce", "Polk", "Reagan", "Roosevelt", "Taft", _
    "Taylor", "Truman", "Tyler", "Van Buren", "Washington", "Wilson"}

Dim items As IEnumerable(Of String) = _
  From p In presidents _
  Skip While p.StartsWith("A")

For Each item As String In items
  Console.WriteLine(item)
Next item
```

In this example, I told the SkipWhile operator to skip elements as long as they started with the string "A". All the remaining elements will be yielded to the output sequence. Here are the results of the previous query:

```
Buchanan
Bush
Carter
...
Van Buren
Washington
Wilson
```

Now, I will try the second SkipWhile overload, which is shown in Listing 4-16.

Listing 4-16. *An Example of the Second SkipWhile Overload*

```
Dim presidents() As String = { _
    "Adams", "Arthur", "Buchanan", "Bush", "Carter", "Cleveland", _
    "Clinton", "Coolidge", "Eisenhower", "Fillmore", "Ford", "Garfield", _
    "Grant", "Harding", "Harrison", "Hayes", "Hoover", "Jackson", _
    "Jefferson", "Johnson", "Kennedy", "Lincoln", "Madison", "McKinley", _
    "Monroe", "Nixon", "Pierce", "Polk", "Reagan", "Roosevelt", "Taft", _
    "Taylor", "Truman", "Tyler", "Van Buren", "Washington", "Wilson"}

Dim items As IEnumerable(Of String) = _
  presidents.SkipWhile(Function(s, i) s.Length > 4 AndAlso i < 10)

For Each item As String In items
  Console.WriteLine(item)
Next item
```

In this example, I am going to skip input elements until the length is no longer greater than four characters or until the tenth element is reached. I will then yield the remaining elements. Here are the results:

```
Bush
Carter
```

```
Cleveland
...
Van Buren
Washington
Wilson
```

In this case, I stopped skipping elements once I hit "Bush", since it was not greater than four characters long, even though its index is only 3.

Concatenation

The concatenation operators allow multiple input sequences of the same type to be concatenated into a single output sequence.

Concat

The Concat operator concatenates two input sequences and yields a single output sequence.

Declarations

The Concat operator has one overload.

The Only Overload of the Concat Operator

```
<ExtensionAttribute> _
Public Shared Function Concat(Of TSource) ( _
    first As IEnumerable(Of TSource), _
    second As IEnumerable(Of TSource) _
) As IEnumerable(Of TSource)
```

In this overload, two sequences of the same type TSource of elements are input, as first and second. An object is returned that, when enumerated, enumerates the first input sequence, yielding each element to the output sequence, followed by enumerating the second input sequence, yielding each element to the output sequence.

Exceptions

ArgumentNullException is thrown if any arguments are Nothing.

Examples

Listing 4-17 is an example using the Concat operator, as well as the Take and Skip operators.

Listing 4-17. *An Example Calling the Concat Operator*

```
Dim presidents() As String = { _
    "Adams", "Arthur", "Buchanan", "Bush", "Carter", "Cleveland", _
    "Clinton", "Coolidge", "Eisenhower", "Fillmore", "Ford", "Garfield", _
    "Grant", "Harding", "Harrison", "Hayes", "Hoover", "Jackson", _
    "Jefferson", "Johnson", "Kennedy", "Lincoln", "Madison", "McKinley", _
```

```
    "Monroe", "Nixon", "Pierce", "Polk", "Reagan", "Roosevelt", "Taft", _
    "Taylor", "Truman", "Tyler", "Van Buren", "Washington", "Wilson"}

Dim items As IEnumerable(Of String) = _
  presidents.Take(5).Concat(presidents.Skip(5))

For Each item As String In items
  Console.WriteLine(item)
Next item
```

This code takes the first five elements from the input sequence, presidents, and concatenates all *but* the first five input elements from the presidents sequence. The results should be a sequence with the identical contents of the presidents sequence, and they are:

```
Adams
Arthur
Buchanan
Bush
Carter
Cleveland
Clinton
Coolidge
Eisenhower
Fillmore
Ford
Garfield
Grant
Harding
Harrison
Hayes
Hoover
Jackson
Jefferson
Johnson
Kennedy
Lincoln
Madison
McKinley
Monroe
Nixon
Pierce
Polk
Reagan
Roosevelt
Taft
Taylor
Truman
Tyler
```

```
Van Buren
Washington
Wilson
```

An alternative technique for concatenating is to call the SelectMany operator on an array of sequences, as shown in Listing 4-18.

Listing 4-18. *An Example Performing Concatention with an Alternative to Using the Concat Operator*

```
Dim presidents() As String = { _
  "Adams", "Arthur", "Buchanan", "Bush", "Carter", "Cleveland", _
  "Clinton", "Coolidge", "Eisenhower", "Fillmore", "Ford", "Garfield", _
  "Grant", "Harding", "Harrison", "Hayes", "Hoover", "Jackson", _
  "Jefferson", "Johnson", "Kennedy", "Lincoln", "Madison", "McKinley", _
  "Monroe", "Nixon", "Pierce", "Polk", "Reagan", "Roosevelt", "Taft", _
  "Taylor", "Truman", "Tyler", "Van Buren", "Washington", "Wilson"}

Dim items = New IEnumerable(Of String) () _
{ _
  presidents.Take(5), _
  presidents.Skip(5) _
}.SelectMany(Function(s) s)

For Each item As String In items
  Console.WriteLine(item)
Next item
```

In this example, I instantiated an array consisting of two sequences: one created by calling the Take operator on the input sequence and another created by calling the Skip operator on the input sequence. Notice that this is similar to the previous example except that I am calling the SelectMany operator on the array of sequences. Also, while the Concat operator only allows two sequences to be concatenated together, since this technique allows an array of sequences, it may be more useful when you need to concatenate more than two sequences together.

Tip When you need to concatenate more than two sequences together, consider using the SelectMany approach.

Of course, none of this would matter if you did not get the same results as calling the Concat operator. Of course, this isn't a problem, since the results are the same:

```
Adams
Arthur
Buchanan
Bush
```

Carter
Cleveland
Clinton
Coolidge
Eisenhower
Fillmore
Ford
Garfield
Grant
Harding
Harrison
Hayes
Hoover
Jackson
Jefferson
Johnson
Kennedy
Lincoln
Madison
McKinley
Monroe
Nixon
Pierce
Polk
Reagan
Roosevelt
Taft
Taylor
Truman
Tyler
Van Buren
Washington
Wilson

Ordering

The ordering operators allow input sequences to be ordered. It is important to notice that both the OrderBy and OrderByDescending operators require an input sequence of type IEnumerable(Of TSource) and return a sequence of type IOrderedEnumerable(Of TSource). You should not pass an IOrderedEnumerable(Of TSource) as the input sequence into the OrderBy or OrderByDescending operators, because subsequent calls to the OrderBy or OrderByDescending operators will not honor the order created by previous calls to the OrderBy or OrderByDescending operators. This means that you should not pass the returned sequence from either the OrderBy or OrderByDescending operators into a subsequent OrderBy or OrderByDescending operator call.

If you need more ordering than is possible with a single call to the OrderBy or OrderByDescending operators, you should subsequently call the ThenBy or ThenByDescending operators. You may chain calls to the ThenBy and ThenByDescending operators to subsequent calls to the ThenBy and ThenByDescending operators, because they accept an IOrderedEnumerable(Of TSource) as their input sequence, return an IOrderedEnumerable(Of TSource) as their output sequence, and will preserve the ordering of previous OrderBy, OrderByDescending, ThenBy, or ThenByDescending operator calls.

For example, this calling sequence is not recommended:

```
inputSequence.OrderBy(Function(s) s.LastName).OrderBy(Function(s) s.FirstName)...
```

Instead, you would use this calling sequence:

```
inputSequence.OrderBy(Function(s) s.LastName).ThenBy(Function(s) s.FirstName)...
```

OrderBy

The OrderBy operator allows an input sequence to be ordered based on a keySelector method that will return a key value for each input element, and an ordered output sequence, IOrderedEnumerable(Of TSource), will be yielded in ascending order based on the values of the returned keys.

The sort performed by the OrderBy operator is *stable*. This means it will preserve the input order of the elements for equal keys. So, if two input elements come into the OrderBy operator in a particular order, and the key values for both elements are equal, the order of the output elements is guaranteed to be maintained.

■**Note** The sorting performed by OrderBy and OrderByDescending is stable.

Declarations

The OrderBy operator has two overloads.

The First Overload of the OrderBy Operator

```
<ExtensionAttribute> _
Public Shared Function OrderBy(Of TSource, TKey) ( _
    source As IEnumerable(Of TSource), _
    keySelector As Func(Of TSource, TKey) _
) As IOrderedEnumerable(Of TSource)
```

In this overload of OrderBy, an input source sequence is passed into the OrderBy operator along with a keySelector delegate, and an object is returned that, when enumerated, enumerates the source input sequence collecting all the elements, passes each element to the keySelector method thereby retrieving each key, and orders the sequence using the keys.

The keySelector method is passed an input element of type TSource and will return the field within the element that is to be used as the key value, of type TKey, for the input element.

Types TSource and TKey may be the same or different types. The type of the value returned by the keySelector method must implement the IComparable interface.

OrderBy has a second overload that looks like the following.

The Second Overload of the OrderBy Operator

```
<ExtensionAttribute> _
Public Shared Function OrderBy(Of TSource, TKey) ( _
    source As IEnumerable(Of TSource), _
    keySelector As Func(Of TSource, TKey), _
    comparer As IComparer(Of TKey) _
) As IOrderedEnumerable(Of TSource)
```

This overload is the same as the first except it allows for a comparer object to be passed. If this version of the OrderBy operator is used, then it is not necessary that type TKey implement the IComparable interface.

Exceptions

ArgumentNullException is thrown if any arguments are Nothing.

Examples

An example of the first overload is shown in Listing 4-19.

Listing 4-19. *An Example Calling the First OrderBy Overload*

```
Dim presidents() As String = { _
  "Adams", "Arthur", "Buchanan", "Bush", "Carter", "Cleveland", _
  "Clinton", "Coolidge", "Eisenhower", "Fillmore", "Ford", "Garfield", _
  "Grant", "Harding", "Harrison", "Hayes", "Hoover", "Jackson", _
  "Jefferson", "Johnson", "Kennedy", "Lincoln", "Madison", "McKinley", _
  "Monroe", "Nixon", "Pierce", "Polk", "Reagan", "Roosevelt", "Taft", _
  "Taylor", "Truman", "Tyler", "Van Buren", "Washington", "Wilson"}

Dim items As IEnumerable(Of String) = _
  presidents.OrderBy(Function(s) s.Length)

For Each item As String In items
  Console.WriteLine(item)
Next item
```

This example orders the presidents by the length of their names. Here are the results:

```
Bush
Ford
Polk
Taft
Adams
Grant
```

Hayes
Nixon
Tyler
Arthur
Carter
Hoover
Monroe
Pierce
Reagan
Taylor
Truman
Wilson
Clinton
Harding
Jackson
Johnson
Kennedy
Lincoln
Madison
Buchanan
Coolidge
Fillmore
Garfield
Harrison
McKinley
Cleveland
Jefferson
Roosevelt
Van Buren
Eisenhower
Washington

Now, I will try an example of the second overload by using my own comparer. Before I explain the code, it might be helpful to examine the IComparer interface.

The IComparer(Of TSource) Interface

```
Public Interface IComparer(Of TSource)
  Function Compare(ByVal x As TSource, ByVal y As TSource) As Integer
End Interface
```

The IComparer interface requires me to implement a single method named Compare. This method will receive two arguments of the same type TSource and will return an Integer that is less than zero if the first argument is less than the second, zero if the two arguments are equal, and greater than zero if the second argument is greater than the first. Notice how the generics added to VB.NET 2.0 come to our aid in this interface and overload.

For this example, to make it clear I am not using any default comparer, I have created a class that implements the IComparer interface, which will order the elements based on their vowel-to-consonant ratios.

My Implementation of the IComparer Interface for an Example Calling the Second OrderBy Overload

```
Public Class MyVowelToConsonantRatioComparer
  Implements IComparer(Of String)

  Public Function Compare(ByVal s1 As String, ByVal s2 As String) As Integer _
    Implements IComparer(Of String).Compare

    Dim vCount1 As Integer = 0
    Dim cCount1 As Integer = 0
    Dim vCount2 As Integer = 0
    Dim cCount2 As Integer = 0

    GetVowelConsonantCount(s1, vCount1, cCount1)
    GetVowelConsonantCount(s2, vCount2, cCount2)

    Dim dRatio1 As Double = CDbl(vCount1)/CDbl(cCount1)
    Dim dRatio2 As Double = CDbl(vCount2)/CDbl(cCount2)

    If dRatio1 < dRatio2 Then
      Return(-1)
    ElseIf dRatio1 > dRatio2 Then
      Return(1)
    Else
      Return(0)
    End If
  End Function

  ' This method is public so my code using this comparer can get the values
  ' if it wants.
  Public Sub GetVowelConsonantCount(ByVal s As String, _
    ByRef vowelCount As Integer, ByRef consonantCount As Integer)
    ' DISCLAIMER:  This code is for demonstration purposes only.
    ' This code treats the letter 'y' or 'Y' as a vowel always,
    ' which linguistically speaking, is probably invalid.

    Dim vowels As String = "AEIOUY"

    ' Initialize the counts.
    vowelCount = 0
    consonantCount = 0
```

```
    ' Convert to uppercase so we are case insensitive.
    Dim sUpper As String = s.ToUpper()

    For Each ch As Char In sUpper
      If vowels.IndexOf(ch) < 0 Then
        consonantCount += 1
      Else
        vowelCount += 1
      End If
    Next ch

    Return
  End Sub
End Class
```

That class contains two methods, Compare and GetVowelConsonantCount. The Compare method is required by the IComparer interface. The GetVowelConsonantCount method exists because I needed it internally in the Compare method so that the number of vowels and consonants for a given input string could be obtained. I also wanted the ability to call that same logic from outside the Compare method so that I could obtain the values for display when I looped through my ordered sequence.

The logic of what my comparer is doing isn't that significant. It is highly unlikely that you will ever need to determine the vowel-to-consonant ratio for a string, much less compare two strings based on that ratio. What is important is how I created a class implementing the IComparer interface by implementing a Compare method. You can see the nitty-gritty implementation of the Compare method by examining the If/ElseIf/Else block at the bottom of the Compare method. As you can see, in that block of code, I return –1, 1, or 0, thereby adhering to the contract of the IComparer interface.

Now, I will call the code, which is shown in Listing 4-20.

Listing 4-20. *An Example Calling the Second OrderBy Overload*

```
Dim presidents() As String = { _
  "Adams", "Arthur", "Buchanan", "Bush", "Carter", "Cleveland", _
  "Clinton", "Coolidge", "Eisenhower", "Fillmore", "Ford", "Garfield", _
  "Grant", "Harding", "Harrison", "Hayes", "Hoover", "Jackson", _
  "Jefferson", "Johnson", "Kennedy", "Lincoln", "Madison", "McKinley", _
  "Monroe", "Nixon", "Pierce", "Polk", "Reagan", "Roosevelt", "Taft", _
  "Taylor", "Truman", "Tyler", "Van Buren", "Washington", "Wilson"}

'  I am going to instantiate my comparer ahead of time so I can keep a
'  reference so I can call the GetVowelConsonantCount() method later
'  for display purposes.
Dim myComp As New MyVowelToConsonantRatioComparer()

Dim namesByVToCRatio As IEnumerable(Of String) = _
  presidents.OrderBy((Function(s) s), myComp)
```

```
For Each item As String In namesByVToCRatio
  Dim vCount As Integer = 0
  Dim cCount As Integer = 0

  myComp.GetVowelConsonantCount(item, vCount, cCount)
  Dim dRatio As Double = CDbl(vCount) / CDbl(cCount)

  Console.WriteLine(item & " - " & dRatio & " - " & vCount & ":" & cCount)
Next item
```

In the preceding example, you can see that I instantiate my comparer before calling the OrderBy operator. I could instantiate it in the OrderBy method call, but then I would not have a reference to it when I want to call it in the For Each loop. Here are the results of this code:

```
Grant - 0.25 - 1:4
Bush - 0.333333333333333 - 1:3
Ford - 0.333333333333333 - 1:3
Polk - 0.333333333333333 - 1:3
Taft - 0.333333333333333 - 1:3
Clinton - 0.4 - 2:5
Harding - 0.4 - 2:5
Jackson - 0.4 - 2:5
Johnson - 0.4 - 2:5
Lincoln - 0.4 - 2:5
Washington - 0.428571428571429 - 3:7
Arthur - 0.5 - 2:4
Carter - 0.5 - 2:4
Cleveland - 0.5 - 3:6
Jefferson - 0.5 - 3:6
Truman - 0.5 - 2:4
Van Buren - 0.5 - 3:6
Wilson - 0.5 - 2:4
Buchanan - 0.6 - 3:5
Fillmore - 0.6 - 3:5
Garfield - 0.6 - 3:5
Harrison - 0.6 - 3:5
McKinley - 0.6 - 3:5
Adams - 0.666666666666667 - 2:3
Nixon - 0.666666666666667 - 2:3
Tyler - 0.666666666666667 - 2:3
Kennedy - 0.75 - 3:4
Madison - 0.75 - 3:4
Roosevelt - 0.8 - 4:5
Coolidge - 1 - 4:4
Eisenhower - 1 - 5:5
Hoover - 1 - 3:3
Monroe - 1 - 3:3
Pierce - 1 - 3:3
```

```
Reagan - 1 - 3:3
Taylor - 1 - 3:3
Hayes - 1.5 - 3:2
```

As you can see, the presidents with the lower vowel-to-consonant ratios come first.

OrderByDescending

This operator is declared and behaves just like the OrderBy operator, except that it orders in descending order.

Declarations

The OrderByDescending operator has two overloads.

The First Overload of the OrderByDescending Operator

```
<ExtensionAttribute> _
Public Shared Function OrderByDescending(Of TSource, TKey) ( _
    source As IEnumerable(Of TSource), _
    keySelector As Func(Of TSource, TKey) _
) As IOrderedEnumerable(Of TSource)
```

This overload of the OrderByDescending operator behaves just like its equivalent OrderBy overload except the order will be descending.

Note The sorting performed by OrderBy and OrderByDescending is stable.

OrderByDescending has a second overload that looks like the following.

The Second Overload of the OrderByDescending Operator

```
<ExtensionAttribute> _
Public Shared Function OrderByDescending(Of TSource, TKey) ( _
    source As IEnumerable(Of TSource), _
    keySelector As Func(Of TSource, TKey), _
    comparer As IComparer(Of TKey) _
) As IOrderedEnumerable(Of TSource)
```

This overload is the same as the first except it allows for a comparer object to be passed. If this version of the OrderByDescending operator is used, it is not necessary that type TKey implement the IComparable interface.

Exceptions

ArgumentNullException is thrown if any arguments are Nothing.

Examples

In the example of the first overload shown in Listing 4-21, I will order the presidents in descending order by their names.

Listing 4-21. *An Example Calling the First Overload of the OrderByDescending Operator*

```
Dim presidents() As String = { _
   "Adams", "Arthur", "Buchanan", "Bush", "Carter", "Cleveland", _
   "Clinton", "Coolidge", "Eisenhower", "Fillmore", "Ford", "Garfield", _
   "Grant", "Harding", "Harrison", "Hayes", "Hoover", "Jackson", _
   "Jefferson", "Johnson", "Kennedy", "Lincoln", "Madison", "McKinley", _
   "Monroe", "Nixon", "Pierce", "Polk", "Reagan", "Roosevelt", "Taft", _
   "Taylor", "Truman", "Tyler", "Van Buren", "Washington", "Wilson"}

Dim items As IEnumerable(Of String) = _
  presidents.OrderByDescending(Function(s) s)

For Each item As String In items
  Console.WriteLine(item)
Next item
```

As you can see, the president names are in descending order:

```
Wilson
Washington
Van Buren
Tyler
Truman
Taylor
Taft
Roosevelt
Reagan
Polk
Pierce
Nixon
Monroe
McKinley
Madison
Lincoln
Kennedy
Johnson
Jefferson
Jackson
Hoover
Hayes
Harrison
Harding
Grant
```

Garfield
Ford
Fillmore
Eisenhower
Coolidge
Clinton
Cleveland
Carter
Bush
Buchanan
Arthur
Adams

Now, I will try an example of the second OrderByDescending overload. I will use the same example that I used for the second overload of the OrderBy operator, except instead of calling the OrderBy operator, I will call the OrderByDescending operator. I will be using the same comparer, MyVowelToConsonantRatioComparer, that I used in that example. The code is shown in Listing 4-22.

Listing 4-22. *An Example Calling the Second Overload of the OrderByDescending Operator*

```
Dim presidents() As String = { _
  "Adams", "Arthur", "Buchanan", "Bush", "Carter", "Cleveland", _
  "Clinton", "Coolidge", "Eisenhower", "Fillmore", "Ford", "Garfield", _
  "Grant", "Harding", "Harrison", "Hayes", "Hoover", "Jackson", _
  "Jefferson", "Johnson", "Kennedy", "Lincoln", "Madison", "McKinley", _
  "Monroe", "Nixon", "Pierce", "Polk", "Reagan", "Roosevelt", "Taft", _
  "Taylor", "Truman", "Tyler", "Van Buren", "Washington", "Wilson"}

' I am going to instantiate my comparer ahead of time so I can keep a
' reference so I can call the GetVowelConsonantCount() method later
' for display purposes.
Dim myComp As New MyVowelToConsonantRatioComparer()

Dim namesByVToCRatio As IEnumerable(Of String) = _
  presidents.OrderByDescending((Function(s) s), myComp)

For Each item As String In namesByVToCRatio
  Dim vCount As Integer = 0
  Dim cCount As Integer = 0

  myComp.GetVowelConsonantCount(item, vCount, cCount)
  Dim dRatio As Double = CDbl(vCount) / CDbl(cCount)

  Console.WriteLine(item & " - " & dRatio & " - " & vCount & ":" & cCount)
Next item
```

This example works just like the equivalent OrderBy example. Here are the results:

```
Hayes - 1.5 - 3:2
Coolidge - 1 - 4:4
Eisenhower - 1 - 5:5
Hoover - 1 - 3:3
Monroe - 1 - 3:3
Pierce - 1 - 3:3
Reagan - 1 - 3:3
Taylor - 1 - 3:3
Roosevelt - 0.8 - 4:5
Kennedy - 0.75 - 3:4
Madison - 0.75 - 3:4
Adams - 0.666666666666667 - 2:3
Nixon - 0.666666666666667 - 2:3
Tyler - 0.666666666666667 - 2:3
Buchanan - 0.6 - 3:5
Fillmore - 0.6 - 3:5
Garfield - 0.6 - 3:5
Harrison - 0.6 - 3:5
McKinley - 0.6 - 3:5
Arthur - 0.5 - 2:4
Carter - 0.5 - 2:4
Cleveland - 0.5 - 3:6
Jefferson - 0.5 - 3:6
Truman - 0.5 - 2:4
Van Buren - 0.5 - 3:6
Wilson - 0.5 - 2:4
Washington - 0.428571428571429 - 3:7
Clinton - 0.4 - 2:5
Harding - 0.4 - 2:5
Jackson - 0.4 - 2:5
Johnson - 0.4 - 2:5
Lincoln - 0.4 - 2:5
Bush - 0.333333333333333 - 1:3
Ford - 0.333333333333333 - 1:3
Polk - 0.333333333333333 - 1:3
Taft - 0.333333333333333 - 1:3
Grant - 0.25 - 1:4
```

These results are the same as the equivalent OrderBy example, except the order is reversed. Now, the presidents are listed by their vowel-to-consonant ratio in descending order.

ThenBy

The ThenBy operator allows an input ordered sequence of type IOrderedEnumerable(Of TSource) to be ordered based on a keySelector method that will return a key value, and an ordered output sequence of type IOrderedEnumerable(Of TSource) will be yielded.

■**Note** Both the `ThenBy` and `ThenByDescending` operators accept a different type of input sequence than most LINQ to Objects deferred query operators. They take an `IOrderedEnumerable(Of TSource)` as the input sequence. This means either the `OrderBy` or `OrderByDescending` operators must be called first to create an `IOrderedEnumerable`, on which you can then call the `ThenBy` or `ThenByDescending` operators.

The sort performed by the `ThenBy` operator is *stable*. This means it will preserve the input order of the elements for equal keys. So, if two input elements come into the `ThenBy` operator in a particular order, and the key values for both elements are equal, the order of the output elements is guaranteed to be maintained.

■**Note** Like `OrderBy` and `OrderByDescending`, `ThenBy` and `ThenByDescending` are stable sorts.

Declarations

The `ThenBy` operator has two overloads.

The First Overload of the ThenBy Operator

```
<ExtensionAttribute> _
Public Shared Function ThenBy(Of TSource, TKey) ( _
    source As IOrderedEnumerable(Of TSource), _
    keySelector As Func(Of TSource, TKey) _
) As IOrderedEnumerable(Of TSource)
```

In this overload of the `ThenBy` operator, an ordered input sequence of type `IOrderedEnumerable(Of TSource)` is passed into the `ThenBy` operator along with a `keySelector` delegate. The `keySelector` method is passed an input element of type `TSource` and will return the field within the element that is to be used as the key value, of type `TKey`, for the input element. Types `TSource` and `TKey` may be the same or different types. The value returned by the `keySelector` method must implement the `IComparable` interface. The `ThenBy` operator will order the input sequence in ascending order based on those returned keys.

There is a second overload defined as follows.

The Second Overload of the ThenBy Operator

```
<ExtensionAttribute> _
Public Shared Function ThenBy(Of TSource, TKey) ( _
    source As IOrderedEnumerable(Of TSource), _
    keySelector As Func(Of TSource, TKey), _
    comparer As IComparer(Of TKey) _
) As IOrderedEnumerable(Of TSource)
```

This overload is the same as the first except it allows for a comparer object to be passed. If this version of the ThenBy operator is used, it is not necessary that type TKey implement the IComparable interface.

Exceptions

ArgumentNullException is thrown if any arguments are Nothing.

Examples

Listing 4-23 shows an example of the first overload.

Listing 4-23. *An Example Calling the First Overload of the ThenBy Operator*

```
Dim presidents() As String = { _
  "Adams", "Arthur", "Buchanan", "Bush", "Carter", "Cleveland", _
  "Clinton", "Coolidge", "Eisenhower", "Fillmore", "Ford", "Garfield", _
  "Grant", "Harding", "Harrison", "Hayes", "Hoover", "Jackson", _
  "Jefferson", "Johnson", "Kennedy", "Lincoln", "Madison", "McKinley", _
  "Monroe", "Nixon", "Pierce", "Polk", "Reagan", "Roosevelt", "Taft", _
  "Taylor", "Truman", "Tyler", "Van Buren", "Washington", "Wilson"}

Dim items As IEnumerable(Of String) = _
  presidents.OrderBy(Function(s) s.Length).ThenBy(Function(s) s)

For Each item As String In items
  Console.WriteLine(item)
Next item
```

This example first orders by the input element length, which in this case is the length of the president's name. It then orders by the element itself. The result is that the names are presented in length order, smallest to largest (ascending), then alphabetically by name, ascending. Here is the proof:

```
Bush
Ford
Polk
Taft
Adams
Grant
Hayes
Nixon
Tyler
Arthur
Carter
Hoover
Monroe
Pierce
Reagan
```

```
Taylor
Truman
Wilson
Clinton
Harding
Jackson
Johnson
Kennedy
Lincoln
Madison
Buchanan
Coolidge
Fillmore
Garfield
Harrison
McKinley
Cleveland
Jefferson
Roosevelt
Van Buren
Eisenhower
Washington
```

For an example of the second ThenBy operator overload, I will again use my
MyVowelToConsonantRatioComparer comparer object that I introduced in the example of
the second OrderBy overload. However, to call ThenBy, I first must call either OrderBy or
OrderByDescending. For this example, I will call OrderBy and order by the number of characters in the name. This way, the names will be ordered ascending by the number of characters,
and then within each grouping of names by length, they will be ordered by their vowel-to-
consonant ratio. The example is shown in Listing 4-24.

Listing 4-24. *An Example of the Second Overload of the ThenBy Operator*

```
Dim presidents() As String = { _
  "Adams", "Arthur", "Buchanan", "Bush", "Carter", "Cleveland", _
  "Clinton", "Coolidge", "Eisenhower", "Fillmore", "Ford", "Garfield", _
  "Grant", "Harding", "Harrison", "Hayes", "Hoover", "Jackson", _
  "Jefferson", "Johnson", "Kennedy", "Lincoln", "Madison", "McKinley", _
  "Monroe", "Nixon", "Pierce", "Polk", "Reagan", "Roosevelt", "Taft", _
  "Taylor", "Truman", "Tyler", "Van Buren", "Washington", "Wilson"}

'  I am going to instantiate my comparer ahead of time so I can keep a
'  reference so I can call the GetVowelConsonantCount() method later
'  for display purposes.
Dim myComp As New MyVowelToConsonantRatioComparer()
```

```
Dim namesByVToCRatio As IEnumerable(Of String) = _
  presidents.OrderBy(Function(n) n.Length).ThenBy((Function(s) s), myComp)

For Each item As String In namesByVToCRatio
  Dim vCount As Integer = 0
  Dim cCount As Integer = 0

  myComp.GetVowelConsonantCount(item, vCount, cCount)
  Dim dRatio As Double = CDbl(vCount) / CDbl(cCount)

  Console.WriteLine(item & " - " & dRatio & " - " & vCount & ":" & cCount)
Next item
```

This code gives the following results:

```
Bush - 0.333333333333333 - 1:3
Ford - 0.333333333333333 - 1:3
Polk - 0.333333333333333 - 1:3
Taft - 0.333333333333333 - 1:3
Grant - 0.25 - 1:4
Adams - 0.666666666666667 - 2:3
Nixon - 0.666666666666667 - 2:3
Tyler - 0.666666666666667 - 2:3
Hayes - 1.5 - 3:2
Arthur - 0.5 - 2:4
Carter - 0.5 - 2:4
Truman - 0.5 - 2:4
Wilson - 0.5 - 2:4
Hoover - 1 - 3:3
Monroe - 1 - 3:3
Pierce - 1 - 3:3
Reagan - 1 - 3:3
Taylor - 1 - 3:3
Clinton - 0.4 - 2:5
Harding - 0.4 - 2:5
Jackson - 0.4 - 2:5
Johnson - 0.4 - 2:5
Lincoln - 0.4 - 2:5
Kennedy - 0.75 - 3:4
Madison - 0.75 - 3:4
Buchanan - 0.6 - 3:5
Fillmore - 0.6 - 3:5
Garfield - 0.6 - 3:5
Harrison - 0.6 - 3:5
McKinley - 0.6 - 3:5
Coolidge - 1 - 4:4
Cleveland - 0.5 - 3:6
Jefferson - 0.5 - 3:6
```

```
Van Buren - 0.5 - 3:6
Roosevelt - 0.8 - 4:5
Washington - 0.428571428571429 - 3:7
Eisenhower - 1 - 5:5
```

As I intended, the names are first ordered by their length, then by their vowel-to-consonant ratio.

ThenByDescending

This operator is defined and behaves just like the ThenBy operator, except that it orders in descending order.

Declarations

The ThenByDescending operator has two overloads.

The First Overload of the ThenByDescending Operator

```
<ExtensionAttribute> _
Public Shared Function ThenByDescending(Of TSource, TKey) ( _
    source As IOrderedEnumerable(Of TSource), _
    keySelector As Func(Of TSource, TKey) _
) As IOrderedEnumerable(Of TSource)
```

This overload of the operator behaves the same as the first overload of the ThenBy operator, except it orders in descending order.

ThenByDescending has a second overload that looks like the following.

The Second Overload of the ThenByDescending Operator

```
<ExtensionAttribute> _
Public Shared Function ThenByDescending(Of TSource, TKey) ( _
    source As IOrderedEnumerable(Of TSource), _
    keySelector As Func(Of TSource, TKey), _
    comparer As IComparer(Of TKey) _
) As IOrderedEnumerable(Of TSource)
```

This overload is the same as the first except it allows for a comparer object to be passed. If this version of the ThenByDescending operator is used, it is not necessary that TKey implement the IComparable interface.

Exceptions

ArgumentNullException is thrown if any arguments are Nothing.

Examples

For my example of the first overload of the ThenByDescending operator, I will use the same basic example I used in the example of the first overload of the ThenBy operator, except I will call ThenByDescending instead of ThenBy. Listing 4-25 shows this example.

Listing 4-25. *An Example Calling the First Overload of the ThenByDescending Operator*

```
Dim presidents() As String = { _
  "Adams", "Arthur", "Buchanan", "Bush", "Carter", "Cleveland", _
  "Clinton", "Coolidge", "Eisenhower", "Fillmore", "Ford", "Garfield", _
  "Grant", "Harding", "Harrison", "Hayes", "Hoover", "Jackson", _
  "Jefferson", "Johnson", "Kennedy", "Lincoln", "Madison", "McKinley", _
  "Monroe", "Nixon", "Pierce", "Polk", "Reagan", "Roosevelt", "Taft", _
  "Taylor", "Truman", "Tyler", "Van Buren", "Washington", "Wilson"}

Dim items As IEnumerable(Of String) = _
  presidents.OrderBy(Function(s) s.Length).ThenByDescending(Function(s) s)

For Each item As String In items
  Console.WriteLine(item)
Next item
```

This produces output where the names within each name length are sorted alphabetically in descending order, which is the reverse order that the ThenBy operator provided:

```
Taft
Polk
Ford
Bush
Tyler
Nixon
Hayes
Grant
Adams
Wilson
Truman
Taylor
Reagan
Pierce
Monroe
Hoover
Carter
Arthur
Madison
Lincoln
Kennedy
Johnson
Jackson
```

```
Harding
Clinton
McKinley
Harrison
Garfield
Fillmore
Coolidge
Buchanan
Van Buren
Roosevelt
Jefferson
Cleveland
Washington
Eisenhower
```

For my example of the second overload of the ThenByDescending operator, which is shown in Listing 4-26, I will use the same example that I did for the second overload of the ThenBy operator, except I will call ThenByDescending instead of ThenBy.

Listing 4-26. *An Example of the Second Overload of the ThenByDescending Operator*

```
Dim presidents() As String = { _
  "Adams", "Arthur", "Buchanan", "Bush", "Carter", "Cleveland", _
  "Clinton", "Coolidge", "Eisenhower", "Fillmore", "Ford", "Garfield", _
  "Grant", "Harding", "Harrison", "Hayes", "Hoover", "Jackson", _
  "Jefferson", "Johnson", "Kennedy", "Lincoln", "Madison", "McKinley", _
  "Monroe", "Nixon", "Pierce", "Polk", "Reagan", "Roosevelt", "Taft", _
  "Taylor", "Truman", "Tyler", "Van Buren", "Washington", "Wilson"}

'  I am going to instantiate my comparer ahead of time so I can keep a
'  reference so I can call the GetVowelConsonantCount() method later
'  for display purposes.
Dim myComp As New MyVowelToConsonantRatioComparer()

Dim namesByVToCRatio As IEnumerable(Of String) = _
  presidents.OrderBy(Function(n) n.Length) _
          .ThenByDescending((Function(s) s), myComp)

For Each item As String In namesByVToCRatio
  Dim vCount As Integer = 0
  Dim cCount As Integer = 0

  myComp.GetVowelConsonantCount(item, vCount, cCount)
  Dim dRatio As Double = CDbl(vCount) / CDbl(cCount)

  Console.WriteLine(item & " - " & dRatio & " - " & vCount & ":" & cCount)
Next item
```

This code provides the following results:

```
Bush - 0.333333333333333 - 1:3
Ford - 0.333333333333333 - 1:3
Polk - 0.333333333333333 - 1:3
Taft - 0.333333333333333 - 1:3
Hayes - 1.5 - 3:2
Adams - 0.666666666666667 - 2:3
Nixon - 0.666666666666667 - 2:3
Tyler - 0.666666666666667 - 2:3
Grant - 0.25 - 1:4
Hoover - 1 - 3:3
Monroe - 1 - 3:3
Pierce - 1 - 3:3
Reagan - 1 - 3:3
Taylor - 1 - 3:3
Arthur - 0.5 - 2:4
Carter - 0.5 - 2:4
Truman - 0.5 - 2:4
Wilson - 0.5 - 2:4
Kennedy - 0.75 - 3:4
Madison - 0.75 - 3:4
Clinton - 0.4 - 2:5
Harding - 0.4 - 2:5
Jackson - 0.4 - 2:5
Johnson - 0.4 - 2:5
Lincoln - 0.4 - 2:5
Coolidge - 1 - 4:4
Buchanan - 0.6 - 3:5
Fillmore - 0.6 - 3:5
Garfield - 0.6 - 3:5
Harrison - 0.6 - 3:5
McKinley - 0.6 - 3:5
Roosevelt - 0.8 - 4:5
Cleveland - 0.5 - 3:6
Jefferson - 0.5 - 3:6
Van Buren - 0.5 - 3:6
Eisenhower - 1 - 5:5
Washington - 0.428571428571429 - 3:7
```

Just as I anticipated, the names are ordered first by ascending length, then by the ratio of their vowels to consonants, descending.

Reverse

The reverse operator outputs a sequence of the same type as the input sequence but in the reverse order.

Declarations

The Reverse operator has one overload.

The Only Overload of the Reverse Operator

```
<ExtensionAttribute> _
Public Shared Function Reverse(Of TSource) ( _
    source As IEnumerable(Of TSource) _
) As IEnumerable(Of TSource)
```

This operator returns an object that, when enumerated, enumerates the elements of the input sequence named TSource and yields elements for the output sequence in reverse order.

Exceptions

ArgumentNullException is thrown if the source argument is Nothing.

Examples

Listing 4-27 is an example of the overload of the Reverse operator.

Listing 4-27. *An Example Calling the Reverse Operator*

```
Dim presidents() As String = { _
  "Adams", "Arthur", "Buchanan", "Bush", "Carter", "Cleveland", _
  "Clinton", "Coolidge", "Eisenhower", "Fillmore", "Ford", "Garfield", _
  "Grant", "Harding", "Harrison", "Hayes", "Hoover", "Jackson", _
  "Jefferson", "Johnson", "Kennedy", "Lincoln", "Madison", "McKinley", _
  "Monroe", "Nixon", "Pierce", "Polk", "Reagan", "Roosevelt", "Taft", _
  "Taylor", "Truman", "Tyler", "Van Buren", "Washington", "Wilson"}

Dim items As IEnumerable(Of String) = presidents.Reverse()

For Each item As String In items
  Console.WriteLine(item)
Next item
```

If this works properly, I should see the presidents in the reverse order of the order in the presidents array. Here are the results of the previous code:

```
Wilson
Washington
Van Buren
...
Bush
Buchanan
Arthur
Adams
```

Join

The join operators perform joins across multiple sequences.

Join

The Join operator performs an inner equijoin on two sequences based on keys extracted from each element in the sequences.

Declarations

The Join operator has two overloads, one of which I will cover.

The First Overload of the Join Operator

```
<ExtensionAttribute> _
Public Shared Function Join(Of TOuter, TInner, TKey, TResult) ( _
    outer As IEnumerable(Of TOuter), _
    inner As IEnumerable(Of TInner), _
    outerKeySelector As Func(Of TOuter, TKey), _
    innerKeySelector As Func(Of TInner, TKey), _
    resultSelector As Func(Of TOuter, TInner, TResult) _
) As IEnumerable(Of TResult)
```

Notice that the first argument of the method is named outer. Since this is an extension method, the sequence we call the Join operator on will be referred to as the outer sequence.

The Join operator will return an object that, when enumerated, will first enumerate the inner sequence of type TInner elements, calling the innerKeySelector method once for each element and storing the element, referenced by its key, in a hash table. Next, the returned object will enumerate the outer sequence of type TOuter elements. As the returned object enumerates each outer sequence element, it will call the outerKeySelector method to obtain its key and retrieve the matching inner sequence elements from the hash table using that key. For each outer sequence element and matching inner sequence element pair, the returned object will call the resultSelector method passing both the outer element and the matching inner element. The resultSelector method will return an instantiated object of type TResult, which the returned object will place in the output sequence of type TResult.

The order of the outer sequence elements will be preserved, as will the order of the inner elements within each outer element.

Exceptions

ArgumentNullException is thrown if any arguments are Nothing.

Examples

For this operator's example, instead of using the presidents array that most examples use, I will use the two common classes defined at the beginning of this chapter, Employee and EmployeeOptionEntry.

Here is an example calling the Join operator using those classes. I have formatted the code in Listing 4-28 a little differently than is typical to make each Join argument more easily readable.

Listing 4-28. *Example Code Calling the Join Operator*

```
Dim employees() As Employee = Employee.GetEmployeesArray()
Dim empOptions() As EmployeeOptionEntry = _
  EmployeeOptionEntry.GetEmployeeOptionEntries()

' Remember, the first argument of the overload is the outer sequence, which will
' be the sequence we call join on.  In this case, the employees array is the outer
' sequence.
Dim employeeOptions = employees _
  .Join( _
    empOptions, _
    Function(e) e.id, _
    Function(o) o.id, _
    Function(e, o) New With { _
      Key .id = e.id, _
      Key .name = String.Format("{0} {1}", e.firstName, e.lastName), _
      Key .options = o.optionsCount})

For Each item In employeeOptions
  Console.WriteLine(item)
Next item
```

In the preceding code, I first obtain a couple arrays of data to join using the two common classes. Because I am calling the Join operator on the employees array, it becomes the outer sequence, and empOptions becomes the inner sequence. Here are the results of the Join operator:

```
{ id = 1, name = Joe Rattz, options = 2 }
{ id = 2, name = William Gates, options = 10000 }
{ id = 2, name = William Gates, options = 10000 }
{ id = 2, name = William Gates, options = 10000 }
{ id = 3, name = Anders Hejlsberg, options = 5000 }
{ id = 3, name = Anders Hejlsberg, options = 7500 }
{ id = 3, name = Anders Hejlsberg, options = 7500 }
{ id = 4, name = David Lightman, options = 1500 }
{ id = 101, name = Kevin Flynn, options = 2 }
```

Notice that resultSelector is creating an anonymous class as the element type for the resulting output sequence. You can detect it is an anonymous class because there is no class name specified in the call to New. Because the type is anonymous, it is a necessity that the resulting output sequence be stored in a variable whose type is specified using the Dim keyword without specifying the type. You cannot specify it is an IEnumerable(Of SomeType), because there is no named type of which to declare it as an IEnumerable.

■**Tip** When the last operator called is returning a sequence of an anonymous type, you must use the Dim keyword without an As type to store the sequence.

GroupJoin

The GroupJoin operator performs a grouped join on two sequences based on keys extracted from each element in the sequences.

The GroupJoin operator works very similarly to the Join operator with the exception that the Join operator passes a single outer sequence element with a single matching inner sequence element to the resultSelector method. This means that multiple matching inner sequence elements for a single outer sequence element result in multiple calls to resultSelector for the outer sequence element. With the GroupJoin operator, all matching inner sequence elements for a specific outer sequence element are passed to resultSelector as a *sequence* of that type of element, resulting in the resultSelector method only being called once for each outer sequence element.

Declarations

The GroupJoin operator has two overloads, one of which I will cover.

The First Overload of the GroupJoin Operator

```
<ExtensionAttribute> _
Public Shared Function GroupJoin(Of TOuter, TInner, TKey, TResult) ( _
    outer As IEnumerable(Of TOuter), _
    inner As IEnumerable(Of TInner), _
    outerKeySelector As Func(Of TOuter, TKey), _
    innerKeySelector As Func(Of TInner, TKey), _
    resultSelector As Func(Of TOuter, IEnumerable(Of TInner), TResult) _
) As IEnumerable(Of TResult)
```

Notice that the first argument of the method is named outer. Since this is an extension method, the sequence the GroupJoin operator is called on will be referred to as the outer sequence.

The GroupJoin operator will return an object that, when enumerated, will first enumerate the inner sequence of type TInner elements, calling the innerKeySelector method once for each element and storing the element, referenced by its key, in a hash table. Next, the returned object will enumerate the outer sequence of type TOuter elements. As the returned object enumerates each outer sequence element, it will call the outerKeySelector method to obtain its key and retrieve the matching inner sequence elements from the hash table using that key. For each outer sequence element, the returned object will call the resultSelector method passing both the outer element and a *sequence* of the matching inner elements so that resultSelector can return an instantiated object of type TResult, which the returned object will place in the output sequence of type TResult.

The order of the outer sequence elements will be preserved, as will the order of the inner elements within each outer element.

Exceptions

ArgumentNullException is thrown if any arguments are Nothing.

Examples

For the GroupJoin example, I will use the same Employee and EmployeeOptionEntry classes that I used in the Join example. My sample code, which appears in Listing 4-29, will join the employees to the options and calculate a sum of the options for each employee using the GroupJoin operator.

Listing 4-29. *An Example of the Covered GroupJoin Operator*

```
Dim employees() As Employee = Employee.GetEmployeesArray()
Dim empOptions() As EmployeeOptionEntry = _
  EmployeeOptionEntry.GetEmployeeOptionEntries()

Dim employeeOptions = employees _
  .GroupJoin( _
    empOptions, _
    Function(e) e.id, _
    Function(o) o.id, _
    Function(e, os) New With { _
      Key .id = e.id, _
      Key .name = String.Format("{0} {1}", e.firstName, e.lastName), _
      Key .options = os.Sum(Function(o) o.optionsCount)})

For Each item In employeeOptions
  Console.WriteLine(item)
Next item
```

The preceding code is almost identical to the example for the Join operator. However, if you examine the second input argument of the lambda expression passed as the resultSelector method, you will notice that I called the input argument o in the Join example, but I am calling it os in this example. This is because, in the Join example, a single employee option object, o, is passed in this argument, but in the GroupJoin example, a *sequence* of employee option objects, os, is being passed. Then, the last member of my instantiated anonymous object is being set to the sum of the sequence of employee option objects' optionsCount members using the Sum operator that I will be covering in the next chapter (since it is not a deferred query operator). For now, you just need to understand that the Sum operator has the ability to calculate the sum of each element or a member of each element in an input sequence.

This code will provide the following results:

```
{ id = 1, name = Joe Rattz, options = 2 }
{ id = 2, name = William Gates, options = 30000 }
{ id = 3, name = Anders Hejlsberg, options = 20000 }
{ id = 4, name = David Lightman, options = 1500 }
{ id = 101, name = Kevin Flynn, options = 2 }
```

Notice that, in these results, there is one record for each employee containing the sum of all of that employee's option records. Contrast this with the Join operator's example where there was a separate record for each of the employee's option records.

Grouping

The grouping operators assist with grouping elements of a sequence together by a common key.

GroupBy

The GroupBy operator is used to group elements of an input sequence.

Declarations

The GroupBy operator has eight overloads, four of which I will cover. All overloads of the GroupBy operator return a sequence of IGrouping(Of TKey, TElement) elements. IGrouping(Of TKey, TElement) is an interface defined as follows:

The IGrouping(Of TKey, TElement) Interface

```
Public Interface IGrouping(Of TKey, TElement)
    Implements IEnumerable(Of TElement), IEnumerable

    ReadOnly Property Key() As TKey
End Interface
```

So, an IGrouping is a sequence of type TElement with a key of type TKey.

The First Overload of the GroupBy Operator

```
<ExtensionAttribute> _
Public Shared Function GroupBy(Of TSource, TKey) ( _
    source As IEnumerable(Of TSource), _
    keySelector As Func(Of TSource, TKey) _
) As IEnumerable(Of IGrouping(Of TKey, TSource))
```

This overload of the GroupBy operator returns an object that when enumerated, enumerates the input source sequence, calls the keySelector method, collects each element with its key, and yields a sequence of IGrouping(Of TKey, TSource) instances, where each IGrouping(Of TKey, TSource) element is a sequence of elements with the same key value. Key values are compared using the default equality comparer, EqualityComparerDefault. Said another way, the return value of the GroupBy method is a sequence of IGrouping objects, each containing a key and a sequence of the elements from the input sequence having that same key.

The order of the IGrouping instances will be in the same order that the keys occurred in the source sequence, and each element in the IGrouping sequence will be in the order that element was found in the source sequence.

The Second Overload of the GroupBy Operator

```
<ExtensionAttribute> _
Public Shared Function GroupBy(Of TSource, TKey) ( _
    source As IEnumerable(Of TSource), _
    keySelector As Func(Of TSource, TKey), _
    comparer As IEqualityComparer(Of TKey) _
) As IEnumerable(Of IGrouping(Of TKey, TSource))
```

This overload of the GroupBy operator is just like the first except instead of using the default equality comparer, EqualityComparerDefault, you provide one.

The Third Overload of the GroupBy Operator

```
<ExtensionAttribute> _
Public Shared Function GroupBy(Of TSource, TKey, TElement) ( _
    source As IEnumerable(Of TSource), _
    keySelector As Func(Of TSource, TKey), _
    elementSelector As Func(Of TSource, TElement) _
) As IEnumerable(Of IGrouping(Of TKey, TElement))
```

This overload of the GroupBy operator is just like the first except, instead of the entire source element being the element in the output IGrouping sequence for its key, you may specify which part of the input element is output with the elementSelector.

The Fourth Overload of the GroupBy Operator

```
<ExtensionAttribute> _
Public Shared Function GroupBy(Of TSource, TKey, TElement) ( _
    source As IEnumerable(Of TSource), _
    keySelector As Func(Of TSource, TKey), _
    elementSelector As Func(Of TSource, TElement), _
    comparer As IEqualityComparer(Of TKey) _
) As IEnumerable(Of IGrouping(Of TKey, TElement))
```

This overload of the GroupBy operator is a combination of the second and third so that you may specify a comparer with the comparer argument, and you may output elements of a different type than the input element type using the elementSelector argument.

Exceptions

ArgumentNullException is thrown if any argument other than the comparer argument is Nothing.

Examples

For my example of the first GroupBy overload, I will use the common EmployeeOptionEntry class. In this example, in Listing 4-30, I am going to group my EmployeeOptionEntry records by id and display them.

Listing 4-30. *An Example of the First Overload of the GroupBy Operator*

```
Dim empOptions() As EmployeeOptionEntry = _
   EmployeeOptionEntry.GetEmployeeOptionEntries()
Dim outerSequence As IEnumerable(Of IGrouping(Of Integer, EmployeeOptionEntry)) = _
   empOptions.GroupBy(Function(o) o.id)

' First enumerate through the outer sequence of IGroupings.
For Each keyGroupSequence As IGrouping(Of Integer, EmployeeOptionEntry) _
    In outerSequence
   Console.WriteLine("Option records for employee: " & keyGroupSequence.Key)

   ' Now enumerate through the grouping's sequence of EmployeeOptionEntry elements.
   For Each element As EmployeeOptionEntry In keyGroupSequence
      Console.WriteLine("id={0} : optionsCount={1} : dateAwarded={2:d}", _
                        element.id, element.optionsCount, element.dateAwarded)
   Next element
Next keyGroupSequence
```

In the preceding code, notice I am enumerating through an outer sequence named outerSequence, where each element is an object implementing IGrouping containing the key, and a sequence of EmployeeOptionEntry elements having that same key.

Here are the results:

```
Option records for employee: 1
id=1 : optionsCount=2 : dateAwarded=12/31/1999
Option records for employee: 2
id=2 : optionsCount=10000 : dateAwarded=6/30/1992
id=2 : optionsCount=10000 : dateAwarded=1/1/1994
id=2 : optionsCount=10000 : dateAwarded=4/1/2003
Option records for employee: 3
id=3 : optionsCount=5000 : dateAwarded=9/30/1997
id=3 : optionsCount=7500 : dateAwarded=9/30/1998
id=3 : optionsCount=7500 : dateAwarded=9/30/1998
Option records for employee: 4
id=4 : optionsCount=1500 : dateAwarded=12/31/1997
Option records for employee: 101
id=101 : optionsCount=2 : dateAwarded=12/31/1998
```

For an example of the second GroupBy overload, let's assume I know that any employee whose id is less than 100 is considered a founder of the company. Those with an id of 100 or greater are not considered founders. My task is to list all option records grouped by the option record's employee founder status. All founders' option records will be grouped together, and all nonfounders' option records will be grouped together.

Now, I need an equality comparer that can handle this key comparison for me. My equality comparer must implement the IEqualityComparer interface. Before examining my comparer, let's take a look at the interface.

The IEqualityComparer(Of T) Interface

```
Public Interface IEqualityComparer(Of T)
    Overloads Function Equals(ByVal x As T, ByVal y As T) As Boolean
    Overloads Function GetHashCode(ByVal x As T) As Integer
End Interface
```

This interface requires me to implement two methods, Equals and GetHashCode. The Equals method is passed two objects of the same type T and returns True if the two objects are considered to be equal or False otherwise. The GetHashCode method is passed a single object and returns a hash code of type Integer for that object.

A hash code is a numerical value, typically mathematically calculated based on some portion of the data in an object, known as the key, for the purpose of uniquely identifying the object. That calculated hash code functions as the index into some data structure to store that object and find it at a later time. Since it is typical for multiple keys to produce the same hash code, thereby making the hash code truly less than unique, it is also necessary to be able to determine if two keys are equal. This is the purpose of the Equals method.

Here is my class implementing the IEqualityComparer interface.

A Class Implmenting the IEqualityComparer Interface for My Second GroupBy Example

```
Public Class MyFounderNumberComparer
  Implements IEqualityComparer(Of Integer)

  Public Overloads Function Equals(ByVal x As Integer, ByVal y As Integer) _
      As Boolean _
    Implements System.Collections.Generic.IEqualityComparer(Of Integer).Equals
    Return (isFounder(x) = isFounder(y))
  End Function

  Public Overloads Function GetHashCode(ByVal obj As Integer) As Integer _
      Implements System.Collections.Generic. _
        IEqualityComparer(Of Integer).GetHashCode
    Dim f As Integer = 1
    Dim nf As Integer = 100
    Dim i As Integer = (If(isFounder(obj), f.GetHashCode(), nf.GetHashCode()))
    Return i
  End Function

  Public Function isFounder(ByVal id As Integer) As Boolean
    Return (id < 100)
  End Function

End Class
```

In addition to the methods required by the interface, I have added a method, isFounder, to determine if an employee is a founder based on our definition. This just makes the code a little easier to understand. I have made that method public so that I can call it from outside the interface, which you will see me do in my example.

My equality comparer is going to consider any integer less than 100 as representing a founder, and if two integers signify either both founders or both nonfounders, they are considered equal. For the purposes of producing a hash code, I return a hash code of 1 for a founder and 100 for a nonfounder so that all founders end up in the same group, and all nonfounders end up in another group.

My GroupBy example code is in Listing 4-31.

Listing 4-31. *An Example of the Second Overload of the GroupBy Operator*

```
' Instead of instantiating the comparer on the fly, I am going
' to keep a reference to it because I will use its isFounder()
' method on the group's key for header display purposes.
Dim comp As New MyFounderNumberComparer()

Dim empOptions() As EmployeeOptionEntry = _
  EmployeeOptionEntry.GetEmployeeOptionEntries()

Dim opts As IEnumerable(Of IGrouping(Of Integer, EmployeeOptionEntry)) = _
  empOptions.GroupBy(Function(o) o.id, comp)

' First enumerate through the sequence of IGroupings.
For Each keyGroup As IGrouping(Of Integer, EmployeeOptionEntry) In opts
  Console.WriteLine( _
    "Option records for: " & _
    (If(comp.isFounder(keyGroup.Key), "founder", "non-founder")))

  ' Now enumerate through the grouping's sequence of EmployeeOptionEntry elements.
  For Each element As EmployeeOptionEntry In keyGroup
    Console.WriteLine( _
      "id={0} : optionsCount={1} : dateAwarded={2:d}", _
      element.id, _
      element.optionsCount, _
      element.dateAwarded)
  Next element
Next keyGroup
```

In the example, I instantiate my equality comparer object ahead of time, as opposed to doing it in the call to the GroupBy method, so that I can use it to call the isFounder method in the For Each loop. Here are the results from this code:

```
Option records for: founder
id=1 : optionsCount=2 : dateAwarded=12/31/1999
id=2 : optionsCount=10000 : dateAwarded=6/30/1992
id=2 : optionsCount=10000 : dateAwarded=1/1/1994
id=3 : optionsCount=5000 : dateAwarded=9/30/1997
id=2 : optionsCount=10000 : dateAwarded=4/1/2003
id=3 : optionsCount=7500 : dateAwarded=9/30/1998
id=3 : optionsCount=7500 : dateAwarded=9/30/1998
```

```
id=4 : optionsCount=1500 : dateAwarded=12/31/1997
Option records for: non-founder
id=101 : optionsCount=2 : dateAwarded=12/31/1998
```

As you can see, all employee options records for an employee whose id is less than 100 are grouped with the founders. Otherwise, they are grouped with the nonfounders.

For an example of the third GroupBy overload, we'll assume we are only interested in getting the dates that the options were awarded for each employee. This code will be very similar to the example for the first overload.

So in Listing 4-32, instead of returning a sequence of groupings of EmployeeOptionEntry objects, I will have groupings of dates.

Listing 4-32. *An Example of the Third Overload of the GroupBy Operator*

```
Dim empOptions() As EmployeeOptionEntry = _
  EmployeeOptionEntry.GetEmployeeOptionEntries()
Dim opts As IEnumerable(Of IGrouping(Of Integer, DateTime)) = _
  empOptions.GroupBy(Function(o) o.id, Function(e) e.dateAwarded)

' First enumerate through the sequence of IGroupings.
For Each keyGroup As IGrouping(Of Integer, DateTime) In opts
  Console.WriteLine("Option records for employee: " & keyGroup.Key)

  ' Now enumerate through the grouping's sequence of DateTime elements.
  For Each [date] As DateTime In keyGroup
    Console.WriteLine([date].ToShortDateString())
  Next [date]
Next keyGroup
```

Notice that in the call to the GroupBy operator, elementSelector, the second argument, is just returning the dateAwarded member. Because I am returning a DateTime, my IGrouping is now for a type of DateTime, instead of EmployeeOptionEntry.

Just as you would expect, I now have the award dates of the options grouped by employee:

```
Option records for employee: 1
12/31/1999
Option records for employee: 2
6/30/1992
1/1/1994
4/1/2003
Option records for employee: 3
9/30/1997
9/30/1998
9/30/1998
Option records for employee: 4
12/31/1997
Option records for employee: 101
12/31/1998
```

For the fourth and final overload, I need to use an elementSelector method and a comparer object, so I will use a combination of the examples for overloads two and three. I want to group the dates of awarded options by whether they were awarded to a founding employee or not, where a founding employee is one whose id is less than 100. That code is in Listing 4-33.

Listing 4-33. *An Example of the Fourth Overload of the GroupBy Operator*

```
' Instead of instantiating the comparer on the fly, I am going
' to keep a reference to it because I will use its isFounder()
' method on the group's key for header display purposes.
Dim comp As New MyFounderNumberComparer()

Dim empOptions() As EmployeeOptionEntry = _
  EmployeeOptionEntry.GetEmployeeOptionEntries()
Dim opts As IEnumerable(Of IGrouping(Of Integer, DateTime)) = _
  empOptions.GroupBy(Function(o) o.id, Function(o) o.dateAwarded, comp)

' First enumerate through the sequence of IGroupings.
For Each keyGroup As IGrouping(Of Integer, DateTime) In opts
  Console.WriteLine("Option records for: " & _
    (If(comp.isFounder(keyGroup.Key), "founder", "non-founder")))

  ' Now enumerate through the grouping's sequence of EmployeeOptionEntry elements.
  For Each [date] As DateTime In keyGroup
    Console.WriteLine([date].ToShortDateString())
  Next [date]
Next keyGroup
```

In the output, we should see just dates grouped by founders and nonfounders:

```
Option records for: founder
12/31/1999
6/30/1992
1/1/1994
9/30/1997
4/1/2003
9/30/1998
9/30/1998
12/31/1997
Option records for: non-founder
12/31/1998
```

Set

The set operators are used to perform mathematical set-type operations on sequences.

■**Tip** The overloads of the set operators that are covered in this chapter do not work properly for DataSets. For use with DataSets please use the overloads that are covered in Chapter 10.

Distinct

The Distinct operator removes duplicate elements from an input sequence.

Declarations

The Distinct operator has two overloads, one of which I will cover.

The First Overload of the Distinct Operator

```
<ExtensionAttribute> _
Public Shared Function Distinct(Of TSource) ( _
    source As IEnumerable(Of TSource) _
) As IEnumerable(Of TSource)
```

This operator returns an object that, when enumerated, enumerates the elements of the input sequence named source and yields any element that is not equal to a previously yielded element. An element is determined to be equal to another element using their GetHashCode and Equals methods.

Isn't it fortuitous that I just covered how and why the GetHashCode and Equals methods are used?

Exceptions

ArgumentNullException is thrown if the source argument is Nothing.

Examples

For this example, I am going to first display the count of the presidents array, next I will concatenate the presidents array with itself, display the count of the resulting concatenated sequence, then call the Distinct operator on that concatenated sequence, and finally display the count of the distinct sequence, which should be the same as the initial presidents array.

To determine the count of the two generated sequences, I will use the Count Standard Query Operator. Since it is a nondeferred operator, I will not cover it in this chapter. I will cover it in the next chapter, though. For now, just be aware that it returns the count of the sequence on which it is called.

The code is in Listing 4-34.

Listing 4-34. *An Example of the Distinct Operator*

```
Dim presidents() As String = { _
  "Adams", "Arthur", "Buchanan", "Bush", "Carter", "Cleveland", _
  "Clinton", "Coolidge", "Eisenhower", "Fillmore", "Ford", "Garfield", _
  "Grant", "Harding", "Harrison", "Hayes", "Hoover", "Jackson", _
  "Jefferson", "Johnson", "Kennedy", "Lincoln", "Madison", "McKinley", _
```

```
  "Monroe", "Nixon", "Pierce", "Polk", "Reagan", "Roosevelt", "Taft", _
  "Taylor", "Truman", "Tyler", "Van Buren", "Washington", "Wilson"}

'  Display the count of the presidents array.
Console.WriteLine("presidents count:  " & presidents.Count())

'  Concatenate presidents with itself.  Now each element should
'  be in the sequence twice.
Dim presidentsWithDupes As IEnumerable(Of String) = presidents.Concat(presidents)
'  Display the count of the concatenated sequence.
Console.WriteLine("presidentsWithDupes count:  " & presidentsWithDupes.Count())

'  Eliminate the duplicates and display the count.
' Note that I use the VB.NET only Distinct query expression syntax here.
Dim presidentsDistinct As IEnumerable(Of String) = _
  From p in presidentsWithDupes _
  Distinct

Console.WriteLine("presidentsDistinct count:  " & presidentsDistinct.Count())
```

If this works as I expect, the count of the elements in the presidentsDistinct sequence should equal the count of the elements in the presidents sequence. Will our results indicate success?

```
presidents count:  37
presidentsWithDupes count:  74
presidentsDistinct count:  37
```

Yes, they do!

Union

The Union operator returns a sequence of the set union of two source sequences.

Declarations

The Union operator has two overloads, one of which I will cover.

The First Overload of the Union Operator

```
<ExtensionAttribute> _
Public Shared Function Union(Of TSource) ( _
    first As IEnumerable(Of TSource), _
    second As IEnumerable(Of TSource) _
) As IEnumerable(Of TSource)
```

This operator returns an object that, when enumerated, first enumerates the elements of the input sequence named first, yielding any element that is not equal to a previously yielded element, then enumerates the second input sequence, again yielding any element that is not equal to a previously yielded element. An element is determined to be equal to another element using their GetHashCode and Equals methods.

Exceptions

ArgumentNullException is thrown if any arguments are Nothing.

Examples

To demonstrate the difference between the Union operator and the Concat operator I covered previously, in the example in Listing 4-35, I will create a first and second sequence from my presidents array that results in the fifth element being duplicated in both sequences. I will then display the count of the presidents array and the first and second sequences, as well as the count of a concatenated and union sequence.

Listing 4-35. *An Example of the Union Operator*

```
Dim presidents() As String = { _
    "Adams", "Arthur", "Buchanan", "Bush", "Carter", "Cleveland", _
    "Clinton", "Coolidge", "Eisenhower", "Fillmore", "Ford", "Garfield", _
    "Grant", "Harding", "Harrison", "Hayes", "Hoover", "Jackson", _
    "Jefferson", "Johnson", "Kennedy", "Lincoln", "Madison", "McKinley", _
    "Monroe", "Nixon", "Pierce", "Polk", "Reagan", "Roosevelt", "Taft", _
    "Taylor", "Truman", "Tyler", "Van Buren", "Washington", "Wilson"}

Dim first As IEnumerable(Of String) = presidents.Take(5)
Dim second As IEnumerable(Of String) = presidents.Skip(4)
'   Since I only skipped 4 elements, the fifth element
'   should be in both sequences.

Dim concat As IEnumerable(Of String) = first.Concat(second)
Dim union As IEnumerable(Of String) = first.Union(second)

Console.WriteLine("The count of the presidents array is: " & presidents.Count())
Console.WriteLine("The count of the first sequence is: " & first.Count())
Console.WriteLine("The count of the second sequence is: " & second.Count())
Console.WriteLine("The count of the concat sequence is: " & concat.Count())
Console.WriteLine("The count of the union sequence is: " & union.Count())
```

If this works properly, the concat sequence should have one more element than the presidents array. The union sequence should contain the same number of elements as the presidents array. The proof, however, is in the pudding:

```
The count of the presidents array is: 37
The count of the first sequence is: 5
The count of the second sequence is: 33
The count of the concat sequence is: 38
The count of the union sequence is: 37
```

Success!

Intersect

The Intersect operator returns the set intersection of two source sequences.

Declarations

The Intersect operator has two overloads, one of which I will cover.

The First Overload of the Intersect Operator

```
<ExtensionAttribute> _
Public Shared Function Intersect(Of TSource) ( _
    first As IEnumerable(Of TSource), _
    second As IEnumerable(Of TSource) _
) As IEnumerable(Of TSource)
```

This operator returns an object that, when enumerated, first enumerates the elements of the input sequence named second, collecting any element that is not equal to a previously collected element. It then enumerates the first input sequence, yielding any element also existing in the collection of elements from the second sequence. An element is determined to be equal to another element using their GetHashCode and Equals methods.

Exceptions

ArgumentNullException is thrown if any arguments are Nothing.

Examples

For my example of the Intersect operator in Listing 4-36, I will use the Take and Skip operators to generate two sequences and get some overlap, just like I did in the Union operator example, where I intentionally duplicated the fifth element. When I call the Intersect operator on those two generated sequences, only the duplicated fifth element should be in the returned intersect sequence. I will display the counts of the presidents array and all the sequences. Lastly, I will enumerate through the intersect sequence displaying each element, which should only be the fifth element of the presidents array.

Listing 4-36. *An Example of the Intersect Operator*

```
Dim presidents() As String = { _
  "Adams", "Arthur", "Buchanan", "Bush", "Carter", "Cleveland", _
  "Clinton", "Coolidge", "Eisenhower", "Fillmore", "Ford", "Garfield", _
  "Grant", "Harding", "Harrison", "Hayes", "Hoover", "Jackson", _
  "Jefferson", "Johnson", "Kennedy", "Lincoln", "Madison", "McKinley", _
  "Monroe", "Nixon", "Pierce", "Polk", "Reagan", "Roosevelt", "Taft", _
  "Taylor", "Truman", "Tyler", "Van Buren", "Washington", "Wilson"}

Dim first As IEnumerable(Of String) = presidents.Take(5)
Dim second As IEnumerable(Of String) = presidents.Skip(4)
```

```
'  Since I only skipped 4 elements, the fifth element
'  should be in both sequences.
```

Dim intersect As IEnumerable(Of String) = first.Intersect(second)

```
Console.WriteLine("The count of the presidents array is: " & presidents.Count())
Console.WriteLine("The count of the first sequence is: " & first.Count())
Console.WriteLine("The count of the second sequence is: " & second.Count())
Console.WriteLine("The count of the intersect sequence is: " & intersect.Count())
```

```
'  Just for kicks, I will display the intersection sequence,
'  which should be just the fifth element.
For Each name As String In intersect
  Console.WriteLine(name)
Next name
```

If this works the way it should, I should have an intersect sequence with just one element containing the duplicated fifth element of the presidents array, "Carter":

```
The count of the presidents array is: 37
The count of the first sequence is: 5
The count of the second sequence is: 33
The count of the intersect sequence is: 1
Carter
```

LINQ rocks! How many times have you needed to perform set-type operations on two collections? Wasn't it a pain? Thanks to LINQ, those days are gone.

Except

The Except operator returns a sequence that contains all the elements of a first sequence that do not exist in a second sequence.

Declarations

The Except operator has two overloads, one of which I will cover.

The First Overload of the Except Operator

```
<ExtensionAttribute> _
Public Shared Function Except(Of TSource) ( _
    first As IEnumerable(Of TSource), _
    second As IEnumerable(Of TSource) _
) As IEnumerable(Of TSource)
```

This operator returns an object that, when enumerated, enumerates the elements of the input sequence named second, collecting any element that is not equal to a previously collected element. It then enumerates the first input sequence, yielding any element from the first sequence *not* existing in the collection of elements from the second sequence. An element is determined to be equal to another element using their `GetHashCode` and `Equals` methods.

Exceptions

`ArgumentNullException` is thrown if any arguments are `Nothing`.

Examples

For this example, I will use the `presidents` array that I use in most of the examples. Imagine a scenario where you have a primary data source, the `presidents` array, with entries that you need to perform some processing on. As you complete the processing of each entry, you want to add it to a collection of processed entries so that if you need to start processing again, you can use the `Except` operator to produce an exception sequence consisting of the primary data source elements, minus the entries from the processed entry collection. You can then process this exception sequence again without the concern of reprocessing an entry.

For this example in Listing 4-37, I will pretend that I have already processed the first four entries. To obtain a sequence containing the first four elements of the `presidents` array, I will just call the `Take` operator on it.

Listing 4-37. *An Example of the Except Operator*

```
Dim presidents() As String = { _
    "Adams", "Arthur", "Buchanan", "Bush", "Carter", "Cleveland", _
    "Clinton", "Coolidge", "Eisenhower", "Fillmore", "Ford", "Garfield", _
    "Grant", "Harding", "Harrison", "Hayes", "Hoover", "Jackson", _
    "Jefferson", "Johnson", "Kennedy", "Lincoln", "Madison", "McKinley", _
    "Monroe", "Nixon", "Pierce", "Polk", "Reagan", "Roosevelt", "Taft", _
    "Taylor", "Truman", "Tyler", "Van Buren", "Washington", "Wilson"}

'  First generate a processed sequence.
Dim processed As IEnumerable(Of String) = presidents.Take(4)

Dim exceptions As IEnumerable(Of String) = presidents.Except(processed)
For Each name As String In exceptions
    Console.WriteLine(name)
Next name
```

In this example, my results should contain the names of the `presidents` array after the fourth element, `"Bush"`:

```
Carter
Cleveland
Clinton
Coolidge
Eisenhower
Fillmore
Ford
Garfield
```

Grant
Harding
Harrison
Hayes
Hoover
Jackson
Jefferson
Johnson
Kennedy
Lincoln
Madison
McKinley
Monroe
Nixon
Pierce
Polk
Reagan
Roosevelt
Taft
Taylor
Truman
Tyler
Van Buren
Washington
Wilson

That worked just as I would have expected.

Conversion

The conversion operators provide a simple and convenient way of converting sequences to other collection types.

Cast

The Cast operator is used to cast every element of an input sequence to an output sequence of the specified type.

Declarations

The Cast operator has one overload.

The Only Overload of the Cast Operator

```
<ExtensionAttribute> _
Public Shared Function Cast(Of TResult) ( _
    source As IEnumerable _
) As IEnumerable(Of TResult)
```

The first thing you should notice about the Cast operator is that its first argument, named source, is of type IEnumerable, not IEnumerable(Of TResult), while most of the deferred Standard Query Operators' first arguments are of type IEnumerable(Of TResult). This is because the Cast operator is designed to be called on classes that implement the IEnumerable interface, as opposed to the IEnumerable(Of TResult) interface. In particular, we are talking about all the legacy .NET collections prior to .NET 2.0 and generics.

You can call the Cast operator on a legacy .NET collection as long as it implements IEnumerable, and an IEnumerable(Of TResult) output sequence will be created. Since most of the Standard Query Operators only work on IEnumerable(Of TResult) type sequences, you must call some method like this one, or perhaps the OfType operator that I will cover next, to get a legacy collection converted to a sequence the Standard Query Operators can be called on. This is important when you're trying to use the Standard Query Operators on legacy collections.

This operator will return an object that, when enumerated, enumerates the source data collection, yielding each element cast to type TResult. If the element cannot be cast to type TResult, an exception will be thrown. Because of this, this operator should only be called when it is known, or to enforce that every element in the sequence can be cast to type TResult.

■Tip When you're trying to perform LINQ queries on legacy collections, don't forget to call Cast or OfType on the legacy collection to create an IEnumerable(Of TResult) sequence that the Standard Query Operators can be called on.

This operator is particularly useful for those times when you want to enforce that a sequence has a specific type and it would be considered a bug to have elements not matching that type.

Exceptions

ArgumentNullException is thrown if the source argument is Nothing. InvalidCastException is thrown if an element in the input source collection cannot be cast to type TResult.

Examples

For this example, I will use my common Employee class's GetEmployeesArrayList method to return a legacy, nongeneric ArrayList.

In Listing 4-38 is some code illustrating how the data type of the elements of an ArrayList get cast to elements in a sequence, IEnumerable(Of TResult).

Listing 4-38. *Code Converting an ArrayList to an IEnumerable(Of TResult) That Can Be Used with the Typical Standard Query Operators*

```
Dim employees As ArrayList = Employee.GetEmployeesArrayList()
Console.WriteLine("The data type of employees is " & employees.GetType().ToString)

Dim seq = employees.Cast(Of Employee)()
Console.WriteLine("The data type of seq is " & seq.GetType().ToString)
```

```
Dim emps = seq.OrderBy(Function(e) e.lastName)
For Each emp As Employee In emps
  Console.WriteLine("{0} {1}", emp.firstName, emp.lastName)
Next emp
```

First, I call the GetEmployeesArrayList method to return an ArrayList of Employee objects, and then I display the data type of the employees variable. Next, I convert that ArrayList to an IEnumerable(Of TResult) sequence by calling the Cast operator, and then I display the data type of the returned sequence. Lastly, I enumerate through that returned sequence to prove that the ordering did indeed work.

Here is the output from the code:

```
The data type of employees is System.Collections.ArrayList
The data type of seq is
System.Linq.Enumerable+<CastIterator>d__aa`1[CH04Console.Module1+Employee]
Kevin Flynn
William Gates
Anders Hejlsberg
David Lightman
Joe Rattz
```

You can see the data type of the employees variable is an ArrayList. It is a little more difficult determining what the data type of seq is. We can definitely see it is different, and it looks like a sequence. We can also see the word CastIterator in its type. Have you noticed that when I discuss the deferred operators that they don't actually return the output sequence but really return an object that, when enumerated, would yield the elements to the output sequence? The seq variable's data type displayed in the previous example is just this kind of object. However, this is an implementation detail and could change.

■**Caution** The Cast operator will attempt to cast each element in the input sequence to the specified type. If any of those elements cannot be cast to the specified type, an InvalidCastException exception will be thrown. If there may be elements of differing types and you wish to prevent an exception from being thrown, use the OfType operator instead.

OfType

The OfType operator is used to build an output sequence containing only the elements that can be successfully cast to a specified type.

Declarations

The OfType operator has one overload.

The Only Overload of the OfType Operator

```
<ExtensionAttribute> _
Public Shared Function OfType(Of TResult) ( _
    source As IEnumerable _
) As IEnumerable(Of TResult)
```

The first thing you should notice about the OfType operator is that, just like the Cast operator, its first argument, named source, is of type IEnumerable, not IEnumerable(Of TResult). Most of the deferred Standard Query Operators' first arguments are of type IEnumerable(Of TResult). This is because the OfType operator is designed to be called on classes that implement the IEnumerable interface, as opposed to the IEnumerable(Of TResult) interface. In particular, we are talking about all the legacy .NET collections prior to .NET 2.0 and generics.

So, you can call the OfType operator on a legacy .NET collection as long as it implements IEnumerable, and an IEnumerable(Of TResult) output sequence will be created. Since most of the Standard Query Operators only work on IEnumerable(Of TResult) type sequences, you must call some method like this one, or perhaps the Cast operator, to get the legacy collection converted to a sequence the Standard Query Operators can be called on. This is important when trying to use the Standard Query Operators on legacy collections.

The OfType operator will return an object that, when enumerated, will enumerate the source sequence, yielding only those elements whose type matches the type specified, TResult.

The OfType operator differs from the Cast operator in that the Cast operator will attempt to cast every element of the input sequence to type TResult and yield it to the output sequence. If the cast fails, an exception is thrown. The OfType operator will only attempt to yield the input element if it *can* be cast to type TResult. Technically, the expression TypeOf e Is TResult, where e is the element, must return True for the element to be yielded to the output sequence.

Because the OfType operator only returns the elements of a sequence that are of a specified type, it is also useful for filtering a sequence of differing types into a sequence of a specific type for which you are searching. For example, perhaps you have a legacy ControlCollection that contains all the controls, of differing control types, on your web page and you want to obtain a sequence containing just the Button controls? The OfType operator can do just that. I will use the OfType operator in Chapter 7, Listing 7-48, to query a sequence of XNode objects to obtain only those elements that are an XElement.

Exceptions

ArgumentNullException is thrown if the source argument is Nothing.

Examples

For the example in Listing 4-39, I am going to create an ArrayList containing objects of my two common classes, Employee and EmployeeOptionEntry. Once I have the ArrayList populated with objects of both classes, I will first call the Cast operator to show how it fails in this circumstance. I will follow that call with a call to the OfType operator showing its prowess in the same situation.

Listing 4-39. *Sample Code Calling the Cast and OfType Operator*

```
Dim al As New ArrayList()
al.Add(New Employee With {.id = 1, .firstName = "Dennis", .lastName = "Hayes"})
al.Add(New Employee With {.id = 2, .firstName = "William", .lastName = "Gates"})
al.Add(New EmployeeOptionEntry With {.id = 1, .optionsCount = 0})
al.Add(New EmployeeOptionEntry With {.id = 2, .optionsCount = 99999999999})
al.Add(New Employee With {.id = 3, .firstName = "Anders", .lastName = "Hejlsberg"})
al.Add(New EmployeeOptionEntry With {.id = 3, .optionsCount = 848475745})


'  First I will demonstrate the Cast Operator's weakness.
Dim items = al.Cast(Of Employee)()

Console.WriteLine("Attempting to use the Cast operator ...")
'  Notice that I am starting the Try after the actual call to the OfType operator.
'  I can get away with that because the operator is deferred.
Try
  For Each item As Employee In items
    Console.WriteLine("{0} {1} {2}", item.id, item.firstName, item.lastName)
  Next item
Catch ex As Exception
  Console.WriteLine("{0}{1}", ex.Message, System.Environment.NewLine)
End Try


'  Now let's try using OfType.
Console.WriteLine("Attempting to use the OfType operator ...")
Dim items2 = al.OfType(Of Employee)()
'  I am so confident, I am not even wrapping in a Try/Catch.
For Each item As Employee In items2
  Console.WriteLine("{0} {1} {2}", item.id, item.firstName, item.lastName)
Next item
```

Once I have the ArrayList created and populated, I call the Cast operator. The next step is to try to enumerate it. This is a necessary step because the Cast operator is deferred. If I never enumerate the results of that query, it will never be performed, and I would not detect a problem. Notice that I wrapped the For Each loop that enumerates the query results with a Try/Catch block. This is necessary in this case, because I know an exception will be thrown since there are objects of two completely different types. Next, I call the OfType operator and enumerate and display its results. Notice my pluck as I brazenly choose not to wrap my For Each loop in a Try/Catch block. Of course, in your real production code, you wouldn't want to ignore the protection a Try/Catch block offers.

Here are the results of this query:

```
Attempting to use the Cast operator ...
1 Dennis Hayes
2 William Gates
Unable to cast object of type 'EmployeeOptionEntry' to type 'Employee'.
```

```
Attempting to use the OfType operator ...
1 Dennis Hayes
2 William Gates
3 Anders Hejlsberg
```

Notice that I was not able to completely enumerate the query results of the Cast operator without an exception being thrown. But, I was able to enumerate the query results of the
OfType operator, and only elements of type Employee were included in the output sequence.

The moral of this story is that if it is feasible that the input sequence contains elements of
more than one data type, prefer the OfType operator to the Cast operator.

■Tip If you are trying to convert a nongeneric collection, such as the legacy collection classes, to an
IEnumerable(Of TResult) type that can be used with the Standard Query Operators operating on that
type, use the OfType operator instead of the Cast operator if it is possible that the input collection could
contain objects of differing types.

AsEnumerable

The AsEnumerable operator simply causes its input sequence of type IEnumerable(Of TSource)
to be returned as type IEnumerable(Of TSource).

Declarations

The AsEnumerable operator has one overload.

The Only Overload of the AsEnumerable Operator

```
<ExtensionAttribute> _
Public Shared Function AsEnumerable(Of TSource) ( _
    source As IEnumerable(Of TSource) _
) As IEnumerable(Of TSource)
```

The preceding overload declares that the AsEnumerable operator operates on an
IEnumerable(Of TSource) named source and returns that same sequence typed as
IEnumerable(Of TSource). It serves no other purpose than changing the output sequence type
at compile time.

This may seem odd since it must be called on an IEnumerable(Of TSource). You may ask,
"Why would you possibly need to convert a sequence of type IEnumerable(Of TSource) to a
sequence of type IEnumerable(Of TSource)?" That would be a good question.

The Standard Query Operators are declared to operate on normal LINQ to Objects
sequences, those collections implementing the IEnumerable(Of TSource) interface. However,
other domain's collections, such as those for accessing a database, could choose to implement
their own sequence type and operators. Ordinarily, when calling a query operator on a collection of one of those types, a collection-specific operator would be called. The AsEnumerable

operator allows the input sequence to be cast as a normal IEnumerable(Of TSource) sequence, allowing a Standard Query Operator method to be called.

For example, when I cover LINQ to SQL in a later part of this book, you will see that LINQ to SQL actually uses its own type of sequence, IQueryable(Of TSource), and implements its own operators. The LINQ to SQL operators will be called on sequences of type IQueryable(Of TSource). When you call the Where method on a sequence of type IQueryable(Of TSource), it is the LINQ to SQL Where method that will get called, not the LINQ to Objects Standard Query Operator Where method. In fact, without the AsEnumerable method, you cannot call a Standard Query Operator on a sequence of type IQueryable(Of TSource). If you try to call one of the Standard Query Operators, you will get an exception unless a LINQ to SQL operator exists with the same name, and the LINQ to SQL operator will be called. With the AsEnumerable operator, you can call it to cast the IQueryable(Of TSource) sequence to an IEnumerable(Of TSource) sequence, thereby allowing Standard Query Operators to be called. This becomes very handy when you need to control in which API an operator is called.

Exceptions

There are no exceptions.

Examples

To better understand this operator, I need a situation where a domain-specific operator is implemented. For that, I need a LINQ to SQL example. I will start with the first LINQ to SQL example in this book from Chapter 1. For your perusal, here is that example.

Reprinted Here for Convenience Is Listing 1-3

```
Dim db As New Northwind _
  ("Data Source=.\SQLEXPRESS;Initial Catalog=Northwind;Integrated Security=SSPI;")

Dim custs = _
  From c In db.Customers _
  Where c.City = "Rio de Janeiro" _
  Select c

For Each cust In custs
  Console.WriteLine("{0}", cust.CompanyName)
Next cust
```

Here are the results of that example:

```
Hanari Carnes
Que Delícia
Ricardo Adocicados
```

For that example to work, you must add the System.Data.Linq.dll assembly to your project, add an Imports statement for the nwind namespace, and add the generated entity classes that I will cover in the LINQ to SQL chapters to your project. Additionally, you may need to tweak the connection string.

Let's assume that I need to reverse the order of the records coming from the database for some reason. I am not concerned because I know there is a Reverse operator that I covered earlier in this chapter. Listing 4-40 shows the previous example modified to call the Reverse operator.

Listing 4-40. *Calling the Reverse Operator*

```
Dim db As New Northwind( _
  "Data Source=.\SQLEXPRESS;Initial Catalog=Northwind;Integrated Security=SSPI;")

Dim custs = ( _
  From c In db.Customers _
  Where c.City = "Rio de Janeiro" _
  Select c).Reverse()

For Each cust In custs
  Console.WriteLine("{0}", cust.CompanyName)
Next cust
```

It seems simple enough. As you can see, my only change is to add the call to the Reverse operator. The code compiles just fine. Here are the results of the example:

```
Unhandled Exception: System.NotSupportedException: The query operator 'Reverse' is
not supported.
...
```

Boy, that seemed like it should have been so simple, what happened? What happened is that there is no Reverse operator for the IQueryable(Of TSource) interface, so the exception was thrown. I need to use the AsEnumerable operator to convert the sequence of type IQueryable(Of TSource) to a sequence of type IEnumerable(Of TSource) so that when I call the Reverse operator, the IEnumerable(Of TSource) Reverse operator gets called. The code modified to do this is in Listing 4-41.

Listing 4-41. *Calling the AsEnumerable Operator Before Calling the Reverse Operator*

```
Dim db As New Northwind( _
  "Data Source=.\SQLEXPRESS;Initial Catalog=Northwind;Integrated Security=SSPI;")

Dim custs = ( _
  From c In db.Customers _
  Where c.City = "Rio de Janeiro" _
  Select c).AsEnumerable().Reverse()

For Each cust In custs
  Console.WriteLine("{0}", cust.CompanyName)
Next cust
```

Now, I am calling the AsEnumerable operator first, followed by the Reverse operator, so the LINQ to Objects Reverse operator will be called. Here are the results:

```
Ricardo Adocicados
Que Delícia
Hanari Carnes
```

Those results are in the reverse order of the initial example, so it worked.

Element

The element operators allow you to retrieve single elements from an input sequence.

DefaultIfEmpty

The DefaultIfEmpty operator returns a sequence containing a default element if the input source sequence is empty.

Declarations

The DefaultIfEmpty operator has two overloads.

The First Overload of the DefaultIfEmpty Operator

```
<ExtensionAttribute> _
Public Shared Function DefaultIfEmpty(Of TSource) ( _
    source As IEnumerable(Of TSource) _
) As IEnumerable(Of TSource)
```

This overload of the DefaultIfEmpty operator returns an object that, when enumerated, enumerates the input source sequence, yielding each element unless the source sequence is empty, in which case it returns a sequence yielding a single element of default(TSource). For reference and nullable types, the default value is Nothing.

Unlike all the other element type operators, notice that DefaultIfEmpty returns a sequence of type IEnumerable(Of TSource) instead of a type TSource. There are additional element type operators, but they are not included in this chapter, because they are not deferred operators.

The second overload allows the default value to be specified.

The Second Overload of the DefaultIfEmpty Operator

```
<ExtensionAttribute> _
Public Shared Function DefaultIfEmpty(Of TSource) ( _
    source As IEnumerable(Of TSource), _
    defaultValue As TSource _
) As IEnumerable(Of TSource)
```

This operator is useful for all the other operators that throw exceptions if the input source sequence is empty. Additionally, this operator is useful in conjunction with the GroupJoin operator for producing left outer joins.

Exceptions

ArgumentNullException is thrown if the source argument is Nothing.

Examples

Listing 4-42 shows the example of the first DefaultIfEmpty overload with an empty sequence. In this example, I will not use the DefaultIfEmpty operator to see what happens. I will search my presidents array for "Jones", return the first element, and if it's not Nothing, output a message.

Listing 4-42. *The First Example for the First Overload of the DefaultIfEmpty Operator, Without Using DefaultIfEmpty*

```
Dim presidents() As String = { _
  "Adams", "Arthur", "Buchanan", "Bush", "Carter", "Cleveland", _
  "Clinton", "Coolidge", "Eisenhower", "Fillmore", "Ford", "Garfield", _
  "Grant", "Harding", "Harrison", "Hayes", "Hoover", "Jackson", _
  "Jefferson", "Johnson", "Kennedy", "Lincoln", "Madison", "McKinley", _
  "Monroe", "Nixon", "Pierce", "Polk", "Reagan", "Roosevelt", "Taft", _
  "Taylor", "Truman", "Tyler", "Van Buren", "Washington", "Wilson"}

Dim jones As String = presidents.Where(Function(n) n.Equals("Jones")).First()
If jones IsNot Nothing Then
  Console.WriteLine("Jones was found")
Else
  Console.WriteLine("Jones was not found")
End If
```

Here are the results:

```
Unhandled Exception: System.InvalidOperationException: Sequence contains no elements
...
```

In the preceding code, the query didn't find any elements equal to "Jones", so an empty sequence was passed to the First operator. The First operator doesn't like empty sequences, so an exception is thrown.

Now, in Listing 4-43, I will call the same code, except I will insert a call to the DefaultIfEmpty operator between the Where operator and the First operator. This way, instead of an empty sequence, a sequence containing a Nothing element will be passed to First.

Listing 4-43. *The Second Example for the First Overload of the DefaultIfEmpty Operator, Using DefaultIfEmpty*

```
Dim presidents() As String = { _
  "Adams", "Arthur", "Buchanan", "Bush", "Carter", "Cleveland", _
  "Clinton", "Coolidge", "Eisenhower", "Fillmore", "Ford", "Garfield", _
  "Grant", "Harding", "Harrison", "Hayes", "Hoover", "Jackson", _
  "Jefferson", "Johnson", "Kennedy", "Lincoln", "Madison", "McKinley", _
  "Monroe", "Nixon", "Pierce", "Polk", "Reagan", "Roosevelt", "Taft", _
  "Taylor", "Truman", "Tyler", "Van Buren", "Washington", "Wilson"}

Dim jones As String = _
  presidents.Where(Function(n) n.Equals("Jones")).DefaultIfEmpty().First()

If jones IsNot Nothing Then
  Console.WriteLine("Jones was found.")
Else
  Console.WriteLine("Jones was not found.")
End If
```

The results now are

```
Jones was not found.
```

For an example of the second overload, I am allowed to specify the default value for an empty sequence, as shown in Listing 4-44.

Listing 4-44. *An Example for the Second Overload of the DefaultIfEmpty Operator*

```
Dim presidents() As String = { _
  "Adams", "Arthur", "Buchanan", "Bush", "Carter", "Cleveland", _
  "Clinton", "Coolidge", "Eisenhower", "Fillmore", "Ford", "Garfield", _
  "Grant", "Harding", "Harrison", "Hayes", "Hoover", "Jackson", _
  "Jefferson", "Johnson", "Kennedy", "Lincoln", "Madison", "McKinley", _
  "Monroe", "Nixon", "Pierce", "Polk", "Reagan", "Roosevelt", "Taft", _
  "Taylor", "Truman", "Tyler", "Van Buren", "Washington", "Wilson"}

Dim name As String = presidents _
  .Where(Function(n) n.Equals("Jones")).DefaultIfEmpty("Missing").First()

Console.WriteLine(name)
```

The results are

```
Missing
```

Next, for one last set of examples, I will perform a left outer join using both the GroupJoin and DefaultIfEmpty operators. I will use my two common classes, Employee and EmployeeOptionEntry. In Listing 4-45 is an example *without* using the DefaultIfEmpty operator.

Listing 4-45. *An Example Without the DefaultIfEmpty Operator*

```
Dim employeesAL As ArrayList = Employee.GetEmployeesArrayList()

'   Add a new employee so one employee will have no EmployeeOptionEntry records.
employeesAL.Add(New Employee With { _
  .id = 102, _
  .firstName = "Michael", _
  .lastName = "Bolton"})

Dim employees() As Employee = employeesAL.Cast(Of Employee)().ToArray()
Dim empOptions() As EmployeeOptionEntry = EmployeeOptionEntry.GetEmployeeOptionEn-
tries()

Dim employeeOptions = employees _
  .GroupJoin( _
    empOptions, _
    Function(e) e.id, _
    Function(o) o.id, _
    Function(e, os) os.Select _
      (Function(o) New With { _
        Key .id = e.id, _
        Key .name = String.Format("{0} {1}", e.firstName, e.lastName), _
        Key .options = If(o IsNot Nothing, o.optionsCount, 0)})) _
  .SelectMany(Function(r) r)

For Each item In employeeOptions
  Console.WriteLine(item)
Next item
```

There are three things I want to point out about this example. First, it is very similar to the example I presented for the GroupJoin operator example when I discussed it. Second, since my common EmployeeOptionEntry class already has a matching object for every employee in the common Employee class, I am getting the ArrayList of employees and adding a new employee, Michael Bolton, to it so that I will have one employee with no matching EmployeeOptionEntry objects. Third, I am not making a call to the DefaultIfEmpty operator in that example.

The results of this query are

```
{ id = 1, name = Joe Rattz, options = 2 }
{ id = 2, name = William Gates, options = 10000 }
{ id = 2, name = William Gates, options = 10000 }
{ id = 2, name = William Gates, options = 10000 }
{ id = 3, name = Anders Hejlsberg, options = 5000 }
{ id = 3, name = Anders Hejlsberg, options = 7500 }
```

```
{ id = 3, name = Anders Hejlsberg, options = 7500 }
{ id = 4, name = David Lightman, options = 1500 }
{ id = 101, name = Kevin Flynn, options = 2 }
```

Please notice that, since there were no matching objects in the EmployeeOptionEntry array for employee Michael Bolton, I got no record for that employee in the output sequence. By using the DefaultIfEmpty operator, I can provide a matching default record, as shown in Listing 4-46.

Listing 4-46. *An Example with the DefaultIfEmpty Operator*

```
Dim employeesAL As ArrayList = Employee.GetEmployeesArrayList()

'  Add a new employee so one employee will have no EmployeeOptionEntry records.
employeesAL.Add(New Employee With { _
  .id = 102, _
  .firstName = "Michael", _
  .lastName = "Bolton"})

Dim employees() As Employee = employeesAL.Cast(Of Employee)().ToArray()
Dim empOptions() As EmployeeOptionEntry = EmployeeOptionEntry.GetEmployeeOptionEn-
tries()

Dim employeeOptions = employees _
  .GroupJoin( _
    empOptions, _
    Function(e) e.id, _
    Function(o) o.id, _
    Function(e, os) os.DefaultIfEmpty() _
      .Select(Function(o) New With { _
        Key .id = e.id, _
        Key .name = String.Format("{0} {1}", e.firstName, e.lastName), _
        Key .options = If(o IsNot Nothing, o.optionsCount, 0)})) _
  .SelectMany(Function(r) r)

For Each item In employeeOptions
  Console.WriteLine(item)
Next item
```

In the preceding example, I am still adding an employee object for Michael Bolton with no matching EmployeeOptionEntry objects. I am now calling the DefaultIfEmpty operator. Here are the results of my resulting left outer join:

```
{ id = 1, name = Joe Rattz, options = 2 }
{ id = 2, name = William Gates, options = 10000 }
{ id = 2, name = William Gates, options = 10000 }
{ id = 2, name = William Gates, options = 10000 }
{ id = 3, name = Anders Hejlsberg, options = 5000 }
```

```
{ id = 3, name = Anders Hejlsberg, options = 7500 }
{ id = 3, name = Anders Hejlsberg, options = 7500 }
{ id = 4, name = David Lightman, options = 1500 }
{ id = 101, name = Kevin Flynn, options = 2 }
{ id = 102, name = Michael Bolton, options = 0 }
```

As you can see, I now have a record for Michael Bolton even though there are no matching EmployeeOptionEntry objects. From the results, you can see Michael Bolton has received no employee options. Indeed, it is no wonder he was always so irritated with that printer.

Generation

The generation operators assist with generating sequences.

Range

The Range operator generates a sequence of integers.

Declarations

The Range operator has one overload.

The Only Overload of the Range Operator

```
Public Shared Function Range ( _
    start As Integer, _
    count As Integer _
) As IEnumerable(Of Integer)
```

A sequence of integers will be generated starting with the value passed as start and continuing for the number of count.

Notice that this is not an extension method and one of the few Standard Query Operators that does not extend IEnumerable(Of T).

■**Note** Range is not an extension method. It is a static method called on System.Linq.Enumerable.

Exceptions

ArgumentOutOfRangeException is thrown if the count is less than zero, or if start plus count minus one is greater than Integer.MaxValue.

Examples

Listing 4-47. *An Example Calling the Range Operator*

```
Dim ints As IEnumerable(Of Integer) = Enumerable.Range(1, 10)
For Each i As Integer In ints
```

```
    Console.WriteLine(i)
Next i
```

Again, I want to stress that I am not calling the Range operator on a sequence. It is a static method of the System.Linq.Enumerable class. There are no surprises here, as the results prove:

```
1
2
3
4
5
6
7
8
9
10
```

Repeat

The Repeat operator generates a sequence by repeating a specified element a specified number of times.

Declarations

The Repeat operator has one overload.

The Only Overload of the Repeat Operator

```
Public Shared Function Repeat(Of TResult) ( _
    element As TResult, _
    count As Integer _
) As IEnumerable(Of TResult)
```

This overload returns an object that, when enumerated, will yield count number of TResult elements.

Notice that this is not an extension method and one of the few Standard Query Operators that does not extend IEnumerable(Of T).

■Note Repeat is not an extension method. It is a static method called on System.Linq.Enumerable.

Exceptions

ArgumentOutOfRangeException is thrown if the count is less than zero.

Examples

In Listing 4-48, I will generate a sequence containing ten elements where each element is the number 2.

Listing 4-48. *Returning a Sequence of Ten Integers All With the Value Two*

```
Dim ints As IEnumerable(Of Integer) = Enumerable.Repeat(2, 10)
For Each i As Integer In ints
  Console.WriteLine(i)
Next i
```

Here are the results of this example:

```
2
2
2
2
2
2
2
2
2
2
```

Empty

The Empty operator generates an empty sequence of a specified type.

Declarations

The Empty operator has one overload.

The Only Overload of the Empty Operator

```
Public Shared Function Empty(Of TResult) As IEnumerable(Of TResult)
```

This overload returns an object that, when enumerated, will return a sequence containing zero elements of type TResult.

Notice that this is not an extension method and one of the few Standard Query Operators that does not extend IEnumerable(Of T).

Note Empty is not an extension method. It is a static method called on System.Linq.Enumerable.

Exceptions

There are no exceptions.

Examples

In Listing 4-49, I generate an empty sequence of type String using the Empty operator and display the Count of the generated sequence, which should be zero since the sequence is empty.

Listing 4-49. *An Example to Return an Empty Sequence of Strings*

```
Dim strings As IEnumerable(Of String) = Enumerable.Empty(Of String)()
For Each s As String In strings
  Console.WriteLine(s)
Next s
Console.WriteLine(strings.Count())
```

Here is the output of the preceding code:

0

Since the sequence is empty, there are no elements to display in the For Each loop, so I added the display of the count of the number of elements in the sequence.

Summary

I know this has been a whirlwind tour of the deferred Standard Query Operators. I have attempted to provide examples for virtually every overload of each deferred operator, instead of just the simplest overload. I always dislike it when books show the simplest form of calling a method but leave it to you to figure out the more complex versions. Hopefully, I will have made calling the more complex overloads simple for you.

Additionally, I hope that by breaking up the Standard Query Operators into those that are deferred and those that are not, I have properly emphasized the significance this can have on your queries.

While this chapter covered the bulk of the Standard Query Operators, in the next chapter I will conclude my coverage of LINQ to Objects with an examination of the nondeferred Standard Query Operators.

■■■

CHAPTER 5

Nondeferred Operators

In the previous chapter, I covered the deferred Standard Query Operators. These are easy to spot because they return either IEnumerable(Of T) or IOrderedEnumerable(Of T). But the deferred operators are only half the Standard Query Operator story. For the full story, I must also cover the nondeferred query operators. A nondeferred operator is easy to spot because it has a return data type other than IEnumerable(Of T) or IOrderedEnumerable(Of T). These nondeferred operators are categorized in this chapter by their purpose.

In order to code and execute the examples in this chapter, you will need to make sure you have Imports statements for all the necessary namespaces. You must also have some common code that the examples share.

Referenced Namespaces

The examples in this chapter will use the System.Linq, System.Collections, and System.Collections.Generic namespaces. Therefore, you should add the following Imports statements to your code if they are not present or included in your project settings:

```
Imports System.Linq
Imports System.Collections
Imports System.Collections.Generic
```

In addition to these namespaces, if you download the companion code, you will see that I have also added an Imports statement for the System.Diagnostics namespace. This will not be necessary if you are typing in the examples from this chapter. It is necessary in the companion code, because I use them to display the name of each function as it runs.

Common Classes

Several of the examples in this chapter require classes to fully demonstrate an operator's behavior. This section describes four classes that will be used by more than one example, beginning with the Employee class.

The Employee class is meant to represent an employee. For convenience, it contains Shared methods to return an ArrayList or array of employees.

The Common Employee Class

```
Public Class Employee
  Public id As Integer
  Public firstName As String
  Public lastName As String

  Public Shared Function GetEmployeesArrayList() As ArrayList
    Dim al As New ArrayList()

    al.Add(New Employee With _
      {.id = 1, .firstName = "Joe", .lastName = "Rattz"})
    al.Add(New Employee With _
      {.id = 2, .firstName = "William", .lastName = "Gates"})
    al.Add(New Employee With _
      {.id = 3, .firstName = "Anders", .lastName = "Hejlsberg"})
    al.Add(New Employee With _
      {.id = 4, .firstName = "David", .lastName = "Lightman"})
    al.Add(New Employee With _
      {.id = 101, .firstName = "Kevin", .lastName = "Flynn"})
  Return (al)
  End Function

  Public Shared Function GetEmployeesArray() As Employee()
    Return (GetEmployeesArrayList().ToArray(GetType(Employee)))
  End Function
End Class
```

The `EmployeeOptionEntry` class represents an award of stock options to a specific employee. For convenience, it contains a `Shared` method to return an array of awarded option entries.

The Common EmployeeOptionEntry Class

```
Public Class EmployeeOptionEntry
  Public id As Integer
  Public optionsCount As Long
  Public dateAwarded As DateTime

  Public Shared Function GetEmployeeOptionEntries() As EmployeeOptionEntry()
    Dim empOptions() As EmployeeOptionEntry = { _
      New EmployeeOptionEntry With { _
        .id = 1, _
        .optionsCount = 2, _
        .dateAwarded = DateTime.Parse("1999/12/31")}, _
      New EmployeeOptionEntry With { _
        .id = 2, _
        .optionsCount = 10000, _
        .dateAwarded = DateTime.Parse("1992/06/30")}, _
```

```
        New EmployeeOptionEntry With { _
          .id = 2, _
          .optionsCount = 10000, _
          .dateAwarded = DateTime.Parse("1994/01/01")}, _
        New EmployeeOptionEntry With { _
          .id = 3, _
          .optionsCount = 5000, _
          .dateAwarded = DateTime.Parse("1997/09/30")}, _
        New EmployeeOptionEntry With { _
          .id = 2, _
          .optionsCount = 10000, _
          .dateAwarded = DateTime.Parse("2003/04/01")}, _
        New EmployeeOptionEntry With { _
          .id = 3, _
          .optionsCount = 7500, _
          .dateAwarded = DateTime.Parse("1998/09/30")}, _
        New EmployeeOptionEntry With { _
          .id = 3, _
          .optionsCount = 7500, _
          .dateAwarded = DateTime.Parse("1998/09/30")}, _
        New EmployeeOptionEntry With { _
          .id = 4, _
          .optionsCount = 1500, _
          .dateAwarded = DateTime.Parse("1997/12/31")}, _
        New EmployeeOptionEntry With { _
          .id = 101, _
          .optionsCount = 2, _
          .dateAwarded = DateTime.Parse("1998/12/31")} _
        }
    Return (empOptions)
  End Function
End Class
```

Several of the operators will accept classes that implement the IEqualityComparer(Of T) interface for the purpose of comparing elements to determine whether they are equal. This is useful for those times when two values may not exactly be equal but you want them to be deemed equal. For example, you may want to be able to ignore case when comparing two strings. However, for this situation, an equality comparison class named StringComparer already exists in the .NET Framework.

Since I cover the IEqualityComparer(Of T) interface in detail in the previous chapter, I will not explain it here.

For my examples, I want an equality comparison class that will know how to check for the equality of numbers in string format. So for example, the strings "17" and "00017" would be considered equal. Here is my MyStringifiedNumberComparer class that does just that.

The Common MyStringifiedNumberComparer Class

```
Public Class MyStringifiedNumberComparer
    Implements IEqualityComparer(Of String)
  Public Overloads Function Equals(ByVal x As String, ByVal y As String) _
      As Boolean Implements IEqualityComparer(Of String).Equals
    Return(GetHashCode(x) = GetHashCode(y))
  End Function

  Public Overloads Function GetHashCode(ByVal obj As String) _
      As Integer Implements IEqualityComparer(Of String).GetHashCode
    Return(Integer.Parse(obj))
  End Function
End Class
```

Notice that this implementation of the IEqualityComparer interface will only work for variables of type String, but that will suffice for this example. Basically, for all comparisons, I just convert all the values from String to Integer. This way "002" gets converted to an integer with a value of 2, so leading zeros do not affect the key value.

For some of the examples in this chapter, I need a class that could have records with non-unique keys. For this purpose, I have created the following Actor class. I will use the birthYear member as the key specifically for this purpose.

The Common Actor Class

```
Public Class Actor
  Public birthYear As Integer
  Public firstName As String
  Public lastName As String

  Public Shared Function GetActors() As Actor()
    Dim actors() As Actor = { _
      New Actor With {.birthYear = 1964, _
        .firstName = "Keanu", .lastName = "Reeves"}, _
      New Actor With {.birthYear = 1968, _
        .firstName = "Owen", .lastName = "Wilson"}, _
      New Actor With {.birthYear = 1960, _
        .firstName = "James", .lastName = "Spader"}, _
      New Actor With {.birthYear = 1964, _
        .firstName = "Sandra", .lastName = "Bullock"} }
    Return (actors)
  End Function
End Class
```

The Nondeferred Operators by Purpose

The nondeferred Standard Query Operators are organized by their purposes in this section.

Conversion

The following conversion operators provide a simple and convenient way of converting sequences to other collection types.

ToArray

The ToArray operator creates an array of type TSource from an input sequence of type TSource.

Declarations

The ToArray operator has one overload.

■**Note** The following declaration is how the .NET Framework defines the ToArray operator. The <ExtensionAttribute> is used internally by the Microsoft .NET Framework and should not be used by any application code. It is not related to the <Extension()> attribute, which is meant to be used in applications. Also note that this is not a case of an evil Microsoft using secret functionality to gain an advantage over competitors. Frameworks typically need flags and functions for internal housekeeping, and this is just one of those occasions. Even though it is only meant for internal use, it is included in the .NET documentation.

The Only Overload of the ToArray Operator

```
<ExtensionAttribute> _
Public Shared Function ToArray(Of TSource) ( _
    source As IEnumerable(Of TSource) _
) As TSource()
```

This operator takes an input sequence named source, of type TSource elements, and returns an array of type TSource elements.

Exceptions

ArgumentNullException is thrown if the source argument is Nothing.

Examples

For an example demonstrating the ToArray operator, I need a sequence of type IEnumerable(Of TSource). I will create a sequence of that type by calling the OfType operator, which I cover in the previous chapter, on an array. Once I have that sequence, I can call the ToArray operator to create an array, as shown in Listing 5-1.

Listing 5-1. *A Code Sample Calling the ToArray Operator*

```
Dim presidents() As String = _
{ _
  "Adams", "Arthur", "Buchanan", "Bush", "Carter", "Cleveland", _
  "Clinton", "Coolidge", "Eisenhower", "Fillmore", "Ford", "Garfield", _
```

```
        "Grant", "Harding", "Harrison", "Hayes", "Hoover", "Jackson", _
        "Jefferson", "Johnson", "Kennedy", "Lincoln", "Madison", "McKinley", _
        "Monroe", "Nixon", "Pierce", "Polk", "Reagan", "Roosevelt", "Taft", _
        "Taylor", "Truman", "Tyler", "Van Buren", "Washington", "Wilson" _
}

Dim names() As String = presidents.OfType(Of String)().ToArray()

For Each name As String In names
    Console.WriteLine(name)
Next name
```

First I convert the presidents array to a sequence of type IEnumerable(Of String) using the OfType operator. Then I convert that sequence to an array using the ToArray operator. Since the ToArray is a nondeferred operator, the query is performed immediately, even prior to enumerating it.

Here is the output when running the previous code:

```
Adams
Arthur
Buchanan
Bush
Carter
Cleveland
Clinton
Coolidge
Eisenhower
Fillmore
Ford
Garfield
Grant
Harding
Harrison
Hayes
Hoover
Jackson
Jefferson
Johnson
Kennedy
Lincoln
Madison
McKinley
Monroe
Nixon
Pierce
Polk
Reagan
Roosevelt
```

```
Taft
Taylor
Truman
Tyler
Van Buren
Washington
Wilson
```

Now, technically, the code in this example is a little redundant. The presidents array is already a sequence, because since .NET 2.0, arrays implement the IEnumerable(Of TSource) interface. So I could have omitted the call to the OfType operator and merely called the ToArray operator on the presidents array. However, I didn't think it would be very impressive to convert an array to an array.

This operator is often useful for caching a sequence so that it cannot change before you can enumerate it. Also, because this operator is not deferred and is executed immediately, multiple enumerations on the array created will always see the same data.

ToList

The ToList operator creates a List of type TSource from an input sequence of type TSource.

Declarations

The ToList operator has one overload.

The Only Overload of the ToList Operator

```
<ExtensionAttribute> _
Public Shared Function ToList(Of TSource) ( _
    source As IEnumerable(Of TSource) _
) As List(Of TSource)
```

This operator takes an input sequence named source, of type TSource elements, and returns a List of type TSource elements.

Exceptions

ArgumentNullException is thrown if the source argument is Nothing.

Examples

Listing 5-2 demonstrates the ToList operator.

Listing 5-2. *A Code Sample Calling the ToList Operator*

```
Dim presidents() As String = _
{ _
  "Adams", "Arthur", "Buchanan", "Bush", "Carter", "Cleveland", _
  "Clinton", "Coolidge", "Eisenhower", "Fillmore", "Ford", "Garfield", _
  "Grant", "Harding", "Harrison", "Hayes", "Hoover", "Jackson", _
```

```
    "Jefferson", "Johnson", "Kennedy", "Lincoln", "Madison", "McKinley", _
    "Monroe", "Nixon", "Pierce", "Polk", "Reagan", "Roosevelt", "Taft", _
    "Taylor", "Truman", "Tyler", "Van Buren", "Washington", "Wilson" _
}
```

Dim names As List(Of String) = presidents.ToList()

```
For Each name As String In names
  Console.WriteLine(name)
Next name
```

In the previous code, I use the same array from the previous example. Unlike the previous example, I do not call the OfType operator to create an intermediate sequence of IEnumerable(Of TSource) because it seems sufficient to convert the presidents array to a List(Of String).

Here are the results:

```
Adams
Arthur
Buchanan
Bush
Carter
Cleveland
Clinton
Coolidge
Eisenhower
Fillmore
Ford
Garfield
Grant
Harding
Harrison
Hayes
Hoover
Jackson
Jefferson
Johnson
Kennedy
Lincoln
Madison
McKinley
Monroe
Nixon
Pierce
Polk
Reagan
Roosevelt
Taft
```

```
Taylor
Truman
Tyler
Van Buren
Washington
Wilson
```

This operator is often useful for caching a sequence so that it cannot change before you can enumerate it. Also, because this operator is not deferred and is executed immediately, multiple enumerations on the List(Of TSource) created will always see the same data.

ToDictionary

The ToDictionary operator creates a Dictionary of type (Of TKey, TSource), or perhaps (Of TKey, TElement) if the call uses the elementSelector argument, from an input sequence of type TSource, where TKey is the type of the key, and TSource is the type of the stored values. Or if the Dictionary is of type (Of TKey, TElement), stored values are of type TElement, which is different than the type of elements in the sequence, which is TSource.

■Note If you are unfamiliar with the .NET Dictionary collection class, it allows elements to be stored that can be retrieved with a key. Each key must be unique, and only one element can be stored for a single key. You index into the Dictionary using the key to retrieve the stored element for that key.

Declarations

The ToDictionary operator has four overloads.

The First Overload of the ToDictionary Operator

```
<ExtensionAttribute> _
Public Shared Function ToDictionary(Of TSource, TKey) ( _
    source As IEnumerable(Of TSource), _
    keySelector As Func(Of TSource, TKey) _
) As Dictionary(Of TKey, TSource)
```

In this overload, a Dictionary of type (Of Key, TSource) is created and returned by enumerating the input sequence named source. The keySelector method delegate is called to specify the key value for each input element, and that key is the element's key into the Dictionary.

Typically, the key would come from each input element or be created from each input element somehow, such as by perhaps calling the ToString or some other transformation type method on each input element. However, it is not necessary for the key returned by the keySelector to come from each input element. The returned key could come from something altogether different such as another data source where the input element was used as the key into that data source to retrieve the key returned by the keySelector.

This version of the operator results in elements in the `Dictionary` being the same type as the elements in the input sequence.

Since this overload does not have a parameter for the specification of an `IEqualityComparer(Of TKey)` object, it defaults to the `EqualityComparer(Of TKey).Default` equality comparison object.

The second `ToDictionary` overload is similar to the first, except it provides the ability to specify an `IEqualityComparer(Of TKey)` equality comparison object. Here is the second overload.

The Second Overload of the ToDictionary Operator

```
<ExtensionAttribute> _
Public Shared Function ToDictionary(Of TSource, TKey) ( _
    source As IEnumerable(Of TSource), _
    keySelector As Func(Of TSource, TKey), _
    comparer As IEqualityComparer(Of TKey) _
) As Dictionary(Of TKey, TSource)
```

This overload provides the ability to specify an `IEqualityComparer(Of TKey)` equality comparison object. This object is used to make comparisons on the key value. So if you add or access an element in the `Dictionary`, it will use this `comparer` to compare the key you specify to the keys already in the `Dictionary` to determine whether it has a match.

A default implementation of the `IEqualityComparer(Of TKey)` interface is provided by `EqualityComparer.Default`. However, if you are going to use the default equality comparison class, there is no reason to even specify the `comparer`, because the previous overload where the `comparer` is not specified defaults to this one anyway. The `StringComparer` class provides a factory for several equality comparison classes, such as one that ignores case. This way, using the keys "Joe" and "joe" evaluates to being the same key.

The third `ToDictionary` overload is just like the first except it allows you to specify an element selector so that the data type of the value stored in the `Dictionary` can be of a different type than the input sequence element.

The Third Overload of the ToDictionary Operator

```
<ExtensionAttribute> _
Public Shared Function ToDictionary(Of TSource, TKey, TElement) ( _
    source As IEnumerable(Of TSource), _
    keySelector As Func(Of TSource, TKey), _
    elementSelector As Func(Of TSource, TElement) _
) As Dictionary(Of TKey, TElement)
```

Through the `elementSelector` argument, you can specify a method delegate that returns a portion of the input element—or a newly created object of an altogether different data type—that you want to be stored in the `Dictionary`.

The fourth overload for the `ToDictionary` operator gives you the best of all worlds. It is a combination of the second and third overloads, which means you can specify an `elementSelector` and a `comparer` object.

The Fourth Overload of the ToDictionary Operator

```
<ExtensionAttribute> _
Public Shared Function ToDictionary(Of TSource, TKey, TElement) ( _
    source As IEnumerable(Of TSource), _
    keySelector As Func(Of TSource, TKey), _
    elementSelector As Func(Of TSource, TElement), _
    comparer As IEqualityComparer(Of TKey) _
) As Dictionary(Of TKey, TElement)
```

This overload allows you to specify the elementSelector and comparer object.

Exceptions

ArgumentNullException is thrown if the source, keySelector, or elementSelector argument is Nothing, or if a key returned by keySelector is Nothing.

ArgumentException is thrown if a keySelector returns the same key for two elements.

Examples

In this example, instead of using the typical presidents array I have been using, I use my common Employee class. I am going to create a dictionary of type Dictionary(Of Integer Employee) where the key of type Integer is the id member of the Employee class, and the Employee object itself is the element stored.

Listing 5-3 is an example calling the ToDictionary operator using the Employee class.

Listing 5-3. *Sample Code Calling the First ToDictionary Operator Overload*

```
Dim eDictionary As Dictionary(Of Integer, Employee) = _
  Employee.GetEmployeesArray().ToDictionary(Function(k) k.id)
Dim e As Employee = eDictionary(2)

Console.WriteLine("Employee whose id = 2 is {0} {1}", e.firstName, e.lastName)
```

I declare my Dictionary to have a key type of Integer, because I will be using the Employee.id field as the key. Since this ToDictionary operator declaration only allows me to store the entire input element, which is an Employee object, as the element in the Dictionary, the Dictionary element type is Employee as well. The Dictionary(Of Integer, Employee) then allows me to look up employees by their employee id providing the performance efficiencies and retrieval convenience of a Dictionary. Here are the results of the previous code:

```
Employee whose id = 2 is William Gates
```

For an example demonstrating the second overload, since the purpose of the second overload is to allow me to specify an equality comparison object of type IEqualityComparer(Of TKey), I need a situation where an equality comparison class would be useful. This is a situation where keys that may not literally be equal will be considered equal by my equality comparison class. I will use a numeric value in string format as the key for this purpose, such as "1". Since sometimes numeric values in string format end up with leading zeros, it is quite feasible that a key for the same data could end up being "1", or "01", or even "00001". Since those string values are not equal, I need an equality comparison class that would know how to determine that they should be considered equal.

First, though, I need a class with a key of type String. For this, I will make a slight modification to the common Employee class that I have been using on occasion. I will create the following Employee2 class that is identical to the Employee class, except that the id member type is now String instead of Integer.

A Class for the Code Sample for the Second Overload of the ToDictionary Operator

```
Public Class Employee2
  Public id As String
  Public firstName As String
  Public lastName As String

  Public Shared Function GetEmployeesArrayList() As ArrayList
    Dim al As New ArrayList()

    al.Add(New Employee2 With _
      {.id = "1", .firstName = "Joe", .lastName = "Rattz"})
    al.Add(New Employee2 With _
      {.id = "2", .firstName = "William", .lastName = "Gates"})
    al.Add(New Employee2 With _
      {.id = "3", .firstName = "Anders", .lastName = "Hejlsberg"})
    al.Add(New Employee2 With _
      {.id = "4", .firstName = "David", .lastName = "Lightman"})
    al.Add(New Employee2 With _
      {.id = "101", .firstName = "Kevin", .lastName = "Flynn"})
    Return (al)
  End Function

  Public Shared Function GetEmployeesArray() As Employee2()
    Return (GetEmployeesArrayList().ToArray(GetType(Employee2)))
  End Function
End Class
```

I have changed the key type to String to demonstrate how an equality comparison class can be used to determine whether two keys are equal, even though they may not literally be equal. In this example, because my keys are now String, I will use my common MyStringifiedNumberComparer class that will know that the key "02" is equal to the key "2".

Now let's look at some code using the Employee2 class and my implementation of IEqualityComparer, shown in Listing 5-4.

Listing 5-4. *Sample Code Calling the Second ToDictionary Operator Overload*

```
'  My dictionary is going to be of type Dictionary(Of string, Employee2) because
'  I am going to use the Employee2.id field as the key, which is of type string,
'  and I am going to store the entire Employee2 object as the element.
```

```
Dim eDictionary As Dictionary(Of String, Employee2) = _
  Employee2.GetEmployeesArray(). _
    ToDictionary(Function(k) k.id, New MyStringifiedNumberComparer())

Dim e As Employee2 = eDictionary("2")
Console.WriteLine("Employee whose id == ""2"" : {0} {1}", e.firstName, e.lastName)

e = eDictionary("000002")
Console.WriteLine _
  ("Employee whose id == ""000002"" : {0} {1}", e.firstName, e.lastName)
```

In this example, I try to access elements in the Dictionary with key values of "2" and "000002". If my equality comparison class works properly, I should get the same element from the Dictionary both times. Here are the results:

```
Employee whose id == "2" : William Gates
Employee whose id == "000002" : William Gates
```

As you can see, I did get the same element from the Dictionary regardless of my String key used for access, as long as each string value parsed to the same integer value.

The third overload allows me to store an element in the dictionary that is a different type than the input sequence element type. For the third overload example, I use the same Employee class that I use in the first overload sample code for ToDictionary. Listing 5-5 is my sample code calling the third ToDictionary overload.

Listing 5-5. *Sample Code Calling the Third ToDictionary Operator Overload*

```
Dim eDictionary As Dictionary(Of Integer, String) = Employee.GetEmployeesArray() _
  .ToDictionary( _
    Function(k) k.id, _
    Function(i) String.Format("{0} {1}", i.firstName, i.lastName))
Dim name As String = eDictionary(2)
Console.WriteLine("Employee whose id = 2 is {0}", name)
```

In this code, I provide a lambda expression that concatenates the firstName and lastName into a String. That concatenated String becomes the value stored in the Dictionary. So while my input sequence element type is Employee, my element data type stored in the dictionary is String. Here are the results of this query:

```
Employee whose id = 2 is William Gates
```

To demonstrate the fourth ToDictionary overload, I will use my Employee2 class and my common MyStringifiedNumberComparer class. Listing 5-6 is my sample code.

Listing 5-6. *Sample Code Calling the Fourth ToDictionary Operator Overload*

```
' My dictionary is going to be of type Dictionary<string, string> because
' I am going to use the Employee.id field as the key, which is of type string,
```

```
'  and I am going to store firstName and lastName concatenated as the value.
Dim eDictionary As Dictionary(Of String, String) = Employee2.GetEmployeesArray() _
  .ToDictionary( _
    Function(k) k.id, _
    Function(i) String.Format("{0} {1}", i.firstName, i.lastName), _
    New MyStringifiedNumberComparer()) ' comparer

Dim name As String = eDictionary("2")
Console.WriteLine("Employee whose id == ""2"" : {0}", name)

name = eDictionary("000002")
Console.WriteLine("Employee whose id == ""000002"" : {0}", name)
```

In the previous code, I provide an elementSelector that specifies a single String as the value to store in the Dictionary, and I provide a custom equality comparison object. The result is that I can use "2" or "000002" to retrieve the element from the Dictionary because of my equality comparison class, and what I get out of the Dictionary is now just a String, which happens to be the employee's lastName appended to the firstName. Here are the results:

```
Employee whose id == "2" : William Gates
Employee whose id == "000002" : William Gates
```

As you can see, indexing into the Dictionary with the key values of "2" and "000002" retrieve the same element.

ToLookup

The ToLookup operator creates a Lookup of type (Of TKey, TSource), or perhaps (Of TKey, TElement), from an input sequence of type TSource, where TKey is the type of the key, and TSource is the type of the stored values. Or if the Lookup is of type (Of TKey, TElement), the stored values are of type TElement, which is different than the type of elements in the sequence, which is TSource.

While all overloads of the ToLookup operator create a Lookup, they return an object that implements the ILookup interface. In this section, I will commonly refer to the object implementing the ILookup interface that is returned as a Lookup.

Note If you are unfamiliar with the .NET Lookup collection class, it allows elements to be stored that can be retrieved with a key. Each key need not be unique, and *multiple* elements can be stored for a single key. You index into the Lookup using the key to retrieve a *sequence* of the stored elements for that key.

Declarations

The ToLookup operator has four overloads.

The First Overload of the ToLookup Operator

```
<ExtensionAttribute> _
Public Shared Function ToLookup(Of TSource, TKey) ( _
    source As IEnumerable(Of TSource), _
    keySelector As Func(Of TSource, TKey) _
) As ILookup(Of TKey, TSource)
```

In this overload, a Lookup of type (Of TKey, TSource) is created and returned by enumerating the input sequence, named source. The keySelector method delegate is called to specify the key value for each input element, and that key is the element's key into the Lookup.

Typically, the key would come from each input element or be created from each input element somehow, such as by perhaps calling the ToString or some other transformation type method on each input element. However, it is not necessary for the key returned by the keySelector to come from each input element. The returned key could come from something altogether different such as another data source where the input element was used as the key into that data source to retrieve the key returned by the keySelector.

This version of the operator results in stored values in the Lookup being the same type as the elements in the input sequence.

Since this overload does not have a parameter for the IEqualityComparer(Of TKey) equality comparison object, it defaults to the EqualityComparer(Of TKey).Default equality comparison class.

The second ToLookup overload is similar to the first, except it provides the ability to specify an IEqualityComparer(Of TKey) equality comparison object. Here is the second overload.

The Second Overload of the ToLookup Operator

```
<ExtensionAttribute> _
Public Shared Function ToLookup(Of TSource, TKey) ( _
    source As IEnumerable(Of TSource), _
    keySelector As Func(Of TSource, TKey), _
    comparer As IEqualityComparer(Of TKey) _
) As ILookup(Of TKey, TSource)
```

This overload provides the ability to specify an IEqualityComparer comparer object. This object is used to make comparisons on the key value. So if you add or access an element in the Lookup, it will use this comparer object to compare the key you specify to the keys already in the Lookup to determine whether there is a match.

A default implementation of the IEqualityComparer(Of TKey) interface is provided by EqualityComparer.Default. However, if you are going to use the default equality comparison class, there is no reason to even specify the equality comparison object because the previous overload where the equality comparison object is not specified defaults to this one anyway. The StringComparer class provides a façade for several equality comparison classes, such as one that ignores case. This way, using the keys "Joe" and "joe" evaluates to being the same key.

The third ToLookup overload is just like the first one except it allows you to specify an element selector so that the data type of the value stored in the Lookup can be of a different type than the input sequence element. Here is the third overload.

The Third Overload of the ToLookup Operator

```
<ExtensionAttribute> _
Public Shared Function ToLookup(Of TSource, TKey, TElement) ( _
        source As IEnumerable(Of TSource), _
        keySelector As Func(Of TSource, TKey), _
        elementSelector As Func(Of TSource, TElement) _
) As ILookup(Of TKey, TElement)
```

Through the elementSelector argument, you can specify a method delegate that returns the portion of the input element—or a newly created object of an altogether different data type—that you want to be stored in the Lookup.

The fourth overload for the ToLookup operator gives you the best of all worlds. It is a combination of the second and third overloads, which means you can specify an elementSelector and a comparer equality comparison object. Here is the fourth overload.

The Fourth Overload of the ToLookup Operator

```
<ExtensionAttribute> _
Public Shared Function ToLookup(Of TSource, TKey, TElement) ( _
        source As IEnumerable(Of TSource), _
        keySelector As Func(Of TSource, TKey), _
        elementSelector As Func(Of TSource, TElement), _
        comparer As IEqualityComparer(Of TKey) _
) As ILookup(Of TKey, TElement)
```

This overload allows you to specify the elementSelector and comparer object.

Exceptions

ArgumentNullException is thrown if the source, keySelector, or elementSelector argument is Nothing or if a key returned by keySelector is Nothing.

Examples

In this example of the first ToLookup overload, instead of using the typical presidents array I have been using, I need a class with elements containing members that can be used as keys but are not unique. For this purpose, I will use my common Actor class.

Listing 5-7 is an example calling the ToLookup operator using the Actor class.

Listing 5-7. *Sample Code Calling the First ToLookup Operator Overload*

```
'  My Lookup is going to be of type ILookup(Integer, Actor) because I am
'  going to use the Actor.birthYear field as the key, which is of type int,
'  and I am going to store the entire Actor object as the stored value.
Dim lookup As ILookup(Of Integer, Actor) = _
  Actor.GetActors().ToLookup(Function(k) k.birthYear)

'  Let's see if I can find the 'one' born in 1964.
Dim actors As IEnumerable(Of Actor) = lookup(1964)
```

```
For Each actor In actors
  Console.WriteLine("{0} {1}", actor.firstName, actor.lastName)
Next actor
```

First, I create the `Lookup` using the `Actor.birthYear` member as the key into the `Lookup`. Next, I index into the `Lookup` using my key, 1964. Then, I enumerate through the returned values. Here are the results:

```
Keanu Reeves
Sandra Bullock
```

Uh-oh, it looks like I got multiple results back. I guess he isn't "the one" after all. It's a good thing I converted this input sequence to a `Lookup` instead of a `Dictionary`, because there were multiple elements with the same key.

For an example demonstrating the second `ToLookup` overload, I will make a slight modification to my common `Actor` class. I will create an `Actor2` class that is identical to the `Actor` class except that the `birthYear` member type is now `String` instead of `Integer`.

A Class for the Second Overload Code Sample of the ToLookup Operator

```
Public Class Actor2
  Public birthYear As String
  Public firstName As String
  Public lastName As String

  Public Shared Function GetActors() As Actor2()
    Dim actors() As Actor2 = { _
      New Actor2 With {.birthYear = "1964", _
        .firstName = "Keanu", .lastName = "Reeves"}, _
      New Actor2 With {.birthYear = "1968", _
        .firstName = "Owen", .lastName = "Wilson"}, _
      New Actor2 With {.birthYear = "1960", _
        .firstName = "James", .lastName = "Spader"}, _
      New Actor2 With {.birthYear = "01964", _
        .firstName = "Sandra", .lastName = "Bullock"} }
      '  The worlds first Y10K compliant date!

    Return(actors)
  End Function
End Class
```

Notice I changed the `birthYear` member to be a `String` for the class. Now I will call the `ToLookup` operator, as shown in Listing 5-8.

Listing 5-8. *Sample Code Calling the Second ToLookup Operator Overload*

```
'  My Lookup is going to be of type ILookup(String, Actor2) because I am
'  going to use the Actor2.birthYear field as the key, which is of type string,
```

```
' and I am going to store the entire Actor2 object as the stored value.
Dim lookup As ILookup(Of String, Actor2) = Actor2.GetActors() _
  .ToLookup(Function(k) k.birthYear, New MyStringifiedNumberComparer())

' Let's see if I can find the 'one' born in 1964.
Dim actors As IEnumerable(Of Actor2) = lookup("0001964")
For Each actor In actors
  Console.WriteLine("{0} {1}", actor.firstName, actor.lastName)
Next actor
```

I am using the same equality comparison object I use in the Dictionary examples. In this case, I convert the input sequence to a Lookup, and I provide an equality comparison object because I know that the key, which is stored as a String, may sometimes contain leading zeros. My equality comparison object knows how to handle that. Here are the results:

```
Keanu Reeves
Sandra Bullock
```

Notice that when I try to retrieve all elements whose key is "0001964", I get back elements whose keys are "1964" and "01964". So I know my equality comparison object works.

For the third overload for the ToLookup operator, I will use the same Actor class that I use in the first overload sample code for ToLookup. Listing 5-9 is my sample code calling the third ToLookup overload.

Listing 5-9. *Sample Code Calling the Third ToLookup Operator Overload*

```
' My Lookup is going to be of type ILookup(Of Integer, String) because I am
' going to use the Actor.birthYear field as the key, which is of type int,
' and I am going to store the firstName and lastName concatenated
' together as the stored value.
Dim lookup As ILookup(Of Integer, String) = _
  Actor.GetActors() _
    .ToLookup( _
      Function(k) k.birthYear, _
      Function(a) String.Format("{0} {1}", a.firstName, a.lastName))

' Let's see if I can find the 'one' born in 1964.
Dim actors As IEnumerable(Of String) = lookup(1964)
For Each actor In actors
  Console.WriteLine("{0}", actor)
Next actor
```

For my elementSelector, I just concatenate the firstName and lastName members. Here are the results:

```
Keanu Reeves
Sandra Bullock
```

Using the elementSelector variation of the ToLookup operator allows me to store a different data type in the Lookup than the input sequence element's data type.

For an example of the fourth ToLookup overload, I will use my Actor2 class and my common MyStringifiedNumberComparer class, as demonstrated in Listing 5-10.

Listing 5-10. *Sample Code Calling the Fourth ToLookup Operator Overload*

```
' My Lookup is going to be of type ILookup<string, string> because I am
' going to use the Actor2.birthYear field as the key, which is of type string,
' and I am going to store the firstName and lastName concatenated together,
' which is a string, as the stored value.
Dim lookup As ILookup(Of String, String) = Actor2 .GetActors() _
  .ToLookup( _
    Function(k) k.birthYear, _
    Function(a) String.Format("{0} {1}", a.firstName, a.lastName), _
    New MyStringifiedNumberComparer())

' Let's see if I can find the 'one' born in 1964.
Dim actors As IEnumerable(Of String) = lookup("0001964")
For Each actor In actors
  Console.WriteLine("{0}", actor)
Next actor
```

Here is the output:

```
Keanu Reeves
Sandra Bullock
```

You can see that I index into the Lookup using a key value different than either of the values retrieved using that key, so I can tell my equality comparison object is working. And instead of storing the entire Actor2 object, I merely store the String I am interested in.

Equality

The following equality operators are used for testing the equality of sequences.

SequenceEqual

The SequenceEqual operator determines whether two input sequences are equal.

Declarations

The SequenceEqual operator has two overloads.

The First Overload of the SequenceEqual Operator

```
<ExtensionAttribute> _
Public Shared Function SequenceEqual(Of TSource) ( _
    first As IEnumerable(Of TSource), _
```

```
    second As IEnumerable(Of TSource) _
) As Boolean
```

This operator enumerates each input sequence in parallel, comparing the elements of each using the System.Object.Equals method. If the elements are all equal, and the sequences have the same number of elements, the operator returns True. Otherwise, it returns False.

The second overload of the operator works just as the first, except an IEqualityComparer (Of TSource) comparer object can be used to determine element equality.

The Second Overload of the SequenceEqual Operator

```
<ExtensionAttribute> _
Public Shared Function SequenceEqual(Of TSource) ( _
    first As IEnumerable(Of TSource), _
    second As IEnumerable(Of TSource), _
    comparer As IEqualityComparer(Of TSource) _
) As Boolean
```

Exceptions

ArgumentNullException is thrown if either argument is Nothing.

Examples

Listing 5-11 is an example.

Listing 5-11. *An Example of the First SequenceEqual Operator Overload*

```
Dim presidents() As String = _
{ _
  "Adams", "Arthur", "Buchanan", "Bush", "Carter", "Cleveland", _
  "Clinton", "Coolidge", "Eisenhower", "Fillmore", "Ford", "Garfield", _
  "Grant", "Harding", "Harrison", "Hayes", "Hoover", "Jackson", _
  "Jefferson", "Johnson", "Kennedy", "Lincoln", "Madison", "McKinley", _
  "Monroe", "Nixon", "Pierce", "Polk", "Reagan", "Roosevelt", "Taft", _
  "Taylor", "Truman", "Tyler", "Van Buren", "Washington", "Wilson" _
}

Dim eq As Boolean = presidents.SequenceEqual(presidents)
Console.WriteLine(eq)
```

And here are the results:

```
True
```

That seems a little cheap, doesn't it? OK, I will make it a little more difficult, as shown in Listing 5-12.

Listing 5-12. *Another Example of the First SequenceEqual Operator Overlaod*

```
Dim presidents() As String = _
{ _
  "Adams", "Arthur", "Buchanan", "Bush", "Carter", "Cleveland", _
  "Clinton", "Coolidge", "Eisenhower", "Fillmore", "Ford", "Garfield", _
  "Grant", "Harding", "Harrison", "Hayes", "Hoover", "Jackson", _
  "Jefferson", "Johnson", "Kennedy", "Lincoln", "Madison", "McKinley", _
  "Monroe", "Nixon", "Pierce", "Polk", "Reagan", "Roosevelt", "Taft", _
  "Taylor", "Truman", "Tyler", "Van Buren", "Washington", "Wilson" _
}
```

```
Dim eq As Boolean = presidents.SequenceEqual(presidents.Take(presidents.Count()))
Console.WriteLine(eq)
```

In the previous code, I use the Take operator to take only the first *N* number of elements of the presidents array and then compare that output sequence back to the original presidents sequence. So in the previous code, if I take all the elements of the presidents array by taking the number of the presidents.Count(), I should get the entire sequence output. Sure enough, here are the results:

```
True
```

OK, that worked as expected. Now, I will take all the elements except the last one by subtracting one from the presidents.Count(), as shown in Listing 5-13.

Listing 5-13. *Yet Another Example of the First SequenceEqual Operator Overload*

```
Dim presidents() As String = _
{ _
  "Adams", "Arthur", "Buchanan", "Bush", "Carter", "Cleveland", _
  "Clinton", "Coolidge", "Eisenhower", "Fillmore", "Ford", "Garfield", _
  "Grant", "Harding", "Harrison", "Hayes", "Hoover", "Jackson", _
  "Jefferson", "Johnson", "Kennedy", "Lincoln", "Madison", "McKinley", _
  "Monroe", "Nixon", "Pierce", "Polk", "Reagan", "Roosevelt", "Taft", _
  "Taylor", "Truman", "Tyler", "Van Buren", "Washington", "Wilson" _
}
```

```
Dim eq As Boolean = presidents _
  .SequenceEqual(presidents. Take(presidents.Count() - 1))
Console.WriteLine(eq)
```

Now, the results should be False, because the two sequences should not even have the same number of elements. The second sequence, the one I passed, should be missing the very last element:

```
False
```

This is going well. Just out of curiosity, let's try one more. Recall that in my discussion of the Take and Skip operators in the previous chapter, I said that when concatenated together properly, they should output the original sequence. I will now give that a try. I will get to use the Take, Skip, Concat, and SequenceEqual operators to prove this statement, as shown in Listing 5-14.

Listing 5-14. *A More Complex Example of the First SequenceEqual Operator Overload*

```
Dim presidents() As String = _
{ _
  "Adams", "Arthur", "Buchanan", "Bush", "Carter", "Cleveland", _
  "Clinton", "Coolidge", "Eisenhower", "Fillmore", "Ford", "Garfield", _
  "Grant", "Harding", "Harrison", "Hayes", "Hoover", "Jackson", _
  "Jefferson", "Johnson", "Kennedy", "Lincoln", "Madison", "McKinley", _
  "Monroe", "Nixon", "Pierce", "Polk", "Reagan", "Roosevelt", "Taft", _
  "Taylor", "Truman", "Tyler", "Van Buren", "Washington", "Wilson" _
}

Dim eq As Boolean = presidents _
  .SequenceEqual(presidents.Take(5).Concat(presidents.Skip(5)))
Console.WriteLine(eq)
```

In this example, I get the first five elements of the original input sequence by calling the Take operator. I then concatenate on the input sequence starting with the sixth element using the Skip and Concat operators. Finally, I determine if that concatenated sequence is equal to the original sequence calling the SequenceEqual operator. What do you think? Let's see:

```
True
```

Cool, it worked! For an example of the second overload, I create two arrays of type String where each element is a number in string form. The elements of the two arrays will be such that when parsed into integers, they will be equal. I use my common MyStringifiedNumberComparer class for this example, shown in Listing 5-15.

Listing 5-15. *An Example of the Second SequenceEqual Operator Overload*

```
Dim stringifiedNums1() As String = { "001", "49", "017", "0080", "00027", "2" }
Dim stringifiedNums2() As String = { "1", "0049", "17", "080", "27", "02" }

Dim eq As Boolean = stringifiedNums1 _
  .SequenceEqual(stringifiedNums2, New MyStringifiedNumberComparer())

Console.WriteLine(eq)
```

In this example, if you examine the two arrays, you can see that if you parse each element from each array into an integer, and then compare the corresponding integers, the two arrays would be considered equal. Let's see if the results indicate that the two sequences are equal:

True

Element

The following element operators allow you to retrieve single elements from an input sequence.

First

The First operator returns the first element of a sequence, or the first element of a sequence matching a predicate, depending on the overload used.

Declarations

The First operator has two overloads.

The First Overload of the First Operator

```
<ExtensionAttribute> _
Public Shared Function First(Of TSource) ( _
    source As IEnumerable(Of TSource) _
) As TSource
```

Using this overload of the First operator enumerates the input sequence named source and returns the first element of the sequence.

The second overload of the First operator allows a predicate to be passed.

The Second Overload of the First Operator

```
<ExtensionAttribute> _
Public Shared Function First(Of TSource) ( _
    source As IEnumerable(Of TSource), _
    predicate As Func(Of TSource, Boolean) _
) As TSource
```

This version of the First operator returns the first element it finds for which the predicate returns True. If no elements cause the predicate to return True, the First operator throws an InvalidOperationException.

Exceptions

ArgumentNullException is thrown if any arguments are Nothing.

InvalidOperationException is thrown if the source sequence is empty, or if the predicate never returns True.

Examples

Listing 5-16 is an example of the first First overload.

Listing 5-16. *Sample Code Calling the First First Operator Overload*

```
Dim presidents() As String = _
{ _
    "Adams", "Arthur", "Buchanan", "Bush", "Carter", "Cleveland", _
    "Clinton", "Coolidge", "Eisenhower", "Fillmore", "Ford", "Garfield", _
    "Grant", "Harding", "Harrison", "Hayes", "Hoover", "Jackson", _
    "Jefferson", "Johnson", "Kennedy", "Lincoln", "Madison", "McKinley", _
    "Monroe", "Nixon", "Pierce", "Polk", "Reagan", "Roosevelt", "Taft", _
    "Taylor", "Truman", "Tyler", "Van Buren", "Washington", "Wilson" _
}

Dim name As String = presidents.First()
Console.WriteLine(name)
```

Here are the results:

Adams

You may be asking yourself how this operator differs from calling the Take operator and passing it 1. The difference is the Take operator returns a *sequence* of elements, even if that sequence only contains a single element. The First operator always returns exactly one *element*, or it throws an exception if there is no first element to return.

Listing 5-17 is some sample code using the second overload of the First operator.

Listing 5-17. *Code Calling the Second First Operator Overload*

```
Dim presidents() As String = _
{ _
    "Adams", "Arthur", "Buchanan", "Bush", "Carter", "Cleveland", _
    "Clinton", "Coolidge", "Eisenhower", "Fillmore", "Ford", "Garfield", _
    "Grant", "Harding", "Harrison", "Hayes", "Hoover", "Jackson", _
    "Jefferson", "Johnson", "Kennedy", "Lincoln", "Madison", "McKinley", _
    "Monroe", "Nixon", "Pierce", "Polk", "Reagan", "Roosevelt", "Taft", _
    "Taylor", "Truman", "Tyler", "Van Buren", "Washington", "Wilson" _
}

Dim name As String = presidents.First(Function(p) p.StartsWith("H"))
Console.WriteLine(name)
```

This should return the first element in the input sequence that begins with the string "H". Here are the results:

Harding

Remember, if either overload of the First operator ends up with no element to return, an InvalidOperationException is thrown. To avoid this, use the FirstOrDefault operator.

FirstOrDefault

The FirstOrDefault operator is similar to the First operator except for how it behaves when an element is not found.

Declarations

The FirstOrDefault operator has two overloads.

The First Overload of the FirstOrDefault Operator

```
<ExtensionAttribute> _
Public Shared Function FirstOrDefault(Of TSource) ( _
    source As IEnumerable(Of TSource) _
) As TSource
```

This version of the FirstOrDefault overload returns the first element found in the input sequence. If the sequence is empty, default(TSource) is returned. For reference and nullable types, the default value is Nothing.

The second overload of the FirstOrDefault operator allows you to pass a predicate to determine which element should be returned.

The Second Overload of the FirstOrDefault Operator

```
<ExtensionAttribute> _
Public Shared Function FirstOrDefault(Of TSource) ( _
    source As IEnumerable(Of TSource), _
    predicate As Func(Of TSource, Boolean) _
) As TSource
```

Exceptions

ArgumentNullException is thrown if any arguments are Nothing.

Examples

Listing 5-18 is an example of the first FirstOrDefault overload where no element is found. I have to get an empty sequence to do this. I'll call Take(0) for this purpose.

Listing 5-18. *Calling the First FirstOrDefault Operator Overload Where an Element Is Not Found*

```
Dim presidents() As String = _
{ _
  "Adams", "Arthur", "Buchanan", "Bush", "Carter", "Cleveland", _
  "Clinton", "Coolidge", "Eisenhower", "Fillmore", "Ford", "Garfield", _
  "Grant", "Harding", "Harrison", "Hayes", "Hoover", "Jackson", _
  "Jefferson", "Johnson", "Kennedy", "Lincoln", "Madison", "McKinley", _
  "Monroe", "Nixon", "Pierce", "Polk", "Reagan", "Roosevelt", "Taft", _
  "Taylor", "Truman", "Tyler", "Van Buren", "Washington", "Wilson" _
}
```

```
Dim name As String = presidents.Take(0).FirstOrDefault()
Console.WriteLine(If(name Is Nothing, "NOTHING", name))
```

Here are the results:

```
NOTHING
```

Listing 5-19 is the same example without the Take(0) call, so an element is found.

Listing 5-19. *Calling the First FirstOrDefault Operator Overload Where an Element Is Found*

```
Dim presidents() As String = _
{ _
  "Adams", "Arthur", "Buchanan", "Bush", "Carter", "Cleveland", _
  "Clinton", "Coolidge", "Eisenhower", "Fillmore", "Ford", "Garfield", _
  "Grant", "Harding", "Harrison", "Hayes", "Hoover", "Jackson", _
  "Jefferson", "Johnson", "Kennedy", "Lincoln", "Madison", "McKinley", _
  "Monroe", "Nixon", "Pierce", "Polk", "Reagan", "Roosevelt", "Taft", _
  "Taylor", "Truman", "Tyler", "Van Buren", "Washington", "Wilson" _
}
```

```
Dim name As String = presidents.FirstOrDefault()
Console.WriteLine(If(name Is Nothing, "NOTHING", name))
```

And finally, here are the results for the code when I find an element:

```
Adams
```

For the second FirstOrDefault overload, I specify that I want the first element that starts with the string "B", as shown in Listing 5-20.

Listing 5-20. *Calling the Second FirstOrDefault Operator Overload Where an Element Is Found*

```
Dim presidents() As String = _
{ _
  "Adams", "Arthur", "Buchanan", "Bush", "Carter", "Cleveland", _
  "Clinton", "Coolidge", "Eisenhower", "Fillmore", "Ford", "Garfield", _
  "Grant", "Harding", "Harrison", "Hayes", "Hoover", "Jackson", _
  "Jefferson", "Johnson", "Kennedy", "Lincoln", "Madison", "McKinley", _
  "Monroe", "Nixon", "Pierce", "Polk", "Reagan", "Roosevelt", "Taft", _
  "Taylor", "Truman", "Tyler", "Van Buren", "Washington", "Wilson" _
}
```

```
Dim name As String = presidents.FirstOrDefault(Function(p) p.StartsWith("B"))
Console.WriteLine(If(name Is Nothing, "NOTHING", name))
```

Here are the results:

Buchanan

Now, I will try that with a predicate that will not find a match, as shown in Listing 5-21.

Listing 5-21. *Calling the Second FirstOrDefault Operator Overload Where an Element Is Not Found*

```
Dim presidents() As String = _
{ _
  "Adams", "Arthur", "Buchanan", "Bush", "Carter", "Cleveland", _
  "Clinton", "Coolidge", "Eisenhower", "Fillmore", "Ford", "Garfield", _
  "Grant", "Harding", "Harrison", "Hayes", "Hoover", "Jackson", _
  "Jefferson", "Johnson", "Kennedy", "Lincoln", "Madison", "McKinley", _
  "Monroe", "Nixon", "Pierce", "Polk", "Reagan", "Roosevelt", "Taft", _
  "Taylor", "Truman", "Tyler", "Van Buren", "Washington", "Wilson" _
}
```

```
Dim name As String = presidents.FirstOrDefault(Function(p) p.StartsWith("Z"))
Console.WriteLine(If(name Is Nothing, "NOTHING", name))
```

Since there is no name in the presidents array beginning with a "Z", here are the results:

```
NOTHING
```

Last

The Last operator returns the last element of a sequence, or the last element of a sequence matching a predicate, depending on the overload used.

Declarations

The Last operator has two overloads.

The First Overload of the Last Operator

```
<ExtensionAttribute> _
Public Shared Function Last(Of TSource) ( _
    source As IEnumerable(Of TSource) _
) As TSource
```

Using this overload, the Last operator enumerates the input sequence named source and returns the last element of the sequence.

The second overload of Last allows a predicate to be passed and looks like this:

The Second Overload of the Last Operator

```
<ExtensionAttribute> _
Public Shared Function Last(Of TSource) ( _
```

```
    source As IEnumerable(Of TSource), _
    predicate As Func(Of TSource, Boolean) _
) As TSource
```

This version of the Last operator returns the last element it finds for which the predicate returns True.

Exceptions

ArgumentNullException is thrown if any arguments are Nothing.

InvalidOperationException is thrown if the source sequence is empty or if the predicate never returns True.

Examples

Listing 5-22 is an example of the first Last overload.

Listing 5-22. *Sample Code Calling the First Last Operator Overload*

```
Dim presidents() As String = _
{ _
    "Adams", "Arthur", "Buchanan", "Bush", "Carter", "Cleveland", _
    "Clinton", "Coolidge", "Eisenhower", "Fillmore", "Ford", "Garfield", _
    "Grant", "Harding", "Harrison", "Hayes", "Hoover", "Jackson", _
    "Jefferson", "Johnson", "Kennedy", "Lincoln", "Madison", "McKinley", _
    "Monroe", "Nixon", "Pierce", "Polk", "Reagan", "Roosevelt", "Taft", _
    "Taylor", "Truman", "Tyler", "Van Buren", "Washington", "Wilson" _
}

Dim name As String = presidents.Last()
Console.WriteLine(name)
```

Here are the results:

```
Wilson
```

The Last operator always returns exactly one *element*, or it throws an exception if there is no last element to return.

Listing 5-23 is some sample code using the second overload of the Last operator.

Listing 5-23. *Calling the Second Last Operator Overload*

```
Dim presidents() As String = _
{ _
    "Adams", "Arthur", "Buchanan", "Bush", "Carter", "Cleveland", _
    "Clinton", "Coolidge", "Eisenhower", "Fillmore", "Ford", "Garfield", _
    "Grant", "Harding", "Harrison", "Hayes", "Hoover", "Jackson", _
    "Jefferson", "Johnson", "Kennedy", "Lincoln", "Madison", "McKinley", _
    "Monroe", "Nixon", "Pierce", "Polk", "Reagan", "Roosevelt", "Taft", _
```

```
    "Taylor", "Truman", "Tyler", "Van Buren", "Washington", "Wilson" _
}
```

```
Dim name As String = presidents.Last(Function(p) p.StartsWith("H"))
Console.WriteLine(name)
```

This should return the last element in the input sequence that begins with the string "H". Here are the results:

Hoover

Remember, if either overload of the Last operator ends up with no element to return, an InvalidOperationException is thrown. To avoid this, use the LastOrDefault operator.

LastOrDefault

The LastOrDefault operator is similar to the Last operator except for how it behaves when an element is not found.

Declarations

The LastOrDefault operator has two overloads.

The First Overload of the LastOrDefault Operator

```
<ExtensionAttribute> _
Public Shared Function LastOrDefault(Of TSource) ( _
    source As IEnumerable(Of TSource) _
) As TSource
```

This version of the LastOrDefault overload returns the last element found in the input sequence. If the sequence is empty, default(TSource) is returned. For reference and nullable types, the default value is Nothing.

The second overload of the LastOrDefault operator allows you to pass a predicate to determine which element should be returned.

The Second Overload of the LastOrDefault Operator

```
<ExtensionAttribute> _
Public Shared Function LastOrDefault(Of TSource) ( _
    source As IEnumerable(Of TSource), _
    predicate As Func(Of TSource, Boolean) _
) As TSource
```

Exceptions

ArgumentNullException is thrown if any arguments are Nothing.

Examples

Listing 5-24 is an example of the first LastOrDefault operator where no element is found. I have to get an empty sequence to do this. I'll call Take(0) for this purpose.

Listing 5-24. *Calling the First LastOrDefault Operator Overload Where an Element Is Not Found*

```
Dim presidents() As String = _
{ _
  "Adams", "Arthur", "Buchanan", "Bush", "Carter", "Cleveland", _
  "Clinton", "Coolidge", "Eisenhower", "Fillmore", "Ford", "Garfield", _
  "Grant", "Harding", "Harrison", "Hayes", "Hoover", "Jackson", _
  "Jefferson", "Johnson", "Kennedy", "Lincoln", "Madison", "McKinley", _
  "Monroe", "Nixon", "Pierce", "Polk", "Reagan", "Roosevelt", "Taft", _
  "Taylor", "Truman", "Tyler", "Van Buren", "Washington", "Wilson" _
}
```

```
Dim name As String = presidents.Take(0).LastOrDefault()
Console.WriteLine(If(name Is Nothing, "NOTHING", name))
```

Here are the results:

```
NOTHING
```

Listing 5-25 is the same example without the Take(0), so an element is found.

Listing 5-25. *Calling the First LastOrDefault Operator Overload Where an Element Is Found*

```
Dim presidents() As String = _
{ _
  "Adams", "Arthur", "Buchanan", "Bush", "Carter", "Cleveland", _
  "Clinton", "Coolidge", "Eisenhower", "Fillmore", "Ford", "Garfield", _
  "Grant", "Harding", "Harrison", "Hayes", "Hoover", "Jackson", _
  "Jefferson", "Johnson", "Kennedy", "Lincoln", "Madison", "McKinley", _
  "Monroe", "Nixon", "Pierce", "Polk", "Reagan", "Roosevelt", "Taft", _
  "Taylor", "Truman", "Tyler", "Van Buren", "Washington", "Wilson" _
}
```

```
Dim name As String = presidents.LastOrDefault()
Console.WriteLine(If(name Is Nothing, "NOTHING", name))
```

And finally, here are the results for the code when I find an element:

```
Wilson
```

For the second overload of the LastOrDefault operator, shown in Listing 5-26, I specify that I want the last element to start with the string "B".

Listing 5-26. *Calling the Second LastOrDefault Operator Overload Where an Element Is Found*

```
Dim presidents() As String = _
{ _
  "Adams", "Arthur", "Buchanan", "Bush", "Carter", "Cleveland", _
  "Clinton", "Coolidge", "Eisenhower", "Fillmore", "Ford", "Garfield", _
  "Grant", "Harding", "Harrison", "Hayes", "Hoover", "Jackson", _
  "Jefferson", "Johnson", "Kennedy", "Lincoln", "Madison", "McKinley", _
  "Monroe", "Nixon", "Pierce", "Polk", "Reagan", "Roosevelt", "Taft", _
  "Taylor", "Truman", "Tyler", "Van Buren", "Washington", "Wilson" _
}
```

```
Dim name As String = presidents.LastOrDefault(Function(p) p.StartsWith("B"))
Console.WriteLine(If(name Is Nothing, "NOTHING", name))
```

Here are the results:

```
Bush
```

Now, I will try that with a predicate that will not find a match, as shown in Listing 5-27.

Listing 5-27. *Calling the Second LastOrDefault Operator Overload Where an Element Is Not Found*

```
Dim presidents() As String = _
{ _
  "Adams", "Arthur", "Buchanan", "Bush", "Carter", "Cleveland", _
  "Clinton", "Coolidge", "Eisenhower", "Fillmore", "Ford", "Garfield", _
  "Grant", "Harding", "Harrison", "Hayes", "Hoover", "Jackson", _
  "Jefferson", "Johnson", "Kennedy", "Lincoln", "Madison", "McKinley", _
  "Monroe", "Nixon", "Pierce", "Polk", "Reagan", "Roosevelt", "Taft", _
  "Taylor", "Truman", "Tyler", "Van Buren", "Washington", "Wilson" _
}
```

```
Dim name As String = presidents.LastOrDefault(Function(p) p.StartsWith("Z"))
Console.WriteLine(If(name Is Nothing, "NOTHING", name))
```

Since there is no name in the presidents array beginning with a "Z", here are the results:

```
NOTHING
```

Single

The Single operator returns the only element of a single element sequence, or the only element of a sequence matching a predicate, depending on the overload used.

Declarations

The Single operator has two overloads.

The First Overload of the Single Operator

```
<ExtensionAttribute> _
Public Shared Function Single(Of TSource) ( _
    source As IEnumerable(Of TSource) _
) As TSource
```

Using this overload, the Single operator enumerates the input sequence named source and returns the only element of the sequence.

The second overload of Single allows a predicate to be passed and looks like this:

The Second Overload of the Single Operator

```
<ExtensionAttribute> _
Public Shared Function Single(Of TSource) ( _
    source As IEnumerable(Of TSource), _
    predicate As Func(Of TSource, Boolean) _
) As TSource
```

This version of the Single operator returns the only element it finds for which the predicate returns True. If no elements cause the predicate to return True, or multiple elements cause the predicate to return True, the Single operator throws an InvalidOperationException.

Exceptions

ArgumentNullException is thrown if any arguments are Nothing.

InvalidOperationException is thrown if the source sequence is empty, or if the predicate never returns True or finds more than one element for which it returns True.

Examples

Listing 5-28 is an example of the first Single overload using the common Employee class.

Listing 5-28. *Sample Code Calling the First Single Operator Overload*

```
'  For the Single call to not throw an exception, I must have a sequence with
'  a single element.  I will use the Where operator to insure this.
Dim emp As Employee = _
  Employee.GetEmployeesArray().Where(Function(e) e.id = 3).Single()

Console.WriteLine("{0} {1}", emp.firstName, emp.lastName)
```

In this example, instead of wanting the query to produce a sequence, I just want a reference to a particular employee. The Single operator is very useful for this as long as you can ensure there will only be a single element in the sequence passed to it. In this case, since I called the Where operator and specified a unique key, I am safe. Here are the results:

Listing 5-29 is some sample code using the second overload of the Single operator.

Listing 5-29. *Code Calling the Second Single Operator Overload*

```
'  For the Single call to not throw an exception, I must have a sequence with
'  a single element.  I will use the Where operator to insure this.
Dim emp As Employee = Employee.GetEmployeesArray().Single(Function(e) e.id = 3)

Console.WriteLine("{0} {1}", emp.firstName, emp.lastName)
```

This code is functionally equivalent to the previous example. Instead of calling the Where operator to ensure a single element is in the sequence, I can provide the same sequence filtering operation in the Single operator itself. This should return the only element in the input sequence whose id is 3. Here are the results:

Remember, if either overload of the Single operator ends up with no element to return, an InvalidOperationException is thrown. To avoid this, use the SingleOrDefault operator.

SingleOrDefault

The SingleOrDefault operator is similar to the Single operator except for how it behaves when an element is not found.

Declarations

The SingleOrDefault operator has two overloads.

The First Overload of the SingleOrDefault Operator

```
<ExtensionAttribute> _
Public Shared Function SingleOrDefault(Of TSource) ( _
    source As IEnumerable(Of TSource) _
) As TSource
```

This version of the operator returns the only element found in the input sequence. If the sequence is empty, default(TSource) is returned. For reference and nullable types, the default value is Nothing. If more than one element is found, an InvalidOperationException is thrown.

The second overload of the SingleOrDefault operator allows you to pass a predicate to determine which element should be returned.

The Second Overload of the SingleOrDefault Operator

```
<ExtensionAttribute> _
Public Shared Function SingleOrDefault(Of TSource) ( _
    source As IEnumerable(Of TSource), _
```

```
    predicate As Func(Of TSource, Boolean) _
) As TSource
```

Exceptions

ArgumentNullException is thrown if any arguments are Nothing.

InvalidOperationException is thrown if the operator finds more than one element for which the predicate returns True.

Examples

Listing 5-30 is an example of the first SingleOrDefault overload where no element is found. I have to get an empty sequence to do this. I'll use the Where operator and provide a key comparison for a key that doesn't exist for this purpose.

Listing 5-30. *Calling the First SingleOrDefault Operator Overload Where an Element Is Not Found*

```
Dim emp As Employee = Employee.GetEmployeesArray().Where(Function(e) e.id = 5) _
  .SingleOrDefault()

Console.WriteLine(If(emp Is Nothing, "NOTHING", _
  String.Format("{0} {1}", emp.firstName, emp.lastName)))
```

I queried for the employee whose id is 5 since I know none exists, so an empty sequence will be returned. Unlike the Single operator, the SingleOrDefault operator handles empty sequences just fine. Here are the results:

```
NOTHING
```

Listing 5-31 is the same example where a single element *is* found. I use the Where operator to provide a sequence with just one element.

Listing 5-31. *Calling the First SingleOrDefault Overload Where an Element Is Found*

```
Dim emp As Employee = Employee.GetEmployeesArray().Where(Function(e) e.id = 4) _
  .SingleOrDefault()

Console.WriteLine(If(emp Is Nothing, "NOTHING", _
  String.Format("{0} {1}", emp.firstName, emp.lastName)))
```

This time I specify an id I know exists. Here are the results for the code when an element is found:

```
David Lightman
```

As you can see, the employee has been found. For the second SingleOrDefault overload, shown in Listing 5-32, I specify an id that I know exists. Instead of using the Where operator, I embed the filter into the SingleOrDefault operator call.

Listing 5-32. *Calling the Second SingleOrDefault Overload Where an Element Is Found*

```
Dim emp As Employee = Employee.GetEmployeesArray() _
  .SingleOrDefault(Function(e) e.id = 4)

Console.WriteLine(If(emp Is Nothing, "NOTHING", _
  String.Format("{0} {1}", emp.firstName, emp.lastName)))
```

This example is functionally equivalent to the previous example except instead of filtering the elements using the Where operator, I filter them by passing a predicate to the SingleOrDefault operator. Here are the results:

```
David Lightman
```

Now, I will try that with a predicate that will not find a match, as shown in Listing 5-33.

Listing 5-33. *Calling the Second SingleOrDefault Overload Where an Element Is Not Found*

```
Dim emp As Employee = Employee.GetEmployeesArray() _
  .SingleOrDefault(Function(e) e.id = 5)

Console.WriteLine(If(emp Is Nothing, "NOTHINIG", _
  String.Format("{0} {1}", emp.firstName, emp.lastName)))
```

Since there is no element whose id is 5, no elements are found. Here are the results:

```
NOTHING
```

While no elements were found in the sequence, the SingleOrDefault operator handled the situation gracefully instead of throwing an exception.

ElementAt

The ElementAt operator returns the element from the source sequence at the specified index.

Declarations

The ElementAt operator has one overload.

The Only Overload of the ElementAt Operator

```
<ExtensionAttribute> _
Public Shared Function ElementAt(Of TSource) ( _
    source As IEnumerable(Of TSource), _
    index As Integer _
) As TSource
```

If the sequence implements IList(Of TSource), the IList interface is used to retrieve the indexed element directly. If the sequence does not implement IList(Of TSource), the sequence is enumerated until the indexed element is reached. An ArgumentOutOfRangeException is thrown if the index is less than zero or greater than or equal to the number of elements in the sequence.

Note In VB.NET, indexes are zero-based. This means the first element's index is zero. The last element's index is the sequence's count minus one.

Exceptions

ArgumentNullException is thrown if the source argument is Nothing.

ArgumentOutOfRangeException is thrown if the index is less than zero or greater than or equal to the number of elements in the sequence.

Examples

Listing 5-34 is an example calling the only overload of the ElementAt operator.

Listing 5-34. *Calling the ElementAt Operator*

```
Dim emp As Employee = Employee.GetEmployeesArray().ElementAt(3)

Console.WriteLine("{0} {1}", emp.firstName, emp.lastName)
```

I specified that I want the element whose index is 3, which is the fourth element. Here are the results of the query:

```
David Lightman
```

ElementAtOrDefault

The ElementAtOrDefault operator returns the element from the source sequence at the specified index.

Declarations

The ElementAtOrDefault operator has one overload.

The Only Overload of the ElementAtOrDefault Operator

```
<ExtensionAttribute> _
Public Shared Function ElementAtOrDefault(Of TSource) ( _
    source As IEnumerable(Of TSource), _
    index As Integer _
) As TSource
```

If the sequence implements IList(Of TSource), the IList interface is used to retrieve the indexed element directly. If the sequence does not implement IList(Of TSource), the sequence will be enumerated until the indexed element is reached.

If the index is less than zero or greater than or equal to the number of elements in the sequence, default(TSource) is returned. For reference and nullable types, the default value is Nothing. This is the behavior that distinguishes it from the ElementAt operator.

Exceptions

ArgumentNullException is thrown if the source argument is Nothing.

Examples

Listing 5-35 is an example calling the ElementAtOrDefault operator when the index is valid.

Listing 5-35. *Calling the ElementAtOrDefault Operator with a Valid Index*

```
Dim emp As Employee = Employee.GetEmployeesArray().ElementAtOrDefault(3)

Console.WriteLine(If(emp Is Nothing, "NOTHING", _
  String.Format("{0} {1}", emp.firstName, emp.lastName)))
```

Here are the results of the query:

```
David Lightman
```

Just as expected, the element at index 3 is retrieved. Now, I will try a query with an invalid index using the code in Listing 5-36.

Listing 5-36. *Calling the ElementAtOrDefault Operator with an Invalid Index*

```
Dim emp As Employee = Employee.GetEmployeesArray() _
  .ElementAtOrDefault(5)

Console.WriteLine(If(emp Is Nothing, "NOTHING", _
  String.Format("{0} {1}", emp.firstName, emp.lastName)))
```

There is no element whose index is 5. Here are the results of the query:

```
NOTHING
```

Quantifiers

The following quantifier operators allow you to perform quantification type operations on input sequences.

Any

The Any operator returns True if any element of an input sequence matches a condition.

Declarations

The Any operator has two overloads.

The First Overload of the Any Operator

```
<ExtensionAttribute> _
Public Shared Function Any(Of TSource) ( _
    source As IEnumerable(Of TSource) _
) As Boolean
```

This overload of the Any operator will return True if the source input sequence contains any elements. The second overload of the Any operator enumerates the source input sequence and returns True if at least one element in the input sequence causes the predicate method delegate to return True. The source input sequence enumeration halts once the predicate returns True.

The Second Overload of the Any Operator

```
<ExtensionAttribute> _
Public Shared Function Any(Of TSource) ( _
    source As IEnumerable(Of TSource), _
    predicate As Func(Of TSource, Boolean) _
) As Boolean
```

Exceptions

ArgumentNullException is thrown if any of the arguments are Nothing.

Examples

First, I will try the case of an empty sequence, as shown in Listing 5-37. I will use the Empty operator I covered in the previous chapter.

Listing 5-37. *First Any Operator Overload Where No Elements Are in the Source Input Sequence*

```
Dim any As Boolean = Enumerable.Empty(Of String)().Any()
Console.WriteLine(any)
```

Here are the results of this code:

```
False
```

Next, I will try the same overload but, this time, with elements in the input sequence, as shown in Listing 5-38.

Listing 5-38. *First Any Operator Overload Where Elements Are in the Source Input Sequence*

```
Dim presidents() As String = _
{ _
  "Adams", "Arthur", "Buchanan", "Bush", "Carter", "Cleveland", _
  "Clinton", "Coolidge", "Eisenhower", "Fillmore", "Ford", "Garfield", _
  "Grant", "Harding", "Harrison", "Hayes", "Hoover", "Jackson", _
  "Jefferson", "Johnson", "Kennedy", "Lincoln", "Madison", "McKinley", _
  "Monroe", "Nixon", "Pierce", "Polk", "Reagan", "Roosevelt", "Taft", _
  "Taylor", "Truman", "Tyler", "Van Buren", "Washington", "Wilson" _
}

Dim any As Boolean = presidents.Any()
Console.WriteLine(any)
```

Here are the results of this code:

```
True
```

For the next example, I use the second overload, first with no elements matching the predicate, as shown in Listing 5-39.

Listing 5-39. *Second Any Operator Overload Where No Elements Cause the Predicate to Return True*

```
Dim presidents() As String = _
{ _
  "Adams", "Arthur", "Buchanan", "Bush", "Carter", "Cleveland", _
  "Clinton", "Coolidge", "Eisenhower", "Fillmore", "Ford", "Garfield", _
  "Grant", "Harding", "Harrison", "Hayes", "Hoover", "Jackson", _
  "Jefferson", "Johnson", "Kennedy", "Lincoln", "Madison", "McKinley", _
  "Monroe", "Nixon", "Pierce", "Polk", "Reagan", "Roosevelt", "Taft", _
  "Taylor", "Truman", "Tyler", "Van Buren", "Washington", "Wilson" _
}

Dim any As Boolean = presidents.Any(Function(s) s.StartsWith("Z"))
Console.WriteLine(any)
```

I specify that I want the presidents that start with the string "Z". Since there are none, an empty sequence will be returned causing the Any operator to return False. The results are as one would expect:

```
False
```

Finally, I try an example of the second overload with a predicate that should return True for at least one element, as shown in Listing 5-40.

Listing 5-40. *Second Any Operator Overload Where at Least One Element Causes the Predicate to Return True*

```
Dim presidents() As String = _
{ _
  "Adams", "Arthur", "Buchanan", "Bush", "Carter", "Cleveland", _
  "Clinton", "Coolidge", "Eisenhower", "Fillmore", "Ford", "Garfield", _
  "Grant", "Harding", "Harrison", "Hayes", "Hoover", "Jackson", _
  "Jefferson", "Johnson", "Kennedy", "Lincoln", "Madison", "McKinley", _
  "Monroe", "Nixon", "Pierce", "Polk", "Reagan", "Roosevelt", "Taft", _
  "Taylor", "Truman", "Tyler", "Van Buren", "Washington", "Wilson" _
}

Dim any As Boolean = presidents.Any(Function(s) s.StartsWith("A"))
Console.WriteLine(any)
```

And finally, here are the results:

```
True
```

All

The All operator returns True if every element in the input sequence matches a condition.

Declarations

The All operator has one overload.

The Only Overload of the All Operator

```
<ExtensionAttribute> _
Public Shared Function All(Of TSource) ( _
    source As IEnumerable(Of TSource), _
    predicate As Func(Of TSource, Boolean) _
) As Boolean
```

The All operator enumerates the source input sequence and returns True only if the predicate returns True for every element in the sequence. Once the predicate returns False, the enumeration will cease.

Exceptions

ArgumentNullException is thrown if any of the arguments are Nothing.

Examples

In Listing 5-41, I begin with a predicate for which I know at least some of the elements will return False.

Listing 5-41. *All Operator Overload Where Not Every Element Causes the Predicate to Return True*

```
Dim presidents() As String = _
{ _
  "Adams", "Arthur", "Buchanan", "Bush", "Carter", "Cleveland", _
  "Clinton", "Coolidge", "Eisenhower", "Fillmore", "Ford", "Garfield", _
  "Grant", "Harding", "Harrison", "Hayes", "Hoover", "Jackson", _
  "Jefferson", "Johnson", "Kennedy", "Lincoln", "Madison", "McKinley", _
  "Monroe", "Nixon", "Pierce", "Polk", "Reagan", "Roosevelt", "Taft", _
  "Taylor", "Truman", "Tyler", "Van Buren", "Washington", "Wilson" _
}
```

```
Dim all As Boolean = presidents.All(Function(s) s.Length > 5)
Console.WriteLine(all)
```

Since I know not every president in the array has a length of more than five characters, I know that predicate will return False for some elements. Here is the output:

```
False
```

Now, I will try a case where I know every element will cause the predicate to return True, as shown in Listing 5-42.

Listing 5-42. *All Operator Overload Where Every Element Causes the Predicate to Return True*

```
Dim presidents() As String = _
{ _
  "Adams", "Arthur", "Buchanan", "Bush", "Carter", "Cleveland", _
  "Clinton", "Coolidge", "Eisenhower", "Fillmore", "Ford", "Garfield", _
  "Grant", "Harding", "Harrison", "Hayes", "Hoover", "Jackson", _
  "Jefferson", "Johnson", "Kennedy", "Lincoln", "Madison", "McKinley", _
  "Monroe", "Nixon", "Pierce", "Polk", "Reagan", "Roosevelt", "Taft", _
  "Taylor", "Truman", "Tyler", "Van Buren", "Washington", "Wilson" _
}
```

```
Dim all As Boolean = presidents.All(Function(s) s.Length > 3)
Console.WriteLine(all)
```

Since I know every president's name has at least four characters, the All operator should return True. Here is the output:

```
True
```

Contains

The Contains operator returns True if any element in the input sequence matches the specified value.

Declarations

The Contains operator has two overloads.

The First Overload of the Contains Operator

```
<ExtensionAttribute> _
Public Shared Function Contains(Of TSource) ( _
    source As IEnumerable(Of TSource), _
    value As TSource _
) As Boolean
```

This overload of the Contains operator first checks the source input sequence to see if it implements the ICollection(Of TSource) interface, and if it does, it calls the Contains method of the sequence's implementation. If the sequence does not implement the ICollection(Of TSource) interface, it enumerates the source input sequence to see if any element matches the specified value. Once it finds an element that does match, the enumeration halts.

The specified value is compared to each element using the EqualityComparer(Of TSource).Default default equality comparison class.

The second overload is like the previous except an IEqualityComparer(Of TSource) object can be specified. If this overload is used, each element in the sequence is compared to the passed value using the passed equality comparison object.

The Second Overload of the Contains Operator

```
<ExtensionAttribute> _
Public Shared Function Contains(Of TSource) ( _
    source As IEnumerable(Of TSource), _
    value As TSource, _
    comparer As IEqualityComparer(Of TSource) _
) As Boolean
```

Exceptions

ArgumentNullException is thrown if the source input sequence is Nothing.

Examples

For an example of the first overload, I begin with a value that I know is not in my input sequence, as shown in Listing 5-43

Listing 5-43. *First Contains Operator Overload Where No Element Matches the Specified Value*

```
Dim presidents() As String = _
{ _
  "Adams", "Arthur", "Buchanan", "Bush", "Carter", "Cleveland", _
  "Clinton", "Coolidge", "Eisenhower", "Fillmore", "Ford", "Garfield", _
  "Grant", "Harding", "Harrison", "Hayes", "Hoover", "Jackson", _
  "Jefferson", "Johnson", "Kennedy", "Lincoln", "Madison", "McKinley", _
  "Monroe", "Nixon", "Pierce", "Polk", "Reagan", "Roosevelt", "Taft", _
```

```
  "Taylor", "Truman", "Tyler", "Van Buren", "Washington", "Wilson" _
}
```

```
Dim contains As Boolean = presidents.Contains("Rattz")
Console.WriteLine(contains)
```

Since there is no element whose value is "Rattz" in the array, the contains variable should be False. Here is the output:

```
False
```

In Listing 5-44, I know an element will match my specified value.

Listing 5-44. *First Contains Operator Overload Where an Element Matches the Specified Value*

```
Dim presidents() As String = _
{ _
  "Adams", "Arthur", "Buchanan", "Bush", "Carter", "Cleveland", _
  "Clinton", "Coolidge", "Eisenhower", "Fillmore", "Ford", "Garfield", _
  "Grant", "Harding", "Harrison", "Hayes", "Hoover", "Jackson", _
  "Jefferson", "Johnson", "Kennedy", "Lincoln", "Madison", "McKinley", _
  "Monroe", "Nixon", "Pierce", "Polk", "Reagan", "Roosevelt", "Taft", _
  "Taylor", "Truman", "Tyler", "Van Buren", "Washington", "Wilson" _
}
```

```
Dim contains As Boolean = presidents.Contains("Hayes")
Console.WriteLine(contains)
```

Since there is an element with the value of "Hayes", the contains variable should be True. Here is the output:

```
True
```

For an example of the second Contains operator overload, I will use my common MyStringifiedNumberComparer class. I will check an array of numbers in string format for a number in string format that is technically unequal to any element in the array, but because I use my equality comparison class, the appropriate element will be found. Listing 5-45 shows the example.

Listing 5-45. *Second Contains Operator Overload Where an Element Matches the Specified Value*

```
Dim stringifiedNums() As String = { "001", "49", "017", "0080", "00027", "2" }
```

```
Dim contains As Boolean = stringifiedNums _
  .Contains("0000002", New MyStringifiedNumberComparer())
```

```
Console.WriteLine(contains)
```

Since I am looking for an element with a value of "0000002", and because my equality comparison object will be used, which will convert that string value as well as all of the sequence elements to an integer before making the comparison, and because my sequence contains the element "2", the contains variable should be True. Let's take a look at the results:

```
True
```

Now, I will try the same example except this time I will query for an element that I know doesn't exist. The code is shown in Listing 5-46.

Listing 5-46. *Second Contains Operator Overload Where an Element Does Not Match the Specified Value*

```
Dim stringifiedNums() As String = { "001", "49", "017", "0080", "00027", "2" }

Dim contains As Boolean = stringifiedNums _
  .Contains("000271", New MyStringifiedNumberComparer())

Console.WriteLine(contains)
```

Since I know that none of the elements when converted to an integer equals 271, I search the array for "000271". Here are the results:

```
False
```

Aggregate

The following aggregate operators allow you to perform aggregate operations on the elements of an input sequence.

Count

The Count operator returns the number of elements in the input sequence.

Declarations

The Count operator has two overloads.

The First Overload of the Count Operator

```
<ExtensionAttribute> _
Public Shared Function Count(Of TSource) ( _
    source As IEnumerable(Of TSource) _
) As Boolean
```

This overload of the Count operator returns the total number of elements in the source input sequence by first checking the input sequence to see if it implements the ICollection(Of TSource) interface, and if so, it obtains the sequence's count using the implementation of that interface. If the source input sequence does not implement the ICollection(Of TSource) interface, it enumerates the entire input sequence counting the number of elements.

The second overload of the Count operator enumerates the source input sequence and counts every element that causes the predicate method delegate to return True.

The Second Overload of the Count Operator

```
<ExtensionAttribute> _
Public Shared Function Count(Of TSource) ( _
    source As IEnumerable(Of TSource), _
    predicate As Func(Of TSource, Boolean) _
) As Boolean
```

Exceptions

ArgumentNullException is thrown if any argument is Nothing.

OverflowException is thrown if the count exceeds the capacity of Integer.MaxValue.

Examples

Listing 5-47 begins with the first overload. How many elements are there in the presidents sequence?

Listing 5-47. *The First Count Operator Overload*

```
Dim presidents() As String = _
{ _
  "Adams", "Arthur", "Buchanan", "Bush", "Carter", "Cleveland", _
  "Clinton", "Coolidge", "Eisenhower", "Fillmore", "Ford", "Garfield", _
  "Grant", "Harding", "Harrison", "Hayes", "Hoover", "Jackson", _
  "Jefferson", "Johnson", "Kennedy", "Lincoln", "Madison", "McKinley", _
  "Monroe", "Nixon", "Pierce", "Polk", "Reagan", "Roosevelt", "Taft", _
  "Taylor", "Truman", "Tyler", "Van Buren", "Washington", "Wilson" _
}

Dim count As Integer = presidents.Count()
Console.WriteLine(count)
```

Here are the results:

37

Now, I will try an example of the second overload, shown in Listing 5-48. I will count the number of presidents beginning with the letter "J".

Listing 5-48. *The Second Count Operator Overload*

```
Dim presidents() As String = _
{ _
```

```
    "Adams", "Arthur", "Buchanan", "Bush", "Carter", "Cleveland", _
    "Clinton", "Coolidge", "Eisenhower", "Fillmore", "Ford", "Garfield", _
    "Grant", "Harding", "Harrison", "Hayes", "Hoover", "Jackson", _
    "Jefferson", "Johnson", "Kennedy", "Lincoln", "Madison", "McKinley", _
    "Monroe", "Nixon", "Pierce", "Polk", "Reagan", "Roosevelt", "Taft", _
    "Taylor", "Truman", "Tyler", "Van Buren", "Washington", "Wilson" _
}

Dim count As Integer = presidents _
    .Count(Function(s) s.StartsWith("J"))
Console.WriteLine(count)
```

The results from this code are the following:

3

So what happens if the count exceeds the capacity of Integer.MaxValue? That's what the LongCount operator is for.

LongCount

The LongCount operator returns the number of elements in the input sequence as a Long.

Declarations

The LongCount operator has two overloads.

The First Overload of the LongCount Operator

```
<ExtensionAttribute> _
Public Shared Function LongCount(Of TSource) ( _
    source As IEnumerable(Of TSource) _
) As Long
```

The first overload of the LongCount operator returns the total number of elements in the source input sequence by enumerating the entire input sequence and counting the number of elements.

The second overload of the LongCount operator enumerates the source input sequence and counts every element that causes the predicate method delegate to return True.

The Second Overload of the LongCount Operator

```
<ExtensionAttribute> _
Public Shared Function LongCount(Of TSource) ( _
    source As IEnumerable(Of TSource), _
    predicate As Func(Of TSource, Boolean) _
) As Long
```

Exceptions

ArgumentNullException is thrown if any argument is Nothing.

Examples

I will begin with an example of the first overload, shown in Listing 5-49. I could just reiterate the same two examples I use for the Count operator, changing the relevant parts to type Long, but that wouldn't be very demonstrative of the operator. Since it isn't feasible for me to have a sequence long enough to require the LongCount operator, I use a Standard Query Operator to generate one. Unfortunately, the generation operators I cover in the previous chapter only allow you to specify the number of elements to generate using an Integer. I have to concat-enate a couple of those generated sequences together to get enough elements to require the LongCount operator.

Listing 5-49. *The First LongCount Operator Overload*

```
Dim count As Long = Enumerable.Range(0, Integer.MaxValue) _
  .Concat(Enumerable.Range(0, Integer.MaxValue)).LongCount()

Console.WriteLine(count)
```

As you can see, I generated two sequences using the Range operator I cover in the previous chapter and concatenated them together using the Concat operator also covered in the previous chapter.

Caution This example takes a long time to run. On my machine, a P4 with 1GB of memory, it took approximately two and a half minutes.

Before you run that example, let me warn you that it takes a long time to run. Don't be surprised if it takes several minutes. After all, it has to generate two sequences, each with 2,147,483,647 elements. Here are the results:

```
4294967294
```

If you try to run that same example using the Count operator, you will get an exception. Now, I will try an example of the second overload. For this example, I use the same basic example as the previous, except I specify a predicate that only returns True for integers greater than 1 and less than 4. This essentially means 2 and 3. Since I have two sequences with the same values, I should get a count of 4, as shown in Listing 5-50.

Listing 5-50. *An Example of the Second LongCount Operator Overload*

```
Dim count As Long = Enumerable.Range(0, Integer.MaxValue) _
  .Concat(Enumerable.Range(0, Integer.MaxValue)) _
  .LongCount(Function(n) n > 1 AndAlso n < 4)

Console.WriteLine(count)
```

This code is pretty much the same as the previous example except I have specified a predicate. This example takes even longer to run than the previous example.

The results from this code are the following:

4

Sum

The Sum operator returns the sum of numeric values contained in the elements of the input sequence.

Declarations

The Sum operator has two basic overloads, each with five overloads for different numeric data types, and each of these have two overloads for nullable and non-nullable numeric types, for a total of twenty overloads.

The First Overload of the Sum Operator

```
<ExtensionAttribute> _
Public Shared Function Sum ( _
    source As IEnumerable(Of Numeric) _
) As Numeric
```

The *Numeric* type must be one of Integer, Long, Single, Double, or Decimal or one of their nullable equivalents, Integer?, Long?, Single?, Double?, or Decimal?.

The first overload of the Sum operator returns the sum of each element in the source input sequence.

An empty sequence will return the sum of zero. The Sum operator will not include values that are equal to Nothing in the result for *Numeric* types that are nullable.

The second overload of the Sum operator behaves like the previous, except it will sum the value selected from each element by the selector method delegate.

The Second Overload of the Sum Operator

```
<ExtensionAttribute> _
Public Shared Function Sum(Of TSource) ( _
    source As IEnumerable(Of TSource), _
    selector As Func(Of TSource, Decimal) _
) As Decimal
```

Exceptions

ArgumentNullException is thrown if any argument is Nothing.

OverflowException is thrown if the sum is too large to be stored in the *Numeric* type if the *Numeric* type is other than Decimal or Decimal?. If the *Numeric* type is Decimal or Decimal?, a positive or negative infinity value is returned.

Examples

I will begin with an example of the first overload, shown in Listing 5-51. First, I generate a sequence of integers using the Range operator, and then, I use the Sum operator to sum them.

Listing 5-51. *An Example of the First Sum Operator Overload*

```
' First I'll generate a sequence of integers.
Dim ints As IEnumerable(Of Integer) = Enumerable.Range(1, 10)

' I'll show you the sequence of integers.
For Each i As Integer In ints
  Console.WriteLine(i)
Next i

Console.WriteLine("--")

' Now, I'll sum them.
Dim sum As Integer = ints.Sum()
Console.WriteLine(sum)
```

Here are the results:

```
1
2
3
4
5
6
7
8
9
10
--
55
```

Now I will try an example of the second overload, shown in Listing 5-52. For this example, I use the common EmployeeOptionEntry class and sum the count of the options for all employees.

Listing 5-52. *An Example of the Second Sum Operator Overload*

```
Dim options As IEnumerable(Of EmployeeOptionEntry) = _
  EmployeeOptionEntry.GetEmployeeOptionEntries()

Dim optionsSum As Long = options.Sum(Function(o) o.optionsCount)
Console.WriteLine("The sum of the employee options is: {0}", optionsSum)
```

Instead of trying to sum the entire element, which makes no sense in this example because it is an employee object, I can use the second overload's element selector to retrieve just the member I am interested in summing, which in this case is the optionsCount member. The results of this code are the following:

```
The sum of the employee options is: 51504
```

Min

The Min operator returns the minimum value of an input sequence.

Declarations

The Min operator has four overloads.

The First Overload of the Min Operator

```
<ExtensionAttribute> _
Public Shared Function Min( _
    source As IEnumerable(Of Numeric) _
) As Numeric
```

The *Numeric* type must be one of Integer, Long, Single, Double, or Decimal or one of their nullable equivalents, Integer?, Long?, Single?, Double?, or Decimal?. The first overload of the Min operator returns the element with the minimum numeric value in the source input sequence.

An empty sequence, or one that contains only values equal to Nothing, will return the value of Nothing for nullable types. For non-nullable types, an InvalidOperationException exception will be thrown.

For the second and fourth overloads, if the element type implements the IComparable(Of TSource) interface, that interface will be used to compare the elements. If the elements do not implement the IComparable(Of TSource) interface, the nongeneric IComparable interface will be used.

The second overload of the Min operator behaves like the previous, except it is for non-*Numeric* types.

The Second Overload of the Min Operator

```
<ExtensionAttribute> _
Public Shared Function Min(Of TSource) ( _
    source As IEnumerable(Of TSource) _
) As TSource
```

The third overload is for *Numeric* types and is like the first, except now a `selector` method delegate can be provided, allowing a member of each element in the input sequence to be compared while searching for the minimum value in the input sequence and returning that minimum value.

The Third Overload of the Min Operator

```
<ExtensionAttribute> _
Public Shared Function Min(Of TSource) ( _
    source As IEnumerable(Of TSource), _
    selector As Func(Of TSource, Numeric) _
) As Numeric
```

The fourth overload is for non-*Numeric* types and is like the second, except now a `selector` method delegate can be provided, allowing a member of each element in the input sequence to be compared while searching for the minimum value in the input sequence and returning that minimum value.

The Fourth Overload of the Min Operator

```
<ExtensionAttribute> _
Public Shared Function Min(Of TSource, TResult) ( _
    source As IEnumerable(Of TSource), _
    selector As Func(Of TSource, TResult) _
) As TResult
```

Exceptions

`ArgumentNullException` is thrown if any argument is `Nothing`.

`InvalidOperationException` is thrown if the `source` sequence is empty for the *Numeric* versions of the overloads if the type `TSource` is non-nullable, such as `Integer`, `Long`, `Single`, `Double`, or `Decimal`. If the types are nullable, that is, `Integer?`, `Long?`, `Single?`, `Double?`, or `Decimal?`, `Nothing` is returned from the operator instead.

Examples

In the example of the first `Min` overload, shown in Listing 5-53, I declare an array of integers and return the minimum from it.

Listing 5-53. *An Example of the First Min Operator Overload*

```
Dim myInts() As Integer = { 974, 2, 7, 1374, 27, 54 }
Dim minInt As Integer = myInts.Min()
Console.WriteLine(minInt)
```

That is a pretty trivial example. The following is the result:

```
2
```

For my example of the second overload, shown in Listing 5-54, I will just call the Min operator on my standard presidents array. This should return the element with the lowest value, alphabetically speaking.

Listing 5-54. *An Example of the Second Min Operator Overload*

```
Dim presidents() As String = _
{ _
  "Adams", "Arthur", "Buchanan", "Bush", "Carter", "Cleveland", _
  "Clinton", "Coolidge", "Eisenhower", "Fillmore", "Ford", "Garfield", _
  "Grant", "Harding", "Harrison", "Hayes", "Hoover", "Jackson", _
  "Jefferson", "Johnson", "Kennedy", "Lincoln", "Madison", "McKinley", _
  "Monroe", "Nixon", "Pierce", "Polk", "Reagan", "Roosevelt", "Taft", _
  "Taylor", "Truman", "Tyler", "Van Buren", "Washington", "Wilson" _
}

Dim minName As String = presidents.Min()
Console.WriteLine(minName)
```

This example provides the following results:

```
Adams
```

While this may be the same output that calling the First operator would provide, this is only because the presidents array is already sequenced alphabetically. Had the array been in some other order, or disordered, the results would have still been Adams.

For the example of the third overload of the Min operator, I use my common Actor class to find the earliest actor birth year by calling the Min operator on the birth year.

Listing 5-55 is the code calling the Min operator.

Listing 5-55. *An Example of the Third Min Operator Overload*

```
Dim oldestActorAge As Integer = Actor.GetActors() _
  .Min(Function(a) a.birthYear)
Console.WriteLine(oldestActorAge)
```

And the birth year of the actor with the most plastic surgery, I mean, the earliest birth year is the following:

```
1960
```

For an example of the fourth `Min` overload, shown in Listing 5-56, I obtain the last name of the actor that would come first alphabetically using my common `Actor` class.

Listing 5-56. *An Example of the Fourth Min Operator Overload*

```
Dim firstAlphabetically As String = Actor.GetActors() _
  .Min(Function(a) a.lastName)
Console.WriteLine(firstAlphabetically)
```

And the Oscar goes to:

```
Bullock
```

Max

The `Max` operator returns the maximum value of an input sequence.

Declarations

The `Max` operator has four overloads.

The First Overload of the Max Operator

```
<ExtensionAttribute> _
Public Shared Function Max ( _
    source As IEnumerable(Of Numeric) _
) As Numeric
```

The *Numeric* type must be one of `Integer`, `Long`, `Single`, `Double`, or `Decimal` or one of their nullable equivalents, `Integer?`, `Long?`, `Single?`, `Double?`, or `Decimal?`. The first overload of the `Max` operator returns the element with the maximum numeric value in the `source` input sequence.

An empty sequence, or one that contains only values that are equal to `Nothing`, will return the value of `Nothing` for nullable types. For non-nullable types, an `InvalidOperationException` exception will be thrown.

For the second and fourth overloads, if the element type implements the `IComparable(Of TSource)` interface, that interface will be used to compare the elements. If the elements do not implement the `IComparable(Of TSource)` interface, the nongeneric `IComparable` interface will be used.

The second overload of the `Max` operator behaves like the previous, except it is for non-*Numeric* types.

The Second Overload of the Max Operator

```
<ExtensionAttribute> _
Public Shared Function Max(Of TSource) ( _
    source As IEnumerable(Of TSource) _
) As TSource
```

The third overload is for *Numeric* types and like the first, except now a `selector` method delegate can be provided, allowing a member of each element in the input sequence to be compared while searching for the maximum value in the input sequence and returning that maximum value.

The Third Overload of the Max Operator

```
<ExtensionAttribute> _
Public Shared Function Max(Of TSource) ( _
    source As IEnumerable(Of TSource), _
    selector As Func(Of TSource, Numeric) _
) As Numeric
```

The fourth overload is for non-*Numeric* types and is like the second, except now a `selector` method delegate can be provided, allowing a member of each element in the input sequence to be compared while searching for the maximum value in the input sequence and returning that maximum value.

The Fourth Overload of the Max Operator

```
<ExtensionAttribute> _
Public Shared Function Max(Of TSource, TResult) ( _
    source As IEnumerable(Of TSource), _
    selector As Func(Of TSource, TResult) _
) As TResult
```

Exceptions

`ArgumentNullException` is thrown if any argument is `Nothing`.

`InvalidOperationException` is thrown if the source sequence is empty for the *Numeric* versions of the overloads if the type `TSource` is non-nullable, such as `Integer`, `Long`, `Single`, `Double`, or `Decimal`. If the types are nullable, such as `Integer?`, `Long?`, `Single?`, `Double?`, or `Decimal?`, `Nothing` is returned from the operator instead.

Examples

As an example of the first `Max` overload, shown in Listing 5-57, I declare an array of integers and return the maximum from it.

Listing 5-57. *An Example of the First Max Operator Overload*

```
Dim myInts() As Integer = { 974, 2, 7, 1374, 27, 54 }
Dim maxInt As Integer = myInts.Max()
Console.WriteLine(maxInt)
```

The results are the following:

1374

For an example of the second overload, shown in Listing 5-58, I just call the Max operator on my standard presidents array.

Listing 5-58. *An Example of the Second Max Operator Overload*

```
Dim presidents() As String = _
{ _
  "Adams", "Arthur", "Buchanan", "Bush", "Carter", "Cleveland", _
  "Clinton", "Coolidge", "Eisenhower", "Fillmore", "Ford", "Garfield", _
  "Grant", "Harding", "Harrison", "Hayes", "Hoover", "Jackson", _
  "Jefferson", "Johnson", "Kennedy", "Lincoln", "Madison", "McKinley", _
  "Monroe", "Nixon", "Pierce", "Polk", "Reagan", "Roosevelt", "Taft", _
  "Taylor", "Truman", "Tyler", "Van Buren", "Washington", "Wilson" _
}

Dim maxName As String = presidents.Max()
Console.WriteLine(maxName)
```

This provides the following results:

Wilson

Again, like I mentioned in the equivalent example for the Min operator, while this example provides the same result that the Last operator would, this is only because the presidents array is already ordered alphabetically.

For the example of the third overload of the Max operator, I use my common Actor class to find the latest actor birth year by calling the Max operator on the birth year.

Listing 5-59 is the code calling the Max operator.

Listing 5-59. *An Example of the Third Max Operator Overload*

```
Dim youngestActorAge As Integer = Actor.GetActors() _
  .Max(Function(a) a.birthYear)
Console.WriteLine(youngestActorAge)
```

And the latest actor birth year in my Actor class is the following:

1968

For an example of the fourth Max overload, shown in Listing 5-60, I will obtain the last name of the actor that would come last alphabetically using the same Actor class as previously.

Listing 5-60. *An Example of the Fourth Max Operator Overload*

```
Dim lastAlphabetically As String = Actor.GetActors() _
    .Max(Function(a) a.lastName)
Console.WriteLine(lastAlphabetically)
```

The results are the following:

```
Wilson
```

Hey, that is the same result I had for my second example where I used the array of the names of the US presidents. How creepy. That Dignan is always up to no good!

Average

The Average operator returns the average of numeric values contained in the elements of the input sequence.

Declarations

The Average operator has two overloads.

The First Overload of the Average Operator

```
<ExtensionAttribute> _
Public Shared Function Average ( _
    source As IEnumerable(Of Numeric) _
) As Numeric
```

The *Numeric* type must be one of Integer, Long, Single, Double, or Decimal or one of their nullable equivalents, Integer?, Long?, Single?, Double?, or Decimal?. If the *Numeric* type is Integer or Long, the *Result* type will be Double. If the *Numeric* type is Integer? or Long?, the *Result* type will be Double?. Otherwise, the *Result* type will be the same as the *Numeric* type.

The first overload of the Average operator enumerates the input source sequence of *Numeric* type elements, creating an average of the elements themselves.

The second overload of the Average operator enumerates the source input sequence and determines the average for the member returned by the selector for every element in the input source sequence.

The Second Overload of the Average Operator

```
<ExtensionAttribute> _
Public Shared Function Average(Of TSource) ( _
    source As IEnumerable(Of TSource), _
    selector As Func(Of TSource, Numeric) _
) As Numeric
```

Exceptions

ArgumentNullException is thrown if any argument is Nothing.

OverflowException is thrown if the sum of the averaged values exceeds the capacity of a Long for *Numeric* types Integer, Integer?, Long, and Long?.

Examples

I will begin with an example of the first overload, shown in Listing 5-61. For this example, I use the Range operator to create a sequence of integers, and then I will average them.

Listing 5-61. *An Example of the First Average Operator Overload*

```
' First build a sequence of integers.
Dim intSequence As IEnumerable(Of Integer) = Enumerable.Range(1, 10)
Console.WriteLine("Here is my sequnece of integers:")
For Each i As Integer In intSequence
  Console.WriteLine(i)
Next i


' Now I'll get the average.
Dim average As Double = intSequence.Average()
Console.WriteLine("Here is the average:  {0}", average)
```

Here are the results:

```
Here is my sequnece of integers:
1
2
3
4
5
6
7
8
9
10
Here is the average:  5.5
```

Now I will try an example of the second overload, which will access a member of the element. For this example, shown in Listing 5-62, I use my common EmployeeOptionEntry class.

Listing 5-62. *An Example of the Second Average Operator Overload*

```
' First, I'll get the sequence of EmployeeOptionEntry objects.
Dim options As IEnumerable(Of EmployeeOptionEntry) = _
  EmployeeOptionEntry.GetEmployeeOptionEntries()
```

```
Console.WriteLine("Here are the employee ids and their options:")
For Each eo As EmployeeOptionEntry In options
  Console.WriteLine("Employee id: {0}, Options: {1}", eo.id, eo.optionsCount)
Next eo

' Now I'll get the average of the options.
Dim optionAverage As Double = options.Average(Function(o) o.optionsCount)
Console.WriteLine("The average of the employee options is: {0}", optionAverage)
```

First, I retrieve the EmployeeOptionEntry objects. Then, I enumerate through the sequence of objects and display each. At the end, I calculate the average and display it. The results of this code are the following:

```
Here are the employee ids and their options:
Employee id:  1,  Options:  2
Employee id:  2,  Options:  10000
Employee id:  2,  Options:  10000
Employee id:  3,  Options:  5000
Employee id:  2,  Options:  10000
Employee id:  3,  Options:  7500
Employee id:  3,  Options:  7500
Employee id:  4,  Options:  1500
Employee id:  101,  Options:  2
The average of the employee options is: 5722.66666666667
```

Aggregate

The Aggregate operator performs a user-specified function on each element of an input sequence, passing in the function's return value from the previous element and returning the return value of the last element.

Declarations

The Aggregate operator has three overloads.

The First Overload of the Aggregate Operator

```
<ExtensionAttribute> _
Public Shared Function Aggregate(Of TSource) ( _
    source As IEnumerable(Of TSource), _
    func As Func(Of TSource, TSource, TSource) _
) As TSource
```

In this version of the overload, the Aggregate operator enumerates through each element of the input source sequence, calling the func method delegate on each, passing the return value from the previous element as the first argument and the element itself as the second argument, and finally, storing the value returned by func into an internal accumulator, which will then be passed to the next element. The first element will be passed itself as the input value to the func method delegate.

The second overload of the Aggregate operator behaves like the first version, except a seed value is provided that will be the input value for the first invocation of the func method delegate instead of the first element.

The Second Overload of the Aggregate Operator

```
<ExtensionAttribute> _
Public Shared Function Aggregate(Of TSource, TAccumulate) ( _
    source As IEnumerable(Of TSource), _
    seed As TAccumulate, _
    func As Func(Of TAccumulate, TSource, TAccumulate) _
) As TAccumulate
```

The third overload of the Aggregate operator takes the result of the aggregate operation and passes it to a function. You can use this function to manage the result according to your needs.

The Third Overload of the Aggregate Operator

```
<ExtensionAttribute> _
Public Shared Function Aggregate(Of TSource, TAccumulate, TResult)( _
    source As IEnumerable(Of TSource), _
    seed As TAccumulate, _
    func As Func(Of TAccumulate, TSource, TAccumulate), _
    resultSelector As Func(Of TAccumulate, TResult) _
) As TResult
```

Exceptions

ArgumentNullException is thrown if the source, func, or resultSelector argument is Nothing.

InvalidOperationException is thrown if the input source sequence is empty, only for the first Aggregate overload, where no seed value is provided.

Examples

I will begin with an example of the first overload, shown in Listing 5-63. In the example, I calculate the factorial for the number 5. A *factorial* is the product of all positive integers less than or equal to some number. The factorial of 5 is the product of all positive integers less than or equal to 5. So, 5!, pronounced *5 factorial*, will be equal to 1 * 2 * 3 * 4 * 5. It looks like I could use the Range operator and the Aggregate operator to calculate this.

Listing 5-63. *An Example of the First Aggregate Overload*

```
' First I need an array of Integers from 1 to N where
' N is the number I want the factorial for.  In this case,
' N will be 5.
```

```
Dim N As Integer = 5
Dim intSequence As IEnumerable(Of Integer) = Enumerable.Range(1, N)


'  I will just output the sequence so all can see it.
For Each item As Integer In intSequence
  Console.WriteLine(item)
Next item


'  Now calculate the factorial and display it.
'  av == aggregated value, e == element
Dim agg As Integer = intSequence.Aggregate(Function(av, e) av * e)
Console.WriteLine("{0}! = {1}", N, agg)
```

In the previous code, I generate a sequence containing the integers from 1 to 5 using the Range operator. After displaying each element in the generated sequence, I call the Aggregate operator passing a lambda expression that multiplies the passed aggregated value with the passed element itself. The following are the results:

```
1
2
3
4
5
5! = 120
```

Caution You should be careful when using this version of the Aggregate operator that the first element doesn't get operated on twice, since it is passed in as the input value and the element for the first element. In the previous example, my first call to my func lambda expression would have passed in 1 and 1. Since I just multiplied these two values, and they are both ones, there is no bad side effect. But if I had added the two values, I would have a sum that included the first element twice. The second overload for this operator will prevent this potential problem.

For the second overload's example, shown in Listing 5-64, I roll my own version of the Sum operator.

Listing 5-64. *An Example of the Second Aggregate Overload*

```
'  Create a sequence of ints from 1 to 10.
Dim intSequence As IEnumerable(Of Integer) = Enumerable.Range(1, 10)


'  I'll just ouput the sequence so all can see it.
For Each item As Integer In intSequence
  Console.WriteLine(item)
```

```
Next item
Console.WriteLine("--")

'  Now calculate the sum and display it.
Dim sum As Integer = intSequence.Aggregate(0, Function(s, i) s + i)
Console.WriteLine(sum)
```

Notice that I passed 0 as the seed for this call to the Aggregate operator. And the envelope please:

```
1
2
3
4
5
6
7
8
9
10
--
55
```

As you can see, I got the exact same results that I did when calling the Sum operator in Listing 5-51.

For the third Aggregate operator overload example I use the same code as in Listing 5-64, except I will divide the aggregation result by the number of elements in the original sequence thereby producing the average. See Listing 5-65.

Listing 5-65. *An Example of the Third Aggregate Overload*

```
'  Create a sequence of ints from 1 to 10.
Dim intSequence As IEnumerable(Of Integer) = Enumerable.Range(1, 10)

'  I'll just ouput the sequence so all can see it.
For Each item As Integer In intSequence
  Console.WriteLine(item)
Next item

'  Now calculate the average and display it.
Dim avg As Double = intSequence.Aggregate(0, _
                                    Function(s, i) s + i, _
                                    Function(r) r / intSequence.Count)

Console.WriteLine("Here is the average:  {0}", avg)
```

The aggregation result r is passed to the function that divides it by the number of elements in the original sequence and returns the result:

```
1
2
3
4
5
6
7
8
9
10
Here is the average:  5.5
```

Notice that I got the same result for this example that I did for Listing 5-61, which was an example of the Average operator. This overload is useful for those times when you would like a little post-aggregation processing.

Summary

Wow, my head is spinning. I hope I didn't lose too many of you so far. I know a lot of the material in this and the previous chapter is a little dry, but these two chapters are packed with the essentials of LINQ. I hope that, as I covered each query operator, you tried to visualize when you might use it. A large part of making LINQ effective for you is having a feel for the operators and what they do. Even if you can't remember every variation of each operator, just knowing they exist and what they can do for you is essential.

From my coverage of LINQ to Objects and the Standard Query Operators, hopefully you can see just how powerful and convenient LINQ is for querying data of all types of in-memory data collections.

With nearly 50 operators to choose from, LINQ to Objects is sure to make your data-querying code more consistent, more reliable, and more expedient to write.

I cannot stress enough that most of the Standard Query Operators work on collections that implement the IEnumerable(Of T) interface, which excludes the legacy .NET collections that implement IEnumerable and are defined in the System.Collections namespace, such as ArrayList. To query data from the legacy collections, please use the Cast and OfType operators. I *know* that some readers will overlook this fact and become frustrated because they have legacy code with an ArrayList or some other legacy collection and cannot find a way to query data from it.

Now that you hopefully have a sound understanding of LINQ to Objects and just what LINQ can do for you, it's time to learn about using LINQ to query and generate XML. This functionality is called LINQ to XML and, not so coincidentally, that is the name of the next part of this book.

PART 3

LINQ to XML

CHAPTER 6

■■■

LINQ to XML Introduction

So you want to be an XML hero? Are you willing to suffer the slings and arrows? Listing 6-1 shows some code that merely creates a trivial XML hierarchy using Microsoft's original XML Document Object Model (DOM) API, which is based on the W3C DOM XML API, demonstrating just how painful that model can be.

Listing 6-1. *A Simple XML Example*

```
Imports System.Xml

' I'll declare some variables I will reuse.
Dim xmlBookParticipant As XmlElement
Dim xmlParticipantType As XmlAttribute
Dim xmlFirstName As XmlElement
Dim xmlLastName As XmlElement

' First, I must build an XML document.
Dim xmlDoc As New XmlDocument()

' I'll create the root element and add it to the document.
Dim xmlBookParticipants As XmlElement = xmlDoc.CreateElement("BookParticipants")
xmlDoc.AppendChild(xmlBookParticipants)

' I'll create a participant and add it to the book participants list.
xmlBookParticipant = xmlDoc.CreateElement("BookParticipant")

xmlParticipantType = xmlDoc.CreateAttribute("type")
xmlParticipantType.InnerText = "Author"
xmlBookParticipant.Attributes.Append(xmlParticipantType)

xmlFirstName = xmlDoc.CreateElement("FirstName")
xmlFirstName.InnerText = "Dennis"
xmlBookParticipant.AppendChild(xmlFirstName)
```

```
xmlLastName = xmlDoc.CreateElement("LastName")
xmlLastName.InnerText = "Hayes"
xmlBookParticipant.AppendChild(xmlLastName)

xmlBookParticipants.AppendChild(xmlBookParticipant)

' I'll create another participant and add it to the book participants list.
xmlBookParticipant = xmlDoc.CreateElement("BookParticipant")

xmlParticipantType = xmlDoc.CreateAttribute("type")
xmlParticipantType.InnerText = "Editor"
xmlBookParticipant.Attributes.Append(xmlParticipantType)

xmlFirstName = xmlDoc.CreateElement("FirstName")
xmlFirstName.InnerText = "Ewan"
xmlBookParticipant.AppendChild(xmlFirstName)

xmlLastName = xmlDoc.CreateElement("LastName")
xmlLastName.InnerText = "Buckingham"
xmlBookParticipant.AppendChild(xmlLastName)

xmlBookParticipants.AppendChild(xmlBookParticipant)

' Now, I'll search for authors and display their first and last name.
Dim authorsList As XmlNodeList = _
  xmlDoc.SelectNodes("BookParticipants/BookParticipant[@type=""Author""]")

For Each node As XmlNode In authorsList
  Dim firstName As XmlNode = node.SelectSingleNode("FirstName")
  Dim lastName As XmlNode = node.SelectSingleNode("LastName")
  Console.WriteLine("{0} {1}", firstName, lastName)
Next node
```

That last line of code, the call to the WriteLine method, is in bold because I will be changing it momentarily. All that code does is build the following XML hierarchy and attempt to display the name of each book participant:

The Desired XML Structure

```
<BookParticipants>
  <BookParticipant type="Author">
    <FirstName>Dennis</FirstName>
    <LastName>Hayes</LastName>
  </BookParticipant>
  <BookParticipant type="Editor">
    <FirstName>Ewan</FirstName>
    <LastName>Buckingham</LastName>
  </BookParticipant>
</BookParticipants>
```

That code is a nightmare to write, understand, and maintain. It is very verbose. Just looking at it, I have no idea what the XML structure should look like. Part of what makes it so cumbersome is that you cannot create an element, initialize it, and attach it to the hierarchy in a single statement. Instead, each element must first be created, then have its `InnerText` member set to the desired value, and finally be appended to some node already existing in the XML document. This must be done for every element and attribute and leads to a lot of code. Additionally, an XML document must first be created because, without it, you cannot even create an element. It is very common to not want an actual XML document, because sometimes just a fragment like the previous is all that is needed. Finally, just look at how many lines of code it takes to generate such a small amount of XML.

Now, let's take a look at the glorious output. I will just press Ctrl+F5:

```
System.Xml.XmlElement System.Xml.XmlElement
```

Oops! It looks like I didn't get the actual text out of the `FirstName` and `LastName` nodes in that `For Each` loop. I'll modify that `Console.WriteLine` method call to get the data:

```
Console.WriteLine("{0} {1}", firstName.ToString(), lastName.ToString())
```

Now prepare to be impressed! Abracadabra, Ctrl+F5:

```
System.Xml.XmlElement System.Xml.XmlElement
```

Heavy sigh.

If chicks really do dig scars, as Keanu Reeves's character suggests in the movie *The Replacements*, they ought to love Extensible Markup Language (XML) developers. I remember the first time I was introduced to XML. Back in 1999, I was contracting for the information technology division of a large corporation. I approached its common architecture group looking for a logging solution for an HP/UX project. I wanted something primarily to roll the log files, saving me the trouble of implementing it myself. Of course, I wanted my logs stored as plain text so I could use the arsenal of UNIX shell commands at my disposal. Instead, I was presented with a logging solution that stored the log messages as XML. They showed me one of their log files. Ouch!

"How am I going to cut[1] that?" I asked. I was told not to worry; they had a GUI application for reading the log files. It sure sounded like fun. Unfortunately, the project was cancelled before we got to the point of logging.

At another company in 2000, it was dictated that we would be using "industry-standard XML" despite the fact that the industry had no standard schema, much less had it committed to XML. But our management was determined that we would be the first, even without a partner to consume it. Is it a standard if you are the only one doing it?

It was clear to me from my experiences that XML was a technology to be reckoned with. Companies were chomping at the bit to get a data format that was easy to share. On paper, XML sounded good, even if the APIs were less than friendly. Every high-tech magazine was

---

1. This is referring to the standard UNIX shell cut command, which allows fields to be cut from a line of text in a text file based on either character position in the line or a common field delimiter such as a tab, a space, or a comma.

singing the praises of XML. Executives were reading it; chief technology officers were believing it, and directors were mandating it. XML was destined to succeed.

Regardless of the battle scars we may have, there is no doubt that XML has become *the* standard for data exchange. And as one of my best friends says when struggling for a compliment for XML, it compresses well.

So the next time you want to turn that young lady's head, let her hear you whisper a sweet something about namespaces, nodes, or attributes. She will be putty in your hands:

```
<PuttyInYourHands>True</PuttyInYourHands>
```

Additional Advantages of LINQ to XML

Microsoft could have given us a new LINQ XML API that only added the ability to perform LINQ queries and been done with it. Fortunately for XML developers, it went the extra mile. In addition to making XML support LINQ queries, Microsoft addressed many of the deficiencies of the standard DOM XML API. After several years of suffering with the W3C DOM XML API, it had become apparent to most developers that many tasks did not seem as simple as they should. When dealing with small fragments of XML, using the W3C DOM required creating an XML document just to create a few elements. Have you ever just built a string so that it looks like XML, rather than using the DOM API because it was such a hassle? I sure have.

Several key deficiencies in the W3C DOM XML API were addressed. A new object model was created. And the result is a far simpler and more elegant method for creating XML trees. Bloated code like that in Listing 6-1 will be an artifact of an API past its prime and left in the wake of LINQ. Creating a full XML tree in a single statement is now a reality thanks to *functional construction*. Functional construction is the term used to describe the ability to construct an entire XML hierarchy in a single statement. That alone makes LINQ to XML worth its weight in gold.

Of course, it wouldn't be a part of LINQ if the new XML API didn't support LINQ queries. In that vein, several new XML-specific query operators, implemented as extension methods, were added. Combining these new XML-specific operators with the LINQ to Objects Standard Query Operators I discuss in Part 2 of this book creates a powerfully elegant solution for finding whatever data you are searching for in an XML tree.

Not only does LINQ support all this, but combine a query with functional construction and you get an XML transformation. LINQ to XML is very flexible.

Cheating the W3C DOM XML API

OK, you are working on your project, and you know some particular data should be stored as XML. In my case, I was developing a general logging class that allowed me to track everything a user does within my ASP.NET web application. I developed the logging class for two purposes. First, I wanted something to be able to prove someone was abusing the system should that ever happen. Second, and most important, when my web application would signal me via email that an exception had occurred, I became frustrated that inevitably the users who triggered the exceptions could never remember what they were doing at the time the exceptions happened. They could never recall the details that lead them to the error.

So I wanted something tracking their every move, at least on the server side. Every different type of action a user would make, such as an invoice query or an order submission, would be considered an *event*. In my database, I had fields that captured the user, the date, the time, the *event* type, and all the common fields you would want. However, it wasn't enough to know they were perhaps querying for an invoice; I had to know what the search parameters were. If they were submitting an order, I needed to know what the part ID was and how many they ordered. Basically, I needed all the data so that I could perform the exact same operation they attempted in order to reproduce the exception condition. Each type of event had different parameter data. I sure did not want a different table for each event type, and I sure did not want my event viewer code to have to hit a zillion different tables to reconstruct the user's actions. I wanted one table to capture it all so that, when viewing the table, I could see every action (event) the user performed. So there I was, confronted with the notion that what I needed was a string of XML data stored in the database that contained the event's parameter data.

There would be no schema defining what the XML looked like, because it was whatever data a particular event needed it to be. If the event was an invoice inquiry across a date range, it might look like this:

```
<StartDate>10/2/2006</StartDate>
<EndDate>10/9/2006</EndDate>
<IncPaid>False</IncPaid>
```

If it was an order submission, it might look like this:

```
<PartId>4754611903</PartId>
<Quantity>12</Quantity>
<DistributionCenter>Atlanta<DistributionCenter>
<ShippingCode>USPS First Class<ShippingCode>
```

I captured whatever fields would be necessary for me to manually reproduce the event. Since the data varied with the event type, this ruled out validating the XML, so there went one benefit of using the DOM XML API.

This event tracker became a first-class support tool, as well as making identifying and resolving bugs much easier. As a side note, it is quite entertaining on those occasions when I get to call a user the next day and announce that the error encountered while trying to pull up invoice number 3847329 the previous day is now fixed. The paranoia that results when users know I know exactly what they did is often reward enough for the tracking code.

Those of you who are already familiar with XML may be looking at those schemas and saying, "Hey, that's not well formed. There's no root node." OK, that's true and is a problem if you use the W3C DOM API. However, I didn't use the W3C DOM API to produce that XML; I used a different XML API. You have probably used it too. It's called the String.Format XML API, and using it looks a little like this:

```
Dim xmlData As String = String.Format( _
  "<StartDate>{0}</StartDate><EndDate>{1}</EndDate><IncPaid>{2}</IncPaid>", _
  startDate.ToShortDateString(), _
  endDate.ToShortDateString(), _
  includePaid.ToString())
```

Yes, I am aware that this is a poor way to create XML data. And, yes, it is prone to bugs. It's certainly easy to spell or set the case of (EndDate vs. endDate, for example) a closing tag differently this way. I even went so far as to create a method so I can pass a parameter list of element names and their data. So my code actually looks a little more like this:

```
Dim xmlData As String = XMLHelper( _
  "StartDate", startDate.ToShortDateString(), _
  "EndDate", endDate.ToShortDateString(), _
  "IncPaid", includePaid.ToString())
```

That XMLHelper method will create a root node for me too. Yet again, this isn't much better. You can see that I did nothing to encode my data in that call. So it was an error down the road before I realized I had better be encoding those data values that got passed.

While using the String.Format method, or any other technique other than the DOM XML API, is a poor substitute for the DOM, the existing API is often too much trouble when dealing with just an XML fragment, as I was in this case.

If you think I am alone in using this approach to create XML, I was recently at a Microsoft seminar, and the presenter demonstrated code that built a string of XML using string concatenation. If only there was a better way. If only LINQ had been available!

Summary

Whenever someone utters the word *LINQ*, the first image that most developers seem to conjure is that of performing a data query. More specifically than that, they seem to want to exclude data sources other than databases. LINQ to XML is here to tell you that LINQ is about XML too—and not just about querying XML.

In this chapter, I showed you some of the pain of dealing with XML when using the existing W3C DOM XML API and some of the traditional cheats to avoid that pain. In the next chapter, I cover the LINQ to XML API. Using this API, I demonstrate how to create XML hierarchies in a fraction of the code possible with the W3C DOM XML API. Just to tease you, I will tell you now that in the next chapter I will create the same XML hierarchy that is created in Listing 6-1 using LINQ to XML, and instead of the 29 lines of code that Listing 6-1 requires to create the hierarchy, LINQ to XML allows me to create that same hierarchy with only 10 lines of code.

Hopefully, by the time you are finished reading the next two chapters, you will agree that LINQ is as revolutionary for XML manipulation as it is for database queries.

CHAPTER 7

The LINQ to XML API

In the previous chapter, I demonstrated creating an XML document using the W3C DOM XML API and just how cumbersome that API can be. I also showed you some of the techniques I have seen used to circumvent the pain it causes.

I also let you in on a seemingly little-known secret about LINQ: the fact that LINQ is not just about data queries, it is also about XML. I told you there was a new XML API on the horizon, and that API is the LINQ to XML API.

Now, there is a better, or at least simpler, way to construct, traverse, manipulate, and query XML, and it's called LINQ to XML. In this chapter, I show you how to create, manipulate, and traverse XML documents using the LINQ to XML API, as well as how to perform searches on an XML object.

For the examples in this chapter, I created a console application. However, before you can leverage this new API, you need to add a reference to your project for the `System.Xml.Linq` assembly if it is not already present.

Note You should be aware that the new VB.NET 2008 XML features such as XML literals, embedded expressions, and axis properties, are part of the VB.NET language, not part of the LINQ to XML API. Therefore, they will not be explained in this chapter since they were covered in Chapter 2. I will, however, be using these VB.NET XML features in some of the examples in this chapter so that you can see them in action while working with the LINQ to XML API.

Referenced Namespaces

The examples in this chapter use the `System.Linq`, `System.Xml.Linq`, and `System.Collections. Generic` namespaces. Therefore, you should add `Imports` statements for these namespaces to your code if they are not already present or included in the list of those automatically included in the project's properties:

```
Imports System.Collections.Generic
Imports System.Linq
Imports System.Xml.Linq
Imports System.Xml
```

In addition to these namespaces, if you download the companion code, you will see that I also added an `Imports` statement for the `System.Diagnostics` namespace. This will not be necessary if you are typing in the examples from this chapter. It is necessary in the downloadable companion code due to some housekeeping code.

Significant API Design Enhancements

After a few years of experience with Microsoft's W3C DOM XML API, several key areas have been identified by Microsoft as inconveniences, annoyances, or weaknesses in the original API. To combat these issues, the following points have been addressed:

- XML tree construction
- Document centricity
- Namespaces and prefixes
- Node value extraction

Each of these problem domains has been a stumbling block to working with XML. Not only have these issues made XML code bloated, and oftentimes unintentionally obfuscated, they needed to be addressed for XML to really work seamlessly with LINQ queries. For example, if you want to use projection to return XML from a LINQ query, it's a bit of a problem if you cannot instantiate an element with a `New` statement. This is a limitation of the existing XML API and had to be addressed in order for LINQ to be practical with XML. Let's take a look at each of these problem areas and how they have been addressed in the new LINQ to XML API.

XML Tree Construction Simplified with Functional Construction

When reading the first sample code of the previous chapter, Listing 6-1, it becomes clear that it is very difficult to determine the XML schema from looking at the code that creates the XML tree. The code is also very verbose. After creating the XML document, we must create some type of XML node such as an element, set its value, and append it to its parent element. However, each of those three steps must be performed individually using the W3C DOM XML API. This leads to an obfuscated schema and a lot of code. The API just doesn't support creating an element, or any other type of node, in place in the XML tree with respect to its parent, and initializing it, all in a single operation.

The LINQ to XML API not only provides the same ability to create the XML tree as the W3C DOM does, but it also provides a new technique known as *functional construction* to create an XML tree. Functional construction allows the schema to be dictated as the XML objects are constructed and the values initialized all at the same time in a single statement. The API accomplishes this by providing constructors for the new API's XML objects that accept either a single object or multiple objects, which specify its value. The type of object, or objects, being added determines where in the schema the added object belongs. The pattern looks like this:

```
Dim o As XMLOBJECT = _
  New XMLOBJECT(OBJECTNAME, _
           XMLOBJECT1, _
```

```
        XMLOBJECT2, _
        ... _
        XMLOBJECTN)
```

> **Note** The preceding code is merely pseudocode meant to illustrate a pattern. None of the classes referenced in the pseudocode actually exist; they just represent some conceptually abstract XML class.

If you add an XML attribute, which is implemented with the LINQ to XML XAttribute class, to an element, implemented with the XElement class, the attribute becomes an attribute of the element. For example, if XMLOBJECT1 in the previous pseudocode is added to the newly created XMLOBJECT named o, and o is an XElement, and XMLOBJECT1 is an XAttribute, XMLOBJECT1 becomes an attribute of XElement o.

If you add an XElement to an XElement, the added XElement becomes a child element of the element to which it is added. So for example, if XMLOBJECT1 is an element and o is an element, XMLOBJECT1 becomes a child element of o.

When we instantiate an XMLOBJECT, as indicated in the previous pseudocode, we can specify its contents by specifying 1 to N XMLOBJECTs. As you will learn later in the section titled "Creating Text with XText," you can even specify its contents to include a string, because that string will be automatically converted to an XMLOBJECT for you.

This makes complete sense and is at the heart of functional construction. Listing 7-1 shows an example.

Listing 7-1. *Using Functional Construction to Create an XML Schema*

```
Dim xBookParticipant As _
  New XElement("BookParticipant", _
    New XElement("FirstName", "Dennis"), _
    New XElement("LastName", "Hayes"))

Console.WriteLine(xBookParticipant.ToString())
```

> **Note** Since this chapter is about the LINQ to XML API, and specifically, this section is about functional construction, I used functional construction in Listing 7-1. It should be noted though that this example could have been simplified by using an XML literal. I covered XML literals in Chapter 2, since they are a VB.NET language enhancement and not part of the LINQ to XML API. I will be using XML literals in some of the examples later in this chapter, as well as functional construction throughout. However, I want to make a clear distinction in your mind between the XML features that exist because they were added to VB.NET, such as XML literals, and those that are part of the LINQ to XML API, such as those features covered in this chapter.

Notice that when I constructed the element named BookParticipant, I passed two XElement objects as its value, each of which becomes a child element. Also notice that when I constructed the FirstName and LastName elements, instead of specifying multiple child objects, as I did when constructing the BookParticipant element, I provided the element's text value. Here are the results of this code:

```
<BookParticipant>
  <FirstName>Dennis</FirstName>
  <LastName>Hayes</LastName>
</BookParticipant>
```

Notice how much easier it is now to visualize the XML schema from the code. Also notice how much less verbose that code is than the first code sample of the previous chapter, Listing 6-1. The LINQ to XML API code necessary to replace the code in Listing 6-1 that actually creates the XML tree is significantly shorter, as shown in Listing 7-2.

Listing 7-2. *Creates the Same XML Tree as Listing 6-1 but with Far Less Code*

```
Dim xBookParticipants As _
  New XElement("BookParticipants", _
    New XElement("BookParticipant", _
      New XAttribute("type", "Author"), _
      New XElement("FirstName", "Dennis"), _
      New XElement("LastName", "Hayes")), _
    New XElement("BookParticipant", _
      New XAttribute("type", "Editor"), _
      New XElement("FirstName", "Ewan"), _
      New XElement("LastName", "Buckingham")))

Console.WriteLine(xBookParticipants.ToString())
```

That is far less code to create and maintain. Also, the schema is fairly ascertainable just reading the code. Here is the output:

```
<BookParticipants>
  <BookParticipant type="Author">
    <FirstName>Dennis</FirstName>
    <LastName>Hayes</LastName>
  </BookParticipant>
  <BookParticipant type="Editor">
    <FirstName>Ewan</FirstName>
    <LastName>Buckingham</LastName>
  </BookParticipant>
</BookParticipants>
```

There is one more additional benefit to the new API that is apparent in the example's results. Please notice that the output is formatted to look like a *tree* of XML. If I output the XML tree created in Listing 6-1, it actually looks like this:

```
<BookParticipants><BookParticipant type="Author"><FirstName>Dennis</FirstName>…
```

Which would you rather read? In the next chapter, when I get to the section on performing LINQ queries that produce XML output, you will see the necessity of functional construction.

Document Centricity Eliminated in Favor of Element Centricity

With the original W3C DOM XML API, you can not simply create an XML element, XmlElement; you must have an XML document, XmlDocument, from which to create it. If you try to instantiate an XmlElement like this

```
Dim xmlBookParticipant As New XmlElement("BookParticipant")
```

you will be greeted with the following compiler error:

```
'System.Xml.XmlElement.Protected Friend Sub New(prefix As String, localName As
String, namespaceURI As String, doc As System.Xml.XmlDocument)' is not accessible in
this context because it is 'Protected Friend'.
```

With the W3C DOM XML API, you can only create an XmlElement by calling an XmlDocument object's CreateElement method like this:

```
Dim xmlDoc As New XmlDocument()
Dim xmlBookParticipant As XmlElement = xmlDoc.CreateElement("BookParticipant")
```

This code compiles just fine. But it is often inconvenient to be forced to create an XML document when you just want to create an XML element. The new LINQ-enabled XML API allows you to instantiate an element itself without creating an XML document:

```
Dim xeBookParticipant As New XElement("BookParticipant")
```

XML elements are not the only XML type of node impacted by this W3C DOM restriction. Attributes, comments, CData sections, processing instructions, and entity references all must be created from an XML document. Thankfully, the LINQ to XML API has made it possible to directly instantiate each of these on the fly.

Of course, nothing prevents you from creating an XML document with the new API. For example, you could create an XML document and add the BookParticipants element and one BookParticipant to it, as shown in Listing 7-3.

Listing 7-3. *Using the LINQ to XML API to Create an XML Document and Add Some Structure to It*

```
Dim xDocument As New XDocument( _
  New XElement("BookParticipants", _
    New XElement("BookParticipant", _
```

```
      New XAttribute("type", "Author"), _
      New XElement("FirstName", "Dennis"), _
      New XElement("LastName", "Hayes"))))

Console.WriteLine(xDocument.ToString())
```

Pressing Ctrl+F5 yields the following results:

```
<BookParticipants>
  <BookParticipant type="Author">
    <FirstName>Dennis</FirstName>
    <LastName>Hayes</LastName>
  </BookParticipant>
</BookParticipants>
```

The XML produced by the previous code is very similar to the XML I created in Listing 6-1, with the exception that I only added one BookParticipant instead of two. This code is much more readable, though, than Listing 6-1, thanks to our new functional construction capabilities. And it is feasible to determine the schema from looking at the code. However, now that XML documents are no longer necessary, I could just leave the XML document out and obtain the same results, as shown in Listing 7-4.

Listing 7-4. *Same Example As the Previous but Without the XML Document*

```
Dim xElement As _
  New XElement("BookParticipants", _
    New XElement("BookParticipant", _
      New XAttribute("type", "Author"), _
      New XElement("FirstName", "Dennis"), _
      New XElement("LastName", "Hayes")))

Console.WriteLine(xElement.ToString())
```

Running the code produces the exact same results as the previous example:

```
<BookParticipants>
  <BookParticipant type="Author">
    <FirstName>Dennis</FirstName>
    <LastName>Hayes</LastName>
  </BookParticipant>
</BookParticipants>
```

In addition to creating XML trees without an XML document, you can do most of the other things that a document requires as well, such as reading XML from a file and saving it to a file.

Names, Namespaces, and Prefixes

To eliminate some of the confusion stemming from names, namespaces, and namespace prefixes, namespace prefixes are out; out of the API that is. With the LINQ to XML API, namespace prefixes get expanded on input and honored on output. On the inside, they no longer exist.

A namespace is used in XML to uniquely identify the XML schema for some portion of the XML tree. A URI is used for XML namespaces because they are already unique to any organization. In several of my code samples, I have created an XML tree that looks like this:

```
<BookParticipants>
  <BookParticipant type="Author">
    <FirstName>Dennis</FirstName>
    <LastName>Hayes</LastName>
  </BookParticipant>
</BookParticipants>
```

Any code that is processing that XML data will be written to expect the BookParticipants node to contain multiple BookParticipant nodes, each of which have a type attribute and a FirstName and LastName node. But what if this code also needs to be able to process XML from another source, and it too has a BookParticipants node but the schema within that node is different from the previous? A namespace will alert the code as to what the schema should look like, thereby allowing the code to handle the XML appropriately.

With XML, every element needs a name. When an element gets created, if its name is specified in the constructor, that name is implicitly converted from a String to an XName object. An XName object consists of a property named NamespaceName of type String, a property named Namespace of type XNamespace, and a property named LocalName of type String, which is the name you provided. Please be aware that the XName class's NamespaceName property is merely a convenience property providing access to the Namespace property's NamespaceName property. That was a mouthful. So, for example, you can create the BookParticipants element like this:

```
Dim xBookParticipants As New XElement("BookParticipants")
```

When you create the element, an XName object gets created with an empty namespace, and a local name of BookParticipants. If you debug the code in VB.NET and examine the xBookParticipants variable in the watch window, you will see that its Name.LocalName property is set to "BookParticipants", and its Name.Namespace.NamespaceName property is set to an empty String, "".

To specify a namespace, you need merely create an XNamespace object and prepend it to the local name you specify like this:

```
Dim MyNameSpace As XNamespace = "http://www.linqdev.com"
Dim xBookParticipants As New XElement(MyNameSpace + "BookParticipants")
```

Now, when you examine the xBookParticipants element in the debugger's watch window, expanding the Name property reveals that the LocalName property is still BookParticipants, but the Namespace.NamespaceName property is set to "http://www.linqdev.com".

It is not necessary to actually use an XNamespace object to specify the namespace. I could have specified it as a hard-coded string literal like this:

```
Dim xBookParticipants As New XElement("{http://www.linqdev.com}" & _
  "BookParticipants")
```

Notice that I enclose the namespace in braces. This clues the XElement constructor into the fact that this portion is the namespace. If you examine the BookParticipants's Name property in the watch window again, you will see that the Name.LocalName and Name.Namespace. NamespaceName properties are both set identically to the same values as the previous example where I used an XNamespace object to create the element.

Keep in mind that when setting the namespace, merely specifying the URI to your company or organization domain may not be enough to guarantee its uniqueness. It only guarantees you won't have any collisions with any other (well-meaning) organization that also plays by the namespace naming convention rules. However, once inside your organization, any other department could have a collision if you provide nothing more than the organization URI. This is where your knowledge of your organization's divisions, departments, and so on, can be quite useful. It would be best if your namespace could extend all the way to some level you have control over. For example, if you work at LINQDev.com and you are creating a schema for the human resources department that will contain information for the pension plan, your namespace might be the following:

```
Dim MyNameSpace As XNamespace = "http://www.linqdev.com/humanresources/pension"
```

So for a final example showing how namespaces are used, I will modify the code from Listing 7-2 to use a namespace, as shown in Listing 7-5.

Listing 7-5. *Modified Version Listing 7-2 with a Namespace Specified*

```
Dim MyNameSpace As XNamespace = "http://www.linqdev.com"

Dim xBookParticipants As _
  New XElement(MyNameSpace + "BookParticipants", _
    New XElement(MyNameSpace + "BookParticipant", _
      New XAttribute("type", "Author"), _
      New XElement(MyNameSpace + "FirstName", "Dennis"), _
      New XElement(MyNameSpace + "LastName", "Hayes")), _
    New XElement(MyNameSpace + "BookParticipant", _
      New XAttribute("type", "Editor"), _
      New XElement(MyNameSpace + "FirstName", "Ewan"), _
      New XElement(MyNameSpace + "LastName", "Buckingham")))

Console.WriteLine(xBookParticipants.ToString())
```

Pressing Ctrl+F5 reveals the following results:

```
<BookParticipants xmlns="http://www.linqdev.com">
  <BookParticipant type="Author">
    <FirstName>Dennis</FirstName>
    <LastName>Hayes</LastName>
  </BookParticipant>
  <BookParticipant type="Editor">
```

```
    <FirstName>Ewan</FirstName>
    <LastName>Buckingham</LastName>
  </BookParticipant>
</BookParticipants>
```

Now any code could read that and know that the schema should match the schema provided by LINQDev.com.

To have control over the namespace prefixes going out, use the XAttribute object to create a prefix as in Listing 7-6.

Listing 7-6. *Specifying a Namespace Prefix*

```
Dim MyNameSpace As XNamespace = "http://www.linqdev.com"

Dim xBookParticipants As _
  New XElement(MyNameSpace + "BookParticipants", _
    New XAttribute(XNamespace.Xmlns + "linqdev", MyNameSpace), _
    New XElement(MyNameSpace + "BookParticipant"))

Console.WriteLine(xBookParticipants.ToString())
```

In the previous code, I am specifying linqdev as the namespace prefix, and I am utilizing the XAttribute object to get the prefix specification into the schema. Here is the output from this code:

```
<linqdev:BookParticipants xmlns:linqdev="http://www.linqdev.com">
  <linqdev:BookParticipant />
</linqdev:BookParticipants>
```

Node Value Extraction

If you read the first code sample of the previous chapter, Listing 6-1, and laughed at my results, which I hope you did, you no doubt have experienced the same issue that prevented me from getting the results I was after—getting the actual value from a node is a bit of a nuisance. If I haven't been working with any XML DOM code for a while, I inevitably end up with an error like the one in Listing 6-1. I just about always forget I have to take the extra step to get the value of the node.

The LINQ to XML API fixes that problem very nicely. First, calling the ToString method of an element outputs the XML string itself, not the object type as it does with the W3C DOM XML API. This is very handy when you want an XML fragment from a certain point in the tree and makes far more sense than outputting the object type. Listing 7-7 shows an example.

Listing 7-7. *Calling the ToString Method on an Element Produces the XML Tree*

```
Dim name As New XElement("Name", "Dennis")
Console.WriteLine(name.ToString())
```

Pressing Ctrl+F5 gives me the following:

```
<Name>Dennis</Name>
```

Wow, that's a nice change. But wait, it gets better. Of course, child nodes are included in the output, and since the WriteLine method doesn't have an explicit overload accepting an XElement, it calls the ToString method for you, as shown in Listing 7-8.

Listing 7-8. *Console.WriteLine Implicitly Calling the ToString Method on an Element to Produce an XML Tree*

```
Dim name As _
  New XElement("Person", _
    New XElement("FirstName", "Dennis"), _
    New XElement("LastName", "Hayes"))

Console.WriteLine(name)
```

And the following is the output:

```
<Person>
  <FirstName>Dennis</FirstName>
  <LastName>Hayes</LastName>
</Person>
```

Even more important, if you cast a node to a data type that its value can be converted to, the value itself will be output. Listing 7-9 shows another example, but I will also print out the node cast to a String.

Listing 7-9. *Casting an Element to Its Value's Data Type Outputs the Value*

```
Dim name As New XElement("Name", "Dennis")
Console.WriteLine(name)
Console.WriteLine(CType(name))
```

Here are the results of this code:

```
<Name>Dennis</Name>
Dennis
```

How slick is that? Now how much would you pay? And there are cast operators provided for String, Integer, Integer?, UInteger, UInteger?, Long, Long?, ULong, ULong?, Boolean, Boolean?, Single, Single?, Double, Double?, Decimal, Decimal?, TimeSpan, TimeSpan?, DateTime, DateTime?, GUID, and GUID?.

Listing 7-10 shows an example of a few different node value types.

Listing 7-10. *Different Node Value Types Retrieved via Casting to the Node Value's Type*

```
Dim count As New XElement("Count", 12)
Console.WriteLine(count)
Console.WriteLine(CType(count, Integer))

Dim smoker As New XElement("Smoker", False)
Console.WriteLine(smoker)
Console.WriteLine(CType(smoker, Boolean))

Dim pi As New XElement("Pi", 3.1415926535)
Console.WriteLine(pi)
Console.WriteLine(CType(pi, Double))
```

And the envelope please!

```
<Count>12</Count>
12
<Smoker>false</Smoker>
False
<Pi>3.1415926535</Pi>
3.1415926535
```

That seems very simple and intuitive. It looks like if I use the LINQ to XML API instead of the W3C DOM XML API, errors like the one in Listing 6-1 of the previous chapter will be a thing of the past.

While all of those examples make obtaining an element's value simple, they are all cases of casting the element to the same data type that its value initially was. This is not necessary. All that is necessary is for the element's value to be able to be converted to the specified data type. Listing 7-11 shows an example where the initial data type is String, but I will obtain its value as a Boolean.

Listing 7-11. *Casting a Node to a Different Data Type Than Its Value's Original Data Type*

```
Dim smoker As New XElement("Smoker", "true")
Console.WriteLine(smoker)
Console.WriteLine(CType(smoker, Boolean))
```

Since I have specified the value of the element to be "true", and since the string "true" can be successfully converted to a Boolean, the code works:

```
<Smoker>true</Smoker>
True
```

Unfortunately, exactly how the values get converted is not specified, but it appears that the conversion methods in the System.Xml.XmlConvert class are used for this purpose. Listing 7-12 demonstrates that this is the case when casting as a Boolean.

Listing 7-12. *Casting to a Boolean Calls the System.Xml.XmlConvert.ToBoolean Method*

```
Try
  Dim smoker As New XElement("Smoker", "Tue")
  Console.WriteLine(smoker)
  Console.WriteLine(CType(smoker, Boolean))
Catch ex As Exception
  Console.WriteLine(ex)
End Try
```

Notice that I intentionally misspell "True" in Listing 7-12 to force an exception in the conversion hoping for a clue to be revealed in the exception that is thrown. Will I be so lucky? Let's press Ctrl+F5 to find out.

```
<Smoker>Tue</Smoker>
System.FormatException: The string 'tue' is not a valid Boolean value.
   at System.Xml.XmlConvert.ToBoolean(String s)
...
```

As you can see, the exception occurred in the call to the System.Xml.XmlConvert.ToBoolean method.

■**Note** You may use the Value property to retrieve the value of an XElement object, as opposed to casting to obtain the value. See Listing 7-13 for an example using the Value property.

The LINQ to XML Object Model

With the new LINQ to XML API comes a new object model containing many new classes that exist in the System.Xml.Linq namespace. One is the static class where the LINQ to XML extension methods live, Extensions; two are comparer classes, XNodeDocumentOrderComparer and XNodeEqualityComparer; and the remaining are used to build your XML trees. Those remaining classes are displayed in the diagram shown in Figure 7-1.

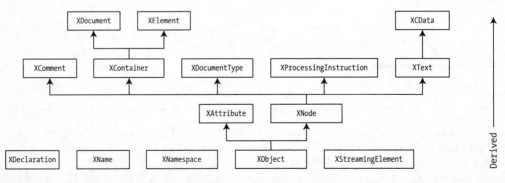

Figure 7-1. *LINQ to XML API object model*

There are some interesting things to notice:

1. Of those remaining classes, three are abstract, XObject, XContainer, and XNode, so you will never be constructing them.

2. An attribute, XAttribute, is not derived from a node, XNode. In fact, it is not a node at all but instead is a totally different type of class that is basically a name-value pair.

3. Streaming elements, XStreamingElement, have no inheritance relationship with elements, XElement.

4. The XDocument and XElement classes are the only classes that have child nodes derived from XNode.

These are the classes you will use to build your XML trees. Most notably, you will use the XElement class, because as I have already discussed, the LINQ to XML API is very element-centric, as opposed to document-centric like the W3C DOM XML API.

Deferred Query Execution, Node Removal, and the Halloween Problem

This section serves as a warning that there are some goblins out there to be leery of. First up is *deferred query execution*. Never forget that many of the LINQ operators defer query execution until absolutely necessary, and this can cause potential side effects.

Another problem to be on the lookout for is the *Halloween problem*. The Halloween problem earned its name because it was first openly discussed among a small group of experts on Halloween. The problem is basically any problem that occurs by changing data that is being iterated over that affects the iteration. It was first detected by database engineers while working on the database optimizer. Their run-in with the problem occurred when their test query was changing the value of a database column that the optimizer they were developing was using as an index. Their test query would retrieve a record based on an index created over one of the table's columns and the query would change the value in that column. Since that column affected the indexing of the record, the record appeared again farther down in the list of records, causing it to be retrieved again in the same query and reprocessed. This caused an endless loop, because every time it was retrieved from the record set, it was updated and moved farther down the record set where it would only be picked up again and processed the same way indefinitely.

You may have seen the Halloween problem yourself even though you may not have known the name for it. Have you ever worked with some sort of collection, iterated through it, and deleted an item, and this caused the iteration to break or misbehave? I have seen this recently working with a major suite of ASP.NET server controls. The suite has a DataGrid server control, and I needed to remove selected records from it. I iterated through the records from start to finish, deleting the ones I needed to, but in doing so, it messed up the pointers being used for the iteration. The result was some records that should not have been deleted were, and some that should have been deleted were not. I called the vendor for support and its solution was to iterate through the records backward. This resolved the problem.

With LINQ to XML, you will most likely run into this problem when removing nodes from an XML tree, although it can occur at other times, so you want to keep this in your mind when you are coding. Let's examine the example in Listing 7-13.

Listing 7-13. *Intentionally Exposing the Halloween Problem*

```
Dim xDocument = _
  <?xml version="1.0"?>
  <BookParticipants>
    <BookParticipant type="Author">
      <FirstName>Dennis</FirstName>
      <LastName>Hayes</LastName>
    </BookParticipant>
    <BookParticipant type="Editor">
      <FirstName>Ewan</FirstName>
      <LastName>Buckingham</LastName>
    </BookParticipant>
  </BookParticipants>

' I'll get a sequence of BookParticipant elements.  I need a sequence of some
' elements to remove to demonstrate the Halloween problem.
Dim elements As IEnumerable(Of XElement) = _
  xDocument.Element("BookParticipants").Elements("BookParticipant")

' Just so you can see the actual source elements in the sequence...
For Each element As XElement In elements
  ' First, we will display the source elements.
  Console.WriteLine( _
    "Source element: {0} : value = {1}", _
    element.Name, element.Value)
Next element
' Ok, I have the BookParticipant elements.

' Now that we have seen the sequence of source elements, I'll enumerate
' through the sequence removing them one at a time.
For Each element As XElement In elements
  ' Now, I'll remove each element.
  Console.WriteLine("Removing {0} = {1} ...", element.Name, element.Value)
  element.Remove()
Next element

Console.WriteLine(xDocument)
```

In the previous code, I first build my XML document using an XML literal. By including the xml declaration, an object of type XDocument is created for me. Had I omitted the xml declaration, an object of type XElement would have been created instead.

Next, I build a sequence of the BookParticipant elements. This is the sequence I will enumerate through, removing elements. Next, I display each element in my sequence so you can see that I do indeed have two BookParticipant elements. I then enumerate through the sequence again, displaying a message that I am removing the element, and I remove the BookParticipant element. I then display the resulting XML document.

If the Halloween problem does not manifest itself, you should see the "Removing ..." message twice; and when the XML document is displayed at the end, you should have an empty BookParticipants element. Here are the results:

```
Source element: BookParticipant : value = DennisHayes
Source element: BookParticipant : value = EwanBuckingham
Removing BookParticipant = DennisHayes ...
<BookParticipants>
  <BookParticipant type="Editor">
    <FirstName>Ewan</FirstName>
    <LastName>Buckingham</LastName>
  </BookParticipant>
</BookParticipants>
```

Just as I anticipated, there are two source BookParticipant elements in the sequence to remove. You can see the first one, Dennis Hayes, gets removed. However, you never see the second one get removed, and when I display the resulting XML document, the last BookParticipant element is still there. The enumeration misbehaved; the Halloween problem got me. Keep in mind that the Halloween problem does not always manifest itself in the same way. Sometimes enumerations may terminate sooner than they should; sometimes they throw exceptions. Their behavior varies depending on exactly what is happening.

I know that you are wondering, what is the solution? The solution for this case is to cache the elements and to enumerate through the cache instead of through the normal enumeration technique, which relies on internal pointers that are getting corrupted by the removal or modification of elements. For this example, I will cache the sequence of elements using one of the Standard Query Operators that is designed for the purpose of caching to prevent deferred query execution problems. I will use the ToArray operator. Listing 7-14 shows the same code as before, except I call the ToArray operator and enumerate on it.

Listing 7-14. *Preventing the Halloween Problem*

```vbnet
Dim xDocument = _
  <?xml version="1.0"?>
  <BookParticipants>
    <BookParticipant type="Author">
      <FirstName>Dennis</FirstName>
      <LastName>Hayes</LastName>
    </BookParticipant>
    <BookParticipant type="Editor">
      <FirstName>Ewan</FirstName>
      <LastName>Buckingham</LastName>
    </BookParticipant>
  </BookParticipants>

' I'll get a sequence of BookParticipant elements.  I need a sequence of some
' elements to remove to demonstrate the Halloween problem.
```

```
Dim elements As IEnumerable(Of XElement) = _
  xDocument.Element("BookParticipants").Elements("BookParticipant")

'  Just so you can see the actual source elements in the sequence...
For Each element As XElement In elements
  ' First, we will display the source elements.
  Console.WriteLine( _
    "Source element: {0} : value = {1}", _
    element.Name, element.Value)
Next element
'  Ok, I have the BookParticipant elements.

'  Now that we have seen the sequence of source elements, I'll enumerate
'  through the sequence removing them one at a time.
For Each element As XElement In elements.ToArray()
  ' Now, I'll remove each element.
  Console.WriteLine("Removing {0} = {1} ...", element.Name, element.Value)
  element.Remove()
Next element

Console.WriteLine(xDocument)
```

This code is identical to the previous example except I call the ToArray operator in the final enumeration where I remove the elements. Here are the results:

```
Source element: BookParticipant : value = DennisHayes
Source element: BookParticipant : value = EwanBuckingham
Removing BookParticipant = DennisHayes ...
Removing BookParticipant = EwanBuckingham ...
<BookParticipants />
```

Notice that this time I got two messages informing me that a BookParticipant element was being removed. Also, when I display the XML document after the removal, I do have an empty BookParticipants element because all the child elements have been removed. The Halloween problem has been foiled!

XML Creation

As I have already discussed, functional construction provided by the LINQ to XML API makes creating an XML tree a breeze compared to the W3C DOM XML API. We will now take a look at creating each of the major XML classes in the LINQ to XML API.

Because the new API is centered on elements, and that is what you will be creating the majority of the time, I cover creating elements with the XElement class first. I then cover the rest of the XML classes in alphabetical order. However, before we begin our examination of creating elements with the XElement class, let's review XML literals, the easiest way to create XML with VB.NET.

Creating XML with XML Literals

The easiest way to create XML in VB.NET is to write it directly into your code! As you have seen in Listings 7-13 and 7-14, creating XML with an XML literal is as easy as assigning an XML tree to a variable. The compiler will translate the XML literal into the appropriate LINQ to XML objects for you.

While using XML literals is incredibly easy when you have a static XML format as in Listings 7-13 and 7-14, combining XML literals with LINQ allows you to dynamically create XML documents on the fly. Thanks to embedded expressions, specified with the `<%= expression %>` syntax, you can render XML content based on the value of the embedded expression. For example, in Listing 7-16, I will use an embedded expression to dynamically generate XML for each object in an array.

While many of the examples in this chapter will not use XML literals so that I can demonstrate the LINQ to XML API, you will see several examples leveraging XML literals so that you can appreciate the power of this new VB.NET feature. For a complete explanation of XML literals and the new XML-specific VB.NET language features, please consult Chapter 2.

Creating Elements with XElement

First, you should keep in mind that with the new API, the `XElement` class is the one you will use most. That said, let's take a look at instantiating an `XElement` object. `XElement` has several constructors, but I am going to examine two of them:

```
Public Sub New (name As XName, content As Object)
Public Sub New (name As XName, ParamArray content As Object())
```

The first constructor is the simplest case where an element has a text value and no child nodes. It's as simple as Listing 7-15.

Listing 7-15. *Creating an Element Using the First Overload*

```
Dim firstName As New XElement("FirstName", "Dennis")
Console.WriteLine(CType(firstName, String))
```

The first argument of the constructor is an `XName` object. As previously mentioned, an `XName` object will be created by implicitly converting the input `String` to an `XName`. The second argument is a single object representing the element's content. In this case, the content is a `String` with the value of `"Dennis"`. The API will convert that `String` literal of `"Dennis"` to an `XText` object for me on the fly. Notice that I am taking advantage of the new node value extraction capabilities to get the value from the `firstName` element variable. That is, I am casting the element to the type of its value, which in this case is a `String`. So the value of the `firstName` element variable will be extracted. Here are the results:

```
Dennis
```

The data type of the single content object is very flexible. It is the data type of the content object that controls its relationship to the element to which it is added. Table 7-1 shows all of the allowed content object data types and how they are handled.

Table 7-1. *LINQ to XML Object to Parent Insertion Behavior Table*

Content Object Data Type	Manner Handled
String	A String object or string literal is automatically converted to an XText object and handled as XText from there.
XText	This object can have either a String or an XText value. It is added as a child node of the element but treated as the element's text content.
XCData	This object can have either a String or an XCData value. It is added as a child node of the element but treated as the element's CData content.
XElement	This object is added as a child element.
XAttribute	This object is added as an attribute.
XProcessingInstruction	This object is added as child content.
XComment	This object is added as child content.
IEnumerable	This object is enumerated and the handling of the object types is applied recursively.
Nothing	This object is ignored. You may be wondering why you would ever want to pass Nothing into the constructor of an element, but it turns out that this can be quite handy for XML transformations.
Any remaining type	The ToString method is called, and the resulting value is treated as String content.

Remember that even though the element's value may be stored as a String, as it would be for *any remaining type*[1] such as an integer, thanks to the new node value extraction facilities you can get it out as the original type. So for example, if when you create the XElement object you specify an Integer as the content object, by casting the node to an Integer, you get the value converted to an Integer for you. As long as you are casting to one of the data types a cast operator is provided for, and as long as the element's value can be converted to the type you are casting to, casting provides a simple way of obtaining the element's value.

The second XElement constructor listed previously is just like the first one, except you can provide multiple objects for the content. This is what makes functional construction so powerful. You need only examine Listing 7-1 or Listing 7-2 to see an example using the second constructor where multiple content objects are provided to the XElement constructor.

For the next example, I will create the standard BookParticipants XML tree that I have been using, but instead of hard-coding the element values with string literals, I will retrieve the data from a LINQ-queryable data source. In this case, the data source will be an array.

First, I need a class that the data can be stored in. Also, since I have types of BookParticipants, I will create an Enum for the different types, as follows:

---

1.   This term is explained in Table 7-1.

An Enum and Class for the Next Example

```vb.net
Public Enum ParticipantTypes
  Author = 0
  Editor
End Enum

Public Class BookParticipant
  Public FirstName As String
  Public LastName As String
  Public ParticipantType As ParticipantTypes
End Class
```

Now, I will build an array of the BookParticipant type and generate an XML tree using a LINQ query to retrieve the data from the array, as shown in Listing 7-16.

Listing 7-16. *Generating an XML Tree with a LINQ Query*

```vb.net
Dim bookParticipants() As BookParticipant = { _
  New BookParticipant With { _
    .FirstName = "Dennis", _
    .LastName = "Hayes", _
    .ParticipantType = ParticipantTypes.Author}, _
  New BookParticipant With { _
    .FirstName = "Ewan", _
    .LastName = "Buckingham", _
    .ParticipantType = ParticipantTypes.Editor}}

Dim xBookParticipants = _
  <BookPartecipants>
    <%= From p In bookParticipants Select _
      <BookPartecipant type=<%= p.ParticipantType %>>
        <FirstName><%= p.FirstName %></FirstName>
        <LastName><%= p.LastName %></LastName>
      </BookPartecipant> _
    %>
  </BookPartecipants>

Console.WriteLine(xBookParticipants)
```

In the previous code, I create an array of BookParticipant objects named bookParticipants. Next, the code queries the values from the bookParticipants array by using an embedded expression containing a LINQ query expression. The code then generates a BookParticipant element for each array element. This example really leverages VB.NET, because it uses an XML literal and an embedded expression, neither of which is available in C#. XML literals and embedded expressions are covered in detail in Chapter 2.

Here is the XML tree generated by the previous code:

```
<BookParticipants>
  <BookParticipant type="Author">
    <FirstName>Dennis</FirstName>
    <LastName>Hayes</LastName>
  </BookParticipant>
  <BookParticipant type="Editor">
    <FirstName>Ewan</FirstName>
    <LastName>Buckingham</LastName>
  </BookParticipant>
</BookParticipants>
```

Imagine trying to do that with the W3C DOM XML API. Actually, you don't have to imagine it; you can just look at Listing 6-1 because that code creates the same XML tree.

Creating Attributes with XAttribute

Unlike the W3C DOM XML API, attributes do not inherit from nodes. An attribute, implemented in LINQ to XML with the XAttribute class, is a name-value pair that is stored in a collection of XAttribute objects belonging to an XElement object.

I can create an attribute and add it to its element on the fly, using functional construction as shown in Listing 7-17.

Listing 7-17. *Creating an Attribute with Functional Construction*

```
Dim xBookParticipant As _
  New XElement("BookParticipant", _
    New XAttribute("type", "Author"))

Console.WriteLine(xBookParticipant)
```

Running this code provides the following results:

```
<BookParticipant type="Author" />
```

Sometimes, however, you can't create the attribute at the same time its element is being constructed. For that, you must instantiate one and then add it to its element as in Listing 7-18.

Listing 7-18. *Creating an Attribute and Adding It to Its Element*

```
Dim xBookParticipant As New XElement("BookParticipant")
Dim xAttribute As New XAttribute("type", "Author")
xBookParticipant.Add(xAttribute)

Console.WriteLine(xBookParticipant)
```

The results are identical:

```
<BookParticipant type="Author" />
```

Notice again how flexible the XElement.Add method is. It accepts any object, applying the same rules for the element's content that are followed when instantiating an XElement. Sweet! Dude!

Creating Comments with XComment

Creating comments with LINQ to XML is trivial. XML comments are implemented in LINQ to XML with the XComment class.

You can create a comment and add it to its element on the fly, using functional construction as in Listing 7-19.

Listing 7-19. *Creating a Comment with Functional Construction*

```
Dim xBookParticipant As _
  New XElement("BookParticipant", _
    New XComment("This person is retired."))

Console.WriteLine(xBookParticipant)
```

Running this code provides the following results:

```
<BookParticipant>
  <!--This person is retired.-->
</BookParticipant>
```

Sometimes, however, you can't create the comment at the same time its element is being constructed. For that, you must instantiate one and then add it to its element as in Listing 7-20.

Listing 7-20. *Creating a Comment and Adding It to Its Element*

```
Dim xBookParticipant As New XElement("BookParticipant")
Dim xComment As New XComment("This person is retired.")
xBookParticipant.Add(xComment)

Console.WriteLine(xBookParticipant)
```

The results are identical:

```
<BookParticipant>
  <!--This person is retired.-->
</BookParticipant>
```

Creating Containers with XContainer

Because XContainer is an abstract class, you cannot instantiate it. Instead, you must instantiate one of its sublcasses, XDocument or XElement. Conceptually, an XContainer is a class that inherits from the XNode class that can contain other classes inheriting from XNode.

Creating Declarations with XDeclaration

With the LINQ to XML API, creating XML document declarations is a simple matter. XML declarations are implemented in LINQ to XML with the XDeclaration class.

Unlike most of the other classes in the LINQ to XML API, declarations are meant to be added to an XML document, not an element. Do you recall though how flexible the constructor was for the XElement class? Any class it wasn't specifically designed to handle would have its ToString method called, and that text would be added to the element as text content. So you can inadvertently add a declaration using the XDeclaration class to an element. But it will not give you the results you are looking for.

■**Caution** While XML declarations apply to an XML document as a whole and should be added to an XML document, an XElement object will gladly accept an XDeclaration object being added to it. However, this will not be the result you are after.

We can create a declaration and add it to an XML document on the fly, using functional construction as in Listing 7-21.

Listing 7-21. *Creating a Declaration with Functional Construction*

```
Dim xDocument As New XDocument( _
    New XDeclaration("1.0", "UTF-8", "yes"), _
    New XElement("BookParticipant"))

Console.WriteLine(xDocument)
```

This code produces the following results:

```
<BookParticipant />
```

Did you notice that the declaration is missing from the output? That's right; the ToString method will omit the declaration. However, if you debug the code and put a watch on the document, you will see that the declaration is there.

Sometimes, however, you can't create the declaration at the same time the document is being constructed. For that, you must instantiate one and then set the document's Declaration property to the instantiated declaration as in Listing 7-22.

Listing 7-22. *Creating a Declaration and Setting the Document's Declaration Property to It*

```
Dim xDocument As New XDocument(New XElement("BookParticipant"))

Dim xDeclaration As New XDeclaration("1.0", "UTF-8", "yes")
xDocument.Declaration = xDeclaration

Console.WriteLine(xDocument)
```

This code produces the following results:

```
<BookParticipant />
```

Again, notice that the declaration does not get output when a document's `ToString` method is called. But just as with the previous example, if you debug the code and examine the document, the declaration is indeed there.

Creating Document Types with XDocumentType

The LINQ to XML API makes creating document type definitions a fairly painless operation. XML document types are implemented in LINQ to XML with the `XDocumentType` class.

Unlike most of the other classes in the LINQ to XML API, document types are meant to be added to an XML document, not an element. Do you recall though how flexible the constructor was for the `XElement` class? Any class it wasn't specifically designed to handle would have its `ToString` method called, and that text would be added to the element as text content. So you can inadvertently add a document type using the `XDocumentType` class to an element. But it will not give you the results you are looking for.

■**Caution** While XML document types apply to an XML document as a whole and should be added to an XML document, an `XElement` object will gladly accept an `XDocumentType` object being added to it. However, this will not be the result you are after.

You can create a document type and add it to an XML document on the fly, using functional construction as in Listing 7-23.

Listing 7-23. *Creating a Document Type with Functional Construction*

```
Dim xDocument As New XDocument( _
  New XDocumentType( _
    "BookParticipants", _
    Nothing, _
    "BookParticipants.dtd", _
    Nothing), _
  New XElement("BookParticipants"))

Console.WriteLine(xDocument)
```

This code produces the following results:

```
<!DOCTYPE BookParticipants SYSTEM "BookParticipants.dtd">
<BookParticipants />
```

Sometimes, however, you can't create the document type at the same time the document is being constructed. For that, you must instantiate one and then add it to the document as in Listing 7-24.

Listing 7-24. *Creating a Document Type and Adding It to a Document*

```vb
Dim xDocument As New XDocument()

Dim documentType As New XDocumentType( _
  "BookParticipants", _
  Nothing, _
  "BookParticipants.dtd", _
  Nothing)

xDocument.Add(documentType, New XElement("BookParticipants"))

Console.WriteLine(xDocument)
```

The following is the result of this code:

```
<!DOCTYPE BookParticipants SYSTEM "BookParticipants.dtd">
<BookParticipants />
```

Notice in the previous code that I did not add any elements prior to adding the document type. If you do add a document type after adding any elements, you will receive the following exception:

```
Unhandled Exception: System.InvalidOperationException: This operation would create
an incorrectly structured document.
...
```

So if you are going to specify a document type after the document's instantiation, make sure you do not specify any elements during the document's instantiation using functional construction or add any elements prior to adding the document type.

Creating Documents with XDocument

I have probably stated this so many times by now that you are sick of hearing it, but with LINQ to XML, it isn't necessary to create an XML document just to create an XML tree or fragment. However, should the need arise, creating an XML document with LINQ to XML is trivial too. XML documents are implemented in LINQ to XML with the XDocument class. Listing 7-25 is an example.

Listing 7-25. *A Simple Example of Creating an XML Document with XDocument*

```
Dim xDocument As New XDocument()
Console.WriteLine(xDocument)
```

This code produces no output, though, because the XML document is empty. The previous example may be a little too trivial, so I will create a document with all the LINQ to XML classes that are specifically designed to be added to an XDocument object, as shown in Listing 7-26.

Listing 7-26. *A Slightly More Complex Example of Creating an XML Document with XDocument*

```
Dim xDocument As New XDocument( _
  New XDeclaration("1.0", "UTF-8", "yes"), _
  New XDocumentType( _
    "BookParticipants", _
    Nothing, _
    "BookParticipants.dtd", _
    Nothing), _
  New XProcessingInstruction( _
    "BookCataloger", _
    "out-of-print"), _
  New XElement( _
    "BookParticipants"))

Console.WriteLine(xDocument)
```

Both the processing instruction and element can be added to elements as well, but I wanted to create an XML document with some meat, so here it is. And I wanted to include a processing instruction so you could see one in action.

The results of this code are the following:

```
<!DOCTYPE BookParticipants SYSTEM "BookParticipants.dtd">
<?BookCataloger out-of-print?>
<BookParticipants />
```

You may have noticed that the declaration is missing. Just as was mentioned with the examples of creating declarations, the document's ToString method omits the declaration from its output. However, if you debug the code and examine the document, you will see that the declaration is there.

Creating Names with XName

As I discussed earlier in this chapter, with LINQ to XML, you have no need to directly create names via the XName object. In fact, the XName class has no public constructors, so there is no way for you to instantiate one. An XName object will get created for you from a string, and optionally a namespace, automatically when an XName object is required.

An XName object consists of a LocalName, which is a String, and a namespace, which is an XNamespace.

Listing 7-27 is some code calling the XElement constructor requiring an XName as its only argument.

Listing 7-27. *Sample Code Where an XName Object Is Created for You*

```
Dim xBookParticipant As New XElement("BookParticipant")
Console.WriteLine(xBookParticipant)
```

In the previous example, I instantiate an XElement object by passing the element's name as a String, so an XName object is created for me with a LocalName of BookParticipant and is assigned to the XElement object's Name property. In this case, no namespace is provided, so the XName object has no namespace.

Pressing Ctrl+F5 reveals the following results:

```
<BookParticipant />
```

I could have specified a namespace with the code in Listing 7-28.

Listing 7-28. *Sample Code Where an XName Object Is Created for You and a Namespace Is Specified*

```
Dim ns As XNamespace = "http://www.linqdev.com/Books"
Dim xBookParticipant As New XElement(ns + "BookParticipant")
Console.WriteLine(xBookParticipant)
```

This code will output this XML:

```
<BookParticipant xmlns="http://www.linqdev.com/Books" />
```

For more information about creating names using the LINQ to XML API, see the section titled "Names, Namespaces, and Prefixes" earlier in this chapter.

Creating Namespaces with XNamespace

In the LINQ to XML API, namespaces are implemented with the XNamespace class. For an example of creating and using a namespace, see the previous example, Listing 7-28. It demonstrates creating a namespace with the XNamespace class.

For more information about creating namespaces using the LINQ to XML API, see the section titled "Names, Namespaces, and Prefixes" earlier in this chapter.

Creating Nodes with XNode

Because XNode is an abstract class, you cannot instantiate it. Instead, you must instantiate one of its subclasses: XComment, XContainer, XDocumentType, XProcessingInstruction, or XText. Conceptually, an XNode is any class that functions as a node in the XML tree.

Creating Processing Instructions with XProcessingInstruction

Processing instructions have never been easier to create than with the LINQ to XML API. With the LINQ to XML API, processing instructions are implemented with the XProcessingInstruction class.

You can create processing instructions at the document or element level. Listing 7-29 shows an example of doing both on the fly using functional construction.

Listing 7-29. *Creating a Processing Instruction at Both the Document and Element Levels*

```
Dim xDocument As New XDocument( _
  New XProcessingInstruction("BookCataloger", "out-of-print"), _
  New XElement("BookParticipants", _
    New XElement("BookParticipant", _
      New XProcessingInstruction("ParticipantDeleter", "delete"), _
      New XElement("FirstName", "Dennis"), _
      New XElement("LastName", "Hayes"))))

Console.WriteLine(xDocument)
```

In the previous code, I added a processing instruction to both the document and the BookParticipant element. Before displaying the results, I want to take a second to point out just how well this functional construction flows. It is a very simple matter to create this XML tree with two processing instructions. Comparing this to my very first sample program in the previous chapter, Listing 6-1, again proves how much the new LINQ to XML API is going to simplify your code. And, lastly, here are the results:

```
<?BookCataloger out-of-print?>
<BookParticipants>
  <BookParticipant>
    <?ParticipantDeleter delete?>
    <FirstName>Dennis</FirstName>
    <LastName>Hayes</LastName>
  </BookParticipant>
</BookParticipants>
```

By now I would presume you can already imagine the code for adding a processing instruction after construction, since it would be just like adding any of the other nodes I have already covered. So instead of boring you with the mundane, Listing 7-30 shows a significantly cooler example of creating and adding a processing instruction after the fact.

Listing 7-30. *A More Complex Example of Adding Processing Instructions After the Document and Element Have Been Constructed*

```
Dim xDocument = _
  <?xml version="1.0"?>
  <BookParticipants>
    <BookParticipant>
```

```
          <FirstName>Dennis</FirstName>
          <LastName>Hayes</LastName>
        </BookParticipant>
      </BookParticipants>

Dim xPI1 As New XProcessingInstruction("BookCataloger", "out-of-print")
xDocument.AddFirst(xPI1)

Dim xPI2 As New XProcessingInstruction("ParticipantDeleter", "delete")

Dim outOfPrintParticipant As XElement = _
  xDocument.<BookParticipants>.<BookParticipant> _
    .Where(Function(e) e.<FirstName>.Value = "Dennis" AndAlso _
                       e.<LastName>.Value = "Hayes") _
    .Single()

outOfPrintParticipant.AddFirst(xPI2)

Console.WriteLine(xDocument)
```

There are several items worth mentioning in this code sample. First, I created the XML document using an XML literal. Because I specified the xml version in the literal, an XDocument is created rather than an XElement. Next, I added a processing instruction to the document. However, here I am using the XElement.AddFirst method to make it the first child node of the document, as opposed to the XElement.Add method, which would just append it to the end of the document's child nodes, which may be too late for any processing instruction to be honored.

In addition, to add a processing instruction to one of the elements, I had to have a reference to it. Here, I used XML literals to query down into the XML tree. Notice that I query into the XDocument's BookParticipants.BookParticipant elements using the XML literal <BookParticipants>.<BookParticipant>. Even cooler is that I can then append a Where operator call after that XML literal to further query the XML where each BookParticipant element's FirstName element equals "Dennis" and the LastName element equals "Hayes". Notice that, yet again, I used XML literals, this time in the lambda expression for the Where operator. Using XML literals and combining LINQ operators with them is a luxury C# developers can only dream of. For full coverage of XML literals, please consult Chapter 2.

Finally, the Where operator returns an IEnumerable(Of T), but I want an XElement object directly. So, in my coverage of the LINQ to Objects deferred Standard Query Operators in Chapter 5, I recall that there is an operator that will return the actual element from a sequence, provided there is only one, and that operator is the Single operator. Once I have the reference to the proper XElement object with that query, it is trivial to add the processing instruction to it and display the results. And, speaking of results, here they are:

```
<?BookCataloger out-of-print?>
<BookParticipants>
  <BookParticipant>
    <?ParticipantDeleter delete?>
    <FirstName>Dennis</FirstName>
```

```
    <LastName>Hayes</LastName>
  </BookParticipant>
</BookParticipants>
```

Creating Streaming Elements with XStreamingElement

Do you recall in Part 2 of this book, "LINQ to Objects," that many of the Standard Query Operators actually defer their work until the time the returned data is enumerated over? If I call some operators that do in fact defer their operation, and I want to project my query's output as XML, I would have a dilemma. On the one hand, I want to take advantage of the deferred nature of the operator since there is no need to do work until it needs to be done. But on the other hand, my LINQ to XML API call will cause the query to execute immediately.

Notice in Listing 7-31 that even though I change the fourth element of the names array when I output my XElement object's value, the XML tree contains the original value. This is because the xNames element was fully created before I changed the names array element.

Listing 7-31. *Immediate Execution of the XML Tree Construction*

```
Dim names() As String = {"John", "Paul", "George", "Pete"}

Dim xNames = _
  <Beatles>
    <%= From n In names Select _
      <Name><%= n %></Name> %>
  </Beatles>

names(3) = "Ringo"

Console.WriteLine(xNames)
```

Before discussing the results of this code, I want to point out just how cool this example is. Notice that I am using an XML literal to create an element whose name is Beatles and whose content is generated by an embedded expression. The embedded expression returns a sequence of XElement objects whose element is named Name. This code produces the following XML tree:

```
<Beatles>
  <Name>John</Name>
  <Name>Paul</Name>
  <Name>George</Name>
  <Name>Pete</Name>
</Beatles>
```

That is pretty awesome. Each XElement object from the sequence becomes a child element. How cool is that? As I mentioned, notice that even though I changed names(3) to "Ringo" prior to outputting the XML, the last element still contains Pete, the original value. This is because the names sequence has to be enumerated in order to construct the XElement object, thereby immediately executing the query.

If I do indeed want the XML tree construction deferred, I need another way to do this, and that is exactly what streaming elements are for. With LINQ to XML, a streaming element is implemented with the XStreamingElement class.

So Listing 7-32 shows the same basic example, except this time I cannot use an XML literal, because I need XStreamingElement objects created instead of XElement objects. Therefore, I will use functional construction instead of XML literals.

Listing 7-32. *Demonstrating the Deferred Execution of the XML Tree Construction by Using the XStreamingElement Class*

```
Dim names() As String = {"John", "Paul", "George", "Pete"}

Dim xNames As New XStreamingElement( _
  "Beatles", From n In names Select New XStreamingElement("Name", n))

names(3) = "Ringo"

Console.WriteLine(xNames)
```

If this works as I have explained, the last Name node's value will now be Ringo and not Pete. But the proof is in the pudding:

```
<Beatles>
  <Name>John</Name>
  <Name>Paul</Name>
  <Name>George</Name>
  <Name>Ringo</Name>
</Beatles>
```

Sorry, Pete, it looks like you have been replaced yet again.

Creating Text with XText

Creating an element with a text value is a pretty simple task. Listing 7-33 is some code doing just that.

Listing 7-33. *Creating an Element and Assigning a String As Its Value*

```
Dim xFirstName As New XElement("FirstName", "Dennis")
Console.WriteLine(xFirstName)
```

This is straightforward, and there are no surprises. Running the code by pressing Ctrl+F5 produces the following results:

```
<FirstName>Dennis</FirstName>
```

What is hidden though is the fact that the string "Dennis" is converted into an XText object, and it is that object that is added to the XElement object. In fact, examining the xFirstName object in the debugger reveals that it contains a single node, an XText object whose value is "Dennis". Since this is all done automatically for you, in most circumstances you will not need to directly construct a text object.

However, should the need arise, you can create a text object by instantiating an XText object as shown in Listing 7-34.

Listing 7-34. *Creating a Text Node and Passing It As the Value of a Created Element*

```
Dim xName As New XText("Dennis")
Dim xFirstName As New XElement("FirstName", xName)
Console.WriteLine(xFirstName)
```

This code produces the exact same output as the previous example, and if we examine the internal state of the xFirstName object, it too is identical to the one created in the previous example:

```
<FirstName>Dennis</FirstName>
```

Creating CData with XCData

Creating an element with a CData value is also pretty simple. Listing 7-35 is an example.

Listing 7-35. *Creating an XCData Node and Passing It As the Value of a Created Element*

```
Dim xErrorMessage As New XElement( _
  "HTMLMessage", New XCData("<H1>Invalid user id or password.</H1>"))

Console.WriteLine(xErrorMessage)
```

This code produces the following output:

```
<HTMLMessage><![CDATA[<H1>Invalid user id or password.</H1>]]></HTMLMessage>
```

As you can see, the LINQ to XML API makes handling CData simple.

XML Output

Of course, creating, modifying, and deleting XML data does no good if you cannot persist the changes. This section contains a few ways to output your XML.

Saving with XDocument.Save()

You can save your XML document using any of several XDocument.Save methods. Here is a list of overloads:

```
Public Sub Save (fileName As String)
Public Sub Save (textWriter As TextWriter)
Public Sub Save (writer As XmlWriter)
Public Sub Save (fileName As String, options As SaveOptions)
Public Sub Save (textWriter As TextWriter, options As SaveOptions)
```

Listing 7-36 is an example where I save the XML document to a file in my project's folder.

Listing 7-36. *Saving a Document with the XDocument.Save Method*

```
Dim xDocument As New XDocument( _
  New XElement("BookParticipants", _
    New XElement("BookParticipant", _
      New XAttribute("type", "Author"), _
      New XAttribute("experience", "first-time"), _
      New XAttribute("language", "English"), _
      New XElement("FirstName", "Dennis"), _
      New XElement("LastName", "Hayes"))))


xDocument.Save("bookparticipants.xml")
```

Notice that I called the Save method on an *object* of type XDocument. This is because the Save methods are instance methods. The Load methods you will read about later in the "XML Input" section are static methods and must be called on the XDocument or XElement *class*.

Here are the contents of the generated bookparticipants.xml file when viewing them in a text editor such as Notepad:

```
<?xml version="1.0" encoding="utf-8"?>
<BookParticipants>
  <BookParticipant type="Author" experience="first-time" language="English">
    <FirstName>Dennis</FirstName>
    <LastName>Hayes</LastName>
  </BookParticipant>
</BookParticipants>
```

That XML document output is easy to read because the version of the Save method that I called is formatting the output. That is, if I call the version of the Save method that accepts a String fileName and a SaveOptions argument, passing a value of SaveOptions.None would give the same results as the previous. Had I called the Save method like this

```
xDocument.Save("bookparticipants.xml", SaveOptions.DisableFormatting)
```

the results in the file would look like this:

```
<?xml version="1.0" encoding="utf-8"?><BookParticipants><BookParticipant type=
"Author" experience="first-time" language="English"><FirstName>Dennis</FirstName>
<LastName>Hayes</LastName></BookParticipant></BookParticipants>
```

This is one single continuous line of text. However, you would have to examine the file in a text editor to see the difference because a browser will format it nicely for you.

Of course, you can use any of the other Save overloads available to output your document as well; it's up to you.

Saving with XElement.Save()

I have said many times that with the LINQ to XML API, creating an XML document is not necessary. And to save your XML to a file, it still isn't. The XElement class has several Save overloads for this purpose:

```
Public Sub Save (fileName As String)
Public Sub Save (textWriter As TextWriter)
Public Sub Save (writer As XmlWriter)
Public Sub Save (fileName As String, options As SaveOptions)
Public Sub Save (textWriter As TextWriter, options As SaveOptions)
```

Listing 7-37 is an example very similar to the previous, except I never even create an XML document.

Listing 7-37. *Saving an Element with the XElement.Save Method*

```
Dim bookParticipants As _
  New XElement("BookParticipants", _
    New XElement("BookParticipant", _
      New XAttribute("type", "Author"), _
      New XAttribute("experience", "first-time"), _
      New XAttribute("language", "English"), _
      New XElement("FirstName", "Dennis"), _
      New XElement("LastName", "Hayes")))

bookParticipants.Save("bookparticipants.xml")
```

And the saved XML looks identical to the previous example where I actually have an XML document:

```
<?xml version="1.0" encoding="utf-8"?>
<BookParticipants>
  <BookParticipant type="Author" experience="first-time" language="English">
    <FirstName>Dennis</FirstName>
    <LastName>Hayes</LastName>
  </BookParticipant>
</BookParticipants>
```

XML Input

Creating and persisting XML to a file does no good if you can't load it back into an XML tree. Here are some techniques to read XML back in.

Loading with XDocument.Load()

Now that you know how to save your XML documents and fragments, you would probably like to know how to load them. You can load your XML document using any of several overloads. Here is a list:

```
Public Shared Function Load (uri As String) As XDocument
Public Shared Function Load (textReader As TextReader ) As XDocument
Public Shared Function Load (reader As XmlReader) As XDocument
Public Shared Function Load (uri As String, options As LoadOptions) As XDocument
Public Shared Function Load (textReader As TextReader, options As LoadOptions) _
  As XDocument
Public Shared Function Load (reader As XmlReader, options As LoadOptions) _
  As XDocument
```

You may notice how symmetrical these overloads are to the XDocument.Save overloads. However, there are a couple differences worth pointing out. First, in the Save overloads, you must call the Save method on an *object* of XDocument or XElement type because the Save method is an instance method. But the Load method is Shared, so you must call it on the XDocument *class* itself. Second, the Save overloads that accept a String are requiring file names to be passed, whereas the Load overloads that accept a String are allowing a URI to be passed.

Additionally, the Load method allows a parameter of type LoadOptions to be specified while loading the XML document. The LoadOptions Enum has the options shown in Table 7-2.

Table 7-2. *The LoadOptions Enumeration*

Option	Description
LoadOptions.None	Use this option to specify that no load options are to be used.
LoadOptions.PreserveWhitespace	Use this option to preserve the whitespace in the XML source, such as blank lines.
LoadOptions.SetLineInfo	Use this option so that you may obtain the line and position of any object inheriting from XObject by using the IXmlLineInfo interface.
LoadOptions.SetBaseUri	Use this option so that you may obtain the base URI of any object inheriting from XObject.

These options can be combined with a bitwise Or operation. However, some options will not work in some contexts. For example, when creating an element or a document by parsing a string, there is no line information available, nor is there a base URI. Or, when creating a document with an XmlReader, there is no base URI.

Listing 7-38 shows an example where I load my XML document created in the previous example, Listing 7-37.

Listing 7-38. *Loading a Document with the XDocument.Load Method*

```vb
Dim xDocument As XDocument = xDocument.Load( _
  "bookparticipants.xml", LoadOptions.SetBaseUri Or LoadOptions.SetLineInfo)

Console.WriteLine(xDocument)

Dim firstName = xDocument...<FirstName>.First()

Console.WriteLine( _
  "FirstName Line:{0} - Position:{1}", _
  (CType(firstName, IXmlLineInfo)).LineNumber, _
  (CType(firstName, IXmlLineInfo)).LinePosition)

Console.WriteLine("FirstName Base URI:{0}", firstName.BaseUri)
```

■**Note** You must either add an `Imports` statement for `System.Xml`, if one is not present, or specify the namespace when referencing the `IXmlLineInfo` interface in your code; otherwise, the `IXmlLineInfo` type will not be found.

This code is loading the same XML file I created in the previous example. After I load and display the document, I obtain a reference for the `FirstName` element using the VB.NET descendant axis property and an XML literal so that I can display the line and position of the element in the source XML document. How can anyone not love those VB.NET axis properties? Then I display the base URI for the element.

Here are the results:

```
<BookParticipants>
  <BookParticipant type="Author" experience="first-time" language="English">
    <FirstName>Dennis</FirstName>
    <LastName>Hayes</LastName>
  </BookParticipant>
</BookParticipants>
FirstName Line:4 - Position:6
FirstName Base URI:file:///C:/Documents and Settings/…/Projects/LINQChapter7/
LINQChapter7/bin/Debug/bookparticipants.xml
```

This output looks just as I would expect, with one possible exception. First, the actual XML document looks fine. I see the line and position of the `FirstName` element, but the line number is causing me concern. It is shown as four, but in the displayed XML document, the `FirstName` element is on the third line. What is that about? If you examine the XML document I loaded, you will see that it begins with the document declaration, which is omitted from the output:

```
<?xml version="1.0" encoding="utf-8"?>
```

This is why the FirstName element is being reported as being on line four.

Loading with XElement.Load()

Just as you could save from either an XDocument or XElement, we can load from either as well. Loading into an element is virtually identical to loading into a document. Here are the overloads available:

```
Public Shared Function Load (uri As String) As XDocument
Public Shared Function Load (textReader As TextReader ) As XDocument
Public Shared Function Load (reader As XmlReader) As XDocument
Public Shared Function Load (uri As String, options As LoadOptions) As XDocument
Public Shared Function Load (textReader As TextReader, options As LoadOptions) _
  As XDocument
Public Shared Function Load (reader As XmlReader, options As LoadOptions) _
  As XDocument
```

These overloads are Shared just like the XDocument.Load overloads, so they must be called from the XElement class directly. Listing 7-39 contains an example loading the same XML file I saved with the XElement.Save method in Listing 7-37.

Listing 7-39. *Loading an Element with the XElement.Load Method*

```
Dim xElement As XElement = xElement.Load("bookparticipants.xml")
Console.WriteLine(xElement)
```

Just as you already expect, the output looks like the following:

```
<BookParticipants>
  <BookParticipant type="Author" experience="first-time" language="English">
    <FirstName>Dennis</FirstName>
    <LastName>Hayes</LastName>
  </BookParticipant>
</BookParticipants>
```

Just as the XDocument.Load method does, the XElement.Load method has overloads that accept a LoadOptions parameter. Please see the description of these in the "Loading with XDocument.Load()" section previously in the chapter.

Parsing with XDocument.Parse() or XElement.Parse()

How many times have you passed XML around in your programs as a String, only to suddenly need to do some serious XML work? Getting the data from a String variable to an XML document type variable always seems like such a hassle. Well, worry yourself no longer. One of my personal favorite features of the LINQ to XML API is the Parse method.

Both the XDocument and XElement classes have a static method named Parse for parsing XML strings. I think by now you probably feel comfortable accepting that if you can parse with the XDocument class, you can probably parse with the XElement class, and vice-versa. And since the LINQ to XML API is all about the elements, baby, I am going to only give you an element example this time.

In the "Saving with XDocument.Save()" section earlier in this chapter, I show the output of the Save method if the LoadOptions parameter is specified as DisableFormatting. The result is a single string of XML. For the example in Listing 7-40, I start with that XML string (after escaping the inner quotes), parse it into an element, and output the XML element to the screen.

Listing 7-40. *Parsing an XML String into an Element*

```
Dim xml As String = _
  "<?xml version=""1.0"" encoding=""utf-8""?><BookParticipants>" & _
  "<BookParticipant type=""Author"" experience=""first-time"" language=" & _
  """""English""><FirstName>Dennis</FirstName><LastName>Hayes</LastName>" & _
  "</BookParticipant></BookParticipants>"

Dim xElement As XElement = xElement.Parse(xml)
Console.WriteLine(xElement)
```

The results are the following:

```
<BookParticipants>
  <BookParticipant type="Author" experience="first-time" language="English">
    <FirstName>Dennis</FirstName>
    <LastName>Hayes</LastName>
  </BookParticipant>
</BookParticipants>
```

How cool is that? Remember the old days when you had to create a document using the W3C DOM XML XmlDocument class? Thanks to the elimination of document centricity, you can turn XML strings into real XML trees in the blink of an eye with one method call.

XML Traversal

XML traversal is primarily accomplished with 4 properties and 11 methods. In this section, I try to mostly use the same code example for each property or method, except I change a single argument on one line when possible. The example in Listing 7-41 builds a full XML document.

Listing 7-41. *A Base Example Subsequent Examples May Be Derived From*

```
Dim xDocument = _
  <?xml version="1.0" encoding="utf-8" standalone="yes"?>
  <?BookCataloger out-of-print?>
  <BookParticipants>
    <BookParticipant type="Author">
```

```
      <FirstName>Dennis</FirstName>
      <LastName>Hayes</LastName>
    </BookParticipant>
    <BookParticipant type="Editor">
      <FirstName>Ewan</FirstName>
      <LastName>Buckingham</LastName>
    </BookParticipant>
  </BookParticipants>

Dim firstParticipant = xDocument...<BookParticipant>(0)

Console.WriteLine(xDocument)
```

First, notice that I used an XML literal to define the XML. Next, I obtained a reference to the first BookParticipant element using the VB.NET 2008 descendant and indexer axis properties. I do this so that I can have a base element from which to do all the traversal. While I did not use the firstParticipant variable in this example, I will in the subsequent traversal examples. The next thing to notice is the argument for the Console.WriteLine method. In this case, I output the document itself. As I progress through these traversal examples, I change that argument to demonstrate how to traverse the XML tree. So here is the output showing the document from the previous example:

```
<?BookCataloger out-of-print?>
<BookParticipants>
  <BookParticipant type="Author">
    <FirstName>Dennis</FirstName>
    <LastName>Hayes</LastName>
  </BookParticipant>
  <BookParticipant type="Editor">
    <FirstName>Ewan</FirstName>
    <LastName>Buckingham</LastName>
  </BookParticipant>
</BookParticipants>
```

Traversal Properties

I will begin my discussion with the primary traversal properties. When directions (up, down, etc.) are specified, they are relative to the element the method is called on. In the subsequent examples, I have obtained a reference to the first BookParticipant element, and it is the base element used for the traversal.

Forward with XNode.NextNode

Traversing forward through the XML tree is accomplished with the NextNode property. Listing 7-42 is an example.

Listing 7-42. *Traversing Forward from an XElement Object via the NextNode Property*

```
Dim xDocument = _
  <?xml version="1.0" encoding="utf-8" standalone="yes"?>
  <?BookCataloger out-of-print?>
  <BookParticipants>
    <BookParticipant type="Author">
      <FirstName>Dennis</FirstName>
      <LastName>Hayes</LastName>
    </BookParticipant>
    <BookParticipant type="Editor">
      <FirstName>Ewan</FirstName>
      <LastName>Buckingham</LastName>
    </BookParticipant>
  </BookParticipants>

Dim firstParticipant = xDocument...<BookParticipant>(0)

Console.WriteLine(firstParticipant.NextNode)
```

Since the base element is the first BookParticipant element, firstParticipant, traversing forward should provide me with the second BookParticipant element. Here are the results:

```
<BookParticipant type="Editor">
  <FirstName>Ewan</FirstName>
  <LastName>Buckingham</LastName>
</BookParticipant>
```

Based on these results I would say I am right on the money. Would you believe me if I told you that if I had accessed the PreviousNode property of the element it would have been Nothing, since it is the first node in its parent's node list? It's true, but I'll leave you the task of proving it to yourself.

Backward with XNode.PreviousNode

If you want to traverse the XML tree backward, use the PreviousNode property. Since there is no previous node for the first participant node, I'll get tricky and access the NextNode property first, obtaining the second participant node, as I did in the previous example, from which I will obtain the PreviousNode. If you got lost in that, I will end up back to the first participant node. That is, I will go forward with NextNode to then go backward with PreviousNode, leaving me where I started. If you have ever heard the expression "taking one step forward and taking two steps back," with just one more access of the PreviousNode property, you could actually do that. LINQ makes it possible. Listing 7-43 is the example.

Listing 7-43. *Traversing Backward from an XElement Object via the PreviousNode Property*

```
Dim xDocument = _
  <?xml version="1.0" encoding="utf-8" standalone="yes"?>
  <?BookCataloger out-of-print?>
  <BookParticipants>
    <BookParticipant type="Author">
      <FirstName>Dennis</FirstName>
      <LastName>Hayes</LastName>
    </BookParticipant>
    <BookParticipant type="Editor">
      <FirstName>Ewan</FirstName>
      <LastName>Buckingham</LastName>
    </BookParticipant>
  </BookParticipants>

Dim firstParticipant = xDocument...<BookParticipant>(0)

Console.WriteLine(firstParticipant.NextNode.PreviousNode)
```

If this works as I expect, I should have the first BookParticipant element's XML:

```
<BookParticipant type="Author">
  <FirstName>Dennis</FirstName>
  <LastName>Hayes</LastName>
</BookParticipant>
```

LINQ to XML actually makes traversing an XML tree fun.

Up to Document with XObject.Document

Obtaining the XML document from an XElement object is as simple as accessing the Document property of the element. So please notice my change to the Console.WriteLine method call, shown in Listing 7-44.

Listing 7-44. *Accessing the XML Document from an XElement Object via the Document Property*

```
Dim xDocument = _
  <?xml version="1.0" encoding="utf-8" standalone="yes"?>
  <?BookCataloger out-of-print?>
  <BookParticipants>
    <BookParticipant type="Author">
      <FirstName>Dennis</FirstName>
      <LastName>Hayes</LastName>
    </BookParticipant>
    <BookParticipant type="Editor">
      <FirstName>Ewan</FirstName>
      <LastName>Buckingham</LastName>
```

```
  </BookParticipant>
 </BookParticipants>

Dim firstParticipant = xDocument...<BookParticipant>(0)

Console.WriteLine(firstParticipant.Document)
```

This will output the document, which is the same output as Listing 7-41, and here is the output to prove it:

```
<?BookCataloger out-of-print?>
<BookParticipants>
  <BookParticipant type="Author">
    <FirstName>Dennis</FirstName>
    <LastName>Hayes</LastName>
  </BookParticipant>
  <BookParticipant type="Editor">
    <FirstName>Ewan</FirstName>
    <LastName>Buckingham</LastName>
  </BookParticipant>
</BookParticipants>
```

Up with XObject.Parent

If you need to go up one level in the tree, it will probably be no surprise that the Parent property will do the job. Changing the node passed to the WriteLine method to what's shown in Listing 7-45 changes the output (as you will see).

Listing 7-45. *Traversing Up from an XElement Object via the Parent Property*

```
Dim xDocument = _
  <?xml version="1.0" encoding="utf-8" standalone="yes"?>
  <?BookCataloger out-of-print?>
  <BookParticipants>
    <BookParticipant type="Author">
      <FirstName>Dennis</FirstName>
      <LastName>Hayes</LastName>
    </BookParticipant>
    <BookParticipant type="Editor">
      <FirstName>Ewan</FirstName>
      <LastName>Buckingham</LastName>
    </BookParticipant>
  </BookParticipants>

Dim firstParticipant = xDocument...<BookParticipant>(0)

Console.WriteLine(firstParticipant.Parent)
```

The output is changed to this:

```
<BookParticipants>
  <BookParticipant type="Author">
    <FirstName>Dennis</FirstName>
    <LastName>Hayes</LastName>
  </BookParticipant>
  <BookParticipant type="Editor">
    <FirstName>Ewan</FirstName>
    <LastName>Buckingham</LastName>
  </BookParticipant>
</BookParticipants>
```

Don't let that fool you either. This is not the entire document. Notice it is missing the processing instruction.

Traversal Methods

To demonstrate the traversal methods, since they return sequences of multiple nodes, I must now change that single Console.WriteLine method call to a For Each loop to output the potential multiple nodes. This will result in the former call to the Console.WriteLine method looking basically like this:

```
For Each node As XNode In firstParticipant.Nodes()
    Console.WriteLine(node)
Next node
```

From example to example, the only thing changing will be the method called on the firstParticipant node in the For Each statement.

Down with XContainer.Nodes()

No, I am not expressing my disdain for nodes. Nor am I stating I am all in favor of nodes, as in being "down for" rock climbing, meaning being excited about the prospect of going rock climbing. I am merely describing the direction of traversal I am about to discuss.

Traversing down an XML tree is easily accomplished with a call to the Nodes method. It will return a sequence of an object's child XNode objects. In case you snoozed through some of the earlier chapters, a sequence is an IEnumerable(Of T), meaning an IEnumerable of some type T. Listing 7-46 is the example.

Listing 7-46. *Traversing Down from an XElement Object via the Nodes Method*

```
Dim xDocument = _
  <?xml version="1.0" encoding="utf-8" standalone="yes"?>
  <?BookCataloger out-of-print?>
  <BookParticipants>
    <BookParticipant type="Author">
      <FirstName>Dennis</FirstName>
      <LastName>Hayes</LastName>
```

```
    </BookParticipant>
    <BookParticipant type="Editor">
      <FirstName>Ewan</FirstName>
      <LastName>Buckingham</LastName>
    </BookParticipant>
  </BookParticipants>

Dim firstParticipant = xDocument...<BookParticipant>(0)

For Each node As XNode In firstParticipant.Nodes()
    Console.WriteLine(node)
Next node
```

Here is the output:

```
<FirstName>Dennis</FirstName>
<LastName>Hayes</LastName>
```

Don't forget, that method is returning all child nodes, not just elements. So any other nodes in the first participant's list of child nodes will be included. This could include comments (XComment), text (XText), processing instructions (XProcessingInstruction), document type (XDocumentType), or elements (XElement). Also notice that it does not include the attribute because an attribute is not a node.

To provide a better example of the Nodes method, let's look at the code in Listing 7-47. It is similar to the base example with some extra nodes thrown in.

Listing 7-47. *Traversing Down from an XElement Object via the Nodes Method with Additional Node Types*

```
Dim xDocument = _
  <?xml version="1.0" encoding="utf-8" standalone="yes"?>
  <?BookCataloger out-of-print?>
  <BookParticipants>
    <BookParticipant type="Author">
      <!--This is a new author.-->
      <?AuthorHandler new?>
      <FirstName>Dennis</FirstName>
      <LastName>Hayes</LastName>
    </BookParticipant>
    <BookParticipant type="Editor">
      <FirstName>Ewan</FirstName>
      <LastName>Buckingham</LastName>
    </BookParticipant>
  </BookParticipants>

Dim firstParticipant = xDocument...<BookParticipant>(0)
```

```
For Each node As XNode In firstParticipant.Nodes()
    Console.WriteLine(node)
Next node
```

This example is different than the previous in that there is now a comment and process-ing instruction added to the first BookParticipant element. Pressing Ctrl+F5 displays the following:

```
<!--This is a new author.-->
<?AuthorHandler new?>
<FirstName>Dennis</FirstName>
<LastName>Hayes</LastName>
```

We can now see the comment and the processing instruction. What if you only want a cer-tain type of node, though, such as just the elements? Do you recall from Chapter 4 the OfType operator? I can use that operator to return only the nodes that are of a specific type, such as XElement. Using the same basic code as Listing 7-47, to return just the elements, I will merely change the For Each line, as shown in Listing 7-48.

Listing 7-48. *Using the OfType Operator to Return Just the Elements*

```
Dim xDocument = _
  <?xml version="1.0" encoding="utf-8" standalone="yes"?>
  <?BookCataloger out-of-print?>
  <BookParticipants>
    <BookParticipant type="Author">
      <!--This is a new author.-->
      <?AuthorHandler new?>
      <FirstName>Dennis</FirstName>
      <LastName>Hayes</LastName>
    </BookParticipant>
    <BookParticipant type="Editor">
      <FirstName>Ewan</FirstName>
      <LastName>Buckingham</LastName>
    </BookParticipant>
  </BookParticipants>

Dim firstParticipant = xDocument...<BookParticipant>(0)

For Each node As XNode In firstParticipant.Nodes().OfType(Of XElement)()
    Console.WriteLine(node)
Next node
```

As you can see, the XComment and XProcessingInstruction objects are still being created. But since I am now calling the OfType operator, the code produces these results:

```
<FirstName>Dennis</FirstName>
<LastName>Hayes</LastName>
```

Are you starting to see how cleverly all the new VB.NET language features and LINQ are coming together? Isn't it cool that we can use that Standard Query Operator to restrict the sequence of XML nodes this way? So if you want to get just the comments from the first BookParticipant element, could you use the OfType operator to do so? Of course you could, and the code would look like Listing 7-49.

Listing 7-49. *Using the OfType Operator to Return Just the Comments*

```
Dim xDocument = _
  <?xml version="1.0" encoding="utf-8" standalone="yes"?>
  <?BookCataloger out-of-print?>
  <BookParticipants>
    <BookParticipant type="Author">
      <!--This is a new author.-->
      <?AuthorHandler new?>
      <FirstName>Dennis</FirstName>
      <LastName>Hayes</LastName>
    </BookParticipant>
    <BookParticipant type="Editor">
      <FirstName>Ewan</FirstName>
      <LastName>Buckingham</LastName>
    </BookParticipant>
  </BookParticipants>

Dim firstParticipant = xDocument...<BookParticipant>(0)

For Each node As XNode In firstParticipant.Nodes().OfType(Of XComment)()
    Console.WriteLine(node)
Next node
```

Here is the output:

```
<!--This is a new author.-->
```

Just to be anticlimactic, can you use the OfType operator to get just the attributes? No, you cannot. This is a trick question. Remember that unlike the W3C DOM XML API, with the LINQ to XML API, attributes are not nodes in the XML tree. They are a sequence of name-value pairs hanging off the element. To get to the attributes of the first BookParticipant node, I would change the code to that in Listing 7-50.

Listing 7-50. *Accessing an Element's Attributes Using the Attributes Method*

```
Dim xDocument = _
  <?xml version="1.0" encoding="utf-8" standalone="yes"?>
  <?BookCataloger out-of-print?>
  <BookParticipants>
    <BookParticipant type="Author">
      <!--This is a new author.-->
```

```
      <?AuthorHandler new?>
      <FirstName>Dennis</FirstName>
      <LastName>Hayes</LastName>
    </BookParticipant>
    <BookParticipant type="Editor">
      <FirstName>Ewan</FirstName>
      <LastName>Buckingham</LastName>
    </BookParticipant>
  </BookParticipants>

Dim firstParticipant = xDocument...<BookParticipant>(0)

For Each attr As XAttribute In firstParticipant.Attributes()
    Console.WriteLine(attr)
Next attr
```

Notice I had to change more than just the property or method of the first BookParticipant element that I was accessing. I also had to change the enumeration variable type to XAttribute, because XAttribute doesn't inherit from XNode. Here are the results:

```
type="Author"
```

Down with XContainer.Elements()

Because the LINQ to XML API is so focused on elements, and that is what we are working with most, Microsoft provides a quick way to get just the elements of an element's child nodes using the Elements method. It is the equivalent of calling the OfType(Of XElement) method on the sequence returned by the Nodes method.

Listing 7-51 is an example that is logically the same as Listing 7-48.

Listing 7-51. *Accessing an Element's Child Elements Using the Elements Method*

```
Dim xDocument = _
  <?xml version="1.0" encoding="utf-8" standalone="yes"?>
  <?BookCataloger out-of-print?>
  <BookParticipants>
    <BookParticipant type="Author">
      <!--This is a new author.-->
      <?AuthorHandler new?>
      <FirstName>Dennis</FirstName>
      <LastName>Hayes</LastName>
    </BookParticipant>
    <BookParticipant type="Editor">
      <FirstName>Ewan</FirstName>
      <LastName>Buckingham</LastName>
    </BookParticipant>
  </BookParticipants>
```

```
Dim firstParticipant = xDocument...<BookParticipant>(0)

For Each node As XNode In firstParticipant.Elements()
    Console.WriteLine(node)
Next node
```

This code produces the exact same results as Listing 7-48:

```
<FirstName>Dennis</FirstName>
<LastName>Hayes</LastName>
```

The Elements method also has an overloaded version that allows you to pass the name of the element you are looking for, as in Listing 7-52.

Listing 7-52. *Accessing Named Child Elements Using the Elements Method*

```
Dim xDocument = _
  <?xml version="1.0" encoding="utf-8" standalone="yes"?>
  <?BookCataloger out-of-print?>
  <BookParticipants>
    <BookParticipant type="Author">
      <!--This is a new author.-->
      <?AuthorHandler new?>
      <FirstName>Dennis</FirstName>
      <LastName>Hayes</LastName>
    </BookParticipant>
    <BookParticipant type="Editor">
      <FirstName>Ewan</FirstName>
      <LastName>Buckingham</LastName>
    </BookParticipant>
  </BookParticipants>

Dim firstParticipant = xDocument...<BookParticipant>(0)

For Each node As XNode In firstParticipant.Elements("FirstName")
    Console.WriteLine(node)
Next node
```

■**Tip** While the purpose of this example is to demonstrate the LINQ to XML API's Elements method, don't forget that you could have accomplished the same result using the VB.NET 2008 child axis property by replacing the Elements method call with firstParticipant.<FirstName>.

This code produces the following:

```
<FirstName>Dennis</FirstName>
```

Down with XContainer.Element()

You may obtain the first child element matching a specified name using the Element method. Instead of a sequence being returned requiring a For Each loop, I will have a single element returned, as shown in Listing 7-53.

Listing 7-53. *Accessing the First Child Element with a Specified Name*

```
Dim xDocument = _
  <?xml version="1.0" encoding="utf-8" standalone="yes"?>
  <?BookCataloger out-of-print?>
  <BookParticipants>
    <BookParticipant type="Author">
      <!--This is a new author.-->
      <?AuthorHandler new?>
      <FirstName>Dennis</FirstName>
      <LastName>Hayes</LastName>
    </BookParticipant>
    <BookParticipant type="Editor">
      <FirstName>Ewan</FirstName>
      <LastName>Buckingham</LastName>
    </BookParticipant>
  </BookParticipants>

Dim firstParticipant = xDocument...<BookParticipant>(0)

Console.WriteLine(firstParticipant.Element("FirstName"))
```

■**Tip** Since the Element method retrieves the first child element matching the specified name, we could have combined the VB.NET 2008 child axis property with the indexer axis property to obtain the same result. Instead of calling the Element method, you could call firstParticipant.<FirstName>(0).

This code outputs the following:

```
<FirstName>Dennis</FirstName>
```

Up Recursively with XNode.Ancestors()

While you can obtain the single parent element using a node's Parent property, you can get a sequence of the ancestor elements using the Ancestors method. This is different in that it recursively traverses up the XML tree instead of stopping one level up, and it only returns elements, as opposed to nodes.

To make this demonstration more clear, I will add a child node to the first book participant's FirstName element. Also, instead of enumerating through the ancestors of the first BookParticipant element, I use an XML literal to reach down two levels to the newly added NickName element. This provides more ancestors to provide greater clarity. The code is shown in Listing 7-54.

Listing 7-54. *Traversing Up from an XElement Object via the Ancestors Method*

```
Dim xDocument = _
  <?xml version="1.0" encoding="utf-8" standalone="yes"?>
  <?BookCataloger out-of-print?>
  <BookParticipants>
    <BookParticipant type="Author">
      <!--This is a new author.-->
      <?AuthorHandler new?>
      <FirstName>Dennis<NickName>Spider</NickName></FirstName>
      <LastName>Hayes</LastName>
    </BookParticipant>
    <BookParticipant type="Editor">
      <FirstName>Ewan</FirstName>
      <LastName>Buckingham</LastName>
    </BookParticipant>
  </BookParticipants>

Dim firstParticipant = xDocument...<BookParticipant>(0)


For Each element As XElement In _
    firstParticipant.<FirstName>.<NickName>.Ancestors()
  Console.WriteLine(element.Name)
Next element
```

Again, please notice I added a child node to the first book participant's FirstName element. This causes the first book participant's FirstName element to have contents that include an XText object equal to the string "Dennis", and to have a child element, NickName. I retrieve the first book participant's FirstName element's NickName element for which to retrieve the ancestors. In addition, notice I used an XElement type variable instead of an XNode type for enumerating through the sequence returned from the Ancestors method. This is so I can access the Name property of the element. Instead of displaying the element's XML as I have done in past examples, I am only displaying the name of each element in the ancestor's sequence. I do this because it would be confusing to display each ancestor's XML, because each would include the previous and it would get very recursive, thereby obscuring the results. That all said, here they are:

```
FirstName
BookParticipant
BookParticipants
```

Just as expected, the code recursively traverses up the XML tree.

Up Recursively with XElement.AncestorsAndSelf()

This method works just like the Ancestors method, except it includes itself in the returned sequence of ancestors. Listing 7-55 is the same example as before, except it calls the AncestorsAndSelf method.

Listing 7-55. *Traversing Up from an XElement Object via the AncestorsAndSelf Method*

```
Dim xDocument = _
  <?xml version="1.0" encoding="utf-8" standalone="yes"?>
  <?BookCataloger out-of-print?>
  <BookParticipants>
    <BookParticipant type="Author">
      <!--This is a new author.-->
      <?AuthorHandler new?>
      <FirstName>Dennis<NickName>Spider</NickName></FirstName>
      <LastName>Hayes</LastName>
    </BookParticipant>
    <BookParticipant type="Editor">
      <FirstName>Ewan</FirstName>
      <LastName>Buckingham</LastName>
    </BookParticipant>
  </BookParticipants>

Dim firstParticipant = xDocument...<BookParticipant>(0)

For Each element As XElement In _
    firstParticipant.<FirstName>.<NickName>.AncestorsAndSelf()
  Console.WriteLine(element.Name)
Next element
```

The results should be the same as when calling the Ancestors method, except I should also see the NickName element's name at the beginning of the output:

```
NickName
FirstName
BookParticipant
BookParticipants
```

Down Recursively with XContainer.Descendants()

In addition to recursively traversing up, you can recursively traverse down with the Descendants method. Again, this method only returns elements. There is an equivalent method named DescendantNodes that will return all descendant nodes. Listing 7-56 is the same code as the previous, except I call the Descendants method on the first book participant element.

Listing 7-56. *Traversing Down from an XElement Object via the Descendants Method*

```
Dim xDocument = _
  <?xml version="1.0" encoding="utf-8" standalone="yes"?>
  <?BookCataloger out-of-print?>
  <BookParticipants>
    <BookParticipant type="Author">
      <!--This is a new author.-->
      <?AuthorHandler new?>
      <FirstName>Dennis<NickName>Spider</NickName></FirstName>
      <LastName>Hayes</LastName>
    </BookParticipant>
    <BookParticipant type="Editor">
      <FirstName>Ewan</FirstName>
      <LastName>Buckingham</LastName>
    </BookParticipant>
  </BookParticipants>

Dim firstParticipant = xDocument...<BookParticipant>(0)

For Each element As XElement In firstParticipant.Descendants()
    Console.WriteLine(element.Name)
Next element
```

The results are the following:

```
FirstName
NickName
LastName
```

As you can see, it traverses all the way to the end of every branch in the XML tree.

■Tip While there is a VB.NET 2008 descendant axis property, it requires that you specify the name of a descendant element to retrieve and will therefore not substitute for the Descendants overload requiring no name that is demonstrated in Listing 7-56. It can, however, substitute for the Descendants overload that accepts an XName parameter.

Down Recursively with XElement.DescendantsAndSelf()

Just as the Ancestors method has an AncestorsAndSelf method variation, so too does the
Descendants method. The DescendantsAndSelf method works just like the Descendants method,
except it also includes the element itself in the returned sequence. Listing 7-57 is the same
example that I used for the Descendants method call, with the exception that now it calls the
DescendantsAndSelf method.

Listing 7-57. *Traversing Down from an XElement Object via the DescendantsAndSelf Method*

```
Dim xDocument = _
  <?xml version="1.0" encoding="utf-8" standalone="yes"?>
  <?BookCataloger out-of-print?>
  <BookParticipants>
    <BookParticipant type="Author">
      <!--This is a new author.-->
      <?AuthorHandler new?>
      <FirstName>Dennis<NickName>Spider</NickName></FirstName>
      <LastName>Hayes</LastName>
    </BookParticipant>
    <BookParticipant type="Editor">
      <FirstName>Ewan</FirstName>
      <LastName>Buckingham</LastName>
    </BookParticipant>
  </BookParticipants>

Dim firstParticipant = xDocument...<BookParticipant>(0)

For Each element As XElement In firstParticipant.DescendantsAndSelf()
  Console.WriteLine(element.Name)
Next element
```

So does the output also include the firstParticipant element's name?

```
BookParticipant
FirstName
NickName
LastName
```

Of course it does.

Forward with XNode.NodesAfterSelf()

For this example, in addition to changing the For Each call, I add a couple of comments to the
BookParticipants element to make the distinction between retrieving nodes and elements
more evident, since XComment is a node but not an element. Listing 7-58 is what the code looks
like for this example.

Listing 7-58. *Traversing Forward from the Current Node Using the NodesAfterSelf Method*

```
Dim xDocument = _
  <?xml version="1.0" encoding="utf-8" standalone="yes"?>
  <?BookCataloger out-of-print?>
  <BookParticipants>
    <!--Begin Of List-->
    <BookParticipant type="Author">
      <FirstName>Dennis</FirstName>
      <LastName>Hayes</LastName>
    </BookParticipant>
    <BookParticipant type="Editor">
      <FirstName>Ewan</FirstName>
      <LastName>Buckingham</LastName>
    </BookParticipant>
    <!--End Of List-->
  </BookParticipants>

Dim firstParticipant = xDocument...<BookParticipant>(0)

For Each node As XNode In firstParticipant.NodesAfterSelf()
    Console.WriteLine(node)
Next node
```

Notice that I added two comments that are siblings of the two BookParticipant elements. This modification to the constructed XML document will be made for the NodesAfterSelf, ElementsAfterSelf, NodesBeforeSelf, and ElementsBeforeSelf examples.

This causes all sibling nodes after the first BookParticipant node to be enumerated. Here are the results:

```
<BookParticipant type="Editor">
  <FirstName>Ewan</FirstName>
  <LastName>Buckingham</LastName>
</BookParticipant>
<!--End Of List-->
```

As you can see, the last comment is included in the output because it is a node. Don't let that output fool you. The NodesAfterSelf method only returns two nodes: the BookParticipant element whose type attribute is Editor and the End Of List comment. Those other nodes, FirstName and LastName are merely displayed because the ToString method is being called on the BookParticipant node.

Keep in mind that this method returns nodes, not just elements. If you want to limit the type of nodes returned, you could use the TypeOf operator as I have demonstrated in previous examples. But if the type you are interested in is elements, there is a method just for that called ElementsAfterSelf.

Forward with XNode.ElementsAfterSelf()

This example uses the same modifications to the XML document made in Listing 7-58 concerning the addition of two comments.

To get a sequence of just the sibling elements after the referenced node, you call the ElementsAfterSelf method, as shown in Listing 7-59.

Listing 7-59. *Traversing Forward from the Current Node Using the ElementsAfterSelf Method*

```
Dim xDocument = _
  <?xml version="1.0" encoding="utf-8" standalone="yes"?>
  <?BookCataloger out-of-print?>
  <BookParticipants>
    <!--Begin Of List-->
    <BookParticipant type="Author">
      <FirstName>Dennis</FirstName>
      <LastName>Hayes</LastName>
    </BookParticipant>
    <BookParticipant type="Editor">
      <FirstName>Ewan</FirstName>
      <LastName>Buckingham</LastName>
    </BookParticipant>
    <!--End Of List-->
  </BookParticipants>

Dim firstParticipant = xDocument...<BookParticipant>(0)

For Each node As XNode In firstParticipant.ElementsAfterSelf()
    Console.WriteLine(node)
Next node
```

The example code with these modifications produces the following results:

```
<BookParticipant type="Editor">
  <FirstName>Ewan</FirstName>
  <LastName>Buckingham</LastName>
</BookParticipant>
```

Notice that the comment is excluded this time because it is not an element. Again, the FirstName and LastName elements are only displayed because they are the content of the BookParticipant element that was retrieved and because the ToString method was called on the element.

Backward with XNode.NodesBeforeSelf()

This example uses the same modifications to the XML document made in Listing 7-58 concerning the addition of two comments.

This method works just like NodesAfterSelf except it retrieves the sibling nodes before the referenced node. In the example code, since the initial reference into the document is the first BookParticipant node, I obtain a reference to the second BookParticipant node using the NextNode property of the first BookParticipant node so that there are more nodes to return, as shown in Listing 7-60.

Listing 7-60. *Traversing Backward from the Current Node*

```
Dim xDocument = _
  <?xml version="1.0" encoding="utf-8" standalone="yes"?>
  <?BookCataloger out-of-print?>
  <BookParticipants>
    <!--Begin Of List-->
    <BookParticipant type="Author">
      <FirstName>Dennis</FirstName>
      <LastName>Hayes</LastName>
    </BookParticipant>
    <BookParticipant type="Editor">
      <FirstName>Ewan</FirstName>
      <LastName>Buckingham</LastName>
    </BookParticipant>
    <!--End Of List-->
  </BookParticipants>

Dim firstParticipant = xDocument...<BookParticipant>(0)

For Each node As XNode In firstParticipant.NextNode.NodesBeforeSelf()
    Console.WriteLine(node)
Next node
```

This modification should result in the return of the first BookParticipant node and the first comment. Here are the results:

```
<!--Begin Of List-->
<BookParticipant type="Author">
  <FirstName>Dennis</FirstName>
  <LastName>Hayes</LastName>
</BookParticipant>
```

Interesting! I was expecting the two nodes that were returned, the comment and the first BookParticipant, to be in the reverse order. I expected the method to start with the referenced node and build a sequence via the PreviousNode property. Perhaps it did indeed do this but then called the Reverse or InDocumentOrder operator. I cover the InDocumentOrder operator in the next chapter. Again, don't let the FirstName and LastName nodes confuse you. The NodesBeforeSelf method did not return those. It is only because the ToString method was called on the first BookParticipant node, by the Console.WriteLine method, that they are displayed.

Backward with XNode.ElementsBeforeSelf()

This example uses the same modifications to the XML document made in Listing 7-58 concerning the addition of two comments.

Just like the NodesAfterSelf method has a companion method named ElementsAfterSelf to return only the elements, so too does the NodesBeforeSelf method. The ElementsBeforeSelf method returns only the sibling elements before the referenced node, as shown in Listing 7-61.

Listing 7-61. *Traversing Backward from the Current Node*

```
Dim xDocument = _
  <?xml version="1.0" encoding="utf-8" standalone="yes"?>
  <?BookCataloger out-of-print?>
  <BookParticipants>
    <!--Begin Of List-->
    <BookParticipant type="Author">
      <FirstName>Dennis</FirstName>
      <LastName>Hayes</LastName>
    </BookParticipant>
    <BookParticipant type="Editor">
      <FirstName>Ewan</FirstName>
      <LastName>Buckingham</LastName>
    </BookParticipant>
    <!--End Of List-->
  </BookParticipants>

Dim firstParticipant = xDocument...<BookParticipant>(0)

For Each node As XNode In firstParticipant.NextNode.ElementsBeforeSelf()
    Console.WriteLine(node)
Next node
```

Notice that again I obtain a reference to the second BookParticipant node via the NextNode property. Will the output contain the comment?

```
<BookParticipant type="Author">
  <FirstName>Dennis</FirstName>
  <LastName>Hayes</LastName>
</BookParticipant>
```

Of course not, because it is not an element.

XML Modification

Modifying XML data is easier than ever with the LINQ to XML API. With just a handful of methods, you can perform all the modifications you could want. Whether it is adding, changing, or deleting nodes or elements, there is a method to get the job done.

As has been stated time and time again, with the LINQ to XML API, you will be working with XElement objects most of the time. Because of this, the majority of these examples are with elements. The LINQ to XML API classes inheriting from XNode are covered first, followed by a section on attributes.

Adding Nodes

In this section on adding nodes to an XML tree, I start with a base example of the code in Listing 7-62.

Listing 7-62. *A Base Example with a Single Book Participant*

```
Dim xDocument = _
  <?xml version="1.0"?>
  <BookParticipants>
    <BookParticipant type="Author">
      <FirstName>Dennis</FirstName>
      <LastName>Hayes</LastName>
    </BookParticipant>
  </BookParticipants>

Console.WriteLine(xDocument)
```

This code produces an XML tree with a single book participant. Here is the code's output:

```
<BookParticipants>
  <BookParticipant type="Author">
    <FirstName>Dennis</FirstName>
    <LastName>Hayes</LastName>
  </BookParticipant>
</BookParticipants>
```

For the different methods to add nodes, I will start with this basic code.

■**Note** While the following examples all add elements, the techniques used to add the elements work for all LINQ to XML classes that inherit from the XNode class.

In addition to the following ways to add nodes, be sure to check out the section "XElement.SetElementValue() on Child XElement Objects" later in this chapter.

XContainer.Add() (AddLast)

The method you will use most to add nodes to an XML tree is the Add method. It appends a node to the end of the specified node's child nodes, hence my AddLast hint in the preceding heading. Listing 7-63 is an example.

Listing 7-63. *Adding a Node to the End of the Specified Node's Child Nodes with Add*

```
Dim xDocument = _
  <?xml version="1.0"?>
  <BookParticipants>
    <BookParticipant type="Author">
      <FirstName>Dennis</FirstName>
      <LastName>Hayes</LastName>
    </BookParticipant>
  </BookParticipants>

xDocument.<BookParticipants>(0). _
  Add(<BookParticipant type="Editor">
        <FirstName>Ewan</FirstName>
        <LastName>Buckingham</LastName>
      </BookParticipant>)

Console.WriteLine(xDocument)
```

In the previous code, you can see I start with the base code and then add a BookParticipant element to the document's BookParticipants element. You can see I used a child axis property and an indexer axis property to obtain the BookParticipants element and added the element to its child nodes using the Add method. Also, please notice that I passed an XML literal into the Add method. This causes the newly added element to be appended to the child nodes:

```
<BookParticipants>
  <BookParticipant type="Author">
    <FirstName>Dennis</FirstName>
    <LastName>Hayes</LastName>
  </BookParticipant>
  <BookParticipant type="Editor">
    <FirstName>Ewan</FirstName>
    <LastName>Buckingham</LastName>
  </BookParticipant>
</BookParticipants>
```

The Add method adds the newly constructed BookParticipant element to the end of the BookParticipants element's child nodes. Additionally, the Add method is every bit as flexible as the XElement constructor and follows the same rules for its arguments, allowing for functional construction had we chosen to use it.

XContainer.AddFirst()

To add a node to the beginning of a node's child nodes, use the AddFirst method. Using the same code as before, except calling the AddFirst method, gives you the code in Listing 7-64.

Listing 7-64. *Adding a Node to the Beginning of the Specified Node's Child Nodes with AddFirst*

```
Dim xDocument = _
  <?xml version="1.0"?>
  <BookParticipants>
    <BookParticipant type="Author">
      <FirstName>Dennis</FirstName>
      <LastName>Hayes</LastName>
    </BookParticipant>
  </BookParticipants>

xDocument.<BookParticipants>(0). _
  AddFirst(<BookParticipant type="Editor">
            <FirstName>Ewan</FirstName>
            <LastName>Buckingham</LastName>
          </BookParticipant>)

Console.WriteLine(xDocument)
```

As one would expect, the newly added `BookParticipant` element will be added to the head of the `BookParticipants` element's child nodes:

```
<BookParticipants>
  <BookParticipant type="Editor">
    <FirstName>Ewan</FirstName>
    <LastName>Buckingham</LastName>
  </BookParticipant>
  <BookParticipant type="Author">
    <FirstName>Dennis</FirstName>
    <LastName>Hayes</LastName>
  </BookParticipant>
</BookParticipants>
```

Can XML manipulation get any easier than this? I submit that it cannot.

XNode.AddBeforeSelf()

To insert a node into a node's list of child nodes in a specific location, obtain a reference to either the node before or the node after where you want to insert, and call either the `AddBeforeSelf` or `AddAfterSelf` method.

I will use the XML tree produced by the Add method example, Listing 7-63, as a starting point and add a new node between the two already existing `BookParticipant` elements. To do this, I must get a reference to the second `BookParticipant` element, as shown in Listing 7-65.

Listing 7-65. *Adding a Node in the Specified Node's Child Nodes with AddBeforeSelf*

```
Dim xDocument = _
  <?xml version="1.0"?>
  <BookParticipants>
    <BookParticipant type="Author">
      <FirstName>Dennis</FirstName>
      <LastName>Hayes</LastName>
    </BookParticipant>
  </BookParticipants>

xDocument.<BookParticipants>(0). _
  Add(<BookParticipant type="Editor">
        <FirstName>Ewan</FirstName>
        <LastName>Buckingham</LastName>
      </BookParticipant>)

xDocument...<BookParticipant>(1). _
  AddBeforeSelf(<BookParticipant type="Technical Editor">
                  <FirstName>Joe</FirstName>
                  <LastName>Rattz</LastName>
                </BookParticipant>)

Console.WriteLine(MyDocument)
```

After adding the second BookParticipant element with the Add method in the previous code, I used the descendant axis property coupled with the indexer axis property to retrieve the second BookParticipant element, the one whose index is 1. Once I have a reference to the proper BookParticipant element, I merely call the AddBeforeSelf method passing it an XML literal, and voilà:

```
<BookParticipants>
  <BookParticipant type="Author">
    <FirstName>Dennis</FirstName>
    <LastName>Hayes</LastName>
  </BookParticipant>
  <BookParticipant type="Technical Editor">
    <FirstName>Joe</FirstName>
    <LastName>Rattz</LastName>
  </BookParticipant>
  <BookParticipant type="Editor">
    <FirstName>Ewan</FirstName>
    <LastName>Buckingham</LastName>
  </BookParticipant>
</BookParticipants>
```

Just as I wanted, I inserted the new BookParticipant before the BookParticipant element whose index was 1.

XNode.AddAfterSelf()

After using the VB.NET XML features to get a reference to the second BookParticipant element in the previous example, the example in Listing 7-66 is sure to be anticlimactic. I will just get a reference to the first BookParticipant element using the normal LINQ to XML API's Element and Elements methods, and add the new BookParticipant element after it using the AddAfterSelf method.

Listing 7-66. *Adding a Node in a Specific Location of the Specified Node's Child Nodes with AddAfterSelf*

```
Dim xDocument = _
  <?xml version="1.0"?>
  <BookParticipants>
    <BookParticipant type="Author">
      <FirstName>Dennis</FirstName>
      <LastName>Hayes</LastName>
    </BookParticipant>
  </BookParticipants>

xDocument.<BookParticipants>(0). _
  Add(<BookParticipant type="Editor">
        <FirstName>Ewan</FirstName>
        <LastName>Buckingham</LastName>
      </BookParticipant>)

xDocument.Element("BookParticipants").Elements("BookParticipant").First(). _
  AddAfterSelf(<BookParticipant type="Technical Editor">
                 <FirstName>Joe</FirstName>
                 <LastName>Rattz</LastName>
               </BookParticipant>)

Console.WriteLine(xDocument)
```

This example just seems trivial after the previous one:

```
<BookParticipants>
  <BookParticipant type="Author">
    <FirstName>Dennis</FirstName>
    <LastName>Hayes</LastName>
  </BookParticipant>
  <BookParticipant type="Technical Editor">
    <FirstName>Joe</FirstName>
    <LastName>Rattz</LastName>
  </BookParticipant>
  <BookParticipant type="Editor">
    <FirstName>Ewan</FirstName>
    <LastName>Buckingham</LastName>
```

```
    </BookParticipant>
  </BookParticipants>
```

Deleting Nodes

Deleting nodes is accomplished with either of two methods: Remove or RemoveAll.

In addition to reading about the following ways to delete nodes, be sure to check out the section "XElement.SetElementValue() on Child XElement Objects" later in this chapter.

XNode.Remove()

The Remove method removes any node, as well as its child nodes and attributes, from an XML tree. In the first example, I construct an XML tree and obtain a reference to the first book participant element as I did in some of the previous examples. I display the XML tree after the construction but before deleting any nodes. I then delete the first BookParticipant element and display the resulting XML tree, as shown in Listing 7-67.

Listing 7-67. *Deleting a Specific Node with Remove*

```
Dim xDocument = _
  <?xml version="1.0" encoding="utf-8" standalone="yes"?>
  <BookParticipants>
    <BookParticipant type="Author">
      <FirstName>Dennis</FirstName>
      <LastName>Hayes</LastName>
    </BookParticipant>
    <BookParticipant type="Editor">
      <FirstName>Ewan</FirstName>
      <LastName>Buckingham</LastName>
    </BookParticipant>
  </BookParticipants>

Dim firstParticipant = xDocument...<BookParticipant>(0)

Console.WriteLine(System.Environment.NewLine + "Before node deletion")
Console.WriteLine(xDocument)

firstParticipant.Remove()

Console.WriteLine(System.Environment.NewLine + "After node deletion")
Console.WriteLine(xDocument)
```

If all goes as planned, I should get the XML tree initially with the first BookParticipant element and subsequently without it:

```
Before node deletion
<BookParticipants>
```

```
      <BookParticipant type="Author">
        <FirstName>Dennis</FirstName>
        <LastName>Hayes</LastName>
      </BookParticipant>
      <BookParticipant type="Editor">
        <FirstName>Ewan</FirstName>
        <LastName>Buckingham</LastName>
      </BookParticipant>
</BookParticipants>

After node deletion
<BookParticipants>
      <BookParticipant type="Editor">
        <FirstName>Ewan</FirstName>
        <LastName>Buckingham</LastName>
      </BookParticipant>
</BookParticipants>
```

As you can see, the first BookParticipant element is gone after the node deletion.

IEnumerable(Of T).Remove()

In the previous case, I call the Remove method on a single XNode object. I can also call Remove on a sequence (IEnumerable(Of T)). Listing 7-68 is an example where I use the Descendants method of the document to recursively traverse all the way down the XML tree, returning only those elements whose name is FirstName by using the Where operator. I then call the Remove method on the resulting sequence.

Listing 7-68. *Deleting a Sequence of Nodes with Remove*

```
Dim xDocument = _
  <?xml version="1.0" encoding="utf-8" standalone="yes"?>
  <BookParticipants>
    <BookParticipant type="Author">
      <FirstName>Dennis</FirstName>
      <LastName>Hayes</LastName>
    </BookParticipant>
    <BookParticipant type="Editor">
      <FirstName>Ewan</FirstName>
      <LastName>Buckingham</LastName>
    </BookParticipant>
  </BookParticipants>

xDocument.Descendants().Where(Function(e) e.Name = "FirstName").Remove()

Console.WriteLine(xDocument)
```

I like this example because I really start to tie all the elements of LINQ together with it. I am using the XDocument.Descendants method to get all the child nodes returned in a sequence, and then I call the Where Standard Query Operator to filter just the ones matching the search criteria, which in this case are elements named FirstName. This returns a sequence that I then call the Remove method on. Sweet! Here are the results:

```
<BookParticipants>
  <BookParticipant type="Author">
    <LastName>Hayes</LastName>
  </BookParticipant>
  <BookParticipant type="Editor">
    <LastName>Buckingham</LastName>
  </BookParticipant>
</BookParticipants>
```

Notice that I no longer have any FirstName elements.

Tip The purpose of this chapter is to examine the LINQ to XML API, and in Listing 7-68, I demonstrated how to remove elements matching a specified name with that API. We'll keep it our secret that, by using the VB.NET 2008 axis properties, we can simply replace the line removing the elements with xDocument...<FirstName>.Remove().

XElement.RemoveAll()

Sometimes, you may want to delete the content of an element but not the element itself. This is what the RemoveAll method is for. Listing 7-69 is an example.

Listing 7-69. *Removing a Node's Content with RemoveAll*

```
Dim xDocument = _
  <?xml version="1.0" encoding="utf-8" standalone="yes"?>
  <BookParticipants>
    <BookParticipant type="Author">
      <FirstName>Dennis</FirstName>
      <LastName>Hayes</LastName>
    </BookParticipant>
    <BookParticipant type="Editor">
      <FirstName>Ewan</FirstName>
      <LastName>Buckingham</LastName>
    </BookParticipant>
  </BookParticipants>

Console.WriteLine(System.Environment.NewLine + "Before removing the content.")
Console.WriteLine(xDocument)
```

```
xDocument.Element("BookParticipants").RemoveAll()

Console.WriteLine(System.Environment.NewLine + "After removing the content.")
Console.WriteLine(xDocument)
```

Here I display the document first before removing the content of the BookParticipants node. Then, I remove the content of the BookParticipants node and display the document again. Since you could be from Missouri, I had better show you the results:

```
Before removing the content.
<BookParticipants>
  <BookParticipant type="Author">
    <FirstName>Dennis</FirstName>
    <LastName>Hayes</LastName>
  </BookParticipant>
  <BookParticipant type="Editor">
    <FirstName>Ewan</FirstName>
    <LastName>Buckingham</LastName>
  </BookParticipant>
</BookParticipants>

After removing the content.
<BookParticipants />
```

Updating Nodes

Several of the subclasses of XNode, such as XElement, XText, and XComment, have a Value property that can be directly updated. Others, such as XDocumentType and XProcessingInstruction, have specific properties that each can be updated. For an element, in addition to modifying the Value property, you can change its value by calling the XElement.SetElementValue or XContainer.ReplaceAll methods covered later in this chapter.

XElement.Value on XElement Objects, XText.Value on XText Objects, and XComment.Value on XComment Objects

Each of these subclasses of XNode has a Value property that can be set to update the node's value. Listing 7-70 demonstrates all of them.

Listing 7-70. *Updating a Node's Value*

```
Dim xDocument = _
  <?xml version="1.0" encoding="utf-8" standalone="yes"?>
  <BookParticipants>
    <BookParticipant type="Author">
      <!--This is a new author.-->
      <FirstName>Dennis</FirstName>
      <LastName>Hayes</LastName>
```

```
      </BookParticipant>
    </BookParticipants>

Dim firstParticipant = xDocument...<BookParticipant>(0)

Console.WriteLine("Before updating nodes:")
Console.WriteLine(xDocument)

'  Now, I'll update an element, a comment, and a text node.
firstParticipant.Element("FirstName").Value = "Spider"

firstParticipant.Nodes().OfType(Of XComment)().Single().Value = _
  "Author of Pro LINQ: Language Integrated Query in VB.Net 2008."

CType(firstParticipant.Element("FirstName").NextNode, XElement) _
  .Nodes().OfType(Of XText)().Single().Value = "Hayes, Jr."

Console.WriteLine("After updating nodes:")
Console.WriteLine(xDocument)
```

In this example, I update the FirstName element first, using its Value property, followed by the comment using its Value property, finally followed by updating the LastName element by accessing its value through its child XText object's Value property. Notice the flexibility LINQ to XML provides for getting references to the different objects I want to update. Just remember that it isn't necessary for me to access the LastName element's value by getting the XText object from its child nodes. I did that merely for demonstration purposes. Other than that, I would have directly accessed its Value property. Here are the results:

```
Before updating nodes:
<BookParticipants>
  <BookParticipant type="Author">
    <!--This is a new author.-->
    <FirstName>Dennis</FirstName>
    <LastName>Hayes</LastName>
  </BookParticipant>
</BookParticipants>
After updating nodes:
<BookParticipants>
  <BookParticipant type="Author">
    <!--Author of Pro LINQ: Language Integrated Query in VB.NET 2008.-->
    <FirstName>Spider</FirstName>
    <LastName>Hayes, Jr.</LastName>
  </BookParticipant>
</BookParticipants>
```

As you can see, all of the node's values are updated.

XDocumentType.Name, XDocumentType.PublicId, XDocumentType.SystemId, and XDocumentType.InternalSubset on XDocumentType Objects

To update a document type node, the XDocumentType class provides four properties for updating its values. Listing 7-71 is some sample code demonstrating this.

Listing 7-71. *Updating the Document Type*

```
'  I will use this to store a reference to the DocumentType for later access.
Dim docType As XDocumentType = _
  New XDocumentType("BookParticipants", Nothing, "BookParticipants.dtd", Nothing)

Dim xDocument As New XDocument(docType, New XElement("BookParticipants"))

Console.WriteLine("Before updating document type:")
Console.WriteLine(xDocument)

docType.Name = "MyBookParticipants"
docType.SystemId = "http://www.somewhere.com/DTDs/MyBookParticipants.DTD"
docType.PublicId = "-//DTDs//TEXT Book Participants//EN"

Console.WriteLine("After updating document type:")
Console.WriteLine(xDocument)
```

Here are the results of this code:

```
Before updating document type:
<!DOCTYPE BookParticipants SYSTEM "BookParticipants.dtd">
<BookParticipants />
After updating document type:
<!DOCTYPE MyBookParticipants PUBLIC "-//DTDs//TEXT Book Participants//EN"
"http://www.somewhere.com/DTDs/MyBookParticipants.DTD">
<BookParticipants />
```

XProcessingInstruction.Target on XProcessingInstruction Objects and XProcessingInstruction.Data on XProcessingInstruction Objects

To update the value of a processing instruction, simply modify the Target and Data properties of the XProcessingInstruction object. Listing 7-72 is an example.

Listing 7-72. *Updating a Processing Instruction*

```
'  I will use this to store a reference for later access.
Dim procInst As XProcessingInstruction = _
  New XProcessingInstruction("BookCataloger", "out-of-print")

Dim xDocument As New XDocument(New XElement("BookParticipants"), procInst)
```

```
Console.WriteLine("Before updating processing instruction:")
Console.WriteLine(xDocument)

procInst.Target = "BookParticipantContactManager"
procInst.Data = "update"

Console.WriteLine("After updating processing instruction:")
Console.WriteLine(xDocument)
```

Now let's take a look at the output:

```
Before updating processing instruction:
<BookParticipants />
<?BookCataloger out-of-print?>
After updating processing instruction:
<BookParticipants />
<?BookParticipantContactManager update?>
```

XElement.ReplaceAll()

The ReplaceAll method is useful for replacing an element's entire subtree of XML. You can pass a simple value, such as a new string or a numeric type; or because there is an overloaded method that accepts multiple objects via the ParamArray keyword, an entire subtree can be changed. The ReplaceAll method also replaces attributes. Listing 7-73 is some sample code.

Listing 7-73. *Using ReplaceAll to Change an Element's Subtree*

```
Dim xDocument = _
  <?xml version="1.0" encoding="utf-8" standalone="yes"?>
  <BookParticipants>
    <BookParticipant type="Author">
      <FirstName>Dennis</FirstName>
      <LastName>Hayes</LastName>
    </BookParticipant>
  </BookParticipants>

Dim firstParticipant = xDocument...<BookParticipant>(0)

Console.WriteLine(System.Environment.NewLine & "Before updating elements:")
Console.WriteLine(xDocument)

firstParticipant.ReplaceAll( _
  <FirstName>Ewan</FirstName>, _
  <LastName>BuckingHam</LastName>)

Console.WriteLine(System.Environment.NewLine & "After updating elements:")
Console.WriteLine(xDocument)
```

Notice that when I replaced the content with the `ReplaceAll` method, I omitted specifying an attribute. Also, please notice that I used the overload that accepts multiple objects and passed it two XML literals. As you would expect, the content is replaced:

```
Before updating elements:
<BookParticipants>
  <BookParticipant type="Author">
    <FirstName>Dennis</FirstName>
    <LastName>Hayes</LastName>
  </BookParticipant>
</BookParticipants>

After updating elements:
<BookParticipants>
  <BookParticipant>
    <FirstName>Ewan</FirstName>
    <LastName>Buckingham</LastName>
  </BookParticipant>
</BookParticipants>
```

Notice that the `BookParticipant` type attribute is now gone. This is interesting in that attributes are not child nodes of an element. But the `ReplaceAll` method replaces them as well.

XElement.SetElementValue() on Child XElement Objects

Don't let this simply named method fool you; it's a powerhouse. It has the ability to add, change, and remove elements. Furthermore, it performs these operations on the child elements of the element you call it on. Stated differently, you call the `SetElementValue` method on a parent element to affect its content, meaning its child elements.

When calling the `SetElementValue` method, you pass it the name of the child element you want to set and the value you want to set it to. If a child element is found by that name, its value is updated, as long as the passed value is not `Nothing`. If the passed value is `Nothing`, that found child element will be removed. If an element by that name is not found, it will be added with the passed value. Wow, what a method!

Also, the `SetElementValue` method will only affect the first child element it finds with the specified name. Any subsequent elements with the same name will not be affected, either by the value being changed to the one passed in or the element being removed, because that passed value is `Nothing`.

Listing 7-74 is an example demonstrating all uses: update, add, and delete.

Listing 7-74. *Using SetElementValue to Update, Add, and Delete Child Elements*

```
Dim xDocument = _
  <?xml version="1.0" encoding="utf-8" standalone="yes"?>
  <BookParticipants>
    <BookParticipant type="Author">
      <FirstName>Dennis</FirstName>
```

```
        <LastName>Hayes</LastName>
      </BookParticipant>
    </BookParticipants>

Dim firstParticipant = xDocument...<BookParticipant>(0)

Console.WriteLine(System.Environment.NewLine & "Before updating elements:")
Console.WriteLine(xDocument)

'  First, I will use XElement.SetElementValue to update the value of an element.
'  Since an element named FirstName is there, its value will be updated to Denny.
firstParticipant.SetElementValue("FirstName", "Denny")

'  Second, I will use XElement.SetElementValue to add an element.
'  Since no element named MiddleInitial exists, one will be added.
firstParticipant.SetElementValue("MiddleInitial", "E")

'  Third, I will use XElement.SetElementValue to remove an element.
'  Setting an element's value to Nothing will remove it.
firstParticipant.SetElementValue("LastName", Nothing)

Console.WriteLine(System.Environment.NewLine & "After updating elements:")
Console.WriteLine(xDocument)
```

As you can see, first I call the SetElementValue method on the firstParticipant element's child element named FirstName. Since an element already exists by that name, its value will be updated. Next, I call the SetElementValue method on the firstParticipant element's child element named MiddleInitial. Since no element exists by that name, the element will be added. Lastly, I call the SetElementValue method on the firstParticipant element's child element named LastName and pass a Nothing. Since a Nothing is passed, the LastName element will be removed. Look at the flexibility that the SetElementValue method provides. I know you can't wait to see the results:

```
Before updating elements:
<BookParticipants>
  <BookParticipant type="Author">
    <FirstName>Dennis</FirstName>
    <LastName>Hayes</LastName>
  </BookParticipant>
</BookParticipants>

After updating elements:
<BookParticipants>
  <BookParticipant type="Author">
    <FirstName>Denny</FirstName>
    <MiddleInitial>E</MiddleInitial>
  </BookParticipant>
</BookParticipants>
```

How cool is that? The `FirstName` element's value was updated, the `MiddleInitial` element was added, and the `LastName` element was removed.

■**Caution** Just because calling the `SetElementValue` method with a value of `Nothing` removes the node, don't make the mistake of thinking that manually setting an element's value to `Nothing` is the same as removing it in the LINQ to XML API. This is merely the behavior of the `SetElementValue` method. If you attempt to set an element's value to `Nothing` using its `Value` property, an exception will be thrown.

XML Attributes

As I previously mentioned, with the LINQ to XML API, attributes are implemented with the `XAttribute` class, and unlike the W3C DOM XML API, they do not inherit from a node. Therefore, they have no inheritance relationship with elements. However, in the LINQ to XML API, they are every bit as easy to work with as elements. Let's take a look.

Attribute Creation

Attributes are created just like elements and most other LINQ to XML classes. This topic is covered in the "Creating Attributes with XAttribute" section previously in this chapter.

Attribute Traversal

Attributes can be traversed using the `XElement.FirstAttribute`, `XElement.LastAttribute`, `XAttribute.NextAttribute`, and `XAttribute.PreviousAttribute` properties and the `XElement.Attribute` and `XElement.Attributes` methods. These are described in the following sections.

Forward with XElement.FirstAttribute

You can gain access to an element's attributes by accessing its first attribute using the element's `FirstAttribute` property. Listing 7-75 is an example.

Listing 7-75. *Accessing an Element's First Attribute with the FirstAttribute Property*

```
Dim xDocument = _
  <?xml version="1.0" encoding="utf-8" standalone="yes"?>
  <BookParticipants>
    <BookParticipant type="Author" experience="first-time" language="English">
      <FirstName>Dennis</FirstName>
      <LastName>Hayes</LastName>
    </BookParticipant>
  </BookParticipants>

Dim firstParticipant = xDocument...<BookParticipant>(0)

Console.WriteLine(firstParticipant.FirstAttribute)
```

This code outputs the following:

```
type="Author"
```

Forward with XAttribute.NextAttribute

To traverse forward through an element's attributes, reference the NextAttribute property on an attribute. Listing 7-76 is an example.

Listing 7-76. *Accessing the Next Attribute with the NextAttribute Property*

```
Dim xDocument = _
  <?xml version="1.0" encoding="utf-8" standalone="yes"?>
  <BookParticipants>
    <BookParticipant type="Author" experience="first-time" language="English">
      <FirstName>Dennis</FirstName>
      <LastName>Hayes</LastName>
    </BookParticipant>
  </BookParticipants>

Dim firstParticipant = xDocument...<BookParticipant>(0)

Console.WriteLine(firstParticipant.FirstAttribute.NextAttribute)
```

Notice I use the FirstAttribute property to obtain a reference to the first attribute and then reference the NextAttribute property on it. Here are the results:

```
experience="first-time"
```

If an attribute's NextAttribute property is Nothing, the attribute is the last attribute of the element.

Backward with XAttribute.PreviousAttribute

To traverse backward through an element's attributes, reference the PreviousAttribute property on an attribute. Listing 7-77 is an example.

Listing 7-77. *Accessing the Previous Attribute with the PreviousAttribute Property*

```
Dim xDocument = _
  <?xml version="1.0" encoding="utf-8" standalone="yes"?>
  <BookParticipants>
    <BookParticipant type="Author" experience="first-time" language="English">
      <FirstName>Dennis</FirstName>
      <LastName>Hayes</LastName>
    </BookParticipant>
  </BookParticipants>
```

```
Dim firstParticipant = xDocument...<BookParticipant>(0)
```

```
Console.WriteLine(firstParticipant.FirstAttribute.NextAttribute.PreviousAttribute)
```

Notice I chain the `FirstAttribute` and `NextAttribute` properties to get a reference to the second attribute from which to go backward. This should take me back to the first attribute. Here are the results:

```
type="Author"
```

And it does! If an attribute's `PreviousAttribute` property is `Nothing`, the attribute is the first attribute of the element.

Backward with XElement.LastAttribute

To get access to the very last attribute of an element so that you can traverse backward through the attributes, use the `LastAttribute` property, as shown in Listing 7-78.

Listing 7-78. *Accessing the Last Attribute with the LastAttribute Property*

```
Dim xDocument = _
  <?xml version="1.0" encoding="utf-8" standalone="yes"?>
  <BookParticipants>
    <BookParticipant type="Author" experience="first-time" language="English">
      <FirstName>Dennis</FirstName>
      <LastName>Hayes</LastName>
    </BookParticipant>
  </BookParticipants>

Dim firstParticipant = xDocument...<BookParticipant>(0)
```

Console.WriteLine(firstParticipant.LastAttribute)

This should output the `language` attribute. Let's see:

```
language="English"
```

Groovy! I have never actually written the word *groovy* before. I had to let the spell-checker spell it for me.

XElement.Attribute()

This method takes the name of an attribute and returns the attribute with the specified name, if one is found. Listing 7-79 is an example.

Listing 7-79. *Accessing an Attribute with the Attribute Method*

```
Dim xDocument = _
  <?xml version="1.0" encoding="utf-8" standalone="yes"?>
  <BookParticipants>
    <BookParticipant type="Author" experience="first-time" language="English">
      <FirstName>Dennis</FirstName>
      <LastName>Hayes</LastName>
    </BookParticipant>
  </BookParticipants>

Dim firstParticipant = xDocument...<BookParticipant>(0)

Console.WriteLine(firstParticipant.Attribute("type").Value)
```

> **Tip** In Listing 7-79, I used the LINQ to XML API `Attribute` method, but don't forget how convenient the VB.NET 2008 attribute axis property is. With it, I could have written `Console.WriteLine(firstParticipant.@type)`. It doesn't get much simpler than that.

Here I use the `Attribute` method to return a reference to the `type` attribute. I then display the attribute's value using its `Value` property. If all goes as expected, the output should be the following:

```
Author
```

Remember, though, instead of obtaining the attribute's value via its `Value` property, I could have just cast the attribute to a `String`.

XElement.Attributes()

We can gain access to all of an element's attributes with its `Attributes` method. This method returns a *sequence* of `XAttribute` objects. Listing 7-80 is an example.

Listing 7-80. *Accessing All of an Element's Attributes with the Attributes Method*

```
Dim xDocument = _
  <?xml version="1.0" encoding="utf-8" standalone="yes"?>
  <BookParticipants>
    <BookParticipant type="Author" experience="first-time" language="English">
      <FirstName>Dennis</FirstName>
      <LastName>Hayes</LastName>
    </BookParticipant>
  </BookParticipants>
```

```
Dim firstParticipant = xDocument...<BookParticipant>(0)

For Each attr As XAttribute In firstParticipant.Attributes()
    Console.WriteLine(attr)
Next attr
```

The output is this:

```
type="Author"
experience="first-time"
language="English"
```

Attribute Modification

There are several methods and properties that can be used to modify attributes. I cover them in this section.

Adding Attributes

As I have pointed out, there is a fundamental difference in the way the W3C DOM XML API handles attributes vs. the way the LINQ to XML API handles them. With the W3C DOM XML API, an attribute is a child node of the node it is an attribute for. With the LINQ to XML API, attributes are *not* child nodes of the node for which they are an attribute. Instead, attributes are name-value pairs that can be accessed via an element's Attributes method or its FirstAttribute property. This is important to remember.

However, working with attributes is very similar to working with elements. The methods and properties for attributes are very symmetrical to those for elements.

The following methods can be used to add an attribute to an element:

- XElement.Add()

- XElement.AddFirst()

- XElement.AddBeforeThis()

- XElement.AddAfterThis()

In the examples provided for each of these methods in the "Adding Nodes" section earlier in this chapter, attributes are added as well. Refer to those examples of adding an attribute. In addition, be sure to check out the section on the XElement.SetAttributeValue method later in this chapter.

Deleting Attributes

Deleting attributes can be accomplished using either the XAttribute.Remove method or the IEnumerable(Of T).Remove method, depending on whether you are trying to delete a single attribute or a sequence of attributes.

In addition to the following ways to delete attributes, be sure to check out the "XElement. SetAttributeValue()" section later in this chapter.

XAttribute.Remove()

Just like the XNode class has a remove method, so too does the XAttribute class. Listing 7-81 is an example.

Listing 7-81. *Removing an Attribute*

```
Dim xDocument = _
  <?xml version="1.0" encoding="utf-8" standalone="yes"?>
  <BookParticipants>
    <BookParticipant type="Author" experience="first-time" language="English">
      <FirstName>Dennis</FirstName>
      <LastName>Hayes</LastName>
    </BookParticipant>
  </BookParticipants>

Dim firstParticipant = xDocument...<BookParticipant>(0)

Console.WriteLine(System.Environment.NewLine & "Before removing attribute:")
Console.WriteLine(xDocument)

firstParticipant.Attribute("type").Remove()

Console.WriteLine(System.Environment.NewLine & "After removing attribute:")
Console.WriteLine(xDocument)
```

As you can see, I use the Attribute method to obtain a reference to the attribute I want to remove, and then I call the Remove method on it. Just so you don't think I am just making this all up, here are the results:

```
Before removing attribute:
<BookParticipants>
  <BookParticipant type="Author" experience="first-time" language="English">
    <FirstName>Dennis</FirstName>
    <LastName>Hayes</LastName>
  </BookParticipant>
</BookParticipants>

After removing attribute:
<BookParticipants>
  <BookParticipant experience="first-time" language="English">
    <FirstName>Dennis</FirstName>
    <LastName>Hayes</LastName>
  </BookParticipant>
</BookParticipants>
```

Notice that the type attribute is now gone.

■**Tip** You may be expecting me to provide an alternate way to delete the attribute using a VB.NET 2008 attribute axis property. However, the attribute axis property returns the attribute's value, not the attribute itself, and since I need a reference to the attribute itself to call the Remove method on, the attribute axis property will not work for me in this circumstance.

IEnumerable(Of T).Remove()

Just as you are able to remove a sequence of nodes using the IEnumerable(Of T).Remove method, you can use the same method to remove all attributes of an element, as shown in Listing 7-82.

Listing 7-82. *Removing All of an Element's Attributes*

```
Dim xDocument = _
  <?xml version="1.0" encoding="utf-8" standalone="yes"?>
  <BookParticipants>
    <BookParticipant type="Author" experience="first-time" language="English">
      <FirstName>Dennis</FirstName>
      <LastName>Hayes</LastName>
    </BookParticipant>
  </BookParticipants>

Dim firstParticipant = xDocument...<BookParticipant>(0)

Console.WriteLine(vbCrLf & "Before removing attributes:")
Console.WriteLine(xDocument)

firstParticipant.Attributes().Remove()

Console.WriteLine(vbCrLf & "After removing attributes:")
Console.WriteLine(xDocument)
```

In the previous example, I call the Attributes method to return the sequence of all attributes of the element the Attributes method is called on, and then I call the Remove method on that returned sequence to remove them all. This seems so simple and intuitive, I wonder if I am wasting your time just covering it. Here are the results:

```
Before removing attributes:
<BookParticipants>
  <BookParticipant type="Author" experience="first-time" language="English">
    <FirstName>Dennis</FirstName>
    <LastName>Hayes</LastName>
  </BookParticipant>
</BookParticipants>
```

```
After removing attributes:
<BookParticipants>
  <BookParticipant>
    <FirstName>Dennis</FirstName>
    <LastName>Hayes</LastName>
  </BookParticipant>
</BookParticipants>
```

Like magic, the attributes are gone.

Updating Attributes

To update the value of an attribute, use the XAttribute.Value property.

Note In addition to using the XAttribute.Value property to update attributes, be sure to check out the "XElement.SetAttributeValue()" section later in the chapter.

Updating the value of an attribute is easily accomplished using its Value property. Listing 7-83 is an example.

Listing 7-83. *Changing an Attribute's Value*

```
Dim xDocument = _
  <?xml version="1.0" encoding="utf-8" standalone="yes"?>
  <BookParticipants>
    <BookParticipant type="Author" experience="first-time" language="English">
      <FirstName>Dennis</FirstName>
      <LastName>Hayes</LastName>
    </BookParticipant>
  </BookParticipants>

Dim firstParticipant = xDocument...<BookParticipant>(0)

Console.WriteLine(vbCrLf & "Before changing attribute's value:")
Console.WriteLine(xDocument)

firstParticipant.Attribute("experience").Value = "beginner"

Console.WriteLine(vbCrLf & "After changing attribute's value:")
Console.WriteLine(xDocument)
```

Notice that I used the Attribute method to obtain a reference to the experience attribute. The results are the following:

```
Before changing attribute's value:
<BookParticipants>
  <BookParticipant type="Author" experience="first-time" language="English">
    <FirstName>Dennis</FirstName>
    <LastName>Hayes</LastName>
  </BookParticipant>
</BookParticipants>

After changing attribute's value:
<BookParticipants>
  <BookParticipant type="Author" experience="beginner" language="English">
    <FirstName>Dennis</FirstName>
    <LastName>Hayes</LastName>
  </BookParticipant>
</BookParticipants>
```

As you can see, the value of the experience attribute has changed from "first-time" to "beginner".

Tip You probably recall that, in the explanation for Listing 7-81, I stated I could not use the VB.NET 2008 attribute axis property because it returned the value of an attribute, not a reference to an attribute. That being the case, it works just perfectly for Listing 7-83, and the line changing the attribute's value could be amended to use the attribute axis property like this: firstParticipant.@experience = "beginner".

XElement.SetAttributeValue()

To be symmetrical with elements, it's only fair that attributes get a SetAttributeValue method every bit as powerful as the SetElementValue method; and they did. The XElement. SetAttributeValue method has the ability to add, delete, and update an attribute.

Passing an attribute name that does *not* exist causes an attribute to be added. Passing a name that exists with a value other than Nothing causes the attribute with that name to have its value updated to the value passed. Passing a name that exists with a Nothing value causes the attribute to be deleted. Listing 7-84 is an example doing all three.

Listing 7-84. *Using SetAttributeValue to Add, Delete, and Update Attributes*

```
Dim xDocument = _
  <?xml version="1.0" encoding="utf-8" standalone="yes"?>
  <BookParticipants>
    <BookParticipant type="Author" experience="first-time">
      <FirstName>Dennis</FirstName>
      <LastName>Hayes</LastName>
    </BookParticipant>
  </BookParticipants>
```

```
Dim firstParticipant = xDocument...<BookParticipant>(0)

Console.WriteLine(vbCrLf & "Before changing the attributes:")
Console.WriteLine(xDocument)

'  This call will update the type attribute's value because an attribute whose
'  name is "type" exists.
firstParticipant.SetAttributeValue("type", "beginner")

'  This call will add an attribute because an attribute with the specified name
'  does not exist.
firstParticipant.SetAttributeValue("language", "English")

'  This call will delete an attribute because an attribute with the specified name
'  exists, and the passed value is Nothing.
firstParticipant.SetAttributeValue("experience", Nothing)

Console.WriteLine(vbCrLf & "After changing the attributes:")
Console.WriteLine(xDocument)
```

As you can see, in this example, first I update an already existing attribute's value, then I add an attribute, and finally I delete an attribute by passing a Nothing value. Here are the results:

```
Before changing the attributes:
<BookParticipants>
  <BookParticipant type="Author" experience="first-time">
    <FirstName>Dennis</FirstName>
    <LastName>Hayes</LastName>
  </BookParticipant>
</BookParticipants>

After changing the attributes:
<BookParticipants>
  <BookParticipant type="beginner" language="English">
    <FirstName>Dennis</FirstName>
    <LastName>Hayes</LastName>
  </BookParticipant>
</BookParticipants>
```

```
firstParticipant.@type = "beginner"
firstParticipant.@language = "English"
firstParticipant.@experience = Nothing
```

XML Annotations

The LINQ to XML API provides the ability to associate a user data object with any class inheriting from the XObject class via annotations. This allows the application developer to assign whatever data type object he wants to an element, document, or any other object whose class is derived from the XObject class. The object could be additional keys for an element's data; it could be an object that will parse the element's contents into itself; or whatever you need.

Adding Annotations with XObject.AddAnnotation()

Adding annotations is accomplished using the XObject.AddAnnotation method. Here is the declaration:

```
Public Sub AddAnnotation (annotation As Object)
```

Accessing Annotations with XObject.Annotation() or XObject.Annotations()

Accessing annotations is accomplished using the XObject.Annotation or XObject.Annotations method. Here are the declarations:

```
Public Function Annotation (type As Type) As Object
Public Function Annotation (Of T As Class) As T
Public Function Annotations (type As Type) As IEnumerable(Of Object)
Public Function Annotations (Of T As Class) As IEnumerable(Of T)
```

Removing Annotations with XObject.RemoveAnnotations()

Removing annotations is accomplished with the XObject.RemoveAnnotations method. There are two overloads:

```
Public Sub RemoveAnnotations (type As Type)
Public Sub RemoveAnnotations (Of T As Class)
```

Annotations Example

To demonstrate annotations, I will create one example that adds, retrieves, and removes annotations. In this example, I will use my typical BookParticipants XML tree. I want a way to associate a handler to each BookParticipant based on its type attribute. In this example, the handler will merely display the element in a type attribute–specific format: one format for authors and another for editors.

First, I need a couple of handler classes, one for authors and another for editors:

```
Public Class AuthorHandler
  Public Sub Display(ByVal element As XElement)
    Console.WriteLine("AUTHOR BIO")
    Console.WriteLine("--------------------------")
    Console.WriteLine("Name:        {0} {1}", element.Element("FirstName").Value, _
      element.Element("LastName").Value)
    Console.WriteLine("Language:    {0}", element.Attribute("language").Value)
    Console.WriteLine("Experience:  {0}", element.Attribute("experience").Value)
    Console.WriteLine("==========================" & System.Environment.NewLine)
  End Sub
End Class


Public Class EditorHandler
  Public Sub Display(ByVal element As XElement)
    Console.WriteLine("EDITOR BIO")
    Console.WriteLine("--------------------------")
    Console.WriteLine("Name:        {0}", element.Element("FirstName").Value)
    Console.WriteLine("             {0}", element.Element("LastName").Value)
    Console.WriteLine("==========================" & System.Environment.NewLine)
  End Sub
End Class
```

There is nothing special here. I just need two handlers that behave differently. In this case, they display the element's data in a slightly different format. Of course, it wouldn't have to just display data. It could do anything you want. Or the annotations might not even be handlers. They might just be some associated data. But in this example, they are handlers.

Because this example is more complex than typical, I will separate sections of the code with explanations, as shown in Listing 7-85.

Listing 7-85. *Adding, Retrieving, and Removing Annotations*

```
Dim xDocument = _
  <?xml version="1.0" encoding="utf-8" standalone="yes"?>
  <BookParticipants>
    <BookParticipant type="Author" experience="first-time" language="English">
      <FirstName>Dennis</FirstName>
      <LastName>Hayes</LastName>
    </BookParticipant>
    <BookParticipant type="Editor">
      <FirstName>Ewan</FirstName>
```

```
      <LastName>Buckingham</LastName>
    </BookParticipant>
  </BookParticipants>

' Display the document for reference.
Console.WriteLine(xDocument)
Console.WriteLine()
```

All I have done at this point is build the typical XML document that I have been using and display it. For the next section of code, I enumerate through the BookParticipants, and for each, I instantiate a handler based on its type attribute and add an annotation to the element for the appropriate handler:

```
' I'll add some annotations based on their type attribute.
For Each e As XElement In xDocument.Element("BookParticipants").Elements()
  If e.@type = "Author" Then
    Dim aHandler As New AuthorHandler()
    e.AddAnnotation(aHandler)
  ElseIf e.Attribute("type").Value = "Editor" Then
    Dim eHandler As New EditorHandler()
    e.AddAnnotation(eHandler)
  End If
Next e
```

Now each BookParticipant element has a handler added as an annotation depending on its type attribute. Please notice that for the comparison of the type attribute to "Author", I used the VB.NET 2008 attribute axis property, but for the comparison to "Editor", I used the LINQ to XML API approach. I did this so you can see just how much convenience VB.NET 2008 is giving you. Now that each element has a handler added via an annotation, I will enumerate through the elements calling the handler by retrieving the element's annotation:

```
' Declare some variables for the handler objects.  I declared additional
' variables because normally, I probably wouldn't be adding the annotations
' and retrieving them in the same place.
Dim aHandler2 As AuthorHandler
Dim eHandler2 As EditorHandler
For Each e As XElement In xDocument...<BookParticipant>
  If e.@type = "Author" Then
    aHandler2 = e.Annotation(Of AuthorHandler)()
    If aHandler2 IsNot Nothing Then
      aHandler2.Display(e)
    End If
  ElseIf e.@type = "Editor" Then
    eHandler2 = e.Annotation(Of EditorHandler)()
    If eHandler2 IsNot Nothing Then
      eHandler2.Display(e)
    End If
  End If
Next e
```

At this point, a display handler will have been called for each element. The display handler called is dependent on the type attribute. You can see I am getting lazier by the code block. Now, I have used the attribute axis property for each comparison of the type attribute, and I have used the VB.NET 2008 descendant axis property to retrieve the BookParticipant elements. Next, I just remove the annotations for each element:

```
'  Now, I'll remove the annotations.
'  This time I will just reuse the handler variables from above.  But normally,
'  this too would probably be done elsewhere.
For Each e As XElement In xDocument...<BookParticipant>
  If e.@type = "Author" Then
    e.RemoveAnnotations(Of AuthorHandler)()
  ElseIf e.@type = "Editor" Then
    e.RemoveAnnotations(Of EditorHandler)()
  End If
Next e
```

That is a fairly long piece of sample code, but it only has four main sections. In the first section, I build the XML document and display it. You have seen this done many times by now. In the second section, I enumerate through the BookParticipant elements, and based on their type attribute, add a handler. In the third section, I enumerate through the BookParticipant elements, and based on their type attribute, retrieve the handler and call the Display method of the handler object. In the fourth section, I enumerate through the BookParticipant elements, removing the annotations.

The thing to remember is that these annotations can be any data object you want to associate with the element.

Finally, here are the results:

```
<BookParticipants>
  <BookParticipant type="Author" experience="first-time" language="English">
    <FirstName>Dennis</FirstName>
    <LastName>Hayes</LastName>
  </BookParticipant>
  <BookParticipant type="Editor">
    <FirstName>Ewan</FirstName>
    <LastName>Buckingham</LastName>
  </BookParticipant>
</BookParticipants>

AUTHOR BIO
-------------------------
Name:       Dennis Hayes
Language:   English
Experience: first-time
=========================
```

```
EDITOR BIO
--------------------------
Name:       Ewan
            Buckingham
==========================
```

What is important to notice in the results is that the different handlers are called based on the element's `type` attribute, using annotations. Of course, the objects you add as annotations could be for any purpose, not just handlers.

XML Events

The LINQ to XML API makes it possible for you to register for events so that you can be notified any time any object inheriting from `XObject` is about to be, or has been, modified.

The first thing you should know is that when you register for an event on an object, the event will be raised on the object if that object, or any descendant object, is changed. This means if you register for an event on the document or root element, any change in the tree will cause your registered method to be called. Because of this, don't make any assumptions about the data type of the object causing the event to be raised. When your registered method is called, the object causing the event to be raised will be passed as the sender of the event, and its data type will be `Object`. Be very careful when casting it, accessing properties on it, or calling its methods. It may not be the type of object you are expecting. I will demonstrate this in Listing 7-86 where the `Object` is actually an `XText` object when I was expecting it to be an `XElement` object.

Lastly, please be aware that constructing XML will not cause events to get raised. How could it? No events could have been registered prior to the construction. Only modifying or deleting already existing XML can cause an event to be raised, and then only if an event has been registered.

XObject.Changing

This event is raised when an object inheriting from `XObject` is about to be changed, but prior to the change. You register for the event by adding an object of type `EventHandler` to the object's `Changing` event like this:

```
AddHandler object.Changing, AddressOf MyHandler
```

where your delegate must match this signature:

```
Public Sub MyChangingEventHandler (ByVal sender As Object, _
                                ByVal cea As XObjectChangeEventArgs)
```

The `sender` object is the object that is about to be changed, which is causing the event to be raised. The change event arguments, `cea`, contain a property named `ObjectChange` of type `XObjectChange` indicating the type of change about to take place: `XObjectChange.Add`, `XObjectChange.Name`, `XObjectChange.Remove`, or `XObjectChange.Value`.

XObject.Changed

This event is raised after an object inheriting from XObject has been changed. You register for the event by adding an object of type EventHandler to the object's Changed event like this:

```
AddHandler object.Changed, AddressOf MyChangedEventHandler
```

where your delegate must match this signature:

```
Public Sub MyChangedEventHandler (ByVal sender As Object, _
                                  ByVal cea As XObjectChangeEventArgs)
```

The sender object is the object that has changed, which caused the event to be raised. The change event arguments, cea, contain a property named ObjectChange of type XObjectChange indicating the type of change that has taken place: XObjectChange.Add, XObjectChange.Name, XObjectChange.Remove, or XObjectChange.Value.

An Event Example

In order to see all the pieces that go together to handle XObject events, an example is necessary. However, before I can show the code to do that, some event handlers are needed, as follows.

This Method Will Be Registered for the Changing Event for an Element

```
Public Sub MyChangingEventHandler(ByVal sender As Object, _
                                  ByVal cea As XObjectChangeEventArgs)
  Console.WriteLine( _
    "Type of object changing: {0}, Type of change: {1}", _
    sender.GetType().Name, cea.ObjectChange)
End Sub
```

I will register the previous method as the event handler for when an element is about to be changed. Now, I need a handler method for after the object has been changed, as follows.

This Method Will Be Registered for the Changed Event for an Element

```
Public Sub MyChangedEventHandler(ByVal sender As Object, _
                                 ByVal cea As XObjectChangeEventArgs)
  Console.WriteLine( _
    "Type of object changed: {0}, Type of change: {1}", _
    sender.GetType().Name, cea.ObjectChange)
End Sub
```

I will register the previous method as the event handler for when an element has been changed.

Earlier, I mentioned that the event will get raised if any descendant object of a registered object is changed. To better demonstrate this, I will also have one additional method that I will register for when the document is changed. Its only purpose is to make it more apparent that the document is also getting a Changed event raised, despite the fact that it is a descendant object several levels down that was changed. That method follows.

This Method Will be Registered for the Changed Event for the XML Document

```
Public Sub DocumentChangedHandler(ByVal sender As Object, _
                                  ByVal cea As XObjectChangeEventArgs)
  Console.WriteLine( _
    "Doc:  Type of object changed: {0}, Type of change: {1}{2}", _
    sender.GetType().Name, cea.ObjectChange, vbCrLf)
End Sub
```

The only significant change between the DocumentChangedHandler method and the MyChangedEventHandler method is that the DocumentChangedHandler method begins the screen output with the prefix "Doc:" to make it clear that it is the handler method being called by the document's Changed event, as opposed to the element's Changed event handler.

Now, let's take a look at the example code shown in Listing 7-86.

Listing 7-86. *XObject Event Handling*

```
Dim xDocument = _
  <?xml version="1.0" encoding="utf-8" standalone="yes"?>
  <BookParticipants>
    <BookParticipant type="Author">
      <FirstName>Dennis</FirstName>
      <LastName>Hayes</LastName>
    </BookParticipant>
    <BookParticipant type="Editor">
      <FirstName>Ewan</FirstName>
      <LastName>Buckingham</LastName>
    </BookParticipant>
  </BookParticipants>

Dim firstParticipant = xDocument...<BookParticipant>(0)

Console.WriteLine("{0}{1}", xDocument, System.Environment.NewLine)
```

There is nothing new so far. As I have done many times, I have created an XML document using an XML literal and displayed the XML document. Notice that also, like many previous examples, I have obtained a reference to the first BookParticipant element. This is the element whose events I will register for:

```
'  First I must register for the event.
AddHandler firstParticipant.Changing, AddressOf MyChangingEventHandler
AddHandler firstParticipant.Changed, AddressOf MyChangedEventHandler
AddHandler xDocument.Changed, AddressOf DocumentChangedHandler
```

Now I have registered with the first BookParticipant element to receive the Changing and Changed events. Additionally, I have registered with the document to receive its Changed event. I am registering for the document's Changed event to demonstrate that you receive events even when it is a descendant object that is changing or changed. Now, it's time to make a change:

```
'  Now. let's make a change.
firstParticipant.Element("FirstName").Value = "Spider"

Console.WriteLine("{0}{1}", xDocument, vbCrLf)
```

All I did was change the value of the first BookParticipant element's FirstName element's value. Then, I displayed the resulting XML document. Let's examine the results:

```
<BookParticipants>
  <BookParticipant type="Author">
    <FirstName>Dennis</FirstName>
    <LastName>Hayes</LastName>
  </BookParticipant>
  <BookParticipant type="Editor">
    <FirstName>Ewan</FirstName>
    <LastName>Buckingham</LastName>
  </BookParticipant>
</BookParticipants>

Type of object changing: XText, Type of change: Remove
Type of object changed: XText, Type of change: Remove
Doc: Type of object changed: XText, Type of change: Remove

Type of object changing: XText, Type of change: Add
Type of object changed: XText, Type of change: Add
Doc: Type of object changed: XText, Type of change: Add

<BookParticipants>
  <BookParticipant type="Author">
    <FirstName>Spider</FirstName>
    <LastName>Hayes</LastName>
  </BookParticipant>
  <BookParticipant type="Editor">
    <FirstName>Ewan</FirstName>
    <LastName>Buckingham</LastName>
  </BookParticipant>
</BookParticipants>
```

You can see the document at the beginning and end of the results, and the FirstName element's value has been changed just as you would expect. What you are interested in here is the output caused by events being raised, which is between the two displays of the XML document. Notice that the type of object being changed is XText. Were you anticipating that? I wasn't. I was expecting to see the type as XElement. It is easy to forget that when you set an element's value to a string literal that an object of type XText is being created automatically in the background for you.

Looking at the event output, it is a little clearer exactly what is happening when you change the element's value. You can see that first, the element's XText value is about to be changed by being removed, and that it is then removed. Next, you see that the document's Changed event is raised as well. This makes it apparent that the order of the events being raised flows upstream.

Next, you see the same progression of events being raised, except this time an XText object is being added. So now you know that when you change the string value of an element, an XText object is removed and then added back.

Trick or Treat, or Undefined?

Do you remember the Halloween problem I discussed earlier in this chapter? Please resist the urge to make changes to the area of the XML tree containing the object for which the current event is raised in your event handlers. Doing so will have an undefined effect on your XML tree and the events that are raised.

Summary

In this chapter, I covered how to use LINQ to XML to create, modify, and traverse XML documents, as well as how to perform LINQ queries on a single XML object. In this demonstration, you hopefully saw that the new API for creating and modifying XML data is not just a luxury but instead is a necessity for performing LINQ queries. You can't very well project data into an XML structure if you can't create an XML element on the fly, initialize its value, and place it in the XML tree in a single statement. The W3C DOM XML API is totally incapable of the flexibility needed to perform a LINQ query, which, as it turns out, is lucky for us because we got an entirely new XML API because of it.

While this chapter was useful for demonstrating how to perform basic LINQ queries on XML data, there was a fairly serious limitation in the LINQ queries that you saw. That is, the queries I performed were always performing the query on a single XML object, such as an element. I was querying the descendants of an element or the ancestors of an element. What do you do if you need to perform a LINQ query on a sequence of elements, such as the descendants of a *sequence* of elements, which are perhaps the descendants of a single element? For this, you need an additional set of XML operators. In the next chapter, I cover the new LINQ to XML operators that were added for just this purpose.

CHAPTER 8

■ ■ ■

LINQ to XML Operators

At this point, we are deep into LINQ to XML, and you are probably starting to wonder, "When are we going to get to the part about queries?" If so, then I say, "Hold on to your null reference there, Shortcake; you have been seeing them." Throughout the previous chapter, I was performing LINQ to XML queries whether they were merely returning all the child elements of an element or obtaining all of the ancestors of a node. Do you remember seeing the XContainer.Elements method? Do you recall any examples where I called the XContainer. Elements method? If so, you saw a LINQ to XML query. As evidence yet again of the seamless integration of LINQ queries into the language, it is sometimes easy to overlook that you are performing a query.

Because many of the class methods I have covered up to this point return a sequence of XML class objects, that is IEnumerable(Of T), where T is one of the LINQ to XML API classes, you can call the Standard Query Operators on the returned sequence, giving you even more power and flexibility.

So there are ways to get a sequence of XML objects from a single XML object, such as the descendants or ancestors of any given element, but what are missing are ways to perform LINQ to XML operations on each object in those sequences. For example, there is no simple way to get a sequence of elements and perform another XML-specific operation on each element in the sequence, such as returning each sequence element's child elements. In other words, thus far, you *can* obtain a sequence of an element's child elements by calling that element's Elements method, but you *cannot* obtain a sequence of an element's child elements' child elements. This is because the Elements method must be called on an XContainer, such as XElement or XDocument, but cannot be called on a *sequence* of XContainer objects. This is where the LINQ to XML operators come in handy.

Introduction to LINQ to XML Operators

The LINQ to XML API extends the LINQ to Objects Standard Query Operators with XML-specific operators. These XML operators are extension methods that are defined in the System. Xml.Linq.Extensions class, which itself is nothing more than a container class for these extension methods.

Each of these XML operators is called on a *sequence* of some LINQ to XML data type and performs some action on each entry in that sequence, such as returning all the ancestors or descendants of the entry.

Virtually every XML operator in this chapter has an equivalent method I covered in the previous chapter. The difference being that the method covered in the previous chapter is called on a single object, and the operator in this chapter is called on a *sequence* of objects. For example, in the previous chapter, I cover the XContainer.Elements method. Its declaration looks like this:

```
Public Function Elements As IEnumerable(Of XElement)
```

In this chapter, I cover the Extensions.Elements operator, and its declaration looks like this:

```
<ExtensionAttribute> _
Public Shared Function Elements (Of T As XContainer) ( _
    source As IEnumerable(Of T)) _
  As IEnumerable(Of XElement)
```

There is a significant difference between the two methods. The first declaration is called on a single object derived from XContainer, while the second declaration is called on a sequence of objects, where each object in the sequence must be derived from XContainer. Please be cognizant of the difference.

In this chapter, to distinguish between the methods covered in the previous chapter and the extension methods covered in this chapter, I typically refer to the extension methods as *operators.*

Now, let's examine each of these operators.

Ancestors

The Ancestors operator can be called on a sequence of nodes and returns a sequence containing the ancestor elements of each source node.

Declarations

The Ancestors operator has two declarations.

The First Ancestors Declaration

```
<ExtensionAttribute> _
Public Shared Function Ancestors (Of T As XNode) ( _
    source As IEnumerable(Of T)) _
  As IEnumerable(Of XElement)
```

This version of the operator can be called on a sequence of nodes, or objects derived from XNode. It returns a sequence of elements containing the ancestor elements of each node in the source sequence.

The Second Ancestors Declaration

```
<ExtensionAttribute> _
Public Shared Function Ancestors (Of T As XNode) ( _
    source As IEnumerable(Of T), name As XName) _
  As IEnumerable(Of XElement)
```

This version is like the first, except a name is passed and only those ancestor elements matching the specified name are returned in the output sequence.

Examples

Listing 8-1 is an example of calling the first `Ancestors` declaration.

Listing 8-1. *An Example of Calling the First Ancestors Declaration*

```
Dim xDocument As XDocument = _
  <?xml version="1.0"?>
  <BookParticipants>
    <BookParticipant type = "Author">
      <FirstName>Dennis</FirstName>
      <LastName>Hayes</LastName>
    </BookParticipant>
    <BookParticipant type = "Editor">
      <FirstName>Ewan</FirstName>
      <LastName>Buckingham</LastName>
    </BookParticipant>
  </BookParticipants>

Dim elements As IEnumerable(Of XElement) = _
  xDocument.Element("BookParticipants").Descendants("FirstName")

'  First, I will display the source elements.
For Each element As XElement In elements
  Console.WriteLine( _
    "Source element: {0} : value = {1}", element.Name, element.Value)
Next element

'  Now, I will display the ancestor elements for each source element.
For Each element As XElement In elements.Ancestors()
  Console.WriteLine("Ancestor element: {0}", element.Name)
Next element
```

In the previous example, I first create an XML document. Next, I generate a sequence of `FirstName` elements. Remember, this `Ancestors` method is called on a sequence of nodes, not on a single node, so I need a sequence on which to call it. Because I want to be able to display the names of the nodes for identification purposes, I actually build a sequence of elements, because elements have names but nodes do not. I then enumerate through the sequence displaying the source elements just so you can see the source sequence. Then, I enumerate on the elements returned from the Ancestors method and display them. Here are the results:

```
Source element: FirstName : value = Dennis
Source element: FirstName : value = Ewan
Ancestor element: BookParticipant
Ancestor element: BookParticipants
Ancestor element: BookParticipant
Ancestor element: BookParticipants
```

As you can see, it displays the two source sequence elements, the two FirstName elements. It then displays the ancestors for each of those two elements.

So using the Ancestors operator, I am able to retrieve all of the ancestor elements for each node in a sequence of nodes. In this case, my sequence is a sequence of elements, but that is alright, because an element is derived from a node. Remember, do not confuse the Ancestors operator that is called on a sequence of nodes, which I just demonstrated, with the Ancestors method I covered in the previous chapter.

Now, this example is not quite as impressive as it could be, because I needed to expand the code for demonstration purposes. For example, I wanted to capture the sequence of FirstName elements, because I wanted to display them so you could see the source elements in the output. So the statement containing the call to the Descendants method and the subsequent For Each block are for this purpose. Then, in the second For Each loop, I call the Ancestors operator and display each ancestor element. In reality, in that second For Each loop, I could have called the Ancestors method from the previous chapter on each element in the sequence of FirstName elements and not even called the Ancestors operator I am demonstrating. Listing 8-2 is an example demonstrating what I could have done, which would have accomplished the same result, but without even using the Ancestors operator.

Listing 8-2. *The Same Results as Listing 8-1 Without Calling the Ancestors Operator*

```
Dim xDocument As XDocument = _
  <?xml version="1.0"?>
  <BookParticipants>
    <BookParticipant type = "Author">
      <FirstName>Dennis</FirstName>
      <LastName>Hayes</LastName>
    </BookParticipant>
    <BookParticipant type = "Editor">
      <FirstName>Ewan</FirstName>
      <LastName>Buckingham</LastName>
    </BookParticipant>
  </BookParticipants>

Dim elements As IEnumerable(Of XElement) = _
  xDocument.Element("BookParticipants").Descendants("FirstName")
```

```
'  First, I will display the source elements.
For Each element As XElement In elements
  Console.WriteLine _
    ("Source element: {0} : value = {1}", element.Name, element.Value)
Next element

For Each element As XElement In elements
  '  Call the Ancestors method on each element.
  For Each e As XElement In element.Ancestors()
    '  Now, I will display the ancestor elements for each source element.
    Console.WriteLine("Ancestor element: {0}", e.Name)
  Next e
Next element
```

The difference between this example and the previous is that, instead of calling the Ancestors *operator* on the elements sequence in the For Each loop, I just loop on each element in the sequence and call the Ancestors *method* on it. In this example, I never call the Ancestors *operator*; I merely call the Ancestors *method* from the previous chapter. This code produces the same output though:

```
Source element: FirstName : value = Dennis
Source element: FirstName : value = Ewan
Ancestor element: BookParticipant
Ancestor element: BookParticipants
Ancestor element: BookParticipant
Ancestor element: BookParticipants
```

However, thanks to the Ancestors operator and the conciseness of LINQ, this query can be combined into a single, more concise statement as demonstrated in Listing 8-3.

Listing 8-3. *A More Concise Example of Calling the First Ancestors Declaration*

```
Dim xDocument As XDocument = _
  <?xml version="1.0"?>
  <BookParticipants>
    <BookParticipant type = "Author">
      <FirstName>Dennis</FirstName>
      <LastName>Hayes</LastName>
    </BookParticipant>
    <BookParticipant type = "Editor">
      <FirstName>Ewan</FirstName>
      <LastName>Buckingham</LastName>
    </BookParticipant>
  </BookParticipants>

For Each element As XElement _
    In xDocument.Element("BookParticipants").Descendants("FirstName").Ancestors()
  Console.WriteLine("Ancestor element: {0}", element.Name)
Next element
```

In this example, I cut right to the chase and call the Ancestors operator on the sequence of elements returned by the Descendants method. So the Descendants method returns a sequence of elements, and the Ancestors operator will return a sequence of elements containing all ancestors of every element in the sequence it is called on.

Since this code is meant to be more concise, it does not display the FirstName elements as the two previous examples did. However, the ancestor elements should be the same. Let's verify that they are:

```
Ancestor element: BookParticipant
Ancestor element: BookParticipants
Ancestor element: BookParticipant
Ancestor element: BookParticipants
```

And they are! In your production code, you would probably opt for a more concise query like the one I just presented. However, in this chapter, the examples will be more verbose, like Listing 8-1, for demonstration purposes.

■Tip We can make Listing 8-3 even more concise if we take advantage of the VB.NET 2008 descendant axis property that I covered in Chapter 2. I could simply replace the For Each statement in the code with:

```
For Each element As XElement In xDocument...<FirstName>.Ancestors()
```

However, since this chapter is about the interaction between the LINQ to XML API methods covered in the previous chapter working together with the LINQ to XML operators covered in this chapter, I will not be using any of the VB.NET 2008 axis properties in this chapter.

To demonstrate the second Ancestors declaration, I will use the same basic code as Listing 8-1, except I will change the call to the Ancestors operator so that it includes the parameter BookParticipant so that I only get the elements matching that name. That code looks like Listing 8-4.

Listing 8-4. *Calling the Second Ancestors Declaration*

```
Dim xDocument As XDocument = _
  <?xml version="1.0"?>
  <BookParticipants>
    <BookParticipant type = "Author">
      <FirstName>Dennis</FirstName>
      <LastName>Hayes</LastName>
    </BookParticipant>
    <BookParticipant type = "Editor">
      <FirstName>Ewan</FirstName>
      <LastName>Buckingham</LastName>
    </BookParticipant>
  </BookParticipants>
```

```
Dim elements As IEnumerable(Of XElement) = _
  xDocument.Element("BookParticipants").Descendants("FirstName")

'  First, I will display the source elements.
For Each element As XElement In elements
  Console.WriteLine ( _
    "Source element: {0} : value = {1}", element.Name, element.Value)
Next element

'  Now, I will display the ancestor elements for each source element.
For Each element As XElement In elements.Ancestors("BookParticipant")
  Console.WriteLine("Ancestor element: {0}", element.Name)
Next element
```

The results now should only include the BookParticipant elements and, of course, the source elements, but the two BookParticipants elements that are displayed in the first declaration's example should now be gone:

```
Source element: FirstName : value = Dennis
Source element: FirstName : value = Ewan
Ancestor element: BookParticipant
Ancestor element: BookParticipant
```

And they are.

AncestorsAndSelf

The AncestorsAndSelf operator can be called on a sequence of elements and returns a sequence containing the ancestor elements of each source element and the source element itself. This operator is just like the Ancestors operator except for the fact that it can only be called on elements, as opposed to nodes, and also includes each source element in the returned sequence of ancestor elements.

Declarations

The AncestorsAndSelf operator has two declarations.

The First AncestorsAndSelf Declaration

```
<ExtensionAttribute> _
Public Shared Function AncestorsAndSelf ( _
    source As IEnumerable(Of XElement)) _
  As IEnumerable(Of XElement)
```

This version of the operator can be called on a sequence of elements and returns a sequence of elements containing each source element itself and its ancestor elements.

The Second AncestorsAndSelf Declaration

```
<ExtensionAttribute> _
Public Shared Function AncestorsAndSelf ( _
    source As IEnumerable(Of XElement), _
    name As XName ) _
  As IEnumerable(Of XElement)
```

This version is like the first, except a name is passed, and only those source elements and its ancestors matching the specified name are returned in the output sequence.

Examples

For an example of the first AncestorsAndSelf declaration, I will use the same basic example I used for the first Ancestors declaration, except I will call the AncestorsAndSelf operator instead of the Ancestors operator, as shown in Listing 8-5.

Listing 8-5. *Calling the First AncestorsAndSelf Declaration*

```
Dim xDocument As XDocument = _
  <?xml version="1.0"?>
  <BookParticipants>
    <BookParticipant type = "Author">
      <FirstName>Dennis</FirstName>
      <LastName>Hayes</LastName>
    </BookParticipant>
    <BookParticipant type = "Editor">
      <FirstName>Ewan</FirstName>
      <LastName>Buckingham</LastName>
    </BookParticipant>
  </BookParticipants>

Dim elements As IEnumerable(Of XElement) = _
  xDocument.Element("BookParticipants").Descendants("FirstName")

'  First, I will display the source elements.
For Each element As XElement In elements
  Console.WriteLine _
    ("Source element: {0} : value = {1}", element.Name, element.Value)
Next element

'  Now, I will display the ancestor elements for each source element.
For Each element As XElement In elements.AncestorsAndSelf()
  Console.WriteLine("Ancestor element: {0}", element.Name)
Next element
```

Just as with the first Ancestors declaration, I first create an XML document. Next, I generate a sequence of FirstName elements. Remember, this AncestorsAndSelf method is called on a sequence of elements, not on a single element, so I need a sequence on which to call it. I then enumerate through the sequence displaying the source elements just so you can see the source sequence. Then, I enumerate on the elements returned from the AncestorsAndSelf method and display them.

If this works as I expect, the results should be the same as the results from the first Ancestors declaration's example, except now the FirstName elements should be included in the output. Here are the results:

```
Source element: FirstName : value = Dennis
Source element: FirstName : value = Ewan
Ancestor element: FirstName
Ancestor element: BookParticipant
Ancestor element: BookParticipants
Ancestor element: FirstName
Ancestor element: BookParticipant
Ancestor element: BookParticipants
```

For an example of the second AncestorsAndSelf declaration, I will use the same basic example that I used in the example for the second Ancestors declaration, except, of course, I will change the call from the Ancestors method to the AncestorsAndSelf method, as shown in Listing 8-6.

Listing 8-6. *Calling the Second AncestorsAndSelf Declaration*

```
Dim xDocument As XDocument = _
  <?xml version="1.0"?>
  <BookParticipants>
    <BookParticipant type = "Author">
      <FirstName>Dennis</FirstName>
      <LastName>Hayes</LastName>
    </BookParticipant>
    <BookParticipant type = "Editor">
      <FirstName>Ewan</FirstName>
      <LastName>Buckingham</LastName>
    </BookParticipant>
  </BookParticipants>

Dim elements As IEnumerable(Of XElement) = _
  xDocument.Element("BookParticipants").Descendants("FirstName")

' First, I will display the source elements.
For Each element As XElement In elements
  Console.WriteLine _
    ("Source element: {0} : value = {1}", element.Name, element.Value)
Next element

' Now, I will display the ancestor elements for each source element.
For Each element As XElement In elements.AncestorsAndSelf("BookParticipant")
  Console.WriteLine("Ancestor element: {0}", element.Name)
Next element
```

Now, I should only receive the elements named BookParticipant. Here are the results:

```
Source element: FirstName : value = Dennis
Source element: FirstName : value = Ewan
Ancestor element: BookParticipant
Ancestor element: BookParticipant
```

Notice that the displayed output from the AncestorsAndSelf method is just the BookParticipant elements, because they are the only elements matching the name I passed. I didn't even get the source elements themselves, because they didn't match the name. So the function worked as defined.

Call me crazy, but this declaration of the operator seems fairly useless to me. How many levels of elements are you going to have in an XML tree with the same name? If you don't answer *at least two*, how will this method ever return the self elements and any ancestor elements? It just doesn't seem likely to me. Yes, I know; I like symmetrical APIs too.

Attributes

The Attributes operator can be called on a sequence of elements and returns a sequence containing the attributes of each source element.

Declarations

The Attributes operator has two declarations.

The First Attributes Declaration

```
<ExtensionAttribute> _
Public Shared Function Attributes ( _
    source As IEnumerable(Of XElement)) _
  As IEnumerable(Of XAttribute)
```

This version of the operator can be called on a sequence of elements and returns a sequence of attributes containing all the attributes for each source element.

The Second Attributes Declaration

```
<ExtensionAttribute> _
Public Shared Function Attributes ( _
    source As IEnumerable(Of XElement), _
    name As XName) _
  As IEnumerable(Of XAttribute)
```

This version of the operator is like the first, except only those attributes matching the specified name will be returned in the sequence of attributes.

Examples

For an example of the first Attributes declaration, I will build the same XML tree I have been building for the previous examples. However, the sequence of source elements I generate will be a little different because I need a sequence of elements with attributes. So I'll generate a sequence of the BookParticipant elements and work from there, as shown in Listing 8-7.

Listing 8-7. *Calling the First Attributes Declaration*

```
Dim xDocument As XDocument = _
  <?xml version="1.0"?>
  <BookParticipants>
    <BookParticipant type = "Author">
      <FirstName>Dennis</FirstName>
      <LastName>Hayes</LastName>
    </BookParticipant>
    <BookParticipant type = "Editor">
      <FirstName>Ewan</FirstName>
      <LastName>Buckingham</LastName>
    </BookParticipant>
  </BookParticipants>

Dim elements As IEnumerable(Of XElement) = _
  xDocument.Element("BookParticipants").Elements("BookParticipant")

'  First, I will display the source elements.
For Each element As XElement In elements
  Console.WriteLine ( _
    "Source element: {0} : value = {1}", element.Name, element.Value)
Next element

'  Now, I will display each source element's attributes.
For Each attribute As XAttribute In elements.Attributes()
  Console.WriteLine("Attribute: {0} : value = {1}", attribute.Name, attribute.Value)
Next attribute
```

Once I obtain the sequence of BookParticipant elements, I display the source sequence. Then, I call the Attributes operator on the source sequence and display the attributes in the sequence returned by the Attributes operator. Here are the results:

```
Source element: BookParticipant : value = DennisHayes
Source element: BookParticipant : value = EwanBuckingham
Attribute: type : value = Author
Attribute: type : value = Editor
```

As you can see, the attributes are retrieved. For an example of the second Attributes declaration, I will use the same basic example as the previous, except I will specify a name that the attributes must match to be returned by the Attributes operator, as shown in Listing 8-8.

Listing 8-8. *Calling the Second Attributes Declaration*

```
Dim xDocument As XDocument = _
  <?xml version="1.0"?>
  <BookParticipants>
    <BookParticipant type = "Author">
      <FirstName>Dennis</FirstName>
      <LastName>Hayes</LastName>
    </BookParticipant>
    <BookParticipant type = "Editor">
      <FirstName>Ewan</FirstName>
      <LastName>Buckingham</LastName>
    </BookParticipant>
  </BookParticipants>

Dim elements As IEnumerable(Of XElement) = _
  xDocument.Element("BookParticipants").Elements("BookParticipant")

'  First, I will display the source elements.
For Each element As XElement In elements
  Console.WriteLine ( _
    "Source element: {0} : value = {1}", element.Name, element.Value)
Next element

'  Now, I will display each source element's attributes.
For Each attribute As XAttribute In elements.Attributes("type")
  Console.WriteLine ( _
    "Attribute: {0} : value = {1}", attribute.Name, attribute.Value)
Next attribute
```

In the previous code, I specify that the attributes must match the name type. So this should return the same output as the previous example. Pressing Ctrl+F5 returns the following:

```
Source element: BookParticipant : value = DennisHayes
Source element: BookParticipant : value = EwanBuckingham
Attribute: type : value = Author
Attribute: type : value = Editor
```

So I did get the results I expected. Had I specified the name as Type so that the first letter is capitalized, the two attributes would not have been displayed because the Attributes operator would not have returned those attributes from the source sequence. That demonstrates the case of when the name doesn't match, as well as the fact that the name is case-sensitive, which isn't that surprising since XML is case-sensitive.

DescendantNodes

The DescendantNodes operator can be called on a sequence of elements and returns a sequence containing the descendant nodes of each element or document.

Declarations

The DescendantNodes operator has one declaration.

The Only DescendantNodes Declaration

```
<ExtensionAttribute> _
Public Shared Function DescendantNodes (Of T As XContainer) ( _
    source As IEnumerable(Of T) ) _
  As IEnumerable(Of XNode)
```

This version can be called on a sequence of elements or documents and returns a sequence of nodes containing each source element's or document's descendant nodes.

This is different from the XContainer.DescendantNodes method in that this method is called on a sequence of elements or documents, as opposed to a single element or document.

Examples

For this example, I will build the same XML tree I have used for the previous examples, except I will also add a comment to the first BookParticipant element. This is to have at least one node get returned that is not an element. When I build my source sequence of elements, I want some elements that have some descendants, so I will build my source sequence with the BookParticipant elements since they have some descendants, as shown in Listing 8-9.

Listing 8-9. *Calling the Only DescendantNodes Declaration*

```
Dim xDocument As XDocument = _
  <?xml version="1.0"?>
  <BookParticipants>
    <BookParticipant type = "Author">
      <!--This is a new author-->
      <FirstName>Dennis</FirstName>
      <LastName>Hayes</LastName>
    </BookParticipant>
    <BookParticipant type = "Editor">
      <FirstName>Ewan</FirstName>
      <LastName>Buckingham</LastName>
    </BookParticipant>
  </BookParticipants>

Dim elements As IEnumerable(Of XElement) = _
  xDocument.Element("BookParticipants").Elements("BookParticipant")

'  First, I will display the source elements.
For Each element As XElement In elements
  Console.WriteLine ( _
    "Source element: {0} : value = {1}", element.Name, element.Value)
Next element
```

```
'  Now, I will display each source element's descendant nodes.
For Each node As XNode In elements.DescendantNodes()
  Console.WriteLine("Descendant node: {0}", node)
Next node
```

As is typical with the examples in this section, I built my XML tree and a source sequence of elements. In this case, the source sequence contains the BookParticipant elements. I then call the DescendantNodes operator on the source sequence and display the results:

```
Source element: BookParticipant : value = DennisHayes
Source element: BookParticipant : value = EwanBuckingham
Descendant node: <!--This is a new author.-->
Descendant node: <FirstName>Dennis</FirstName>
Descendant node: Dennis
Descendant node: <LastName>Hayes</LastName>
Descendant node: Hayes
Descendant node: <FirstName>Ewan</FirstName>
Descendant node: Ewan
Descendant node: <LastName>Buckingham</LastName>
Descendant node: Buckingham
```

Notice that not only did I get my descendant elements, I got my comment node as well. Also notice that for each element in the XML document, I ended up with two nodes. For example, there is a node whose value is "<FirstName>Dennis</FirstName>" and a node whose value is "Dennis". The first node in the pair is the FirstName element. The second node is the XText node for that element. I bet you had forgotten about those automatically created XText objects. I know I did, but there they are.

DescendantNodesAndSelf

The DescendantNodesAndSelf operator can be called on a sequence of elements and returns a sequence containing each source element itself and each source element's descendant nodes.

Declarations

The DescendantNodesAndSelf operator has one declaration.

The Only DescendantNodesAndSelf Declaration

```
<ExtensionAttribute> _
Public Shared Function DescendantNodesAndSelf ( _
    source As IEnumerable(Of XElement)) _
  As IEnumerable(Of XNode)
```

This version is called on a sequence of elements and returns a sequence of nodes containing each source element itself and each source element's descendant nodes.

Examples

For this example, I will use the same example used for the DescendantNodes operator, except I
will call the DescendantNodesAndSelf operator, as shown in Listing 8-10.

Listing 8-10. *Calling the Only DescendantNodesAndSelf Declaration*

```
Dim xDocument As XDocument = _
  <?xml version="1.0"?>
  <BookParticipants>
    <BookParticipant type = "Author">
      <!--This is a new author-->
      <FirstName>Dennis</FirstName>
      <LastName>Hayes</LastName>
    </BookParticipant>
    <BookParticipant type = "Editor">
      <FirstName>Ewan</FirstName>
      <LastName>Buckingham</LastName>
    </BookParticipant>
  </BookParticipants>

Dim elements As IEnumerable(Of XElement) = _
  xDocument.Element("BookParticipants").Elements("BookParticipant")

' First, I will display the source elements.
For Each element As XElement In elements
  Console.WriteLine ( _
    "Source element: {0} : value = {1}", element.Name, element.Value)
Next element

' Now, I will display each source element's descendant nodes.
For Each node As XNode In elements.DescendantNodesAndSelf()
  Console.WriteLine("Descendant node: {0}", node)
Next node
```

So the question is, will the output be the same as the output for the DescendantNodes
example except that the source elements will be included too? You bet:

```
Source element: BookParticipant : value = DennisHayes
Source element: BookParticipant : value = EwanBuckingham
Descendant node: <BookParticipant type="Author">
  <!--This is a new author.-->
  <FirstName>Dennis</FirstName>
  <LastName>Hayes</LastName>
</BookParticipant>
Descendant node: <!--This is a new author.-->
Descendant node: <FirstName>Dennis</FirstName>
Descendant node: Dennis
Descendant node: <LastName>Hayes</LastName>
Descendant node: Hayes
```

```
Descendant node: <BookParticipant type="Editor">
  <FirstName>Ewan</FirstName>
  <LastName>Buckingham</LastName>
</BookParticipant>
Descendant node: <FirstName>Ewan</FirstName>
Descendant node: Ewan
Descendant node: <LastName>Buckingham</LastName>
Descendant node: Buckingham
```

Not only did I get the BookParticipant elements themselves and their descendants, I got the single node that is not an element, the comment. This is in contrast to the Descendants and DescendantsAndSelf operators I cover next, which will omit the nodes that are not elements.

Descendants

The Descendants operator can be called on a sequence of elements or documents and returns a sequence of elements containing each source element's or document's descendant elements.

Declarations

The Descendants operator has two declarations.

The First Descendants Declaration

```
<ExtensionAttribute> _
Public Shared Function Descendants (Of T As XContainer) ( _
    source As IEnumerable(Of T)) _
  As IEnumerable(Of XElement)
```

This version is called on a sequence of elements or documents and returns a sequence of elements containing each source element's or document's descendant elements.

This is different from the XContainer.Descendants method in that this method is called on a sequence of elements or documents, as opposed to a single element or document.

The Second Descendants Declaration

```
<ExtensionAttribute> _
Public Shared Function Descendants (Of T As XContainer) ( _
    source As IEnumerable(Of T), name As XName) _
  As IEnumerable(Of XElement)
```

This version is like the first, except only those elements matching the specified name are returned in the output sequence.

Examples

For the example of the first declaration, I will basically use the same example I used for the DescendantNodes operator, except I will call the Descendants operator instead. The output should be the same, except there should not be any nodes that are not elements. This means you should not see the comment in the output. Listing 8-11 shows the code.

Listing 8-11. *Calling the First Descendants Declaration*

```
Dim xDocument As XDocument = _
  <?xml version="1.0"?>
  <BookParticipants>
    <BookParticipant type = "Author">
      <!--This is a new author-->
      <FirstName>Dennis</FirstName>
      <LastName>Hayes</LastName>
    </BookParticipant>
    <BookParticipant type = "Editor">
      <FirstName>Ewan</FirstName>
      <LastName>Buckingham</LastName>
    </BookParticipant>
  </BookParticipants>

Dim elements As IEnumerable(Of XElement) = _
  xDocument.Element("BookParticipants").Elements("BookParticipant")

' First, I will display the source elements.
For Each element As XElement In elements
  Console.WriteLine( _
    "Source element: {0} : value = {1}", element.Name, element.Value)
Next element

' Now, I will display each source element's descendant elements.
For Each element As XElement In elements.Descendants()
  Console.WriteLine("Descendant element: {0}", element)
Next element
```

This example is basically like all of the previous except you should only see the descendant elements of the two BookParticipant elements. The results of this example are the following:

```
Source element: BookParticipant : value = DennisHayes
Source element: BookParticipant : value = EwanBuckingham
Descendant element: <FirstName>Dennis</FirstName>
Descendant element: <LastName>Hayes</LastName>
Descendant element: <FirstName>Ewan</FirstName>
Descendant element: <LastName>Buckingham</LastName>
```

Comparing these results to that of the DescendantNodes operator example, I notice some differences I did not initially anticipate. Sure, the descendants are labeled as elements instead of nodes, and the comment is not there, but additionally, the descendant nodes such as Dennis and Hayes are missing as well. Oh yeah, those nodes are not elements either; they are XText objects. The LINQ to XML API handles the text nodes so seamlessly that it is easy to forget about them.

For an example of the second declaration, I will use the same code as the first example except I specify a name that the descendant elements must match to be returned by the second declaration of the Descendants operator, as shown in Listing 8-12.

Listing 8-12. *Calling the Second Descendants Declaration*

```
Dim xDocument As XDocument = _
  <?xml version="1.0"?>
  <BookParticipants>
    <BookParticipant type = "Author">
      <!--This is a new author-->
      <FirstName>Dennis</FirstName>
      <LastName>Hayes</LastName>
    </BookParticipant>
    <BookParticipant type = "Editor">
      <FirstName>Ewan</FirstName>
      <LastName>Buckingham</LastName>
    </BookParticipant>
  </BookParticipants>

Dim elements As IEnumerable(Of XElement) = _
  xDocument.Element("BookParticipants").Elements("BookParticipant")

' First, I will display the source elements.
For Each element As XElement In elements
  Console.WriteLine( _
    "Source element: {0} : value = {1}", element.Name, element.Value)
Next element

' Now, I will display each source element's descendant elements.
For Each element As XElement In elements.Descendants("LastName")
  Console.WriteLine("Descendant element: {0}", element)
Next element
```

The results of this example are the following:

```
Source element: BookParticipant : value = DennisHayes
Source element: BookParticipant : value = EwanBuckingham
Descendant element: <LastName>Hayes</LastName>
Descendant element: <LastName>Buckingham</LastName>
```

As you would expect, only the LastName elements are returned.

DescendantsAndSelf

The DescendantsAndSelf operator can be called on a sequence of elements and returns a sequence containing each source element and its descendant elements.

Declarations

The DescendantsAndSelf operator has two declarations.

The First DescendantsAndSelf Declaration

```
<ExtensionAttribute> _
Public Shared Function DescendantsAndSelf ( _
    source As IEnumerable(Of XElement)) _
  As IEnumerable(Of XElement)
```

This version is called on a sequence of elements and returns a sequence of elements containing each source element and its descendant elements.

The Second DescendantsAndSelf Declaration

```
<ExtensionAttribute> _
Public Shared Function DescendantsAndSelf ( _
    source As IEnumerable(Of XElement), _
    name As XName) _
  As IEnumerable(Of XElement)
```

This version is like the first, except only those elements matching the specified name are returned in the output sequence.

Examples

For this example, I will use the same code as the example for the first declaration of the Descendants operator, except I will call the DescendantsAndSelf operator, as shown in Listing 8-13.

Listing 8-13. *Calling the First DescendantsAndSelf Declaration*

```
Dim xDocument As XDocument = _
  <?xml version="1.0"?>
  <BookParticipants>
    <BookParticipant type = "Author">
      <!--This is a new author-->
      <FirstName>Dennis</FirstName>
      <LastName>Hayes</LastName>
    </BookParticipant>
    <BookParticipant type = "Editor">
      <FirstName>Ewan</FirstName>
      <LastName>Buckingham</LastName>
    </BookParticipant>
  </BookParticipants>

Dim elements As IEnumerable(Of XElement) = _
  xDocument.Element("BookParticipants").Elements("BookParticipant")
```

```
'  First, I will display the source elements.
For Each element As XElement In elements
  Console.WriteLine( _
    "Source element: {0} : value = {1}", element.Name, element.Value)
Next element

'  Now, I will display each source element's descendant elements.
For Each element As XElement In elements.DescendantsAndSelf()
  Console.WriteLine("Descendant element: {0}", element)
Next element
```

Now, you should see all the descendant elements and the source elements themselves. The results of this example are the following:

```
Source element: BookParticipant : value = DennisHayes
Source element: BookParticipant : value = EwanBuckingham
Descendant element: <BookParticipant type="Author">
  <!--This is a new author.-->
  <FirstName>Dennis</FirstName>
  <LastName>Hayes</LastName>
</BookParticipant>
Descendant element: <FirstName>Dennis</FirstName>
Descendant element: <LastName>Hayes</LastName>
Descendant element: <BookParticipant type="Editor">
  <FirstName>Ewan</FirstName>
  <LastName>Buckingham</LastName>
</BookParticipant>
Descendant element: <FirstName>Ewan</FirstName>
Descendant element: <LastName>Buckingham</LastName>
```

So the output is the same as the first declaration for the Descendants operator, except it does include the source elements themselves, the BookParticipant elements. Don't let the existence of the comment in the results fool you. It is not there because the comment was returned by the DescendantsAndSelf operator; it is there because I display the BookParticipant element, which was returned by the operator.

For the second DescendantsAndSelf declaration, I will use the same example as the first declaration, except I specify a name the element must match to be returned, as shown in Listing 8-14.

Listing 8-14. *Calling the Second DescendantsAndSelf Declaration*

```
Dim xDocument As XDocument = _
  <?xml version="1.0"?>
  <BookParticipants>
    <BookParticipant type = "Author">
      <!--This is a new author-->
      <FirstName>Dennis</FirstName>
```

```
      <LastName>Hayes</LastName>
    </BookParticipant>
    <BookParticipant type = "Editor">
      <FirstName>Ewan</FirstName>
      <LastName>Buckingham</LastName>
    </BookParticipant>
  </BookParticipants>

Dim elements As IEnumerable(Of XElement) = _
  xDocument.Element("BookParticipants").Elements("BookParticipant")

'  First, I will display the source elements.
For Each element As XElement In elements
  Console.WriteLine( _
    "Source element: {0} : value = {1}", element.Name, element.Value)
Next element

'  Now, I will display each source element's descendant elements.
For Each element As XElement In elements.DescendantsAndSelf("LastName")
  Console.WriteLine("Descendant element: {0}", element)
Next element
```

The results of this example are the following:

```
Source element: BookParticipant : value = DennisHayes
Source element: BookParticipant : value = EwanBuckingham
Descendant element: <LastName>Hayes</LastName>
Descendant element: <LastName>Buckingham</LastName>
```

The results include only the descendant elements that match the name I specified. There isn't much evidence that I called the DescendantsAndSelf operator, as opposed to the Descendants operator, since the source elements were not returned due to their name not matching the specified name. Again, as with all the operators that return elements from multiple levels of the XML tree that accept a name argument that the elements must match to be returned, it just doesn't seem likely that you will need the AndSelf versions of the operators, because you probably wouldn't have that many levels of elements having the same name.

Elements

The Elements operator can be called on a sequence of elements or documents and returns a sequence of elements containing each source element's or document's child elements.

This operator is different than the Descendants operator, because the Elements operator returns only the immediate child elements of each element in the source sequence of elements, whereas the Descendants operator recursively returns all child elements until the end of each tree is reached.

Declarations

The Elements operator has two declarations.

The First Elements Declaration

```
<ExtensionAttribute> _
Public Shared Function Elements (Of T As XContainer) ( _
    source As IEnumerable(Of T)) _
  As IEnumerable(Of XElement)
```

This version is called on a sequence of elements or documents and returns a sequence of elements containing each source element's or document's child elements.

This is different from the XContainer.Elements method in that this method is called on a sequence of elements or documents, as opposed to a single element or document.

The Second Elements Declaration

```
<ExtensionAttribute> _
Public Shared Function Elements (Of T As XContainer) ( _
    source As IEnumerable(Of T), _
    name As XName) _
  As IEnumerable(Of XElement)
```

This version is like the first, except only those elements matching the specified name are returned in the output sequence.

Examples

By now, you probably know the drill. For an example of the first declaration, I will use the same basic example as the DescendantsAndSelf operator used, except I will call the Elements operator instead, as shown in Listing 8-15.

Listing 8-15. *Calling the First Elements Declaration*

```
Dim xDocument As XDocument = _
  <?xml version="1.0"?>
  <BookParticipants>
    <BookParticipant type = "Author">
      <!--This is a new author-->
      <FirstName>Dennis</FirstName>
      <LastName>Hayes</LastName>
    </BookParticipant>
    <BookParticipant type = "Editor">
      <FirstName>Ewan</FirstName>
      <LastName>Buckingham</LastName>
    </BookParticipant>
  </BookParticipants>
```

```
Dim elements As IEnumerable(Of XElement) = _
  xDocument.Element("BookParticipants").Elements("BookParticipant")

'  First, I will display the source elements.
For Each element As XElement In elements
  Console.WriteLine( _
    "Source element: {0} : value = {1}", element.Name, element.Value)
Next element

'  Now, I will display each source element's elements.
For Each element As XElement In elements.Elements()
  Console.WriteLine("Child element: {0}", element)
Next element
```

As in the previous examples, I build my XML tree, obtain a sequence of source elements, display each source element, retrieve a sequence of each source element's child elements, and display the child elements:

```
Source element: BookParticipant : value = DennisHayes
Source element: BookParticipant : value = EwanBuckingham
Child element: <FirstName>Dennis</FirstName>
Child element: <LastName>Hayes</LastName>
Child element: <FirstName>Ewan</FirstName>
Child element: <LastName>Buckingham</LastName>
```

That example returns all child elements. To retrieve just those matching a specific name, I use the second declaration of the Elements operator, as shown in Listing 8-16.

Listing 8-16. *Calling the Second Elements Declaration*

```
Dim xDocument As XDocument = _
  <?xml version="1.0"?>
  <BookParticipants>
    <BookParticipant type = "Author">
      <!--This is a new author-->
      <FirstName>Dennis</FirstName>
      <LastName>Hayes</LastName>
    </BookParticipant>
    <BookParticipant type = "Editor">
      <FirstName>Ewan</FirstName>
      <LastName>Buckingham</LastName>
    </BookParticipant>
  </BookParticipants>

Dim elements As IEnumerable(Of XElement) = _
  xDocument.Element("BookParticipants").Elements("BookParticipant")
```

```
'  First, I will display the source elements.
For Each element As XElement In elements
  Console.WriteLine( _
    "Source element: {0} : value = {1}", element.Name, element.Value)
Next element

'  Now, I will display each source element's elements.
For Each element As XElement In elements.Elements("LastName")
  Console.WriteLine("Child element: {0}", element)
Next element
```

Now, I should only get the child elements matching the name LastName:

```
Source element: BookParticipant : value = DennisHayes
Source element: BookParticipant : value = EwanBuckingham
Child element: <LastName>Hayes</LastName>
Child element: <LastName>Buckingham</LastName>
```

That works just as expected.

InDocumentOrder

The InDocumentOrder operator can be called on a sequence of nodes and returns a sequence containing each source node sorted in document order.

Declarations

The InDocumentOrder operator has one declaration.

The Only InDocumentOrder Declaration

```
<ExtensionAttribute> _
Public Shared Function InDocumentOrder (Of T As XNode) ( _
    source As IEnumerable(Of T)) _
  As IEnumerable(Of T)
```

This version is called on a sequence of a specified type, which must be nodes or some type derived from nodes, and returns a sequence of that same type containing each source node in document order.

Examples

This is a fairly odd operator. For this example, I need a source sequence of nodes. Since I want to see some nodes that are not elements in addition to elements, I will build a sequence of nodes that are the child nodes of the BookParticipant elements. I do this because one of them has a comment, which is a node but not an element. My source is shown in Listing 8-17.

Listing 8-17. *Calling the Only InDocumentOrder Declaration*

```
Dim xDocument As XDocument = _
  <?xml version="1.0"?>
  <BookParticipants>
    <BookParticipant type = "Author">
      <!--This is a new author-->
      <FirstName>Dennis</FirstName>
      <LastName>Hayes</LastName>
    </BookParticipant>
    <BookParticipant type = "Editor">
      <FirstName>Ewan</FirstName>
      <LastName>Buckingham</LastName>
    </BookParticipant>
  </BookParticipants>

Dim nodes As IEnumerable(Of XNode) = _
  xDocument.Element("BookParticipants") _
    .Elements("BookParticipant"). Nodes().Reverse()


'  First, I will display the source nodes.
For Each node As XNode In nodes
  Console.WriteLine("Source node: {0}", node)
Next node


'  Now, I will display each source nodes's child nodes.
For Each node As XNode In nodes.InDocumentOrder()
  Console.WriteLine("Ordered node: {0}", node)
Next node
```

As you can see in the previous code, I build my XML tree. When I retrieve my source sequence, I get the BookParticipant element's child nodes by calling the Nodes operator, and then I call the Reverse Standard Query Operator. If you recall from Part 2 of this book about LINQ to Objects, the Reverse operator will return a sequence where entries in the input sequence have had their order reversed. So now I have a sequence of nodes that are not in the original order. I take this additional step of altering the order so that when I call the InDocumentOrder operator, a difference can be detected. Then, I display the disordered source nodes, call the InDocumentOrder operator, and display the results. Here they are:

```
Source node: <LastName>Buckingham</LastName>
Source node: <FirstName>Ewan</FirstName>
Source node: <LastName>Hayes</LastName>
Source node: <FirstName>Dennis</FirstName>
Source node: <!--This is a new author.-->
Ordered node: <!--This is a new author.-->
Ordered node: <FirstName>Dennis</FirstName>
Ordered node: <LastName>Hayes</LastName>
```

```
Ordered node: <FirstName>Ewan</FirstName>
Ordered node: <LastName>Buckingham</LastName>
```

As you can see, the source nodes are in the reverse order that I built them in, and the ordered nodes are back in the original order. Cool but odd.

Nodes

The Nodes operator can be called on a sequence of elements or documents and returns a sequence of nodes containing each source element's or document's child nodes.

This operator is different than the DescendantNodes operator in that the Nodes operator only returns the immediate child elements of each element in the source sequence of elements, whereas the DescendantNodes operator recursively returns all child nodes until the end of each tree is reached.

Declarations

The Nodes operator has one declaration.

The Only Nodes Declaration

```
<ExtensionAttribute> _
Public Shared Function Nodes (Of T As XContainer) ( _
    source As IEnumerable(Of T)) As _
  IEnumerable(Of XNode)
```

This version is called on a sequence of elements or documents and returns a sequence of nodes containing each source element's or document's child nodes.

This is different from the XContainer.Nodes method in that this method is called on a sequence of elements or documents, as opposed to a single element or document.

Examples

For this example, I will build my typical XML tree and build a source sequence of BookParticipant elements. I will display each of them, and then I will return the child nodes of each source element and display them, as shown in Listing 8-18.

Listing 8-18. *Calling the Only Nodes Declaration*

```
Dim xDocument As XDocument = _
  <?xml version="1.0"?>
  <BookParticipants>
    <BookParticipant type = "Author">
      <!--This is a new author-->
      <FirstName>Dennis</FirstName>
      <LastName>Hayes</LastName>
    </BookParticipant>
    <BookParticipant type = "Editor">
```

```
      <FirstName>Ewan</FirstName>
      <LastName>Buckingham</LastName>
    </BookParticipant>
  </BookParticipants>

Dim elements As IEnumerable(Of XElement) = _
  xDocument.Element("BookParticipants").Elements("BookParticipant")

'  First, I will display the source elements.
For Each element As XElement In elements
  Console.WriteLine( _
    "Source element: {0} : value = {1}", element.Name, element.Value)
Next element

'  Now, I will display each source element's child nodes.
For Each node As XNode In elements.Nodes()
  Console.WriteLine("Child node: {0}", node)
Next node
```

Since this operator returns the child nodes, as opposed to elements, the output should have the comment of the first BookParticipant element in the results:

```
Source element: BookParticipant : value = DennisHayes
Source element: BookParticipant : value = EwanBuckingham
Child node: <!--This is a new author.-->
Child node: <FirstName>Dennis</FirstName>
Child node: <LastName>Hayes</LastName>
Child node: <FirstName>Ewan</FirstName>
Child node: <LastName>Buckingham</LastName>
```

The results display each source element's child nodes. Notice that because only the immediate child nodes are retrieved, I didn't get the XText nodes that are children of each FirstName and LastName element, as I did in the DescendantNodes operator example.

Remove

The Remove operator can be called on a sequence of nodes or attributes to remove them. This method will cache a copy of the nodes or attributes in a List to eliminate the Halloween problem discussed in the previous chapter.

Declarations

The Remove operator has two declarations.

The First Remove Declaration

```
<ExtensionAttribute> _
Public Shared Sub Remove( _
  source As IEnumerable(Of XAttribute))
```

This version is called on a sequence of attributes and removes all attributes in the source sequence.

The Second Remove Declaration

```
<ExtensionAttribute> _
Public Shared Sub Remove (Of T As XNode) ( _
  source As IEnumerable(Of T))
```

This version is called on a sequence of a specified type, which must be nodes or some type derived from nodes, and removes all nodes in the source sequence.

Examples

Since the first declaration is for removing attributes, I need a sequence of attributes. So I will build my standard XML tree and retrieve a sequence of the BookParticipant element's attributes. I will display each source attribute and then call the Remove operator on the sequence of source attributes. Just to prove it worked, I will display the entire XML document, and the attributes will be gone, as shown in Listing 8-19.

Listing 8-19. *Calling the First Remove Declaration*

```
Dim xDocument As XDocument = _
  <?xml version="1.0"?>
  <BookParticipants>
    <BookParticipant type = "Author">
      <!--This is a new author-->
      <FirstName>Dennis</FirstName>
      <LastName>Hayes</LastName>
    </BookParticipant>
    <BookParticipant type = "Editor">
      <FirstName>Ewan</FirstName>
      <LastName>Buckingham</LastName>
    </BookParticipant>
  </BookParticipants>

Dim attributes As IEnumerable(Of XAttribute) = _
  xDocument.Element("BookParticipants").Elements("BookParticipant").Attributes()

'  First, I will display the source attributes.
For Each attribute As XAttribute In attributes
  Console.WriteLine( _
```

```
        "Source attribute: {0} : value = {1}", _
        attribute.Name, _
        attribute.Value)
Next attribute
```

attributes.Remove()

```
'  Now, I will display the XML document.
Console.WriteLine(xDocument)
```

Will it work? Let's see:

```
Source attribute: type : value = Author
Source attribute: type : value = Editor
<BookParticipants>
  <BookParticipant>
  <!--This is a new author.-->
  <FirstName>Dennis</FirstName>
  <LastName>Hayes</LastName>
  </BookParticipant>
  <BookParticipant>
  <FirstName>Ewan</FirstName>
  <LastName>Buckingham</LastName>
  </BookParticipant>
</BookParticipants>
```

So far, all is good. Now, I'll try the second declaration. For this example, instead of merely obtaining a sequence of nodes and removing them, I'll show something that might be a little more interesting. I'll get a sequence of the comments of some particular elements and remove just those, as shown in Listing 8-20.

Listing 8-20. *Calling the Second Remove Declaration*

```
Dim xDocument As XDocument = _
  <?xml version="1.0"?>
  <BookParticipants>
    <BookParticipant type = "Author">
      <!--This is a new author-->
      <FirstName>Dennis</FirstName>
      <LastName>Hayes</LastName>
    </BookParticipant>
    <BookParticipant type = "Editor">
      <FirstName>Ewan</FirstName>
      <LastName>Buckingham</LastName>
    </BookParticipant>
  </BookParticipants>
```

```
Dim comments As IEnumerable(Of XComment) = _
  xDocument.Element("BookParticipants").Elements("BookParticipant") _
    .Nodes().OfType(Of XComment)()

' First, I will display the source comments.
For Each comment As XComment In comments
  Console.WriteLine("Source comment: {0}", comment)
Next comment

comments.Remove()

' Now, I will display the XML document.
Console.WriteLine(xDocument)
```

In this example, when building my source sequence, I retrieve the child nodes of each BookParticipant element. I could just call the Remove operator on that sequence, and then all the child nodes of each BookParticipant element would be gone. But instead, to spice it up, I call the OfType Standard Query Operator. If you recall from Part 2 of this book on LINQ to Objects, this operator will return only the objects in the input sequence matching the type specified. By calling the OfType operator and specifying a type of XComment, I get a sequence of just the comments. Then, I call the Remove method on the comments. The results should be that the original document is missing the one comment that it initially had:

```
Source comment: <!--This is a new author.-->
<BookParticipants>
  <BookParticipant type="Author">
  <FirstName>Dennis</FirstName>
  <LastName>Hayes</LastName>
  </BookParticipant>
  <BookParticipant type="Editor">
  <FirstName>Ewan</FirstName>
  <LastName>Buckingham</LastName>
  </BookParticipant>
</BookParticipants>
```

That worked like a charm. Look how handy the OfType operator is and how I can integrate it into the LINQ to XML query. That seems like it could be very useful.

Summary

In the previous chapter, I covered the new LINQ to XML API that allows you to create, modify, save, and load XML trees. Notice I said *trees* as opposed to *documents*, because with LINQ to XML, documents are no longer a requirement. In that chapter, I demonstrated how to query a single node or element for nodes and elements hierarchically related to it. In this chapter, I covered doing the same thing with sequences of nodes or elements using the LINQ to XML operators. I hope I have made it clear how to perform elementary queries on XML trees using LINQ to XML. I believe that this new XML API will prove to be quite useful for querying XML data. In particular, the way the Standard Query Operators can be mingled with LINQ to XML operators lends itself to quite elegant and powerful queries.

At this point, I have covered just about all there is to know about the building blocks needed for performing LINQ to XML queries. In the next chapter, I provide some slightly more complex queries and cover some of the remaining XML necessities such as validation and transformation.

CHAPTER 9

■ ■ ■

Additional XML Capabilities

In the previous two chapters, I demonstrated how to create, modify, and traverse XML data with the LINQ to XML API. I also demonstrated the building blocks for creating powerful XML queries. I hope by now you would agree that LINQ to XML will handle about 90 percent of your XML needs, but what about the remaining 10 percent? Let's see if we can get that percentage higher. If Microsoft added schema validation, transformations, and XPath query capability, what percentage of your use cases would that achieve?

While I have covered the new LINQ to XML API and how to perform the most basic of queries with it, I have yet to demonstrate slightly more complex, real-world queries. In this chapter, I provide some examples that will hopefully make querying XML with the LINQ to XML API seem trivial, including some that use the query expression syntax for those of you who prefer it.

Additionally, the new LINQ to XML API just wouldn't be complete without a few additional capabilities such as transformation and validation. In this chapter, I cover these LINQ to XML leftovers, as well as any other good-to-know information.

Specifically, I cover how to perform transformations with XSLT and without. I demonstrate how to validate an XML document against a schema, and I even present an example performing an XPath-style query.

Referenced Namespaces

Examples in this chapter reference the System.Xml, System.Xml.Schema, System.Xml.Xsl, and System.Xml.XPath namespaces, in addition to the typical LINQ and LINQ to XML namespaces, System.Linq and System.Xml.Linq. Therefore, you will want to add Imports statements for these if they are not already present or included in the project settings:

```
Imports System.Linq
Imports System.Xml
Imports System.Xml.Linq
Imports System.Xml.Schema
Imports System.Xml.XPath
Imports System.Xml.Xsl
```

Queries

In the previous LINQ to XML chapters, I demonstrated the core principles needed to perform XML queries using LINQ to XML. However, most of the examples are specifically designed to demonstrate an operator or a property. In this section, I want to provide some examples that are more solution oriented.

No Reaching

In the previous chapters, many of the examples would reach down into the XML hierarchy to obtain a reference to a particular element by calling the `Element` or `Elements` operators recursively until the desired element was reached.

For instance, many of the examples contained lines such as this:

```
Dim elements As IEnumerable(Of XElement) = _
  MyDocument.Element("BookParticipants").Elements("BookParticipant")
```

In this statement, I start at the document level, then obtain its child element named `BookParticipants`, then obtain its child elements named `BookParticipant`. However, it is not necessary to reach down through each level like that. Instead, I could simply write the code as shown in Listing 9-1.

Listing 9-1. *Obtaining Elements Without Reaching*

```
Dim xDocument As XDocument = _
  <?xml version="1.0"?>
  <BookParticipants>
    <BookParticipant type = "Author">
      <FirstName>Dennis</FirstName>
      <LastName>Hayes</LastName>
    </BookParticipant>
    <BookParticipant type = "Editor">
      <FirstName>Ewan</FirstName>
      <LastName>Buckingham</LastName>
    </BookParticipant>
  </BookParticipants>
```

```
Dim elements As IEnumerable(Of XElement) = _
  xDocument.Descendants("BookParticipant")
```

```
For Each element As XElement In elements
  Console.WriteLine("Element: {0} : value = {1}", element.Name, element.Value)
Next element
```

In this example, I obtain every descendant element in the document named `BookParticipant`. Since I am not reaching into a specific branch of the XML tree, it is necessary that I know the schema because I could get back elements from a branch I do not want. However, in many cases, including this one, it works just fine. Here are the results:

```
Element: BookParticipant : value = DennisHayes
Element: BookParticipant : value = EwanBuckingham
```

Tip Don't forget the VB.NET 2008 descendant axis property that I covered in Chapter 2. You can also use the descendant axis property to retrieve those same elements by replacing the line calling the `Descendants` method with `xDocument...<BookParticipant>`. While I demonstrated many of the VB.NET 2008 XML enhancements in the previous LINQ to XML chapters, I will stick to LINQ to XML API method calls in this chapter so that you can appreciate the API itself. Admittedly, this is difficult since the VB.NET design team made such great language enhancements for XML.

However, I might not want all of the `BookParticipant` elements; perhaps I need to restrict the returned elements? Listing 9-2 is an example returning just the elements whose `FirstName` element's value is `"Ewan"`:

Listing 9-2. *Obtaining Restricted Elements Without Reaching*

```
Dim xDocument As XDocument = _
  <?xml version="1.0"?>
  <BookParticipants>
    <BookParticipant type = "Author">
      <FirstName>Dennis</FirstName>
      <LastName>Hayes</LastName>
    </BookParticipant>
    <BookParticipant type = "Editor">
      <FirstName>Ewan</FirstName>
      <LastName>Buckingham</LastName>
    </BookParticipant>
  </BookParticipants>

Dim elements As IEnumerable(Of XElement) = _
  xDocument _
    .Descendants("BookParticipant") _
    .Where(Function(e) e.Element("FirstName").Value = "Ewan")

  'The above statement can also be written as below.
  'See the note below for more info
    '.Where(Function(e) CType(e.Element("FirstName"), String) = "Ewan")

For Each element As XElement In elements
  Console.WriteLine("Element: {0} : value = {1}", element.Name, element.Value)
Next element
```

This time, I appended a call to the `Where` operator.

■**Note** You can retrieve an XML element's value by accessing its `Value` property or by converting it with the `CType` function to any data type its value can be converted to, which in this case is `String`.

Here are the results:

```
Element: BookParticipant : value = EwanBuckingham
```

Of course, sometimes you need to control the order. This time, so that I have more than one returned element so the order matters, I will change the `Where` operator lambda expression so that both elements will be returned. To make it interesting, I will query on the `type` attribute, and I will try this one in query expression syntax, as shown in Listing 9-3.

Listing 9-3. *Obtaining Restricted Elements Without Reaching While Ordering and Using Query Expression Syntax*

```
Dim xDocument As XDocument = _
  <?xml version="1.0"?>
  <BookParticipants>
    <BookParticipant type = "Author">
      <FirstName>Dennis</FirstName>
      <LastName>Hayes</LastName>
    </BookParticipant>
    <BookParticipant type = "Editor">
      <FirstName>Ewan</FirstName>
      <LastName>Buckingham</LastName>
    </BookParticipant>
  </BookParticipants>

Dim elements As IEnumerable(Of XElement) = _
  From e In xDocument.Descendants("BookParticipant") _
  Where e.Attribute("type").Value <> "Illustrator" _
  Order By e.Element("LastName").Value _
  Select e

For Each element As XElement In elements
  Console.WriteLine("Element: {0} : value = {1}", element.Name, element.Value)
Next element
```

In this example, I still query for the document's `BookParticipant` elements but only retrieve the ones whose `type` attribute is not `Illustrator`. In this case, that is all of the `BookParticipant` elements. I then order them by each element's `LastName` element. Here are the results:

```
Element: BookParticipant : value = EwanBuckingham
Element: BookParticipant : value = DennisHayes
```

A Complex Query

So far, all the example queries have been very trivial, so before I leave the topic of queries, I want to provide one complex query. For this example, I will use sample data suggested by the W3C specifically for XML query use case testing.

The example in Listing 9-4 contains data from three different XML documents. In my example code, I create each document using a VB.NET 2008 XML literal for each of the W3C's suggested XML documents. Since this is a complex example, I will explain as I go.

The first step is to create the documents from the XML.

Listing 9-4. *A Complex Query Featuring a Three-Document Join with Query Expression Syntax*

```
Dim users As XDocument = _
  <?xml version="1.0"?>
  <users>
    <user_tuple>
      <userid>U01</userid>
      <name>Tom Jones</name>
      <rating>B</rating>
    </user_tuple>
    <user_tuple>
      <userid>U02</userid>
      <name>Mary Doe</name>
      <rating>A</rating>
    </user_tuple>
    <user_tuple>
      <userid>U03</userid>
      <name>Dee Linquent</name>
      <rating>D</rating>
    </user_tuple>
    <user_tuple>
      <userid>U04</userid>
      <name>Roger Smith</name>
      <rating>E</rating>
    </user_tuple>
    <user_tuple>
      <userid>U05</userid>
      <name>Jack Sprat</name>
      <rating>B</rating>
    </user_tuple>
    <user_tuple>
      <userid>U06</userid>
      <name>Rip Van Winkle</name>
      <rating>B</rating>
    </user_tuple>
  </users>
```

```
Dim items As XDocument = _
  <?xml version="1.0"?>
  <items>
    <item_tuple>
      <itemno>1001</itemno>
      <description>Red Bicycle</description>
      <offered_by>U01</offered_by>
      <start_date>1999-01-05</start_date>
      <end_date>1999-01-20</end_date>
      <reserve_price>40</reserve_price>
    </item_tuple>
    <item_tuple>
      <itemno>1002</itemno>
      <description>Motorcycle</description>
      <offered_by>U02</offered_by>
      <start_date>1999-02-11</start_date>
      <end_date>1999-03-15</end_date>
      <reserve_price>500</reserve_price>
    </item_tuple>
    <item_tuple>
      <itemno>1003</itemno>
      <description>Old Bicycle</description>
      <offered_by>U02</offered_by>
      <start_date>1999-01-10</start_date>
      <end_date>1999-02-20</end_date>
      <reserve_price>25</reserve_price>
    </item_tuple>
    <item_tuple>
      <itemno>1004</itemno>
      <description>Tricycle</description>
      <offered_by>U01</offered_by>
      <start_date>1999-02-25</start_date>
      <end_date>1999-03-08</end_date>
      <reserve_price>15</reserve_price>
    </item_tuple>
    <item_tuple>
      <itemno>1005</itemno>
      <description>Tennis Racket</description>
      <offered_by>U03</offered_by>
      <start_date>1999-03-19</start_date>
      <end_date>1999-04-30</end_date>
      <reserve_price>20</reserve_price>
    </item_tuple>
    <item_tuple>
      <itemno>1006</itemno>
      <description>Helicopter</description>
      <offered_by>U03</offered_by>
```

```
        <start_date>1999-05-05</start_date>
        <end_date>1999-05-25</end_date>
        <reserve_price>50000</reserve_price>
      </item_tuple>
      <item_tuple>
        <itemno>1007</itemno>
        <description>Racing Bicycle</description>
        <offered_by>U04</offered_by>
        <start_date>1999-01-20</start_date>
        <end_date>1999-02-20</end_date>
        <reserve_price>200</reserve_price>
      </item_tuple>
      <item_tuple>
        <itemno>1008</itemno>
        <description>Broken Bicycle</description>
        <offered_by>U01</offered_by>
        <start_date>1999-02-05</start_date>
        <end_date>1999-03-06</end_date>
        <reserve_price>25</reserve_price>
      </item_tuple>
    </items>

Dim bids As XDocument = _
  <?xml version="1.0"?>
  <bids>
    <bid_tuple>
      <userid>U02</userid>
      <itemno>1001</itemno>
      <bid>35</bid>
      <bid_date>1999-01-07</bid_date>
    </bid_tuple>
    <bid_tuple>
      <userid>U04</userid>
      <itemno>1001</itemno>
      <bid>40</bid>
      <bid_date>1999-01-08</bid_date>
    </bid_tuple>
    <bid_tuple>
      <userid>U02</userid>
      <itemno>1001</itemno>
      <bid>45</bid>
      <bid_date>1999-01-11</bid_date>
    </bid_tuple>
    <bid_tuple>
      <userid>U04</userid>
      <itemno>1001</itemno>
      <bid>50</bid>
```

```
        <bid_date>1999-01-13</bid_date>
    </bid_tuple>
    <bid_tuple>
      <userid>U02</userid>
      <itemno>1001</itemno>
      <bid>55</bid>
      <bid_date>1999-01-15</bid_date>
    </bid_tuple>
    <bid_tuple>
      <userid>U01</userid>
      <itemno>1002</itemno>
      <bid>400</bid>
      <bid_date>1999-02-14</bid_date>
    </bid_tuple>
    <bid_tuple>
      <userid>U02</userid>
      <itemno>1002</itemno>
      <bid>600</bid>
      <bid_date>1999-02-16</bid_date>
    </bid_tuple>
    <bid_tuple>
      <userid>U03</userid>
      <itemno>1002</itemno>
      <bid>800</bid>
      <bid_date>1999-02-17</bid_date>
    </bid_tuple>
    <bid_tuple>
      <userid>U04</userid>
      <itemno>1002</itemno>
      <bid>1000</bid>
      <bid_date>1999-02-25</bid_date>
    </bid_tuple>
    <bid_tuple>
      <userid>U02</userid>
      <itemno>1002</itemno>
      <bid>1200</bid>
      <bid_date>1999-03-02</bid_date>
    </bid_tuple>
    <bid_tuple>
      <userid>U04</userid>
      <itemno>1003</itemno>
      <bid>15</bid>
      <bid_date>1999-01-22</bid_date>
    </bid_tuple>
    <bid_tuple>
      <userid>U05</userid>
      <itemno>1003</itemno>
```

```
      <bid>20</bid>
      <bid_date>1999-02-03</bid_date>
    </bid_tuple>
    <bid_tuple>
      <userid>U01</userid>
      <itemno>1004</itemno>
      <bid>40</bid>
      <bid_date>1999-03-05</bid_date>
    </bid_tuple>
    <bid_tuple>
      <userid>U03</userid>
      <itemno>1007</itemno>
      <bid>175</bid>
      <bid_date>1999-01-25</bid_date>
    </bid_tuple>
    <bid_tuple>
      <userid>U05</userid>
      <itemno>1007</itemno>
      <bid>200</bid>
      <bid_date>1999-02-08</bid_date>
    </bid_tuple>
    <bid_tuple>
      <userid>U04</userid>
      <itemno>1007</itemno>
      <bid>225</bid>
      <bid_date>1999-02-12</bid_date>
    </bid_tuple>
  </bids>
```

This sample data is basically meant to represent an Internet auction-type site and the data it would have. There are documents for users, items, and bids.

For my query, I want to produce a list of each bid greater than $50. In the results, I want to see the date and price of the bid as well as the user placing the bid and the item number and item description. Here is the query:

```
Dim biddata = _
  From b In bids.Descendants("bid_tuple") _
  Where (CDbl(b.Element("bid"))) > 50 _
  Join u In users.Descendants("user_tuple") _
  On b.Element("userid").Value Equals u.Element("userid").Value _
  Join i In items.Descendants("item_tuple") _
  On b.Element("itemno").Value Equals i.Element("itemno").Value _
  Select New With { _
    .Item = b.Element("itemno").Value, _
    .Description = i.Element("description").Value, _
    .User = u.Element("name").Value, _
    .Date = b.Element("bid_date").Value, _
    .Price = (CDbl(b.Element("bid")))}
```

OK, that is a complex query. The first step is that I query for the descendants named bid_tuple in the bids document using the Descendants method. Next, I perform a Where statement for elements that have a child element named bid whose value is greater than 50. This is so I only retrieve the bids that are greater than $50. It may seem a little unusual that I am performing a Where statement this soon in the query. I actually could have called the Where statement farther down in the query, just before the Select statement call. However, this means I would have retrieved and performed a join against the users and items XML documents even for bids not greater than $50, which is not necessary. By filtering the results set as soon as possible, I have reduced the workload for the remainder of the query, thereby leading to better performance.

Once I have filtered the results set to just the bids that are greater than $50, I join those bids on the users XML document by the commonly named userid element so that I can obtain the user's name. At this point, I have the bids and users joined for the bids greater than $50.

Next, I join the results on the items XML document by the commonly named itemno element so that I can obtain the item's description. At this point, I have the bids, users, and items joined.

The next step is to simply select an anonymous class containing the joined element's child elements I am interested in.

My next step is to display a header:

```
Console.WriteLine("{0,-12} {1,-12} {2,-6} {3,-14} {4,10}", _
  "Date", "User", "Item", "Description", "Price")

Console.WriteLine("=========================================================")
```

There is nothing special about that. All that is left is to enumerate the sequence and display each bid:

```
For Each bd In biddata
  Console.WriteLine("{0,-12} {1,-12} {2,-6} {3,-14} {4,10:C}", _
    bd.Date, _
    bd.User, _
    bd.Item, _
    bd.Description, _
    bd.Price)
Next bd
```

That part is trivial. Actually, all but the query itself is trivial. Are you ready to see the results? I know I am:

Date	User	Item	Description	Price
1999-01-15	Mary Doe	1001	Red Bicycle	$55.00
1999-02-14	Tom Jones	1002	Motorcycle	$400.00
1999-02-16	Mary Doe	1002	Motorcycle	$600.00
1999-02-17	Dee Linquent	1002	Motorcycle	$800.00
1999-02-25	Roger Smith	1002	Motorcycle	$1,000.00
1999-03-02	Mary Doe	1002	Motorcycle	$1,200.00

```
1999-01-25   Dee Linquent   1007   Racing Bicycle   $175.00
1999-02-08   Jack Sprat     1007   Racing Bicycle   $200.00
1999-02-12   Roger Smith    1007   Racing Bicycle   $225.00
```

OK, come on, you have to admit that is pretty spectacular, don't you think? I just joined three XML documents in a single query.

Surely you now see the power of LINQ to XML. Are you starting to see why LINQ to XML is my favorite part of LINQ? Now how much would you pay? But wait, there's more!

Transformations

With LINQ to XML, you can perform XML transformations using two completely different approaches. The first approach is to use XSLT via the bridge classes, XmlReader and XmlWriter. The second approach is to use LINQ to XML to perform the transformation itself by functionally constructing the target XML document and embedding a LINQ to XML query on the source XML document.

Using XSLT provides the benefit that it is a standard XML technology. Tools already exist to assist with writing, debugging, and testing XSLT transformations. Additionally, because it already exists, you may have XSLT documents and can leverage them in new code using LINQ to XML. There is a world full of existing XSLT documents from which to choose. Additionally, using XSLT for your transformations is just more dynamic. Unlike using the LINQ to XML functional construction approach, you do not have to recompile code to change the transformation. Merely changing the XSLT document allows you to modify the transformation at runtime. Lastly, XSLT is a known technology with many developers having expertise that may be able to assist you. At least in the early days of LINQ, this may not be available if you take the functional construction approach.

Using the functional construction approach does not really buy you much. It does allow you to perform XML transformations knowing nothing more than LINQ to XML. So if you do not already know XSLT, and your transformation needs are modest, this may be a fine approach for you. Also, while functional construction is less convenient than merely modifying an XSLT document, having to recompile code to modify a transformation could be said to add security. Someone cannot simply muck with an outside document to modify the transformation. So for those times when you think you are pushing the limits by using Sarbanes-Oxley as the excuse for not doing something, blame it on the fact that you cannot simply change the transformation without a code overhaul. Or if you are in the medical field and you don't think you can get away with blaming HIPAA one more time, transformation via functional construction may just be the obstacle you need on which to blame a lack of agility.

Transformations Using XSLT

To perform an XML transformation using XSLT, you will utilize the XmlWriter and XmlReader bridge classes that you will obtain from the XDocument classes' CreateWriter and CreateReader methods, respectively.

Because the example shown in Listing 9-5 requires a bit of explanation, I will explain it as I go. First, I will specify the transformation style sheet.

■**Note** The following example requires an `Imports` statement for the `System.IO` namespace.

Listing 9-5. *Transforming an XML Document with XSLT*

```
Imports System.IO
Dim xsl As String = _
  "<xsl:stylesheet version='1.0' " & vbCrLf & _
  "xmlns:xsl='http://www.w3.org/1999/XSL/Transform'>" & vbCrLf & _
  "    <xsl:template match='//BookParticipants'>" & vbCrLf & _
  "      <html>" & vbCrLf & _
  "        <body>" & vbCrLf & _
  "        <h1>Book Participants</h1>" & vbCrLf & _
  "        <table>" & vbCrLf & _
  "          <tr align='left'>" & vbCrLf & _
  "            <th>Role</th>" & vbCrLf & _
  "            <th>First Name</th>" & vbCrLf & _
  "            <th>Last Name</th>" & vbCrLf & _
  "          </tr>" & vbCrLf & _
  "          <xsl:apply-templates></xsl:apply-templates>" & vbCrLf & _
  "        </table>" & vbCrLf & _
  "        </body>" & vbCrLf & _
  "      </html>" & vbCrLf & _
  "    </xsl:template>" & VBCrLf & _
  "    <xsl:template match='BookParticipant'>" & vbCrLf & _
  "      <tr>" & vbCrLf & _
  "        <td><xsl:value-of select='@type'/></td>" & vbCrLf & _
  "        <td><xsl:value-of select='FirstName'/></td>" & vbCrLf & _
  "        <td><xsl:value-of select='LastName'/></td>" & vbCrLf & _
  "      </tr>" & vbCrLf & _
  "    </xsl:template>" & vbCrLf & _
  "  </xsl:stylesheet>"
```

There is nothing earth shattering here. I am just specifying some XSL to create some HTML to display my typical book participant XML as an HTML table. Next, I will create my XML document with the book participants:

```
Dim xDocument As XDocument = _
  <?xml version="1.0"?>
  <BookParticipants>
    <BookParticipant type = "Author">
      <FirstName>Dennis</FirstName>
      <LastName>Hayes</LastName>
    </BookParticipant>
    <BookParticipant type = "Editor">
      <FirstName>Ewan</FirstName>
      <LastName>Buckingham</LastName>
```

```
</BookParticipant>
</BookParticipants>
```

This is just my typical XML. Now is where the magic happens. I need to create a new XDocument for the transformed version. Then, from that document, I will create an XmlWriter, instantiate an XslCompiledTransform object, load the transform object with the transformation style sheet, and transform my input XML document into the output XmlWriter:

```
Dim transformedDoc As New XDocument()
Using writer As XmlWriter = transformedDoc.CreateWriter()
  Dim transform As New XslCompiledTransform()
  transform.Load(XmlReader.Create(New StringReader(xsl)))
  transform.Transform(xDocument.CreateReader(), writer)
End Using
Console.WriteLine(transformedDoc)
```

Of course, after all that, I display the transformed version of the document. As you can see, I use both bridge classes, XmlWriter and XmlReader, to perform the transformation. Here are the results:

```
<html>
  <body>
    <h1>Book Participants</h1>
    <table>
      <tr align="left">
      <th>Role</th>
      <th>First Name</th>
      <th>Last Name</th>
      </tr>
      <tr>
      <td>Author</td>
      <td>Dennis</td>
      <td>Hayes</td>
      </tr>
      <tr>
      <td>Editor</td>
      <td>Ewan</td>
      <td>Buckingham</td>
      </tr>
    </table>
  </body>
</html>
```

Transformations Using Functional Construction

While the LINQ to XML API does support XSLT transformations, there are some very effective ways to produce transformations using the LINQ to XML API itself. Logically speaking, a transformation can be as simple as combining a functionally constructed XML tree with an embedded XML query.

■**Tip** Combine functional construction with an embedded XML LINQ query to perform a transformation.

I will explain XML transformations via an example. In many of the examples in the LINQ to XML chapters, I have worked with the following XML tree:

```
<BookParticipants>
  <BookParticipant type="Author">
    <FirstName>Dennis</FirstName>
    <LastName>Hayes</LastName>
  </BookParticipant>
  <BookParticipant type="Editor">
    <FirstName>Ewan</FirstName>
    <LastName>Buckingham</LastName>
  </BookParticipant>
</BookParticipants>
```

Let's pretend that I need to transform this XML tree to this:

```
<MediaParticipants type="book">
  <Participant Role="Author" Name="Dennis Hayes" />
  <Participant Role="Editor" Name="Ewan Buckingham" / >
</MediaParticipants>
```

To accomplish this transformation, I will use functional construction with an embedded query. With this approach, you basically functionally construct a new document matching the desired output XML tree structure while obtaining the needed data from the original source XML document by performing a LINQ to XML query. It is the desired output XML tree structure that drives your functional construction and query logic.

Because this task is slightly more complex than some of the previous LINQ to XML examples, I will explain this one as I go. The code is shown in Listing 9-6.

Listing 9-6. *Transforming an XML Document*

```
Dim xDocument As XDocument = _
  <?xml version="1.0"?>
  <BookParticipants>
    <BookParticipant type = "Author">
      <FirstName>Dennis</FirstName>
      <LastName>Hayes</LastName>
    </BookParticipant>
    <BookParticipant type = "Editor">
      <FirstName>Ewan</FirstName>
      <LastName>Buckingham</LastName>
```

```
    </BookParticipant>
  </BookParticipants>
```

```
Console.WriteLine("Here is the original XML document:")
Console.WriteLine("{0}{1}{1}", xDocument, vbCrLf)
```

The previous code simply creates the original source XML document that I am going to transform and displays it. Next, I need to build the new document and root element:

```
Dim xTransDocument As New XDocument( _
  New XElement("MediaParticipants", _
```

Remember, my desired output XML tree structure is driving my functional construction. At this point, I have the document and root element, MediaParticipants. Next, I need to add the type attribute to the root element:

```
    New XAttribute("type", "book"), _
```

The type attribute and its value do not exist in the source XML document. This would be hard-coded, or possibly configured, in my program logic, which is safe because I already know this code is for a book; otherwise, this code would not be getting called.

Now, I have the MediaParticipants' type attribute handled. Next up, I need to generate a Participant element for each BookParticipant element in the original XML. To do this, I will query the original XML document for its BookParticipant elements:

```
    xDocument.Element("BookParticipants").Elements("BookParticipant") _
```

Now, I have a returned sequence of the BookParticipant elements. Next, I need to generate a Participant element for each BookParticipant element and populate its attributes. I will use projection via the Select operator to construct the Participant elements:

```
      .Select(Function(e) New XElement("Participant", _
```

Next, I construct the two attributes, Role and Name, for each Participant element by getting their values from the BookParticipant element:

```
        New XAttribute("Role", e.Attribute("type").Value), _
        New XAttribute("Name", e.Element("FirstName").Value & " " & _
          e.Element("LastName").Value)))))
```

Last, I display the transformed XML document:

```
Console.WriteLine("Here is the transformed XML document:")
Console.WriteLine(xTransDocument)
```

Let's see if this outputs what I am looking for:

```
Here is the original XML document:
<BookParticipants>
  <BookParticipant type="Author">
    <FirstName>Dennis</FirstName>
    <LastName>Hayes</LastName>
  </BookParticipant>
```

```
  <BookParticipant type="Editor">
    <FirstName>Ewan</FirstName>
    <LastName>Buckingham</LastName>
  </BookParticipant>
</BookParticipants>
```

```
Here is the transformed XML document:
<MediaParticipants type="book">
  <Participant Role="Author" Name="Dennis Hayes" />
  <Participant Role="Editor" Name="Ewan Buckingham" />
</MediaParticipants>
```

Wow, that went great! I got the exact output I was looking for. Not bad for using nothing more than LINQ to XML.

Tips On XML Transformations Using LINQ

There are a few tips to pass on when it comes to performing XML transformations with the LINQ to XML API. While you may not have a need for these, there is no reason not to point them out.

Simplify Complex Tasks with Helper Methods

There is no requirement that every bit of code needed to perform a transformation or query actually exist in the transformation code itself. It is possible to create helper methods that carry out more complex transformation chores.

Here is some code demonstrating how you can create a helper method to break up a more complex task:

A Helper Method to Transform an XML Document

```
Function Helper() As IEnumerable(Of XElement)
  Dim elements() As XElement = {<Element>A</Element>, <Element>B</Element>}
  Return(elements)
End Function
```

In Listing 9-7, I begin the construction of an XML tree. It creates the root node, named RootElement, in the call to the constructor itself. To create the child nodes, it calls a helper method named Helper. It isn't important what the helper method is doing specifically, it just matters that it is helping me build some part of my XML tree and that the call to the method can be embedded in the functional construction of the XML tree.

Listing 9-7. *Using a Helper Method to Transform an XML Document*

```
Dim xElement As New XElement("RootElement", Helper())
Console.WriteLine(xElement)
```

Here are the results of this code:

```
<RootElement>
  <Element>A</Element>
  <Element>B</Element>
</RootElement>
```

Remember, as I discussed in Chapter 7, the XElement constructor knows how to handle IEnumerable(Of T), which happens to be the returned data type of my Helper method. How cool is that?

Suppressing Node Construction with Nothing

There may be times when you want to suppress some nodes from being constructed for one reason or another. Perhaps some essential data is missing from the source that causes you to want to omit an element from being created, or perhaps the data is such that you want to skip it.

Back in the "Creating Elements with XElement" section of Chapter 7 when I described the constructor for XElement, I mentioned that you could pass Nothing as an object value for an element's content and that this can be handy when performing transformations. Suppressing node construction is what it is handy for.

As an example, I will first build a sequence of elements. I will then begin constructing a new XML tree based on that sequence. However, if an input element's value is "A", then I don't want to create an output element for that input element. I will pass its value as Nothing to make that happen. The code is in Listing 9-8.

Listing 9-8. *Suppressing Node Construction with Nothing*

```
Dim elements As IEnumerable(Of XElement) = _
  New XElement() _
    {<Element>A</Element>, _
     <Element>B</Element>}

Dim xElement As New XElement( _
  "RootElement", _
  elements.Select(Function(e) If(e.Value <> "A", _
    New XElement(e.Name, e.Value), Nothing)))

Console.WriteLine(xElement)
```

As you can see in the previous code, I do build an input source sequence of elements. I then construct the root element and enumerate through the input source sequence. Then, using the Select operator, as long as the input element's value is not equal to "A", I construct an XElement object using the input element. If the input element's value is equal to "A", I return Nothing. The XElement constructor knows how to handle Nothing; it ignores it. The result is that any element whose value is equal to "A" is eliminated from the output XML tree.

Here are the results:

```
<RootElement>
  <Element>B</Element>
</RootElement>
```

Notice that the element "A" is missing. Of course, there are other ways to implement this same logic without using Nothing. For example, I could have just used the Where operator to filter out the elements whose value is equal to "A". But I wanted to show you the affect of using Nothing in a very simple example.

There are other ways to use this same concept. Perhaps I have some XML to generate that would cause me to have an empty element in some instances that I would prefer not exist. Consider the code in Listing 9-9.

Listing 9-9. *An Example That Generates an Empty Element*

```
Dim elements As IEnumerable(Of XElement) = _
  New XElement() { _
    <BookParticipant>
      <Name>Dennis Hayes</Name>
      <Book>Pro LINQ: Language Integrated Query in VB 2008</Book>
    </BookParticipant>, _
    <BookParticipant>
      <Name>John Q. Public</Name>
    </BookParticipant>}

Dim xElement As New XElement("BookParticipants", _
                             elements.Select(Function(e) New XElement( _
                               e.Name, _
                                 New XElement(e.Element("Name").Name, _
                                             e.Element("Name").Value), _
                                 New XElement("Books", e.Elements("Book")))))

Console.WriteLine(xElement)
```

In the previous code, in the first statement, I generate a sequence of BookParticipant elements, two to be precise. Notice that some of the BookParticipant elements have Book child elements, such as the BookParticipant with the Name child element whose value is "Dennis Hayes", and some have no Book elements, such as the BookParticipant whose Name child element is "John Q. Public".

In the second statement, I build an XML tree using the sequence of elements I obtained. In the XML tree, I create an element with the same name as the source sequence, which will be BookParticipant. I then make the participant's name a child element, and I create a list of Books for each participant. Here is the output from this code:

```
<BookParticipants>
  <BookParticipant>
    <Name>Dennis Hayes</Name>
    <Books>
      <Book>Pro LINQ: Language Integrated Query in VB 2008</Book>
    </Books>
  </BookParticipant>
  <BookParticipant>
    <Name>John Q. Public</Name>
    <Books />
  </BookParticipant>
</BookParticipants>
```

The XML is just as I would expect based on the code, but notice that the Books element for the second BookParticipant is empty. What if you didn't want an empty Books element if there were no Book elements? You could use Nothing to suppress the Books element as well, with the correct operator. In Listing 9-10, I make a slight change to the code that produces the XML.

Listing 9-10. *An Example That Prevents an Empty Element*

```
Dim elements As IEnumerable(Of XElement) = _
  New XElement() { _
    <BookParticipant>
      <Name>Dennis Hayes</Name>
      <Book>Pro LINQ: Language Integrated Query in VB 2008</Book>
    </BookParticipant>, _
    <BookParticipant>
      <Name>John Q. Public</Name>
    </BookParticipant>}

Dim xElement As New XElement("BookParticipants", _
                            elements.Select(Function(e) New XElement( _
                              e.Name, _
                                New XElement(e.Element("Name").Name, _
                                             e.Element("Name").Value), _
                                If(e.Elements("Book").Any(), _
                                  New XElement("Books", _
                                    e.Elements("Book")), Nothing))))

Console.WriteLine(xElement)
```

The significant change in the previous code is in bold. Instead of just creating a Books element and specifying all the existing Book elements as its content, I use the Any Standard Query Operator combined with the ternary If operator to create the Books element only if there are in fact any Book elements.

VB.NET 2008 has a new `If` operator with three arguments, a `Boolean`, and two state-ments. If the first argument evaluates to `True`, the second argument is executed, and its value returned. If the first argument evaluates to `False`, the third argument is executed, and its value is returned. Note that this a bit different from the VB.NET `IIf` function. The `IIf` function returns the same value as the three argument `If` operator, but the `IIf` function executes *both* statements, *regardless* of which value finally gets returned. See the VB.NET documentation for more information.

If there are no `Book` elements, the `If` operator returns `Nothing`, and the `XElement` construc-tor knows to just ignore `Nothing`, thereby eliminating the creation of the `Books` element. This can be very handy. Here are the results after the modification:

```
<BookParticipants>
  <BookParticipant>
    <Name>Dennis Hayes</Name>
    <Books>
      <Book>Pro LINQ: Language Integrated Query in VB 2008</Book>
    </Books>
  </BookParticipant>
  <BookParticipant>
    <Name>John Q. Public</Name>
  </BookParticipant>
</BookParticipants>
```

As you can see, the second `BookParticipant` element no longer has an empty `Books` ele-ment, as it did in the previous example.

Handling Multiple Peer Nodes While Remaining Flat

Sometimes when making an XML transformation, you know exactly how many of each type of output element you are going to want. But what happens if there are several known elements as well as a variable number of repeating elements all at the same level in the tree for each entry in the source XML? Let's say I have the following XML:

What I Want My Source XML to Look Like

```
<BookParticipants>
  <BookParticipant type="Author">
    <FirstName>Dennis</FirstName>
    <LastName>Hayes</LastName>
    <Nickname>SCCatman</Nickname>
    <Nickname>Null Pointer</Nickname>
  </BookParticipant>
  <BookParticipant type="Editor">
    <FirstName>Ewan</FirstName>
    <LastName>Buckingham</LastName>
  </BookParticipant>
</BookParticipants>
```

What if I want to flatten the structure so that the BookParticipants root node only contains repeating sets of FirstName, LastName, and Nickname elements, instead of those elements being contained in a child BookParticipant element? I would like for the target XML to look like this:

What I Want the XML to Look Like After Transformation

```
<BookParticipants>
  <!- BookParticipant  -->
  <FirstName>Dennis</FirstName>
  <LastName>Hayes</LastName>
  <Nickname>SCCatman</Nickname>
  <Nickname>Null Pointer</Nickname>
  <!- BookParticipant  -->
  <FirstName>Ewan</FirstName>
  <LastName>Buckingham</LastName>
</BookParticipants>
```

The comments are not necessary, but they make it easier for humans to know what they are looking at. Plus, without them, if you looked farther down in the list, it might be confusing as to whether the FirstName or LastName comes first, causing a human to think that there is a BookParticipant named Ewan Hayes when there really isn't.

Because this example is more complex, I will explain it as I go. Let's take a look at the example code in Listing 9-11 to make this transformation.

Listing 9-11. *Handling Multiple Peer Nodes While Maintaining a Flat Structure*

```
Dim xDocument As XDocument = _
  <?xml version="1.0"?>
  <BookParticipants>
    <BookParticipant type="Author">
      <FirstName>Dennis</FirstName>
      <LastName>Hayes</LastName>
      <Nickname>SCCatman</Nickname>
      <Nickname>Null Pointer</Nickname>
    </BookParticipant>
    <BookParticipant type="Editor">
      <FirstName>Ewan</FirstName>
      <LastName>Buckingham</LastName>
    </BookParticipant>
  </BookParticipants>

Console.WriteLine("Here is the original XML document:")
Console.WriteLine("{0}{1}{1}", xDocument, vbCrLf)
```

At this point, I have built the source XML tree and displayed it. It does indeed match the XML I specified previously as the source. Now I just have to transform the source XML:

```
Dim xTransDocument As New XDocument(New XElement("BookParticipants", _
  xDocument.Element("BookParticipants").Elements("BookParticipant") _
```

Here is where the challenge occurs. I am about to use projection via the Select opera-tor to create an object in which I will contain the comment, first name, last name, and any nicknames. But what object type should I create? I could create an element and make the comment, the first name, and the remainder child elements of it, but that would expand the XML tree by adding a level. So I must create something that will not add a level to the XML tree. An array of objects will work for this, because in VB.NET 2008, an array implements IEnumerable(Of T), thereby making the array of objects work just like a sequence. As you hopefully recall from Chapter 7, when an IEnumerable is passed into an XElement constructor as its content, the sequence is enumerated and each object in the sequence is applied to the element being constructed. I will use an array initializer to populate that array with the com-ment, first name, last name, and any nicknames:

```
.Select(Function(e) New Object() { _
  New XComment(" BookParticipant "), _
  New XElement("FirstName", e.Element("FirstName").Value), _
  New XElement("LastName", e.Element("LastName").Value), _
  e.Elements("Nickname")}))))
```

```
Console.WriteLine("Here is the transformed XML document:")
Console.WriteLine(xTransDocument)
```

At this point, I have projected an array containing a comment, a FirstName element, a LastName element, and however many Nickname elements there are in the source XML. Finally, I display the transformed XML document.

This example is actually quite complex. Notice that my array of objects includes an XComment object, two XElement objects, and an IEnumerable(Of XElement). By projecting a newly instantiated array as the return value of the Select operator, a sequence of Object(), IEnumerable(Of Object()), is being returned as the content of the newly constructed BookParticipants element.

In this case, each object in that sequence is an array of objects, where the array contains the comment, FirstName and LastName elements, and the sequence of Nickname elements. Because, as I just mentioned, an array of objects does not inject a level into the XML tree, the array adds its elements directly into the BookParticipants element.

This may be confusing, so let's take a look at the results:

```
Here is the original XML document:
<BookParticipants>
  <BookParticipant type="Author">
    <FirstName>Dennis</FirstName>
    <LastName>Hayes</LastName>
    <Nickname>SCCatman</Nickname>
    <Nickname>Null Pointer</Nickname>
  </BookParticipant>
  <BookParticipant type="Editor">
    <FirstName>Ewan</FirstName>
```

```
      <LastName>Buckingham</LastName>
  </BookParticipant>
</BookParticipants>
```

```
Here is the transformed XML document:
<BookParticipants>
  <!-- BookParticipant -->
  <FirstName>Dennis</FirstName>
  <LastName>Hayes</LastName>
  <Nickname>SCCatman</Nickname>
  <Nickname>Null Pointer</Nickname>
  <!-- BookParticipant -->
  <FirstName>Ewan</FirstName>
  <LastName>Buckingham</LastName>
</BookParticipants>
```

The transformed XML matches the specification exactly. Bravo! The real nifty part of this example is how I project an array of objects, a non-XML class, to create peer XML elements without inflicting a level of XML to the tree.

Validation

An XML API would just not be complete without the ability to validate XML. So LINQ to XML has the ability to validate an XML document against an XML schema.

The Extension Methods

LINQ to XML has addressed the need for validation by creating the System.Xml.Schema. Extensions static class, which contains the validation methods. These validation methods are implemented as extension methods.

Declarations

Here is a list of some of the validation method declarations available in the System.Xml. Schema.Extensions class:

```
<ExtensionAttribute> _
Public Shared Sub Validate ( _
  source As XDocument, _
  schemas As XmlSchemaSet, _
  validationEventHandler As ValidationEventHandler)
```

```
<ExtensionAttribute> _
Public Shared Sub Validate ( _
  source As XDocument, _
  schemas As XmlSchemaSet, _
```

```
    validationEventHandler As ValidationEventHandler, _
    addSchemaInfo As Boolean)


<ExtensionAttribute> _
Public Shared Sub Validate ( _
    source As XElement, _
    partialValidationType As XmlSchemaObject, _
    schemas As XmlSchemaSet, _
    validationEventHandler As ValidationEventHandler)


<ExtensionAttribute> _
Public Shared Sub Validate ( _
    source As XElement, _
    partialValidationType As XmlSchemaObject, _
    schemas As XmlSchemaSet, _
    validationEventHandler As ValidationEventHandler, _
    addSchemaInfo As Boolean)


<ExtensionAttribute> _
Public Shared Sub Validate ( _
    source As XAttribute, _
    partialValidationType As XmlSchemaObject, _
    schemas As XmlSchemaSet, _
    validationEventHandler As ValidationEventHandler)


<ExtensionAttribute> _
Public Shared Sub Validate ( _
    source As XAttribute, _
    partialValidationType As XmlSchemaObject, _
    schemas As XmlSchemaSet, _
    validationEventHandler As ValidationEventHandler, _
    addSchemaInfo As Boolean)
```

There are two declarations for each object type the method can be called on. These object types are XDocument, XElement, and XAttribute. The second declaration for each object type merely adds a Boolean argument specifying whether schema information should be added to the XElement and XAttribute objects after validation. The first method for each object type, the ones without the Boolean arguments, are the same as passing False for the addSchemaInfo argument. In this case, no schema information would be added to the LINQ to XML objects after validation.

To obtain the schema information for an XElement or XAttribute object, call the GetSchemaInfo method on the object. If the schema information is not added because either the first declaration is called or the second declaration is called and False is passed for the addSchemaInfo argument, the GetSchemaInfo method will return Nothing. Otherwise, it will return an object that implements IXmlSchemaInfo. That object will contain properties named SchemaElement, which will return an XmlSchemaElement object, and SchemaAttribute, which will return an XmlSchemaAttribute object, assuming the element or attribute is valid. These objects can be used to obtain additional information about the schema.

It is important to note that the schema information is not available *during* validation, only after validation has completed. This means you cannot obtain the schema information in your validation event handler. Calling the `GetSchemaInfo` method will return `Nothing` in your validation event handler. This also means that the validation must complete and that you must not throw an exception in your validation event handler if you wish to have access to the schema information.

■Tip Schema information is not available during validation, only after. Calling the `GetSchemaInfo` method in your validation event-handling code will return `Nothing`.

Notice that the `Validate` method declarations for elements and attributes require that you pass an `XmlSchemaObject` as one of the arguments. This means that you must have already validated the document that they are in.

Lastly, if you pass `Nothing` for the `ValidationEventHandler` argument, an exception of type `XmlSchemaValidationException` will be thrown should a validation error occur. This will be the simplest approach to validate an XML document.

Obtaining an XML Schema

Odds are good that if you are interested in validating your XML document, you either have, or know how to produce, an XSD schema file. Just in case you don't, I will demonstrate how to let the .NET Framework do it for you. Let's examine the example in Listing 9-12.

Listing 9-12. *Creating an XSD Schema by Inferring It from an XML Document*

```
Dim xDocument As XDocument = _
  <?xml version="1.0"?>
  <BookParticipants>
    <BookParticipant type="Author">
      <FirstName>Dennis</FirstName>
      <LastName>Hayes</LastName>
    </BookParticipant>
    <BookParticipant type="Editor">
      <FirstName>Ewan</FirstName>
      <LastName>Buckingham</LastName>
    </BookParticipant>
  </BookParticipants>

Console.WriteLine("Here is the source XML document:")
Console.WriteLine("{0}{1}{1}", xDocument, vbCrLf)

xDocument.Save("bookparticipants.xml")
```

```
Dim infer As New XmlSchemaInference()
Dim schemaSet As XmlSchemaSet = _
  infer.InferSchema(New XmlTextReader("bookparticipants.xml"))

Using w As XmlWriter = XmlWriter.Create("bookparticipants.xsd")
  For Each schema As XmlSchema In schemaSet.Schemas()
    schema.Write(w)
  Next schema
End Using

Dim newDocument As XDocument = XDocument.Load("bookparticipants.xsd")
Console.WriteLine("Here is the schema:")
Console.WriteLine("{0}{1}{1}", newDocument, vbCrLf)
```

In the previous code, I first create my typical XML document that I have been using in many of the examples and display it for your inspection. Then, I save the XML document to disk. Next, I instantiate an XmlSchemaInference object and create an XmlSchemaSet by calling the InferSchema method on the XmlSchemaInference object. I create a writer and enumerate through the set of schemas, writing each to the bookparticipants.xsd file. Last, I load in the generated XSD schema file and display it. Here are the results:

```
Here is the source XML document:
<BookParticipants>
  <BookParticipant type="Author">
    <FirstName>Dennis</FirstName>
    <LastName>Hayes</LastName>
  </BookParticipant>
  <BookParticipant type="Editor">
    <FirstName>Ewan</FirstName>
    <LastName>Buckingham</LastName>
  </BookParticipant>
</BookParticipants>


Here is the schema:
<xs:schema attributeFormDefault="unqualified" elementFormDefault=
"qualified" xmlns:xs="http://www.w3.org/2001/XMLSchema">
  <xs:element name="BookParticipants">
    <xs:complexType>
      <xs:sequence>
        <xs:element maxOccurs="unbounded" name="BookParticipant">
          <xs:complexType>
            <xs:sequence>
              <xs:element name="FirstName" type="xs:string" />
              <xs:element name="LastName" type="xs:string" />
            </xs:sequence>
            <xs:attribute name="type" type="xs:string" use="required" />
```

```
          </xs:complexType>
        </xs:element>
      </xs:sequence>
    </xs:complexType>
  </xs:element>
</xs:schema>
```

Obtaining the schema this way is not too painful. I will use this generated XSD schema file named bookparticipants.xsd in the validation examples. Also, you should notice that I use the XmlSchemaSet class in that example, which is used in the validation examples as well.

Examples

For the first example, I will demonstrate the simplest means of validating an XML document, which will be the approach many developers will take. To do this, I merely specify Nothing as the ValidationEventHandler argument, as shown in Listing 9-13.

Listing 9-13. *Validating an XML Document with Default Validation Event Handling*

```
Dim xDocument As XDocument = _
  <?xml version="1.0"?>
  <BookParticipants>
    <BookParticipant type="Author">
      <FirstName>Dennis</FirstName>
      <MiddleInitial>E</MiddleInitial>
      <LastName>Hayes</LastName>
    </BookParticipant>
    <BookParticipant type="Editor">
      <FirstName>Ewan</FirstName>
      <LastName>Buckingham</LastName>
    </BookParticipant>
  </BookParticipants>

Console.WriteLine("Here is the source XML document:")
Console.WriteLine("{0}{1}{1}", xDocument, vbCrLf)

Dim schemaSet As New XmlSchemaSet()
schemaSet.Add(Nothing, "bookparticipants.xsd")

Try
  xDocument.Validate(schemaSet, Nothing)
  Console.WriteLine("Document validated successfully.")
Catch ex As XmlSchemaValidationException
  Console.WriteLine("Exception occurred: {0}", ex.Message)
  Console.WriteLine("Document validated unsuccessfully.")
End Try
```

In this example, I construct my typical XML document, except I add a `MiddleInitial` element to intentionally make the document invalid. I am using the schema I inferred in the previous example. Notice that for the `ValidationEventHandler` argument for the `Validate` method that I passed a value of `Nothing`. This means that if a validation error occurs, an exception of type `XmlSchemaValidationException` will automatically be thrown. Here are the results:

```
Here is the source XML document:

<BookParticipants>
  <BookParticipant type="Author">
    <FirstName>Dennis</FirstName>
    <MiddleInitial>E</MiddleInitial>
    <LastName>Hayes</LastName>
  </BookParticipant>
  <BookParticipant type="Editor">
    <FirstName>Ewan</FirstName>
    <LastName>Buckingham</LastName>
  </BookParticipant>
</BookParticipants>


Exception occurred: The element 'BookParticipant' has invalid child element
'MiddleInitial'. List of possible elements expected: 'LastName'.
Document validated unsuccessfully.
```

That worked like a charm. It was also very simple. Not too bad.

For the next example, I will validate my typical XML document, the one I used to infer the schema, against the schema I obtained by inference. Of course, since the schema was inferred from this very XML document, it should work. However, for this example, I will need a `ValidationEventHandler` method. Let's take a look at the one I am going to use.

My ValidationEventHandler

```
Private Sub MyValidationEventHandler( _
    ByVal o As Object, _
    ByVal vea As ValidationEventArgs)

  Console.WriteLine( _
    "A validation error occurred processing object type {0}.", _
    o.GetType().Name)

  Console.WriteLine(vea.Message)
  Throw (New Exception(vea.Message))
End Sub
```

In that handler, I really don't do much except display the problem and throw an exception. Of course, the handling is completely up to my handler. It isn't required to throw an exception. I could choose to implement it so that it handles validation errors more gracefully, perhaps choosing to ignore any or specific errors.

Let's examine an example using that handler, as shown in Listing 9-14.

Listing 9-14. *Successfully Validating an XML Document Against an XSD Schema*

```
Dim xDocument As XDocument = _
  <?xml version="1.0"?>
  <BookParticipants>
    <BookParticipant type="Author">
      <FirstName>Dennis</FirstName>
      <LastName>Hayes</LastName>
    </BookParticipant>
    <BookParticipant type="Editor">
      <FirstName>Ewan</FirstName>
      <LastName>Buckingham</LastName>
    </BookParticipant>
  </BookParticipants>

Console.WriteLine("Here is the source XML document:")
Console.WriteLine("{0}{1}{1}", xDocument, vbCrLf)

Dim schemaSet As New XmlSchemaSet()
schemaSet.Add(Nothing, "bookparticipants.xsd")

Try
  xDocument.Validate(schemaSet, AddressOf MyValidationEventHandler)
  Console.WriteLine("Document validated successfully.")
Catch ex As XmlSchemaValidationException
  Console.WriteLine("Exception occurred: {0}", ex.Message)
  Console.WriteLine("Document validated unsuccessfully.")
End Try
```

In the example, I create my typical XML document and display it to the console. Next, I instantiate an XmlSchemaSet object and add the inferred schema file I created using the Add method. Next, I merely call the Validate extension method on the XML document passing it the schema set and my validation event-handling method. Notice that I wrap the call to the Validate method in a Try/Catch block for safety's sake. Let's look at the results:

```
Here is the source XML document:
<BookParticipants>
  <BookParticipant type="Author">
    <FirstName>Dennis</FirstName>
    <LastName>Hayes</LastName>
  </BookParticipant>
  <BookParticipant type="Editor">
    <FirstName>Ewan</FirstName>
    <LastName>Buckingham</LastName>
```

```
    </BookParticipant>
</BookParticipants>
```

```
Document validated successfully.
```

As you can see, the XML document is successfully validated. Now, let's try an example, shown in Listing 9-15, where the document is invalid.

Listing 9-15. *Unsuccessfully Validating an XML Document Against an XSD Schema*

```
Dim xDocument As XDocument = _
  <?xml version="1.0"?>
  <BookParticipants>
    <BookParticipant type="Author" language="English">
      <FirstName>Dennis</FirstName>
      <LastName>Hayes</LastName>
    </BookParticipant>
    <BookParticipant type="Editor">
      <FirstName>Ewan</FirstName>
      <LastName>Buckingham</LastName>
    </BookParticipant>
  </BookParticipants>

Console.WriteLine("Here is the source XML document:")
Console.WriteLine("{0}{1}{1}", xDocument, vbCrLf)

Dim schemaSet As New XmlSchemaSet()
schemaSet.Add(Nothing, "bookparticipants.xsd")

Try
  xDocument.Validate(schemaSet, AddressOf MyValidationEventHandler)
  Console.WriteLine("Document validated successfully.")
Catch ex As Exception
  Console.WriteLine("Exception occurred: {0}", ex.Message)
  Console.WriteLine("Document validated unsuccessfully.")
End Try
```

This code is identical to the previous example, except I added an additional attribute, language. Since the schema doesn't specify this attribute, the XML document is not valid. Here are the results:

```
Here is the source XML document:
<BookParticipants>
  <BookParticipant type="Author" language="English">
    <FirstName>Dennis</FirstName>
    <LastName>Hayes</LastName>
  </BookParticipant>
```

```
   <BookParticipant type="Editor">
     <FirstName>Ewan</FirstName>
     <LastName>Buckingham</LastName>
   </BookParticipant>
 </BookParticipants>
```

```
A validation error occurred processing object type XAttribute.
The 'language' attribute is not declared.
Exception occurred: The 'language' attribute is not declared.
Document validated unsuccessfully.
```

For my next example, I will need an event handler that does not throw an exception. Here it is:

```
Private Sub MyValidationEventHandler2( _
    ByVal o As Object, _
    ByVal vea As ValidationEventArgs)

  Console.WriteLine( _
    "A validation error occurred processing object type {0}.", _
    o.GetType().Name)

  Console.WriteLine("{0}{1}", vea.Message, vbCrLf)
  Valid = False
End Sub
```

Also, for these examples to work, I need a global variable to track the status of the validation:

```
Private Valid as Boolean = True
```

Now, I'll try an example specifying to add the schema information, as shown in Listing 9-16.

Listing 9-16. *Unsuccessfully Validating an XML Document Against an XSD Schema and Specifying to Add Schema Information*

```
Dim xDocument As XDocument = _
  <?xml version="1.0"?>
  <BookParticipants>
    <BookParticipant type="Author">
      <FirstName>Dennis</FirstName>
      <MiddleName>Eugene</MiddleName>
      <LastName>Hayes</LastName>
    </BookParticipant>
    <BookParticipant type="Editor">
      <FirstName>Ewan</FirstName>
      <LastName>Buckingham</LastName>
```

```
      </BookParticipant>
    </BookParticipants>

Console.WriteLine("Here is the source XML document:")
Console.WriteLine("{0}{1}{1}", xDocument, System.Environment.NewLine)

Dim schemaSet As New XmlSchemaSet()
schemaSet.Add(Nothing, "bookparticipants.xsd")
Valid = True
xDocument.Validate(schemaSet, AddressOf MyValidationEventHandler2, True)

For Each element As XElement In xDocument.Descendants()
  Console.WriteLine( _
    "Element {0} is {1}", _
    element.Name, _
    element.GetSchemaInfo().Validity)

  Dim se As XmlSchemaElement = element.GetSchemaInfo().SchemaElement
  If se IsNot Nothing Then
    Console.WriteLine( _
      "Schema element {0} must have " & _
        "MinOccurs = {1} and MaxOccurs = {2}{3}", _
      se.Name, _
      se.MinOccurs, _
      se.MaxOccurs, _
      System.Environment.NewLine)
  Else
    '  Invalid elements will not have a SchemaElement.
    Console.WriteLine()
  End If
Next element
```

This example starts like the previous. It creates an XML document. This time, though, I added an additional element for the first BookParticipant: MiddleName and removed the language attribute. This is invalid because it is not specified in the schema I am validating against. Unlike the previous example, I specify for the Validate method to add the schema information. Also, unlike the previous example, I am not throwing an exception in my validation event-handling code. As you may recall, I mentioned previously that the validation must complete to have the schema information added, so your handler must not throw an exception. Therefore, I also removed the Try/Catch block and modified MyValidationEventHandler2 so that it does not throw any exceptions.

After the validation completes, I am enumerating all the elements in the document and displaying whether they are valid. Additionally, I obtain the SchemaElement object from the added schema information. Notice that I make sure the SchemaElement property is not Nothing, because if the element is not valid, the SchemaElement property may be Nothing. After all, the element may not be valid because it is not in the schema, so how could there be schema information? The same applies to the SchemaAttribute property for invalid attributes. Once I have a SchemaElement object, I display its Name, MinOccurs, and MaxOccurs properties.

Here are the results:

```
Here is the source XML document:
<BookParticipants>
  <BookParticipant type="Author">
    <FirstName>Dennis</FirstName>
    <MiddleName>Eugene</MiddleName>
    <LastName>Hayes</LastName>
  </BookParticipant>
  <BookParticipant type="Editor">
    <FirstName>Ewan</FirstName>
    <LastName>Buckingham</LastName>
  </BookParticipant>
</BookParticipants>


A validation error occurred processing object type XElement.
The element 'BookParticipant' has invalid child element 'MiddleName'. List of
possible elements expected: 'LastName'.

Element BookParticipants is Invalid
Schema element BookParticipants must have MinOccurs = 1 and MaxOccurs = 1

Element BookParticipant is Invalid
Schema element BookParticipant must have MinOccurs = 1 and MaxOccurs =
79228162514264337593543950335

Element FirstName is Valid
Schema element FirstName must have MinOccurs = 1 and MaxOccurs = 1

Element MiddleName is Invalid

Element LastName is NotKnown

Element BookParticipant is Valid
Schema element BookParticipant must have MinOccurs = 1 and MaxOccurs =
79228162514264337593543950335

Element FirstName is Valid
Schema element FirstName must have MinOccurs = 1 and MaxOccurs = 1

Element LastName is Valid
Schema element LastName must have MinOccurs = 1 and MaxOccurs = 1
```

There are no real surprises in this output. Notice that the MaxOccurs property value for the BookParticipant element is a very large number. This is because in the schema, the maxOccurs attribute is specified to be "unbounded".

For the final pair of validation examples, I will use one of the Validate method declarations that apply to validating elements. The first thing you will notice about these are that they have an argument that requires an XmlSchemaObject to be passed. This means the document must have already been validated. This seems odd. This is for a scenario where we have already validated once and need to revalidate a portion of the XML tree.

For this scenario, imagine I load an XML document and validate it to start. Next, I have allowed a user to update the data for one of the book participants and now need to update the XML document to reflect the user's changes, and I want to validate that portion of the XML tree again, after the updates. This is where the Validate method declarations of the elements and attributes can come in handy.

Because this example, shown in Listing 9-17, is more complex than some of the previous examples, I will explain it as I go. First, to be a little different, and because I need an expanded schema to facilitate an edit to the XML tree, I will define the schema programmatically instead of loading it from a file, as I have in the previous examples.

Listing 9-17. *Successfully Validating an XML Element*

```
Dim schema = _
  <?xml version="1.0" encoding="utf-8"?>
  <xs:schema attributeFormDefault="unqualified" elementFormDefault="qualified"
    xmlns:xs="http://www.w3.org/2001/XMLSchema">
    <xs:element name="BookParticipants">
      <xs:complexType>
        <xs:sequence>
          <xs:element maxOccurs="unbounded" name="BookParticipant">
            <xs:complexType>
              <xs:sequence>
                <xs:element name="FirstName" type="xs:string" />
                <xs:element minOccurs="0" name="MiddleInitial"
                  type="xs:string" />
                <xs:element name="LastName" type="xs:string" />
              </xs:sequence>
              <xs:attribute name="type" type="xs:string" use="required" />
            </xs:complexType>
          </xs:element>
        </xs:sequence>
      </xs:complexType>
    </xs:element>
  </xs:schema>

Dim schemaSet As New XmlSchemaSet()
schemaSet.Add("", XmlReader.Create(New StringReader(schema.ToString())))
```

In the previous code, I merely copied the schema from the file that I have been using. I also added a MiddleInitial element between the FirstName and LastName elements. Notice that I specify the minOccurs attribute as 0 so the element is not required. Next, I create a schema set from the schema. Next, it's time to create an XML document:

```
Dim xDocument As XDocument = _
  <?xml version="1.0"?>
  <BookParticipants>
    <BookParticipant type="Author">
      <FirstName>Dennis</FirstName>
      <LastName>Hayes</LastName>
    </BookParticipant>
    <BookParticipant type="Editor">
      <FirstName>Ewan</FirstName>
      <LastName>Buckingham</LastName>
    </BookParticipant>
  </BookParticipants>

Console.WriteLine("Here is the source XML document:")
Console.WriteLine("{0}{1}{1}", xDocument, System.Environment.NewLine)
```

There is nothing new here. I just created the same document I usually do for the examples and displayed it. Now I will validate the document:

Valid = True
```
xDocument.Validate(schemaSet, AddressOf MyValidationEventHandler2, True)

Console.WriteLine( _
  "Document validated {0}.{1}", _
  If(Valid, "successfully", "unsuccessfully"), vbCrLf)
```

Notice that I validate a little differently than I have in previous examples. I initialize a Boolean to True, representing whether the document is valid. Inside the validation handler, I set it to False. So if a validation error occurs, Valid will be set to False. I then check the value of Valid after validation to determine whether the document is valid and display its validity. In this example, the document is valid at this point.

Now, it's time to imagine that I am allowing a user to edit any particular book participant. The user has edited the book participant whose first name is "Dennis". So I obtain a reference for that element, update it, and revalidate it after the update:

```
Dim bookParticipant As XElement = xDocument.Descendants("BookParticipant") _
  .Where(Function(e) e.Element("FirstName").Value.Equals("Dennis")).First()

bookParticipant.Element("FirstName").AddAfterSelf( _
  New XElement("MiddleInitial", "E"))
```

Valid = True
```
bookParticipant.Validate( _
  bookParticipant.GetSchemaInfo().SchemaElement, _
  schemaSet, _
  AddressOf MyValidationEventHandler2, _
  True)
```

```
Console.WriteLine( _
  "Element validated {0}.{1}", _
  If(Valid, "successfully", "unsuccessfully"), vbCrLf)
```

As you can see, I initialize Valid to True and call the Validate method, this time on the BookParticipant element instead of the entire document. Inside the validation event handler, I set Valid to False. After validation of the BookParticipant element, I display its validity. Here are the results:

```
Here is the source XML document:
<BookParticipants>
  <BookParticipant type="Author">
    <FirstName>Dennis</FirstName>
    <LastName>Hayes</LastName>
  </BookParticipant>
  <BookParticipant type="Editor">
    <FirstName>Ewan</FirstName>
    <LastName>Buckingham</LastName>
  </BookParticipant>
</BookParticipants>


Document validated successfully.

Element validated successfully.
```

As you can see, the validation of the element is successful. For the final example, I have the same code, except this time, when I update the BookParticipant element, I will create a MiddleName element, as opposed to MiddleInitial, which is not valid. Listing 9-18 is the code.

Listing 9-18. *Unsuccessfully Validating an XML Element*

```
Dim schema = _
  <?xml version='1.0' encoding='utf-8'?>
  <xs:schema attributeFormDefault='unqualified' elementFormDefault='qualified'
    xmlns:xs='http://www.w3.org/2001/XMLSchema'>
    <xs:element name='BookParticipants'>
      <xs:complexType>
        <xs:sequence>
          <xs:element maxOccurs='unbounded' name='BookParticipant'>
            <xs:complexType>
              <xs:sequence>
                <xs:element name='FirstName' type='xs:string' />
                <xs:element minOccurs='0' name='MiddleInitial'
                  type='xs:string' />
                <xs:element name='LastName' type='xs:string' />
              </xs:sequence>
```

```vb
                  <xs:attribute name='type' type='xs:string' use='required' />
               </xs:complexType>
            </xs:element>
         </xs:sequence>
      </xs:complexType>
   </xs:element>
</xs:schema>

Dim schemaSet As New XmlSchemaSet()
schemaSet.Add("", XmlReader.Create(New StringReader(schema.ToString())))

Dim xDocument As XDocument = _
   <?xml version="1.0"?>
   <BookParticipants>
     <BookParticipant type="Author">
       <FirstName>Dennis</FirstName>
       <LastName>Hayes</LastName>
     </BookParticipant>
     <BookParticipant type="Editor">
       <FirstName>Ewan</FirstName>
       <LastName>Buckingham</LastName>
     </BookParticipant>
   </BookParticipants>

Console.WriteLine("Here is the source XML document:")
Console.WriteLine("{0}{1}{1}", xDocument, System.Environment.NewLine)

Valid = True
xDocument.Validate(schemaSet, AddressOf MyValidationEventHandler2, True)

Console.WriteLine( _
   "Document validated {0}.{1}", _
   If(Valid, "successfully", "unsuccessfully"), vbCrLf)

Dim bookParticipant As XElement = xDocument.Descendants("BookParticipant") _
   .Where(Function(e) e.Element("FirstName").Value.Equals("Dennis")).First()

bookParticipant.Element("FirstName"). _
   AddAfterSelf(New XElement("MiddleName", "Eugene"))

Valid = True
bookParticipant.Validate( _
   bookParticipant.GetSchemaInfo().SchemaElement, _
   schemaSet, _
   AddressOf MyValidationEventHandler2, _
   True)
```

```
Console.WriteLine( _
  "Element validated {0}.{1}", _
  If(Valid, "successfully", "unsuccessfully"), vbCrLf)
```

This code is identical to the previous example except instead of adding a `MiddleInitial` element, I added a `MiddleName` element that is invalid. Here are the results:

```
Here is the source XML document:
<BookParticipants>
  <BookParticipant type="Author">
    <FirstName>Dennis</FirstName>
    <LastName>Hayes</LastName>
  </BookParticipant>
  <BookParticipant type="Editor">
    <FirstName>Ewan</FirstName>
    <LastName>Buckingham</LastName>
  </BookParticipant>
</BookParticipants>


Document validated successfully.

A validation error occurred processing object type XElement.
The element 'BookParticipant' has invalid child element 'MiddleName'. List of
possible elements expected: 'MiddleInitial, LastName'.

Element validated unsuccessfully.
```

As you can see, the element is no longer valid. Now, this example may seem a little hokey because I said to imagine a user is editing the document. No developer in their right mind would create a user interface that would intentionally allow a user to create edits that would be invalid. But imagine if that user is in reality some other process on the XML document. Perhaps you passed the XML document to someone else's program to make some update and you know they personally have it in for you and are seeking your personal destruction. Now it may make sense to revalidate. You know you can't trust them.

XPath

If you are accustomed to using XPath, you can also gain some XPath query capabilities thanks to the `System.Xml.XPath.Extensions` class in the `System.Xml.XPath` namespace. This class adds XPath search capability via extension methods.

Declarations

Here is a list of some of the method declarations available in the `System.Xml.XPath.Extensions` class:

```vbnet
<ExtensionAttribute> _
Public Shared Function CreateNavigator ( _
  node As XNode _
) As XPathNavigator

<ExtensionAttribute> _
Public Shared Function CreateNavigator ( _
  node As XNode, _
  nameTable As XmlNameTable _
) As XPathNavigator


<ExtensionAttribute> _
Public Shared Function XPathEvaluate ( _
  node As XNode, _
  expression As String _
) As Object

<ExtensionAttribute> _
Public Shared Function XPathEvaluate ( _
  node As XNode, _
  expression As String, _
  resolver As IXmlNamespaceResolver _
) As Object


<ExtensionAttribute> _
Public Shared Function XPathSelectElement ( _
  node As XNode, _
  expression As String _
) As XElement

<ExtensionAttribute> _
Public Shared Function XPathSelectElement ( _
  node As XNode, _
  expression As String, _
  resolver As IXmlNamespaceResolver _
) As XElement


<ExtensionAttribute> _
Public Shared Function XPathSelectElements ( _
  node As XNode, _
  expression As String _
) As IEnumerable(Of XElement)
```

```
<ExtensionAttribute> _
Public Shared Function XPathSelectElements ( _
  node As XNode, _
  expression As String, _
  resolver As IXmlNamespaceResolver _
) As IEnumerable(Of XElement)
```

Examples

Using these extension methods, it is possible to query a LINQ to XML document using XPath search expressions. Listing 9-19 is an example.

Listing 9-19. *Querying XML with XPath Syntax*

```
Dim xDocument As XDocument = _
  <?xml version="1.0"?>
  <BookParticipants>
    <BookParticipant type = "Author">
      <FirstName>Dennis</FirstName>
      <LastName>Hayes</LastName>
    </BookParticipant>
    <BookParticipant type = "Editor">
      <FirstName>Ewan</FirstName>
      <LastName>Buckingham</LastName>
    </BookParticipant>
  </BookParticipants>

Dim bookParticipant As XElement = xDocument.XPathSelectElement( _
  "//BookParticipants/BookParticipant[FirstName='Dennis']")

Console.WriteLine(bookParticipant)
```

As you can see, I created my typical XML document. I didn't display the document this time though. I called the XPathSelectElement method on the document and provided an XPath search expression to find the BookParticipant element whose FirstName element's value is "Dennis". Here are the results:

```
<BookParticipant type="Author">
  <FirstName>Dennis</FirstName>
  <LastName>Hayes</LastName>
</BookParticipant>
```

Using the XPath extension methods, you can obtain a reference to a System.Xml.XPath. XPathNavigator object to navigate your XML document, perform an XPath query to return an element or a sequence of elements, or evaluate an XPath query expression.

Summary

At this point, if you came into this chapter without any knowledge of XML, I can only assume you are overwhelmed. If you did have a basic understanding of XML, but not of LINQ to XML, I hope I have made this understandable for you. The power and flexibility of the LINQ to XML API is quite intoxicating.

While writing this chapter and creating the examples, I would find myself lulled into a state of XML euphoria, a state without the underlying desire to avoid using "real" XML, only to find myself back at my day job planning on taking advantage of the simplicity LINQ to XML offers, despite the fact that my work project cannot use it because it has not been released yet. So many times I thought, if I could just use functional construction to whip up this piece of XML, only to find the reality of the situation causing me to use my standby XML library, the String.Format method.

Don't chastise me for taking the easy way out. As I previously mentioned, I was at a Microsoft seminar where the presenter demonstrated code that built XML in a similar manner.

Having written the many examples in this chapter and the previous LINQ to XML chapters, I can't tell you how excited I will be to actually use the LINQ to XML API in my real production code. The fact is that with LINQ to XML, because XML creation is largely based on elements rather than documents coupled with the capability of functional construction, creating XML is painless. It might even be fun. Combine the easy creation with the intuitive traversal and modification, and it becomes a joy to work with, considering the alternatives.

Having all this ease of use working with XML piled on top of a powerfully flexible query language makes LINQ to XML my personal favorite part of LINQ. If you find yourself dreading XML or intimidated to work with it, I think you will find the LINQ to XML API quite pleasant.

PART 4

LINQ to DataSet

CHAPTER 10

■ ■ ■

LINQ to DataSet Operators

While I haven't covered LINQ to SQL yet, let me mention at this time that to utilize LINQ to SQL for a given database, source code classes must be generated for that database and compiled, or a mapping file must be created. This means that performing LINQ queries with LINQ to SQL on a database unknown until runtime is not possible. Additionally, LINQ to SQL only works with Microsoft SQL Server. What is a developer to do?

The LINQ to DataSet operators allow a developer to perform LINQ queries on a DataSet, and since a DataSet can be obtained using normal ADO.NET SQL queries, LINQ to DataSet allows LINQ queries over *any* database that can be queried with ADO.NET. This provides a far more dynamic database-querying interface than LINQ to SQL.

You may be wondering, under what circumstances would you not know the database until runtime? It is true that for the typical application, the database is known while the application is being developed, and therefore LINQ to DataSet is not as necessary. But what about a database utility type application? For example, consider an application such as SQL Server Enterprise Manager. It doesn't know what databases are going to be installed on the server until runtime. The Enterprise Manager application allows you to examine whatever databases are installed on the server, with whatever tables are in a specified database. There is no way the Enterprise Manager application developer could generate the LINQ to SQL classes at compile time for *your* database. This is when LINQ to DataSet becomes a necessity.

While this part of the book is named "LINQ to DataSet," you will find that the added operators are really pertaining to DataTable, DataRow, and DataColumn objects. Don't be surprised that you don't see DataSet objects referenced often in this chapter. It is understood that in real-life circumstances, your DataTable objects will almost always come from DataSet objects. However, for the purpose of database independence, brevity, and clarity, I have intentionally created simple DataTable objects programmatically, rather than retrieve them from a database, for most of the examples.

The LINQ to DataSet operators consist of several special operators from multiple assemblies and namespaces that allow the developer to do the following:

- Perform set operations on sequences of DataRow objects.

- Retrieve and set DataColumn values.

- Obtain a LINQ standard IEnumerable(Of T) sequence from a DataTable so Standard Query Operators may be called.

- Copy modified sequences of DataRow objects to a DataTable.

In addition to these LINQ to DataSet operators, once you have called the AsEnumerable operator, you can call the LINQ to Objects Standard Query Operators on the returned sequence of DataRow objects, resulting in even more power and flexibility.

Assembly References

For the examples in this chapter, you will need to add references to your project for the System.Data.dll and System.Data.DataSetExtensions.dll assembly DLLs, if they have not already been added.

Referenced Namespaces

To use the LINQ to DataSet operators, your program will need to have an Imports statement for the System.Linq and System.Data namespaces, if they are not automatically included in your project settings:

```
Imports System.Data
Imports System.Linq
```

This will allow your code to find the LINQ to DataSet operators.

Common Code for the Examples

Virtually every example in this chapter will require a DataTable object on which to perform LINQ to DataSet queries. In real production code, you would typically obtain these DataTable objects by querying a database. However, for some of these examples, I present situations where the data conditions in a typical database table will not suffice. For example, I need duplicate records to demonstrate the Distinct method. Rather than jump through hoops trying to manipulate the database to contain the data I may need, I programmatically create a DataTable containing the specific data I desire for each example. This also relieves you of the burden of having a database for testing the majority of these examples.

Since I will not actually be querying a database for the DataTable objects, and to make creating the DataTable objects easy, I generate them from an array of objects of a predefined class. For the predefined class, I use the Student class.

A Simple Class with Two Public Members

```
Class Student
  Public Id As Integer
  Public Name As String
End Class
```

You should just imagine that I am querying a table named Students where each record is a student, and the table contains two columns: Id and Name.

To make creation of the DataTable simple, and to prevent obscuring the relevant details of each example, I use a common method to convert an array of Student objects into a DataTable object. This allows the data to easily vary from example to example. Here is that common method.

Converting an Array of Student Objects to a DataTable

```
Function GetDataTable(ByVal students() As Student) As DataTable
  Dim table As New DataTable()

  table.Columns.Add("Id", GetType(Int32))
  table.Columns.Add("Name", GetType(String))

  For Each student As Student In students
    table.Rows.Add(student.Id, student.Name)
  Next student

  Return (table)
End Function
```

There isn't anything complex in this method. I just instantiate a `DataTable` object, add two columns, and add a row for each element in the passed `students` array.

For many of the examples of the LINQ to DataSet operators, I need to display a `DataTable` for the results of the code to be clear. While the actual data in the `DataTable` varies, the code needed to display the `DataTable` object's header will not. Instead of repeating this code throughout all the examples, I create the following method and call it in any example needing to display a `DataTable` header.

The OutputDataTableHeader Method

```
Sub OutputDataTableHeader( _
    ByVal dt As DataTable, _
    ByVal columnWidth As Integer)
  Dim format As String = String.Format("{0}0,-{1}{2}", "{", columnWidth, "}")

  ' Display the column headings.
  For Each column As DataColumn In dt.Columns
    Console.Write(format, column.ColumnName)
  Next column
  Console.WriteLine()
  For Each column As DataColumn In dt.Columns
    For i As Integer = 0 To columnWidth - 1
      Console.Write("=")
    Next i
  Next column
  Console.WriteLine()
End Sub
```

The purpose of the method is to output the header of a `DataTable` in a tabular form.

DataRow Set Operators

As you may recall, in the LINQ to Objects API, there are a handful of Standard Query Operators that exist for the purpose of making sequence set-type comparisons. I am referring to the Distinct, Except, Intersect, Union, and SequenceEqual operators. Each of these operators performs a set operation on two sequences.

For each of these set-type operators, determining sequence element equality is necessary to perform the appropriate set operation. These operators perform element comparisons by calling the GetHashCode and Equals methods on the elements. For a DataRow, this results in a reference comparison, which is not the desired behavior. This will result in the incorrect determination of element equality, thereby causing the operators to return erroneous results. Because of this, each of these operators has an additional declaration that I omitted in the LINQ to Objects chapters. This additional declaration allows an IEqualityComparer object to be provided as an argument. Conveniently, a comparer object has been provided for us specifically for these versions of the operators, System.Data.DataRowComparer.Default. This comparer class is in the System.Data namespace in the System.Data.Entity.dll assembly. This comparer determines element equality by comparing the number of columns and the static data type of each column, and using the IComparable interface on the column's dynamic data type if that type implements the interface; otherwise, it calls the System.Object's static Equals method.

Each of these additional operator declarations is defined in the System.Linq.Enumerable static class just as the other declarations of these operators are.

In this section, I provide some examples to illustrate the incorrect and, more importantly, correct way to make these sequence comparisons when working with DataSet objects.

Distinct

The Distinct operator removes duplicate rows from a sequence of objects. It returns an object that, when enumerated, enumerates a source sequence of objects and returns a sequence of objects with the duplicate rows removed. Typically, this operator determines duplicates by calling each element's data type's GetHashCode and Equals methods. However, for DataRow type objects and other reference types, the operator compares the equality of the references and not the DataRow or object being referenced. This causes all rows to be considered different, even if all the fields are the same. I will discuss this further in the next chapter.

Because of this, I am going to call the additional declaration and provide the System. Data.DataRowComparer.Default comparer object, so the element equality will be properly determined. With it, a row is deemed to be a duplicate by comparing DataRow objects using the number of columns in a row and the static data type of each column, and then using the IComparable interface on each column if its dynamic data type implements the IComparable interface, or calling the static Equals method in System.Object if it does not.

Declarations

The Distinct operator has one declaration I will cover.

The Distinct Declaration

```
<ExtensionAttribute> _
Public Function Distinct(Of TSource) ( _
    source As IEnumerable(Of TSource), _
    comparer As IEqualityComparer(Of TSource)) _
  As IEnumerable(Of TSource)
```

Examples

In the first example, I create a DataTable from an array of Student objects using my common GetDataTable method, and the array will have one duplicate in it. The record whose Id is equal to 1 is repeated in the array. I then display the DataTable. This proves that the record is in the DataTable twice. Then I remove any duplicate rows by calling the Distinct operator and display the DataTable again, showing that the duplicate row has been removed. Listing 10-1 shows the code.

Listing 10-1. *The Distinct Operator with an Equality Comparer*

```
Dim students() As Student = { _
  New Student With {.Id = 1, .Name = "Dennis Hayes"}, _
  New Student With {.Id = 6, .Name = "Ulyses Hutchens"}, _
  New Student With {.Id = 19, .Name = "Bob Tanko"}, _
  New Student With {.Id = 45, .Name = "Erin Doutensal"}, _
  New Student With {.Id = 1, .Name = "Dennis Hayes"}, _
  New Student With {.Id = 12, .Name = "Bob Mapplethorpe"}, _
  New Student With {.Id = 17, .Name = "Anthony Adams"}, _
  New Student With {.Id = 32, .Name = "Dignan Stephens"}}

Dim dt As DataTable = GetDataTable(students)

Console.WriteLine("{0}Before calling Distinct(){0}", System.Environment.NewLine)

OutputDataTableHeader(dt, 15)

For Each dataRow As DataRow In dt.Rows
  Console.WriteLine( _
    "{0,-15}{1,-15}", _
    dataRow.Field(Of Integer)(0), _
    dataRow.Field(Of String)(1))
Next dataRow

Dim distinct As IEnumerable(Of DataRow) = _
  dt.AsEnumerable().Distinct(DataRowComparer.Default)

Console.WriteLine( _
  "{0}After calling Distinct(){0}", System.Environment.NewLine)
```

```
OutputDataTableHeader(dt, 15)

For Each dataRow As DataRow In distinct
  Console.WriteLine( _
    "{0,-15}{1,-15}", _
    dataRow.Field(Of Integer)(0), _
    dataRow.Field(Of String)(1))
Next dataRow
```

Notice that I use the AsEnumerable operator to get a sequence of DataRow objects from the DataTable because that is what I must call the Distinct operator on. Also notice that in the students array, the record with an Id equal to 1 is repeated.

You no doubt noticed that I call a method named Field on the DataRow object. For now, just understand that this is a helper method that makes obtaining a DataColumn object's value from a DataRow more convenient. I cover the Field(Of T) operator in depth later in the "DataRow Field Operators" section of this chapter.

Here are the results:

```
Before calling Distinct()

Id        Name
==============================
1         Dennis Hayes
6         Ulyses Hutchens
19        Bob Tanko
45        Erin Doutensal
1         Dennis Hayes
12        Bob Mapplethorpe
17        Anthony Adams
32        Dignan Stephens

After calling Distinct()

Id        Name
==============================
1         Dennis Hayes
6         Ulyses Hutchens
19        Bob Tanko
45        Erin Doutensal
12        Bob Mapplethorpe
17        Anthony Adams
32        Dignan Stephens
```

Notice that in the results, before I call the Distinct operator, the record whose Id is 1 is repeated, and that after calling the Distinct operator, the second occurrence of that record has been removed.

For a second example, I am going to demonstrate the results if I had called the `Distinct` operator without specifying the comparer object. The code is shown in Listing 10-2.

Listing 10-2. *The Distinct Operator Without an Equality Comparer*

```
Dim students() As Student = { _
  New Student With {.Id = 1, .Name = "Dennis Hayes"}, _
  New Student With {.Id = 6, .Name = "Ulyses Hutchens"}, _
  New Student With {.Id = 19, .Name = "Bob Tanko"}, _
  New Student With {.Id = 45, .Name = "Erin Doutensal"}, _
  New Student With {.Id = 1, .Name = "Dennis Hayes"}, _
  New Student With {.Id = 12, .Name = "Bob Mapplethorpe"}, _
  New Student With {.Id = 17, .Name = "Anthony Adams"}, _
  New Student With {.Id = 32, .Name = "Dignan Stephens"}}

Dim dt As DataTable = GetDataTable(students)

Console.WriteLine("{0}Before calling Distinct(){0}", System.Environment.NewLine)

OutputDataTableHeader(dt, 15)

For Each dataRow As DataRow In dt.Rows
  Console.WriteLine( _
    "{0,-15}{1,-15}", _
    dataRow.Field(Of Integer)(0), _
    dataRow.Field(Of String)(1))
Next dataRow

Dim distinct As IEnumerable(Of DataRow) = dt.AsEnumerable().Distinct()

Console.WriteLine("{0}After calling Distinct(){0}", System.Environment.NewLine)

OutputDataTableHeader(dt, 15)

For Each dataRow As DataRow In distinct
  Console.WriteLine( _
    "{0,-15}{1,-15}", _
    dataRow.Field(Of Integer)(0), _
    dataRow.Field(Of String)(1))
Next dataRow
```

The only difference between this code and the previous example is that the call to the `Distinct` operator does not have an equality comparer provided. Will it remove the duplicate row? Let's take a look:

```
Before calling Distinct()

Id      Name
==============================
1       Dennis Hayes
6       Ulyses Hutchens
19      Bob Tanko
45      Erin Doutensal
1       Dennis Hayes
12      Bob Mapplethorpe
17      Anthony Adams
32      Dignan Stephens

After calling Distinct()

Id      Name
==============================
1       Dennis Hayes
6       Ulyses Hutchens
19      Bob Tanko
45      Erin Doutensal
1       Dennis Hayes
12      Bob Mapplethorpe
17      Anthony Adams
32      Dignan Stephens
```

No, it did not remove the duplicate. As you can now see, these two examples are comparing rows differently.

Except

The Except operator produces a sequence of DataRow objects that are in the first sequence of DataRow objects that do not exist in the second sequence of DataRow objects. The operator returns an object that, when enumerated, enumerates the second sequence of DataRow objects collecting the unique elements, followed by enumerating the first sequence of DataRow objects, removing those elements from the collection that also occur in the second sequence and returning the results as they are generated.

To determine that elements from the same sequence are unique, and that one element in one sequence is or is not equal to an element in the other sequence, the operator must be able to determine whether two elements are equal. Typically, this operator determines element equality by calling each element's data type's GetHashCode and Equals methods. However, for DataRow type objects, this would cause an incorrect result.

Because I am going to call the additional declaration and provide the System.Data. DataRowComparer.Default comparer object, the element equality will be properly determined. With it, a row is deemed to be a duplicate by comparing DataRow objects using the number of columns in a row and the static data type of each column, and then using the IComparable interface on each column if its dynamic data type implements the `IComparable` interface, or calling the static `Equals` method in `System.Object` if it does not.

Declarations

The `Except` operator has one declaration that I will cover.

The Except Declaration

```
<ExtensionAttribute> _
Public Function Except(Of TSource) ( _
    first As IEnumerable(Of TSource), _
    second As IEnumerable(Of TSource), _
    comparer As IEqualityComparer(Of TSource)) _
  As IEnumerable(Of TSource)
```

Examples

In this example, I call the `Except` operator twice. The first time, I pass the `System.Data.DataRowComparer.Default` comparer object, so the results of the first query with the `Except` operator should be correct. The second time I call the `Except` operator, I will not pass the comparer object. This causes the results of that query to be incorrect. Listing 10-3 shows the code.

Listing 10-3. *The Except Operator With and Without the Comparer Object*

```
Dim students() As Student = { _
  New Student With {.Id = 1, .Name = "Dennis Hayes"}, _
  New Student With {.Id = 7, .Name = "Anthony Adams"}, _
  New Student With {.Id = 13, .Name = "Stacy Sinclair"}, _
  New Student With {.Id = 72, .Name = "Dignan Stephens"}}

Dim students2() As Student = { _
  New Student With {.Id = 5, .Name = "Abe Henry"}, _
  New Student With {.Id = 7, .Name = "Anthony Adams"}, _
  New Student With {.Id = 29, .Name = "Future Man"}, _
  New Student With {.Id = 72, .Name = "Dignan Stephens"}}

Dim dt1 As DataTable = GetDataTable(students)
Dim seq1 As IEnumerable(Of DataRow) = dt1.AsEnumerable()
Dim dt2 As DataTable = GetDataTable(students2)
Dim seq2 As IEnumerable(Of DataRow) = dt2.AsEnumerable()

Dim except As IEnumerable(Of DataRow) = _
  seq1.Except(seq2, System.Data.DataRowComparer.Default)

Console.WriteLine( _
  "{0}Results of Except() with comparer{0}", System.Environment.NewLine)
```

```
OutputDataTableHeader(dt1, 15)

For Each dataRow As DataRow In except
  Console.WriteLine( _
    "{0,-15}{1,-15}", _
    dataRow.Field(Of Integer)(0), _
    dataRow.Field(Of String)(1))
Next dataRow

except = seq1.Except(seq2)

Console.WriteLine( _
  "{0}Results of Except() without comparer{0}", _
  System.Environment.NewLine)

OutputDataTableHeader(dt1, 15)

For Each dataRow As DataRow In except
  Console.WriteLine( _
    "{0,-15}{1,-15}", _
    dataRow.Field(Of Integer)(0), _
    dataRow.Field(Of String)(1))
Next dataRow
```

There isn't much to this example. I basically create two DataTable objects that are populated from the Student arrays. I create sequences from each DataTable object by calling the
AsEnumerable method. I then call the Except operator on the two sequences and display the
results of each. As you can see, the first time I call the Except operator, I pass the System.Data.
DataRowComparer.Default comparer object. The second time I do not.

Let's look at the results of that code by pressing Ctrl+F5:

```
Results of Except() with comparer

Id          Name
==============================
1           Dennis Hayes
13          Stacy Sinclair

Results of Except() without comparer

Id          Name
==============================
1           Dennis Hayes
7           Anthony Adams
13          Stacy Sinclair
72          Dignan Stephens
```

As you can see, the Except operator called with the System.Data.DataRowComparer.Default comparer object is able to properly determine the element equality for the two sequences, whereas the Except operator without the comparer object does not identify any elements from the two sequences as being equal, which is not the desired behavior for this operator.

Intersect

The Intersect operator produces a sequence of DataRow objects that is the intersection of two sequences of DataRow objects. It returns an object that when enumerated enumerates the second sequence of DataRow objects collecting the unique elements, followed by enumerating the first sequence of DataRow objects, returning those elements occurring in both sequences as they are generated.

To determine that elements from the same sequence are unique, and that one element in one sequence is or is not equal to an element in the other sequence, the operator must be able to determine whether two elements are equal. Typically, this operator determines element equality by calling each element's data type's GetHashCode and Equals methods. However, for DataRow type objects, this would cause an incorrect result.

Because I am going to call the additional declaration and provide the System.Data.DataRowComparer.Default comparer object, the element equality will be properly determined. With it, a row is deemed to be a duplicate by comparing DataRow objects using the number of columns in a row and the static data type of each column, and then using the IComparable interface on each column if its dynamic data type implements the IComparable interface, or calling the static Equals method in System.Object if it does not.

Declarations

The Intersect operator has one declaration I will cover.

The Intersect Declaration

```
<ExtensionAttribute> _
Public Function Intersect(Of TSource) ( _
    first As IEnumerable(Of TSource), _
    second As IEnumerable(Of TSource), _
    comparer As IEqualityComparer(Of TSource)) _
  As IEnumerable(Of TSource)
```

Examples

In this example, I use the same basic code I use in the Except example, except I will change the operator calls from Except to Intersect. Listing 10-4 shows that code.

Listing 10-4. *The Intersect Operator With and Without the Comparer Object*

```
Dim students() As Student = { _
    New Student With {.Id = 1, .Name = "Dennis Hayes"}, _
    New Student With {.Id = 7, .Name = "Anthony Adams"}, _
    New Student With {.Id = 13, .Name = "Stacy Sinclair"}, _
    New Student With {.Id = 72, .Name = "Dignan Stephens"} }
```

```
Dim students2() As Student = { _
  New Student With {.Id = 5, .Name = "Abe Henry"}, _
  New Student With {.Id = 7, .Name = "Anthony Adams"}, _
  New Student With {.Id = 29, .Name = "Future Man"}, _
  New Student With {.Id = 72, .Name = "Dignan Stephens"} }

Dim dt1 As DataTable = GetDataTable(students)
Dim seq1 As IEnumerable(Of DataRow) = dt1.AsEnumerable()
Dim dt2 As DataTable = GetDataTable(students2)
Dim seq2 As IEnumerable(Of DataRow) = dt2.AsEnumerable()

Dim intersect As IEnumerable(Of DataRow) = _
  seq1.Intersect(seq2, System.Data.DataRowComparer.Default)

Console.WriteLine( _
  "{0}Results of Intersect() with comparer{0}", _
  System.Environment.NewLine)

OutputDataTableHeader(dt1, 15)

For Each dataRow As DataRow In intersect
  Console.WriteLine( _
    "{0,-15}{1,-15}", _
    dataRow.Field(Of Integer)(0), _
    dataRow.Field(Of String)(1))
Next dataRow

intersect = seq1.Intersect(seq2)

Console.WriteLine( _
  "{0}Results of Intersect() without comparer{0}", _
  System.Environment.NewLine)

OutputDataTableHeader(dt1, 15)

For Each dataRow As DataRow In intersect
  Console.WriteLine( _
    "{0,-15}{1,-15}", _
    dataRow.Field(Of Integer)(0), _
    dataRow.Field(Of String)(1))
Next dataRow
```

There is nothing new here. I create a couple of DataTable objects from the two Student arrays and obtain sequences from them. I then call the Intersect operator first with the comparer object and then without. I display the results after each Intersect call. Let's look at the results of that code by pressing Ctrl+F5:

Results of Intersect() with comparer

```
Id        Name
===============================
7         Anthony Adams
72        Dignan Stephens
```

Results of Intersect() without comparer

```
Id        Name
===============================
```

As you can see, the Intersect operator with the comparer is able to properly determine the element equality from the two sequences, whereas the Intersect operator without the comparer did not identify any elements from the two sequences as being equal, which is not the desired behavior for this operator.

Union

The Union operator produces a sequence of DataRow objects that is the union of two sequences of DataRow objects. It returns an object that, when enumerated, enumerates the first sequence of DataRow objects, followed by the second sequence of DataRow objects, yielding any element that has not already been yielded.

To determine that elements have already been yielded, the operator must be able to determine whether two elements are equal. Typically, this operator determines element equality by calling each element's data type's GetHashCode and Equals methods. However, for DataRow type objects, this would cause an incorrect result.

Because I am going to call the additional declaration and provide the System.Data.DataRowComparer.Default comparer object, the element equality will be properly determined. With it, a row is deemed to be a duplicate by comparing DataRow objects using the number of columns in a row and the static data type of each column, and then using the IComparable interface on each column if its dynamic data type implements the IComparable interface, or calling the static Equals method in System.Object if it does not.

Declarations

The Union operator has one declaration that I will cover.

The Union Declaration

```
<ExtensionAttribute> _
Public Function Union(Of TSource) ( _
    first As IEnumerable(Of TSource), _
    second As IEnumerable(Of TSource), _
    comparer As IEqualityComparer(Of TSource)) _
  As IEnumerable(Of TSource)
```

Examples

In this example, I use the same basic code I use in the Intersect example, except I will change
the operator calls from Intersect to Union. Listing 10-5 shows that code.

Listing 10-5. *The Union Operator With and Without the Comparer Object*

```
Dim students() As Student = { _
  New Student With {.Id = 1, .Name = "Dennis Hayes"}, _
  New Student With {.Id = 7, .Name = "Anthony Adams"}, _
  New Student With {.Id = 13, .Name = "Stacy Sinclair"}, _
  New Student With {.Id = 72, .Name = "Dignan Stephens"}}

Dim students2() As Student = { _
  New Student With {.Id = 5, .Name = "Abe Henry"}, _
  New Student With {.Id = 7, .Name = "Anthony Adams"}, _
  New Student With {.Id = 29, .Name = "Future Man"}, _
  New Student With {.Id = 72, .Name = "Dignan Stephens"}}

Dim dt1 As DataTable = GetDataTable(students)
Dim seq1 As IEnumerable(Of DataRow) = dt1.AsEnumerable()
Dim dt2 As DataTable = GetDataTable(students2)
Dim seq2 As IEnumerable(Of DataRow) = dt2.AsEnumerable()

Dim union As IEnumerable(Of DataRow) = _
  seq1.Union(seq2, System.Data.DataRowComparer.Default)

Console.WriteLine( _
  "{0}Results of Union() with comparer{0}", _
  System.Environment.NewLine)

OutputDataTableHeader(dt1, 15)

For Each dataRow As DataRow In union
  Console.WriteLine( _
    "{0,-15}{1,-15}", _
    dataRow.Field(Of Integer)(0), _
    dataRow.Field(Of String)(1))
Next dataRow

union = seq1.Union(seq2)

Console.WriteLine( _
  "{0}Results of Union() without comparer{0}", _
  System.Environment.NewLine)

OutputDataTableHeader(dt1, 15)
```

```
For Each dataRow As DataRow In union
  Console.WriteLine( _
    "{0,-15}{1,-15}", _
    dataRow.Field(Of Integer)(0), _
    dataRow.Field(Of String)(1))
Next dataRow
```

Again, there is nothing new here. I create a couple of DataTable objects from the two Student arrays and obtain sequences from them. I then call the Union operator first with the comparer object and then without. I display the results after each Union call. Here are the results:

```
Results of Union() with comparer

Id        Name
==============================
1         Dennis Hayes
7         Anthony Adams
13        Stacy Sinclair
72        Dignan Stephens
5         Abe Henry
29        Future Man


Results of Union() without comparer

Id        Name
==============================
1         Dennis Hayes
7         Anthony Adams
13        Stacy Sinclair
72        Dignan Stephens
5         Abe Henry
7         Anthony Adams
29        Future Man
72        Dignan Stephens
```

Notice that the results of the Union operator with the comparer object are correct, but the results of the Union operator without the comparer object are not.

SequenceEqual

The SequenceEqual operator compares two sequences of DataRow objects to determine whether they are equal. It enumerates two source sequences, comparing the corresponding DataRow objects. If the two source sequences have the same number of records, and if all the corresponding DataRow objects are equal, True is returned. Otherwise, the two sequences are not equal, and False is returned.

This operator must be able to determine whether two elements are equal. Typically, this operator determines element equality by calling each element's data type's GetHashCode and Equals methods. However, for DataRow type objects, this would cause an incorrect result.

Because I am going to call the additional declaration and provide the System.Data. DataRowComparer.Default comparer object, the element equality will be properly determined. With it, a row is deemed to be a duplicate by comparing DataRow objects using the number of columns in a row and the static data type of each column, and then using the IComparable interface on each column if its dynamic data type implements the IComparable interface, or calling the static Equals method in System.Object if it does not.

Declarations

The SequenceEqual operator has one declaration I will cover.

The SequenceEqual Declaration

```
<ExtensionAttribute> _
Public Function SequenceEqual(Of TSource) ( _
    first As IEnumerable(Of TSource), _
    second As IEnumerable(Of TSource), _
    comparer As IEqualityComparer(Of TSource)) _
  As Boolean
```

Examples

In this example of the SequenceEqual operator, I build two identical sequences of DataRow objects and compare them first with the SequenceEqual operator with a comparer object followed by a comparison with the SequenceEqual operator without a comparer object. Because of the way equality comparisons are handled by the two different operator calls, the SequenceEqual operator call with the comparer object returns that the two sequences are equal, while the SequenceEqual operator call without the comparer object returns that the two sequences are not equal. Listing 10-6 shows the code.

Listing 10-6. *The SequenceEqual Operator With and Without a Comparer Object*

```
Dim students() As Student = { _
  New Student With {.Id = 1, .Name = "Dennis Hayes"}, _
  New Student With {.Id = 7, .Name = "Anthony Adams"}, _
  New Student With {.Id = 13, .Name = "Stacy Sinclair"}, _
  New Student With {.Id = 72, .Name = "Dignan Stephens"}}

Dim dt1 As DataTable = GetDataTable(students)
Dim seq1 As IEnumerable(Of DataRow) = dt1.AsEnumerable()
Dim dt2 As DataTable = GetDataTable(students)
Dim seq2 As IEnumerable(Of DataRow) = dt2.AsEnumerable()
```

```
Dim equal As Boolean = _
  seq1.SequenceEqual(seq2, System.Data.DataRowComparer.Default)
Console.WriteLine("SequenceEqual() with comparer : {0}", equal)

equal = seq1.SequenceEqual(seq2)
Console.WriteLine("SequenceEqual() without comparer : {0}", equal)
```

There's not much to discuss here except that the first call should indicate that the two sequences are equal, while the second should indicate that they are not. The results are exactly as expected:

```
SequenceEqual() with comparer : True
SequenceEqual() without comparer : False
```

DataRow Field Operators

In addition to the `DataRow`-specific comparer class for the set-type operators, there is a need for some `DataRow`-specific operators. These operators are defined in the `System.Data.DataSetExtensions.dll` assembly, in the static `System.Data.DataRowExtensions` class.

You have no doubt noticed that in virtually every example thus far, I have used the `Field(Of T)` operator to extract a `DataColumn` object's value from a `DataRow`. There are two purposes for this operator: correct equality comparisons and `Nothing` value handling.

With `DataRow` objects, we have a problem. Their `DataColumn` values do not get compared properly for equality when they are accessed with the `DataRow` object's indexer if the column is a value-type. The reason is that because the column's data type could be any type, the indexer returns an object of type `System.Object`. This allows the indexer to return an integer, a string, or whatever data type is necessary for that column. This means that if a column is of type `Integer`, it is a value-type, and it must get *packaged* into an object of type `Object`. This packaging is known in the Microsoft .NET Framework as *boxing*. Pulling the value-type back out of the object is known as *unboxing*. This boxing is where the problem lies.

Let's take a look at some sample code. First, let's take the example of comparing an integer literal to another integer literal of the same value, as shown in Listing 10-7.

Listing 10-7. *Comparing 3 to 3*

```
Console.WriteLine("(3 = 3) is {0}.", (3 = 3))
```

The following is the result of this code:

```
(3 = 3) is True.
```

There is absolutely no surprise there. But what happens when an integer gets boxed? Let's examine the code in Listing 10-8 and look at the results.

Listing 10-8. *Comparing 3 Converted to an Object to Another 3 Converted to an Object Using the = Operator*

```
Console.WriteLine( _
  "CType(3, Object) = CType(3, Object) is {0}.", _
  (CType(3, Object) = CType(3, Object)))
```

If we set `Option Strict Off`, we get the following results:

```
CType(3, Object) = CType(3, Object) is True.
```

Again, everything is fine. Or is it? We do get the correct answer, which is good, but we have `Option Strict Off`, which disables strong type checking; this is bad. Setting `Option Strict Off` prevents the compiler from warning us when we unintentionally do a narrowing conversion, such as assigning a `Double` value to an `Integer` variable. Most experts recommend always programming with `Option Strict On` to help prevent errors.

With `Option Strict On`, which it should be, Listing 10-8 gives the following compiler error:

```
Option Strict On disallows operands of type Object for operator '='. Use the 'Is'
operator to test for object identity.
```

So, what to do? Set `Option Strict Off`? No, we should take the compiler's advice to use the `Is` operator; then, the code will look like Listing 10-9.

Listing 10-9. *Comparing 3 Converted to an Object to Another 3 Converted to an Object Using the Is Operator*

```
Console.WriteLine( _
  "CType(3, Object) Is CType(3, Object) is {0}.", _
  (CType(3, Object) Is CType(3, Object)))
```

Here is the output:

```
((Object)3 Is (Object)3) is False.
```

What is the difference? This code creates two objects. Both objects contain the value of 3. The two objects are different, but the values they contain are identical. In many languages, including C#, the = or == operator compares the two objects and finds them to be different objects. VB is smart enough to realize that you probably want to compare the contents in the containers, rather than the containers themselves, so, in Listing 10-8 with `Option Strict Off`, it compares the values in each container for you and finds the contents identical.

Setting `Option Strict On` prevents VB from making this assumption about what the programmer wants, and rather than give possibly unexpected results, the compiler generates an error. However, taking the compiler's advice and using the `Is` operator as I did in Listing 10-9 yields the wrong results.

The difference between comparing values and comparing objects is important to us here because of the way `DataColumns` are handled. When you access `DataColumn` objects using the

DataRow object's indexer, if any of the columns are a value-type, the column values will get boxed, and the results you get if you compare them will depend on the state of Option Strict.

To demonstrate this, I'll create a more complex example that actually uses DataColumn objects. In this example, I have two arrays, each of a different class type. One is the same basic array of students I have been using. The other is an array of class designations with foreign keys into the students array. Here is the StudentClass class.

A Simple Class with Two Public Properties

```
Class StudentClass
  Public Id As Integer
  Public ClassYear As String
End Class
```

Now that I have a different class type, I am going to need another method to convert this array to an object of type DataTable. Here is that method:

```
Private Function GetDataTable2(ByVal studentClasses() As StudentClass) _
    As DataTable
  Dim table As New DataTable()

  table.Columns.Add("Id", GetType(Integer))
  table.Columns.Add("ClassYear", GetType(String))

  For Each studentClass As StudentClass In studentClasses
    table.Rows.Add(studentClass.Id, studentClass.ClassYear)
  Next studentClass

  Return (table)
End Function
```

This method is nothing more than a copy of the existing common GetTableData method that has been modified to work with arrays of StudentClass objects. Obviously, if you were going to be working from arrays in real production code, you would want something more abstract than creating a method for each class type for which you need a DataTable object. Perhaps a generic extension method would be a nice approach. But as I mentioned at the beginning of the examples, you will typically be performing LINQ to DataSet queries on data from databases, not arrays, so I won't worry about that here.

For the example, I'll build a sequence of DataRow objects from each array and try to join them using their common Id column, which I will retrieve by indexing into the DataRow with the column name, which is Id. Listing 10-10 shows the code.

Listing 10-10. *Joining Two Value-Type Columns by Indexing into the DataRow*

```
Dim students() As Student = { _
  New Student With {.Id = 1, .Name = "Dennis Hayes"}, _
  New Student With {.Id = 7, .Name = "Anthony Adams"}, _
  New Student With {.Id = 13, .Name = "Stacy Sinclair"}, _
  New Student With {.Id = 72, .Name = "Dignan Stephens"}}
```

```vbnet
Dim classDesignations() As StudentClass = { _
  New StudentClass With {.Id = 1, .ClassYear = "Sophmore"}, _
  New StudentClass With {.Id = 7, .ClassYear = "Freshman"}, _
  New StudentClass With {.Id = 13, .ClassYear = "Graduate"}, _
  New StudentClass With {.Id = 72, .ClassYear = "Senior"}}

Dim dt1 As DataTable = GetDataTable(students)
Dim seq1 As IEnumerable(Of DataRow) = dt1.AsEnumerable()
Dim dt2 As DataTable = GetDataTable2(classDesignations)
Dim seq2 As IEnumerable(Of DataRow) = dt2.AsEnumerable()

Dim anthonysClass As String = ( _
  From s In seq1 _
  Where s.Field(Of String)("Name") = "Anthony Adams" _
  From c In seq2 _
  Where c("Id") = s("Id") _
  Select CStr(c("ClassYear"))).SingleOrDefault()

Console.WriteLine("Anthony's Class is: {0}", _
  If(anthonysClass IsNot Nothing, anthonysClass, "Nothing"))
```

There are a couple of things worth pointing out about that query. First, notice the line that is bold. There, I am indexing into the DataRow object to get the columns' values. Since the column value data types are integers, they will get boxed, which means there will be a problem determining equality. Additionally, you can see that I am using the Field(Of T) operator in this example when I compare the Name field to the name "Anthony Adams". Ignore this for now. Just realize that I am calling the Field(Of T) operator to prevent any equality comparison problem from occurring with the Name field while I am in the midst of demonstrating the boxing problem with the Id field. Also, notice that this query is combining the query expression syntax with the standard dot notation syntax. As you can see, I am performing a join on the two DataTable objects too.

With Option Strict On, I get the following compiler error:

```
Option Strict On disallows operands of type Object for operator '='. Use the 'Is'
operator to test for object identity.
```

With Option Strict Off, I get the following output:

```
Anthony's Class is: Freshman
```

But as I keep saying, setting Option Strict Off is a bad idea. If I leave Option Strict On, and take the compiler's advice to change the line to

```vbnet
Where c("Id") Is s("Id") _
```

I get the following output:

```
Anthony's Class is: Nothing
```

The String anthonysClass is Nothing because the join failed to find a record in seq2 that had an equal value for the Id field. This is because of the boxing of the Id field when it is retrieved using the DataRow indexer. Now, the better way is to handle the unboxing yourself in VB.NET by changing the line

```
Where c("Id") = s("Id") _
```

to

```
Where CInt(c("Id")) = CInt(s("Id")) _
```

Listing 10-11 is the entire example with that line replaced.

Listing 10-11. *Using Casting to Make the Test for Equality Correct*

```
Dim students() As Student = { _
    New Student With {.Id = 1, .Name = "Dennis Hayes"}, _
    New Student With {.Id = 7, .Name = "Anthony Adams"}, _
    New Student With {.Id = 13, .Name = "Stacy Sinclair"}, _
    New Student With {.Id = 72, .Name = "Dignan Stephens"}}

Dim classDesignations() As StudentClass = { _
    New StudentClass With {.Id = 1, .ClassYear = "Sophmore"}, _
    New StudentClass With {.Id = 7, .ClassYear = "Freshman"}, _
    New StudentClass With {.Id = 13, .ClassYear = "Graduate"}, _
    New StudentClass With {.Id = 72, .ClassYear = "Senior"}}

Dim dt1 As DataTable = GetDataTable(students)
Dim seq1 As IEnumerable(Of DataRow) = dt1.AsEnumerable()
Dim dt2 As DataTable = GetDataTable2(classDesignations)
Dim seq2 As IEnumerable(Of DataRow) = dt2.AsEnumerable()


Dim anthonysClass As String = CStr(( _
    From s In seq1 _
    Where s.Field(Of String)("Name") = "Anthony Adams" _
    From c In seq2 _
    Where CInt(c("Id")) = CInt(s("Id")) _
    Select c("ClassYear")).SingleOrDefault())

Console.WriteLine("Anthony's Class is: {0}", _
  If(anthonysClass IsNot Nothing, anthonysClass, "Nothing"))
```

Now, we can have Option Strict On and get the result we want, as we can see in the following output:

```
Anthony's Class is: Freshman
```

It does not matter if we have Option Strict On or Option Strict Off, we get the same output.

So that solves the boxing problem. However, there is still one other problem. When you attempt to retrieve a column's value using the DataRow object's indexer, remember, the column's value gets returned as an object of type Object. To compare it to any value or assign it to a variable will require casting it to another data type as I did previously by casting it to an Integer. Since DataSet objects use DBNull.Value as the value for a column that is Nothing, if that column's value is DBNull.Value, casting it to another data type will throw an exception.

Fortunately, LINQ to DataSet has made both of these problems—boxed value comparisons and Nothing handling—disappear, thanks to the Field(Of T) and SetField(Of T) operators. Listing 10-12 shows the previous example using the Field(Of T) operator.

Listing 10-12. *Using the Field Operator*

```
Dim students() As Student = { _
  New Student With {.Id = 1, .Name = "Dennis Hayes"}, _
  New Student With {.Id = 7, .Name = "Anthony Adams"}, _
  New Student With {.Id = 13, .Name = "Stacy Sinclair"}, _
  New Student With {.Id = 72, .Name = "Dignan Stephens"}}

Dim classDesignations() As StudentClass = { _
  New StudentClass With {.Id = 1, .ClassYear = "Sophmore"}, _
  New StudentClass With {.Id = 7, .ClassYear = "Freshman"}, _
  New StudentClass With {.Id = 13, .ClassYear = "Graduate"}, _
  New StudentClass With {.Id = 72, .ClassYear = "Senior"}}

Dim dt1 As DataTable = GetDataTable(students)
Dim seq1 As IEnumerable(Of DataRow) = dt1.AsEnumerable()
Dim dt2 As DataTable = GetDataTable2(classDesignations)
Dim seq2 As IEnumerable(Of DataRow) = dt2.AsEnumerable()

Dim anthonysClass As String = ( _
  From s In seq1 _
  Where s.Field(Of String)("Name") = "Anthony Adams" _
  From c In seq2 _
  Where c.Field(Of Integer)("Id") = s.Field(Of Integer)("Id") _
  Select CStr(c("ClassYear"))).SingleOrDefault()

Console.WriteLine("Anthony's Class is: {0}", _
  If(anthonysClass IsNot Nothing, anthonysClass, "Nothing"))
```

This code is the same as the previous example except I call the Field(Of T) operator instead of casting the field as an Integer Here are the results:

```
Anthony's Class is: Freshman
```

Field(Of T)

As I just demonstrated in Listing 10-12, the Field(Of T) operator allows you to obtain the value of a column from a DataRow object and handles the casting of DBNull.Value and boxed value comparison problems I previously discussed.

Declarations

The Field operator has six declarations.

The first declaration returns the column's value for the DataColumn and version specified.

The First Field Declaration

```
<ExtensionAttribute> _
Public Function Field(Of T) ( _
    row As DataRow, _
    column As DataColumn, _
    version As DataRowVersion) _
  As T
```

The second declaration returns the column's value for the column with the name and version specified.

The Second Field Declaration

```
<ExtensionAttribute> _
Public Function Field(Of T) ( _
    row As DataRow, _
    columnName As String, _
    version As DataRowVersion) _
  As T
```

The third declaration returns the column's value for the column with the ordinal and version specified.

The Third Field Declaration

```
<ExtensionAttribute> _
Public Function Field(Of T) ( _
    row As DataRow, _
    columnIndex As Integer, _
    version As DataRowVersion) _
  As T
```

The fourth declaration returns the column's current value only for the DataColumn specified.

The Fourth Field Declaration

```
<ExtensionAttribute> _
Public Function Field(Of T) ( _
    row As DataRow, _
    column As DataColumn) _
  As T
```

The fifth declaration returns the column's current value only for the column with the specified name.

The Fifth Field Declaration

```
<ExtensionAttribute> _
Public Function Field(Of T) ( _
    row As DataRow, _
    columnName As String) _
  As T
```

The sixth declaration returns the column's current value only for the column with the specified ordinal.

The Sixth Field Declaration

```
<ExtensionAttribute> _
Public Function Field(Of T) ( _
    row As DataRow, _
    columnIndex As Integer) _
  As T
```

As you may have noticed, the first three declarations allow you to specify which DataRowVersion of the DataColumn object's value you want to retrieve.

Examples

At this point, you have seen the Field(Of T) operator called many times and in different ways. But just so you can see each declaration in action, Listing 10-13 shows a trivial example of each.

Listing 10-13. *An Example of Each Field Operator Declaration*

```
Dim students() As Student = { _
  New Student With {.Id = 1, .Name = "Dennis Hayes"}, _
  New Student With {.Id = 7, .Name = "Anthony Adams"}, _
  New Student With {.Id = 13, .Name = "Stacy Sinclair"}, _
  New Student With {.Id = 72, .Name = "Dignan Stephens"}}

Dim dt1 As DataTable = GetDataTable(students)
Dim seq1 As IEnumerable(Of DataRow) = dt1.AsEnumerable()
```

```vbnet
Dim id As Integer

' Using declaration 1.
id = ( _
  From s In seq1 _
  Where s.Field(Of String)("Name") = "Anthony Adams" _
  Select s.Field(Of Integer)(dt1.Columns(0), DataRowVersion.Current)).Single()
Console.WriteLine("Anthony's Id retrieved with declaration 1 is: {0}", id)

' Using declaration 2.
id = ( _
  From s In seq1 _
  Where s.Field(Of String)("Name") = "Anthony Adams" _
  Select s.Field(Of Integer)("Id", DataRowVersion.Current)).Single()
Console.WriteLine("Anthony's Id retrieved with declaration 2 is: {0}", id)

' Using declaration 3.
id = ( _
  From s In seq1 _
  Where s.Field(Of String)("Name") = "Anthony Adams" _
  Select s.Field(Of Integer)(0, DataRowVersion.Current)).Single()
Console.WriteLine("Anthony's Id retrieved with declaration 3 is: {0}", id)

' Using declaration 4.
id = ( _
  From s In seq1 _
  Where s.Field(Of String)("Name") = "Anthony Adams" _
  Select s.Field(Of Integer)(dt1.Columns(0))).Single()
Console.WriteLine("Anthony's Id retrieved with declaration 4 is: {0}", id)

' Using declaration 5.
id = ( _
  From s In seq1 _
  Where s.Field(Of String)("Name") = "Anthony Adams" _
  Select s.Field(Of Integer)("Id")).Single()
Console.WriteLine("Anthony's Id retrieved with declaration 5 is: {0}", id)

' Using declaration 6.
id = ( _
  From s In seq1 _
  Where s.Field(Of String)("Name") = "Anthony Adams" _
  Select s.Field(Of Integer)(0)).Single()
Console.WriteLine("Anthony's Id retrieved with declaration 6 is: {0}", id)
```

Nothing here is very significant. I declare the array of students and create a DataTable object from it just like in most examples. Next I obtain a sequence of DataRow objects. I then work my way through each Field(Of T) operator declaration, one by one, using each to obtain the field named Id. Notice that in each query of the Id field, I am also using the Field(Of T) operator in the Where operator portion of the query. Here are the results:

```
Anthony's Id retrieved with declaration 1 is: 7
Anthony's Id retrieved with declaration 2 is: 7
Anthony's Id retrieved with declaration 3 is: 7
Anthony's Id retrieved with declaration 4 is: 7
Anthony's Id retrieved with declaration 5 is: 7
Anthony's Id retrieved with declaration 6 is: 7
```

Before moving on to the SetField(Of T) operator, I want to provide an example demonstrating one of the declarations that allows you to specify the DataRowVersion of the DataColumn object's value to retrieve. To provide an example, I will have to modify one of the DataColumn object's values using the SetField(Of T) operator. Although I haven't discussed the SetField(Of T) operator yet, just ignore it for now. I will be covering it in the next section.

Also, since this chapter is meant to explain the LINQ to DataSet operators and is not meant to be a detailed discussion of how the DataSet class works, I will only briefly cover a couple of additional DataSet methods I am calling in the example. Listing 10-14 is the code.

Listing 10-14. *The Field Operator Declaration with a Specified DataRowVersion*

```
Dim students() As Student = { _
  New Student With {.Id = 1, .Name = "Dennis Hayes"}, _
  New Student With {.Id = 7, .Name = "Anthony Adams"}, _
  New Student With { .Id = 13, .Name = "Stacy Sinclair"}, _
  New Student With { .Id = 72, .Name = "Dignan Stephens"}}

Dim dt1 As DataTable = GetDataTable(students)
Dim seq1 As IEnumerable(Of DataRow) = dt1.AsEnumerable()

Dim row As DataRow = ( _
  From s In seq1 _
  Where s.Field(Of String)("Name") = "Anthony Adams" _
  Select s).Single()

row.AcceptChanges()
row.SetField("Name", "George Oscar Bluth")

Console.WriteLine( _
  "Original value = {0} : Current value = {1}", _
  row.Field(Of String)("Name", DataRowVersion.Original), _
  row.Field(Of String)("Name", DataRowVersion.Current))

row.AcceptChanges()
Console.WriteLine( _
  "Original value = {0} : Current value = {1}", _
  row.Field(Of String)("Name", DataRowVersion.Original), _
  row.Field(Of String)("Name", DataRowVersion.Current))
```

In this example, I obtain a sequence from the array of students as I typically do. I then query for a single DataRow object on which I can make some changes. The first code of interest is the AcceptChanges method that I call after obtaining the DataRow object. I call this method to make the DataRow object accept the current value for each DataColumn object within it as the original version. Without that, there would be no original version of the DataColumn objects' values, and merely attempting to access the field's original version causes an exception to be thrown. In this way, the DataRow object is ready to begin tracking DataColumn object value changes. I need this to be able to obtain different DataRowVersion versions of the DataRow object's DataColumn values.

Once I call the AcceptChanges method the first time, I set a field using the SetField operator. I then display the original version and current version of the Name DataColumn value to the console. At this point, the original version should be "Anthony Adams", and the current version should be "George Oscar Bluth". This allows you to see the different versions you can obtain from a DataRow object.

Then, just to make it interesting, I call the AcceptChanges method a second time and again display the original and current version of the DataColumn object's value. This time, the original and current version values should both be "George Oscar Bluth", because I have told the DataRow object to accept the changes as the current version. Let's examine the results:

```
Original value = Anthony Adams : Current value = George Oscar Bluth
Original value = George Oscar Bluth : Current value = George Oscar Bluth
```

That works like a charm. Remember, though, without calling the AcceptChanges method the first time, I could have changed the value of the DataColumn object all day long, and there would not have been an original version.

You may recall that I mentioned that one of the additional benefits of using the Field(Of T) operator is that it also nicely handles the situation when fields are Nothing. Let's take a look at the example in Listing 10-15 where a student's name has a Nothing value, but I am not using the Field(Of T) operator.

Listing 10-15. *An Example Without the Field Operator When There Is a Nothing Value Present*

```
Dim students() As Student = { _
  New Student With {.Id = 1, .Name = "Dennis Hayes"}, _
  New Student With { .Id = 7, .Name = Nothing}, _
  New Student With { .Id = 13, .Name = "Stacy Sinclair"}, _
  New Student With { .Id = 72, .Name = "Dignan Stephens"} }

Dim dt1 As DataTable = GetDataTable(students)
Dim seq1 As IEnumerable(Of DataRow) = dt1.AsEnumerable()

Dim name As String = seq1.Where( _
  Function(student) student.Field(Of Integer)("Id") = 7) _
    .Select(Function(student) CStr(student("Name"))).Single()

Console.WriteLine("Student's name is '{0}'", name)
```

That is a fairly simple example. Notice that I initialized the Name member of the Student record of the student whose Id is 7 to Nothing. Also notice that instead of using the Field(Of T) operator, I just index into the DataRow and convert the value to a String. Let's take a look at the results:

```
Unhandled Exception: System.InvalidCastException: Conversion from type 'DBNull' to
type 'String' is not valid.
…
```

So what happened? What happened is that the DataColumn object's value is DBNull, and you can't convert that to a String. There are some rather verbose solutions I could take to alleviate this complication, but this is what the Field(Of T) operator is designed to simplify for you. Let's take a look at the same example, except this time I use the Field(Of T) operator to obtain the DataColumn object's value. Listing 10-16 is the code.

Listing 10-16. *An Example with the Field Operator When There Is a Nothing Value Present*

```
Dim students() As Student = { _
  New Student With {.Id = 1, .Name = "Dennis Hayes"}, _
  New Student With { .Id = 7, .Name = Nothing}, _
  New Student With { .Id = 13, .Name = "Stacy Sinclair"}, _
  New Student With { .Id = 72, .Name = "Dignan Stephens"} }

Dim dt1 As DataTable = GetDataTable(students)
Dim seq1 As IEnumerable(Of DataRow) = dt1.AsEnumerable()

Dim name As String = seq1.Where( _
  Function(student) student.Field(Of Integer)("Id") = 7) _
    .Select(Function(student) student.Field(Of String)("Name")).Single()

Console.WriteLine("Student's name is '{0}'", name)
```

OK, this is the same code except I use the Field(Of T) operator instead of casting it to a String. Let's look at the results:

```
Student's name is ''
```

This is much easier to deal with.

SetField(Of T)

Just as with the *retrieval* of DataColumn objects, Nothing adversely affects the *setting* of DataColumn objects. To assist with this issue, the SetField(Of T) operator was created. It handles the case where a DataColumn object's value is set with a nullable data type whose value is Nothing.

Declarations

The SetField(Of T) operator has three declarations.

The first declaration allows you to set a column's current value for the DataColumn specified.

The First SetField Declaration

```
<ExtensionAttribute> _
Public Sub SetField(Of T) ( _
    row As DataRow, _
    column As DataColumn, _
    value As T)
```

The second declaration allows you to set a column's current value for the column with the specified name.

The Second SetField Declaration

```
<ExtensionAttribute> _
Public Sub SetField(Of T) ( _
    row As DataRow, _
    columnName As String, _
    value As T)
```

The third declaration allows you to set a column's current value for the column with the specified ordinal.

The Third SetField Declaration

```
<ExtensionAttribute> _
Public Sub SetField(Of T) ( _
    row As DataRow, _
    columnIndex As Integer, _
    value As T)
```

Examples

As an exampleof the SetField(Of T) operator, shown in Listing 10-17, first, I display the sequence of DataRow objects that contain the students. Next, I query one of the students by name from the sequence of DataRow objects and change that name using the SetField(Of T) operator. I then display the sequence of DataRow objects after the change has been made. Rinse and repeat for each declaration.

Listing 10-17. *An Example of Each SetField Operator Declaration*

```
Dim students() As Student = { _
  New Student With {.Id = 1, .Name = "Dennis Hayes"}, _
  New Student With {.Id = 7, .Name = "Anthony Adams"}, _
  New Student With {.Id = 13, .Name = "Stacy Sinclair"}, _
  New Student With {.Id = 72, .Name = "Dignan Stephens"} }
```

```vbnet
Dim dt1 As DataTable = GetDataTable(students)
Dim seq1 As IEnumerable(Of DataRow) = dt1.AsEnumerable()

Console.WriteLine( _
  "{0}Results before calling any declaration:", vbCrLf)

For Each dataRow As DataRow In seq1
  Console.WriteLine("Student Id = {0} is {1}", _
    dataRow.Field(Of Integer)("Id"), _
    dataRow.Field(Of String)("Name"))
Next dataRow

Dim MyRow As DataRow

' Using declaration 1.
MyRow = (From s In seq1 Where s.Field(Of String)("Name") = "Anthony Adams" _
  Select s).Single()
MyRow.SetField(dt1.Columns(1), "George Oscar Bluth")

Console.WriteLine("{0}Results after calling declaration 1:", vbCrLf)

For Each dataRow As DataRow In seq1
  Console.WriteLine("Student Id = {0} is {1}", dataRow.Field(Of Integer)("Id"), _
    dataRow.Field(Of String)("Name"))
Next dataRow

' Using declaration 2.
MyRow = ( _
  From s In seq1 Where s.Field(Of String)("Name") = "George Oscar Bluth" _
    Select s).Single()
MyRow.SetField("Name", "Michael Bluth")

Console.WriteLine("{0}Results after calling declaration 2:", vbCrLf)

For Each dataRow As DataRow In seq1
  Console.WriteLine("Student Id = {0} is {1}", dataRow.Field(Of Integer)("Id"), _
    dataRow.Field(Of String)("Name"))
Next dataRow

' Using declaration 3.
MyRow = (From s In seq1 Where s.Field(Of String)("Name") = "Michael Bluth" _
  Select s).Single()
MyRow.SetField(1, "Tony Wonder")

Console.WriteLine("{0}Results after calling declaration 3:", vbCrLf)
```

```
For Each dataRow As DataRow In seq1
  Console.WriteLine("Student Id = {0} is {1}", dataRow.Field(Of Integer)("Id"), _
    dataRow.Field(Of String)("Name"))
Next dataRow
```

This code is not quite as bad as it looks. After I obtain the sequence of students and display them, there is a block of code that gets repeated three times, once for each declaration. Each block contains a LINQ query that retrieves the field and updates its value, displays a header line to the console, and then displays each row in the sequence to the console to show the change just made to the field.

There are a couple noteworthy things in this example. In each LINQ query where I query the DataRow on its Name field, again, I am mixing query expression syntax and standard dot notation syntax in the query. Also, I am using the Field(Of T) operator to find the record that I am going to set with the SetField(Of T) operator. After obtaining the sequence of DataRow objects of students, I work my way through the SetField(Of T) operator declarations one by one. Throughout the example, I query the previously changed element by its value and change it again. For example, for the first declaration, I just query the element whose Name field is "Anthony Adams" and set it to "George Oscar Bluth". For the second declaration, I query the element whose Name field is "George Oscar Bluth" and change it to something else, which I will query for on the next declaration. Of course, after each element value update, I display the sequence to the console so you can verify that the element's value did indeed change.

Here are the results:

```
Results before calling any declaration:
Student Id = 1 is Dennis Hayes
Student Id = 7 is Anthony Adams
Student Id = 13 is Stacy Sinclair
Student Id = 72 is Dignan Stephens

Results after calling declaration 1:
Student Id = 1 is Dennis Hayes
Student Id = 7 is George Oscar Bluth
Student Id = 13 is Stacy Sinclair
Student Id = 72 is Dignan Stephens

Results after calling declaration 2:
Student Id = 1 is Dennis Hayes
Student Id = 7 is Michael Bluth
Student Id = 13 is Stacy Sinclair
Student Id = 72 is Dignan Stephens

Results after calling declaration 3:
Student Id = 1 is Dennis Hayes
Student Id = 7 is Tony Wonder
Student Id = 13 is Stacy Sinclair
Student Id = 72 is Dignan Stephens
```

As you can see, the Name field of the appropriate element is updated each time.

DataTable Operators

In addition to the DataRow-specific operators in the DataRowExtensions class, there is a need for some DataTable-specific operators. These operators are defined in the System.Data.Entity. dll assembly, in the static System.Data.DataTableExtensions class.

AsEnumerable

I am guessing that you are probably surprised to see the AsEnumerable operator here. In fact, you may be surprised to learn that there is an AsEnumerable operator specifically for the DataTable class that returns a sequence of DataRow objects. If so, I am pleased because it means you were not wondering throughout this whole chapter why I had not mentioned it yet. After all, I have called it in virtually every example.

Yes, if you look in the System.Data.DataTableExtensions static class, you will see there is an AsEnumerable operator. The purpose of this operator is to return a sequence of type IEnumerable(Of DataRow) from a DataTable object.

Declarations

The AsEnumerable operator has one declaration.

The AsEnumerable Declaration

```
<ExtensionAttribute> _
Public Function AsEnumerable ( _
    source As DataTable) _
  As EnumerableRowCollection(Of DataRow)
```

This operator when called on a DataTable object returns a sequence of DataRow objects. This is typically the first step of performing a LINQ to DataSet query on a DataSet object's DataTable. By calling this operator, you can obtain a sequence, an IEnumerable(Of T) where T happens to be a DataRow, thereby allowing you to call the many LINQ operators that may be called on an IEnumerable(Of T) type sequence.

■**Note** We can use the AsEnumerable operator because EnumerableRowCollection(Of DataRow) implements IEnumerable(Of T) where T is DataRow.

Examples

There is no shortage of examples in this chapter. Since calling the AsEnumerable operator is the first step to perform a LINQ to DataSet query, virtually every example in this chapter is calling the AsEnumerable operator. Therefore, there is no need to provide one here.

CopyToDataTable(Of DataRow)

Now that you know how to query and modify the DataColumn values of a DataRow, you might just be interested in getting that sequence of modified DataRow objects into a DataTable. The CopyToDataTable operator exists for this very purpose.

Declarations

The CopyToDataTable operator has three declarations, I cover the first two here. The third declaration is the same as the second, except that it also takes a delegate that handles errors during the fill as a fourth argument.

This first declaration is called on an IEnumerable(Of DataRow) and returns a DataTable. This is used to create a new DataTable object from a sequence of DataRow objects.

The First CopyToDataTable Declaration

```
<ExtensionAttribute> _
Public Shared Function CopyToDataTable(Of T As DataRow) ( _
    source As IEnumerable(Of T))
  As DataTable
```

The first declaration establishes original versions for each field for you automatically without you needing to call the AcceptChanges method.

The second declaration is called on an IEnumerable(Of DataRow) of the source DataTable to update an already existing destination DataTable based on the LoadOption value specified.

The Second CopyToDataTable Declaration

```
<ExtensionAttribute> _
Public Sub CopyToDataTable(Of T As DataRow) (
  source As IEnumerable(Of T), _
  table As DataTable, _
  options As LoadOption)
```

The value of the LoadOption argument passed informs the operator whether the *original* column values only should be changed, the *current* column values only should be changed, or both. This is helpful for managing the DataTable's changes. The following are the available values for LoadOption:

- OverwriteChanges: Both the current value and original value will be updated for each column.

- PreserveChanges: Only the original value will be updated for each column.

- Upsert: Only the current value will be updated for each column.

This LoadOption argument has now created a bit of a problem, though. Notice that the description of each possible value refers to updating the values of a column. This, of course, means updating the columns of a record already in the destination DataTable. How would the CopyToDataTable operator possibly know which record already in the destination DataTable corresponds to a record in the source DataTable? In other words, when it tries to copy a record from the source DataTable to the destination DataTable and has to honor the LoadOption parameter, how does it know whether it should just add the record from the source DataTable or update an already existing record in the destination DataTable? The answer is that it doesn't, unless it is aware of primary key fields in the DataTable.

Therefore, for this declaration of the CopyToDataTable operator to work properly, the destination DataTable object must have the appropriate fields specified as the primary key fields. Without specifying primary keys, this declaration will result in appending all the records from the source DataTable to the destination DataTable.

There is one additional complication to be cognizant of when working with this declaration of the operator. Since, by using this declaration, you are possibly interested in original vs. current version values of fields, do not forget that with this declaration of the CopyToDataTable operator, a field doesn't have an original version unless the AcceptChanges method has been called. Attempting to access the original version when one does not exist causes an exception to be thrown. However, you can call the HasVersion method on each DataRow object before attempting to access the original version to determine if there is an original version to prevent this type of exception.

Examples

As an example of the first CopyToDataTable operator declaration, I will simply modify a field in a DataTable, create a new DataTable from the modified DataTable by calling the CopyToDataTable operator, and then display the contents of the new DataTable. Listing 10-18 is the code.

Listing 10-18. *Calling the First Declaration of the CopyToDataTable Operator*

```
Dim students() As Student = { _
  New Student With { .Id = 1, .Name = "Dennis Hayes"}, _
  New Student With { .Id = 7, .Name = "Anthony Adams"}, _
  New Student With { .Id = 13, .Name = "Stacy Sinclair"}, _
  New Student With { .Id = 72, .Name = "Dignan Stephens"} }

Dim dt1 As DataTable = GetDataTable(students)

Console.WriteLine("Original DataTable:")
For Each dataRow As DataRow In dt1.AsEnumerable()
  Console.WriteLine( _
    "Student Id = {0} is {1}", _
    dataRow.Field(Of Integer)("Id"), _
    dataRow.Field(Of String)("Name"))
Next dataRow

Dim MyRow As DataRow
MyRow = ( _
  From s In dt1.AsEnumerable() _
    Where s.Field(Of String)("Name") = "Anthony Adams" _
    Select s).Single()

MyRow.SetField("Name", "George Oscar Bluth")
```

```
Dim newTable As DataTable = dt1.AsEnumerable().CopyToDataTable()

Console.WriteLine("{0}New DataTable:", System.Environment.NewLine)
For Each dataRow As DataRow In newTable.AsEnumerable()
  Console.WriteLine( _
    "Student Id = {0} is {1}", _
    dataRow.Field(Of Integer)("Id"), _
    dataRow.Field(Of String)("Name"))
Next dataRow
```

As I said, first, I create a `DataTable` from my array of students as I typically do in the previous examples. I then display the contents of that `DataTable` to the console. Next, I modify the `Name` field in one of the `DataRow` objects. Then, I create a new `DataTable` by calling the `CopyToDataTable` operator. Last, I display the contents of the newly created `DataTable`.

Are you ready for the final countdown? Poof!

```
Original DataTable:
Student Id = 1 is Dennis Hayes
Student Id = 7 is Anthony Adams
Student Id = 13 is Stacy Sinclair
Student Id = 72 is Dignan Stephens

New DataTable:
Student Id = 1 is Dennis Hayes
Student Id = 7 is George Oscar Bluth
Student Id = 13 is Stacy Sinclair
Student Id = 72 is Dignan Stephens
```

As you can see, not only do I have data in the new `DataTable`, it is the modified version, just as you would expect.

For the next example, I want to demonstrate the second declaration of the `CopyToDataTable` operator. As you may recall, I mentioned that for the `LoadOption` argument to work properly, primary keys must be established on the destination `DataSet`. For this example, I will *not* establish those so you can see the behavior. Because this example is a little more complex, I describe this one as I go. Listing 10-19 is the code.

Listing 10-19. *Calling the Second Declaration of the CopyToDataTable Operator When Primary Keys Are Not Established*

```
Dim students() As Student = { _
  New Student With {.Id = 1, .Name = "Dennis Hayes"}, _
  New Student With {.Id = 7, .Name = "Anthony Adams"}, _
  New Student With {.Id = 13, .Name = "Stacy Sinclair"}, _
  New Student With {.Id = 72, .Name = "Dignan Stephens"} }

Dim dt1 As DataTable = GetDataTable(students)
Dim newTable As DataTable = dt1.AsEnumerable().CopyToDataTable()
```

There is little new so far. I created what will be my source `DataTable` from the `students` array. I created my destination `DataTable` by calling the `CopyToDataTable` operator on the source `DataTable`. Notice that because I called the first declaration of the `CopyToDataTable` operator, I do not need to call the `AcceptChanges` method on the destination `DataTable`. This is important to be cognizant of because, in the next segment of code, I reference the original version of the `Name` field. If it were not for the fact that the first declaration of the `CopyToDataTable` operator establishes the original versions of fields for you, an exception would be thrown since the original version would not exist.

```
Console.WriteLine("Before upserting DataTable:")
For Each dataRow As DataRow In newTable.AsEnumerable()
  Console.WriteLine( _
    "Student Id = {0} : original {1} : current {2}", _
    dataRow.Field(Of Integer)("Id"), _
    dataRow.Field(Of String)("Name", DataRowVersion.Original), _
    dataRow.Field(Of String)("Name", DataRowVersion.Current))
Next dataRow
```

There is nothing of significance here except that I reference the original version of the `Name` field in the record, and no exception is thrown when doing so because this declaration of the `CopyToDataTable` operator established the original version for me.

```
dim MyRow As DataRow

MyRow = (From s In dt1.AsEnumerable() _
  Where s.Field(Of String)("Name") = "Anthony Adams" Select s).Single()
MyRow.SetField("Name", "George Oscar Bluth")

dt1.AsEnumerable().CopyToDataTable(newTable, LoadOption.Upsert)
```

This is the most exciting code segment of this example. Notice that I change the value of the `Name` field for one of the records in the source `DataTable` using the `SetField(Of T)` operator. Next, I call the `CopyToDataTable` operator specifying that a `LoadOption.Upsert` type of copy should occur, meaning update only the current version. This causes a problem, though: since I have called the second `CopyToDataTable` operator declaration, which doesn't establish original versions for records inserted into the database, and I haven't called the `AcceptChanges` method, if I attempt to access the original versions on inserted records, an exception will be thrown. I will have to use the `HasVersion` method to prevent this from happening if any records are inserted. Since I have not specified any primary keys, I *know* that all of the records in the source table will be inserted into the destination table.

```
Console.WriteLine("{0}After upserting DataTable:", System.Environment.NewLine)
For Each dataRow As DataRow In newTable.AsEnumerable()
  Console.WriteLine( _
    "Student Id = {0} : original {1} : current {2}", _
    dataRow.Field(Of Integer)("Id"), _
    If(dataRow.HasVersion(DataRowVersion.Original), _
      dataRow.Field(Of String) _
        ("Name", DataRowVersion.Original), _
```

```
        "-does not exist-"), _
    dataRow.Field(Of String) ("Name", DataRowVersion.Current))
Next dataRow
```

In this code segment, I merely display the DataTable content to the console. Now, the interesting thing about this example is that, since I do not specify any primary keys for the destination table, when the copy occurs, no records will be deemed the same, so all the copied records from the source DataTable will be appended to the destination DataTable.

Also, notice that I only access the original version of the field's data if the HasVersion method returns True indicating that there is an original version. Here are the results:

```
Before upserting DataTable:
Student Id = 1 : original Dennis Hayes : current Dennis Hayes
Student Id = 7 : original Anthony Adams : current Anthony Adams
Student Id = 13 : original Stacy Sinclair : current Stacy Sinclair
Student Id = 72 : original Dignan Stephens : current Dignan Stephens

After upserting DataTable:
Student Id = 1 : original Dennis Hayes : current Dennis Hayes
Student Id = 7 : original Anthony Adams : current Anthony Adams
Student Id = 13 : original Stacy Sinclair : current Stacy Sinclair
Student Id = 72 : original Dignan Stephens : current Dignan Stephens
Student Id = 1 : original -does not exist- : current Dennis Hayes
Student Id = 7 : original -does not exist- : current George Oscar Bluth
Student Id = 13 : original -does not exist- : current Stacy Sinclair
Student Id = 72 : original -does not exist- : current Dignan Stephens
```

Notice that several records are now duplicated because I don't specify any primary keys in the destination DataTable. Even the record I actually updated is in the DataTable twice now.

You may be wondering, since I made such a big deal about calling the HasVersion method since the AcceptChanges method was not called, why not just call the AcceptChanges method? You could do that, but if you did, all of the fields' current version values would have become their original version values, and you would not have been able to tell which records had changed. For these examples, I want the original version values and current version values to be distinguishable when a record is changed.

The solution to the problem in the previous example is to specify the primary keys for the destination DataTable. Listing 10-20 is the same example as the previous, except this time I specify the primary keys.

Listing 10-20. *Calling the Second Declaration of the CopyToDataTable Operator When Primary Keys Are Established*

```
Dim students() As Student = { _
    New Student With {.Id = 1, .Name = "Dennis Hayes"}, _
    New Student With {.Id = 7, .Name = "Anthony Adams"}, _
    New Student With {.Id = 13, .Name = "Stacy Sinclair"}, _
    New Student With {.Id = 72, .Name = "Dignan Stephens"} }
```

```vb
Dim dt1 As DataTable = GetDataTable(students)
Dim newTable As DataTable = dt1.AsEnumerable().CopyToDataTable()
newTable.PrimaryKey = New DataColumn() { newTable.Columns(0) }

Console.WriteLine("Before upserting DataTable:")
For Each dataRow As DataRow In newTable.AsEnumerable()
  Console.WriteLine( _
    "Student Id = {0} : original {1} : current {2}", _
    dataRow.Field(Of Integer)("Id"), _
    dataRow.Field(Of String)("Name", DataRowVersion.Original), _
    dataRow.Field(Of String)("Name", DataRowVersion.Current))
Next dataRow

Dim MyRow As DataRow
MyRow =( From s In dt1.AsEnumerable() _
  Where s.Field(Of String)("Name") = "Anthony Adams" Select s).Single()
MyRow.SetField("Name", "George Oscar Bluth")

dt1.AsEnumerable().CopyToDataTable(newTable, LoadOption.Upsert)

Console.WriteLine("{0}After upserting DataTable:", System.Environment.NewLine)
For Each dataRow As DataRow In newTable.AsEnumerable()
  Console.WriteLine("Student Id = {0} : original {1} : current {2}", _
    dataRow.Field(Of Integer)("Id"), _
    If(dataRow.HasVersion(DataRowVersion.Original), _
        dataRow.Field(Of String) _
          ("Name", DataRowVersion.Original), _
        "-does not exist-"), _
    dataRow.Field(Of String) _
      ("Name", DataRowVersion.Current))
Next dataRow
```

The only difference between this example and the previous is that I add the line setting the primary key on the new DataTable named newTable. Here are the results:

```
Before upserting DataTable:
Student Id = 1 : original Dennis Hayes : current Dennis Hayes
Student Id = 7 : original Anthony Adams : current Anthony Adams
Student Id = 13 : original Stacy Sinclair : current Stacy Sinclair
Student Id = 72 : original Dignan Stephens : current Dignan Stephens

After upserting DataTable:
Student Id = 1 : original Dennis Hayes : current Dennis Hayes
Student Id = 7 : original Anthony Adams : current George Oscar Bluth
Student Id = 13 : original Stacy Sinclair : current Stacy Sinclair
Student Id = 72 : original Dignan Stephens : current Dignan Stephens
```

Now this is more like it. Notice that now, the student whose Id is 7 had the name "Anthony Adams" but now his name is "George Oscar Bluth". This is exactly what I am looking for.

Summary

In this chapter, I showed you how to use all the IEnumerable operators for set-type operations with DataRow objects and how to get and set field values using the Field(Of T) and SetField(Of T) operators. I also showed you what can go wrong if you do not use the DataRow specific set-type operator declarations. Combining the LINQ to Objects Standard Query Operators with these DataSet-specific operators allows one to create powerful LINQ queries for DataSet objects.

In the next chapter, I wrap up the LINQ to DataSet part of this book by covering how to query typed DataSets with LINQ, as well as provide a real database example of a LINQ to DataSet query.

CHAPTER 11

■ ■ ■

Additional DataSet Capabilities

In the previous chapter, I provided numerous examples querying DataTable objects that would naturally come from typical DataSets in a real-world development environment. For the sake of simplicity, though, I programmatically created the DataTable objects using a static array declaration. However, there is more to DataSet queries than just creating DataTable objects from statically declared arrays.

Also, the examples in the previous chapter were all performed on untyped DataSets. Sometimes, you may find you have a need to query a typed DataSet. LINQ to DataSet can do that too.

In this chapter, I address these issues and show you how to make the most of LINQ to DataSet. I begin with a discussion of querying typed DataSets with LINQ to DataSet. Then, since I pointed out that there is more to querying DataSets than programmatically creating DataTable objects, I follow up with a real-world example of querying a database with LINQ to DataSet.

Required Namespaces

The examples in this chapter reference classes in the System.Data, System.Data.SqlClient, and System.Linq namespaces. If Imports statements do not already exist in your code, you should add them like this:

```
Imports System.Data
Imports System.Data.SqlClient
Imports System.Linq
```

Typed DataSets

Typed DataSets can be queried using LINQ, just as untyped DataSets can. However, typed DataSets make your LINQ query code simpler and easier to read. When querying a typed Data-Set, because there is a class for the DataSet, you may access the table and column names using the typed DataSet object's class properties instead of indexing into the Tables collection or using the Field(Of T) and SetField(Of T) operators.

So instead of accessing a DataSet object's table named Students like this

```
Dim Students As DataTable = dataSet.Tables("Students")
```

you can access it like this:

```
Dim Students As DataTable = dataSet.Students
```

Instead of obtaining a field's value like this

```
dataRow.Field(Of String)("Name")
```

you can obtain it like this:

```
dataRow.Name
```

This certainly makes the code more readable and maintainable.

Before looking at an example, we need to create a typed DataSet. Here are the steps to do so:

1. Right-click your project in the Solution Explorer window.

2. Choose the Add/New Item menu option in the context menu.

3. Expand the Categories tree on the Add New Item dialog box that opens. Select the Data node in the tree. Select the DataSet template in the list of Data Templates. Edit the Name of the DataSet file to StudentsDataSet.xsd, and click the Add button.

4. You should now see the DataSet Designer. Put your mouse pointer over the toolbox, and drag a DataTable onto the DataSet Designer.

5. Right-click the title bar of the DataTable you just added, and select the Properties menu option from the context menu.

6. Edit the Name of the DataTable to Students in the Properties window.

7. Right-click the DataTable again, and select the Add/Column menu option from the context menu.

8. Edit the newly added DataColumn Name to Id, and change the DataType to System.Int32.

9. Right-click the DataTable again, and select the Add/Column menu option from the context menu.

10. Edit the newly added DataColumn Name to Name.

11. Save the file.

I have now created a typed DataSet named StudentsDataSet. The StudentsDataSet typed DataSet contains a DataTable named Students that contains two data columns of type DataColumn, one named Id of type Int32 and one named Name of type String. I can use this typed DataSet to perform LINQ queries, and because the DataSet is typed, I can access the DataRow fields as first-class object members. Let's take a look at an example.

Now that I have a typed DataSet, I can perform LINQ queries on it, as shown in Listing 11-1.

Listing 11-1. *An Example of a Typed DataSet Query*

```
Dim studentsDataSet As New StudentsDataSet()
studentsDataSet.Students.AddStudentsRow(1, "Dennis Hayes")
studentsDataSet.Students.AddStudentsRow(7, "Ruth Weinstein")
```

```
studentsDataSet.Students.AddStudentsRow(13, "Kerry Ayres")
studentsDataSet.Students.AddStudentsRow(72, "George McCurdy")

Dim name As String = _
   studentsDataSet.Students.Where(Function(student) student.Id = 7).Single().Name

Console.WriteLine(name)
```

In this example, I instantiate a `StudentsDataSet` object and add four student records where each record is one of the array elements as in most examples in the previous chapter. In most production code, you would not be doing this part because, more than likely, you would be obtaining your data from a database.

Once my typed DataSet is populated, I perform a query on it. Notice that I access the `Students` DataTable as a property on the `StudentsDataSet` object. Also, notice in the `Where` operator's lambda expression that I directly access the `Id` property on the element, which happens to be a `DataRow`, as opposed to calling the `Field` property on the `DataRow`. I can do this because the DataSet is typed. Also notice that when I obtain the singular `DataRow` object by calling the `Single` operator, I can directly access the `Name` property on it, again because the DataSet is typed.

Here are the results:

Ruth Weinstein

Isn't that cool? Typed DataSets make working with DataSets as easy as working with normal class objects and class object properties.

Putting It All Together

I wanted the examples in the previous chapter to be easy for someone trying to learn how to query with the LINQ to DataSet API. I wanted the time you spend working with any examples to be focused on LINQ. I didn't want you to have to struggle with getting a database or getting your connection string correct. But, before we leave *this* chapter, I want to provide a more complete example—one that is actually getting a DataSet from a database because this is most likely how you will obtain a DataSet in your real-life code.

I must admit that creating a reasonable-size example that gets data from a database and uses the LINQ to DataSet API to any degree feels very contrived. After all, I am going to perform a SQL query on data in a database using ADO.NET to obtain a DataSet, then turn right around and query that data again using LINQ to DataSet, all within several lines of code. In real life, some would ask, "Why not just change the SQL query to get exactly what you need in the first place?" To them I say, "Play along!" What I need here is a scenario to explain away the silliness.

In my scenario, I work for a company named Northwind. If ever there was a less than subtle hint at the database I will be using, that was it. My company has an already existing application that queries our database for orders. This particular application performs various analyses on which employees sold items to which customers and to what countries the orders were shipped. So the application is already downloading the employees, customers, and shipping countries for all orders into a DataSet. My task is to perform one more analysis on that already queried data. I am required to produce a unique list of each employee who sold to each company for all orders that were shipped to Germany.

In this example, I instantiate a SqlDataAdapter followed by a DataSet and call the SqlDataAdapter object's Fill method to populate the DataSet. In this scenario, this would have already been done because this existing application is already doing it. So the DataSet object would be passed into my code. But since I don't have a full-blown application, I will just do it in the example. After I obtain the DataSet object with the results of the SQL query, all I have to do for my task is perform a LINQ to DataSet query and display the results. Listing 11-2 is the code.

Listing 11-2. *Putting It All Together*

```
Dim connectionString As String = _
  "Data Source=.\SQLEXPRESS;Initial Catalog=Northwind;Integrated Security=SSPI;"

Using dataAdapter As New SqlDataAdapter( _
  "SELECT O.EmployeeID, E.FirstName + ' ' + E.LastName as EmployeeName," & _
  "  O.CustomerID, C.CompanyName, O.ShipCountry" & _
  "  FROM Orders O" & _
  "  JOIN Employees E on O.EmployeeID = E.EmployeeID" & _
  "  JOIN Customers C on O.CustomerID = C.CustomerID", connectionString)

  Using dataSet As New DataSet()
    dataAdapter.Fill(dataSet, "EmpCustShip")

    '  All code prior to this comment is legacy code.

    Dim ordersQuery = dataSet.Tables("EmpCustShip").AsEnumerable() _
      .Where(Function(r) r.Field(Of String)("ShipCountry").Equals("Germany")) _
      .Distinct(System.Data.DataRowComparer.Default) _
      .OrderBy(Function(r) r.Field(Of String)("EmployeeName")) _
      .ThenBy(Function(r) r.Field(Of String)("CompanyName"))

    For Each dataRow In ordersQuery
      Console.WriteLine( _
        "{0,-20} {1,-20}", dataRow.Field(Of String)("EmployeeName"), _
        dataRow.Field(Of String)("CompanyName"))
    Next dataRow
  End Using
End Using
```

As you can see, I am connecting to the Northwind database. You may need to tweak the connection string for your needs.

Notice that in the previous query, I use the AsEnumerable, Distinct, and Field(Of T) operators I covered in the previous chapter and the Where, OrderBy, and ThenBy operators from the LINQ to Objects API together to create the exact query I want. You really have to admire the way this stuff all plays together so nicely. If the query is doing what I need it to do, I should get a list of each employee who sold an order to each company where that order was shipped to

Germany in alphabetical order by employee name and company name, and with no duplicate rows. Here are the results:

```
Andrew Fuller     Die Wandernde Kuh
Andrew Fuller     Königlich Essen
Andrew Fuller     Lehmanns Marktstand
Andrew Fuller     Morgenstern Gesundkost
Andrew Fuller     Ottilies Käseladen
Andrew Fuller     QUICK-Stop
Andrew Fuller     Toms Spezialitäten
Anne Dodsworth     Blauer See Delikatessen
Anne Dodsworth     Königlich Essen
Anne Dodsworth     Lehmanns Marktstand
Anne Dodsworth     QUICK-Stop
...
Steven Buchanan   Frankenversand
Steven Buchanan   Morgenstern Gesundkost
Steven Buchanan   QUICK-Stop
```

Notice that for each employee on the left, no company is repeated on the right. This is important because it is once again demonstrating the necessity of the LINQ to DataSet API set-type operators. As a test, change the call to the Distinct operator in the previous code so that the DataRowComparer.Default comparer is not specified, and you will see that you get duplicates.

Just so you can see another example using query expression syntax, Listing 11-3 is the same example again, but with the aforementioned syntax.

Listing 11-3. *Putting It All Together with Query Expression Syntax*

```
Dim connectionString As String = _
  "Data Source=.\SQLEXPRESS;Initial Catalog=Northwind;Integrated Security=SSPI;"

Using dataAdapter As New SqlDataAdapter( _
  "SELECT O.EmployeeID, E.FirstName + ' ' + E.LastName as EmployeeName, " & _
    "O.CustomerID, C.CompanyName, O.ShipCountry " & _
  "FROM Orders O JOIN Employees E on O.EmployeeID = E.EmployeeID " & _
  "JOIN Customers C on O.CustomerID = C.CustomerID", connectionString)

  Using dataSet As New DataSet()
    dataAdapter.Fill(dataSet, "EmpCustShip")

    ' All code prior to this comment is legacy code.

    Dim ordersQuery = _
      (From r In dataSet.Tables("EmpCustShip").AsEnumerable() _
       Where r.Field(Of String)("ShipCountry").Equals("Germany") _
       Order By r.Field(Of String)("EmployeeName"), _
```

```
        r.Field(Of String)("CompanyName") _
      Select r) _
      .Distinct(System.Data.DataRowComparer.Default)

    For Each dataRow In ordersQuery
      Console.WriteLine("{0,-20} {1,-20}", _
        dataRow.Field(Of String)("EmployeeName"), _
        dataRow.Field(Of String)("CompanyName"))
    Next dataRow
  End Using
End Using
```

Now, the query is using query expression syntax. While it was my goal to make the query functionally the same as the previous, I was not able to do this. VB.NET has compiler support for the Distinct operator, but it takes no parameters, and thus only uses the default comparer, which, as noted previously, does not really work with DataRow objects. Because of this, I cannot make that call in the query expression syntax portion of the query. As you can see, I did call it at the end of the query, and I will end up with the same results from this query.

However, there is a performance difference between the query in Listing 11-3 and the query in Listing 11-2. In Listing 11-2, the Distinct operator is called just after the Where operator, so duplicate records are eliminated from the results set prior to ordering them. In Listing 11-3, the Distinct operator is not called until the end, so the duplicate records are still there during the ordering of the results set. This means records are being sorted that will be eliminated once the Distinct operator is called. This is unnecessary work, but unavoidable if you wish to use query expression syntax for this query.

Summary

As covered in this chapter, not only can you query normal DataSets with LINQ to DataSet but you can query typed DataSets. Typed DataSets make your code easier to maintain and more readable, and LINQ to DataSet makes querying those typed DataSets a breeze. I also demonstrated a more real-world LINQ to DataSet query that queried the Northwind database.

The LINQ to DataSet API adds yet another domain to those available for LINQ queries. With all the existing code already utilizing DataSets, LINQ to DataSet promises to be easy to retrofit into your legacy .NET code, thereby making it easier than ever to query data from a DataSet.

One benefit that the LINQ to DataSet API has over the LINQ to SQL API is the fact that no database class code needs to be generated and compiled ahead of time to perform LINQ to DataSet queries. This makes LINQ to DataSet more dynamic and suitable for database-type utilities where the databases will be unknown until runtime.

By providing the AsEnumerable operator to create sequences from DataTable objects, using the LINQ to Objects Standard Query Operators becomes possible, adding even more power to the arsenal of query capabilities.

For the LINQ to DataSet API, operators have been added for the key classes of the DataSet: DataTable, DataRow, and DataColumn. One must not forget the issue that makes the new set-type operator prototypes for the Distinct, Union, Intersect, Except, and SequenceEqual operators necessary: the problem that DataRows have being compared for equality. So when working with DataSets, DataTables, and DataRows, always opt for the LINQ to DataSet set-type opera-tor prototypes for the `Distinct`, `Union`, `Intersect`, `Except`, and `SequenceEqual` operators where the equality comparer object is specified instead of the prototype versions without an equality comparer object being specified.

Last, when obtaining a column's value, use the `Field(Of T)` and `SetField(Of T)` operators to eliminate issues with comparisons for equality and `Nothing` values.

One thing became apparent while working with the LINQ to DataSet API. I had totally underestimated the power and utility of DataSets. They offer so much in the way of a cached, relational data store. And while they already offer somewhat limited search facilities, with the LINQ to DataSet API, those limitations have been removed. You now have LINQ to query your DataSets with, and that makes coding just that much easier.

PART 5

LINQ to SQL

CHAPTER 12

■ ■ ■

LINQ to SQL Introduction

Listing 12-1. *A Simple Example Updating the ContactName of a Customer in the Northwind Database*

```vb
'  Create a DataContext.
Dim db As New Northwind( _
   "Data Source=.\SQLEXPRESS;Initial Catalog=Northwind;Integrated Security=SSPI;")

'  Retrieve customer LAZYK.
Dim cust As Customer = ( _
   From c In db.Customers _
   Where c.CustomerID = "LAZYK" _
   Select c).Single()

'  Update the contact name.
cust.ContactName = "Ned Plimpton"

Try
   '  Save the changes.
   db.SubmitChanges()
   '  Detect concurrency conflicts.
Catch e1 As ChangeConflictException
   '  Resolve conflicts.
   db.ChangeConflicts.ResolveAll(RefreshMode.KeepChanges)
End Try
```

■ **Note** This example requires generation of entity classes, which I will cover later in this chapter. It also requires adding a reference to the System.Data.Linq.dll, and adding an `Imports System.Data.Linq` statement.

In Listing 12-1, I used LINQ to SQL to query the record whose CustomerID field is "LAZYK" from the Northwind database Customers table and to return a `Customer` object representing that record. I then updated the `Customer` object's `ContactName` property and saved the change to the Northwind database by calling the SubmitChanges method. That's not much code considering it is also detecting concurrency conflicts and resolving them if they occur.

Run Listing 12-1 by pressing Ctrl+F5. There is no console output, but if you check the database, you should see that the ContactName for customer LAZYK is now "Ned Plimpton".

■**Note** This example makes a change to the data in the database without changing it back. The original value of the ContactName for customer LAZYK is "John Steel". You should change this back so that no subsequent examples behave improperly. You could change it manually, or you could just change the example code to set it back, and run the example again.

This book uses an extended version of the Northwind database. Please read the section in this chapter titled "Obtaining the Appropriate Version of the Northwind Database" for details.

Introducing LINQ to SQL

At this point, I have discussed using LINQ with in-memory data collections and arrays, XML, and DataSets. Now, I will move on to what many seem to feel is the most compelling reason to use LINQ, LINQ to SQL. I say that because when I look at the MSDN forum for LINQ, the majority of the posts seem to focus on LINQ to SQL. I think many developers are overlooking the significance of LINQ as a general-purpose query language and the multitude of ways it can be utilized. Hopefully, I have convinced you of this already through the previous chapters.

LINQ to SQL is an application programming interface (API) for working with SQL Server databases. In the current world of object-oriented programming languages, there is a mismatch between the programming language and the relational database. When writing an application, we model classes to represent real-world objects such as customers, accounts, policies, and flights. We need a way to persist these objects so that when the application is restarted, these objects and their data are not lost. However, most production-caliber databases are still relational and store their data as records in tables, not as objects. A customer class may contain multiple addresses and phone numbers stored in collections that are child properties of that customer class; once persisted, this data will most likely be stored in multiple tables, such as a customer table, an address table, and a phone table.

Additionally, the data types supported by the application language differ from the database data types. Developers left to their own devices are required to write code that knows how to load a customer object from all of the appropriate tables, as well as save the customer object back to the appropriate tables, handling the data type conversion between the application language and the database. This is a tedious, and often error-prone, process. Because of this object-relational mapping (ORM) problem, often referred to as the *object-relational impedance mismatch,* a plethora of prewritten ORM software solutions have been designed through the years. LINQ to SQL is Microsoft's entry-level LINQ-enabled ORM implementation for SQL Server.

Notice that I said "for SQL Server." LINQ to SQL is exclusive to SQL Server. LINQ, however, is not, and hopefully, other database vendors are or will be at work implementing their own LINQ APIs. I personally would like to see a LINQ to DB2 API, and I am sure many others would like to see LINQ to Oracle, LINQ to MySQL, LINQ to Sybase, and perhaps others.

■**Note** LINQ to SQL only works with SQL Server 2000 and later, SQL Express, and SQL Compact Edition 3.5 and later. To use LINQ with other databases, additional LINQ APIs will need to be written by the appropriate database vendors. Until then, or perhaps as an alternative, consider using LINQ to DataSet.

You may have also noticed that I said LINQ to SQL is an *entry-level* ORM implementation. If you find it is not powerful or flexible enough to meet your requirements, you may want to investigate LINQ to Entities. While I do not cover LINQ to Entities in this book, it is alleged to be more powerful and flexible than LINQ to SQL. Be aware, though, that the increase in power comes coupled with additional complexity. Also, LINQ to Entities is not as mature as LINQ to SQL.

At this point, you may be wondering, what is the catch? In what ways would LINQ to SQL not be powerful enough for my application? LINQ to SQL's most significant limitation, other than being limited to the SQL Server database, is that it really only supports a one-to-one mapping between your business classes and your database tables. So, if you need a single business class mapped to multiple tables, you will probably find LINQ to SQL too limiting for your needs. Or, if you need the ability to map multiple classes to a single table, you will probably be disappointed. LINQ to SQL does have very limited support for a "many classes to one table" scenario based on class inheritance that I cover in the entity class inheritance section of Chapter 18. However, in all honesty, LINQ to SQL's implementation of multiple classes mapped to a single table seems so limited, I consider it to be more of a hack that seems to have been developed for some specific corner case Microsoft had in mind. If however, a one-to-one mapping between business classes and database tables works for you, you will be pleasantly surprised how quickly LINQ to SQL can get you working with your database.

Most ORM tools attempt to abstract the physical database into business objects. With that abstraction, we sometimes lose the ability to perform SQL-like queries, which is a large part of the attraction to relational databases. This is what separates LINQ to SQL from many of its contemporaries. We get not only the convenience of business objects that are mapped to the database but a full-blown query language, similar to the already familiar SQL, thrown in to boot.

■**Tip** LINQ to SQL is an entry-level ORM tool that permits powerful SQL-like queries.

In addition to providing LINQ query capabilities, as long as your query returns LINQ to SQL *entity objects*, as opposed to returning single fields, named nonentity classes, or anonymous classes, LINQ to SQL also provides change tracking and database updates, complete with optimistic concurrency conflict detection and resolution, and transactional integrity.

In Listing 12-1, I first had to instantiate an instance of the Northwind class. That class is derived from the DataContext class, and I will cover this class in depth in Chapter 16. For now, consider it a supercharged database connection. It also handles updating the database for us, as you can see when I later call the SubmitChanges method on it. Next, I retrieved a single customer from the Northwind database into a Customer object. That Customer object is an instantiation of the Customer class, which is an entity class that either had to be written or generated. In this case, the Customer class was generated for me by the SqlMetal utility, as was the Northwind class for that matter. After retrieving the customer, I updated one of the Customer object's properties, ContactName, and called the SubmitChanges method to persist the modified contact name to the database. Please notice that I wrapped the call to the SubmitChanges method in a Try/Catch block and specifically caught the ChangeConflictException exception. This is for handling concurrency conflicts, which I will cover in detail in Chapter 17.

Before you can run this example or any of the others in this chapter, you will need to create entity classes for the Northwind database. Please read the section in this chapter titled "Prerequisites for Running the Examples" to guide you through creation of the necessary entity classes.

LINQ to SQL is a complex subject, and to provide any example requires involving many LINQ to SQL elements. In the first example at the beginning of this chapter, I am utilizing a derived DataContext class, which is the Northwind class; an entity class, which is the Customer class; concurrency conflict detection and resolution; and database updates via the SubmitChanges method. I can't possibly explain all these concepts simultaneously. So, I need to give you some background on each of these components before I begin so that you will have a basic understanding of the foundation of LINQ to SQL. Rest assured that I will cover each of these concepts in agonizing detail later in the subsequent LINQ to SQL chapters.

The DataContext

The DataContext is the class that establishes a connection to a database. It also provides several services that provide identity tracking, change tracking, and change processing. I'll cover each of these services in more detail in Chapter 16. For now, just know that it is the DataContext class that is connecting us to the database, monitoring what we have changed, and updating the database when we call its SubmitChanges method.

It is typical with LINQ to SQL to use a class derived from the DataContext class. The name of the derived class typically is the same as the database it is mapped to. I will often refer to that derived class in the LINQ to SQL chapters as [Your]DataContext, because its name is dependent on the database for which it is being created.

In my examples, my derived DataContext class will be named Northwind, because it was generated by the SqlMetal command-line tool, and SqlMetal names the generated, derived DataContext class after the database for which it is generated.

This derived DataContext class, [Your]DataContext, will typically have a Table(Of T) public property for each database table you have mapped in the database, where T will be the type of the *entity class* that is instantiated for each retrieved record from that particular database table. The data type Table(Of T) is a specialized collection. For example, since there is a Customers table in the Northwind database, my Northwind class derived from the DataContext class will have a Table(Of Customer) named Customers. This means that I can access the records in the Customers database table by directly accessing the Customers property of type Table(Of Customer) in my Northwind class. You can see an example of this in the first example in this chapter, Listing 12-1, where I coded db.Customers. That code is querying the records in the Customers table of the Northwind database.

Entity Classes

LINQ to SQL involves using entity classes, where each entity class is typically mapped to a single database table. However, using entity class inheritance mapping, it is possible to map an entire class hierarchy to a single table under special circumstances. You can read more about this in Chapter 18. So, we have entity classes mapping to database tables, and the entity class properties get mapped to table columns. This entity class-to-table and property-to-column mapping is the essence of LINQ to SQL.

■**Note** The essence of LINQ to SQL is mapping entity classes to database tables and entity class properties to database table columns.

This mapping can occur directly in class source files by decorating classes with the appropriate attributes, or it can be specified with an external XML mapping file. By using an external XML mapping file, the LINQ-to-SQL–specific bits can be kept external to the source code. This could be very handy if you don't have source code or want to keep the code separated from LINQ to SQL. For the majority of examples in the LINQ to SQL chapters, I will be using entity classes that have been generated by the SQLMetal command-line tool. SQLMetal generates the entity classes with the LINQ to SQL mapping bits right in the source module it generates. These mapping bits are in the form of attributes and attribute properties.

You will be able to detect the existence of entity classes in my examples when you see classes or objects that have the singular form of a Northwind database table name. For example, in Listing 12-1, I use a class named `Customer`. Because *Customer* is the singular form of *Customers*, and the Northwind database has a table named Customers, this is your clue that the `Customer` class is an entity class for the Northwind database's Customers table.

The SqlMetal command-line tool has an option called `/pluralize` that causes the entity classes to be named in the singular form of the database table name. Had I not specified the `/pluralize` option when generating my entity classes, my entity class would be named `Customers`, as opposed to `Customer`, because the name of the table is Customers. I mention this in case you get confused reading other writings about LINQ to SQL. Depending on how the author ran the SqlMetal tool and what options were specified, the entity class names may be plural or singular.

Associations

An *association* is the term used to designate a primary key to foreign key relationship between two entity classes. In a one-to-many relationship, the result of an association is that the parent class, the class containing the primary key, contains a collection of the child classes, the classes having the foreign key. That collection is stored in a private member variable of type `EntitySet(Of T)`, where `T` will be the type of the child entity class.

For example, in the `Customer` entity class generated by the SqlMetal command-line tool for the Northwind database, there is a private member of type `EntitySet(Of [Order])` named `_Orders` that contains all of the `Order` objects for a specific `Customer` object:

```
Private _Orders As EntitySet(Of [Order])
```

■**Note** SqlMetal puts brackets ([ ]) around [Order] to distinguish it from the SQL Order operator.

SqlMetal also generated a public property named `Orders` to be used for accessing the private `_Orders` collection.

On the other end of the relationship, the child, which is the class containing the foreign key, contains a reference to the parent class, since that is a many-to-one relationship. That reference is stored in a private member variable of type `EntityRef(Of T)`, where `T` is the type of the parent class.

In the generated `Northwind` entity classes, the `Order` entity class contains a private member variable of type `EntityRef(Of Customer)` named `_Customer`:

```
Private _Customer As EntityRef(Of Customer)
```

Again, the SqlMetal tool also generated a public property named `Customer` to provide access to the parent reference.

The association, primary and foreign keys, as well as the direction of the relationship are all defined by attributes and attribute properties in the generated entity classes' source module.

The benefit gained by the association is the ability to access a parent's child classes, and therefore database records, as easily as accessing a property of the parent class. Likewise, accessing a child's parent class is as easy as accessing a property of the child class.

Concurrency Conflict Detection

One of the valuable services that the `DataContext` is performing for you is change processing. When you try to update the database by calling the `DataContext` object's `SubmitChanges` method, it is automatically performing optimistic concurrency conflict detection.

If a conflict is detected, a `ChangeConflictException` exception is thrown. Any time you call the `SubmitChanges` method, you should wrap that call in a `Try/Catch` block and catch the `ChangeConflictException` exception. This is the proper way to detect concurrency conflicts.

You can see an example of this in Listing 12-1. I will go into painstaking detail about concurrency conflict detection and resolution in Chapter 17. Many of the examples in this and the following LINQ to SQL chapters will not provide concurrency conflict detection or resolution for the sake of brevity and clarity. In your real code, you should always do both.

Concurrency Conflict Resolution

Once a concurrency conflict has been detected, the next step will be to resolve the concurrency conflict. This can be done in multiple ways. In Listing 12-1, I do it the simplest way by calling the `ResolveAll` method of the `ChangeConflicts` collection of the derived `DataContext` class when the `ChangeConflictException` exception is caught.

Again, in many of the examples in the LINQ to SQL chapters, I will not have code to either detect the concurrency conflicts or to resolve them, but you should always have code handling this in your real production code.

As I mentioned in the previous section, I will cover concurrency conflict resolution in detail in Chapter 17.

Prerequisites for Running the Examples

Since virtually all of the examples in this and the following LINQ to SQL chapters use Micro-soft's sample *extended* Northwind database, we will need entity classes and mapping files for the Northwind database.

Obtaining the Appropriate Version of the Northwind Database

Unfortunately, the standard Microsoft Northwind database is missing a few things I will need to fully show off LINQ to SQL, such as table-valued and scalar-valued functions. Therefore, instead of using the standard Northwind database, I will use an extended version of it that Microsoft initially distributed to demonstrate LINQ.

You may obtain the extended version of the Northwind database in the Book Extras sec-tion of this book's page at the Apress web site:

```
http://www.apress.com/book/view/1430216441
```

Or, you may obtain it at Joe Rattz's web site, LINQDev.com. Look for the section titled Obtain the Northwind Database:

```
http://www.linqdev.com
```

If you download it from LINQDev.com, make sure you download the extended version.

To run all the examples in the LINQ to SQL chapters of this book, you will need to down-load this extended version of the Northwind database.

Generating the Northwind Entity Classes

Because I have not yet covered how to generate entity classes in detail, I am going to tell you how to generate them without providing much explanation. However, I will cover the details thoroughly in Chapter 13.

To generate the entity classes, you must have the extended version of the Northwind data-base that I discussed in the previous section.

Open a Visual Studio command prompt. To do so, look in your Microsoft Visual Studio 2008 menu for a submenu named Visual Studio Tools for an item named Visual Studio 2008 Command Prompt, and select it. Once the command prompt opens, change your current directory to whatever directory in which you desire to create your entity classes and external mapping file. I am going to change my directory to the root of the C: drive:

```
cd \
```

If you are going to generate your entity classes using the Northwind database files without first attaching the database to them, use the following command:

```
sqlmetal /namespace:nwind /code:Northwind.vb /pluralize /functions /sprocs /views
<path to Northwind MDF file>
```

■**Caution** Pay particular attention to the MDF file name and its case as you specify it on the command line. The name and case of the `DataContext` derived class that is generated will match the file name that is passed on the command line, not the physical file name itself. If you deviate from a `DataContext`-derived class name of `Northwind`, none of the examples will work without modification. Therefore, it is critical that you pass the Northwind database file name as `[path]\Northwind.mdf`, not northwind.mdf, NorthWind.mdf, or any other variation of the name.

To create entity classes from a file named Northwind.mdf, enter the following command:

```
sqlmetal /namespace:nwind /code:Northwind.vb /pluralize /functions /sprocs /views
"C:\Northwind.mdf"
```

■**Note** When you run SqlMetal, you may get a warning about a mapping between `DbType` `'Decimal(38,2)` and `System.Decimal` possibly causing data loss. You may ignore it. We don't use the stored procedure that causes the error, and even if we did, the overflow would be unlikely to happen. The curious can check out the sidebar on the next page for more information.

Running this command will cause an entity class module named Northwind.vb to be created for you in the current directory.

If you are going to generate your entity classes from the Northwind database that is already attached to your SQL Server, use the following command:

```
sqlmetal /server:<server> /user:<user> /password:<password> /database:Northwind
/namespace:nwind /code:Northwind.vb /pluralize /functions /sprocs /views
```

To create entity classes from an attached database named Northwind, enter the following command:

```
sqlmetal /server:.\SQLExpress /database:Northwind /namespace:nwind
/code:Northwind.vb /pluralize /functions /sprocs /views
```

■**Note** Depending on your environment, you may need to specify a user with the `/user:[username]` option and a password with the `/password:[password]` option on the command line in the preceding example. Please read the section titled "SQLMetal" in Chapter 13 for more details.

The command entered using either of these approaches tells SqlMetal to generate the source code into a file named Northwind.vb in the current directory. I will cover all the program's options in the next chapter. Copy the generated Northwind.vb file into your project by adding it as an existing item.

You may now utilize LINQ to SQL on the Northwind database using the entity classes contained in the Northwind.vb file.

Tip Be cautious of making changes to the generated entity class source file. You may find you need to regenerate it at some later point, causing you to lose any changes. You may desire to add business logic by adding methods to the entity classes. Instead of modifying the generated file, consider taking advantage of VB.NET 2005 partial classes to keep the added properties and methods in a separate source module.

WHAT'S UP WITH THE SQLMETAL WARNING?

When running SqlMetal, you will probably get the following warning:

```
Warning DBML1008: Mapping between DbType 'Decimal(38,2)' and
Type 'System.Decimal' in Column 'TotalPurchase' of Type 'SalesByCategoryResult'
may cause data loss when loading from the database.
```

This warning is the result of mapping a SQL Server Decimal(38,2) data type that is returned by the stored procedure to a .NET System.Decimal data type. Since the .NET data type is smaller than the SQL Server data type, an overflow can occur, resulting in a loss of data. In our case, it is unlikely to be an issue, but something of which you should always be conscious.

This example illustrates the impedance mismatch problem that exists between databases and programming languages. The database has a data type that can store more data than our language's equivalent data type can. This is one of those ugly impedance mismatch details raising its ugly head that the LINQ to SQL design team at Microsoft could not safely resolve or hide, so they provided us with a warning.

Another point of interest is that the version of SqlMetal that came with the original release of Visual Studio 2008 (V1.00.21022) does not generate this error; it first appears in SqlMetal SP1 (V1.00.30729).

Generating the Northwind XML Mapping File

I will also need to generate a mapping file that some of the examples will use. Again, I will use SqlMetal for this purpose. So, from the same command line and path, execute the following command:

```
sqlmetal /map:northwindmap.xml /code:nwind.vb "C:\Northwind.mdf" /pluralize
/functions /sprocs /views /namespace:nwind
```

Again, pay close attention to the casing used to specify the MDF file. This will generate a file named northwindmap.xml into the current directory.

Importing the Generated Code

The namespace for the generated code needs to be compatible with the namespace in the main code. There are three ways to achieve this. First, when you generate the code, you can specify the namespace you will be using in your main code. Second, you can add an

Imports statement to your code to reference the generated code; this is how I will deal with namespaces in the examples. Third, you may omit the namespace when generating the code. VB will assume this code is in the default namespace for the project. Also, if you are using this code in a module, and you specified a namespace when generating your entity classes, you must prefix the namespace with the project name

```
Imports [Your Project Name].nwind
```

where [Your Project Name] is the name of your project, for example:

```
Imports Ch12.nwind
```

If you are importing the generated code into classes (as opposed to modules), simply importing the namespace should be sufficient:

```
Imports nwind
```

Using the LINQ to SQL API

In order to use the LINQ to SQL API, you will need to add the System.Data.Linq.dll assembly to your project if it is not already there. Also, if they do not already exist, you will need to add Imports statements to your source module for the System.Linq and System.Data.Linq namespaces like this:

```
Imports System.Data.Linq
Imports System.Linq
```

Additionally, for the examples, you may need to add an Imports statement for the namespace the entity classes were generated into, as discussed previously.

IQueryable(Of T)

You will see that in many of the LINQ to SQL examples in this chapter and the subsequent LINQ to SQL chapters, I work with sequences of type IQueryable(Of T), where T is the type of an entity class. These are the type of sequences that are typically returned by LINQ to SQL queries. They will often appear to work just like an IEnumerable(Of T) sequence, and that is no coincidence. The IQueryable(Of T) interface extends the IEnumerable(Of T) interface. Here is the definition of IQueryable(Of T):

```
Public Interface IQueryable(Of T) _
  Implements IEnumerable(Of T), IQueryable, IEnumerable
```

Because of this inheritance, you can treat an IQueryable(Of T) sequence like an IEnumerable(Of T) sequence.

Some Common Methods

As you will soon see, many of the examples in the LINQ to SQL chapters can become complex very quickly. Demonstrating a concurrency conflict requires making changes to the database external to LINQ to SQL. Sometimes, I need to retrieve data externally of LINQ to SQL too. To highlight the LINQ to SQL code and to eliminate as many of the trivial details as possible, while at the same time providing real working examples, I have created some common methods to use in many of the examples.

Be sure to add these common methods to your source modules as appropriate when testing the examples in the LINQ to SQL chapters.

GetStringFromDb()

A common function that will come in handy is one to obtain a simple string from the database using standard ADO.NET. This will allow me to examine what is actually in the database, as opposed to what LINQ to SQL is showing me.

GetStringFromDb: A Function for Retrieving a String Using ADO.NET

```
Private Function GetStringFromDb( _
    ByVal sqlConnection As System.Data.SqlClient.SqlConnection, _
    ByVal sqlQuery As String) As String
  If sqlConnection.State <> System.Data.ConnectionState.Open Then
    sqlConnection.Open()
  End If
  Dim result As String = Nothing

  Using sqlCommand As New System.Data.SqlClient.SqlCommand(sqlQuery, sqlConnection)
    Using sqlDataReader As System.Data.SqlClient.SqlDataReader = _
        sqlCommand.ExecuteReader()

      If (Not sqlDataReader.Read()) Then
        Throw (New Exception(String.Format( _
          "Unexpected exception executing query [{0}].", sqlQuery)))
      Else
        If (Not sqlDataReader.IsDBNull(0)) Then
          result = sqlDataReader.GetString(0)
        End If
      End If

    End Using
  End Using

  Return (result)
End Function
```

To call the GetStringFromDb function, a SqlConnection and a String containing a SQL query are passed into the method. The method verifies that the connection is open, and if the connection is not open, the method opens it.

Next, a SqlCommand is created by passing the query and connection into the constructor. Then, a SqlDataReader is obtained by calling the ExecuteReader method on the SqlCommand. The SqlDataReader is read by calling its Read method, and if data was read and the returned first column's value is not null, the returned first column value is retrieved with the GetString method.

ExecuteStatementInDb()

Sometimes, I will need to execute nonquery SQL statements such as insert, update, and delete in ADO.NET to modify the state of the database external to LINQ to SQL. For that purpose, I have created the ExecuteStatementInDb method:

ExecuteStatementInDb: A Method for Executing Inserts, Updates, and Deletes in ADO.NET

```
Private Sub ExecuteStatementInDb(ByVal cmd As String)
  Dim connection As String = _
    "Data Source=.\SQLEXPRESS;Initial Catalog=Northwind;" & _
    "Integrated Security=SSPI;"

  Using sqlConn As New System.Data.SqlClient.SqlConnection(connection)
    Using sqlComm As New System.Data.SqlClient.SqlCommand(cmd)

      sqlComm.Connection = sqlConn
      sqlConn.Open()
      Console.WriteLine( _
        "Executing SQL statement against database with ADO.NET ...")
      sqlComm.ExecuteNonQuery()
      Console.WriteLine("Database updated.")

    End Using
  End Using
End Sub
```

To call the ExecuteStatementInDb method, a String is passed containing a SQL command. A SqlConnection is created followed by a SqlCommand. The SqlConnection is assigned to the SqlCommand. The SqlConnection is then opened, and the SQL command is executed by calling the SqlCommand object's ExecuteNonQuery method.

Summary

In this chapter, I have introduced you to LINQ to SQL and some of its most basic terminology, such as DataContext objects, entity classes, associations, and concurrency conflict detection and resolution.

I also showed you how to generate your entity classes and external mapping file for the extended Northwind database. These entity classes will be used extensively throughout the LINQ to SQL examples.

Last, I provided a couple of common methods that many of the examples in the subsequent LINQ to SQL chapters will rely on.

The next step is to arm you with some tips and show you how to use the necessary tools to leverage LINQ to SQL, and this is exactly what the next chapter is about.

■ ■ ■

CHAPTER 13

LINQ to SQL Tips and Tools

In the previous chapter, I introduced you to LINQ to SQL and most of its terminology. I showed you how to generate the entity classes that most of the examples in the LINQ to SQL chapters will require. I also provided some common methods that many of the examples in these chapters will leverage.

In this chapter, I will present some tips that I hope you will find useful while working with LINQ to SQL. I will also show you some of the tools that make LINQ to SQL such a pleasure to use.

Introduction to LINQ to SQL Tips and Tools

Now would be a good time to remind you that before you can run the examples in this chapter, you must have met the prerequisites. First, you must have the extended Northwind database and already generated the entity classes for it. Please review the section in Chapter 12 titled "Prerequisites for Running the Examples" to ensure that you have the appropriate database and generated entity classes.

In this chapter, because I will be demonstrating code that utilizes entity classes generated by both SqlMetal and the Object Relational Designer, I will not specify an `Imports` statement for the `nwind` namespace in the examples. Instead, I will explicitly specify the namespace where it's needed for the `nwind` classes. This is necessary in this chapter to control which `Customer` entity class is getting referenced in each specific example. Since, by default, the Object Relational Designer generates a namespace that is the same as your project, and since the examples will already exist in your project's namespace, you will not need to specify the namespace for the designer-generated entity classes, but you will for the SqlMetal-generated entity classes.

■**Note** Unlike most of the LINQ to SQL chapters, do not specify an `Imports` statement for the `nwind` namespace for the examples in this chapter.

Tips

It's early in the LINQ to SQL chapters, and keeping with my style, I am going to jump the gun and give you some tips requiring information I have yet to discuss. So if this section makes little sense to you, my work is done! After all, I want you to know about these tips *before* you need them, not after you have learned them the hard way.

Use the DataContext.Log Property

Now would be a good time to remind you of some of the LINQ-to-SQL-specific tips I provided in Chapter 1. One of those tips titled "The DataContext Log" discussed how you could use the DataContext object's Log property to display what the translated SQL query will be. This can be very useful not only for debugging purposes but for performance analysis. You may find that your LINQ to SQL queries are getting translated into very inefficient SQL queries. Or, you may find that due to *deferred loading* of associated entity classes, you are making many more SQL queries than is necessary. The DataContext.Log property will reveal this type of information to you.

To take advantage of this feature, you merely assign the DataContext.Log property to a System.IO.TextWriter object, such as Console.Out.

Listing 13-1 contains an example.

Listing 13-1. *An Example Using the DataContext.Log Property*

```
Dim db As New nwind.Northwind( _
  "Data Source=.\SQLEXPRESS;" & _
  "Initial Catalog=Northwind;" & _
  "Integrated Security=SSPI;")

db.Log = Console.Out

Dim custs = From c In db.Customers _
  Where c.Region Is "WA" _
  Select New With {Key .Id = c.CustomerID, Key .Name = c.ContactName}

For Each cust In custs
  Console.WriteLine("{0} - {1}", cust.Id, cust.Name)
Next cust
```

Since I will be demonstrating both SqlMetal-generated and Object Relational Designer–generated entity classes in this chapter, there will be two Customer classes that exist for the examples. As I mentioned earlier, I did not include an Imports statement for the examples so that the entity classes such as Customer would not be ambiguous. Therefore, I have to specify the namespace nwind for the Northwind class in Listing 13-1, since I am using the SqlMetal-generated entity class code for this example.

As you can see, in Listing 13-1, I simply assign Console.Out to my Northwind DataContext object's Log property. Here are the results of Listing 13-1:

```
SELECT [t0].[CustomerID] AS [Id], [t0].[ContactName] AS [Name]
FROM [dbo].[Customers] AS [t0]
WHERE [t0].[Region] = @p0
-- @p0: Input NVarChar (Size = 2; Prec = 0; Scale = 0) [WA]
-- Context: SqlProvider(Sql2008) Model: AttributedMetaModel Build: 3.5.30729.1

LAZYK - John Steel
TRAIH - Helvetius Nagy
WHITC - Karl Jablonski
```

This allows us to see exactly what the generated SQL query looks like. Notice that the generated SQL statement is not merely formatting a string; it is using parameters. So by using LINQ to SQL, we automatically get protection from SQL injection attacks.

■**Caution** If you see in your results that the name associated with customer LAZYK is Ned Plimpton instead of John Steel as I show in the preceding example, you probably ran Listing 12-1 without setting the data back as I recommended. You may want to resolve this now before any further examples are affected.

In later chapters, I will demonstrate how to use this logging feature to detect and resolve potential performance issues.

Use the GetChangeSet() Method

You can use the DataContext object's GetChangeSet method to obtain all entity objects containing changes that need to be persisted to the database when the SubmitChanges method is called. This is useful for logging and debugging purposes. This method is also fully documented in Chapter 16.

Consider Using Partial Classes or Mapping Files

Without a doubt, one of the bigger hassles of using any ORM tool is going to be managing changes to the database. If you keep all your business class logic and LINQ to SQL logic in the same modules, you may be creating a maintenance headache for yourself down the road once the database changes. Consider leveraging partial classes by adding your business logic to a separate module than the generated entity class modules. By using partial classes to keep your LINQ to SQL database attributes separate from your business logic, you will minimize the need to add code back to any generated entity class code.

Alternatively, you could have your business classes and your LINQ to SQL entity mapping decoupled by using an external XML mapping file. This is an XML file that maps business objects to the database without relying on LINQ to SQL attributes. You can read more about mapping files in the section titled "XML External Mapping File Schema" in Chapter 15 and in the DataContext constructor section of Chapter 16.

Consider Using Partial Methods

Partial methods are lightweight events that allow you to hook into certain events that occur in entity classes. The beauty of partial methods is that if you do not take advantage of them by implementing the body of a partial method, there is no overhead, and no code is emitted by the compiler to call them.

I will discuss how partial methods are used in entity classes in the section named "Calling the Appropriate Partial Methods" in Chapter 15.

Tools

Just as there are some tips I want to make you aware of before you actually need them, there are some tools that can make your life easier. Again, I may be bringing these up before they make sense to you, but I want you to be aware of them and how they can facilitate and accelerate your adoption of LINQ to SQL.

SqlMetal

While I have yet to discuss the different ways to create the entity classes necessary to use LINQ to SQL with a database, you should know that the easiest way to generate all entity classes for an entire database, if you do not already have business classes, is with the SqlMetal program. You can find this tool in the `Program Files\Microsoft SDKs\Windows\v6.0A\bin` directory (note that the `v6.0A` part of the path will vary with the version number). SqlMetal allows you to specify a database, and it will generate all the necessary and nifty parts of LINQ to SQL entity classes. SqlMetal is a command-line tool, and there is no user interface for it.

To see the options available for the SqlMetal program, open a Visual Studio command prompt. To do so, look in your Microsoft Visual Studio 2008 menu for a submenu named Visual Studio Tools for an item named Visual Studio 2008 Command Prompt, and select it.

Once the command prompt is open, type the following command, and press Enter:

```
SqlMetal
```

This command will cause the program's template and options to be displayed:

```
Microsoft (R) Database Mapping Generator 2008 version 1.00.30729
for Microsoft (R) .NET Framework version 3.5
Copyright (C) Microsoft Corporation. All rights reserved.

SqlMetal [options] [<input file>]

  Generates code and mapping for the LINQ to SQL component of the .NET framework.
SqlMetal can:
  - Generate source code and mapping attributes or a mapping file from a database.
  - Generate an intermediate dbml file for customization from the database.
  - Generate code and mapping attributes or mapping file from a dbml file.

Options:
  /server:<name>          Database server name.
```

/database:<name>	Database catalog on server.
/user:<name>	Login user ID (default: use Windows Authentication).
/password:<password>	Login password (default: use Windows Authentication).
/conn:<connection string>	Database connection string. Cannot be used with /server, /database, /user or /password options.
/timeout:<seconds>	Timeout value to use when SqlMetal accesses the database (default: 0 which means infinite).
/views	Extract database views.
/functions	Extract database functions.
/sprocs	Extract stored procedures.
/dbml[:file]	Output as dbml. Cannot be used with /map option.
/code[:file]	Output as source code. Cannot be used with /dbml option.
/map[:file]	Generate mapping file, not attributes. Cannot be used with /dbml option.
/language:<language>	Language for source code: VB or C# (default: derived from extension on code file name).
/namespace:<name>	Namespace of generated code (default: no namespace).
/context:<type>	Name of data context class (default: derived from database name).
/entitybase:<type>	Base class of entity classes in the generated code (default: entities have no base class).
/pluralize	Automatically pluralize or singularize class and member names using English language rules.
/serialization:<option>	Generate serializable classes: None or Unidirectional (default: None).
/provider:<type>	Provider type: SQLCompact, SQL2000, SQL2005, or SQL2008. (default: provider is determined at run time).
<input file>	May be a SqlExpress mdf file, a SqlCE sdf file, or a dbml intermediate file.

Create code from SqlServer:
```
SqlMetal /server:myserver /database:northwind /code:nwind.cs /namespace:nwind
```

Generate intermediate dbml file from SqlServer:
```
SqlMetal /server:myserver /database:northwind /dbml:northwind.dbml
        /namespace:nwind
```

Generate code with external mapping from dbml:
```
SqlMetal /code:nwind.cs /map:nwind.map northwind.dbml
```

Generate dbml from a SqlCE sdf file:
```
SqlMetal /dbml:northwind.dbml northwind.sdf
```

Generate dbml from SqlExpress local server:
```
SqlMetal /server:.\sqlexpress /database:northwind /dbml:northwind.dbml
```

Generate dbml by using a connection string in the command line:
```
SqlMetal /conn:"server='myserver'; database='northwind'" /dbml:northwind.dbml
```

As you can see, it even provides a few examples too. Unfortunately, the examples are for C#, but all you have to do is replace the .cs with .vb to convert them, as I have done in the following examples. Most of the options are fairly self-explanatory, but for those that aren't, Table 13-1 provides a summary.

Table 13-1. *SqlMetal Command-Line Options*

Option / Example	Description
/server:<name> /server:.\SQLExpress	This option allows you to specify the name of the database server to connect to. If omitted, SqlMetal will default to localhost/sqlexpress. To have SqlMetal generate entity classes from an MDF file, omit this option and the /database option, and specify the pathed MDF file name at the end of the command.
/database:<name> /database:Northwind	This is the name of the database on the specified server for which to generate entity classes. To have SqlMetal generate entity classes from an MDF file, omit this option and the /server option, and specify the pathed MDF file name at the end of the command.
/user:<name> /user:sa	This is the user account used to log into the specified database when connecting to create the entity classes.
/password:<password> /password:143021644	This is the password used for the specified user account to log into the specified database when connecting to create the entity classes.
/conn:<connection string> /conn:"Data Source=.\SQLEXPRESS; Initial Catalog=Northwind; Integrated Security=SSPI;"	This is a connection string to the database. You may use this instead of specifying the /server, /database, /user, and /password options.
/timeout:<seconds> /timeout:120	This option allows you to specify the time-out value in seconds for SqlMetal to use when generating the entity classes. Omitting this option will cause SqlMetal to default to 0, which means never time out. This option does not control the time-out your generated DataContext will use for LINQ to SQL queries. If you want to control the time-out for that, consider setting the CommandTimeout property of the DataContext class, or for even more granular control, call the DataContext.GetCommand method to set the time-out for a specific query. See Listing 16-29 in Chapter 16 for an example doing this.
/views /views	Specify this option to have SqlMetal generate the necessary Table(Of T) properties and entity classes to support the specified database's views.

Option / Example	Description
/functions /functions	Specify this option to have SqlMetal generate methods to call the specified database's user-defined functions.
/sprocs /sprocs	Specify this option to have SqlMetal generate methods to call the specified database's stored procedures.
/dbml[:file] /dbml:Northwind.dbml	This option specifies the file name for a DBML intermediate file. The purpose of generating this file is so that you can control class and property names of the generated entity classes. You would generate the DBML intermediate file with this option, edit the file, and then create a source code module by calling SqlMetal on the intermediate DBML file and specifying the /code option. Alternatively, you could load the DBML intermediate file created with this option into the Object Relational Designer, edit the file in the designer using its GUI, and allow the designer to generate the necessary source code. This option cannot be used with the /map option.
/code[:file] /code:Northwind.vb	This is the file name for SqlMetal to create containing the derived DataContext and entity classes in the specified programming language. This option cannot be used with the /dbml option. Interestingly, if you specify both the /code and /map options in the same invocation of SqlMetal, you will get code generated without LINQ to SQL attributes. Of course, you would also use the generated map with the generated code to be able to use LINQ to SQL.
/map[:file] /map:northwindmap.xml	This option specifies that SqlMetal should generate an XML external mapping file, in addition to a source code module specified by the /code option. If you specify the /map option, you must also specify the /code option. This XML external mapping file can then be loaded when instantiating the DataContext. This allows LINQ to SQL to be used without any actual LINQ to SQL source code being compiled with your code. Interestingly, when you specify the /map and /code options in the same invocation of SqlMetal, you get code generated without LINQ to SQL attributes. Of course, you would also use the generated map with the generated code to be able to use LINQ to SQL.
/language:<language> language:VB	This option defines for which programming language SqlMetal is to generate the code. The valid options are currently csharp, C#, and VB. Omitting this option will cause SqlMetal to derive the language from the specified code file name's extension.
/namespace:<name> /namespace:nwind	This dictates the namespace that the generated derived DataContext and entity classes will live in.
/context:<type> /context:Northwind	This specifies the name of the generated class that will be derived from the DataContext class. If this option is omitted, the class name will be the same as the database for which the code was generated.

Continued

Table 13-1. *Continued*

Option / Example	Description
/entitybase:<type> /entitybase:MyEntityClassBase	This specifies the name of a class for SqlMetal to specify as the base class for all generated entity classes. If this option is omitted, the generated entity classes will not be derived from any class.
/pluralize /pluralize	This option causes SqlMetal to retain the plural names for tables but to singularize the entity class names mapped to those tables. So, for a database table named Customers, the entity class generated will be named Customer (singular), and a Table(Of Customer) will be generated named Customers (plural). In this way, a Customer object exists in a Customers table. Grammatically speaking, this sounds correct. Without specifying this option, the entity class will be named Customers (plural), and the Table(Of Customers) will be named Customers (plural). This means a Customers object will exist in the Customers table. Grammatically speaking, this sounds incorrect.
/serialization:<option> /serialization:None	This option specifies whether SqlMetal should generate serialization attributes for the classes. The choices are None and Unidirectional. If this option is not specified, SqlMetal will default to None.
/provider:<type> /provider:Sql2005	This option is used to specify the database provider class. The valid values are SqlCompact, Sql2000, Sql2005, and Sql2008. Each of these values maps to a provider class in the System.Data.Linq.SqlClient namespace. SqlMetal will append *Provider* to the end of the value specified to build the provider class name and generate a Provider attribute specifying that provider class name.

Notice that the /dbml, /code, and /map options may be specified without providing a file name. If a file name is not specified, the generated code or XML will be output to the console.

■**Note** SqlMetal Builder is an open source GUI to SqlMetal that can be downloaded from http:// sourceforge.net/projects/SqlMetalBuilder. See Figure 13-1 for a screen shot. Also note that this is an open source project, so if the URL has changed, try searching the Internet for *SqlMetal Builder*.

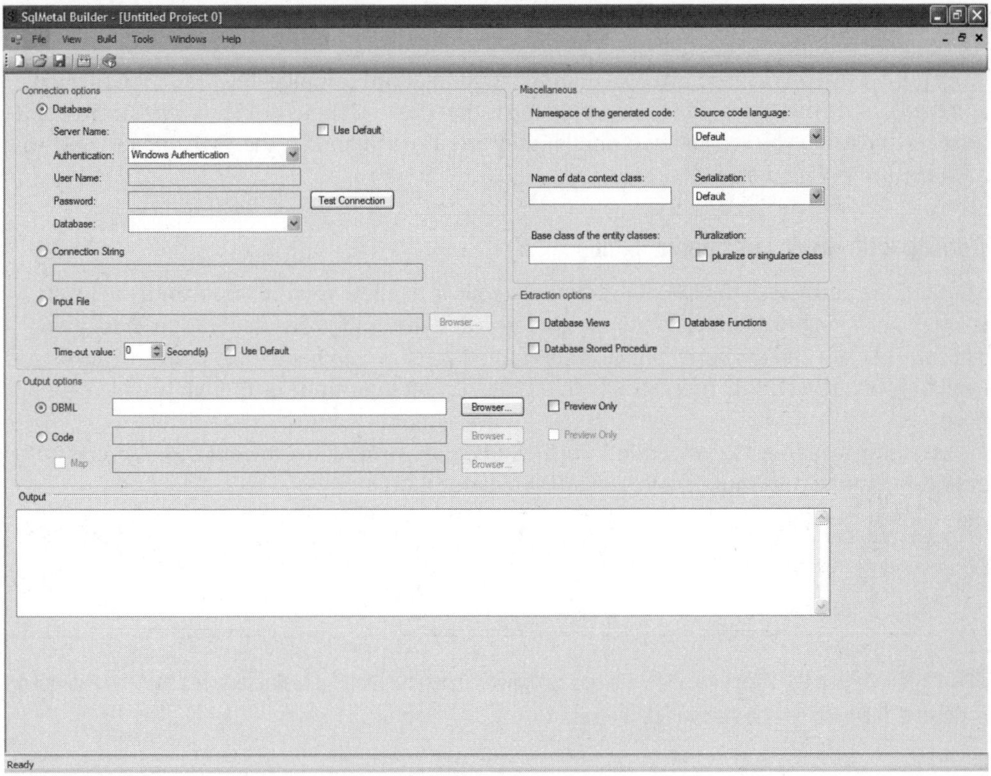

Figure 13-1. *A screen shot of SqlMetal Builder*

XML Mapping File vs. DBML Intermediate File

One of the confusing aspects of using SqlMetal is that it allows you to specify two different types of XML files to produce. One is created by specifying the /map option, and the other is created by specifying the /dbml option.

The difference between these two files is that the /map option creates an XML external mapping file intended to be loaded when the DataContext is instantiated. The /map option is an alternative to generating, or writing by hand, a source module containing LINQ to SQL attributes that you compile. With this approach, your source code never has any database-specific LINQ to SQL code compiled with or linked to it. This allows for somewhat dynamic consumption of a database, since you do not need any pregenerated and compiled code. I say it is "somewhat dynamic," because your code has to know the names of tables and fields; otherwise, it wouldn't even know what to query. The XML external mapping file instructs LINQ to SQL as to what tables, columns, and stored procedures exist with which it can interact and to what classes, class properties, and methods they should be mapped.

The /dbml option creates an intermediate DBML (XML) file for the purpose of allowing you to edit it to control class and property names for the soon-to-be-generated entity classes. You would then generate a source code module by running SqlMetal again, this time against the DBML file instead of the database, and specifying the /code option. Or, you can load the

DBML intermediate file into the Object Relational Designer, edit it in the designer, and allow the designer to generate the necessary entity class source code.

Another reason that the two XML files that SqlMetal can produce, the XML mapping file and the DBML intermediate file, are confusing is that their schemas are fairly similar. So don't be surprised when you see just how similar they are. The schema for the XML mapping file will be discussed in Chapter 15.

Working with DBML Intermediate Files

As I said, the purpose of the DBML intermediate file is to allow you the opportunity to insert yourself between the database schema extraction and the entity class generation so that you can control class and property names. Therefore, if you have no need to do that, you have no need to generate a DBML intermediate file. That said, let's continue as though you have the need.

Assuming you have the extended Northwind database attached to your SQL Server database, here is how you would create the intermediate DBML file:

```
SqlMetal /server:.\SQLExpress /database:Northwind /pluralize /sprocs /functions
/views /dbml:Northwind.dbml
```

■**Note** Specifying the /server and /database options when running SqlMetal requires that the extended Northwind database be attached to SQL Server.

Additionally, you may need to specify the appropriate /user and /password options so that SqlMetal can connect to the database.

Or, if you prefer, you can generate the DBML intermediate file from an MDF file:

```
SqlMetal /pluralize /sprocs /functions /views /dbml:Northwind.dbml
"C:\Northwind.mdf"
```

■**Note** Generating the DBML intermediate file from an MDF file may cause the MDF database file to be attached to SQL Server with the name C:\NORTHWIND.MDF or something similar. You should rename the database to *Northwind* inside SQL Server Enterprise Manager or SQL Server Management Studio so that the examples work properly.

Either of these two approaches should produce an identical DBML intermediate file. I specified only those options relevant for reading the database and producing the DBML file. Options such as /language and /code are only relevant when creating the source code module.

Once you have edited your intermediate XML file, here is how you would produce the source code module:

```
SqlMetal /namespace:northwind /code:Northwind.vb Northwind.dbml
```

The options I specified in that execution of SqlMetal are relevant when generating the source code.

DBML Intermediate File Schema

If you decide to take the route of creating the DBML intermediate file so that you can edit it and then generate your entity class mappings from that, you will need to know the schema and what the element and attribute names mean.

Because the schema is subject to change, please consult the Microsoft documentation for the DBML intermediate file schema for the most recent schema definition and explanation. Once you understand the schema, you could choose to manually edit the DBML intermediate file to control entity class and property names and then generate the entity class source code with SqlMetal from your edited DBML intermediate file.

Or, even better, you can load the generated DBML intermediate file into Visual Studio's Object Relational Designer and edit it there. This will give you a GUI for maintaining your O/R model and free you from the necessity of knowing and understanding the schema. I will describe how to edit your O/R model in the next section.

The Object Relational Designer

In addition to the SqlMetal tool, there is also a graphical user tool for generating entity classes that runs inside of Visual Studio. This tool is called the Object Relational Designer, but you will commonly see it referred to as the LINQ to SQL Designer, the O/R Designer, or even DLinq Designer. SqlMetal is designed to generate entity classes for all tables in a database, despite the fact that you do have the ability to be selective by generating an intermediate DBML file, modifying it, and generating entity classes from it. Furthermore, SqlMetal is a command-line utility. For a more selective approach with a graphical user interface, the Object Relational Designer is just the ticket. I will refer to the Object Relational Designer as *the designer* in this chapter.

The designer gives the developer drag-and-drop design-time entity class modeling. You needn't worry; the designer does most of the difficult work for you. You get the easy parts of selecting the database tables you want modeled and, if it suits you, editing entity class and entity class property names. Of course, you still have the option of doing all the modeling manually in the designer if you desire ultimate control.

Creating Your LINQ to SQL Classes File

The first step to use the designer is to create a file of LINQ to SQL classes by right-clicking your project and selecting Add/New Item from the pop-up context menu. After doing that, the Add New Item dialog box will open. Select the LINQ to SQL Classes template from the list of installed templates. Edit the name to whatever you choose. The name of the database you will be modeling is typically a good choice for the LINQ to SQL Classes file name. The extension for a LINQ to SQL Classes file is .dbml. For this example, I will use Nwnd.dbml for the name of the file, because using *nwind* or *Northwind* will conflict with other names in the samples.

Click the Add button once you have named the file. You will then be presented with a blank window. This is your designer canvas. Figure 13-2 shows the designer canvas.

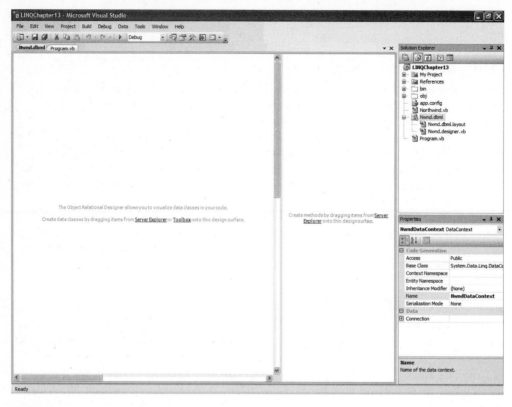

Figure 13-2. *The Object Relational Designer canvas*

If you click the canvas and examine the Properties window, you will see a property named Name. The value of the Name property will be the name of the generated DataContext class. Because I named my LINQ to SQL Classes file Nwnd.dbml, the Name property's value will default to NwndDataContext, which is just fine. You could change it if you wanted to, but for this discussion, I will leave it as it is.

If you examine the Solution Explorer, you will see that you now have a file nested under Nwnd.dbml named Nwnd.designer.vb. If you open this file, you will see that it contains very little code at this point. Basically, it will contain the constructors for the new DataContext class it is deriving for you named NwndDataContext.

■Note Designer files, references, and other files are by default not displayed by VB.NET in the Solution Explorer. To display them, click the Show All Files button in the Solution Explorer toolbar.

Connecting the DataContext to the Database

The next step is to add a connection to the appropriate database server containing the Northwind database in the Server Explorer window if one does not already exist.

■Tip If you do not see the Server Explorer window, select Server Explorer from the Visual Studio View menu.

To add a connection to the database, right-click the Data Connections node in the Server Explorer window, and choose the Add Connection menu item to open the Choose Data Source dialog box shown in Figure 13-3. Select Microsoft SQL Server. If you have been to this screen before and selected "Always use this selection", this dialog box will be skipped, and you will go directly to the Add Connection dialog box shown in Figure 13-4. The "Data source" entry field will default to Microsoft SQL Server (SqlClient), which is what we want.

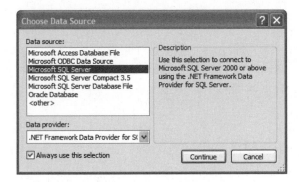

Figure 13-3. *The Choose Data Source dialog box*

Configure the appropriate settings for your Northwind database in the Add Connection dialog box. You may want to click the Test Connection button to make sure you have properly configured the connection.

Once you have the connection properly configured, click the OK button. You should now have a node representing your Northwind database connection under the Data Connections node in the Server Explorer. You may now access the Northwind database in the designer.

Before proceeding, make sure you are viewing the Nwnd.dbml file in the Visual Studio editor.

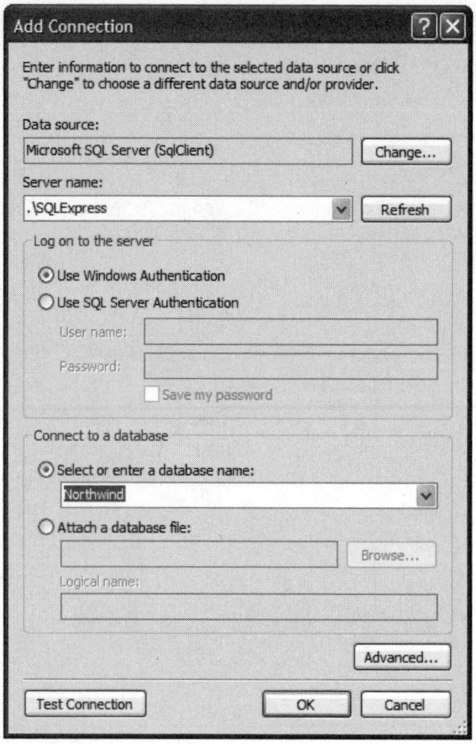

Figure 13-4. *The Add Connection dialog box*

Adding an Entity Class

Find your Northwind database in the list of Data Connections in the Server Explorer window. Expand the Tables node, and you should be presented with a list of tables in the Northwind database. Entity classes are created by dragging tables from the Table list in the Server Explorer window to the designer canvas.

From the Server Explorer, drag the Customers table to the designer canvas. You have just instructed the designer to create an entity class for the Customers table named Customer. Your canvas should look like Figure 13-5.

You may have to resize some of the panes to be able to see everything clearly. By dragging the Customers table to the designer canvas, the source code for the Customer entity class is added to the Nwnd.designer.vb source file. Once you build your project, which we will do in a few moments, you can begin using the Customer entity class to access and update data in the Northwind database. It's just that simple!

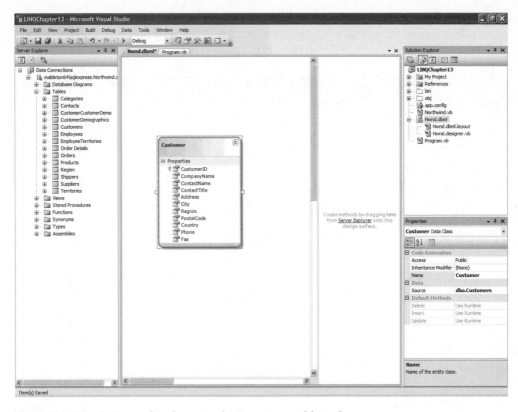

Figure 13-5. *The designer after dragging the Customers table to the canvas*

However, before I build the project and write code utilizing the generated entity classes, I want to create a few more bits necessary to reap all the benefits of LINQ to SQL. Now, from the Server Explorer, drag the Orders table to the canvas. You may need to move it around the canvas to get it to a desirable location. You have now instructed the designer to create an entity class for the Orders table named Order. Your canvas should look something like Figure 13-6.

You may notice that, in Figure 13-4, there is no longer a pane on the right side of the canvas that existed in the previous figures of the designer. This window is the Methods pane. I closed that pane by right-clicking the canvas and selecting the Hide Methods Pane context menu item. To open the Methods pane, right-click the canvas, and select the Show Methods Pane context menu item. I will leave the Methods pane closed so that more of the canvas is visible.

Looking at the canvas, you will see a dashed line connecting the Customer class to the Order class. That dashed line represents the relationship, referred to as an association in LINQ to SQL, between the Customers and Orders tables, as defined by the FK_Orders_Customers foreign key constraint that exists in the Northwind database. That line being there indicates that the designer will also be creating the necessary association in the entity classes to support the relationship between those two entity classes. The existence of that association will allow you to obtain a reference to a collection of a customer's orders by referencing a property on a Customer object and to obtain a reference to an order's customer by referencing a property on an Order object.

If you do not want the association to be generated, you may select the dashed line representing the association and delete it by pressing the Delete key or by right-clicking the dashed line and selecting the Delete menu option from the context menu.

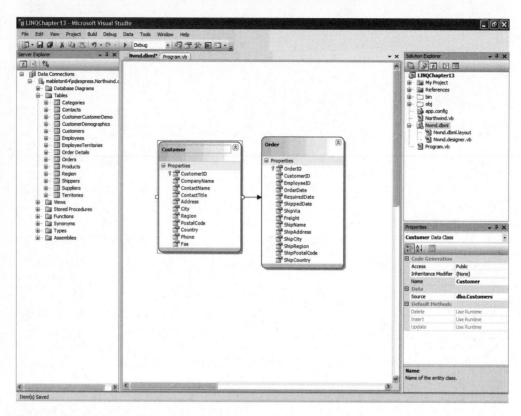

Figure 13-6. *The designer after dragging the Orders table to the canvas*

Using the Designer-Generated Entity Classes

You are now ready to use the entity classes the designer generated for you. Listing 13-2 contains an example querying the Northwind database for the customers whose city is London.

Listing 13-2. *An Example Using the Designer-Generated Entity Classes*

```
Dim db As New NwndDataContext()

Dim custs As IQueryable(Of Customer) = _
  From c In db.Customers _
  Where c.City = "London" _
  Select c

For Each c As Customer In custs
  Console.WriteLine("{0} has {1} orders.", c.CompanyName, c.Orders.Count)
Next c
```

This looks like my other examples with an exception. Please notice that I did not specify any connection information when instantiating the NwndDataContext object. This is because the designer generated my NwndDataContext class with a parameterless constructor that gets the connection information from the project's settings file named app.config. It was even kind enough to set the value for me in the settings file. Here is what the generated parameterless constructor looks like:

The Designer-Generated DataContext Constructor

```
Public Sub New()
  MyBase.New( _
    Global.Ch13Console.My.MySettings.Default.NorthwindConnectionString, _
    mappingSource)
  OnCreated
End Sub
```

Notice in the preceding code that I am able to access the retrieved customer's orders by referencing a Customer object's Orders property. This is because of the association that the designer created automatically for me. How cool is that? Here are the results of Listing 13-2:

```
Around the Horn has 13 orders.
B's Beverages has 10 orders.
Consolidated Holdings has 3 orders.
Eastern Connection has 8 orders.
North/South has 3 orders.
Seven Seas Imports has 9 orders.
```

Editing the Entity Class Model

Naturally, you may want to have some control over entity class names, entity class properties (entity class settings), entity class property (entity class member) names, and entity class property (entity class member) properties (settings). OK Microsoft, can you make the naming any more confusing? Did you really need to call the members of classes "properties," knowing that in Visual Studio you call the settings "properties" too?

The flexibility and ease of use for controlling the names of entity classes and their properties is what makes the designer so attractive. It's all drag and drop, point and click, man!

Editing the Entity Class Name

You can edit the entity class name by double-clicking the name on the canvas or by selecting the entity class on the canvas and editing the Name property in the Properties window.

Editing the Entity Class's Properties (Entity Class Settings)

You can edit the properties, as in settings, of the entity class by selecting the entity class on the canvas and editing the appropriate properties in the Properties window, of which the entity class name is one. You have the ability to edit the database table name in which these entities are stored; the insert, update, and delete override methods; and other properties.

Editing an Entity Class Property (Entity Class Member) Name

You can edit the name of an entity class property, as in entity class member, by triple-clicking the property name on the canvas. I wasn't aware that there was such a thing as triple-clicking either, but that's what it appears to be responding to. Or, you can select the entity class property on the canvas and edit the Name property in the Properties window.

Editing an Entity Class Property's (Entity Class Member's) Properties (Settings)

You can edit an entity class property's properties by selecting the property on the canvas and editing the appropriate property in the Properties window, of which the entity class property name is one. This is where you will find all the properties that correspond to the entity class attribute properties, such as Name and UpdateCheck, for the Column entity class attribute. I will discuss the entity class attributes in detail in Chapter 15.

Adding Objects to the Entity Class Model

Dragging and dropping an entity class on the canvas is simple enough, as long as you have a table in a database in the Server Explorer. There are times when you may not have this luxury. Perhaps you are defining the entity class first and plan to generate the database by calling the CreateDatabase method on the DataContext. Or, perhaps you are going to be taking advantage of entity class inheritance, and there is no existing table to map to.

Adding New Entity Classes

One way to add new entity classes to your entity class model is to drag them from the tables of a database in your Server Explorer window, as I did in the previous section. Another way you can create a new entity class is by dragging the Object Relational Designer Class object in the Visual Studio Toolbox onto the canvas. Edit the name, and set the entity class's properties as described in the previous section. You can also add a new entity class to the model by right-clicking the designer canvas, and selecting Add and then Class.

Adding New Entity Class Properties (Members)

You can add new entity class properties (members) by right-clicking the entity class in the designer and selecting the Property menu item in the Add context menu. Once the property has been added to the entity class, follow the directions for editing an entity class property's properties in the section above named "Editing an Entity Class Property's (Entity Class Member's) Properties (Settings)."

Adding a New Association

Instead of using drag and drop to create an association, like you did when adding a new entity class from the Visual Studio Toolbox, you create an association by clicking the Association object in the toolbox followed by clicking the parent entity class, the *one* side of the one-to-many relationship, followed by clicking the child entity class, the *many* side of the one-to-many relationship. Each of the two classes needs to have the appropriate property before you add the association so that you can map the primary key on the *one* side to the foreign key on the *many* side. Once you have selected the second class, the *many* class, of the association by clicking it, the Association Editor dialog box will open allowing you to map the property of the *one* class to its corresponding property of the *many* class. You can also add a new association to the model by right-clicking the designer canvas and selecting Add and then Association.

Once you have mapped the properties and dismissed the Association Editor dialog box, you will see a dotted line connecting the parent to the child entity class.

Select the association by clicking the dotted line, and set the appropriate association properties in the Properties window. Refer to the descriptions of the `Association` attribute and its properties in Chapter 15 for more information about the association properties.

Adding a New Inheritance Relationship

You may use the Object Relational Designer to model inheritance relationships too. Adding an inheritance relationship works just like adding a new association. Select the Inheritance object in the Visual Studio Toolbox, and click the entity class that will be the derived class, followed by the entity class that will be the base class. Make sure to set all appropriate entity class properties as defined by the `InheritanceMapping` and `Column` entity class attributes, which I cover in Chapter 15. You can also add a new inheritance relationship to the model by right-clicking the designer canvas, and selecting Add and then Inheritance.

Adding Stored Procedures and User-Defined Functions

To have the designer generate the code necessary to call stored procedures or user-defined functions, drag the stored procedure or user-defined function from the Server Explorer to the Methods pane of the designer. I will demonstrate this in the next section.

Overriding the Insert, Update, and Delete Methods

In Chapter 14, I will discuss overriding the insert, update, and delete methods used by LINQ to SQL when making changes to an entity class object. You can override the default methods by adding specific methods to an entity class. If you take this approach, be sure to use partial classes, so you are not modifying any generated code. I will demonstrate how to do this in Chapter 14.

However, overriding the insert, update, and delete methods is easily accomplished in the designer too. Let's assume you have a stored procedure named InsertCustomer that will insert a new customer record into the Northwind database's Customer table. Here is the stored procedure I will use:

The InsertCustomer Stored Procedure

```
CREATE PROCEDURE dbo.InsertCustomer
  (
  @CustomerID        nchar(5),
  @CompanyName       nvarchar(40),
  @ContactName       nvarchar(30),
  @ContactTitle      nvarchar(30),
  @Address           nvarchar(60),
  @City              nvarchar(15),
  @Region            nvarchar(15),
  @PostalCode        nvarchar(10),
```

```
    @Country            nvarchar(15),
    @Phone              nvarchar(24),
    @Fax                nvarchar(24)
    )
AS
    INSERT INTO Customers
    (
      CustomerID,
      CompanyName,
      ContactName,
      ContactTitle,
      Address,
      City,
      Region,
      PostalCode,
      Country,
      Phone,
      Fax
    )
    VALUES
    (
      @CustomerID,
      @CompanyName,
      @ContactName,
      @ContactTitle,
      @Address,
      @City,
      @Region,
      @PostalCode,
      @Country,
      @Phone,
      @Fax
    )
```

Note The InsertCustomer stored procedure is not part of the extended Northwind database. I manually added it for this demonstration.

To override the `Customer` entity class's insert method, first make sure the Methods pane is visible. If it is not, right-click the canvas, and select the Show Methods Pane context menu item. Next, open the Server Explorer window in Visual Studio if it is not already open. Find and expand the Stored Procedures node in the appropriate database node in the tree. Your Visual Studio should look very similar to Figure 13-7.

Once you have found your stored procedure, simply drag it to the Methods pane, which is the window to the right of the entity class model. Figure 13-8 shows Visual Studio after I have dragged the InsertCustomer stored procedure to the Methods pane.

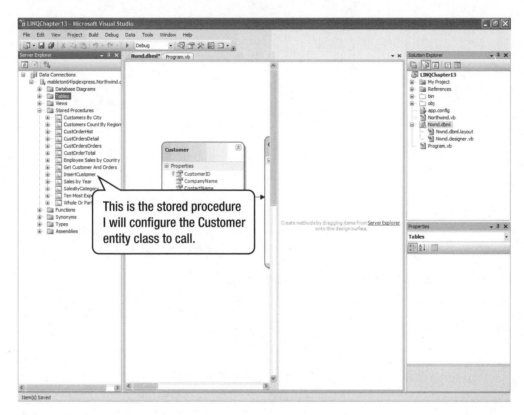

Figure 13-7. *Finding the stored procedure*

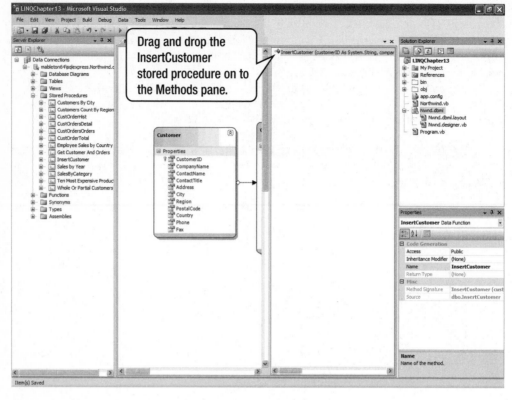

Figure 13-8. *Dropping the stored procedure on the Methods pane*

Dragging a stored procedure from the Server Explorer window to the Methods pane is the way you instruct the designer to generate the code necessary to call the stored procedure from LINQ to SQL. This is also the same way you instruct the designer to generate the code for a user-defined function too.

Making the stored procedure accessible from LINQ to SQL is the first step to having the insert, update, or delete operation call a stored procedure instead of the default method. The next step is to override one of those operations to call the now accessible stored procedure.

Now that the InsertCustomer stored procedure is in the Methods pane, select the Customer class in the designer canvas and examine the Properties window for the Customer class. You will now see a list of the Default Methods. Select the Insert method by clicking it. You will now be presented with the ellipses (…) selection button as is displayed in Figure 13-9.

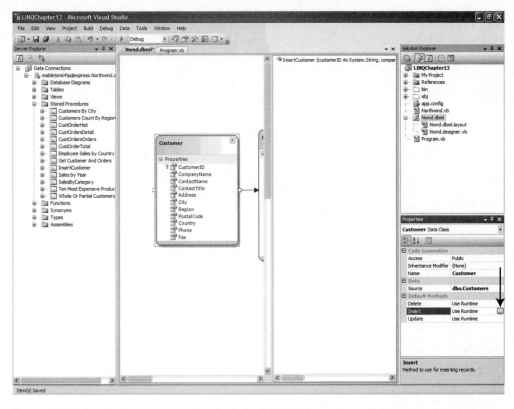

Figure 13-9. *Select the Insert method in the Default Methods category of the Properties window.*

Now, simply click the ellipses selection button to display the Configure Behavior dialog box. Select the Customize radio button, and select the InsertCustomer stored procedure from the drop-down list. Map the Method Arguments on the left to the appropriate Customer Class Properties on the right, as illustrated in Figure 13-10.

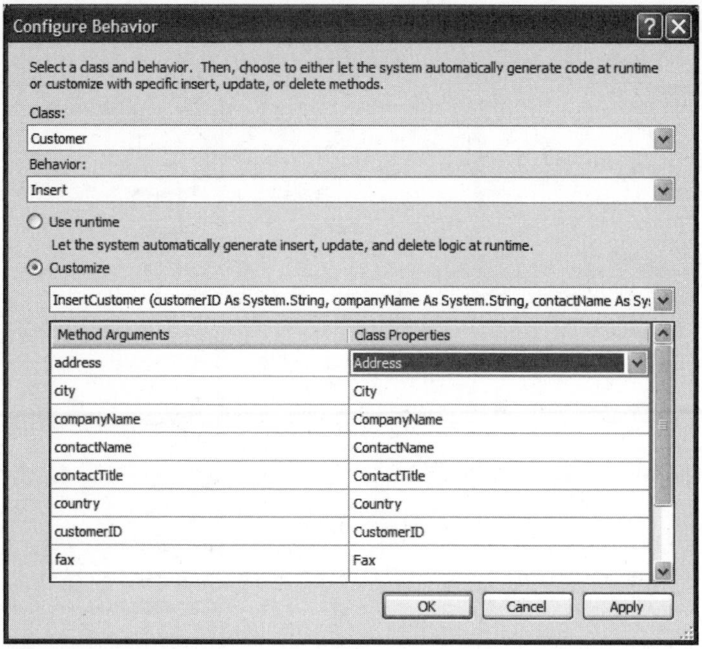

Figure 13-10. *Mapping Method Arguments to Class Properties*

Amazingly, all my method arguments were already mapped by default to the appropriate class properties. Nice!

Once you have mapped all of the method arguments, click the OK button. You are now ready to insert Customer records using the InsertCustomer stored procedure. In Listing 13-3, I will create a new customer using the InsertCustomer stored procedure.

Listing 13-3. *Creating a Customer Record with the Default Insert Method Overridden*

```
Dim db As New NwndDataContext()

db.Log = Console.Out

Dim cust As Customer = New Customer With { _
  .CustomerID = "EWICH", _
  .CompanyName = "Every 'Wich Way", _
  .ContactName = "Vickey Rattz", _
  .ContactTitle = "Owner", _
  .Address = "105 Chip Morrow Dr.", _
  .City = "Alligator Point", _
  .Region = "FL", _
  .PostalCode = "32346", _
  .Country = "USA", _
  .Phone = "(800) EAT-WICH", _
  .Fax = "(800) FAX-WICH"}
```

```
db.Customers.InsertOnSubmit(cust)

db.SubmitChanges()

Dim customer As Customer = _
  db.Customers.Where(Function(c) c.CustomerID = "EWICH").First()
Console.WriteLine( _
  "{0} - {1}", _
  customer.CompanyName, _
  customer.ContactName)

' Restore the database.
db.Customers.DeleteOnSubmit(cust)
db.SubmitChanges()
```

Notice that I am not specifying any namespace on the Customer class that I reference; therefore, I will be using the Customer class that exists in the same namespace as the project, which is the designer-generated Customer class.

There is nothing special in Listing 13-3. I merely instantiate a DataContext, which in this case is the designer-generated NwndDataContext. I then create a new Customer object and insert it into the Customers Table(Of T) property. Next, I call the SubmitChanges method to persist the new customer to the database. Then, I query for that customer from the database and display it to the console just to prove the record was indeed inserted into the database table. The very last things I do are delete the customer by calling the DeleteOnSubmit method and persist to the database by calling the SubmitChanges method, so the database is left in the same state it was initially so that subsequent examples will run properly and so that this example can be run multiple times.

Let's examine the output of Listing 13-3:

```
EXEC @RETURN_VALUE = [dbo].[InsertCustomer] @CustomerID = @p0, @CompanyName = @p1,
@ContactName = @p2, @ContactTitle = @
p3, @Address = @p4, @City = @p5, @Region = @p6, @PostalCode = @p7, @Country = @p8,
@Phone = @p9, @Fax = @p10
-- @p0: Input NChar (Size = 5; Prec = 0; Scale = 0) [EWICH]
-- @p1: Input NVarChar (Size = 15; Prec = 0; Scale = 0) [Every 'Wich Way]
-- @p2: Input NVarChar (Size = 12; Prec = 0; Scale = 0) [Vickey Rattz]
-- @p3: Input NVarChar (Size = 5; Prec = 0; Scale = 0) [Owner]
-- @p4: Input NVarChar (Size = 19; Prec = 0; Scale = 0) [105 Chip Morrow Dr.]
-- @p5: Input NVarChar (Size = 15; Prec = 0; Scale = 0) [Alligator Point]
-- @p6: Input NVarChar (Size = 2; Prec = 0; Scale = 0) [FL]
-- @p7: Input NVarChar (Size = 5; Prec = 0; Scale = 0) [32346]
-- @p8: Input NVarChar (Size = 3; Prec = 0; Scale = 0) [USA]
-- @p9: Input NVarChar (Size = 14; Prec = 0; Scale = 0) [(800) EAT-WICH]
-- @p10: Input NVarChar (Size = 14; Prec = 0; Scale = 0) [(800) FAX-WICH]
-- @RETURN_VALUE: Output Int (Size = 0; Prec = 0; Scale = 0) [Null]
-- Context: SqlProvider(Sql2008) Model: AttributedMetaModel Build: 3.5.30729.1
```

```
SELECT TOP (1) [t0].[CustomerID], [t0].[CompanyName], [t0].[ContactName],
[t0].[ContactTitle], [t0].[Address], [t0].[City],
[t0].[Region], [t0].[PostalCode], [t0].[Country], [t0].[Phone], [t0].[Fax]
FROM [dbo].[Customers] AS [t0]
WHERE [t0].[CustomerID] = @p0
-- @p0: Input NVarChar (Size = 5; Prec = 0; Scale = 0) [EWICH]
-- Context: SqlProvider(Sql2008) Model: AttributedMetaModel Build: 3.5.30729.1

Every 'Wich Way - Vickey Rattz
DELETE FROM [dbo].[Customers] WHERE ([CustomerID] = @p0) AND ([CompanyName] = @p1)
AND ([ContactName] = @p2) AND ([Conta
ctTitle] = @p3) AND ([Address] = @p4) AND ([City] = @p5) AND ([Region] = @p6) AND
([PostalCode] = @p7) AND ([Country] =
@p8) AND ([Phone] = @p9) AND ([Fax] = @p10)
-- @p0: Input NChar (Size = 5; Prec = 0; Scale = 0) [EWICH]
-- @p1: Input NVarChar (Size = 15; Prec = 0; Scale = 0) [Every 'Wich Way]
-- @p2: Input NVarChar (Size = 12; Prec = 0; Scale = 0) [Vickey Rattz]
-- @p3: Input NVarChar (Size = 5; Prec = 0; Scale = 0) [Owner]
-- @p4: Input NVarChar (Size = 19; Prec = 0; Scale = 0) [105 Chip Morrow Dr.]
-- @p5: Input NVarChar (Size = 15; Prec = 0; Scale = 0) [Alligator Point]
-- @p6: Input NVarChar (Size = 2; Prec = 0; Scale = 0) [FL]
-- @p7: Input NVarChar (Size = 5; Prec = 0; Scale = 0) [32346]
-- @p8: Input NVarChar (Size = 3; Prec = 0; Scale = 0) [USA]
-- @p9: Input NVarChar (Size = 14; Prec = 0; Scale = 0) [(800) EAT-WICH]
-- @p10: Input NVarChar (Size = 14; Prec = 0; Scale = 0) [(800) FAX-WICH]
-- Context: SqlProvider(Sql2008) Model: AttributedMetaModel Build: 3.5.30729.1
```

While it is a little difficult to see with all of the output, a SQL insert statement was not created. Instead, the InsertCustomer stored procedure was called. The designer makes it very easy to override the insert, update, and delete methods for an entity class.

Use SqlMetal and the O/R Designer Together

Because SqlMetal's DBML intermediate file format shares the same XML schema as the Object Relational Designer's format, it is completely possible to use them together.

For example, you could generate a DBML intermediate file for a database using SqlMetal, and then load that file into the O/R Designer to tweak any entity class or entity class property names you desire. This approach provides a simple way to generate entity classes for an entire database, yet makes it simple to modify what you would like.

Another example where this interchangeability can be useful is for overriding the insert, update, and delete operations that are performed to make changes to the database for an entity class. You can generate the DBML intermediate file for your database with SqlMetal but then load the file into the designer and modify the insert, update, and delete methods, as was described in the section in this chapter about the Object Relational Designer.

Summary

As is typical of my style, much of the information in this chapter may seem premature, since I have yet to actually discuss entity classes or the `DataContext` class. However, I just can't, in good conscience, allow you to continue without you knowing some of these tips and tools that are available for LINQ to SQL development. Refer to these tips once you have the foundation to more fully understand them.

Remember that there are two tools for modeling your entity classes. The first, SqlMetal, is a command-line tool better suited to generating entity classes for an entire database. The second tool, the Object Relational Designer, often referred to as the LINQ to SQL Designer, is a GUI drag-and-drop entity class-modeling tool that runs inside Visual Studio. It is better suited for iterative and new development. But, as I pointed out, these two tools work well together. Your best path may be to start with SqlMetal to generate your entity classes for your entire database and maintain your entity classes with the Object Relational Designer.

Now that I have provided some tips, covered the LINQ to SQL tools, and you have had the opportunity to create your entity classes, in Chapter 14, I will show you how to perform the most common database operations you will utilize on a regular basis.

■ ■ ■

LINQ to SQL Database Operations

In this chapter, I will discuss and demonstrate how all of the typical database operations are performed with LINQ to SQL. Specifically, I will cover how to perform

- Inserts
- Queries
- Updates
- Deletes

After I discuss the standard database operations, I will demonstrate how you can override the default insert, update, and delete methods an entity class uses to persist changes to the database.

The last topic I will cover is the automatic translation of LINQ to SQL queries, including what to be mindful of when writing queries.

In order to discuss the standard database operations, I will have to refer to the DataContext and relevant entity classes. I am aware that I have not provided much detail yet as to how entity classes and the DataContext class work, but they will be covered in subsequent chapters. I will discuss entity classes in Chapter 15 and the DataContext in Chapter 16. For now, just remember that the DataContext manages the connection to the database, and it manages the entity class objects. An entity class object represents a specific database record in object form.

Prerequisites for Running the Examples

To run the examples in this chapter, you will need to have obtained the extended version of the Northwind database and generated entity classes for it. Please read and follow the section in Chapter 12 titled "Prerequisites for Running the Examples."

Some Common Methods

Additionally, to run the examples in this chapter, you will need some common methods that will be utilized by the examples. Please read and follow the section in Chapter 12 titled "Some Common Methods."

Using the LINQ to SQL API

To run the examples in this chapter, you may need to add the appropriate references and Imports statements to your project. Please read and follow the section in Chapter 12 titled "Using the LINQ to SQL API."

Standard Database Operations

While I will be covering the details of performing LINQ to SQL queries in detail in subsequent LINQ to SQL chapters, I want to give you a glimpse of how to perform the rudimentary database operations without the complexity of the complications. These examples are meant to merely demonstrate the basic concepts. As such, they will not include error checking or exception handling.

For example, since many of the basic operations I will discuss make changes to the database, those that make changes should detect and resolve concurrency conflicts. But, for the sake of simplicity, these examples will not demonstrate these principles. However, in Chapter 17, I will discuss concurrency conflict detection and resolution.

Inserts

Instantiating an entity class, such as the Customer class, is not enough to perform an insert into the database. An entity object must also either be inserted into a table collection of type Table(Of T), where T is the type of the entity class stored in the table, or be added to an EntitySet(Of T) on an entity object already being tracked by the DataContext, where T is the type of an entity class.

The first step to insert a record into a database is to create a DataContext. That is the first step for every LINQ to SQL query. Second, an entity object is instantiated from an entity class. Third, that entity object is inserted into the appropriate table collection. And fourth, the SubmitChanges method is called on the DataContext.

Listing 14-1 contains an example of inserting a record into the database.

Listing 14-1. *Inserting a Record by Inserting an Entity Object into Table(Of T)*

```
'  1.  Create the DataContext.
Dim db As New Northwind("Data Source=.\SQLEXPRESS;Initial Catalog=Northwind;" & _
   "Integrated Security=SSPI;")

'  2.  Instantiate an entity object.
Dim cust As Customer = New Customer With _
{ _
  .CustomerID = "LAWN", _
  .CompanyName = "Lawn Wranglers", _
  .ContactName = "Mr. Abe Henry", _
  .ContactTitle = "Owner", _
  .Address = "1017 Maple Leaf Way", _
  .City = "Ft. Worth", _
  .Region = "TX", _
  .PostalCode = "76104", _
```

```
    .Country = "USA", _
    .Phone = "(800) MOW-LAWN", _
    .Fax = "(800) MOW-LAWO"}

'   3.  Add the entity object to the Customers table.
db.Customers.InsertOnSubmit(cust)

'   4.  Call the SubmitChanges method.
db.SubmitChanges()

'   5.  Query the record.
Dim customer As Customer = _
  db.Customers.Where(Function(c) c.CustomerID = "LAWN").First()
Console.WriteLine("{0} - {1}", customer.CompanyName, customer.ContactName)

'   This part of the code merely resets the database so the example can be
'   run more than once.
Console.WriteLine("Deleting the added customer LAWN.")
db.Customers.DeleteOnSubmit(cust)
db.SubmitChanges()
```

There really isn't much to this example. First, I instantiate a Northwind object so that I have a DataContext for the Northwind database. Second, I instantiate a Customer object and populate it using the new object initialization feature of VB.NET 2008. Third, I insert the instantiated Customer object into the Customers table, of type Table(Of Customer), in the Northwind DataContext class. Fourth, I call the SubmitChanges method to persist the newly created Customer object to the database. Fifth, I query the customer back out of the database just to prove it was inserted.

■Note If you run this example, a new record will be temporarily added to the Northwind Customers table for customer LAWN. Please notice that after the newly added record is queried and displayed, it is then deleted. I do this so that the example can be run more than once and so the newly inserted record does not affect subsequent examples. Any time one of my examples changes the database, the database needs to be returned to its original state so that no examples are impacted. If any example that modifies the database is unable to complete for some reason, you should manually reset the database to its original state.

Here are the results of Listing 14-1.

```
Lawn Wranglers - Mr. Abe Henry
Deleting the added customer LAWN.
```

As you can see from the output, the inserted record was found in the database.

Alternatively, to insert a record into the database, we can add a new instance of an entity class to an already existing entity object being tracked by the DataContext object as demonstrated in Listing 14-2.

Listing 14-2. *Inserting a Record into the Northwind Database by Adding It to EntitySet(Of T)*

```
Dim db As New Northwind("Data Source=.\SQLEXPRESS;Initial Catalog=Northwind;" & _
  "Integrated Security=SSPI;")

Dim cust As Customer = ( _
  From c In db.Customers _
  Where c.CustomerID = "LONEP" _
  Select c).Single()

'  Used to query record back out.
Dim now As DateTime = DateTime.Now

Dim order As Order = New Order With { _
  .CustomerID = cust.CustomerID, _
  .EmployeeID = 4, .OrderDate = now, _
  .RequiredDate = DateTime.Now.AddDays(7), _
  .ShipVia = 3, .Freight = New Decimal(24.66), _
  .ShipName = cust.CompanyName, _
  .ShipAddress = cust.Address, _
  .ShipCity = cust.City, _
  .ShipRegion = cust.Region, _
  .ShipPostalCode = cust.PostalCode, _
  .ShipCountry = cust.Country}

cust.Orders.Add(order)

db.SubmitChanges()

Dim orders As IEnumerable(Of Order) = db.Orders _
  .Where(Function(o) o.CustomerID = "LONEP" AndAlso o.OrderDate.Value = now)

For Each o As Order In orders
  Console.WriteLine("{0} {1}", o.OrderDate, o.ShipName)
Next o

'  This part of the code merely resets the database so the example can be
'  run more than once.
db.Orders.DeleteOnSubmit(order)
db.SubmitChanges()
```

■Note You may find it odd that in Listing 14-1 I call the `InsertOnSubmit` method, but in Listing 14-2, I call the `Add` method. This discrepancy is caused by the fact that those methods are called on two different object types. In Listing 14-1, the `InsertOnSubmit` method is called on an object of type `Table(Of T)`. In Listing 14-2, the `Add` method is called on an object of type `EntitySet(Of T)`.

In Listing 14-2, I created a `Northwind DataContext`, retrieved a customer, and added a newly constructed `order` entity object to the `Orders EntitySet(Of Order)` of the `Customer` entity object. I then queried for the new record and displayed it to the console.

■Note Again, please notice that at the end of the example I am deleting, via the `DeleteOnSubmit` method, the order record added to the Orders table. If the example code does not complete, you will need to manually delete this record to maintain the state of the database for the subsequent examples.

In case this example doesn't seem to be doing anything significantly different than Listing 14-1, in Listing 14-1, the inserted object, which was a `Customer`, was inserted into a variable of type `Table(Of Customer)`. In Listing 14-2, the inserted object, which is an `Order`, is added to a variable of type `EntitySet(Of Order)`.

Here are the results of Listing 14-2.

```
12/22/2008 12:11:53 AM Lonesome Pine Restaurant
```

This output proves that the order record was indeed inserted into the database.

Inserting Attached Entity Objects

One of the niceties of inserting records is that the `DataContext` detects any associated dependent entity class objects that are attached so that they will be persisted too when the `SubmitChanges` method is called. By dependent, I mean any entity class object containing a foreign key to the inserted entity class object. Listing 14-3 contains an example.

Listing 14-3. *Adding Attached Records*

```
Dim db As New Northwind("Data Source=.\SQLEXPRESS;Initial Catalog=Northwind;" & _
    "Integrated Security=SSPI;")

Dim cust As Customer = New Customer With { _
    .CustomerID = "LAWN", _
    .CompanyName = "Lawn Wranglers", _
    .ContactName = "Mr. Abe Henry", _
    .ContactTitle = "Owner", _
    .Address = "1017 Maple Leaf Way", _
```

```
    .City = "Ft. Worth", _
    .Region = "TX", _
    .PostalCode = "76104", _
    .Country = "USA", _
    .Phone = "(800) MOW-LAWN", _
    .Fax = "(800) MOW-LAWO"}

cust.Orders.Add(New Order With { _
    .CustomerID = "LAWN", _
    .EmployeeID = 4, _
    .OrderDate = DateTime.Now, _
    .RequiredDate = DateTime.Now.AddDays(7), _
    .ShipVia = 3, _
    .Freight = New Decimal(24.66), _
    .ShipName = "Lawn Wranglers", _
    .ShipAddress = "1017 Maple Leaf Way", _
    .ShipCity = "Ft. Worth", _
    .ShipRegion = "TX", _
    .ShipPostalCode = "76104", _
    .ShipCountry = "USA"})

db.Customers.InsertOnSubmit(cust)
db.SubmitChanges()

Dim customer As Customer = _
    db.Customers.Where(Function(c) c.CustomerID = "LAWN").First()

Console.WriteLine("{0} - {1}", customer.CompanyName, customer.ContactName)
For Each order As Order In customer.Orders
    Console.WriteLine("{0} - {1}", order.CustomerID, order.OrderDate)
Next order

'  This part of the code merely resets the database so the example can be
'  run more than once.
db.Orders.DeleteOnSubmit(cust.Orders.First())
db.Customers.DeleteOnSubmit(cust)
db.SubmitChanges()
```

In Listing 14-3, I created a new Customer object and added a newly instantiated Order to its Orders collection. Even though I only inserted the Customer object cust into the Customers table, and specifically, I do not add the orders to the Orders table, because the new Order is attached to the new Customer, the new Order will be persisted in the database when the SubmitChanges method is called.

There is one additional point I would like to make about this example. Please notice that, in the cleanup code at the end of Listing 14-3, I call the DeleteOnSubmit method for both the new Order and the new Customer. In this case, I only delete the first Order, but since the Customer was new, I know this is the only Order. It is necessary that I manually delete the orders, because while new attached associated entity objects are automatically inserted into the database when a parent entity object is inserted, the same is not true when deleting an entity object. Deleting a parent entity object will not cause any attached entity objects to automatically be deleted from the database. Had I not deleted the orders manually, an exception would have been thrown. I will discuss this in more detail in the "Deletes" section of this chapter.

Let's take a look at the output of Listing 14-3 by pressing Ctrl+F5.

```
Lawn Wranglers - Mr. Abe Henry
LAWN - 6/7/2009 6:05:07 PM
```

From this output, you can see that the new `Customer`, and its associated `Order`, was indeed inserted into the database, albeit temporarily because of the database restoration code at the end of the example.

Queries

Performing LINQ to SQL queries is about like performing any other LINQ query with a few exceptions. I will cover the exceptions very shortly.

To perform a LINQ to SQL query, I need to first create a `DataContext`. Then I can perform the query on a table in that `DataContext`, as Listing 14-4 demonstrates.

Listing 14-4. *Performing a Simple LINQ to SQL Query on the Northwind Database*

```
Dim db As New Northwind("Data Source=.\SQLEXPRESS;Initial Catalog=Northwind;" & _
  "Integrated Security=SSPI;")

Dim cust As Customer = ( _
  From c In db.Customers _
  Where c.CustomerID Is "LONEP" _
  Select c).Single()
```

When that code is executed, the customer whose `CustomerID` is `"LONEP"` will be retrieved into the `cust` variable. You should be aware, though, as was mentioned in Chapter 5, that the `Single` Standard Query Operator will throw an exception if the sequence it is called on contains no matching elements. So, using this code, you must know that customer `"LONEP"` exists. In reality, the `SingleOrDefault` Standard Query Operator provides better protection for the possibility of no record matching the `Where` clause.

There are a couple additional points worth mentioning in this example. First, notice that the query is using VB.NET syntax when comparing the `CustomerID` to `"LONEP"`. This is evidenced by the fact that double quotes are used to contain the string `"LONEP"` as opposed to single quotes that SQL syntax requires. Also, the VB.NET equality test operator "Is" is used instead of the SQL equality test operator "=". This demonstrates the fact that the query is indeed integrated into the language, since after all, this is what LINQ is named for: Language Integrated Query. Note that I could have used "=" instead of "Is," but then you may not have believed it really was a VB.NET expression. Second, notice that I am mixing both query expression syntax and standard dot notation syntax in this query. The query expression syntax portion is contained within parentheses, and the `Single` operator is called using standard dot notation syntax.

Now, here is a question for you. I have discussed deferred query execution many times in the book so far. The question is, will just executing the preceding code cause the query to actually be performed? Don't forget to consider deferred query execution when selecting your answer. The answer is yes; the Single Standard Query Operator will cause the query to actually execute. Had I left off that operator call and merely returned the query minus the call to the Single operator, the query would not have executed.

Listing 14-4 provides no screen output, so just for verification that the code does indeed retrieve the appropriate customer, Listing 14-5 is the same code, plus output to the console has been added to display the customer that is retrieved.

Listing 14-5. *Performing the Same Query with Console Output*

```
Dim db As New Northwind("Data Source=.\SQLEXPRESS;Initial Catalog=Northwind;" & _
  "Integrated Security=SSPI;")

Dim cust As Customer = ( _
  From c In db.Customers _
  Where c.CustomerID Is "LONEP" _
  Select c).Single()

Console.WriteLine("{0} - {1}", cust.CompanyName, cust.ContactName)
```

Here is the output for Listing 14-5.

```
Lonesome Pine Restaurant - Fran Wilson
```

Exceptions to the Norm

Earlier I mentioned that LINQ to SQL queries are like typical LINQ queries with some exceptions. Now I will discuss the exceptions.

LINQ to SQL Queries Return an IQueryable(Of T)

While LINQ queries performed on arrays and collections return sequences of type IEnumerable(Of T), a LINQ to SQL query that returns a sequence, returns a sequence of type IQueryable(Of T). Listing 14-6 contains an example of a query returning a sequence of type IQueryable(Of T).

Listing 14-6. *A Simple LINQ to SQL Query Returning an IQueryable(Of T) Sequence*

```
Dim db As New Northwind("Data Source=.\SQLEXPRESS;Initial Catalog=Northwind;" & _
  "Integrated Security=SSPI;")

Dim custs As IQueryable(Of Customer) = _
  From c In db.Customers _
  Where c.City = "London" _
  Select c
```

```
For Each cust As Customer In custs
  Console.WriteLine("Customer: {0}", cust.CompanyName)
Next cust
```

As you can see, the return type for this query is IQueryable(Of Customer). Here are the results of Listing 14-6.

```
Customer: Around the Horn
Customer: B's Beverages
Customer: Consolidated Holdings
Customer: Eastern Connection
Customer: North/South
Customer: Seven Seas Imports
```

However, as I stated in Chapter 12, since IQueryable(Of T) extends IEnumerable(Of T), you can typically treat a sequence of type IQueryable(Of T) as though it were a sequence of type IEnumerable(Of T). If you are trying to treat an IQueryable(Of T) sequence like an IEnumerable(Of T) sequence and you are having trouble, don't forget the AsEnumerable operator.

LINQ to SQL Queries Are Performed on Table(Of T) Objects

While most normal LINQ queries are performed on arrays or collections that implement the IEnumerable(Of T) or IEnumerable interfaces, a LINQ to SQL query is performed on classes that implement the IQueryable(Of T) interface, such as the Table(Of T) class.

This means that LINQ to SQL queries have additional query operators available, as well as the Standard Query Operators, since IQueryable(Of T) implements IEnumerable(Of T).

LINQ to SQL Queries Are Translated to SQL

As I discussed in Chapter 2, because LINQ to SQL queries return sequences of type IQueryable(Of T), they are not compiled into .NET intermediate language code the way that normal LINQ queries are. Instead, they are converted into expression trees, which allows them to be evaluated as a single unit, and translated to appropriate and optimal SQL statements. Please read the section titled "SQL Translation" at the end of this chapter to learn more about the SQL translation that takes place with LINQ to SQL queries.

LINQ to SQL Queries Are Executed in the Database

Unlike normal LINQ queries which are executed in local machine memory, LINQ to SQL queries are translated to SQL calls and actually executed in the database. There are ramifications because of this, such as the way projections are handled, which cannot actually occur in the database since the database knows nothing about your entity classes, or any other classes for that matter.

Also, since the query actually executes in the database, and the database doesn't have access to your application code, what you can do in a query must be translated and is therefore limited in some ways based on the translator's capabilities. You can't just embed a call to a method you wrote in a lambda expression and expect SQL Server to know what to do with the call. Because of this, it is good to know what can be translated, what it will be translated to, and what happens when it cannot be translated.

Associations

Querying for an associated entity object in LINQ to SQL is as simple as accessing a property of an entity object. This is because an entity object contains a property providing a reference to the associated entity object, or it contains a property that provides a reference to a collection of associated entity objects.

If the associated entity object is the *many* (child) side of a one-to-many relationship, the associated *many* entity object will be stored in a collection of associated *many* entity objects, where the type of the collection is EntitySet(Of T), and T is the type of the *many* entity class. This collection can be accessed with a property of the *one* entity object.

If the associated entity object is the *one* (parent) side of a one-to-many relationship, a reference to the *one* entity object will be provided by a property of type EntityRef(Of T), where T is the type of the *one* entity class. This reference to the *one* entity object will be a property of the *many* entity object.

For example, consider the case of the Customer and Order entity classes that were generated for the Northwind database. A customer may have many orders, but an order can have but one customer. In this example, the Customer class is the *one* side of the one-to-many relationship between the Customer and Order entity classes. The Order class is the *many* side of the one-to-many relationship. Therefore, a Customer object's orders can be referenced by a property, typically named Orders, of type EntitySet(Of Order) in the Customer class. An Order object's customer can be referenced with a property, typically named Customer, of type EntityRef(Of Customer) in the Order class (see Figure 14-1).

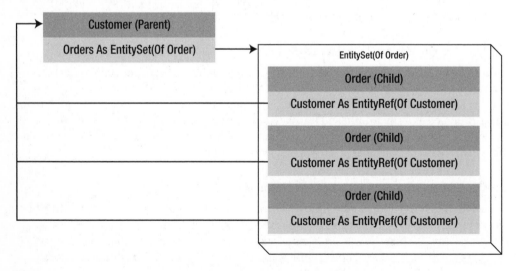

Figure 14-1. *A parent and child entity class association relationship*

If you have a difficult time remembering which end of the relationship is stored in which variable type, just remember that a child has one parent, so therefore it is stored in a single *reference*. So, the child stores the associated parent in a variable of type EntityRef(Of T). Since a parent can have many children, it needs to store the references to the children in a *collection*. So, the parent stores the references to the children in a variable of type EntitySet(Of T).

Classes are associated by specifying the Association attribute on the class property that contains the reference to the associated class in the entity class definition. Since both the parent and child have a class property referencing the other, the Association attribute is specified in both the parent and child entity classes. I will discuss the Association attribute in depth in Chapter 15.

Listing 14-7 is an example where I query for certain customers and display the retrieved customers and each of their orders.

Listing 14-7. *Using an Association to Access Related Data*

```
Dim db As New Northwind("Data Source=.\SQLEXPRESS;Initial Catalog=Northwind;" & _
  "Integrated Security=SSPI;")

Dim custs As IQueryable(Of Customer) = _
  From c In db.Customers _
  Where c.Country = "UK" AndAlso c.City = "London" _
  Order By c.CustomerID _
  Select c

For Each cust As Customer In custs
  Console.WriteLine("{0} - {1}", cust.CompanyName, cust.ContactName)
  For Each order As Order In cust.Orders
    Console.WriteLine("    {0} {1}", order.OrderID, order.OrderDate)
  Next order
Next cust
```

As you can see, I enumerate through each customer, display the customer, enumerate through each customer's orders, and display them. I never even specified that I wanted orders in the query. Here are the truncated results for Listing 14-7.

```
Around the Horn - Thomas Hardy
    10355 11/15/1996 12:00:00 AM
    10383 12/16/1996 12:00:00 AM
    10453 2/21/1997 12:00:00 AM
    10558 6/4/1997 12:00:00 AM
    10707 10/16/1997 12:00:00 AM
    10741 11/14/1997 12:00:00 AM
    10743 11/17/1997 12:00:00 AM
    10768 12/8/1997 12:00:00 AM
    10793 12/24/1997 12:00:00 AM
    10864 2/2/1998 12:00:00 AM
    10920 3/3/1998 12:00:00 AM
    10953 3/16/1998 12:00:00 AM
    11016 4/10/1998 12:00:00 AM
...
Consolidated Holdings - Elizabeth Brown
```

```
10435 2/4/1997 12:00:00 AM
10462 3/3/1997 12:00:00 AM
10848 1/23/1998 12:00:00 AM
```
...

You may be thinking that is pretty cool. The orders are there, yet I never even explicitly queried for them. At this point, you might be thinking, isn't this terribly inefficient if I never access the customer's orders?

The answer is no. The reason is that the orders were not actually retrieved until they were referenced. Had the code not accessed the Orders property of the customer, they would have never been retrieved. This is known as *deferred loading*, which should not be confused with deferred query execution, which I have already discussed.

Deferred Loading

Deferred loading is the term used to describe the type of loading in which records are not actually loaded from the database until absolutely necessary, which is when they are first referenced; hence, the loading of the records is deferred.

In Listing 14-7, had I not referenced the Orders member variable, the orders would never have been retrieved from the database. That's pretty slick. For most situations, deferred loading is a good thing. It prevents needless queries from occurring and unnecessary data from eating up network bandwidth.

However, a problem can occur. Listing 14-8 is the same as Listing 14-7 except I have turned on the logging feature provided by the DataContext.Log object to reveal the problem.

Listing 14-8. *An Example Demonstrating Deferred Loading*

```
Dim db As New Northwind("Data Source=.\SQLEXPRESS;Initial Catalog=Northwind;" & _
  "Integrated Security=SSPI;")

Dim custs As IQueryable(Of Customer) = _
  From c In db.Customers _
  Where c.Country = "UK" AndAlso c.City = "London" _
  Order By c.CustomerID _
  Select c

'  Turn on the logging.
db.Log = Console.Out

For Each cust As Customer In custs
  Console.WriteLine("{0} - {1}", cust.CompanyName, cust.ContactName)
  For Each order As Order In cust.Orders
    Console.WriteLine("    {0} {1}", order.OrderID, order.OrderDate)
  Next order
Next cust
```

I will run the example by pressing Ctrl+F5. I am going to severely truncate the output.

```
SELECT [t0].[CustomerID], [t0].[CompanyName], [t0].[ContactName],
[t0].[ContactTitle], [t0].[Address], [t0].[City], [t0]
[Region], [t0].[PostalCode], [t0].[Country], [t0].[Phone], [t0].[Fax]
FROM [dbo].[Customers] AS [t0]
WHERE ([t0].[Country] = @p0) AND ([t0].[City] = @p1)
ORDER BY [t0].[CustomerID]
-- @p0: Input NVarChar (Size = 2; Prec = 0; Scale = 0) [UK]
-- @p1: Input NVarChar (Size = 6; Prec = 0; Scale = 0) [London]
-- Context: SqlProvider(Sql2008) Model: AttributedMetaModel Build: 3.5.30729.1
```

Around the Horn - Thomas Hardy
```
SELECT [t0].[OrderID], [t0].[CustomerID], [t0].[EmployeeID], [t0].[OrderDate],
[t0].[RequiredDate], [t0].[ShippedDate],
[t0].[ShipVia], [t0].[Freight], [t0].[ShipName], [t0].[ShipAddress],
[t0].[ShipCity], [t0].[ShipRegion], [t0].[ShipPosta
lCode], [t0].[ShipCountry]
FROM [dbo].[Orders] AS [t0]
WHERE [t0].[CustomerID] = @p0
-- @p0: Input NVarChar (Size = 5; Prec = 0; Scale = 0) [AROUT]
-- Context: SqlProvider(Sql2008) Model: AttributedMetaModel Build: 3.5.30729.1
```

```
    10355 11/15/1996 12:00:00 AM
    10383 12/16/1996 12:00:00 AM
    10453 2/21/1997 12:00:00 AM
    10558 6/4/1997 12:00:00 AM
    10707 10/16/1997 12:00:00 AM
    10741 11/14/1997 12:00:00 AM
    10743 11/17/1997 12:00:00 AM
    10768 12/8/1997 12:00:00 AM
    10793 12/24/1997 12:00:00 AM
    10864 2/2/1998 12:00:00 AM
    10920 3/3/1998 12:00:00 AM
    10953 3/16/1998 12:00:00 AM
    11016 4/10/1998 12:00:00 AM
```
B's Beverages - Victoria Ashworth
```
SELECT [t0].[OrderID], [t0].[CustomerID], [t0].[EmployeeID], [t0].[OrderDate],
[t0].[RequiredDate], [t0].[ShippedDate],
[t0].[ShipVia], [t0].[Freight], [t0].[ShipName], [t0].[ShipAddress],
[t0].[ShipCity], [t0].[ShipRegion], [t0].[ShipPosta
lCode], [t0].[ShipCountry]
FROM [dbo].[Orders] AS [t0]
WHERE [t0].[CustomerID] = @p0
-- @p0: Input NVarChar (Size = 5; Prec = 0; Scale = 0) [BSBEV]
-- Context: SqlProvider(Sql2008) Model: AttributedMetaModel Build: 3.5.30729.1
```

```
    10289 8/26/1996 12:00:00 AM
    10471 3/11/1997 12:00:00 AM
```

```
     10484 3/24/1997 12:00:00 AM
     10538 5/15/1997 12:00:00 AM
     10539 5/16/1997 12:00:00 AM
     10578 6/24/1997 12:00:00 AM
     10599 7/15/1997 12:00:00 AM
     10943 3/11/1998 12:00:00 AM
     10947 3/13/1998 12:00:00 AM
     11023 4/14/1998 12:00:00 AM
Consolidated Holdings - Elizabeth Brown
...
```

I have marked the SQL queries in bold to make them stand out from the customer and order output data. In the first SQL query, you can see that a query is created to query the customers, and you can see that nothing in the query is querying the Orders table. Then you can see that the company name and contact name for the first company are displayed, and then another SQL query is output. In that second SQL query, you can see that the Orders table is queried with a specific customer's CustomerID in the Where clause. So, a query is generated and executed just for the specific customer that I just displayed to the console. Next, you will see a list of orders displayed for that previously listed customer, followed by the next customer. Next, another SQL query appears for a specific customer's orders.

As you can see, a separate query is performed to retrieve each customer's orders. The orders are not queried, and therefore not loaded, until the Orders EntityRef(Of T) variable is referenced in the second For Each loop, which is immediately after the customer information is displayed to the console. Because the orders are not retrieved until they are referenced, their loading is deferred.

Since a separate query is generated and performed for each customer, potentially, a lot of SQL queries will be going back and forth to the database. This could be a performance problem.

Because I wrote the code, I know that I am going to access the orders for the customers I retrieve. In this case, it may provide better performance if I *could* retrieve the orders when I retrieve the customers. What I need is *immediate loading*.

Immediate Loading with the DataLoadOptions Class

While deferred loading is the default behavior for associated classes, we do have the ability to perform immediate loading. Immediate loading causes associated classes to be loaded prior to being referenced. This may provide performance benefits. We can use the DataLoadOptions class's LoadWith(Of T) operator to instruct the DataContext to immediately load the associated class specified in the LoadWith(Of T) operator's lambda expression. By using the LoadWith(Of T) operator, when the query is actually executed, not only will the primary class be retrieved, so will the specified associated class.

In Listing 14-9, I will use the same basic example code as in Listing 14-8 except I will instantiate a DataLoadOptions object, call the LoadWith(Of T) operator on that DataLoadOptions object, passing the Orders member as a class to immediately load when a Customer object is loaded, and assign the DataLoadOptions object to the Northwind DataContext. Also, to eliminate any doubt that the associated classes, the orders, are being loaded prior to being referenced, I will omit the code that enumerates through the customer's orders, so there will be no reference to them.

Listing 14-9. *An Example Demonstrating Immediate Loading Using the DataLoadOptions Class*

```
Dim db As New Northwind("Data Source=.\SQLEXPRESS;Initial Catalog=Northwind;" & _
  "Integrated Security=SSPI;")

Dim dlo As New DataLoadOptions()
dlo.LoadWith(Of Customer)(Function(c) c.Orders)
db.LoadOptions = dlo

Dim custs As IQueryable(Of Customer) = ( _
  From c In db.Customers _
  Where c.Country = "UK" AndAlso c.City = "London" _
  Order By c.CustomerID _
  Select c)

' Turn on the logging.
db.Log = Console.Out

For Each cust As Customer In custs
  Console.WriteLine("{0} - {1}", cust.CompanyName, cust.ContactName)
Next cust
```

Again, the only differences between this listing and Listing 14-8 are the instantiation of the DataLoadOptions object, the call to the LoadWith(Of T) operator, the assignment of the DataLoadOptions object to the Northwind DataContext, and the removal of any reference to each customer's orders. In the call to the LoadWith(Of T) operator, I instruct the DataLoadOptions to immediately load Orders whenever a Customer object is loaded. Now, let's take a look at the output of Listing 14-9.

```
SELECT [t0].[CustomerID], [t0].[CompanyName], [t0].[ContactName],
[t0].[ContactTitle], [t0].[Address], [t0].[City], [t0][Region], [t0].[PostalCode],
[t0].[Country], [t0].[Phone], [t0].[Fax], [t1].[OrderID],
[t1].[CustomerID] AS [CustomerID2], [t1].[EmployeeID], [t1].[OrderDate],
[t1].[RequiredDate], [t1].[ShippedDate], [t1].[ShipVia], [t1].[Freight],
[t1].[ShipName], [t1].[ShipAddress], [t1].[ShipCity], [t1].[ShipRegion],
[t1].[ShipPostalCode], [t1].[ShipCountry], (
    SELECT COUNT(*)
    FROM [dbo].[Orders] AS [t2]
    WHERE [t2].[CustomerID] = [t0].[CustomerID]
    ) AS [value]
FROM [dbo].[Customers] AS [t0]
LEFT OUTER JOIN [dbo].[Orders] AS [t1] ON [t1].[CustomerID] = [t0].[CustomerID]
WHERE ([t0].[Country] = @p0) AND ([t0].[City] = @p1)
ORDER BY [t0].[CustomerID], [t1].[OrderID]
-- @p0: Input NVarChar (Size = 2; Prec = 0; Scale = 0) [UK]
-- @p1: Input NVarChar (Size = 6; Prec = 0; Scale = 0) [London]
-- Context: SqlProvider(Sql2008) Model: AttributedMetaModel Build: 3.5.30729.1
```

Around the Horn - Thomas Hardy
B's Beverages - Victoria Ashworth
Consolidated Holdings - Elizabeth Brown
Eastern Connection - Ann Devon
North/South - Simon Crowther
Seven Seas Imports - Hari Kumar

Just like in the output of Listing 14-8, in the output for Listing 14-9, I have marked the SQL queries with bold type. I am really not interested in the output of the customers; I want to see the SQL queries that were executed.

As you can see, a single SQL query was executed to retrieve all the customers matching my query's Where clause. You can also see that, despite the fact that I never even referenced a customer's orders, the single SQL query joined each customer retrieved with that customer's orders. Since the orders were loaded prior to being referenced, their loading was not deferred and therefore is considered to be immediate. Instead of having a number of SQL queries equal to one (for the customers), plus the number of customers (for each customer's orders), there is a single SQL query. If there are a lot of customers, this can make a huge difference.

Using the DataLoadOptions class, you are not limited to the immediate loading of a single associated class or a single hierarchical level of class. However, immediately loading more than one associated class does affect the way immediate loading works.

When Immediate Loading Is Not So Immediate

When classes are not loaded until they are referenced, their loading is said to be deferred. If they are loaded prior to being referenced, their loading is said to be immediate. However, sometimes, immediate is not as immediate as other times.

With the code in Listing 14-9, we saw that, by specifying an associated class as the argument to the DataLoadOptions class's LoadWith(Of T) method, we could get immediate loading to cause the orders to be loaded along with the customers. Not only is this not deferred, since it was prior to them being referenced, it was indeed immediate. If we call the LoadWith(Of T) method multiple times to have multiple classes loaded immediately, only one of the classes will be joined with the original entity class, and the others will be loaded upon referencing that original entity class. When this happens, since the associated classes not joined with the original entity class are still loaded prior to being referenced, they are still considered immediately loaded, but a separate query is still made for them as you reference each original entity class. In this way, while their loading is still considered to be immediate, it feels less immediate than when they are joined.

The decision as to which associated classes should be joined vs. which should just be loaded prior to being referenced is made by LINQ to SQL. It is an optimized decision based on general principles applied to your entity class model, though; it is not an optimization made by the database. It will join the association lowest in the hierarchy of the immediately loaded classes. This will be more easily understood when I get to the section about immediately loading a hierarchy of associated classes.

To better understand this behavior, I will discuss this for each approach where more than one association is immediately loaded. The two approaches are loading multiple associated classes of the original entity class and loading a hierarchy of associated classes.

Immediate Loading of Multiple Associated Classes

With the DataLoadOptions class, it is possible to instruct it to immediately load multiple associated classes of an entity class.

Notice that in Listing 14-9, the generated SQL query made no reference to the customer's associated customer demographics. Had I referenced the customer demographics on the retrieved customers, additional SQL statements would have been executed for each customer whose customer demographics were referenced.

In Listing 14-10, I will instruct the DataLoadOptions to immediately load the customer's customer demographics as well as its orders.

Listing 14-10. *Immediately Loading Multiple EntitySets*

```
Dim db As New Northwind("Data Source=.\SQLEXPRESS;Initial Catalog=Northwind;" & _
  "Integrated Security=SSPI;")

Dim dlo As New DataLoadOptions()
dlo.LoadWith(Of Customer)(Function(c) c.Orders)
dlo.LoadWith(Of Customer)(Function(c) c.CustomerCustomerDemos)
db.LoadOptions = dlo

Dim custs As IQueryable(Of Customer) = ( _
  From c In db.Customers _
  Where c.Country = "UK" AndAlso c.City = "London" _
  Order By c.CustomerID _
  Select c)

'  Turn on the logging.
db.Log = Console.Out

For Each cust As Customer In custs
  Console.WriteLine("{0} - {1}", cust.CompanyName, cust.ContactName)
Next cust
```

In Listing 14-10, I am not only specifying to immediately load the orders but to immediately load the customer's customer demographics as well. Notice that nowhere am I actually referencing either. So, any loading of these associated classes is immediate as opposed to deferred. I am really not interested in the returned data so much as the executed SQL statements. Let's examine the output of Listing 14-10.

```
SELECT [t0].[CustomerID], [t0].[CompanyName], [t0].[ContactName],
[t0].[ContactTitle], [t0].[Address], [t0].[City], [t0] [Region], [t0].[PostalCode],
[t0].[Country], [t0].[Phone], [t0].[Fax],[t1].[CustomerID] AS [CustomerID2],
[t1].[CustomerTypeID], (
    SELECT COUNT(*)
    FROM [dbo].[CustomerCustomerDemo] AS [t2]
    WHERE [t2].[CustomerID] = [t0].[CustomerID]
    ) AS [value]
FROM [dbo].[Customers] AS [t0]
```

```
LEFT OUTER JOIN [dbo].[CustomerCustomerDemo] AS [t1] ON [t1].[CustomerID] =
[to].[CustomerID]
WHERE ([to].[Country] = @p0) AND ([to].[City] = @p1)
ORDER BY [to].[CustomerID], [t1].[CustomerTypeID]
-- @p0: Input NVarChar (Size = 2; Prec = 0; Scale = 0) [UK]
-- @p1: Input NVarChar (Size = 6; Prec = 0; Scale = 0) [London]
-- Context: SqlProvider(Sql2008) Model: AttributedMetaModel Build: 3.5.30729.1

SELECT [to].[OrderID], [to].[CustomerID], [to].[EmployeeID], [to].[OrderDate],
[to].[RequiredDate], [to].[ShippedDate],
[to].[ShipVia], [to].[Freight], [to].[ShipName], [to].[ShipAddress],
[to].[ShipCity], [to].[ShipRegion], [to].[ShipPostalCode], [to].[ShipCountry]
FROM [dbo].[Orders] AS [to]
WHERE [to].[CustomerID] = @x1
-- @x1: Input NChar (Size = 5; Prec = 0; Scale = 0) [AROUT]
-- Context: SqlProvider(Sql2008) Model: AttributedMetaModel Build: 3.5.30729.1

Around the Horn - Thomas Hardy
SELECT [to].[OrderID], [to].[CustomerID], [to].[EmployeeID], [to].[OrderDate],
[to].[RequiredDate], [to].[ShippedDate],[to].[ShipVia], [to].[Freight],
[to].[ShipName], [to].[ShipAddress], [to].[ShipCity], [to].[ShipRegion],
[to].[ShipPostalCode], [to].[ShipCountry]
FROM [dbo].[Orders] AS [to]
WHERE [to].[CustomerID] = @x1
-- @x1: Input NChar (Size = 5; Prec = 0; Scale = 0) [BSBEV]
-- Context: SqlProvider(Sql2008) Model: AttributedMetaModel Build: 3.5.30729.1

B's Beverages - Victoria Ashworth
...
```

As you can see in the SQL queries that were generated, the customer demographics were joined with the customers when they were queried, but a separate SQL query was generated to load each customer's orders. That separate query for orders was performed when each customer was actually referenced, which is in the For Each statement. Notice that in the output, the query for the orders of a customer is output *before* the customer information is displayed to the console.

Since neither the customer demographics nor the orders are referenced in the code, other than when calling the LoadWith(Of T) method, since they were in fact loaded, the loading is not deferred and is therefore immediate. However, it certainly feels like the customer demographics are a little more immediate than the orders.

Immediate Loading of Hierarchical Associated Classes

In the previous section, I discussed how to cause multiple associated entity classes to be immediately loaded. In this section, I will discuss how to cause a hierarchy of associated entity classes to be immediately loaded. To demonstrate this, in Listing 14-11, I will make the query not only immediately load the orders but each order's order details.

Listing 14-11. *Immediate Loading of a Hierarchy of Entity Classes*

```
Dim db As New Northwind("Data Source=.\SQLEXPRESS;Initial Catalog=Northwind;" & _
  "Integrated Security=SSPI;")

Dim dlo As New DataLoadOptions()
dlo.LoadWith(Of Customer)(Function(c) c.Orders)
dlo.LoadWith(Of Order)(Function(o) o.OrderDetails)
db.LoadOptions = dlo

Dim custs As IQueryable(Of Customer) = ( _
  From c In db.Customers _
  Where c.Country = "UK" AndAlso c.City = "London" _
  Order By c.CustomerID _
  Select c)

' Turn on the logging.
db.Log = Console.Out

For Each cust As Customer In custs
  Console.WriteLine("{0} - {1}", cust.CompanyName, cust.ContactName)
  For Each order As Order In cust.Orders
    Console.WriteLine("    {0} {1}", order.OrderID, order.OrderDate)
  Next order
Next cust
```

Notice that, in Listing 14-11, I am immediately loading the customer's orders, and for each order, I am immediately loading its order details. Here is the output for Listing 14-11.

```
SELECT [t0].[CustomerID], [t0].[CompanyName], [t0].[ContactName],
[t0].[ContactTitle], [t0].[Address], [t0].[City], [t0]
[Region], [t0].[PostalCode], [t0].[Country], [t0].[Phone], [t0].[Fax]
FROM [dbo].[Customers] AS [t0]
WHERE ([t0].[Country] = @p0) AND ([t0].[City] = @p1)
ORDER BY [t0].[CustomerID]
-- @p0: Input NVarChar (Size = 2; Prec = 0; Scale = 0) [UK]
-- @p1: Input NVarChar (Size = 6; Prec = 0; Scale = 0) [London]
-- Context: SqlProvider(Sql2008) Model: AttributedMetaModel Build: 3.5.30729.1

SELECT [t0].[OrderID], [t0].[CustomerID], [t0].[EmployeeID], [t0].[OrderDate],
[t0].[RequiredDate], [t0].[ShippedDate],
[t0].[ShipVia], [t0].[Freight], [t0].[ShipName], [t0].[ShipAddress],
[t0].[ShipCity], [t0].[ShipRegion], [t0].[ShipPosta
lCode], [t0].[ShipCountry], [t1].[OrderID] AS [OrderID2], [t1].[ProductID],
[t1].[UnitPrice], [t1].[Quantity], [t1].[Discount], (
    SELECT COUNT(*)
    FROM [dbo].[Order Details] AS [t2]
    WHERE [t2].[OrderID] = [t0].[OrderID]
```

```
      ) AS [value]
FROM [dbo].[Orders] AS [t0]
LEFT OUTER JOIN [dbo].[Order Details] AS [t1] ON [t1].[OrderID] = [t0].[OrderID]
WHERE [t0].[CustomerID] = @x1
ORDER BY [t0].[OrderID], [t1].[ProductID]
-- @x1: Input NChar (Size = 5; Prec = 0; Scale = 0) [AROUT]
-- Context: SqlProvider(Sql2008) Model: AttributedMetaModel Build: 3.5.30729.1


Around the Horn - Thomas Hardy
      10355 11/15/1996 12:00:00 AM
      10383 12/16/1996 12:00:00 AM
      10453 2/21/1997 12:00:00 AM
      10558 6/4/1997 12:00:00 AM
      10707 10/16/1997 12:00:00 AM
      10741 11/14/1997 12:00:00 AM
      10743 11/17/1997 12:00:00 AM
      10768 12/8/1997 12:00:00 AM
      10793 12/24/1997 12:00:00 AM
      10864 2/2/1998 12:00:00 AM
      10920 3/3/1998 12:00:00 AM
      10953 3/16/1998 12:00:00 AM
      11016 4/10/1998 12:00:00 AM
SELECT [t0].[OrderID], [t0].[CustomerID], [t0].[EmployeeID], [t0].[OrderDate],
[t0].[RequiredDate], [t0].[ShippedDate],
[t0].[ShipVia], [t0].[Freight], [t0].[ShipName], [t0].[ShipAddress],
[t0].[ShipCity], [t0].[ShipRegion], [t0].[ShipPosta
lCode], [t0].[ShipCountry], [t1].[OrderID] AS [OrderID2], [t1].[ProductID],
[t1].[UnitPrice], [t1].[Quantity], [t1].[Discount], (
      SELECT COUNT(*)
      FROM [dbo].[Order Details] AS [t2]
      WHERE [t2].[OrderID] = [t0].[OrderID]
      ) AS [value]
FROM [dbo].[Orders] AS [t0]
LEFT OUTER JOIN [dbo].[Order Details] AS [t1] ON [t1].[OrderID] = [t0].[OrderID]
WHERE [t0].[CustomerID] = @x1
ORDER BY [t0].[OrderID], [t1].[ProductID]
-- @x1: Input NChar (Size = 5; Prec = 0; Scale = 0) [BSBEV]
-- Context: SqlProvider(Sql2008) Model: AttributedMetaModel Build: 3.5.30729.1


B's Beverages - Victoria Ashworth
...
```

Again, I am not interested in the retrieved data, merely the executed SQL statements. Notice that this time, the query for the customers joined neither the orders nor the order details. Instead, as each customer was referenced, an additional SQL query was made that joined the orders and order details. Since neither was referenced, they were still loaded prior to being referenced and are still considered to be immediately loaded.

From this example, you can see that LINQ to SQL does perform the single join for the association at the lowest level in the hierarchy of the immediately loaded files, as I previously mentioned.

Filtering and Ordering

While I am discussing the DataLoadOptions class, I want you to be aware of its AssociateWith method, which can be used to both filter associated child objects and order them.

In Listing 14-8, I retrieve some customers and enumerate through them displaying the customer and its orders. You can see in the results that the orders' dates are in ascending order. To demonstrate how the AssociateWith method can be used to both filter associated classes and order them, in Listing 14-12 I will do both.

Listing 14-12. *Using the DataLoadOptions Class to Filter and Order*

```
Dim db As New Northwind("Data Source=.\SQLEXPRESS;Initial Catalog=Northwind;" & _
  "Integrated Security=SSPI;")

Dim dlo As New DataLoadOptions()
dlo.AssociateWith(Of Customer)(Function(c) _
  From o In c.Orders _
  Where o.OrderID < 10700 _
  Order By o.OrderDate Descending)
db.LoadOptions = dlo

Dim custs As IQueryable(Of Customer) = _
  From c In db.Customers _
  Where c.Country = "UK" AndAlso c.City = "London" _
  Order By c.CustomerID _
  Select c

For Each cust As Customer In custs
  Console.WriteLine("{0} - {1}", cust.CompanyName, cust.ContactName)
  For Each order As Order In cust.Orders
    Console.WriteLine("   {0} {1}", order.OrderID, order.OrderDate)
  Next order
Next cust
```

Notice that in Listing 14-12, I embed a query for the lambda expression passed to the AssociateWith method. In that query, I filter out all records where the OrderID is not less than 10700, and I sort the orders by OrderDate in descending order. Let's examine the results of Listing 14-12.

```
Around the Horn - Thomas Hardy
    10558 6/4/1997 12:00:00 AM
    10453 2/21/1997 12:00:00 AM
    10383 12/16/1996 12:00:00 AM
    10355 11/15/1996 12:00:00 AM
```

```
B's Beverages - Victoria Ashworth
    10599 7/15/1997 12:00:00 AM
    10578 6/24/1997 12:00:00 AM
    10539 5/16/1997 12:00:00 AM
    10538 5/15/1997 12:00:00 AM
    10484 3/24/1997 12:00:00 AM
    10471 3/11/1997 12:00:00 AM
    10289 8/26/1996 12:00:00 AM
Consolidated Holdings - Elizabeth Brown
    10462 3/3/1997 12:00:00 AM
    10435 2/4/1997 12:00:00 AM
Eastern Connection - Ann Devon
    10532 5/9/1997 12:00:00 AM
    10400 1/1/1997 12:00:00 AM
    10364 11/26/1996 12:00:00 AM
North/South - Simon Crowther
    10517 4/24/1997 12:00:00 AM
Seven Seas Imports - Hari Kumar
    10547 5/23/1997 12:00:00 AM
    10523 5/1/1997 12:00:00 AM
    10472 3/12/1997 12:00:00 AM
    10388 12/19/1996 12:00:00 AM
    10377 12/9/1996 12:00:00 AM
    10359 11/21/1996 12:00:00 AM
```

As you can see in the preceding results, only the orders whose OrderID is less than 10700 are returned, and they are returned in descending order by date.

Coincidental Joins

One of the benefits of associations is that they are, in effect, performing joins for us automatically. When we query customers from the Northwind database, each customer has a collection of orders that is accessible via the Customer object's Orders property. So, retrieving orders for customers is automatic. Normally, you would have to perform a join to get that type of behavior. The reverse is also true. When we retrieve orders, the Order class has a Customer property that references the appropriate customer.

While we have this automatic join happening, it is, as the late painter Bob Ross would say, merely a happy little accident. The join happens because when we have an object, say a child object, that has a relationship to another object, say a parent object, we *expect* to be able to access it via a reference in the initial, child object.

For example, when working with XML, when we have a reference to a node, we expect to be able to obtain a reference to its parent by the child node having a member variable that references the parent. We don't expect to have to perform a query on the entire XML structure and provide the child node as a search key. Also, when we have a reference to a node, we expect to be able to access its children with a reference on the node itself as well.

So, while the automatic join is certainly convenient, the implementation has more to do with the nature of object relationships, and our expectations of how they *should* behave, than an intentional effort to make joins happen automatically. In this way, the joins are really coincidental.

Joins

I just discussed the fact that many relationships in the database are specified to be associations, and that we can access the associated objects by simply accessing a class member. However, only those relationships that are defined using foreign keys will get mapped this way. Since every type of relationship is not defined using foreign keys, you will sometimes need to explicitly join tables.

Inner Joins

We can perform an inner equijoin by using the `Join` operator. As is typical with an inner join, any records in the outer results set will be omitted if a matching record does not exist in the inner results set. Listing 14-13 contains an example.

Listing 14-13. *Performing an Inner Join*

```
Dim db As New Northwind("Data Source=.\SQLEXPRESS;Initial Catalog=Northwind;" & _
  "Integrated Security=SSPI;")

Dim entities = From s In db.Suppliers _
               Join c In db.Customers On s.City Equals c.City _
               Select New With _
               { _
                 .SupplierName = s.CompanyName, _
                 .CustomerName = c.CompanyName, _
                 .City = c.City _
               }

For Each e In entities
  Console.WriteLine("{0}: {1} - {2}", e.City, e.SupplierName, e.CustomerName)
Next e
```

In Listing 14-13, I performed an inner join on the suppliers and the customers. If a customer record doesn't exist with the same city as a supplier, the supplier record will be omitted from the results set. Here are the results of Listing 14-13.

```
London: Exotic Liquids - Around the Horn
London: Exotic Liquids - B's Beverages
London: Exotic Liquids - Consolidated Holdings
London: Exotic Liquids - Eastern Connection
London: Exotic Liquids - North/South
London: Exotic Liquids - Seven Seas Imports
Sao Paulo: Refrescos Americanas LTDA - Comércio Mineiro
Sao Paulo: Refrescos Americanas LTDA - Familia Arquibaldo
Sao Paulo: Refrescos Americanas LTDA - Queen Cozinha
Sao Paulo: Refrescos Americanas LTDA - Tradiçao Hipermercados
```

```
Berlin: Heli Süßwaren GmbH & Co. KG - Alfred Futterkiste
Paris: Aux joyeux ecclésiastiques - Paris spécialités
Paris: Aux joyeux ecclésiastiques - Spécialités du monde
Montréal: Ma Maison - Mère Paillarde
```

As you can see, despite the fact that some suppliers are in the output with multiple matching customers, some suppliers are not in the list at all. This is because there were no customers in the same city as the missing suppliers. If we need to still see the supplier regardless of whether there is a matching customer or not, we need to perform an outer join.

Outer Joins

In Chapter 4, I discussed the DefaultIfEmpty Standard Query Operator and mentioned that it can be used to perform outer joins. In Listing 14-14, I will use the Into clause to direct the matching Join results into a temporary sequence that I will subsequently call the DefaultIfEmpty operator on. This way, if the record is missing from the joined results, a default value will be provided. I will use the DataContext logging feature so we can see the generated SQL statement.

Listing 14-14. *Performing an Outer Join*

```
Dim db As New Northwind("Data Source=.\SQLEXPRESS;Initial Catalog=Northwind;" & _
  "Integrated Security=SSPI;")

db.Log = Console.Out

Dim entities = From s In db.Suppliers _
            Group Join c In db.Customers On s.City Equals c.City _
            Into temp = Group _
            From t In temp.DefaultIfEmpty() _
            Select New With _
            { _
              .SupplierName = s.CompanyName, _
              .CustomerName = t.CompanyName, _
              .City = s.City _
            }

For Each e In entities
  Console.WriteLine("{0}: {1} - {2}", e.City, e.SupplierName, e.CustomerName)
Next e
```

Notice that in the Join statement in Listing 14-14, I direct the join results into the temporary sequence named temp. That temporary sequence name can be whatever you want, as long as it doesn't conflict with any other name or keyword. Then I perform a subsequent query on the results of the temp sequence passed to the DefaultIfEmpty operator. Even though I haven't covered it yet, the DefaultIfEmpty operator called in Listing 14-14 is not the same operator that was discussed in Chapter 4. As I will explain shortly, LINQ to SQL queries are translated into SQL statements, and those SQL statements are executed by the database. SQL Server has no way to call the DefaultIfEmpty Standard Query Operator. Instead, that operator call will be translated into the appropriate SQL statement. This is why I wanted the DataContext logging to be enabled.

Also, notice that I access the city name from the Suppliers table instead of the temp collection. I did this because I know there will always be a record for the supplier, but for suppliers without a matching customer, there will be no city in the joined results in the temp collection. This is different than the previous example of the inner join where I obtained the city from the joined table. In that example, it didn't matter which of the tables I got the city from, because if a matching customer record didn't exist, there would be no record anyway since an inner join was performed.

Let's look at the results of Listing 14-14.

```
SELECT [t0].[CompanyName] AS [SupplierName], [t1].[CompanyName] AS [CustomerName],
[t0].[City]
FROM [dbo].[Suppliers] AS [t0]
LEFT OUTER JOIN [dbo].[Customers] AS [t1] ON [t0].[City] = [t1].[City]
-- Context: SqlProvider(Sql2008) Model: AttributedMetaModel Build: 3.5.30729.1


London: Exotic Liquids - Around the Horn
London: Exotic Liquids - B's Beverages
London: Exotic Liquids - Consolidated Holdings
London: Exotic Liquids - Eastern Connection
London: Exotic Liquids - North/South
London: Exotic Liquids - Seven Seas Imports
New Orleans: New Orleans Cajun Delights -
Ann Arbor: Grandma Kelly's Homestead -
Tokyo: Tokyo Traders -
Oviedo: Cooperativa de Quesos 'Las Cabras' -
Osaka: Mayumi's -
Melbourne: Pavlova, Ltd. -
Manchester: Specialty Biscuits, Ltd. -
Göteborg: PB Knäckebröd AB -
Sao Paulo: Refrescos Americanas LTDA - Comércio Mineiro
Sao Paulo: Refrescos Americanas LTDA - Familia Arquibaldo
Sao Paulo: Refrescos Americanas LTDA - Queen Cozinha
Sao Paulo: Refrescos Americanas LTDA - Tradiçao Hipermercados
Berlin: Heli Süßwaren GmbH & Co. KG - Alfreds Futterkiste
Frankfurt: Plutzer Lebensmittelgroßmärkte AG -
Cuxhaven: Nord-Ost-Fisch Handelsgesellschaft mbH -
Ravenna: Formaggi Fortini s.r.l. -
Sandvika: Norske Meierier -
Bend: Bigfoot Breweries -
Stockholm: Svensk Sjöföda AB -
Paris: Aux joyeux ecclésiastiques - Paris spécialités
Paris: Aux joyeux ecclésiastiques - Spécialités du monde
Boston: New England Seafood Cannery -
Singapore: Leka Trading -
```

```
Lyngby: Lyngbysild -
Zaandam: Zaanse Snoepfabriek -
Lappeenranta: Karkki Oy -
Sydney: G'day, Mate -
Montréal: Ma Maison - Mère Paillarde
Salerno: Pasta Buttini s.r.l. -
Montceau: Escargots Nouveaux -
Annecy: Gai pâturage -
Ste-Hyacinthe: Forêts d'érables -
```

As you can see in the output of Listing 14-14, I got at least one record for every supplier, and you can see that some suppliers do not have a matching customer, thereby proving the outer join was performed. But, if there is any doubt, you can see the actual generated SQL statement and that clearly is performing an outer join.

To Flatten or Not to Flatten

In the examples in Listing 14-13 and Listing 14-14, I projected my query results into a flat structure. By this, I mean an object was created from an anonymous class where each field requested is a member of that anonymous class. Contrast this with the fact that, instead of creating a single anonymous class containing each field I wanted, I could have created an anonymous class composed of a Supplier object and matching Customer object. In that case, there would be the topmost level of the anonymous class, and a lower level containing a Supplier object and either a Customer object or the default value provided by the DefaultIfEmpty operator, which would be Nothing.

If I take the flat approach, as I did in the two previous examples, because the projected output class is not an entity class, I will not be able to perform updates to the output objects by having the DataContext object manage persisting the changes to the database for me. This is fine for data that will not be changed. However, sometimes you may be planning on allowing updates to the retrieved data. In this case, using the nonflat approach would allow you to make changes to the retrieved objects and have the DataContext object manage the persistence. I will cover this in more depth in Chapter 16. For now, let's just take a look at Listing 14-15, which contains an example that isn't flat.

Listing 14-15. *Returning Nonflat Results so the DataContext Can Manage Persistence*

```
Dim db As New Northwind("Data Source=.\SQLEXPRESS;Initial Catalog=Northwind;" & _
  "Integrated Security=SSPI;")

Dim entities = _
  From s In db.Suppliers _
  Group Join c In db.Customers On s.City Equals c.City Into temp = Group _
  From t In temp.DefaultIfEmpty() _
  Select New With {Key s, Key t}

For Each e In entities
  Console.WriteLine( _
    "{0}: {1} - {2}", _
```

```
    e.s.City, e.s.CompanyName, _
  If(e.t IsNot Nothing, e.t.CompanyName, ""))
Next e
```

In Listing 14-15, instead of returning the query results into a flat anonymous object with a member for each desired field, I return the query results in an anonymous object composed of the Supplier and potentially Customer entity objects. Also notice that in the Console. WriteLine method call, I still have to be concerned that the temporary result can be a Nothing if no matching Customer object exists. Let's take a look at the results of Listing 14-15.

```
London: Exotic Liquids - Around the Horn
London: Exotic Liquids - B's Beverages
London: Exotic Liquids - Consolidated Holdings
London: Exotic Liquids - Eastern Connection
London: Exotic Liquids - North/South
London: Exotic Liquids - Seven Seas Imports
New Orleans: New Orleans Cajun Delights -
Ann Arbor: Grandma Kelly's Homestead -
Tokyo: Tokyo Traders -
Oviedo: Cooperativa de Quesos 'Las Cabras' -
Osaka: Mayumi's -
Melbourne: Pavlova, Ltd. -
Manchester: Specialty Biscuits, Ltd. -
Göteborg: PB Knäckebröd AB -
Sao Paulo: Refrescos Americanas LTDA - Comércio Mineiro
Sao Paulo: Refrescos Americanas LTDA - Familia Arquibaldo
Sao Paulo: Refrescos Americanas LTDA - Queen Cozinha
Sao Paulo: Refrescos Americanas LTDA - Tradiçao Hipermercados
Berlin: Heli Süßwaren GmbH & Co. KG - Alfreds Futterkiste
Frankfurt: Plutzer Lebensmittelgroßmärkte AG -
Cuxhaven: Nord-Ost-Fisch Handelsgesellschaft mbH -
Ravenna: Formaggi Fortini s.r.l. -
Sandvika: Norske Meierier -
Bend: Bigfoot Breweries -
Stockholm: Svensk Sjöföda AB -
Paris: Aux joyeux ecclésiastiques - Paris spécialités
Paris: Aux joyeux ecclésiastiques - Spécialités du monde
Boston: New England Seafood Cannery -
Singapore: Leka Trading -
Lyngby: Lyngbysild -
Zaandam: Zaanse Snoepfabriek -
Lappeenranta: Karkki Oy -
Sydney: G'day, Mate -
Montréal: Ma Maison - Mère Paillarde
Salerno: Pasta Buttini s.r.l. -
Montceau: Escargots Nouveaux -
Annecy: Gai pâturage -
Ste-Hyacinthe: Forêts d'érables -
```

In the output for Listing 14-15, you can see that some suppliers do not have customers in their cities. Unlike the sequence of anonymous objects returned by the query in Listing 14-14, the anonymous objects returned by the query in Listing 14-15 contain entity objects of type Supplier and Customer. Because these are entity objects, I can take advantage of the services provided by the DataContext to manage the changes to them, and their persistence to the database.

Deferred Query Execution

I know by now you have probably read my explanation of deferred query execution a dozen times. But, being neurotic, I am always paranoid that you may have skipped some pertinent part of a previous chapter. In this case, I am concerned you might have missed the explanation of deferred query execution.

Deferred query execution refers to the fact that a LINQ query of any type—be it a LINQ to SQL query, a LINQ to XML query, or a LINQ to Objects query—may not actually be executed at the time it is defined. Take the following query, for example:

```
Dim custs As IQueryable(Of Customer) = _
  From c In db.Customers _
  Where c.Country = "UK" _
  Select c
```

The database query is not actually performed when this statement is executed; it is merely defined and assigned to the variable custs. The query will not be performed until the custs sequence is enumerated. This has several repercussions.

Repercussions of Deferred Query Execution

One repercussion of deferred query execution is that your query can contain errors that will cause exceptions but only when the query is actually performed, not when defined. This can be very misleading when you step over the query in the debugger and all is well, but then, farther down in the code, an exception is thrown when enumerating the query sequence. Or, perhaps you call another operator on the query sequence that results in the query sequence being enumerated.

Another repercussion is that, since the SQL query is performed when the query sequence is enumerated, enumerating it multiple times results in the SQL query being performed multiple times. This could certainly hamper performance. The way to prevent this is by calling one of the Standard Query Operator conversion operators, ToArray(Of T), ToList(Of T), ToDictionary(Of T, K), or ToLookup(Of T, K), on a sequence. Each of these operators will convert the sequence on which it is called to a data structure of the type specified, which in effect, caches the results for you. You can then enumerate that new data structure repeatedly without causing the SQL query to be performed again and the results potentially changing.

Taking Advantage of Deferred Query Execution

One advantage of deferred query execution is that performance can be improved while at the same time allowing you to reuse previously defined queries. Since the query is executed every time the query sequence is enumerated, you can define it once and enumerate it over and over, whenever the situation warrants. And, if the code flow takes some path that doesn't need to actually examine the query results by enumerating them, performance is improved because the query is never actually executed.

Another of the benefits of deferred query execution is that, since the query isn't actually performed by merely defining it, we can append additional operators programmatically as needed. Imagine an application that allows the user to query customers. Also imagine that the user can filter the queried customers. Picture one of those filter-type interfaces that have a drop-down list for each column in the customer table. There is a drop-down list for the City column and another for the Country column. Each drop-down list has every city and country from all Customer records in the database. At the top of each drop-down list is an [ALL] option, which is the default for its respective database column. If the user hasn't changed the setting of either of those drop-down lists, no additional Where clause is appended to the query for the respective column. Listing 14-16 contains an example programmatically building a query for such an interface.

Listing 14-16. *Programmatically Building a Query*

```
Dim db As New Northwind("Data Source=.\SQLEXPRESS;Initial Catalog=Northwind;" & _
  "Integrated Security=SSPI;")

'  Turn on the logging.
db.Log = Console.Out

'  Pretend the values below are not hard-coded, but instead, obtained by accessing
'  a drop-down list's selected value.
Dim dropdownListCityValue As String = "Cowes"
Dim dropdownListCountryValue As String = "UK"

Dim custs As IQueryable(Of Customer) = ( _
  From c In db.Customers _
  Select c)

If (Not dropdownListCityValue.Equals("[ALL]")) Then
  custs = _
    From c In custs _
    Where c.City = dropdownListCityValue _
    Select c
End If

If (Not dropdownListCountryValue.Equals("[ALL]")) Then
  custs = _
    From c In custs _
    Where c.Country = dropdownListCountryValue _
    Select c
End If

For Each cust As Customer In custs
  Console.WriteLine("{0} - {1} - {2}", cust.CompanyName, cust.City, cust.Country)
Next cust
```

In Listing 14-16, I simulate obtaining the user-selected city and country from their drop-down lists, and only if they are not set to "[ALL]", I append an additional Where operator to the query. Because the query is not actually performed until the sequence is enumerated, I can programmatically build it, a portion at a time.

Let's take a look at the results of Listing 14-16.

```
SELECT [t0].[CustomerID], [t0].[CompanyName], [t0].[ContactName],
[t0].[ContactTitle], [t0].[Address], [t0].[City], [t0]
.[Region], [t0].[PostalCode], [t0].[Country], [t0].[Phone], [t0].[Fax]
FROM [dbo].[Customers] AS [t0]
WHERE ([t0].[Country] = @p0) AND ([t0].[City] = @p1)
-- @p0: Input NVarChar (Size = 2; Prec = 0; Scale = 0) [UK]
-- @p1: Input NVarChar (Size = 5; Prec = 0; Scale = 0) [Cowes]
-- Context: SqlProvider(Sql2008) Model: AttributedMetaModel Build: 3.5.30729.1

Island Trading - Cowes - UK
```

Notice that since I specified that the selected city was Cowes and the selected country was UK, I got the records for the customers in Cowes in the United Kingdom. Also notice that there is a single SQL statement that was performed. Because the query's execution is deferred until it is actually needed, I can continue to append to the query to further restrict it, or perhaps order it, without the expense of multiple SQL queries taking place.

You can see that both of the filter criteria, the city and country, do appear in the Where clause of the executed SQL statement.

For another test, in Listing 14-17, I'll change the value of the dropdownListCityValue variable to "[ALL]" and see what the executed SQL statement looks like then and what the results are. Since the default city of "[ALL]" is specified, the SQL query shouldn't even restrict the results set by the city.

Listing 14-17. *Programmatically Building Another Query*

```
Dim db As New Northwind("Data Source=.\SQLEXPRESS;Initial Catalog=Northwind;" & _
    "Integrated Security=SSPI;")

' Turn on the logging.
db.Log = Console.Out

' Pretend the values below are not hard-coded, but instead, obtained by accessing
' a drop-down list's selected value.
Dim dropdownListCityValue As String = "[ALL]"
Dim dropdownListCountryValue As String = "UK"

Dim custs As IQueryable(Of Customer) = ( _
  From c In db.Customers _
  Select c)
```

```
If (Not dropdownListCityValue.Equals("[ALL]")) Then
  custs = _
    From c In custs _
    Where c.City = dropdownListCityValue _
    Select c
End If

If (Not dropdownListCountryValue.Equals("[ALL]")) Then
  custs = _
    From c In custs _
    Where c.Country = dropdownListCountryValue _
    Select c
End If

For Each cust As Customer In custs
  Console.WriteLine("{0} - {1} - {2}", cust.CompanyName, cust.City, cust.Country)
Next cust
```

Let's examine the output of Listing 14-17.

```
SELECT [t0].[CustomerID], [t0].[CompanyName], [t0].[ContactName],
[t0].[ContactTitle], [t0].[Address], [t0].[City], [t0] [Region], [t0].[PostalCode],
[t0].[Country], [t0].[Phone], [t0].[Fax]
FROM [dbo].[Customers] AS [t0]
WHERE [t0].[Country] = @p0
-- @p0: Input NVarChar (Size = 2; Prec = 0; Scale = 0) [UK]
-- Context: SqlProvider(Sql2008) Model: AttributedMetaModel Build: 3.5.30729.1

Around the Horn - London - UK
B's Beverages - London - UK
Consolidated Holdings - London - UK
Eastern Connection - London - UK
Island Trading - Cowes - UK
North/South - London - UK
Seven Seas Imports - London - UK
```

You can see that the Where clause of the SQL statement no longer specifies the city, which is exactly what I wanted. You can also see in the output results that there are now customers from different cities in the United Kingdom.

Of course, you can always append a call to the ToArray(Of T), ToList(Of T), ToDictionary(Of T, K), or ToLookup(Of T, K) Standard Query Operators to force the query to execute when you want.

I hope you can see that deferred query execution can be your friend. I also hope by now that you can see the usefulness of the DataContext.Log.

The SQL IN Statement with the Contains Operator

One of the SQL query capabilities that early incarnations of LINQ to SQL lacked was the ability to perform a SQL IN statement, such as the one in the following SQL query:

A SQL Query with an IN Statement

```
SELECT *
FROM Customers
WHERE (City IN ('London', 'Madrid'))
```

To alleviate this problem, Microsoft added the Contains operator. This operator is used differently, though, than may be immediately obvious. To me, it seems to work backward of the way I would expect an implementation of the SQL IN statement to work. I would expect to be able to say some member of an entity class must be IN some set of values. Instead, it works in the opposite manner. Let's take a look at Listing 14-18 where I demonstrate the Contains operator.

Listing 14-18. *The Contains Operator*

```
Dim db As New Northwind("Data Source=.\SQLEXPRESS;Initial Catalog=Northwind;" & _
    "Integrated Security=SSPI;")

db.Log = Console.Out

Dim cities() As String = { "London", "Madrid" }

Dim custs As IQueryable(Of Customer) = _
    db.Customers.Where(Function(c) cities.Contains(c.City))

For Each cust As Customer In custs
    Console.WriteLine("{0} - {1}", cust.CustomerID, cust.City)
Next cust
```

As you can see in Listing 14-18, instead of writing the query so that the customer's city must be in some set of values, you write the query so that some set of values contains the customer's city. In the case of Listing 14-18, I create an array of cities named cities. In my query, I then call the Contains operator on the cities array and pass it the customer's city. If the cities array contains the customer's city, true will be returned to the Where operator and that will cause the Customer object to be included in the output sequence.

Let's take a look at the output of Listing 14-18.

```
SELECT [t0].[CustomerID], [t0].[CompanyName], [t0].[ContactName],
[t0].[ContactTitle], [t0].[Address], [t0].[City], [t0]
[Region], [t0].[PostalCode], [t0].[Country], [t0].[Phone], [t0].[Fax]
FROM [dbo].[Customers] AS [t0]
WHERE [t0].[City] IN (@p0, @p1)
-- @p0: Input NVarChar (Size = 6; Prec = 0; Scale = 0) [London]
```

```
-- @p1: Input NVarChar (Size = 6; Prec = 0; Scale = 0) [Madrid]
-- Context: SqlProvider(Sql2008) Model: AttributedMetaModel Build: 3.5.30729.1

AROUT - London
BOLID - Madrid
BSBEV - London
CONSH - London
EASTC - London
FISSA - Madrid
NORTS - London
ROMEY - Madrid
SEVES - London
```

Looking at the generated SQL statement, you can see that the Contains operator was translated into a SQL IN statement.

Updates

Making database updates with LINQ to SQL is as easy as changing properties on an object, calling the DataContext object's SubmitChanges method, and handling any concurrency conflicts that may occur. Don't let the concurrency conflict handling intimidate you; there are several options for handling conflicts, and none of them are too painful. I will cover detecting and handling conflicts in detail in Chapter 17.

Of course, this simplicity is only true if you have properly written entity classes that are mapped to the database properly and maintain graph consistency. For more information about mapping the entity classes to the database, read the section titled "Entity Class Attributes and Attribute Properties" in Chapter 15. For more information about graph consistency, read the section titled "Graph Consistency" in that same chapter. However, SqlMetal and the Object Relational Designer handle all of the necessary plumbing to make all this just happen.

For a simple example of making an update to the database, you merely need to look at the first example in Chapter 12, Listing 12-1.

Updating Associated Classes

By design, LINQ to SQL allows you to update either side of associated classes to remove the relationship between them. You could update a parent object's reference to one of its children, or you could update that child's reference to the parent. Obviously, the references at each end of that relationship must be updated, but *you* only need to update one side or the other.

It is not LINQ to SQL that keeps your object model's graph consistent when updating one side; it is the responsibility of the entity class to make this happen. Please read the section titled "Graph Consistency" in Chapter 15 for more information on how this should be implemented.

However, SqlMetal and the Object Relational Designer handle this for you if you allow them to create your entity classes.

Updating a Child's Parent Reference

Since we can update either side of the relationship, we could choose to update a child's parent reference. So, as an example, let's see how I would change the employee that gets credit for an order in the Northwind database by examining Listing 14-19. Because this example is more complex than many of the others, I will explain it as I go.

Listing 14-19. *Changing a Relationship by Assigning a New Parent*

```
Dim db As New Northwind("Data Source=.\SQLEXPRESS;Initial Catalog=Northwind;" & _
  "Integrated Security=SSPI;")

Dim order As Order = ( _
  From o In db.Orders _
  Where o.EmployeeID = 5 _
  Order By o.OrderDate Descending _
  Select o).First()

'  Save off the current employee so I can reset it at the end.
Dim origEmployee As Employee = order.Employee
```

In the preceding code, after obtaining the DataContext, I query for the most recent order of the employee whose EmployeeID is 5 by ordering that person's orders by date in descending order and calling the First operator. This will provide me the most recent order. Next, just so I will have a reference to the original employee this order was credited to, so that I can restore it at the end of the example, I save the reference in a variable named origEmployee.

```
Console.WriteLine("Before changing the employee.")
Console.WriteLine( _
  "OrderID = {0} : OrderDate = {1} : EmployeeID = {2}", _
  order.OrderID, order.OrderDate, order.Employee.EmployeeID)
```

Next, I display a line to the console letting you know I haven't changed the employee for the retrieved order yet, followed by displaying the order's ID, date, and credited employee to the screen. We should see that the order is credited to employee 5, since that is the employee I queried to obtain the order.

```
Dim emp As Employee = ( _
  From e In db.Employees _
  Where e.EmployeeID = 9 _
  Select e).Single()

'  Now I will assign the new employee to the order.
order.Employee = emp

db.SubmitChanges()
```

Next, I query for some other employee, the one whose EmployeeID is 9, that I then set to be the credited employee for the previously queried order. Then, I persist the changes by calling the SubmitChanges method.

Now, to prove the change was really made at both ends, I could just show you the credited employee for the queried order, but that would be anticlimactic, since you just saw me set the Employee property of the order, and it wouldn't really prove to you that the change was made on the employee side of the relationship. It would be much more satisfying for me to find the order I just changed in the new employee's collection of orders, so that is what I will do.

```
Dim order2 As Order = ( _
  From o In emp.Orders _
  Where o.OrderID = order.OrderID _
  Select o).First()
```

In the preceding code, I query for the order I changed by its OrderID in the new employee's Orders. If it is found, that will prove the relationship between the employee and order was updated on both ends of the relationship.

```
Console.WriteLine("{0}After changing the employee.", System.Environment.NewLine)
Console.WriteLine( _
  "OrderID = {0} : OrderDate = {1} : EmployeeID = {2}", _
  order2.OrderID, order2.OrderDate, order2.Employee.EmployeeID)
```

In the preceding code, I merely display to the console that I am about to display the order after changing it to the new employee emp. I then display that order. We should see that its employee is the employee whose EmployeeID is 9. Prior to the change, the EmployeeID was 5.

```
' Now I need to reverse the changes so the example can be run multiple times.
order.Employee = origEmployee
db.SubmitChanges()
```

The last two lines of code, as well as the line that saves the order's original employee, are merely for resetting the database so the example can be run multiple times.

Now, let's examine the output for Listing 14-19.

```
Before changing the employee.
OrderID = 11043 : OrderDate = 4/22/1998 12:00:00 AM : EmployeeID = 5

After changing the employee.
OrderID = 11043 : OrderDate = 4/22/1998 12:00:00 AM : EmployeeID = 9
```

As you can see, the employee for the order before the change was the employee whose EmployeeID is 5. After the change of the order's credited employee, the order's credited EmployeeID is 9. What is significant is that I didn't just display the order's credited employee on the same order variable, order. I retrieved that order from the employee whose EmployeeID is 9. This proves that the order was indeed changed on the employee side of the relationship.

In this example, I updated the child object's parent reference, where the child was the order and the parent was the employee. There is yet another approach I could have taken to achieve the same result. I could have updated the parent object's child reference.

Updating a Parent's Child Reference

Another approach to changing the relationship between two objects is to remove the child object from the parent object's EntitySet(Of T) collection and add it to a different parent's EntitySet(Of T) collection. In Listing 14-20, I will remove the order from the employee's collection of orders. Because this example is similar to Listing 14-19, I will be far briefer in the explanation, but the significant differences will be in bold.

Listing 14-20. *Changing a Relationship by Removing and Adding a Child to a Parent's EntitySet*

```
Dim db As New Northwind("Data Source=.\SQLEXPRESS;Initial Catalog=Northwind;" & _
  "Integrated Security=SSPI;")

Dim order As Order = ( _
  From o In db.Orders _
  Where o.EmployeeID = 5 _
  Order By o.OrderDate Descending _
  Select o).First()

'  Save off the current employee so I can reset it at the end.
Dim origEmployee As Employee = order.Employee

Console.WriteLine("Before changing the employee.")
Console.WriteLine( _
  "OrderID = {0} : OrderDate = {1} : EmployeeID = {2}", order.OrderID, _
  order.OrderDate, order.Employee.EmployeeID)

Dim emp As Employee = ( _
  From e In db.Employees _
  Where e.EmployeeID = 9 _
  Select e).Single()

'  Remove the order from the original employee's Orders.
origEmployee.Orders.Remove(order)

'  Now add it to the new employee's orders.
emp.Orders.Add(order)

db.SubmitChanges()

Console.WriteLine("{0}After changing the employee.", System.Environment.NewLine)
Console.WriteLine( _
  "OrderID = {0} : OrderDate = {1} : EmployeeID = {2}", _
  order.OrderID, order.OrderDate, order.Employee.EmployeeID)

'  Now I need to reverse the changes so the example can be run multiple times.
order.Employee = origEmployee
db.SubmitChanges()
```

In Listing 14-20, I retrieve the most recent order for the employee whose `EmployeeID` is 5, and I save off the retrieved order's employee in `origEmployee` so that I can restore it at the end of the example. Next, I display the order before the employee is changed. Then, I retrieve the employee whose `EmployeeID` is 9 and store the reference in the variable named `emp`. At this point, this code is the same as Listing 14-19.

Then, I remove the order from the original employee's collection of orders and add it to the new employee's collection of orders. I then call the `SubmitChanges` method to persist the changes to the database. Next, I display the order after the changes to the console. Last, I restore the order to its original condition so the example can be run more than once.

Let's examine the results of Listing 14-20.

```
Before changing the employee.
OrderID = 11043 : OrderDate = 4/22/1998 12:00:00 AM : EmployeeID = 5

After changing the employee.
OrderID = 11043 : OrderDate = 4/22/1998 12:00:00 AM : EmployeeID = 9
```

Deletes

To delete a record from a database using LINQ to SQL, you must delete the entity object from the `Table(Of T)` of which it is a member with the `Table(Of T)` object's `DeleteOnSubmit` method. Then, of course, you must call the `SubmitChanges` method. Listing 14-21 contains an example.

■**Caution** Unlike all the other examples in this chapter, this example will not restore the database at the end. This is because one of the tables involved contains an identity column, and it is not a simple matter to programmatically restore the data to its identical state prior to the example executing. Therefore, before running this example, make sure you have a backup of your database that you can restore from. If you downloaded the zipped extended version of the Northwind database, after running this example, you could just detach the Northwind database, re-extract the database files, and reattach the database.

Listing 14-21. *Deleting a Record by Deleting It from Its Table(Of T)*

```
Dim db As New Northwind("Data Source=.\SQLEXPRESS;Initial Catalog=Northwind;" & _
  "Integrated Security=SSPI;")

' Retrieve a customer to delete.
Dim customer As Customer = ( _
  From c In db.Customers _
  Where c.CompanyName = "Alfreds Futterkiste" _
  Select c).Single()

db.OrderDetails.DeleteAllOnSubmit( _
  customer.Orders.SelectMany(Function(o) o.OrderDetails))
```

```
db.Orders.DeleteAllOnSubmit(customer.Orders)
db.Customers.DeleteOnSubmit(customer)

db.SubmitChanges()

Dim customer2 As Customer = ( _
  From c In db.Customers _
  Where c.CompanyName = "Alfreds Futterkiste" _
  Select c).SingleOrDefault()

Console.WriteLine( _
  "Customer {0} found.",If(customer2 IsNot Nothing, "is", "is not"))
```

This example is pretty straightforward, but there are some interesting facets to it. First, since the Orders table contains a foreign key to the Customers table, you cannot delete a customer without first deleting the customer's orders. And, since the Order Details table contains a foreign key to the Orders table, you cannot delete an order without first deleting the order's order details. So, to delete a customer, I must first delete the order details for all of the orders for the customer, and then I can delete all the orders, and finally I can delete the customer.

Deleting all the orders is not difficult thanks to the DeleteAllOnSubmit operator that can delete a sequence of orders, but deleting all the order details for each order is a little trickier. Of course, I could enumerate through all the orders and call the DeleteAllOnSubmit operator on each order's sequence of order details, but that would be boring. Instead, I call the SelectMany operator to take a sequence of sequences of order details to create a single concatenated sequence of order details that I then pass to the DeleteAllOnSubmit operator. Man, it's like I am drunk on the power of LINQ.

After deleting the order details, orders, and the customer, I merely call the SubmitChanges method. To prove the customer is actually gone, I query for it and display a message to the console.

Let's take a look at the output of Listing 14-21.

```
Customer is not found.
```

That's not very exciting output, but it does prove the customer no longer exists. While the point of Listing 14-21 is to demonstrate that to delete an entity object you must delete it from the appropriate Table(Of T), I think the example became a cheerleader for the SelectMany operator as well.

■**Note** Remember that this example did not restore the database at the end, so you should manually restore it now.

Deleting Attached Entity Objects

Unlike when an attached associated dependent entity object was automatically inserted into the database by the DataContext when the dependent entity object's associated parent object was inserted, as happened in Listing 14-3, our attached dependent entity objects are not automatically deleted if the parent entity object is deleted. By dependent, I mean the entity objects containing the foreign key. You saw this fully demonstrated in Listing 14-21, where I had to delete the Order Details records before the Orders records and the Orders records before the Customers record.

So, for example, with the Northwind database, if you attempt to delete an order, its order details will not automatically be deleted. This will cause a foreign key constraint violation when you attempt to delete the order. Therefore, before you can delete an entity object, you must delete all its attached associated child entity objects.

For examples of this, please examine Listing 14-21 and Listing 14-3. In each of these listings, I had to delete the associated attached entity objects before I could delete their parent object.

Deleting Relationships

To delete a relationship between two entity objects in LINQ to SQL, you merely reassign the entity object's reference to the related object to a different object or Nothing. By assigning the reference to Nothing, the entity object will have no relationship to an entity of that type. However, removing the relationship altogether by assigning the reference to Nothing will not delete the record itself. Remember, to actually delete a record, its corresponding entity object must be deleted from the appropriate Table(Of T). Listing 14-22 contains an example of removing the relationship.

Listing 14-22. *Removing a Relationship Between Two Entity Objects*

```vb
Dim db As New Northwind("Data Source=.\SQLEXPRESS;Initial Catalog=Northwind;" & _
  "Integrated Security=SSPI;")

'  Retrieve an order to unrelate.
Dim order As Order = ( _
  From o In db.Orders _
  Where o.OrderID = 11043 _
  Select o).Single()

'  Save off the original customer so I can set it back.
Dim c As Customer = order.Customer

Console.WriteLine("Orders before deleting the relationship:")
For Each ord As Order In c.Orders
  Console.WriteLine("OrderID = {0}", ord.OrderID)
Next ord

'  Remove the relationship to the customer.
order.Customer = Nothing
db.SubmitChanges()
```

```
Console.WriteLine("{0}Orders after deleting the relationship:", vbCrLf)
For Each ord As Order In c.Orders
  Console.WriteLine("OrderID = {0}", ord.OrderID)
Next ord

'  Restore the database back to its original state.
order.Customer = c
db.SubmitChanges()
```

In Listing 14-22, I query a specific order, the one whose OrderID is 11043. I then save that order's customer, so I can restore it at the end of the example. I next display all of that customer's orders to the console and assign the retrieved order's customer to null and call the SubmitChanges method to persist the changes to the database. Then, I display all the customer's orders again, and this time, the order whose OrderID is 11043 is gone. Let's examine the output for Listing 14-22.

```
Orders before deleting the relationship:
OrderID = 10738
OrderID = 10907
OrderID = 10964
OrderID = 11043

Orders after deleting the relationship:
OrderID = 10738
OrderID = 10907
OrderID = 10964
```

As you can see, once I remove the relationship to the customer for the order whose OrderID is 11043, the order is no longer in the customer's collection of orders.

Overriding Database Modification Statements

If you have been thinking that using LINQ to SQL in your environment is not possible, perhaps because of requirements to utilize stored procedures for all modifications to the database, then you would be interested in knowing that the actual code that gets called to make the updates, including inserts and deletes, can be overridden.

Overriding the code called to insert, update, and delete is as simple as defining the appropriately named *partial* method with the appropriate signature. When you override this way, the DataContext change processor will then call your partial method implementation for the database update, insert, or delete. Here is yet another way Microsoft is taking advantage of partial methods. You get the ability to hook into the code but with no overhead if you don't.

You must be aware, though, that if you take this approach, you will be responsible for concurrency conflict detection. Please read Chapter 17 thoroughly before accepting this responsibility.

When you define these override methods, it is the name of the partial method and the entity type of the method's parameters that instruct the DataContext to call your override methods. Let's take a look at the method declarations you must define to override the insert, update, and delete methods.

Overriding the Insert Method

You may override the method called to insert a record in the database by implementing a partial method declared as

```
Partial Private Sub Insert[EntityClassName] (ByVal instance As T)
```

where [EntityClassName] is the name of the entity class whose insert method is being overridden, and type T is that entity class.

Here is an example of the declaration to override the insert method for the Shipper entity class:

```
Partial Private Sub InsertShipper(ByVal instance As Shipper)
```

Overriding the Update Method

You may override the method called to update a record in the database by implementing a partial method declared as

```
Partial Private Sub Update[EntityClassName](ByVal instance As T)
```

where [EntityClassName] is the name of the entity class whose update method is being overridden, and type T is that entity class.

Here is an example of the declaration to override the update method for the Shipper entity class:

```
Partial Private Sub UpdateShipper(ByVal instance As Shipper)
```

Overriding the Delete Method

You may override the method called to delete a record in the database by implementing a partial method declared as

```
Partial Private Sub Delete[EntityClassName](ByVal instance As T)
```

where [EntityClassName] is the name of the entity class whose delete method is being overridden, and type T is that entity class.

Here is an example of the declaration to override the delete method for the Shipper entity class:

```
Partial Private Sub DeleteShipper(ByVal instance As Shipper)
```

Example

For an example demonstrating overriding the insert, update, and delete methods, instead of modifying my generated entity class file, I am going to create a new file for my override partial methods so that if I ever need to regenerate my entity class file, I will not lose my override partial methods. I have named my file NorthwindExtended.vb. Here is what it will look like:

My NorthwindExtended.vb File with Database Update Override Methods

```
Imports System
Imports System.Data.Linq

Namespace nwind
  Partial Public Class Northwind
      Inherits DataContext
    Private Sub InsertShipper(ByVal instance As Shipper)
      Console.WriteLine( _
        "Insert override method was called for shipper {0}.", instance.CompanyName)
    End Sub

    Private Sub UpdateShipper(ByVal instance As Shipper)
      Console.WriteLine( _
        "Update override method was called for shipper {0}.", instance.CompanyName)
    End Sub

    Private Sub DeleteShipper(ByVal instance As Shipper)
      Console.WriteLine( _
        "Delete override method was called for shipper {0}.", instance.CompanyName)
    End Sub
  End Class
End Namespace
```

■**Note** You will have to add the file containing this partial class definition to your Visual Studio project.

The first thing to notice about the override code is the fact that the override methods are partial methods defined at the DataContext level. They are not defined in the entity class they pertain to.

As you can see, my override methods aren't doing anything except for informing me that they are getting called. In many situations, the override will be for the purpose of calling a stored procedure, but this is up to the developer.

Now, let's take a look at Listing 14-23, which contains code that will cause my override methods to be called.

Listing 14-23. *An Example Where the Update, Insert, and Delete Methods Are Overridden*

```
Dim db As New Northwind("Data Source=.\SQLEXPRESS;Initial Catalog=Northwind;" & _
  "Integrated Security=SSPI;")
```

```
Dim ship As Shipper = ( _
  From s In db.Shippers _
  Where s.ShipperID = 1 _
  Select s).Single()

ship.CompanyName = "Jiffy Shipping"

Dim newShip As Shipper = New Shipper With { _
  .ShipperID = 4, _
  .CompanyName = "Vickey Rattz Shipping", _
  .Phone = "(800) SHIP-NOW"}

db.Shippers.InsertOnSubmit(newShip)

Dim deletedShip As Shipper = ( _
  From s In db.Shippers _
  Where s.ShipperID = 3 _
  Select s).Single()

db.Shippers.DeleteOnSubmit(deletedShip)

db.SubmitChanges()
```

In Listing 14-23, first I retrieve the shipper whose `ShipperID` is 1, and update a field. Then, I insert another shipper, Vickey Rattz Shipping, and delete yet another, the one whose `ShipperID` is 3. Of course, since my override methods are getting called, and they only display a message to the console, none of these changes are actually persisted to the database. Here are the results of Listing 14-23.

```
Update override method was called for shipper Jiffy Shipping.
Insert override method was called for shipper Vickey Rattz Shipping.
Delete override method was called for shipper Federal Shipping.
```

From the results, you can see each of my override methods is called. Now the question becomes, what if you want to override the insert, update, and delete methods, but you also want the default behavior to occur?

Because the code required would conflict with my partial methods for the previous example, I will not provide a working example of this, but I will explain how to do it. In your partial method implementations for the insert, update, and delete methods, you merely call the `DataContext.ExecuteDynamicInsert`, `DataContext.ExecuteDynamicUpdate`, or `DataContext.ExecuteDynamicDelete` method, respectively, to get the default method behavior.

For example, if for the previous example, I want my log messages to be called *and* I want the normal LINQ to SQL code to be called to actually handle the persistence to the database, I could change my partial method implementations to the following:

Overriding the Insert, Update, and Delete Methods Plus Calling the Default Behavior

```
Namespace nwind
  Partial Public Class Northwind
      Inherits DataContext
    Private Sub InsertShipper(ByVal instance As Shipper)
      Console.WriteLine( _
        "Insert override method was called for shipper {0}.", instance.CompanyName)
      Me.ExecuteDynamicInsert(instance)
    End Sub

    Private Sub UpdateShipper(ByVal instance As Shipper)
      Console.WriteLine( _
        "Update override method was called for shipper {0}.", instance.CompanyName)
      Me.ExecuteDynamicUpdate(instance)
    End Sub

    Private Sub DeleteShipper(ByVal instance As Shipper)
      Console.WriteLine( _
        "Delete override method was called for shipper {0}.", instance.CompanyName)
      Me.ExecuteDynamicDelete(instance)
    End Sub
  End Class
End Namespace
```

■**Note** If you run this code against the extended Northwind database, you will get an exception when the code tries to delete the shipper, because there are orders that reference this shipper.

Notice that in each of the partial methods I call the appropriate ExecuteDynamicInsert, ExecuteDynamicUpdate, or ExecuteDynamicDelete method. Now, I can extend the behavior when an entity class is called, I can modify it, or I can even create a wrapper for the existing default behavior. LINQ to SQL is very flexible.

Overriding in the Object Relational Designer

Don't forget, as I covered in Chapter 13, you can override the insert, update, and delete methods using the Object Relational Designer.

Considerations

Don't forget that when you override the update, insert, and delete methods, you take responsibility for performing concurrency conflict detection. This means you should be very familiar with how the currently implemented concurrency conflict detection works. For example, the way Microsoft has implemented it is to specify all relevant fields involved in update checks in the Where clause of the update statement. The logic then checks to see how many records were updated by the statement. If the number of records updated is not one, they know there was a concurrency conflict. You should follow a similar pattern, and if a concurrency conflict is detected, you must throw a ChangeConflictException exception. Be sure to read Chapter 17 before attempting to override these methods.

SQL Translation

When writing LINQ to SQL queries, you may have noticed that when specifying expressions such as Where clauses, the expressions are in the native programming language, as opposed to SQL. After all, this is part of the goal of LINQ, language integration. For this book, the expressions are in VB.NET. If you haven't noticed, shame on you.

For example, in Listing 14-2, I have a query that looks like this:

An Example of a LINQ to SQL Query

```
Dim cust As Customer = ( _
  From c In db.Customers _
  Where c.CustomerID = "LONEP" _
  Select c).Single ()
```

Notice that the expression in the Where clause is indeed VB.NET syntax, as opposed to SQL syntax that would look more like this:

An Example of an Invalid LINQ to SQL Query

```
Dim cust As Customer = ( _
  From c In db.Customers _
  Where c.CustomerID = 'LONEP' _
  select c).Single()
```

Notice that instead of enclosing the string literal in double quotes (""), single quotes (' ') enclose it. In SQL, this would be a string, but in VB.NET, this causes the rest of the line to be interpreted as a comment. One of the goals of LINQ is to allow developers to program in their native programming languages. Remember, LINQ stands for Language Integrated Query. However, since the database won't be executing VB.NET expressions, your VB.NET expressions must be translated to valid SQL. Therefore, your queries must be translated to SQL.

Right off the bat, this means that what you can do does have limitations. But, in general, the translation is pretty good. Rather than attempt to recreate a reference similar to the MSDN help for this translation process and what can and cannot be translated, I want to show you what to expect when your LINQ to SQL query cannot be translated.

First, be aware that the code may compile. Don't be caught off guard because your query compiled. A failed translation may not actually reveal itself until the time the query is actually performed. Because of deferred query execution, this also means the line of code defining the query may execute just fine. Only when the query is actually performed does the failed translation rear its ugly head, and it does so in the form of an exception similar to this:

Unhandled Exception: System.NotSupportedException: Method 'System.String
TrimEnd(Char[])' has no supported translation to SQL.
...

That is a pretty clear error message. Let's examine the code in Listing 14-24 that produces this exception.

Listing 14-24. *A LINQ to SQL Query That Cannot Be Translated*

```
Dim db As New Northwind("Data Source=.\SQLEXPRESS;Initial Catalog=Northwind;" & _
  "Integrated Security=SSPI;")

Dim custs As IQueryable(Of Customer) = _
  From c In db.Customers _
  Where c.CustomerID.TrimEnd("K"c) = "LAZY" _
  Select c

For Each c As Customer In custs
  Console.WriteLine("{0}", c.CompanyName)
Next c
```

Notice that the TrimEnd method that caused the translation exception is called on the database field, not my local string literal. In Listing 14-25, I'll reverse the side I call the TrimEnd method on, and see what happens.

Listing 14-25. *A LINQ to SQL Query That Can Be Translated*

```
Dim db As New Northwind("Data Source=.\SQLEXPRESS;Initial Catalog=Northwind;" & _
  "Integrated Security=SSPI;")

Dim custs As IQueryable(Of Customer) = _
  From c In db.Customers _
  Where c.CustomerID = "LAZY".TrimEnd("K"c) _
  Select c

For Each c As Customer In custs
  Console.WriteLine("{0}", c.CompanyName)
Next c
```

The output of Listing 14-25 looks like this:

OK, you got me; there is no output. But that is fine because this is the appropriate output for the query, and no SQL translation exception is thrown.

So, calling an unsupported method on a database column causes the exception, while calling that same method on the passed parameter is just fine. This makes sense. LINQ to SQL would have no problem calling the TrimEnd method on our parameter, because it can do this prior to binding the parameter to the query, which occurs in our process environment. Calling the TrimEnd method on the database column would have to be done in the database, and that means, instead of calling the method in our process environment, that call must be translated to a SQL statement that can be passed to the database and executed. Since the TrimEnd method is not supported for SQL translation, the exception is thrown.

One thing to keep in mind is that if you do need to call an unsupported method on a database column, perhaps you can instead call a method that has the mutually opposite effect on the parameter? Say, for example, you want to call the ToUpper method on the database column, and it's not supported; perhaps you could call the ToLower method on the parameter instead. However, in this case, the ToUpper method is supported so the point is moo, like a cow's opinion. Also, you must insure that the method you do call does indeed have a mutually opposite effect. In this case, the database column could have mixed case, so calling the ToLower method would still not have exactly the opposite effect. If your database column contained the value "Smith" and your parameter was "SMITH", and you were checking for equality, calling the ToUpper method on the database column would work and give you a match. However, if the ToUpper method were not supported, trying to reverse the logic by calling the ToLower method on the parameter would still not yield a match.

You may be wondering how you would know that the TrimEnd method is not supported by SQL translation. Because the nature of which primitive types and methods are supported is so dynamic and subject to change, it is beyond the scope of this book to attempt to document them all. There are also a lot of restrictions and disclaimers to the translation. I suspect SQL translation will be an ongoing effort for Microsoft. For you to know what is supported, you should consult the MSDN documentation titled ".NET Framework Function Translation" for LINQ to SQL. However, as you can see from the previous examples, it is pretty easy to tell when a method is not supported.

Summary

I know this chapter is a whirlwind tour of standard database operations using LINQ to SQL. I hope I kept the examples simple enough to allow you to focus on the basic steps necessary to perform inserts, queries, updates, and deletes to the database. I also pointed out the ways that LINQ to SQL queries differ from LINQ to Objects queries.

Bear in mind that any LINQ to SQL code that changes the database should detect and resolve concurrency conflicts. However, for the sake of clarity, none of the examples in this chapter did so. I will cover concurrency conflicts thoroughly in Chapter 17 though, so don't be too disappointed.

In addition to understanding how to perform these basic operations on entity objects, it is also important to understand how this affects an object's associated entity objects. Remember, when you insert an entity object into the database, any attached objects will be added automatically for you. However, this does not apply to deletes. To delete a parent entity object in an association relationship, you must first delete the child entity objects to prevent an exception from being thrown.

Next, I demonstrated how you can override the default methods generated to modify your entity object's corresponding database records. This allows a developer to control how database changes are made, which facilitates stored procedures being used.

Finally, I covered the fact that LINQ to SQL queries must be translated to SQL statements. It is important to never forget that this translation takes place, and this does somewhat restrict what can be done.

I know that so far in this book, I have mentioned entity classes repeatedly yet not discussed them in any depth. It's high time I rectify this state of affairs. So, in the next chapter, Chapter 15, I plan to bore you to tears with them.

LINQ to SQL Entity Classes

In the previous LINQ to SQL chapters, I have mentioned entity classes numerous times but have yet to fully define or describe them. In this chapter, I will rectify this shortcoming.

In this chapter, I will define entity classes, as well as discuss the different ways they can be created. I will also inform you of the complexities you become responsible for should you decide to create your own entity classes.

But before we can begin the fun stuff, there are some prerequisites you must meet to be able to run the examples in this chapter.

Prerequisites for Running the Examples

In order to run the examples in this chapter, you will need to have obtained the extended version of the Northwind database and generated entity classes for it. Please read and follow the instructions in the section in Chapter 12 titled "Prerequisites for Running the Examples."

Entity Classes

Classes that are mapped to a SQL Server database using LINQ to SQL are known as *entity classes*. An instantiated object of an entity class is an entity of that type, and I will refer to it as an *entity object*. Entity classes are normal VB.NET classes with additional LINQ to SQL attributes specified. Alternatively, rather than adding attributes, entity classes can be created by providing an XML mapping file when instantiating the DataContext object. Those attributes or mapping file entries dictate how the entity classes are to be mapped to a SQL Server database when using LINQ to SQL.

By using these entity classes, we can query and update the database using LINQ to SQL.

Creating Entity Classes

Entity classes are the basic building blocks utilized when performing LINQ to SQL queries. In order to begin using LINQ to SQL, entity classes are required. There are two ways to obtain entity classes; you can generate them, as I demonstrate in Chapter 12 and Chapter 13, or you can write them by hand. And, there is no reason you cannot do a combination of both.

If you do not already have business classes for the entities stored in the database, generating the entity classes is probably the best approach. If you already have an object model, writing the entity classes may be the best approach.

If you are starting a project from scratch, I would recommend that you consider modeling the database first and generate the entity classes from the database. This will allow you to leverage the generated entity classes, which will alleviate the burden of writing them correctly, which is not necessarily trivial.

Generating Entity Classes

So far in this book, I have only demonstrated generating entity classes, which is the simplest way to obtain them. In Chapter 12, I demonstrate how to generate the entity classes for the Northwind database, so you can try the examples in the LINQ to SQL chapters of this book. In Chapter 13, I discuss in detail how you can generate entity classes using either the command-line tool named SqlMetal or the GUI tool named the Object Relational Designer.

SqlMetal is very simple to use but does not provide any options for controlling the naming of the generated entity classes barring producing an intermediate XML file, editing it, and generating entity classes from it. Also, it generates entity classes for all tables in the specified database and for all fields in each table, barring the same labor-intensive procedure I previously described. This gives you little control of the names of your entity classes and their properties. The Object Relational Designer may take longer to create a complete object model for a database, but it allows you to specify exactly which tables and fields for which you want to generate entity classes, as well as allowing you to specify the names of the entity classes and their properties. I have already discussed SqlMetal and the Object Relational Designer in Chapter 13, so refer to that chapter for more details about using either of these two tools.

If you generate entity classes for a database, nothing requires you to interact with every table's entity class. You could choose to use an entity class for one table but not another. Additionally, there is no reason you cannot add business functionality to the generated entity classes. For example, a Customer class was generated by SqlMetal in Chapter 12. There is no reason that business methods or nonpersisted class properties cannot be added to this Customer class. However, if you do this, make sure you do not actually modify the generated entity class code. Instead, create another Customer class module, and take advantage of the fact that entity classes are generated as partial classes. Partial classes are a great addition to VB.NET and make it easier than ever to separate functionality into separate modules. This way, if the entity class gets regenerated for any reason, you will not lose your added methods or properties.

Writing Entity Classes By Hand

Writing entity classes by hand is the more difficult approach. It requires a solid understanding of the LINQ to SQL attributes or the external mapping schema. However, writing entity classes by hand is a great way to really learn LINQ to SQL.

Where writing entity classes by hand really pays off is for already existing classes. You may have an existing application with an already implemented object model. It wouldn't be very beneficial to generate entity classes from a database, since you already have your object model used by the application.

The solution is to add the necessary attributes to your existing object model or to create a mapping file. Thanks to the flexibility of LINQ to SQL, it is not necessary that your classes match the name of the table they are persisted in or that the names of the properties of the class match the column names in the table. This means that previously implemented classes can now be modified to persist to a SQL Server database.

To create entity classes by hand using attributes, you will need to add the appropriate attributes to your classes, be they existing business classes or new classes created specifically as entity classes. Read the section titled "Entity Class Attributes and Attribute Properties" in this chapter for a description of the available attributes and properties.

To create entity classes by using an external mapping file, you will need to create an XML file that conforms to the schema discussed in the section titled "XML External Mapping File Schema" later in this chapter. Once you have this external mapping file, you will use the appropriate `DataContext` constructor when instantiating the `DataContext` object to load the mapping file. There are two constructors that allow you to specify an external mapping file.

Additional Responsibilities of Entity Classes

Unfortunately, when writing entity classes by hand, it is not adequate to only understand the attributes and attribute properties. You must also know about some of the additional responsibilities of entity classes.

For example, when writing entity classes by hand, you should be aware of the need for change notifications and how to implement them. You also must ensure graph consistency between your parent and child classes.

These additional responsibilities are all taken care of for you when using SqlMetal or the Object Relational Designer, but if you are creating your entity classes yourself, you must add the necessary code.

Change Notifications

Later, in Chapter 16, I will discuss change tracking. It turns out that change tracking is not very elegant or efficient without assistance from the entity classes themselves. If your entity classes are generated by SqlMetal or the Object Relational Designer, you can relax because these tools will take care of these inefficiencies by implementing code to participate in change notifications when they generate your entity classes. But if you are writing your entity classes, you need to understand change notifications and potentially implement the code to participate in the change notifications.

Entity classes have the option of whether they participate in change notifications or not. If they do not participate in change notifications, the `DataContext` provides change tracking by keeping two copies of each entity object; one with the original values, and one with the current values. It creates the copies the first time an entity is retrieved from the database when change tracking begins. However, you can make change tracking more efficient by making your hand-written entity classes implement the change notification interfaces, `System.ComponentModel.INotifyPropertyChanging` and `System.ComponentModel.INotifyPropertyChanged`.

As I will do often in the LINQ to SQL chapters, I will refer to the code that was generated by SqlMetal to show you the quintessential way to handle some situation. In this case, I will refer to the SqlMetal-generated code to handle change notifications. To implement the `INotifyPropertyChanging` and `INotifyPropertyChanged` interfaces, I need to do four things.

First, I need to define my entity class so that it implements the `INotifyPropertyChanging` and `INotifyPropertyChanged` interfaces.

From the Generated Customer Entity Class

```
<Table(Name:="dbo.Customers")> _
Partial Public Class Customer
```

```
    Implements System.ComponentModel.INotifyPropertyChanging, _
    System.ComponentModel.INotifyPropertyChanged
...
End Class
```

Because the entity class implements these two interfaces, the DataContext will know to register two event handlers for two events I will discuss in just a few paragraphs.

You can also see that the Table attribute is specified in the preceding code. I will be displaying the related attributes for context purposes in this section, but I will not be explaining them, though I will discuss them in detail later in this chapter. For now, just pretend like they are not there.

Second, I need to declare a Private Shared variable of type PropertyChangingEventArgs and pass String.Empty to its constructor.

From the Generated Customer Entity Class

```
<Table(Name:="dbo.Customers")> _
Partial Public Class Customer
    Implements System.ComponentModel.INotifyPropertyChanging, _
    System.ComponentModel.INotifyPropertyChanged

  Private Shared emptyChangingEventArgs As PropertyChangingEventArgs = _
    New PropertyChangingEventArgs(String.Empty)
  ...
End Class
```

The emptyChangingEventArgs object will be passed to one of the previously mentioned event handlers when the appropriate event is raised.

Third, I need to add two Public Event members, one of type System.ComponentModel. PropertyChangingEventHandler named PropertyChanging, and one of type System. ComponentModel.PropertyChangedEventHandler named PropertyChanged to the entity class.

From the Generated Customer Entity Class

```
<Table(Name:="dbo.Customers")> _
Partial Public Class Customer
    Implements System.ComponentModel.INotifyPropertyChanging, _
    System.ComponentModel.INotifyPropertyChanged

  Private Shared emptyChangingEventArgs As PropertyChangingEventArgs = _
    New PropertyChangingEventArgs(String.Empty)
  ...
  Public Event PropertyChanging As PropertyChangingEventHandler _
    Implements System.ComponentModel.INotifyPropertyChanging.PropertyChanging

  Public Event PropertyChanged As PropertyChangedEventHandler _
    Implements System.ComponentModel.INotifyPropertyChanged.PropertyChanged
  ...
End Class
```

When the DataContext object initiates change tracking for an entity object, the DataContext object will register event handlers with these two events if the entity class implements the two change notification interfaces. If not, it will make a copy of the entity object as I previously mentioned.

Fourth, every time a mapped entity class property is changed, I need to raise the PropertyChanging event prior to changing the property and raise the PropertyChanged event after changing the property.

While it is not necessary that I implement raising the events the following way, for conciseness, SqlMetal generates SendPropertyChanging and SendPropertyChanged methods for you.

From the Generated Customer Entity Class

```
Protected Overridable Sub SendPropertyChanging()
  If ((Me.PropertyChangingEvent Is Nothing) = false) Then
    RaiseEvent PropertyChanging(Me, emptyChangingEventArgs)
  End If
End Sub

Protected Overridable Sub SendPropertyChanged(ByVal propertyName As [String])
  If ((Me.PropertyChangedEvent Is Nothing) = false) Then
    RaiseEvent PropertyChanged(Me, New PropertyChangedEventArgs(propertyName))
  End If
End Sub
```

Notice that in the raising of the PropertyChanged event, a new PropertyChangedEventArgs object is created and passed the name of the specific property that has been changed. This lets the DataContext object know exactly which property has been changed. So when the SendPropertyChanging method is called, it raises the PropertyChanging event, which results in the event handler the DataContext object registered being called. This same pattern and flow also applies to the SendPropertyChanged method and PropertyChanged event.

Of course, you could choose to embed similar logic in your code instead of creating methods that are reused, but that would be more of a hassle and create more code to maintain.

Then, in each property's Set method, I must call the two methods SendPropertyChanging and SendPropertyChanged just prior to and after changing a property.

From the Generated Customer Entity Class

```
<Column(Storage:="_ContactName", DbType:="NVarChar(30)")> _
Public Property ContactName() As String
  Get
    Return Me._ContactName
  End Get
  Set
    If (String.Equals(Me._ContactName, value) = false) Then
      Me.OnContactNameChanging(value)
      Me.SendPropertyChanging
      Me._ContactName = value
      Me.SendPropertyChanged("ContactName")
```

```
      Me.OnContactNameChanged
    End If
  End Set
End Property
```

Again, notice that in the call to the SendPropertyChanged method, the name of the property is passed, which in this case is ContactName. Once the SendPropertyChanged method is called, the DataContext object knows the ContactName property has been changed for this entity object.

I must also see to it that the appropriate events are raised in the Set methods for properties that represent an association. So, on the *many* side of a one-to-many association, I need to add the following code that is bold:

From the Order Class Since Customer Has No EntityRef(Of T) Properties

```
<Association(Name:="FK_Orders_Customers", Storage:="_Customer", _
  ThisKey:="CustomerID", OtherKey:="CustomerID", IsForeignKey:=true)> _
Public Property Customer() As Customer
  Get
    Return Me._Customer.Entity
  End Get
  Set
    Dim previousValue As Customer = Me._Customer.Entity
    If ((Object.Equals(previousValue, value) = false) _
        OrElse (Me._Customer.HasLoadedOrAssignedValue = false)) Then
      Me.SendPropertyChanging
      If ((previousValue Is Nothing) = false) Then
        Me._Customer.Entity = Nothing
        previousValue.Orders.Remove(Me)
      End If
      Me._Customer.Entity = value
      If ((value Is Nothing) = false) Then
        value.Orders.Add(Me)
        Me._CustomerID = value.CustomerID
      Else
        Me._CustomerID = CType(Nothing, String)
      End If
      Me.SendPropertyChanged("Customer")
    End If
  End Set
End Property
```

and, on the *one* side of a one-to-many association, I need the following code that is bold:

From the Generated Customer Entity Class

```
Public Sub New()
  ...
  Me._Orders = New EntitySet(Of [Order])( _
```

```
    AddressOf Me.attach_Orders, _
    AddressOf Me.detach_Orders)
  ...
End Sub
...
Private Sub attach_Orders(ByVal entity As [Order])
  Me.SendPropertyChanging()
  entity.Customer = Me
End Sub

Private Sub detach_Orders(ByVal entity As [Order])
  Me.SendPropertyChanging()
  entity.Customer = Nothing
End Sub
```

By implementing change notification in the manner just described, we can make change tracking more efficient. Now, the DataContext object knows when and which entity class properties are changed.

When we call the SubmitChanges method, the DataContext object merely forgets the original values of the properties, the current property values effectively become the original property values, and change tracking starts over. The SubmitChanges method is covered in detail in Chapter 16.

Of course, as I previously mentioned, if you allow SqlMetal or the Object Relational Designer to create your entity classes, you are relieved of these complexities, because they handle all this plumbing code for you. It is only when writing entity classes by hand that you need to be concerned with implementing change notifications.

Graph Consistency

In mathematics, when nodes are connected together, the network created by the connections is referred to as a *graph*. In the same way, the network representing the connections created by classes referencing other classes is also referred to as a graph. When you have two entity classes that participate in a relationship, meaning an Association has been created between them, since they each have a reference to the other, a graph exists.

When you are modifying a relationship between two entity objects, such as a Customer and an Order, the references on each side of the relationship must be properly updated so that each entity object properly references or no longer references the other. This is true whether you are creating the relationship or removing it. Since LINQ to SQL defines that the programmer writing code that utilizes entity classes need only modify one side of the relationship, something has to handle updating the other side, and LINQ to SQL doesn't do that for us.

It is the responsibility of the entity class to handle updating the other side of the relationship. If you allowed SqlMetal or the Object Relational Designer to generate your entity classes, you are set because they do this for you. But, when you create your own entity classes, it is the entity class developer who must implement the code to make this happen.

By insuring that each side of the relationship is properly updated, the graph remains consistent. Without it, the graph becomes inconsistent, and chaos ensues. A Customer may be related to an Order, but the Order might be related to a different Customer or no Customer at all. This makes navigation impossible and is an unacceptable situation.

Fortunately, Microsoft provides a pattern we can use to make sure our entity classes properly implement graph consistency. Let's take a look at their implementation generated for the Northwind database by SqlMetal.

From the Generated Customer Entity Class

```
Public Sub New()
  ...
  Me._Orders = New EntitySet(Of [Order])( _
    AddressOf Me.attach_Orders, _
    AddressOf Me.detach_Orders)
  ...
End Sub
...
Private Sub attach_Orders(ByVal entity As [Order])
  Me.SendPropertyChanging()
  entity.Customer = Me
End Sub

Private Sub detach_Orders(ByVal entity As [Order])
  Me.SendPropertyChanging()
  entity.Customer = Nothing
End Sub
```

In this example, the Customer class will be the parent class, or the *one* side of the one-to-many relationship. The Order class will be the child class, or the *many* side of the one-to-many relationship.

In the preceding code, we can see that in the constructor of the parent class Customer, when the EntitySet(Of T) member for our child class collection _Orders is initialized, two Action(Of T) delegate objects are passed into the constructor.

The first Action(Of T) delegate object is passed a delegate to a callback method that will handle assigning the current Customer object, referenced with the Me keyword, as the Customer of the Order that will be passed into the callback method. In the preceding code, the callback method I am referring to is the attach_Orders method.

The second parameter to the EntitySet(Of T) constructor is an Action(Of T) delegate object that is passed a delegate to a callback method that will handle removing the assignment of the passed Order object's Customer. In the preceding code, the callback method I am referring to is the detach_Orders method.

Even though the preceding code is in the parent class Customer, the assignment of the child class Order to the Customer is actually being handled by the Order object's Customer property. You can see that in both the attach_Orders and detach_Orders methods; all they really do is change the Order object's Customer property. You can see the entity.Customer property being set to Me and Nothing, respectively, to attach the current Customer and detach the currently assigned Customer. In the Get and Set methods for the child class, Order is where all the heavy lifting will be done to maintain graph consistency. We have effectively pawned off the real work to the child class this way. In the parent class, that is all there is to maintaining graph consistency.

However, before I proceed, notice that in the attach_Orders and detach_Orders methods, change notifications are being raised by calling the SendPropertyChanging methods.

Now, let's take a look at what needs to be done in the child class of the parent-to-child relation to maintain graph consistency.

From the Generated Order Entity Class

```
<Association(Name:="FK_Orders_Customers", Storage:="_Customer", _
  ThisKey:="CustomerID", OtherKey:="CustomerID", IsForeignKey:=true)> _
Public Property Customer() As Customer
  Get
    Return Me._Customer.Entity
  End Get
  Set
    Dim previousValue As Customer = Me._Customer.Entity
    If ((Object.Equals(previousValue, value) = false) _
        OrElse (Me._Customer.HasLoadedOrAssignedValue = false)) Then
      Me.SendPropertyChanging
      If ((previousValue Is Nothing) = false) Then
        Me._Customer.Entity = Nothing
        previousValue.Orders.Remove(Me)
      End If
      Me._Customer.Entity = value
      If ((value Is Nothing) = false) Then
        value.Orders.Add(Me)
        Me._CustomerID = value.CustomerID
      Else
        Me._CustomerID = CType(Nothing, String)
      End If
      Me.SendPropertyChanged("Customer")
    End If
  End Set
End Property
```

In the preceding code, we are only concerned with the Customer property's Set method, especially since the parent side of the relationship put the burden of maintaining graph consistency on it. Because this method gets so complicated, I will present the code as I describe it.

```
  Set
    Dim previousValue As Customer = Me._Customer.Entity
```

You can see that in the first line of the Set method code, a copy of the original Customer assigned to the Order is saved as previousValue. Don't let the fact that the code is referencing Me._Customer.Entity confuse you. Remember that the _Customer member variable is actually an EntityRef(Of Customer), not a Customer. So, to get the actual Customer object, the code must reference the EntityRef(Of T) object's Entity property. Since the EntityRef(Of T) is for a Customer, the type of Entity will be Customer; casting is not necessary. I just love the generics added to VB.NET 2005, don't you?

```
If ((Object.Equals(previousValue, value) = false)  _
    OrElse (Me._Customer.HasLoadedOrAssignedValue = false)) Then
```

Next, the preceding line of code checks to see if the Customer currently being assigned to the Order via the passed value parameter is not the same Customer that is already assigned to the Order, because if it is, there is nothing that needs to be done unless the Customer has not been loaded or assigned a value yet. Not only is this logically sensible, when I get to the recursive nature of how this code works, this line of code will become very important, as it is what will cause the recursion to stop.

```
Me.SendPropertyChanging()
```

In the preceding line of code, the SendPropertyChanging method is called to raise the change notification event.

```
If ((previousValue Is Nothing) = false) Then
```

Next, the code determines if a Customer object, the parent object, is already assigned to the Order object, the child object, by comparing the previousValue to Nothing. Remember, at this point, the Order object's Customer is still the same as the previousValue variable.

If a Customer is assigned to the Order—meaning the previousValue, which represents the assigned Customer, is not Nothing—the code needs to set the Order object's Customer EntityRef(Of T) object's Entity property to Nothing in the following line:

```
Me._Customer.Entity = Nothing
```

The Entity property is set to Nothing in the preceding line of code to halt the recursion that will be set in motion in the next line of code. Since the Order object's Customer property's Entity property is now Nothing and doesn't reference the actual Customer object, but the Customer object's Orders property still contains this Order in its collection, the graph is inconsistent at this moment in time.

In the next line of code, the Remove method is called on the Customer object's Orders property and the current Order is passed as the Order to be removed.

```
previousValue.Orders.Remove(Me)
End If
```

Calling the Remove method will cause the Customer class's detach_Orders method to get called and passed the Order that is to be removed. In the detach_Orders method, the passed Order object's Customer property is set to Nothing. To refresh your memory, here is what the detach_Orders method looks like:

This Code Is a Separate Method Listed Here for Your Convenience

```
Private Sub detach_Orders(ByVal entity As [Order])
  Me.SendPropertyChanging
  entity.Customer = Nothing
End Sub
```

When the detach_Orders method is called, the passed Order has its Customer property set to Nothing. This causes the passed Order object's Customer property's Set method to be called, which is the method that invoked the code that invoked the detach_Orders method, so the very method that started this process of removing the Order gets called recursively, and the value of Nothing is passed as the value to the Set method. The flow of execution is now in a recursed call to the Customer Set method.

The detach_Orders Method Causes the Set Method to Be Called Recursively

```
Set
  Dim previousValue As Customer = Me._Customer.Entity
  If ((Object.Equals(previousValue, value) = false) _
       OrElse (Me._Customer.HasLoadedOrAssignedValue = false)) Then
```

In the second line of the Set method, the passed value is checked, and if it is equal to the currently assigned Customer property's Entity property, this recursed call to the Set method returns without doing anything. Because in the previous line of code of the first, nonrecursed Set method call the Customer property's Entity property was set to Nothing, and because Nothing was passed as the value in the detach_Orders method, they are indeed equal: the recursed invocation of the Set method exits without doing anything more, and the flow of control returns back to the first invocation of the Set method. This is what I meant in a previous paragraph when I said the Entity property was set to Nothing to halt recursion. Now, take a break while I get some aspirin.

So, once the recursed call to the Set method returned, flow returns to the last line in the initial invocation of the Set method I was discussing.

This Line of Code Is Repeated from a Previous Snippet for Your Convenience

```
      previousValue.Orders.Remove(Me)
  End If
```

Once the Orders.Remove method has completed, the Customer object's Orders property no longer contains a reference to this Order, therefore the graph is now consistent again.

Obviously if you are planning to write your entity classes, you should plan to spend some time in the debugger on this. Just put breakpoints in the detach_Orders method and the Set method, and watch what happens.

Next, the Order object's Customer object's Entity property is assigned to be the new Customer object that was passed to the Set method in the value parameter.

```
  Me._Customer.Entity = value
```

After all, this is the Customer property's Set method. We were trying to assign the Order to a new Customer. And again, at this point, the Order has a reference to the newly assigned Customer, but the newly assigned Customer does not have a reference to the Order, so the graph is no longer consistent.

Next, the code checks to see if the Customer being assigned to the Order is not Nothing, because if it is not, the newly assigned Customer needs to be assigned to the Order.

```
  If ((value Is Nothing) = false) Then
```

If the Customer object passed in the value parameter is not Nothing, add the current Order to the passed Customer object's collection of Order objects.

```
      value.Orders.Add(Me)
```

When the Order is added to the passed Customer object's Orders collection in the preceding line, the delegate that was passed to the callback method in the Customer object's EntitySet(Of T) constructor will be called. So, the result of making the assignment is that the Customer object's attach_Orders method gets called.

This, in turn, will assign the current Order object's Customer to the passed Customer resulting in the Order object's Customer property's Set method being called again. The code recurses into the Set method just like it did before. However, just two code statements prior to the previous code statement, and before we recursed, the Order object's Customer property's Entity property was set to the new Customer, and this is the Customer who is passed to the Set method by the attach_Orders method. Again, the Set method code is called recursively, and eventually the second line of code, which is listed next, is called.

The Following Line of Code Is from Another Invocation of the Set Method

```
If ((Object.Equals(previousValue, value) = false) _
    OrElse (Me._Customer.HasLoadedOrAssignedValue = false)) Then
```

Since the Order object's current Customer object, which is now stored in previousValue, and the value parameter are the same, the Set method returns without doing anything more, and the recursed call is over.

In the next line of code, the current Order object's CustomerID member is set to the new Customer object's CustomerID.

```
Me._CustomerID = value.CustomerID
```

If the newly assigned Customer is Nothing, then the code merely sets the Order object's CustomerID member to the default value of the member's data type, which in this case is a String.

```
Else
  Me._CustomerID = CType(Nothing, String)
End If
```

If the CustomerID member had been of type Integer, the code would have set it to CType(Nothing, Integer).

In the very last line of the code, the SendPropertyChanged method is called and passed the name of the property being changed to raise the change notification event.

```
Me.SendPropertyChanged("Customer")
End If
```

This pattern is relevant for one-to-many relationships. For a one-to-one relationship, each side of the relationship would be implemented as the child side was in this example, with a couple of changes. Since in a one-to-one relationship there is no logical parent or child, let's pretend that the relationship between customers and orders is one-to-one. This will give me a name to use to reference each class since parent and child no longer apply.

If you are writing the entity classes by hand and the relationship between the Customer class and Order class is one-to-one, then each of those classes will contain a property that is of type EntityRef(Of T) where type T is the other entity class. The Customer class will contain an EntityRef(Order) and the Order class will contain an EntityRef(Of Customer). Since neither class contains an EntitySet(Of T), there are no calls to the Add and Remove methods that exist in the pattern for one-to-many relationships as I previously described.

So, assuming a one-to-one relationship between orders and customers, the Order class Customer property Set method would look basically like it does previously, except, when we are removing the assignment of the current Order to the original Customer. Since that original Customer has a single Order, we will not be removing the current Order from a collection of Order objects; we will merely be assigning the Customer object's Order property to Nothing.

So instead of this line of code

```
previousValue.Orders.Remove(Me)
```

we would have this line of code:

```
previousValue.Order = Nothing
```

Likewise, when we assign the current Order to the new Customer, since it has a single Order, instead of calling the Add method on a collection of Order objects, we merely assign the new Customer object's Order property to the current Order.

So instead of this line of code

```
value.Orders.Add(Me)
```

we would have this line of code:

```
value.Order = Me
```

As you can see, handling graph consistency is not trivial, and it gets confusing fast. Fortunately, there are two tools that take care of all of this for you. Their names are SqlMetal and the Object Relational Designer. For maintaining graph consistency and properly implementing change notifications, they are worth their weight in, uh, metal. Perhaps the command-line tool should have been named SQLGold, but I suspect that the metal portion of the name came from the term *metalanguage*.

Calling the Appropriate Partial Methods

When Microsoft added partial methods to make extending generated code, such as entity classes, easier, they threw a little bit more responsibility your way if you are going to implement your entity classes yourself.

There are several partial methods you should declare in your hand-written entity classes:

```
Partial Private Sub OnLoaded()
Partial Private Sub OnValidate(ByVal action As System.Data.Linq.ChangeAction)
Partial Private Sub OnCreated()
Partial Private Sub On[Property]Changing(ByVal value As [Type])
Partial Private Sub On[Property]Changed()
```

You should have a pair of On[Property]Changing and On[Property]Changed methods for each entity class property.

For the OnLoaded and OnValidate methods, you do not need to add calls anywhere in your entity class code for them; they will be called by the DataContext for you.

You should add code to call the OnCreated method inside your entity class's constructor like this:

Calling the OnCreated Partial Method

```
Public Sub New()
  OnCreated()
  ...
End Sub
```

Then, for each mapped entity class property, you should add a call to the On[Property] Changing and On[Property]Changed methods just prior to and just after a change to the entity class property like this:

An Entity Class Property Set Method Calling the On[Property]Changing and On[Property] Changed Methods

```
<Column(Storage:="_CompanyName", DbType:="NVarChar(40) NOT NULL", _
  CanBeNull:=false)> _
Public Property CompanyName() As String
  Get
    Return Me._CompanyName
  End Get
  Set
    If (String.Equals(Me._CompanyName, value) = false) Then
      Me.OnCompanyNameChanging(value)
      Me.SendPropertyChanging
      Me._CompanyName = value
      Me.SendPropertyChanged("CompanyName")
      Me.OnCompanyNameChanged
    End If
  End Set
End Property
```

Notice that the On[Property]Changing method is called before the SendPropertyChanging method is called, and the On[Property]Changed method is called after the SendPropertyChanged method.

By declaring and calling these partial methods, you are giving other developers easy extensibility with no performance cost should they choose to not take advantage of it. That's the beauty of partial methods.

EntityRef(Of T) Complications

While the private class member data type for an associated class is of type EntityRef(Of T), the public property for that private class member must return the type of the entity class, not EntityRef(Of T).

Let's take a look at the way SqlMetal generates the property for an EntityRef(Of T) private member.

A Public Property for a Class Member Returning the Entity Class Type Instead of EntityRef(Of T)

```
<Table(Name:="dbo.Orders")>  _
Partial Public Class [Order]
    Implements System.ComponentModel.INotifyPropertyChanging, _
    System.ComponentModel.INotifyPropertyChanged
  ...
  Private _Customer As EntityRef(Of Customer)
  ...
  <Association(Name:="FK_Orders_Customers", Storage:="_Customer", _
    ThisKey:="CustomerID", OtherKey:="CustomerID", IsForeignKey:=true)>  _
  Public Property Customer() As Customer
    Get
      Return Me._Customer.Entity
    End Get
    Set
      ...
    End Set
  End Property
  ...
End Class
```

As you can see, even though the private class member is of type EntityRef(Of Customer), the Customer property returns the type Customer, not EntityRef(Of Customer). This is important because any reference in a query to type EntityRef(Of T) will not get translated into SQL.

EntitySet(Of T) Complications

While public properties for private class members of type EntityRef(Of T) should return a type T instead of EntityRef(Of T), the same is not true for public properties for private class members of type EntitySet(Of T). Let's take a look at the code SqlMetal generated for a private class member of type EntitySet(Of T).

An EntitySet(Of T) Private Class Member and Its Property

```
<Table(Name:="dbo.Customers")>  _
Partial Public Class Customer
    Implements System.ComponentModel.INotifyPropertyChanging, _
    System.ComponentModel.INotifyPropertyChanged
  ...
  Private _Orders As EntitySet(Of [Order])
  ...
  <Association(Name:="FK_Orders_Customers", Storage:="_Orders", _
    ThisKey:="CustomerID", OtherKey:="CustomerID", DeleteRule:="NO ACTION")>  _
  Public Property Orders() As EntitySet(Of [Order])
    Get
      Return Me._Orders
    End Get
    Set
```

```
      Me._Orders.Assign(value)
    End Set
  End Property
  ...
End Class
```

As you can see, the property return type is `EntitySet(Order)`, just like the private class member type. Since `EntitySet(Of T)` implements the `ICollection(Of T)` interface, you may have the property return the type of `ICollection(Of T)` if you would like to hide the implementation details.

Another complication to keep in mind when writing your own entity classes is that when you write a public setter for an `EntitySet(Of T)` property, you should use its `Assign` method, as opposed to merely assigning the passed value to the `EntitySet(Of T)` class member. This will allow the entity object to continue using the original collection of associated entity objects, since the collection may already be getting tracked by the `DataContext` object's change tracking service.

Looking at the previous example code again, as you can see, instead of assigning the member variable `this._Orders` to the value of variable `value`, it calls the `Assign` method.

Entity Class Attributes and Attribute Properties

Entity classes are defined by the attributes and attribute properties that map the entity class to a database table and the entity class properties to database table columns. Attributes define the existence of a mapping, and the attribute properties provide the specifics on how to map. For example, it is the `Table` attribute that defines that a class is mapped to a database table, but it is the `Name` property that specifies the database table name to which to map the class.

There is no better way to understand the attributes and attribute properties, and how they work, than by examining the attributes generated by the experts. So, we will analyze the `Customer` entity object generated by SqlMetal.

Here is a portion of the `Customer` entity class:

A Portion of the SqlMetal-Generated Customer Entity Class

```
<Table(Name:="dbo.Customers")> _
Partial Public Class Customer
    Implements System.ComponentModel.INotifyPropertyChanging, _
    System.ComponentModel.INotifyPropertyChanged
  ...
  <Column(Storage:="_CustomerID", DbType:="NChar(5) NOT NULL", _
    CanBeNull:=false, IsPrimaryKey:=true)> _
  Public Property CustomerID() As String
    Get
      Return Me._CustomerID
    End Get
    Set(ByVal value As String)
      If (String.Equals(Me._CustomerID, value) = false) Then
```

```
        Me.OnCustomerIDChanging(value)
        Me.SendPropertyChanging()
        Me._CustomerID = value
        Me.SendPropertyChanged("CustomerID")
        Me.OnCustomerIDChanged()
      End If
    End Set
  End Property
  ...
  <Association(Name:="FK_Orders_Customers", Storage:="_Orders", _
    ThisKey:="CustomerID", OtherKey:="CustomerID", DeleteRule:="NO ACTION")> _
  Public Property Orders() As EntitySet(Of [Order])
    Get
      Return Me._Orders
    End Get
    Set
      Me._Orders.Assign(value)
    End Set
  End Property
  ...
End Class
```

For the sake of brevity, I have omitted all of the parts of the entity class except those containing LINQ to SQL attributes. I have also eliminated any redundant attributes.

And here is a portion containing a stored procedure and user-defined function:

A Portion Containing a Stored Procedure and User-Defined Function

```
<FunctionAttribute(Name:="dbo.Get Customer And Orders"), _
  ResultType(GetType(GetCustomerAndOrdersResult1)), _
  ResultType(GetType(GetCustomerAndOrdersResult2))> _
Public Function GetCustomerAndOrders( _
  <Parameter(Name:="CustomerID", DbType:="NChar(5)")> _
  ByVal customerID As String) As IMultipleResults
  ...
End Function


<FunctionAttribute(Name:="dbo.MinUnitPriceByCategory", IsComposable:=true)> _
Public Function MinUnitPriceByCategory(<Parameter(DbType:="Int")> _
  ByVal categoryID As System.Nullable(Of Integer)) _
    As <Parameter(DbType:="Money")> System.Nullable(Of Decimal)
  ...
End Function
```

In the preceding code fragments, the attributes are in bold type. I listed these code fragments to provide context for the discussion of attributes.

Database

The Database attribute specifies for a derived DataContext class the default name of the mapped database if the database name is not specified in the connection information when the DataContext is instantiated. If the Database attribute is not specified and the database is not specified in the connection information, the name of the derived DataContext class will be assumed to be the name of the database with which to connect.

So for clarity, the order of precedence for where the database name comes from, in highest priority order, follows:

1. The connection information provided when the derived DataContext class is instantiated

2. The database name specified in the Database attribute

3. The name of the derived DataContext class

Here is the relevant portion of the SqlMetal-generated derived DataContext class named Northwind:

From the SqlMetal-Generated Northwind Class

```
Partial Public Class Northwind
    Inherits System.Data.Linq.DataContext
```

As you can see, the Database attribute is not specified in the generated Northwind class that derives from the DataContext class. Since this class was generated by Microsoft, I assume this is intentional. If you were going to specify the Database attribute, and you wanted it to default to a database named NorthwindTest, the code should look like this:

The Database Attribute

```
<Database(Name:="NorthwindTest")> _
Partial Public Class Northwind
    Inherits System.Data.Linq.DataContext
```

I cannot necessarily see a reason to omit specifying the Database attribute. Perhaps it is because if you specify the database in the connection information, that will override the derived DataContext class name and the Database attribute. Perhaps they thought if you don't specify the database name in the connection information, the derived DataContext class name will be used, and that is satisfactory.

I thought about this and came to the conclusion that I personally don't like the idea of the generated class derived from DataContext connecting to a database by default. I cringe at the thought of running an application, perhaps accidentally, that has not yet been configured and having it default to a database. That sounds like a potentially painful mistake just waiting to happen. In fact, I might just advocate specifying a Database attribute with an intentionally ludicrous name just to prevent it from connecting to a default database. Perhaps something like this:

A Derived DataContext Class Highly Unlikely to Actually Connect to a Database by Default

```
<Database(Name:=" goopeygobezileywag")>
Partial Public Class Northwind
    Inherits System.Data.Linq.DataContext
```

I can't see that connecting to a database unless I have specified one in the connection information passed to the DataContext during instantiation.

Name (String)

The Name attribute property is a String that specifies the name of the database with which to connect if the database name is not specified in the connection information when the class derived from the DataContext class is instantiated. If the Name attribute property is not specified, and the database name is not specified in the connection information, the name of the derived DataContext class will be assumed to be the name of the database with which to connect.

Table

It is the Table attribute that specifies in which database table an entity class is to be persisted. The entity class name does not necessarily need to be the same as the table. Here is the relevant portion of the entity class:

The Table Attribute

```
<Table(Name:="dbo.Customers")> _
Partial Public Class Customer
    Implements System.ComponentModel.INotifyPropertyChanging, _
    System.ComponentModel.INotifyPropertyChanged
```

Notice that the Table attribute is specifying the name of the database table by specifying the Name attribute property. If the name of the entity class is the same as the name of the database table, the Name attribute property can be omitted, as the class name will be the default table name to which it is mapped.

In this example, because I specified the pluralize option when I used SqlMetal to generate my Northwind entity classes, the database table name, Customers, is converted to its singular form, Customer, for the class name. Since the class name does not match the database table name, the Name property must be specified.

Name (String)

The Name attribute property is a String that specifies the name of the table to which to map this entity class. If the Name attribute property is not specified, the entity class name will be mapped to a database table of the same name by default.

Column

The Column attribute defines that an entity class property is mapped to a database field. Here is the relevant portion of the entity class:

The Column Attribute

```
Private _CustomerID As String
...
<Column(Storage:="_CustomerID", DbType:="NChar(5) NOT NULL", _
  CanBeNull:=false, IsPrimaryKey:=true)> _
Public Property CustomerID() As String
```

In this example, because the Storage attribute property is specified, LINQ to SQL can directly access the private member variable _CustomerID, bypassing the public property accessor CustomerID. If the Storage attribute property is not specified, the public accessors will be used. This can be useful for bypassing special logic that may exist in your public property accessors.

You can see that the database type for this field is specified by the DbType attribute property as an NCHAR that is five characters long. Because the CanBeNull attribute property is specified with a value of false, this field's value in the database cannot be NULL, and because the IsPrimaryKey attribute property is specified with a value of true, this is a primary key column for a record in the database.

It is not necessary for every property of an entity class to be mapped to the database. You may have runtime data properties that you would not want to persist to the database, and this is perfectly fine. For those properties, you just wouldn't specify the Column attribute.

You can also have persisted columns that are read-only. This is accomplished by mapping the column and specifying the Storage attribute property to reference the private member variable but not implementing the Set method of the class property. The DataContext can still access the private member, but since there is no Set method for the entity class property, no one can change it.

AutoSync (AutoSync Enum)

The AutoSync attribute property is an AutoSync Enum that instructs the runtime to retrieve the mapped column's value after an insert or update database operation. The possible values are Default, Always, Never, OnInsert, and OnUpdate. I am going to let you guess which one is used by default. According to Microsoft documentation, the default behavior is Never.

This attribute property setting is overridden when either IsDbGenerated or IsVersion is set to true.

CanBeNull (Boolean)

The CanBeNull attribute property is a Boolean that specifies if the mapped database column's value can be NULL. This attribute property defaults to true.

DbType (String)

The DbType attribute property is a String that specifies the data type of the column in the database to which this entity class property is mapped. If the DbType attribute property is not specified, the database column type will be inferred from the data type of the entity class property. This attribute property is only used to define the column if the CreateDatabase method is called.

Expression (String)

The `Expression` attribute property is a `String` that defines a computed column in the database. It is only used if the `CreateDatabase` method is called. This attribute property defaults to `String.Empty`.

IsDbGenerated (Boolean)

The `IsDbGenerated` attribute property is a `Boolean` specifying that the database table column that the entity class property is mapped to is automatically generated by the database. If a primary key is specified with its `IsDbGenerated` attribute property set to `true`, the class property's `DbType` attribute property must be set to include the `IDENTITY` keyword.

An entity class property whose `IsDbGenerated` attribute property is set to `true` will be immediately synchronized after a record is inserted into the database regardless of the `AutoSync` attribute property setting, and the entity class property's synchronized value will be visible in the entity class property once the `SubmitChanges` method has successfully completed. This attribute property defaults to `false`.

IsDiscriminator (Boolean)

The `IsDiscriminator` attribute property is a `Boolean` that specifies that the mapped entity class property is the entity class property that stores the discriminator value for entity class inheritance. This attribute property defaults to `false`. Please read the section about the `InheritanceMapping` attribute later in this chapter, and the section titled "Entity Class Inheritance" in Chapter 18 for more information.

IsPrimaryKey (Boolean)

The `IsPrimaryKey` attribute property is a `Boolean` specifying whether the database table column that this entity class property is mapped to is part of the database table's primary key. Multiple class properties may be specified to be part of the primary key. In that case, all of the mapped database columns act as a composite primary key. For an entity object to be updateable, at least one entity class property must have an attribute property `IsPrimaryKey` set to `true`. Otherwise, the entity objects mapped to this table will be read-only. This attribute property defaults to `false`.

IsVersion (Boolean)

The `IsVersion` attribute property is a `Boolean` that specifies that the mapped database column is either a version number or a timestamp that provides version information for the record. By specifying the `IsVersion` attribute property and setting its value to `true`, the mapped database column will be incremented if it is a version number and updated if it is a timestamp, whenever the database table record is updated.

An entity class property whose `IsVersion` attribute property is set to `true` will be immediately synchronized after a record is inserted or updated in the database regardless of the `AutoSync` attribute property setting, and the entity class property's synchronized value will be visible in the entity class property once the `SubmitChanges` method has successfully completed. This attribute property defaults to `false`.

Name (String)

The Name attribute property is a String that specifies the name of the table column to which to map this entity class property. If the Name attribute property is not specified, the entity class property will be mapped to a database table column of the same name by default.

Storage (String)

The Storage attribute property is a String that specifies the private member variable that the entity class property's value is stored in. This allows LINQ to SQL to bypass the property's public accessors and any business logic they contain and allows it to directly access the private member variable. If the Storage attribute property is not specified, the property's public accessors will be used by default.

UpdateCheck (UpdateCheck Enum)

The UpdateCheck attribute property is an UpdateCheck Enum that controls how optimistic concurrency detection behaves for the entity class property and its mapped database column if no entity class mapped property has an attribute property of IsVersion set to true. The three possible values are UpdateCheck.Always, UpdateCheck.WhenChanged, and UpdateCheck.Never. If no entity class property has an attribute property of IsVersion set to true, the value of the UpdateCheck attribute property will default to Always. You may read Chapter 17 for more information about this attribute property and its effect.

Association

The Association attribute is used to define relationships between two tables, such as a primary key to foreign key relationship. In this context, the entity whose mapped table contains the primary key is referred to as the parent, and the entity whose mapped table contains the foreign key is the child. Here are the relevant portions of two entity classes containing an association:

The Association from the Parent (Customer) Entity Class

```
<Association(Name:="FK_Orders_Customers", Storage:="_Orders", _
  ThisKey:="CustomerID", OtherKey:="CustomerID", DeleteRule:="NO ACTION")> _
Public Property Orders() As EntitySet(Of [Order])
```

The Association from the Child (Order) Entity Class

```
<Association(Name:="FK_Orders_Customers", Storage:="_Customer", _
  ThisKey:="CustomerID", OtherKey:="CustomerID", IsForeignKey:=true)> _
Public Property Customer() As Customer
```

For this discussion of the Association attribute and its properties, I am using the Customer entity class as the parent example, and the Order entity class as the child example. Therefore, I have provided the relevant Association attributes that exist in both the Customer and Order entity classes.

When discussing the Association attribute properties, some attribute properties will pertain to the class in which the Association attribute exists, and other attribute properties will pertain to the other associated entity class. In this context, the class in which the Association attribute exists is referred to as the *source* class, and the other associated entity class is the *target* class. So, if I am discussing the attribute properties for the Association attribute that is specified in the Customer entity class, the Customer entity class is the source class and the Order entity class is the target. If I am discussing the attribute properties for the Association attribute that is specified in the Order entity class, the Order entity class is the source class and the Customer entity class is the target.

The Association attribute defines that the source entity class, Customer, has a relationship to the target entity class, Order.

In the preceding examples, the Name attribute property is specified to provide a name for the relationship. The Name attribute property's value corresponds to the name of the foreign key constraint in the database and will be used to create the foreign key constraint if the CreateDatabase method is called. The Storage attribute property is also specified. Specifying the Storage attribute property allows LINQ to SQL to bypass the property's public accessors to get access to the entity class property's value.

With associations of the primary key to foreign key variety, an entity class that is the parent in the relationship will store the reference to the child entity class in an EntitySet(Of T) collection since there may be many children. The entity class that is the child will store the reference to the parent entity class in an EntityRef(Of T), since there will be only one. Please read the sections titled "EntitySet(Of T)" and "EntityRef(Of T)" later in this chapter, and "Deferred Loading" and "Immediate Loading with the DataLoadOptions Class" in Chapter 14 for more information about associations and their characteristics.

DeleteOnNull (Boolean)

The DeleteOnNull attribute property is a Boolean that, if set to true, specifies that an entity object that is on the child side of an association should be deleted if the reference to its parent is set to Nothing.

This attribute property's value is inferred by SqlMetal if there is a "Cascade" Delete Rule specified for the foreign key constraint in the database and the foreign key column does not allow NULL.

DeleteRule (String)

The DeleteRule attribute property is a String that specifies the Delete Rule for a foreign key constraint. It is only used by LINQ to SQL when the constraint is created in the database by the CreateDatabase method.

The possible values are "NO ACTION", "CASCADE", "SET NULL", and "SET DEFAULT". Consult your SQL Server documentation for the definition of each.

IsForeignKey (Boolean)

The IsForeignKey attribute property is a Boolean that, if set to true, specifies that the source entity class is the side of the relationship containing the foreign key; therefore it is the child side of the relationship. This attribute property defaults to false.

In the Association attribute examples shown previously for the Customer and Order entity classes, because the Association attribute specified for the Order entity class contains the IsForeignKey attribute property whose value is set to true, the Order class is the child class in this relationship.

IsUnique (Boolean)

The IsUnique attribute property is a Boolean that, if true, specifies that a uniqueness constraint exists on the foreign key, indicating a one-to-one relationship between the two entity classes. This attribute property defaults to false.

Name (String)

The Name attribute property is a String that specifies the name of the foreign key constraint. This will be used to create the foreign key constraint if the CreateDatabase method is called. It is also used to differentiate multiple relationships between the same two entities. In that case, if both sides of the parent and child relationship specify a name, they must be the same.

If you do not have multiple relationships between the same two entity classes, and you do not call the CreateDatabase method, this attribute property is not necessary. There is no default value for this attribute property.

OtherKey (String)

The OtherKey attribute property is a String that is a comma-delimited list of all of the entity class properties of the target entity class that make up the key, either primary or foreign, depending on which side of the relationship the target entity is. If this attribute property is not specified, the primary key members of the target entity class are used by default.

It is important to realize that the Association attribute specified on each side of the association relationship, Customer and Order, specify where both sides' keys are located. The Association attribute specified in the Customer entity class specifies which Customer entity class properties contain the key for the relationship and which Order entity class properties contain the key for the relationship. Likewise, the Association attribute specified in the Order entity class specifies which Order entity class properties contain the key for the relationship and which Customer entity class properties contain the key for the relationship.

It often may not look as though each side always specifies both sides' key locations. Because typically on the parent side of the relationship the table's primary key is the key used, the ThisKey attribute property need not be specified, since the primary key is the default. And on the child side, the OtherKey attribute property need not be specified, because the parent's primary key is the default. Therefore, it is common to see the OtherKey attribute property specified only on the parent side and the ThisKey attribute property specified on the child side. But because of the default values, both the parent and child know the keys on both sides.

Storage (String)

The Storage attribute property is a String that specifies the private member variable that the entity class property's value is stored in. This allows LINQ to SQL to bypass the entity class property's public accessors and directly access the private member variable. This allows any business logic in the accessors to be bypassed. If the Storage attribute property is not specified, the property's public accessors will be used by default.

Microsoft recommends that both members of an association relationship be entity class properties with separate entity class member variables for data storage and for the Storage attribute property to be specified.

ThisKey (String)

The ThisKey attribute property is a String that is a comma-delimited list of all of the entity class properties of the source entity class that make up the key, either primary or foreign, depending on which side of the relationship the source entity is, which is determined by the IsForeignKey attribute property. If the ThisKey attribute property is not specified, the primary key members of the source entity class are used by default.

Since the example Association attribute shown previously for the Customer entity class does not contain the IsForeignKey attribute property, we know that the Customer entity class is the parent side of the relationship, the side containing the primary key. Because the Association attribute does not specify the ThisKey attribute property, we know the Customer table's primary key value will become the foreign key in the associated table, Orders.

Because the Association attribute shown previously for the Order entity class specifies the IsForeignKey attribute with a value of true, we know the Orders table will be the side of the association containing the foreign key. And, because the Association attribute does specify the ThisKey attribute property with a value of CustomerID, we know that the CustomerID column of the Orders table will be where the foreign key is stored.

It is important to realize that the Association attribute specified on each side of the association relationship, Customer and Order, specifies where both sides' keys are located. The Association attribute specified in the Customer entity class specifies which Customer entity class properties contain the key for the relationship and which Order entity class properties contain the key for the relationship. Likewise, the Association attribute specified in the Order entity class specifies which Order entity class properties contain the key for the relationship and which Customer entity class properties contain the key for the relationship.

It often may not look as though each side always specifies both sides' key locations. Because typically on the parent side of the relationship, the table's primary key is the key used, the ThisKey attribute property need not be specified since the primary key is the default. And on the child side, the OtherKey attribute property need not be specified, because the parent's primary key is the default. Therefore, it is common to see the OtherKey attribute property specified only on the parent side and the ThisKey attribute property specified on the child side. But because of the default values, both the parent and child know the keys on both sides.

FunctionAttribute

The FunctionAttribute attribute defines that an entity class method, when called, will call a stored procedure or scalar-valued or table-valued user-defined function. Here is the relevant portion of the derived DataContext class for a stored procedure:

A FunctionAttribute Attribute Mapping a Method to a Stored Procedure in the Northwind Database

```
<FunctionAttribute(Name:="dbo.Get Customer And Orders"), _
  ResultType(GetType(GetCustomerAndOrdersResult1)), _
  ResultType(GetType(GetCustomerAndOrdersResult2))> _
Public Function GetCustomerAndOrders( _
  <Parameter(Name:="CustomerID", DbType:="NChar(5)")> _
  ByVal customerID As String) As IMultipleResults
  ...
End Function
```

From this, we can see that there is a method named GetCustomerAndOrders that will call the stored procedure named "Get Customer And Orders". We know the method is being mapped to a stored procedure as opposed to a user-defined function because the IsComposable attribute property is not specified and therefore defaults to false, thereby mapping the method to a stored procedure. We can also see that it returns multiple result shapes, because there are two ResultType attributes specified.

Writing your derived DataContext class so that it can call a stored procedure is not quite as trivial as mapping an entity class to a table. In addition to the appropriate attributes being specified, you must also call the appropriate version of the DataContext class's ExecuteMethodCall method. You will read about this method in Chapter 16.

Of course, as is typical, this is only necessary when writing your own DataContext class, because SqlMetal and the Object Relational Designer do it for you.

The relevant portion of the derived DataContext class for a user-defined function follows:

A FunctionAttribute Attribute Mapping a Method to a User-Defined Function in the Northwind Database

```
<FunctionAttribute(Name:="dbo.MinUnitPriceByCategory", IsComposable:=true)> _
Public Function MinUnitPriceByCategory(<Parameter(DbType:="Int")> _
  ByVal categoryID As System.Nullable(Of Integer)) _
  As <Parameter(DbType:="Money")> System.Nullable(Of Decimal)
  ...
End Function
```

From this, we can see that there is a method named MinUnitPriceByCategory that will call the user-defined function named "MinUnitPriceByCategory". We know the method is being mapped to a user-defined function, as opposed to a stored procedure, because the IsComposable attribute property is set to true. We can also see from the return Parameter attribute's DbType attribute property that the user-defined function will return a value of type Money.

Writing your derived DataContext class so that it can call a user-defined function is not quite as trivial as mapping an entity class to a table. In addition to the appropriate attributes being specified, you must also call the DataContext class's ExecuteMethodCall method for scalar-valued user-defined functions or the CreateMethodCallQuery method for table-valued user-defined functions. You will read about these methods in Chapter 16 as well.

Of course, as is typical, this is only necessary when writing your own DataContext class, because SqlMetal and the Object Relational Designer do it for you.

IsComposable (Boolean)

The IsComposable attribute property is a Boolean that specifies whether the mapped function is calling a stored procedure or a user-defined function. If the value of IsComposable is true, the method is being mapped to a user-defined function. If the value of IsComposable is false, the method is being mapped to a stored procedure. This attribute property's value defaults to false if it is not specified, so a method mapped with the FunctionAttribute attribute defaults to a stored procedure if the IsComposable attribute property is not specified.

Name (String)

The Name attribute property is a String that specifies the actual name of the stored procedure or user-defined function in the database. If the Name attribute property is not specified, the name of the stored procedure or user-defined function is assumed to be the same as the name of the entity class method.

ResultType

The ResultType attribute maps the data type returned by a stored procedure to a .NET class in which to store the returned data. Stored procedures that return multiple shapes will specify multiple ResultType attributes in their respective order.

ResultType Attributes from the Northwind Class

```
<FunctionAttribute(Name:="dbo.Get Customer And Orders"), _
  ResultType(GetType(GetCustomerAndOrdersResult1)), _
  ResultType(GetType(GetCustomerAndOrdersResult2))> _
Public Function GetCustomerAndOrders( _
  <Parameter(Name:="CustomerID", DbType:="NChar(5)")> _
  ByVal customerID As String) As IMultipleResults
  ...
End Function
```

From the preceding code, we can tell that the stored procedure this method is mapped to will first return a shape of type GetCustomerAndOrdersResult1 followed by a shape of type GetCustomerAndOrdersResult2. SqlMetal is kind enough to even generate entity classes for GetCustomerAndOrdersResult1 and GetCustomerAndOrdersResult2.

Parameter

The Parameter attribute maps a method parameter to a parameter of a database stored procedure or user-defined function. It is also used to map the returned data type from a scalar-valued user-defined function. Here is the relevant portion of the derived DataContext class:

A Parameter Attribute from the Northwind Class

```
<FunctionAttribute(Name:="dbo.Get Customer And Orders"), _
  ResultType(GetType(GetCustomerAndOrdersResult1)), _
  ResultType(GetType(GetCustomerAndOrdersResult2))> _
Public Function GetCustomerAndOrders( _
  <Parameter(Name:="CustomerID", DbType:="NChar(5)")> _
  ByVal customerID As String) As IMultipleResults
  ...
End Function
```

From this, we can see that the GetCustomerAndOrders method, which is mapped to a database stored procedure named "Get Customer And Orders", passes the stored procedure a parameter of type NChar(5).

The `Parameter` attribute is also used to map a scalar-valued user-defined function's returned data type.

A Parameter Attribute Mapped To a Scalar-Valued User-Defined Function's Returned Type

```
<FunctionAttribute(Name:="dbo.MinUnitPriceByCategory", IsComposable:=true)> _
Public Function MinUnitPriceByCategory(<Parameter(DbType:="Int")> _
  ByVal categoryID As System.Nullable(Of Integer)) _
  As <Parameter(DbType:="Money")> System.Nullable(Of Decimal)
  ...
End Function
```

In the preceding code, we can tell that the user-defined function being called will return a value of type `Money` because of the returned `Parameter` attribute and its specified `DbType` attribute property.

DbType (String)

The `DbType` attribute property is a `String` that specifies the database data type and modifiers of the database stored procedure or user-defined function parameter.

Name (String)

The `Name` attribute property is a `String` that specifies the actual name of the parameter of the stored procedure or user-defined function. If the `Name` attribute property is not specified, the name of the database stored procedure or user-defined function parameter is assumed to be the same as the name of the entity class method parameter.

InheritanceMapping

The `InheritanceMapping` attribute is used to map a *discriminator code* to a base class or subclass of that base class. A discriminator code is the value of an entity class property's mapped database table's column for the entity class property specified as the discriminator, which is defined as the entity class property whose `IsDiscriminator` attribute property is set to `True`.

Note If you have a high degree of attention to detail, you may have noticed that when I just referenced the `IsDiscriminator` attribute property's value, I referenced its value as `True` with the first letter in uppercase, whereas prior to this point, I have used lowercase `true`. The difference is that, in the previous parts of this chapter, I was discussing the SqlMetal-generated code. SqlMetal uses lowercase `true` and `false` in the generated code. Since the code I am now discussing is hand-written, and since it is more natural in VB.NET to use uppercase `True` and `False`, I will use the uppercase spelling in this hand-written code.

For an example, let's examine an `InheritanceMapping` attribute.

An InheritanceMapping Attribute

```
<Table(), _
  InheritanceMapping(Code := "G", Type := GetType(Shape), IsDefault := True), _
  InheritanceMapping(Code := "S", Type := GetType(Square)), _
  InheritanceMapping(Code := "R", Type := GetType(Rectangle))> _
```

The preceding InheritanceMapping attribute defines that if a database record has the value "G" in the discriminator column, which means its discriminator code is "G", instantiate that record as a Shape object using the Shape class. Because the IsDefault attribute property is set to True, if the discriminator code of a record doesn't match any of the InheritanceMapping attributes' Code values, that record will be instantiated as a Shape object using the Shape class.

To use inheritance mapping, when a base entity class is declared, one of its entity class properties is given the Column attribute property of IsDiscriminator, and that property's value is set to True. This means that the value of this column will determine, by discrimination, which class, be it the base class or one of its subclasses, a database table record is an instance of. An InheritanceMapping attribute is specified on the base class for each of its subclasses, as well as one for the base class itself. Of those InheritanceMapping attributes, one and only one must be given an attribute property of IsDefault with a value of True. This is so a database table record whose discriminator column does not match any of the discriminator codes specified in any of the InheritanceMapping attributes can be instantiated into a class. It is probably most common for the base class's InheritanceMapping attribute to be specified as the default InheritanceMapping attribute.

Again, all of the InheritanceMapping attributes are specified on the base class only and associate a discriminator code to the base class or one of its subclasses.

Since the Northwind database does not contain any tables used in this way, I will provide three example classes.

Some Example Classes Demonstrating Inheritance Mapping

```
<Table(), _
  InheritanceMapping(Code := "G", Type := GetType(Shape), IsDefault := True), _
  InheritanceMapping(Code := "S", Type := GetType(Square)), _
  InheritanceMapping(Code := "R", Type := GetType(Rectangle))> _
Public Class Shape
  <Column(IsPrimaryKey := True, IsDbGenerated := True, _
    DbType := "Int NOT NULL IDENTITY")> _
  Public Id As Integer

  <Column(IsDiscriminator := True, DbType := "NVarChar(2)")> _
  Public ShapeCode As String

  <Column(DbType := "Int")> _
  Public StartingX As Integer

  <Column(DbType := "Int")> _
  Public StartingY As Integer
End Class
```

```
Public Class Square
    Inherits Shape
  <Column(DbType := "Int")> _
  Public Width As Integer
End Class

Public Class Rectangle
    Inherits Square
  <Column(DbType := "Int")> _
  Public Length As Integer
End Class
```

Here, you can see that I have mapped the Shape class to a table, and since I didn't specify the Name attribute property, the Shape class will be mapped by default to a table named Shape.

Next, you will see three InheritanceMapping attributes. The first one defines that if the value of a database Shape table record's discriminator column is "G", then that record should be instantiated as a Shape object using the Shape class. For my purposes, I chose "G" for *generic*, meaning it is a generic undefined shape. Since it is the ShapeCode property in the Shape class that is the discriminator, meaning it has an attribute property of IsDiscriminator set to True, if a record has a ShapeCode value of "G", that record will get instantiated into a Shape object.

Also, you can see that the first InheritanceMapping attribute has the IsDefault attribute property set to True, so if the value of a Shape record's ShapeCode column matches none of the discriminator codes specified—"G", "S", and "R"—the default mapping is used and the record will be instantiated as a Shape object.

The second InheritanceMapping attribute associates a discriminator code of "S" to the Square class. So, if a record in the database Shape table has a ShapeCode of "S", then that record will be instantiated into a Square object.

The third InheritanceMapping attribute associates a discriminator code of "R" to the Rectangle class. So, if a record in the database Shape table has a ShapeCode of "R", then that record will be instantiated into a Rectangle object.

Any record with a ShapeCode different than those specified will get instantiated into a Shape object, because Shape is the default class as specified with the IsDefault attribute property.

■**Note** Inheritance mapping is discussed and examples are provided in Chapter 18.

Code (Object)

The Code attribute property specifies what the discriminator code is for the mapping to the specified class, which will be specified by the Type attribute property.

IsDefault (Boolean)

The IsDefault attribute property is a Boolean that specifies which InheritanceMapping attribute should be used if a database table record's discriminator column doesn't match any of the discriminator codes specified in any of the InheritanceMapping attributes.

Type (Type)

The Type attribute property specifies the class type to instantiate the record as, when the discriminator column matches the mapped discriminator code.

Data Type Compatibility

Some of the entity class attributes have a DbType attribute property where you can specify the database column data type. This attribute property is only used when the database is created with the CreateDatabase method. Since the mapping between .NET data types and SQL Server data types is not one-to-one, you will need to specify the DbType attribute property if you plan on calling the CreateDatabase method.

Because the .NET Common Language Runtime (CLR) data types that are used in your LINQ code are not the same data types that the database uses, you should refer to the MSDN documentation for SQL-CLR Type Mapping (LINQ to SQL). There is a matrix in that documentation that defines the behavior when converting between CLR data types and SQL data types. If you have trouble locating this information, see the section titled "Additional LINQ to SQL Resources" on my web site at www.linqdev.com. There you will find a link to the MSDN documentation.

You should be aware that some data type conversions are not supported, and others can cause a loss of data depending on the data types involved and the direction of the conversion.

However, I think that you will find the conversions work fine most of the time, and this will not typically be an issue. While writing the examples for the LINQ to SQL chapters, I never encountered an issue caused by the data type conversions. Of course, you should use common sense. If you are trying to map obviously incompatible types, such as a .NET numeric data type to a SQL character data type, you should expect some issues.

XML External Mapping File Schema

As I discuss in the section on SqlMetal in Chapter 13, not only can you map classes to the database with entity classes, you can also use an XML external mapping file. You will learn how to use the XML external mapping file when I cover the constructors for the DataContext class in Chapter 16.

Also, as I discuss in Chapter 13, the easiest way to obtain an XML external mapping file is to call the SqlMetal program and specify the /map option, and one will be generated for you. However, if you intend to create the mapping file manually, you will need to know the schema.

Please refer to the MSDN documentation for the external mapping schema titled "External Mapping Reference (LINQ to SQL)". If you have trouble locating this information, see the section titled "Additional LINQ to SQL Resources" on my web site at www.linqdev.com. There you will find a link to the MSDN documentation.

Projecting into Entity Classes vs. Nonentity Classes

When performing LINQ to SQL queries, you have two options for projecting the returned results. You can project the results into an entity class, or you can project the results into a nonentity class, which could be a named or anonymous class. There is a major difference between projecting into an entity class vs. a nonentity class.

When projecting into an entity class, that entity class gains the benefit of the DataContext object's identity tracking, change tracking, and change processing services. You may make changes to an entity class and persist them to the database with the SubmitChanges method.

When projecting into a nonentity class, barring one specialized exception, you do not get the benefits of the DataContext object's identity tracking, change tracking, and change processing services. This means you cannot change the nonentity class and have it persist using LINQ to SQL. This only makes sense, since the class will not have the necessary attributes or a mapping file to map the class to the database. And, if it does have the attributes or a mapping file, then by definition it *is* an entity class.

Here is an example of a query that projects into an entity class:

Projecting into an Entity Class Provides DataContext Services

```
Dim custs As IEnumerable(Of Customer) = _
  From c In db.Customers _
  Select c
```

After that query, I could make changes to any of the Customer entity objects in the custs sequence, and I would be able to persist them by calling the SubmitChanges method.

Here is an example of a query that projects into a nonentity class:

Projecting into a Nonentity Class Does Not Provide DataContext Services

```
Dim custs = _
  From c In db.Customers _
  Select New With {Key .Id = c.CustomerID, Key .Name = c.ContactName}
```

By projecting into the anonymous class, I will not be able to persist any changes I make to each object in the custs sequence by calling the SubmitChanges method.

I mentioned that there is one specialized exception concerning gaining the benefits of identity tracking, change tracking, and change processing when projecting into nonentity classes. This exception occurs when the class projected into *contains* members that are entity classes. Listing 15-1 contains an example.

Listing 15-1. *Projecting into a Nonentity Class Containing Entity Classes*

```
Dim db As New Northwind("Data Source=.\SQLEXPRESS;Initial Catalog=Northwind;" & _
    "Integrated Security=SSPI;")

Dim cusorders = _
  From o In db.Orders _
  Where o.Customer.CustomerID = "CONSH" _
  Order By o.ShippedDate Descending _
  Select New With {Key .Customer = o.Customer, Key .Order = o}

'  Grab the first order.
Dim firstOrder As Order = cusorders.First().Order
```

```
'  Now, let's save off the first order's shipcountry so I can reset it later.
Dim MyshipCountry As String = firstOrder.ShipCountry
Console.WriteLine("Order is originally shipping to {0}", MyshipCountry)

'  Now, I'll change the order's ship country from UK to USA.
firstOrder.ShipCountry = "USA"
db.SubmitChanges()

'  Query to see that the country was indeed changed.
Dim country As String = ( _
    From o In db.Orders _
    Where o.Customer.CustomerID = "CONSH" _
    Order By o.ShippedDate Descending _
    Select o.ShipCountry).FirstOrDefault()

Console.WriteLine("Order is now shipping to {0}", country)

'  Reset the order in the database so example can be re-run.
firstOrder.ShipCountry = MyshipCountry
db.SubmitChanges()
```

In Listing 15-1, I query for the orders whose customer is "CONSH". I project the returned orders into an anonymous type containing the Customer and each Order. The anonymous class itself does not receive the DataContext services such as identity tracking, change tracking, and change processing, but its components Customer and Order do, because they are entity classes. I then perform another query on the previous query's results to get the first Order. I then save a copy of the Order object's original ShipCountry, so I can restore it at the end of the example, and I display the original ShipCountry to the screen. Next, I change the ShipCountry on the Order and save the change by calling the SubmitChanges method. Then, I query the ShipCountry for this order from the database again and display it just to prove that it was indeed changed in the database. This proves that the SubmitChanges method worked, and that the entity class components of my anonymous type did gain the services of the DataContext object. Then, I reset the ShipCountry back to the original value and save so that the example can be run again and no subsequent examples will be affected.

Here are the results of Listing 15-1:

```
Order is originally shipping to UK
Order is now shipping to USA
```

Listing 15-1 is an example where I projected the query results into a nonentity class type, but because it was composed of an entity class, I was able to gain the benefits of identity tracking, change tracking, and change processing by the DataContext.

There is one interesting note about the preceding code. You will notice that the query that obtains a reference to the first Order is in bold. I did this to catch your attention. Notice that I call the First operator before selecting the portion of the sequence element I am interested in, the Order member. I do this for performance enhancement, because in general, the faster you can narrow the results, the better the performance.

Prefer Object Initialization to Parameterized Construction When Projecting

You are free to project into classes prior to the end of the query for subsequent query operations, but when you do, prefer object initialization to parameterized construction. To understand why, let's take a look at Listing 15-2, which uses object initialization in the projection.

Listing 15-2. *Projecting Using Object Initialization*

```
Dim db As New Northwind("Data Source=.\SQLEXPRESS;Initial Catalog=Northwind;" & _
    "Integrated Security=SSPI;")

db.Log = Console.Out

Dim contacts = _
  From c in db.Customers _
  Where c.City = "Buenos Aires" _
  Select New With { .Name = c.ContactName, .Phone = c.Phone }

Dim orderedContacts = From co In contacts Order By co.Name

For Each contact In orderedContacts
  Console.WriteLine("{0} - {1}", contact.Name, contact.Phone)
Next contact
```

Notice that, in Listing 15-2, I projected into an anonymous class and used object initialization to populate the anonymous objects that get created. Let's take a look at the output of Listing 15-2:

```
SELECT [t0].[ContactName] AS [Name], [t0].[Phone]
FROM [dbo].[Customers] AS [t0]
WHERE [t0].[City] = @p0
ORDER BY [t0].[ContactName]
-- @p0: Input NVarChar (Size = 12; Prec = 0; Scale = 0) [Buenos Aires]
-- Context: SqlProvider(Sql2008) Model: AttributedMetaModel Build: 3.5.30729.1

Patricio Simpson - (1) 135-5555
Sergio Gutiérrez - (1) 123-5555
Yvonne Moncada - (1) 135-5333
```

I am not even interested in the output of the query's results. I really want to see the SQL query that was generated. "So," you ask, "why the need for the For Each loop?" Because without it, due to query execution being deferred, the query would not actually execute.

The significant parts of the LINQ to SQL query for this discussion are the Select and Order By statements. In my LINQ to SQL query, I instruct the query to create a member in the anonymous class named Name that is populated with the ContactName field from the Customers table. I then tell the query to sort by the Name member of the anonymous object into which I projected. The DataContext object has all of that information passed to it. The object initialization is effectively mapping a source field, ContactName, from the Customer class to the destination field, Name, in the anonymous class, and the DataContext object is privy to that mapping. From that information, it is able to know that I am effectively sorting the Customers by the ContactName field, so it can generate the SQL query to do just that. When you look at the generated SQL query, you can see that is exactly what it is doing.

Now, let's take a look at what happens when I project into a named class using parameterized construction. First, I will need a named class. I will use this one:

The Named Class Used in Listing 15-3

```
Public Class CustomerContact
  Public Name As String
  Public Phone As String

  Public Sub New(ByVal name As String, ByVal phone As String)
    Me.Name = name
    Me.Phone = phone
  End Sub
End Class
```

Notice that there is a single constructor that takes two parameters, name and phone. Now, let's take a look at the same code as is in Listing 15-2, except in Listing 15-3, the code will be modified to project into the CustomerContact class using parameterized construction.

Listing 15-3. *Projecting Using Parameterized Construction*

```
Dim db As New Northwind("Data Source=.\SQLEXPRESS;Initial Catalog=Northwind;" & _
    "Integrated Security=SSPI;")

db.Log = Console.Out

Dim contacts = _
  From c In db.Customers _
  Where c.City = "Buenos Aires" _
  Select New CustomerContact(c.ContactName, c.Phone)

Dim orderedContacts = From co In contacts Order By co.Name

For Each contact In orderedContacts
  Console.WriteLine("{0} - {1}", contact.Name, contact.Phone)
Next contact
```

Again, I am focusing on the Select and Order By statements. As you can see in Listing 15-3, instead of projecting into an anonymous class, I am projecting into the CustomerContact class. And, instead of using object initialization to initialize the created objects, I am using a parameterized constructor. This code compiles just fine, but what happens when I run the example? The following exception is thrown:

```
Unhandled Exception: System.NotSupportedException: The member
'Chapter15.Module1+CustomerContact.Name' has no supported translation to SQL.
```

So, what happened? Looking at the preceding LINQ to SQL query, ask yourself, "How does the DataContext know which field in the Customer class gets mapped to the CustomerContact. Name member that I am trying to order by?" In Listing 15-2, because I passed it the field names of the anonymous class, it knew the source field in the Customer class was ContactName, and it knew the destination field in the anonymous class was Name. In Listing 15-3, that mapping does not occur in the LINQ to SQL query, it happens in the constructor of the CustomerContact class, which the DataContext is not privy to. Therefore, it has no idea what field in the source class, Customer, to order by when it generates the SQL statement. And that spells trouble.

However, it is safe to use parameterized construction so long as nothing in the query after the projection references the named class's members, as Listing 15-4 demonstrates.

Listing 15-4. *Projecting Using Parameterized Construction Without Referencing Members*

```
Dim db As New Northwind("Data Source=.\SQLEXPRESS;Initial Catalog=Northwind;" & _
    "Integrated Security=SSPI;")

db.Log = Console.Out

Dim contacts = From c In db.Customers _
  Where c.City = "Buenos Aires" _
  Select New CustomerContact(c.ContactName, c.Phone)

For Each contact In contacts
  Console.WriteLine("{0} - {1}", contact.Name, contact.Phone)
Next contact
```

In Listing 15-4, since the query does not attempt to reference members of the named class into which the query projected the query results using parameterized construction, I am safe. Here are the results of Listing 15-4:

```
SELECT [t0].[ContactName] AS [name], [t0].[Phone] AS [phone]
FROM [dbo].[Customers] AS [t0]
WHERE [t0].[City] = @p0
-- @p0: Input NVarChar (Size = 12; Prec = 0; Scale = 0) [Buenos Aires]
-- Context: SqlProvider(Sql2008) Model: AttributedMetaModel Build: 3.5.30729.1

Patricio Simpson - (1) 135-5555
Yvonne Moncada - (1) 135-5333
Sergio Gutiérrez - (1) 123-5555
```

It should come as no surprise that the problem caused by referencing class members for classes projected into using parameterized construction also afflicts queries when using standard dot notation syntax too. Listing 15-5 is an example using standard dot notation syntax with the last projection using parameterized construction, but because a subsequent part of the query references the named class members, the query throws an exception.

Listing 15-5. *Projecting Using Parameterized Construction Referencing Members*

```
Dim db As New Northwind("Data Source=.\SQLEXPRESS;Initial Catalog=Northwind;" & _
    "Integrated Security=SSPI;")

db.Log = Console.Out

Dim contacts = db.Customers _
  .Where(Function(c) c.City = "Buenos Aires") _
  .Select(Function(c) New CustomerContact(c.ContactName, c.Phone)) _
  .OrderBy(Function(c) c.Name)

For Each contact In contacts
    Console.WriteLine("{0} - {1}", contact.Name, contact.Phone)
Next contact
```

The query in Listing 15-5 is very similar to the query in Listing 15-4 except I am using standard dot notation syntax instead of query expression syntax, and I have tacked a call to the OrderBy operator onto the end of the query. I am using parameterized construction in the final projection, but this doesn't work because the OrderBy operator is referencing a member of the named class. Here are the results of Listing 15-5:

```
Unhandled Exception: System.NotSupportedException: The member
'Ch15Console.Module1+CustomerContact.Name' has no supported translation to SQL.
...
```

Because of these complexities, I recommend using object initialization instead of parameterized construction whenever possible.

Extending Entity Classes with Partial Methods

One of the problems early adopting LINQ developers complained of was their inability to know what is happening inside an entity class. During the incubation period of LINQ, there was no way for a developer to know, programmatically speaking, when an entity class object's property is being changed or when the entity class itself is being created except by modifying the generated entity class code, which we all know is a no-no. Any modifications to the generated entity class code will be lost the next time that code needs to be regenerated, so that just isn't feasible. Fortunately, the engineers at Microsoft were listening.

In Chapter 2, I told you about partial methods, and this is where partial methods become incredibly useful. Microsoft determined where in the lifetime of an entity class developers were most likely interested in being notified and added calls to partial methods.

Here is a list of the supported partial methods that are called:

The Supported Partial Methods for an Entity Class

```
Partial Private Sub OnLoaded()
Partial Private Sub OnValidate(ByVal action As System.Data.Linq.ChangeAction)
Partial Private Sub OnCreated()
Partial Private Sub On[Property]Changing(ByVal value As [Type])
Partial Private Sub On[Property]Changed()
```

The last two methods listed will have the name of a property where I show "[Property]", and the property's data type where I have "[Type]". To demonstrate some of the partial methods supported by entity classes, I will add the following class code for the Contact entity class:

An Additional Declaration for the Contact Class to Implement Some Partial Methods

```
Namespace nwind
  Partial Public Class Contact
    Private Sub OnLoaded()
      Console.WriteLine("OnLoaded() called.")
    End Sub

    Private Sub OnCreated()
      Console.WriteLine("OnCreated() called.")
    End Sub

    Private Sub OnCompanyNameChanging(ByVal value As String)
      Console.WriteLine("OnCompanyNameChanging() called.")
    End Sub

    Private Sub OnCompanyNameChanged()
      Console.WriteLine("OnCompanyNameChanged() called.")
    End Sub
  End Class
End Namespace
```

Notice that I specified the namespace as nwind. This is necessary because the namespace for my declaration of the class must match the namespace of the class I am extending. Because I specified the namespace nwind when I generated my entity classes with SqlMetal, I must declare my Partial Contact class to be in the nwind namespace too. In your real production code, you would probably want to create a separate module in which to keep this partial class declaration.

Notice that I have provided implementations for the OnLoaded, OnCreated, OnCompanyNameChanging, and OnCompanyNameChanged methods. All they do is display a message to the console though. You can, of course, do what you want in your implementations.

Now, let's take a look at some code demonstrating the partial methods. In Listing 15-6, I query a Contact record from the database and change its CompanyName property.

Listing 15-6. *Querying a Class with Implemented Partial Methods*

```
Dim db As New Northwind("Data Source=.\SQLEXPRESS;Initial Catalog=Northwind;" & _
    "Integrated Security=SSPI;")

Dim contact As Contact = db.Contacts _
  .Where(Function(c) c.ContactID = 11) _
  .SingleOrDefault()
Console.WriteLine("CompanyName = {0}", contact.CompanyName)

contact.CompanyName = "Joe's House of Booze"
Console.WriteLine("CompanyName = {0}", contact.CompanyName)
```

There is nothing special about the preceding code except for the fact that I have implemented some of the partial methods that entity classes support. First, I query a contact and display its company's name to the console. Then, I change the contact's company name and display it again to the console. Let's press Ctrl+F5 to see the output:

```
OnCreated() called.
OnLoaded() called.
CompanyName = B's Beverages
OnCompanyNameChanging() called.
OnCreated() called.
OnCompanyNameChanged() called.
CompanyName = Joe's House of Booze
```

As you can see, the OnCreated method was called, followed by the OnLoaded method. At this point, the record has been retrieved from the database and loaded into a Contact entity object. You can then see the output of the company's name I sent to the console. Next, the OnCompanyNameChanging method is called, followed by the only surprise to me, another call to the OnCreated method. Obviously, the DataContext is creating another Contact entity object as part of its change tracking procedure. Next, the OnCompanyNameChanged method is called, followed by my output of the new company name to the console.

This demonstrates how you can extend entity classes using partial methods without modifying the generated code.

Important System.Data.Linq API Classes

There are a handful of classes in the System.Data.Linq namespace that you will use on a regular basis when using LINQ to SQL. The following section is meant to provide a brief overview of these classes, their purposes, and where they fit in the scheme of LINQ to SQL.

EntitySet(Of T)

An entity class on the *one* side of a one-to-many relationship stores its associated *many* entity classes in a class member of type EntitySet(Of T) where type T is the type of the associated entity class.

Since, in the Northwind database, the relationship between Customers and Orders is one-to-many, in the `Customer` class, the `Orders` are stored in an `EntitySet(Of Order)`.

```
Private _Orders As EntitySet(Of [Order])
```

The `EntitySet(Of T)` class is a special collection used by LINQ to SQL. It implements the `IEnumerable(Of T)` interface, which allows you to perform LINQ queries on it. It also implements the `ICollection(Of T)` interface.

EntityRef(Of T)

An entity class on the *many* side of a one-to-many relationship stores its associated *one* entity class in a class member of type `EntityRef(Of T)` where type `T` is the type of the associated entity class.

Since in the Northwind database, the relationship between Customers and Orders is one-to-many, the `Customer` is stored in an `EntityRef(Of Customer)` in the `Order` class.

```
Private _Customer As EntityRef(Of Customer)
```

Entity

When we are referencing an associated entity class that is on the *one* side of a one-to-many or one-to-one relationship, we tend to think of the member variable as being the same type as the entity class. For example, when we refer to an `Order` object's `Customer`, we tend to think the `Customer` object is stored in a `Customer` class member of the `Order` class. You should remember though that, in reality, the `Customer` is stored in an `EntityRef(Of Customer)`. Should you need to actually reference the `Customer` object referenced by the `EntityRef(Of Customer)` member, it can be referenced using the `EntityRef(Of Customer)` object's `Entity` property.

There are times when it is important to be cognizant of this fact, such as when writing your own entity classes. If you look at the `Order` class generated by SqlMetal, you will notice that the public property `Get` and `Set` methods for the `Customer` property use the `EntityRef(Of Customer)` object's `Entity` property to reference the `Customer`.

A Public Property Using the EntityRef(Of T).Entity Property to Access the Actual Entity Object

```
Private _Customer As EntityRef(Of Customer)
...
Public Property Customer() As Customer
  Get
    Return Me._Customer.Entity
  End Get
  Set
    Dim previousValue As Customer = Me._Customer.Entity
    ...
  End Set
End Property
```

HasLoadedOrAssignedValue

This property is a `Boolean` that lets you know if an entity class property stored in an `EntityRef(Of T)` has been assigned a value or if one has been loaded into it.

It is typically used in the `Set` methods for references to the *one* side of a one-to-many association to prevent the entity class property containing the *one* side's ID from becoming inconsistent with the `EntityRef(Of T)` containing the reference to the *one*.

For example, let's look at the `Set` methods for the `Order` entity class properties `CustomerID` and `Customer`.

The CustomerID Set Method

```
Public Property CustomerID() As String
  Get
    Return Me._CustomerID
  End Get
  Set
    If (String.Equals(Me._CustomerID, value) = false) Then
      If Me._Customer.HasLoadedOrAssignedValue Then
        Throw New System.Data.Linq.ForeignKeyReferenceAlreadyHasValueException
      End If
      Me.OnCustomerIDChanging(value)
      Me.SendPropertyChanging
      Me._CustomerID = value
      Me.SendPropertyChanged("CustomerID")
      Me.OnCustomerIDChanged
    End If
  End Set
End Property
```

Notice that in the `Set` method for the `CustomerID` property, if the `EntityRef(Of T)` storing the `Customer` has the `HasLoadedOrAssignedValue` property set to `True`, an exception is thrown. This prevents a developer from changing the `CustomerID` of an `Order` entity object if that `Order` already has a `Customer` entity assigned to it. We cannot cause the `Order` entity object's `CustomerID` and `Customer` to become inconsistent due to this safeguard.

Contrast this with the fact that in the `Set` method for the `Customer` property, the `Customer` reference can be assigned if the `HasLoadedOrAssignedValue` property is set to `False`.

The Customer Set Method

```
Public Property Customer() As Customer
  Get
    Return Me._Customer.Entity
  End Get
  Set
    Dim previousValue As Customer = Me._Customer.Entity
    If ((Object.Equals(previousValue, value) = false) _
        OrElse (Me._Customer.HasLoadedOrAssignedValue = false)) Then
      Me.SendPropertyChanging
```

```
        If ((previousValue Is Nothing) = false) Then
          Me._Customer.Entity = Nothing
          previousValue.Orders.Remove(Me)
        End If
        Me._Customer.Entity = value
        If ((value Is Nothing) = false) Then
          value.Orders.Add(Me)
          Me._CustomerID = value.CustomerID
        Else
          Me._CustomerID = CType(Nothing, String)
        End If
        Me.SendPropertyChanged("Customer")
      End If
    End Set
  End Property
End Property
```

Checking the HasLoadedOrAssignedValue property in each of these Set methods prevents the developer from causing the reference to become inconsistent between the CustomerID and the Customer references.

Table(Of T)

This is the data type LINQ to SQL uses to interface with a table or view in a SQL Server database. Typically, the derived DataContext class, often referred to as [Your]DataContext in the LINQ to SQL chapters, will have a public property of type Table(Of T), where type T is an entity class, for each database table mapped in the derived DataContext.

So to reference the Customers database table of the Northwind database, there will typically be a public property of type Table(Of Customer) named Customers in the derived DataContext. It would look like this:

A Table(Of T) Property for the Customers Database Table

```
Public ReadOnly Property Customers() As System.Data.Linq.Table(Of Customer)
  Get
    Return Me.GetTable(Of Customer)
  End Get
End Property
```

Table(Of T) implements the IQueryable(Of T) interface, which itself implements IEnumerable(Of T). This means you can perform LINQ to SQL queries on it. This is the initial data source for most LINQ to SQL queries.

IExecuteResult

When a stored procedure or user-defined function is called with the ExecuteMethodCall method, the results are returned in an object implementing the IExecuteResult interface, like this:

The ExecuteMethodCall Method Returns an IExecuteResult

```
Dim result As IExecuteResult = Me.ExecuteMethodCall(...)
```

The IExecuteResult interface provides one property named ReturnValue and one method named GetParameterValue for accessing the returned value and output parameters, respectively.

ReturnValue

All stored procedure results other than output parameters and scalar-valued user-defined function results are returned via the IExecuteResult.ReturnValue variable.

To obtain access to the return value of a stored procedure or scalar-valued user-defined function, you reference the returned object's ReturnValue member. Your code should look something like this:

Accessing the Returned Value from a Stored Procedure Returning an Integer

```
Dim result As IExecuteResult = Me.ExecuteMethodCall(...)
Return CType(result.ReturnValue,Integer)
```

In Chapter 16, I will discuss the ExecuteMethodCall method and provide an example returning a stored procedure's returned integer.

If a stored procedure is returning data other than its return value, the ReturnValue variable will implement either the ISingleResult(Of T) or IMultipleResults interface, whichever is appropriate depending on how many data shapes are returned from the stored procedure.

GetParameterValue

To obtain access to a stored procedure's output parameters, you call the GetParameterValue method on the returned object, passing the method the zero-based index number of the parameter for which you want the value. Assuming the stored procedure is returning the CompanyName in the third parameter, your code should look something like this:

Accessing the Returned Parameters from a Stored Procedure

```
Dim result As IExecuteResult = _
  Me.ExecuteMethodCall(..., param1, param2, companyName)
Dim CompanyName As String = CType(result.GetParameterValue(2),String)
```

In Chapter 16, I will discuss the ExecuteMethodCall method and provide an example accessing a stored procedure's output parameters.

ISingleResult(Of T)

When a stored procedure returns its results in a single shape, the results are returned in an object that implements the ISingleResult(Of T) interface, where T is an entity class. That returned object implementing ISingleResult(Of T) is the IExecuteResult.ReturnValue variable. Your code should look similar to this:

Accessing the Returned Results When There Is One Shape

```
Dim result As IExecuteResult = Me.ExecuteMethodCall(...)
Dim results As ISingleResult(Of CustOrdersOrdersResult) = _
  CType(result.ReturnValue, ISingleResult(Of CustOrdersOrdersResult))
```

Notice that I simply cast the IExecuteResult object's ReturnValue member to an ISingleResult(Of T) to get access to the results.

Since ISingleResult(Of T) inherits from IEnumerable(Of T), the good news is that you access the returned results just as you would any other LINQ sequence.

Accessing the Results from ISingleResult(Of T)

```
For Each cust As CustomersByCityResult In results

  ...
Next
```

In Chapter 16, I will discuss the ExecuteMethodCall method and provide an example accessing a stored procedure's results when the stored procedure returns a single shape.

ReturnValue

The ISingleResult(Of T) interface provides a ReturnValue property that works just as it does in the IExecuteResult interface. Please read the previous section for the IExecuteResult ReturnValue property to understand how to access this property.

IMultipleResults

When a stored procedure returns its results in multiple shapes, the results are returned in an object that implements the IMultipleResults interface. That returned object implementing IMultipleResults is the IExecuteResult.ReturnValue variable. Your code should look similar to this:

Accessing the Returned Results When There Are Multiple Shapes

```
Dim result As IExecuteResult = Me.ExecuteMethodCall(...)
Dim results As IMultipleResults = CType(result.ReturnValue, IMultipleResults)
```

To obtain access to the multiple shapes that are returned, call the IMultipleResults. GetResult(Of T) method I discuss below.

In Chapter 16, I will discuss the ExecuteMethodCall method and provide an example accessing a stored procedure's results when the stored procedure returns multiple shapes.

The IMultipleResults interface provides one property named ReturnValue for accessing the stored procedure's returned value and one method named GetResult(Of T) for retrieving an IEnumerable(Of T) for each returned shape where type T is an entity class corresponding to the shape.

ReturnValue

The IMultipleResults interface provides a ReturnValue property that works just as it does in the IExecuteResults interface. Please read the previous section for the IExecuteResults ReturnValue property to understand how to access this property.

GetResult(Of T)

The IMultipleResults interface provides a GetResult(Of T) method where type T represents the data type storing the shape returned. The GetResult(Of T) method is used to obtain the repeating records of the specified result shape, and the records are returned in an IEnumerable(Of T) where T is the entity class used to store the shape record. Your code should look something like this:

Accessing Multiple Shapes Returned by a Stored Procedure

```
<FunctionAttribute(Name:="A Stored Procedure"), _
 ResultType(GetType(Shape1)), _
 ResultType(GetType(Shape2))> _
...
Dim result As IExecuteResult = Me.ExecuteMethodCall(...)
Dim results As IMultipleResults = CType(result.ReturnValue, IMultipleResults)

For Each x As Shape1 In results.GetResult(Of Shape1)()
  ...
Next x

For Each y As Shape2 In results.GetResult(Of Shape2)()
  ...
Next y
```

I have included the attributes that would be before the method containing this code so that you can see the context of the ResultType attributes and the shapes that are returned by the stored procedure.

In the preceding code, I know that records that will be mapped to data type Shape1 will be returned by the stored procedure first, followed by records mapped to data type Shape2. So I enumerate through the IEnumerable(Of Shape1) sequence that is returned from the first call to the GetResult(Of T) method first, followed by enumerating through the IEnumerable(Of Shape2) sequence that is returned by the second call to the GetResult(Of T) method. It is important that I know Shape1 records are returned first, followed by Shape2 records, and that I retrieve them with the GetResult(Of T) method in that same order.

In Chapter 16, I will discuss the ExecuteMethodCall method and provide an example accessing a stored procedure's returned multiple shapes.

Summary

This chapter provided an in-depth examination of LINQ to SQL entity classes, the complications of writing your own, and their attributes and attribute properties.

It is important to remember that if you write your own entity classes, you will be responsible for implementing change notifications and ensuring graph consistency. These are not trivial details and can become complex to implement. Fortunately, as I have pointed out in this chapter, both SqlMetal and the Object Relational Designer take care of these complications for you.

Also, to write your own entity classes, you must have a thorough knowledge of the entity class attributes and their properties. I covered each of these in this chapter and provided the quintessential implementation of each by discussing the SqlMetal generated entity classes for the Northwind database.

I also covered the benefits of projecting your query results into entity classes as opposed to nonentity classes. If you have no need to modify the data and persist the changes, nonentity classes are generally fine. But if you want to be able to change the data that is returned and persist it back to the database, projecting into entity classes is the way to go.

Last, I discussed some of the often-used classes in the `System.Data.Linq` namespace and how they are used by LINQ to SQL.

At this point, you should be an expert on the anatomy of entity classes. I have discussed them in depth and explained to you the generated code. Of course, these entity classes are typically referenced by a class derived from the `DataContext` class, which I have yet to discuss in detail. Therefore, in the next chapter, I will discuss the `DataContext` class in painful detail.

CHAPTER 16

The DataContext

In most of the previous LINQ to SQL chapters, I reference the DataContext class but have yet to fully explain it. In this chapter, I remedy this oversight.

In this chapter, I explain the DataContext class, what it can do for you, and how to make the most of it. I discuss all of its major methods and provide examples of each. Understanding the DataContext class is necessary to successfully employ LINQ to SQL, and by the time you have read this chapter, you should be a master of the DataContext class.

Prerequisites for Running the Examples

In order to run the examples in this chapter, you will need to have obtained the extended version of the Northwind database and generated entity classes for it. Please read and follow the section in Chapter 12 titled "Prerequisites for Running the Examples."

Some Common Methods

Additionally, to run the examples in this chapter, you will need some common methods that will be utilized by the examples. Please read and follow the section in Chapter 12 titled "Some Common Methods."

Using the LINQ to SQL API

To run the examples in this chapter, you may need to add the appropriate references and Imports statements to your project. Please read and follow the section in Chapter 12 titled "Using the LINQ to SQL API."

Additionally, for some of the examples in this chapter, you will also need to add an Imports statement for the System.Data.Linq.Mapping namespace like this:

```
Imports System.Data.Linq.Mapping
```

[Your]DataContext Class

While I haven't covered it yet, one of the LINQ to SQL classes you will frequently use is the System.Data.Linq.DataContext class. This is the class you will use to establish your database connection. When creating or generating entity classes, it is common for a class to be created that derives from the DataContext class. This derived class will typically take on the name of the database it will be connecting to. Since I am using the Northwind database for the examples in this chapter, my derived database class will be named Northwind. However, since the name of the derived class changes with the database being used, the name of the class will vary from code to code. For ease of reference in the LINQ to SQL chapters, I will often refer to this derived class as the [Your]DataContext class. This is your clue that I am talking about your created or generated class that is derived from the DataContext class.

The DataContext Class

It is the DataContext class that handles your connection to the database. It also handles database queries, updates, inserts, identity tracking, change tracking, change processing, transactional integrity, and even database creation.

The DataContext class translates your queries of entity classes into SQL statements that are performed on the connected database.

Deriving [Your]DataContext class from the DataContext class gives [Your]DataContext class access to a host of common database methods, such as ExecuteQuery, ExecuteCommand, and SubmitChanges. In addition to these inherited methods, [Your]DataContext class will contain properties of type System.Data.Linq.Table(Of T) for each table and view in the database for which you desire to use LINQ to SQL, where each type T is an entity class mapped to a particular table or view.

For example, let's take a look at the Northwind class that was generated for me by the SqlMetal tool. It is the [Your]DataContext class for the Northwind database. Here is what a portion of mine looks like, with the noteworthy portions in bold:

A Portion of the Generated Northwind Class

```
Partial Public Class Northwind
   Inherits System.Data.Linq.DataContext

...

Public Sub New(ByVal connection As String)
   MyBase.New(connection, mappingSource)
   OnCreated
End Sub

Public Sub New(ByVal connection As System.Data.IDbConnection)
   MyBase.New(connection, mappingSource)
   OnCreated
End Sub

Public Sub New( _
    ByVal connection As String, _
    ByVal mappingSource As System.Data.Linq.Mapping.MappingSource)
   MyBase.New(connection, mappingSource)
```

```
    OnCreated
End Sub

Public Sub New( _
    ByVal connection As System.Data.IDbConnection, _
    ByVal mappingSource As System.Data.Linq.Mapping.MappingSource)
    MyBase.New(connection, mappingSource)
    OnCreated
End Sub

...

Public ReadOnly Property Customers() As System.Data.Linq.Table(Of Customer)
    Get
        Return Me.GetTable(Of Customer)
    End Get
End Property

...

End Class
```

As you can see, this class does indeed inherit from the DataContext class. You can also see that there are four constructors. Each of the public constructors correlates to one of the DataContext constructors. Each [Your]DataContext constructor calls the base DataContext class's equivalent constructor in the initializer, and in the body of the constructor, the only code is a call to the OnCreated partial method. This allows the consuming developer to implement an OnCreated partial method and for that developer's implementation to be called every time a [Your]DataContext object is instantiated.

Also in the Northwind class, there is a property named Customers of type Table(Of Customer) where type Customer is an entity class. It is the Customer entity class that is mapped to the Northwind database's Customers table.

It is not necessary to actually write code that uses the [Your]DataContext class. It is totally possible to work with the standard DataContext class. However, using the [Your]DataContext class does make writing the code more convenient. For example, if you use the [Your]DataContext class, each table is a property that can be accessed directly off the [Your]DataContext object. Listing 16-1 contains an example.

Listing 16-1. *An Example Demonstrating Table Access with a Property*

```
Dim db As New Northwind( _
    "Data Source=.\SQLEXPRESS;Initial Catalog=Northwind;Integrated Security=SSPI;")

Dim query As IQueryable(Of Customer) = _
    From cust In db.Customers _
    Where cust.Country = "USA" _
    Select cust
```

```
For Each c As Customer In query
  Console.WriteLine("{0}", c.CompanyName)
Next c
```

■**Note** You may need to tweak the connection strings in the examples in this chapter for them to work.

In the preceding code, since I connect using the [Your]DataContext class, Northwind, I can access the customers Table(Of Customer) as a property, Customers, of the [Your]DataContext class. Here are the results of the code:

```
Great Lakes Food Market
Hungry Coyote Import Store
Lazy K Kountry Store
Let's Stop N Shop
Lonesome Pine Restaurant
Old World Delicatessen
Rattlesnake Canyon Grocery
Save-a-lot Markets
Split Rail Beer & Ale
The Big Cheese
The Cracker Box
Trail's Head Gourmet Provisioners
White Clover Markets
```

If, instead, I connect using the DataContext class itself, I must use the GetTable(Of T) method of the DataContext object, as in Listing 16-2.

Listing 16-2. *An Example Demonstrating Table Access with the GetTable(Of T) Method*

```
Dim dc As New DataContext( _
  "Data Source=.\SQLEXPRESS;Initial Catalog=Northwind;Integrated Security=SSPI;")

Dim query As IQueryable(Of Customer) = _
  From cust In dc.GetTable(Of Customer)() _
  Where cust.Country = "USA" _
  Select cust

For Each c As Customer In query
  Console.WriteLine("{0}", c.CompanyName)
Next c
```

This code gives me the same results though:

```
Great Lakes Food Market
Hungry Coyote Import Store
Lazy K Kountry Store
Let's Stop N Shop
Lonesome Pine Restaurant
Old World Delicatessen
Rattlesnake Canyon Grocery
Save-a-lot Markets
Split Rail Beer & Ale
The Big Cheese
The Cracker Box
Trail's Head Gourmet Provisioners
White Clover Markets
```

So using the [Your]DataContext class is merely a convenience, but one worth taking advantage of whenever possible.

The DataContext Class Implements IDisposable

The DataContext class implements the IDisposable interface, and because of this, it should be treated properly as a disposable object. This means that if you create a new class that is composed of a DataContext or [Your]DataContext class, meaning there is a *has-a* relationship between your new class and the DataContext or [Your]DataContext class, the new class should implement the IDisposble interface too. Designing classes to properly implement the IDisposable interface is beyond the scope of this book, but many resources online delve into this topic, and it's covered in great detail in *Accelerated VB 2008* by Guy Fouché and Trey Nash (Apress, 2008).

Another benefit of the DataContext class implementing the IDisposable interface is that you can now utilize a Using statement to manage the DataContext or [Your]DataContext object. Many of the examples in this chapter don't really need the protection offered by the Using statement because they are so simple and exit immediately at the end of the code, but I will begin to take advantage of the Using statement anyway. While this will be unnecessary for most of these examples, it will hopefully help reinforce the habit for both you and me.

Primary Purposes

In addition to all the methods I cover in this chapter, the DataContext class provides three main services: identity tracking, change tracking, and change processing.

Identity Tracking

One of the issues that LINQ to SQL is designed to overcome is referred to as the *object-relational impedance mismatch*. This term refers to the inherent difficulties caused by the fact that the most commonly used databases are relational, while most modern programming languages are object oriented. Because of this difference, problems arise.

One such manifestation of the object-relational impedance mismatch is the way we expect identity to behave. If we query the same record from a database in multiple places in our code, we expect that the returned data will be stored in different locations in memory. We expect that modifying a record's fields in one part of the code will not affect that same record's fields that were retrieved in another part of the code. We expect this because we know that retrieved data is stored in different variables living at different addresses in memory.

Contrast this with the way we expect objects to behave. We expect that when we have an object in memory, say a Customer object, all places in the code having a reference to that same customer will actually have a reference to the same location in memory. If we update that Customer object's Name property in one location of our program, we expect the customer we have a reference to in another part of the code will have the new name.

The DataContext class identity tracking service is what provides this behavior for us. When a record is queried from the database for the first time since the instantiation of the DataContext object, that record is recorded in an identity table using its primary key, and an entity object is created and stored in a cache. Subsequent queries that determine that the same record should be returned will first check the identity table, and if the record exists in the identity table, the already existing entity object will be returned from the cache. That is an important concept to understand, so I will reiterate it in a slightly different way. When a query is executed, if a record in the database matches the search criteria, *and* its entity object is already cached, the already cached entity object is returned. This means that the actual data returned by the query may not be the same as the record in the database. The query determines *which* entities will be returned based on data in the database. But the DataContext object's identity tracking service determines *what* data is returned. This can lead to a problem I call the *results set cache mismatch.*

The Results Set Cache Mismatch

While working on some of the examples for this book, I spotted some behavior I found to be quite odd. A Microsoft developer told me this behavior was correct and intentional. I can't help but wonder if they really Schruted this one.

I have yet to see this behavior named in any way, so I will dub it the "results set cache mismatch." Since I am a firm believer in trying before you buy, you may use that phrase free 30 times, but after that, please send me a royalty check.

The results set cache mismatch can occur when a record in the database is inconsistent with that same record's entity object in your DataContext object's cache. When you perform a query, the actual database is queried for records matching the query. If a record in the database matches the search criteria for the query, that record's entity object will be included in the returned results set. However, if a record from the results set is already cached in the DataContext object's cache of entity objects, the cached entity object will be returned by the query, as opposed to reading the latest version from the database.

The result is that if you have an entity object cached in your DataContext, and another context updates a field for that entity object's record in the database, and you perform a LINQ query specifying that field in the search criteria so that it matches the new value in the database, the record will be included in the results set. However, since you already have it cached, you get the cached entity object returned with the field not matching your search criteria.

It will probably be clearer if I provide a specific example. What I will do is first query for a specific customer that I know will not match the search criteria I will provide for a subsequent query. I will use customer LONEP. The region for customer LONEP is OR, so I will search for customers whose region is WA. I will then display those customers whose region is WA. Next, I will update the region for customer LONEP to WA using ADO.NET, just as if some other context did it externally to my process. At this point, LONEP will have a region of OR in my entity object but WA in the database. Next, I will perform that very same query again to retrieve all the customers whose region is WA. When you look in the code, you will not see the query defined again though. You will merely see me enumerate through the returned sequence of custs. Remember that, because of deferred query execution, I need only enumerate the results to cause the query to be executed again. Since the region for LONEP is WA in the database, that record will be included in the results set. But, since that record's entity object is already cached, it will be the cached entity object that is returned, and that object still has a region of OR. I will then display each returned entity object's region. When customer LONEP is displayed, its region will be OR, despite the fact that my query specified it wanted customers whose region is WA. Listing 16-3 provides the code to demonstrate this mismatch.

Listing 16-3. *An Example Demonstrating the Results Set Cache Mismatch*

```
Using db As New Northwind( _
  "Data Source=.\SQLEXPRESS;Initial Catalog=Northwind;Integrated Security=SSPI")

  ' Let's get a customer to modify that will be outside our query of region == 'WA'.
  Dim cust As Customer = ( _
    From c In db.Customers _
    Where c.CustomerID = "LONEP" _
    Select c).Single()

  Console.WriteLine( _
    "Customer {0} has region = {1}.{2}", _
    cust.CustomerID, cust.Region, _
    System.Environment.NewLine)

  '  Ok, LONEP's region is OR.

  '  Now, let's get a sequence of customers from 'WA', which will not include LONEP
  '  since his region is OR.
  Dim custs As IEnumerable(Of Customer) = ( _
    From c In db.Customers _
    Where c.Region Is "WA" _
    Select c)

  Console.WriteLine("Customers from WA before ADO.NET change - start ...")
  For Each c As Customer In custs
    '  Display each entity object's Region.
    Console.WriteLine("Customer {0}'s region is {1}.", c.CustomerID, c.Region)
  Next c
  Console.WriteLine( _
    "Customers from WA before ADO.NET change - end.{0}", _
    System.Environment.NewLine)
```

```
'  Now I will change LONEP's region to WA, which would have included it
'  in that previous query's results.

'  Change the customers' region through ADO.NET.
Console.WriteLine("Updating LONEP's region to WA in ADO.NET...")
  ExecuteStatementInDb( _
  "update Customers set Region = 'WA' " & _
  "where CustomerID = 'LONEP'")
Console.WriteLine("LONEP's region updated.{0}", System.Environment.NewLine)

Console.WriteLine("So LONEP's region is WA in database, but ...")
Console.WriteLine( _
  "Customer {0} has region = {1} in entity object.{2}", _
  cust.CustomerID, _
  cust.Region, _
  vbCrLf)

'  Now, LONEP's region is WA in database, but still OR in entity object.

'  Now, let's perform the query again.
'  Display the customers' entity object's region again.
Console.WriteLine("Query entity objects after ADO.NET change - start ...")
For Each c As Customer In custs
  '  Display each entity object's Region.
  Console.WriteLine("Customer {0}'s region is {1}.", c.CustomerID, c.Region)
Next c
Console.WriteLine( _
  "Query entity objects after ADO.NET change - end.{0}", _
  System.Environment.NewLine)

'  We need to reset the changed values so that the code can be run
'  more than once.
Console.WriteLine("{0}Resetting data to original values.", vbCrLf)
  ExecuteStatementInDb( _
  "update Customers set Region = 'OR' where CustomerID = 'LONEP'")
End Using
```

Notice that in Listing 16-3, instead of simply instantiating a Northwind object, I have utilized a Using statement to manage the Northwind object for me. This way, once the End Using statement is reached at the end of the code, the Northwind object will be disposed of deterministically. Of course, the reality is that in this example, since the code ended anyway, the same result would have been achieved once the program exits, even without the Using statement. Here are the results:

```
Customer LONEP has region = OR.

Customers from WA before ADO.NET change - start ...
Customer LAZYK's region is WA.
```

```
Customer TRAIH's region is WA.
Customer WHITC's region is WA.
Customers from WA before ADO.NET change - end.

Updating LONEP's region to WA in ADO.NET...
Executing SQL statement against database with ADO.NET ...
Database updated.
LONEP's region updated.

So LONEP's region is WA in database, but ...
Customer LONEP has region = OR in entity object.

Query entity objects after ADO.NET change - start ...
Customer LAZYK's region is WA.
Customer LONEP's region is OR.
Customer TRAIH's region is WA.
Customer WHITC's region is WA.
Query entity objects after ADO.NET change - end.


Resetting data to original values.
Executing SQL statement against database with ADO.NET ...
Database updated.
```

As you can see, even though I queried for customers in WA, LONEP is included in the results despite the fact that its region is OR. Sure, it's true that in the database LONEP has a region of WA, but it does not in the object I have a reference to in my code. Is anyone else getting a queasy feeling?

Another manifestation of this behavior is the fact that inserted entities cannot be queried back out and deleted entities can be, prior to calling the SubmitChanges method. Again, this is because of the fact that even though we have inserted an entity, when the query executes, the results set is determined by what is in the actual database, not the DataContext object's cache. Since the changes have not been submitted, the inserted entity is not yet in the database. The opposite applies to deleted entities. Listing 16-4 contains an example demonstrating this behavior.

Listing 16-4. *Another Example Demonstrating the Results Set Cache Mismatch*

```
Using db As New Northwind( _
  "Data Source=.\SQLEXPRESS;Initial Catalog=Northwind;Integrated Security=SSPI")

  Console.WriteLine("First I will add customer LAWN.")
  db.Customers.InsertOnSubmit( _
    New Customer With { _
      .CustomerID = "LAWN", _
      .CompanyName = "Lawn Wranglers", _
      .ContactName = "Mr. Abe Henry", _
```

```vbnet
          .ContactTitle = "Owner", _
          .Address = "1017 Maple Leaf Way", _
          .City = "Ft. Worth", _
          .Region = "TX", _
          .PostalCode = "76104", _
          .Country = "USA", _
          .Phone = "(800) MOW-LAWN", _
          .Fax = "(800) MOW-LAWO"})

  Console.WriteLine("Next I will query for customer LAWN.")
  Dim cust As Customer = ( _
    From c In db.Customers _
    Where c.CustomerID = "LAWN" _
    Select c).SingleOrDefault()

  Console.WriteLine( _
    "Customer LAWN {0}.{1}", _
    If(cust Is Nothing, "does not exist", "exists"), _
    vbCrLf)

  Console.WriteLine("Now I will delete customer LONEP")
  cust = ( _
    From c In db.Customers _
    Where c.CustomerID = "LONEP" _
    Select c).SingleOrDefault()
  db.Customers.DeleteOnSubmit(cust)

  Console.WriteLine("Next I will query for customer LONEP.")
  cust = ( _
    From c In db.Customers _
    Where c.CustomerID = "LONEP" _
    Select c).SingleOrDefault()

  Console.WriteLine( _
    "Customer LONEP {0}.{1}", _
    If(cust Is Nothing, "does not exist", "exists"), _
    vbCrLf)

  ' No need to reset database since SubmitChanges() was not called.
End Using
```

In the previous code, I insert a customer, LAWN, and then query to see if it exists. I then delete a different customer, LONEP, and query to see if it exists. I do all this without calling the SubmitChanges method so that the cached entity objects have not been persisted to the database. Here are the results of this code:

First I will add customer LAWN.
Next I will query for customer LAWN.
Customer LAWN does not exist.

Now I will delete customer LONEP
Next I will query for customer LONEP.
Customer LONEP exists.

The Microsoft developer who told me that this was intentional behavior stated that the data retrieved by a query is stale the moment you retrieve it and that the data cached by the DataContext is not meant to be cached for long periods of time. If you need better isolation and consistency, he recommended you wrap it all in a transaction. Please read the section titled "Pessimistic Concurrency" in Chapter 17 to see an example doing this.

Change Tracking

Once the identity tracking service creates an entity object in its cache, change tracking begins for that object. Change tracking works by storing the original values of an entity object. Change tracking for an entity object continues until you call the SubmitChanges method. Calling the SubmitChanges method causes the entity objects' changes to be saved to the database, the original values to be forgotten, and the changed values to become the original values. This allows change tracking to start over.

This works fine as long as the entity objects are retrieved from the database. However, merely creating a new entity object by instantiating it will not provide any identity or change tracking until the DataContext is aware of its existence. To make the DataContext aware of the entity object's existence, simply insert the entity object into one of the Table(Of T) properties. For example, in my Northwind class, I have a Table(Of Customer) property named Customers. I can call the InsertOnSubmit method on the Customers property to insert the entity object, a Customer, into the Table(Of Customer). When this is done, the DataContext will begin identity and change tracking on that entity object. Here is example code inserting a customer:

```
db.Customers.InsertOnSubmit( _
  New Customer With { _
    .CustomerID = "LAWN", _
    .CompanyName = "Lawn Wranglers", _
    .ContactName = "Mr. Abe Henry", _
    .ContactTitle = "Owner", _
    .Address = "1017 Maple Leaf Way", _
    .City = "Ft. Worth", _
    .Region = "TX", _
    .PostalCode = "76104", _
    .Country = "USA", _
    .Phone = "(800) MOW-LAWN", _
    .Fax = "(800) MOW-LAWO"})
```

Once I call the InsertOnSubmit method, identity and change tracking for customer LAWN begins.

Initially, I found change tracking a little confusing. Understanding the basic concept is simple enough, but feeling comfortable about how it was working did not come easy. Understanding change tracking becomes even more important if you are writing your entity classes by hand. Be sure to read the section titled "Change Notifications" in Chapter 15 to gain an even more complete understanding of how change tracking works.

Change Processing

One of the more significant services the `DataContext` provides is change tracking for entity objects. When you insert, change, or delete an entity object, the `DataContext` is monitoring what is happening. However, no changes are actively being propagated to the database. The changes are cached by the `DataContext` until you call the `SubmitChanges` method.

When you call the `SubmitChanges` method, the `DataContext` object's change processor manages the update of the database. First, the change processor will insert any newly inserted entity objects to its list of tracked entity objects. Next, it will order all changed entity objects based on their dependencies resulting from foreign keys and unique constraints. Then, if no transaction is in scope, it will create a transaction so that all SQL commands carried out during this invocation of the `SubmitChanges` method will have transactional integrity. It uses SQL Server's default isolation level of `ReadCommitted`, which means that the data read will not be physically corrupted and only committed data will be read, but since the lock is shared, nothing prevents the data from being changed before the end of the transaction. Last, it enumerates through the ordered list of changed entity objects, creates the necessary SQL statements, and executes them.

If any errors occur while enumerating the changed entity objects, if the `SubmitChanges` method is using a `ConflictMode` of `FailOnFirstConflict`, the enumeration process aborts, and the transaction is rolled back, undoing all changes to the database, and an exception is thrown. If a `ConflictMode` of `ContinueOnConflict` is specified, all changed entity objects will be enumerated and processed despite any conflicts that occur, while the `DataContext` builds a list of the conflicts. But again, the transaction is rolled back, undoing all changes to the database, and an exception is thrown. However, while the changes have not persisted to the database, all of the entity objects' changes still exist in the entity objects. This gives the developer the opportunity to try to resolve the problem and to call the `SubmitChanges` method again.

If all the changes are made to the database successfully, the transaction is committed, and the change tracking information for the changed entity objects is deleted, so that change tracking can restart fresh.

The DataContext Lifetime

One of the questions that gets asked regularly is how long a `DataContext` object should be kept alive and utilized. As I mentioned in "The Results Set Cache Mismatch" section, data retrieved and cached by the `DataContext` is considered stale the moment it is retrieved. This means the longer you keep a `DataContext` object alive, the more stale data it contains. Not only does this create additional overhead, it creates a greater likelihood of a results set cache mismatch occurring. Therefore it is highly recommended to keep `DataContext` objects as short-lived as possible.

I would recommend creating a `DataContext` object each time it is needed and then allowing it to go out of scope after the `SubmitChanges` method has been called. Of course every situation is different, so this is a judgment call. I would not create a single `DataContext` object and try to use it for the lifetime of a desktop application. A good rule of thumb would be that a DataContext object should live for seconds, not minutes or hours.

Some developers may be tempted to keep a DataContext object alive for longer periods of time and rely on the Refresh method that I will cover at the end of this chapter to prevent results set cache mismatches from occurring. I think this would be a poor approach because then you are left with the decision of how often and when you should call the Refresh method. Would you call it every time you use the DataContext object? Unnecessarily calling the Refresh method will cause all of the cached data to be refreshed from the database. This could lead to big performance issues if a DataContext lives long enough. That is a large price to pay just to eliminate the cost of instantiating a DataContext.

DataContext() and [Your]DataContext()

The DataContext class is typically derived from to create the [Your]DataContext class. It exists for the purpose of connecting to the database and handling all database interaction. You will use one of the following constructors to instantiate a DataContext or [Your]DataContext object.

Declarations

The DataContext constructor has four declarations I will cover.

The First DataContext Constructor Declaration

```
Public Sub New (fileOrServerOrConnection As String)
```

This declaration of the constructor takes an ADO.NET connection string and is probably the one you will use the majority of the time. This declaration is the one used by most of the LINQ to SQL examples in this book.

The Second DataContext Constructor Declaration

```
Public Sub New (connection As IDbConnection)
```

Because System.Data.SqlClient.SqlConnection inherits from System.Data.Common. DbConnection, which implements System.Data.IDbConnection, you can instantiate a DataContext or [Your]DataContext with a SqlConnection that you have already created. This declaration of the constructor is useful when mixing LINQ to SQL code with already existing ADO.NET code.

The Third DataContext Constructor Declaration

```
Public Sub New (fileOrServerOrConnection As String, mapping As MappingSource)
```

This declaration of the constructor is useful when you don't have a [Your]DataContext class, and instead have an XML mapping file. Sometimes, you may have an already existing business class to which you cannot add the appropriate LINQ to SQL attributes. Perhaps you don't even have the source code for it. You can generate a mapping file with SqlMetal or write one by hand to work with an already existing business class, or any other class for that matter. You provide a normal ADO.NET connection string to establish the connection.

The Fourth DataContext Constructor Declaration

```
Public Sub New (connection As IDbConnection, mapping As MappingSource)
```

This declaration allows you to create a LINQ to SQL connection from an already existing ADO.NET connection and to provide an XML mapping file. This version of the declaration is useful for those times when you are combining LINQ to SQL code with already existing ADO. NET code, and you don't have entity classes decorated with attributes.

Examples

For an example of the first DataContext constructor declaration, in Listing 16-5, I will connect to a physical .mdf file using an ADO.NET type connection string.

Listing 16-5. *The First DataContext Constructor Declaration Connecting to a Database File*

```
Using dc As New DataContext("c:\Northwind.mdf")
  Dim query As IQueryable(Of Customer) = _
    From cust In dc.GetTable(Of Customer)() _
    Where cust.Country = "USA" _
    Select cust

  For Each c As Customer In query
    Console.WriteLine("{0}", c.CompanyName)
  Next c
End Using
```

■**Note** You will need to modify the path passed to the DataContext constructor so that it can find your .mdf file.

I merely provide the path to the .mdf file to instantiate the DataContext object. Since I am creating a DataContext and not a [Your]DataContext object, I must call the GetTable(Of T) method to access the customers in the database. Here are the results:

```
Great Lakes Food Market
Hungry Coyote Import Store
Lazy K Kountry Store
Let's Stop N Shop
Lonesome Pine Restaurant
Old World Delicatessen
Rattlesnake Canyon Grocery
Save-a-lot Markets
Split Rail Beer & Ale
The Big Cheese
The Cracker Box
```

Trail's Head Gourmet Provisioners
White Clover Markets

Next, I want to demonstrate the same basic code, except this time, in Listing 16-6, I will use my [Your]DataContext class, which in this case is the Northwind class.

Listing 16-6. *The First [Your]DataContext Constructor Declaration Connecting to a Database File*

```
Using db As New Northwind("C:\Northwind.mdf")
  Dim query As IQueryable(Of Customer) = _
    From cust In db.Customers _
    Where cust.Country = "USA" _
    Select cust

  For Each c As Customer In query
    Console.WriteLine("{0}", c.CompanyName)
  Next c
End Using
```

Notice that instead of calling the GetTable(Of T) method, I simply reference the Customers property to access the customers in the database. Unsurprisingly, this code provides the same results:

Great Lakes Food Market
Hungry Coyote Import Store
Lazy K Kountry Store
Let's Stop N Shop
Lonesome Pine Restaurant
Old World Delicatessen
Rattlesnake Canyon Grocery
Save-a-lot Markets
Split Rail Beer & Ale
The Big Cheese
The Cracker Box
Trail's Head Gourmet Provisioners
White Clover Markets

For the sake of completeness, I will provide one more example of the first declaration but this time use a connection string to actually connect to a SQL Express database server containing the attached Northwind database. And, because my normal practice will be to use the [Your]DataContext class, I will use it in Listing 16-7.

Listing 16-7. *The First [Your]DataContext Constructor Declaration Connecting to a Database*

```
Using db As New Northwind( _
  "Data Source=.\SQLEXPRESS;Initial Catalog=Northwind;Integrated Security=SSPI")
```

```
Dim query As IQueryable(Of Customer) = _
  From cust In db.Customers _
  Where cust.Country = "USA" _
  Select cust

For Each c As Customer In query
  Console.WriteLine("{0}", c.CompanyName)
Next c
End Using
```

And the results are still the same:

```
Great Lakes Food Market
Hungry Coyote Import Store
Lazy K Kountry Store
Let's Stop N Shop
Lonesome Pine Restaurant
Old World Delicatessen
Rattlesnake Canyon Grocery
Save-a-lot Markets
Split Rail Beer & Ale
The Big Cheese
The Cracker Box
Trail's Head Gourmet Provisioners
White Clover Markets
```

Since the second declaration for the DataContext class is useful when combining LINQ to SQL code with ADO.NET code, that is what my next example, Listing 16-8, will do. First, I will create a SqlConnection and insert a record in the Customers table using it. Then, I will use the SqlConnection to instantiate a [Your]DataContext class. I will query the Customers table with LINQ to SQL and display the results. Lastly, using ADO.NET, I will delete the record from the Customers table I inserted, query the Customers table one last time using LINQ to SQL, and display the results.

Listing 16-8. *The Second [Your]DataContext Constructor Declaration Connecting with a Shared ADO.NET Connection*

```
Using db As New Northwind( _
  "Data Source=.\SQLEXPRESS;Initial Catalog=Northwind;Integrated Security=SSPI")

Dim cmd As String = _
  "insert into Customers values ('LAWN', 'Lawn Wranglers', " & _
  "  'Mr. Abe Henry', 'Owner', '1017 Maple Leaf Way', 'Ft. Worth', 'TX', " & _
  "  '76104', 'USA', '(800) MOW-LAWN', '(800) MOW-LAWO')"

using sqlComm As New System.Data.SqlClient.SqlCommand(cmd)
```

```vb
    sqlComm.Connection = sqlConn

    sqlConn.Open()
    '  Insert the record.
    sqlComm.ExecuteNonQuery()

    Dim db As New Northwind(sqlConn)

    Dim query As IQueryable(Of Customer) = _
      From cust In db.Customers _
      Where cust.Country = "USA" _
      Select cust

    Console.WriteLine("Customers after insertion, but before deletion.")
    For Each c As Customer In query
      Console.WriteLine("{0}", c.CompanyName)
    Next c

    sqlComm.CommandText = "delete from Customers where CustomerID = 'LAWN'"
    '  Delete the record.
    sqlComm.ExecuteNonQuery()

    Console.WriteLine("{0}{0}Customers after deletion.", vbCrLf)
    For Each c As Customer In query
      Console.WriteLine("{0}", c.CompanyName)
    Next c
  End Using
End Using
```

Notice that I only defined the LINQ query once, but I caused it to be performed twice by enumerating the returned sequence twice. Remember, due to deferred query execution, the definition of the LINQ query does not actually result in the query being performed. The query is only performed when the results are enumerated. This is demonstrated by the fact that the results differ between the two enumerations. Listing 16-8 also shows a nice integration of ADO.NET and LINQ to SQL and just how well they can play together. Here are the results:

```
Customers after insertion, but before deletion.
Great Lakes Food Market
Hungry Coyote Import Store
Lawn Wranglers
Lazy K Kountry Store
Let's Stop N Shop
Lonesome Pine Restaurant
Old World Delicatessen
Rattlesnake Canyon Grocery
Save-a-lot Markets
Split Rail Beer & Ale
The Big Cheese
```

```
The Cracker Box
Trail's Head Gourmet Provisioners
White Clover Markets


Customers after deletion.
Great Lakes Food Market
Hungry Coyote Import Store
Lazy K Kountry Store
Let's Stop N Shop
Lonesome Pine Restaurant
Old World Delicatessen
Rattlesnake Canyon Grocery
Save-a-lot Markets
Split Rail Beer & Ale
The Big Cheese
The Cracker Box
Trail's Head Gourmet Provisioners
White Clover Markets
```

For an example of the third declaration, I won't even use the Northwind entity classes. Pretend I don't even have them. Instead, I will use a `Customer` class I have written by hand and an abbreviated mapping file. In truth, my hand-written `Customer` class is the SqlMetal-generated `Customer` class that I have gutted to remove all LINQ to SQL attributes. Let's take a look at my hand-written `Customer` class:

My Hand-Written Customer Class

```
Namespace Linqdev
  Partial Public Class Customer
    Private CustomerID As String
    Private CompanyName As String
    Private ContactName As String
    Private ContactTitle As String
    Private Address As String
    Private City As String
    Private Region As String
    Private PostalCode As String
    Private Country As String
    Private Phone As String
    Private Fax As String

    Public Sub New()
    End Sub

    Public Property CustomerID() As String
      Get
```

```vb
      Return Me._CustomerID
    End Get
    Set(ByVal value As String)
      If (Me._CustomerID <> value) Then
        Me._CustomerID = value
      End If
    End Set
End Property

Public Property CompanyName() As String
  Get
      Return Me._CompanyName
    End Get
    Set(ByVal value As String)
      If (Me._CompanyName <> value) Then
        Me._CompanyName = value
      End If
    End Set
End Property

Public Property ContactName() As String
  Get
      Return Me._ContactName
    End Get
    Set(ByVal value As String)
      If (Me._ContactName <> value) Then
        Me.ContactName = value
      End If
    End Set
End Property

Public Property ContactTitle() As String
  Get
      Return Me._ContactTitle
    End Get
    Set(ByVal value As String)
      If (Me._ContactTitle <> value) Then
        Me.ContactTitle = value
      End If
    End Set
End Property

Public Property Address() As String
  Get
      Return Me._Address
    End Get
    Set(ByVal value As String)
```

```vbnet
      If (Me._Address <> value) Then
        Me._Address = value
      End If
    End Set
  End Property

  Public Property City() As String
    Get
      Return Me._City
    End Get
    Set(ByVal value As String)
      If (Me._City <> value) Then
        Me._City = value
      End If
    End Set
  End Property

  Public Property Region() As String
    Get
      Return Me._Region
    End Get
    Set(ByVal value As String)
      If (Me._Region <> value) Then
        Me._Region = value
      End If
    End Set
  End Property

  Public Property PostalCode() As String
    Get
      Return Me._PostalCode
    End Get
    Set(ByVal value As String)
      If (Me._PostalCode <> value) Then
        Me.PostalCode = value
      End If
    End Set
  End Property

  Public Property Country() As String
    Get
      Return Me._Country
    End Get
    Set(ByVal value As String)
      If (Me._Country <> value) Then
        Me._Country = value
      End If
```

```
        End Set
      End Property

      Public Property Phone() As String
        Get
          Return Me._Phone
        End Get
        Set(ByVal value As String)
          If (Me._Phone <> value) Then
            Me._Phone = value
          End If
        End Set
      End Property

      Public Property Fax() As String
        Get
          Return Me._Fax
        End Get
        Set(ByVal value As String)
          If (Me._Fax <> value) Then
            Me._Fax = value
          End If
        End Set
      End Property
    End Class
End Namespace
```

Now, this is probably the worst hand-written entity class of all time. I don't handle change notifications, and I have deleted many of the portions of code that would make this a well-behaved entity class. Please read Chapter 15 to learn how to write well-behaved entity classes.

Notice that I have specified that this class lives in the Linqdev namespace. This is important, because not only will I need to specify this in my example code to differentiate between this Customer class and the one in the nwind namespace, but this namespace must also be specified in the external mapping file.

What is important for this example, though, is that there is a property for each database field mapped in the external mapping file. Now, let's take a look at the external mapping file I will be using for this example:

An Abbreviated External XML Mapping File

```xml
<?xml version="1.0" encoding="utf-8"?>
<Database Name="Northwind"
  xmlns="http://schemas.microsoft.com/linqtosql/mapping/2007">
  <Table Name="dbo.Customers" Member="Customers">
    <Type Name="Chapter16.Linqdev.Customer">
      <Column Name="CustomerID" Member="CustomerID" Storage="_CustomerID"
        DbType="NChar(5) NOT NULL" CanBeNull="false" IsPrimaryKey="true" />
      <Column Name="CompanyName" Member="CompanyName" Storage="_CompanyName"
```

```
                 DbType="NVarChar(40) NOT NULL" CanBeNull="false" />
         <Column Name="ContactName" Member="ContactName" Storage="_ContactName"
             DbType="NVarChar(30)" />
         <Column Name="ContactTitle" Member="ContactTitle" Storage="_ContactTitle"
             DbType="NVarChar(30)" />
         <Column Name="Address" Member="Address" Storage="_Address"
             DbType="NVarChar(60)" />
         <Column Name="City" Member="City" Storage="_City" DbType="NVarChar(15)" />
         <Column Name="Region" Member="Region" Storage="_Region"
             DbType="NVarChar(15)" />
         <Column Name="PostalCode" Member="PostalCode" Storage="_PostalCode"
             DbType="NVarChar(10)" />
         <Column Name="Country" Member="Country" Storage="_Country"
             DbType="NVarChar(15)" />
         <Column Name="Phone" Member="Phone" Storage="_Phone" DbType="NVarChar(24)" />
         <Column Name="Fax" Member="Fax" Storage="_Fax" DbType="NVarChar(24)" />
     </Type>
   </Table>
</Database>
```

■**Note** Notice that the line `<Type Name="`**Chapter16**`.Linqdev.Customer">` includes my project's name, `Chapter16`, in the namespace. Don't forget that, by default, Visual Studio sets the project's root namespace to be the same as the name of the project. Because the `Customer` class I will be mapping to is defined in my project with an explicit namespace of `Linqdev`, the fully qualified class name is `Chapter16.Linqdev.Customer`, and the fully qualified class name must be specified in the external mapping file. If I were mapping to a class defined outside of my project, like a third-party class for example, the class's fully qualified class name would not include my project's root namespace, and the type specified in the external mapping file would need to reflect that.

Notice that I have specified that the `Customer` class this mapping applies to is in the `Linqdev` namespace.

I have placed this XML in a file named abbreviatednorthwindmap.xml and placed that file in my `bin\Debug` directory.

In Listing 16-9 I will use this hand-written `Customer` class and external mapping file to perform a LINQ to SQL query without using any attributes.

Listing 16-9. *The Third DataContext Constructor Declaration Connecting to a Database and Using a Mapping File*

```
Dim mapPath As String = "abbreviatednorthwindmap.xml"
Dim nwindMap As XmlMappingSource = _
  XmlMappingSource.FromXml(System.IO.File.ReadAllText(mapPath))
```

```
Using db As New DataContext( _
  "Data Source=.\SQLEXPRESS;Initial Catalog=Northwind;Integrated Security=SSPI;", _
  nwindMap)

  Dim query As IQueryable(Of Linqdev.Customer) = _
    From cust In db.GetTable(Of Linqdev.Customer)() _
    Where cust.Country = "USA" _
    Select cust

  For Each c As Linqdev.Customer In query
    Console.WriteLine("{0}", c.CompanyName)
  Next c
End Using
```

■**Note** I placed the abbreviatednorthwindmap.xml file in my Visual Studio project's bin\Debug directory for this example, since I am compiling and running with the Debug configuration.

As you can see, I instantiate the XmlMappingSource object from the mapping file and pass that XmlMappingSource into the DataContext constructor. Also notice that I cannot simply access the Customers Table(Of Customer) property in my DataContext object for the LINQ to SQL query, because I am using the base DataContext class, as opposed to my [Your]DataContext class, and it doesn't exist.

Also notice that everywhere I reference the Customer class I also explicitly state the Linqdev namespace just to be sure I am not using the SqlMetal-generated Customer class that most of the other examples are using.

Here are the results of Listing 16-9:

```
Great Lakes Food Market
Hungry Coyote Import Store
Lazy K Kountry Store
Let's Stop N Shop
Lonesome Pine Restaurant
Old World Delicatessen
Rattlesnake Canyon Grocery
Save-a-lot Markets
Split Rail Beer & Ale
The Big Cheese
The Cracker Box
Trail's Head Gourmet Provisioners
White Clover Markets
```

While this example uses a crude Customer class missing most of the code that makes a class a well-behaved entity class, I wanted to show you one example using a mapping file and a class without LINQ to SQL attributes.

■**Note** If you get an exception saying "Mapping Problem: Cannot find type 'Chapter16.Linqdev.Customer' from mapping.", check to make sure that the type specified in the external mapping file is consistent with your project's root namespace. You can determine your project's root namespace by examining the Root Namespace field on the Application tab of your project's Properties.

The fourth declaration is merely a combination of the second and third declarations, and Listing 16-10 contains an example.

Listing 16-10. *The Fourth DataContext Constructor Declaration Connecting to a Database with a Shared ADO.NET Connection and Using a Mapping File*

```
Using sqlConn As New System.Data.SqlClient.SqlConnection( _
  "Data Source=.\SQLEXPRESS;Initial Catalog=Northwind;Integrated Security=SSPI;")

  Dim cmd As String = _
    "insert into Customers values ('LAWN', 'Lawn Wranglers', " _
    "  'Mr. Abe Henry', 'Owner', '1017 Maple Leaf Way', 'Ft. Worth', 'TX', " _
    "  '76104', 'USA', '(800) MOW-LAWN', '(800) MOW-LAWO')"

  Using  sqlComm As New System.Data.SqlClient.SqlCommand(cmd)

    sqlComm.Connection = sqlConn

    sqlConn.Open()
    '  Insert the record.
    sqlComm.ExecuteNonQuery()

    Dim mapPath As String = "abbreviatednorthwindmap.xml"
    Dim nwindMap As XmlMappingSource = _
      XmlMappingSource.FromXml(System.IO.File.ReadAllText(mapPath))

    Dim db As New DataContext(sqlConn, nwindMap)

    Dim query As IQueryable(Of Linqdev.Customer) = _
      From cust In db.GetTable(Of Linqdev.Customer)() _
      Where cust.Country = "USA" _
      Select cust

    Console.WriteLine("Customers after insertion, but before deletion.")
    For Each c As Linqdev.Customer In query
      Console.WriteLine("{0}", c.CompanyName)
    Next c
```

```
    sqlComm.CommandText = "delete from Customers where CustomerID = 'LAWN'"
    ' Delete the record.
    sqlComm.ExecuteNonQuery()

    Console.WriteLine("{0}{0}Customers after deletion.", vbCrLf)
    For Each c As Linqdev.Customer In query
      Console.WriteLine("{0}", c.CompanyName)
    Next c
  End Using
End Using
```

Listing 16-10 depends on the `Linqdev.Customer` class and abbreviatednorthwindmap.xml external mapping file just at Listing 16-9 does.

This is a nice example of using LINQ to SQL to query a database without attribute-decorated entity class code and integrating with ADO.NET code. And, the results are just as we would expect:

```
Customers after insertion, but before deletion.
Great Lakes Food Market
Hungry Coyote Import Store
Lawn Wranglers
Lazy K Kountry Store
Let's Stop N Shop
Lonesome Pine Restaurant
Old World Delicatessen
Rattlesnake Canyon Grocery
Save-a-lot Markets
Split Rail Beer & Ale
The Big Cheese
The Cracker Box
Trail's Head Gourmet Provisioners
White Clover Markets


Customers after deletion.
Great Lakes Food Market
Hungry Coyote Import Store
Lazy K Kountry Store
Let's Stop N Shop
Lonesome Pine Restaurant
Old World Delicatessen
Rattlesnake Canyon Grocery
Save-a-lot Markets
Split Rail Beer & Ale
The Big Cheese
The Cracker Box
Trail's Head Gourmet Provisioners
White Clover Markets
```

As you can see from the previous examples, getting a connected DataContext or [Your] DataContext is not difficult.

■**Note** Here too, if you get an exception saying "Mapping Problem: Cannot find type 'Chapter16.Linqdev. Customer' from mapping.", check to make sure that the type specified in the external mapping file is consistent with your project's root namespace. You can determine your project's root namespace by examining the Root Namespace field on the Application tab of your project's Properties.

Creating Mapping Sources

In Listings 16-9 and 16-10, the mapping source was loaded from an XML string using the FromXml method. You should be aware that you may also create your mapping source, XmlMappingSource, from an XmlReader, a Stream, or a URL. While I won't provide an example of each, I will share the declarations of each method for obtaining an XmlMappingSource:

```
Public Shared Function FromXml (xml As String) As XmlMappingSource
Public Shared Function FromReader (reader As XmlReader) As XmlMappingSource
Public Shared Function FromStream (stream As Stream) As XmlMappingSource
Public Shared Function FromUrl (url As String) As XmlMappingSource
```

SubmitChanges()

The DataContext will cache all changes made to entity objects until the SubmitChanges method is called. The SubmitChanges method will initiate the change processor, and the changes to entity objects will be persisted to the database.

If an ambient transaction is not available for the DataContext object to enlist with during the SubmitChanges method call, a transaction will be created, and all changes will be made within the transaction. This way if one transaction fails, all database changes can be rolled back.

If concurrency conflicts occur, a ChangeConflictException will be thrown, allowing you the opportunity to try to resolve any conflicts and resubmit. And, what is really nice is that the DataContext contains a ChangeConflicts collection that provides a ResolveAll method to do the resolution for you. How cool is that?

Concurrency conflicts are covered in excruciating detail in Chapter 17.

Declarations

The SubmitChanges method has two declarations I will cover.

The First SubmitChanges Declaration

```
void SubmitChanges()
```

This declaration of the method takes no arguments and defaults to FailOnFirstConflict for the ConflictMode.

The Second SubmitChanges Declaration

```
void SubmitChanges(ConflictMode failureMode)
```

This declaration of the method allows you to specify the ConflictMode. The possible values are ConflictMode.FailOnFirstConflict and ConflictMode.ContinueOnConflict.

ConflictMode.FailOnFirstConflict behaves just as it sounds, causing the SubmitChanges method to throw a ChangeConflictException on the very first conflict that occurs.

ConflictMode.ContinueOnConflict attempts to make all the database updates so that they may all be reported and resolved at once when the ChangeConflictException is thrown.

Conflicts are counted in terms of the number of records conflicting, not the number of fields conflicting. So multiple conflicting fields from the same record only cause a single conflict.

Examples

Since many of the examples in Chapter 14 call the SubmitChanges method, a trivial example of this method is probably old hat to you by now. Instead of boring you with another basic example calling the SubmitChanges method to merely persist changes to the database, I want to get a little more complex.

For an example of the first SubmitChanges declaration, I want to prove to you that the changes are not made to the database until the SubmitChanges method is called. Because this example is more complex than many of the previous examples, I will explain it as I go. Listing 16-11 contains the example.

Listing 16-11. *An Example of the First SubmitChanges Declaration*

```
Using sqlConn As New System.Data.SqlClient.SqlConnection( _
    "Data Source=.\SQLEXPRESS;Initial Catalog=Northwind;Integrated Security=SSPI;")

  sqlConn.Open()

  Dim sqlQuery As String = _
      "select ContactTitle from Customers where CustomerID = 'LAZYK'"
  Dim originalTitle As String = GetStringFromDb(sqlConn, sqlQuery)
  Dim title As String = originalTitle
  Console.WriteLine("Title from database record: {0}", title)

  Using db As New Northwind(sqlConn)

    Dim c As Customer = ( _
      From cust In db.Customers _
      Where cust.CustomerID = "LAZYK" _
      Select cust).Single()
    Console.WriteLine("Title from entity object : {0}", c.ContactTitle)
```

In the previous code, I create an ADO.NET database connection and open it. Next, I query the database for the LAZYK customer's ContactTitle using my common GetStringFromDb method and display it. Then, I create a Northwind object using the ADO.NET database connection, query the same customer using LINQ to SQL, and display their ContactTitle. At this point, the ContactTitle of each should match.

```
Console.WriteLine(String.Format("{0}Change the title to " & _
  "'Director of Marketing' in the entity object:", vbCrLf))
c.ContactTitle = "Director of Marketing"

title = GetStringFromDb(sqlConn, sqlQuery)
Console.WriteLine("Title from database record: {0}", title)

Dim c2 As Customer = ( _
  From cust In db.Customers _
  Where cust.CustomerID = "LAZYK" _
  Select cust).Single()
Console.WriteLine("Title from entity object : {0}", c2.ContactTitle)
```

In the previous code, I change the ContactTitle of the customer's LINQ to SQL entity object. Then, I query the ContactTitle from the database and the entity object again and display them. This time, the ContactTitle values should not match, because the change has not yet been persisted to the database.

```
db.SubmitChanges()
Console.WriteLine( _
  String.Format("{0}SubmitChanges() method has been called.", vbCrLf))

title = GetStringFromDb(sqlConn, sqlQuery)
Console.WriteLine("Title from database record: {0}", title)

Console.WriteLine("Restoring ContactTitle back to original value ...")
c.ContactTitle = originalTitle
db.SubmitChanges()
Console.WriteLine("ContactTitle restored.")
  End Using
End Using
```

In the previous code, I call the SubmitChanges method and then retrieve the ContactTitle from the database to display again. This time, the value from the database should be updated, because the SubmitChanges method has persisted the change to the database.

Last, I set the ContactTitle back to the original value and persist it to the database using the SubmitChanges method to restore the database back to its original state so this example can be run multiple times and no other examples will be affected.

That code is doing a lot, but its intent is to prove that the changes made to the entity object are not persisted to the database until the SubmitChanges method is called. When you see a call to the GetStringFromDb method, it is retrieving the ContactTitle directly from the database using ADO.NET. Here are the results:

```
Title from database record: Marketing Manager
Title from entity object : Marketing Manager
```

Change the title to 'Director of Marketing' in the entity object:
Title from database record: Marketing Manager
Title from entity object : Director of Marketing

SubmitChanges() method has been called.
Title from database record: Director of Marketing
Restoring ContactTitle back to original value ...
ContactTitle restored.

As you can see in the previous results, the ContactTitle's value is not changed in the database until the SubmitChanges method is called.

For an example of the second SubmitChanges declaration, I will intentionally induce concurrency errors on two records by updating them with ADO.NET between the time I query the records with LINQ to SQL, and the time I try to update them with LINQ to SQL. I will create *two* record conflicts to demonstrate the difference between ConflictMode.FailOnFirstConflict and ConflictMode.ContinueOnConflict.

Also, you will see code toward the bottom that will reset the ContactTitle values back to their original values in the database. This is to allow the code to be run multiple times. If, while running the code in the debugger, you prevent the entire code from running, you may need to manually reset these values.

In the first example of the second declaration of the SubmitChanges method, Listing 16-12, I will set the ConflictMode to ContinueOnConflict so that you can see it handle multiple conflicts first. Because this example is complex, I will explain it a portion at a time.

Listing 16-12. *The Second SubmitChanges Declaration Demonstrating ContinueOnConflict*

```
Using db As New Northwind( _
  "Data Source=.\SQLEXPRESS;Initial Catalog=Northwind;Integrated Security=SSPI;")

  Console.WriteLine("Querying for the LAZYK Customer with LINQ.")
  Dim cust1 As Customer = ( _
    From c In db.Customers _
    Where c.CustomerID = "LAZYK" _
    Select c).Single()

  Console.WriteLine("Querying for the LONEP Customer with LINQ.")
  Dim cust2 As Customer = ( _
    From c In db.Customers _
    Where c.CustomerID = "LONEP" _
    Select c).Single()

  Dim cmd As String = _
    "update Customers set ContactTitle = 'Director of Marketing' " & _
    "  where CustomerID = 'LAZYK'; " & _
    "update Customers set ContactTitle = 'Director of Sales' " & _
    "  where CustomerID = 'LONEP'"
  ExecuteStatementInDb(cmd)
```

Next, in the preceding code, I update the ContactTitle value in the database for both customers using my ExecuteStatementInDb common method, which uses ADO.NET to make the changes. At this point, I have created the potential for concurrency conflicts for each record.

```
Console.WriteLine("Change ContactTitle in entity objects for LAZYK and LONEP.")
cust1.ContactTitle = "Vice President of Marketing"
cust2.ContactTitle = "Vice President of Sales"
```

In the previous code, I update the ContactTitle for each customer so that when I call the SubmitChanges method in the next portion of code, the DataContext object's change processor will try to persist the changes for these two customers and detect the concurrency conflicts.

```
Try
    Console.WriteLine("Calling SubmitChanges() ...")
    db.SubmitChanges(ConflictMode.ContinueOnConflict)
    Console.WriteLine("SubmitChanges() called successfully.")
```

In the previous code, I call the SubmitChanges method. This will cause the DataContext change processor to try to persist these two customers, but since the value for each customer's ContactTitle will be different in the database than when initially loaded from the database, a concurrency conflict will be detected.

```
Catch ex As ChangeConflictException
    Console.WriteLine( _
        "Conflict(s) occurred calling SubmitChanges(): {0}", ex.Message)

    For Each objectConflict As ObjectChangeConflict In db.ChangeConflicts
        Console.WriteLine( _
            "Conflict for {0} occurred.", _
            (CType(objectConflict.Object, Customer)).CustomerID)

        For Each memberConflict _
            As MemberChangeConflict _
            In ObjectConflict.MemberConflicts
            Console.WriteLine( _
                "  LINQ value = {0}{1}  Database value = {2}", _
                memberConflict.CurrentValue, _
                vbCrLf, _
                memberConflict.DatabaseValue)
        Next memberConflict
    Next objectConflict
End Try
```

In the preceding code, I catch the ChangeConflictException exception. This is where things get interesting. Notice that first I enumerate the ChangeConflicts collection of the DataContext object, db. This collection will store ObjectChangeConflict objects. Notice that an ObjectChangeConflict object has a property named Object that references the actual entity object that the concurrency conflict occurred during the persistence thereof. I simply cast that Object member as the data type of the entity class to reference property values of the entity object. In this case, I access the CustomerID property.

Then, for each `ObjectChangeConflict` object, I enumerate through its collection of `MemberChangeConflict` objects and display the information from each that I am interested in. In this case, I display the LINQ value and the value from the database.

```
Console.WriteLine("{0}Resetting data to original values.", vbCrLf)
cmd = _
  "update Customers set ContactTitle = 'Marketing Manager' " & _
  "  where CustomerID = 'LAZYK'; " & _
  "update Customers set ContactTitle = 'Sales Manager' " & _
  "  where CustomerID = 'LONEP'"
ExecuteStatementInDb(cmd)
End Using
```

In the previous code, I simply restore the database back to its original state so the example can be run multiple times.

That is a lot of code to demonstrate this. Keep in mind that none of this enumeration through the various conflict collections is necessary. I am merely demonstrating how you would do it and showing some of the conflict information available, should you care.

Also, please notice that I am doing nothing in this example to resolve the conflicts. I am merely reporting them.

Here are the results of the code:

```
Querying for the LAZYK Customer with LINQ.
Querying for the LONEP Customer with LINQ.
Executing SQL statement against database with ADO.NET ...
Database updated.
Change ContactTitle in entity objects for LAZYK and LONEP.
Calling SubmitChanges() ...
Conflict(s) occurred calling SubmitChanges(): 2 of 2 updates failed.
Conflict for LAZYK occurred.
  LINQ value = Vice President of Marketing
  Database value = Director of Marketing
Conflict for LONEP occurred.
  LINQ value = Vice President of Sales
  Database value = Director of Sales

Resetting data to original values.
Executing SQL statement against database with ADO.NET ...
Database updated.
```

As you can see, there were two conflicts, one for each of the two records for which I created a conflict. This demonstrates that the change processor did *not* stop trying to persist the changes to the database after the first conflict. This is because I passed a `ConflictMode` of `ContinueOnConflict` when I called the `SubmitChanges` method.

Listing 16-13 is the same code except I pass a `ConflictMode` of `FailOnFirstConflict` when I call the `SubmitChanges` method.

Listing 16-13. *The Second SubmitChanges Declaration Demonstrating FailOnFirstConflict*

```
Using db As New Northwind( _
  "Data Source=.\SQLEXPRESS;Initial Catalog=Northwind;Integrated Security=SSPI;")

  Console.WriteLine("Querying for the LAZYK Customer with LINQ.")
  Dim cust1 As Customer = ( _
    From c In db.Customers _
    Where c.CustomerID = "LAZYK" _
    Select c).Single()

  Console.WriteLine("Querying for the LONEP Customer with LINQ.")
  Dim cust2 As Customer = ( _
    From c In db.Customers _
    Where c.CustomerID = "LONEP" _
    Select c).Single()

  Dim cmd As String = _
    "update Customers set ContactTitle = 'Director of Marketing' " & _
    "  where CustomerID = 'LAZYK'; " & _
    "update Customers set ContactTitle = 'Director of Sales' " & _
    "  where CustomerID = 'LONEP'"
  ExecuteStatementInDb(cmd)

  Console.WriteLine("Change ContactTitle in entity objects for LAZYK and LONEP.")
  cust1.ContactTitle = "Vice President of Marketing"
  cust2.ContactTitle = "Vice President of Sales"

  Try
    Console.WriteLine("Calling SubmitChanges() ...")
    db.SubmitChanges(ConflictMode.FailOnFirstConflict)
    Console.WriteLine("SubmitChanges() called successfully.")
  Catch ex As ChangeConflictException
    Console.WriteLine( _
      "Conflict(s) occurred calling SubmitChanges(): {0}", ex.Message)

  For Each objectConflict As ObjectChangeConflict In db.ChangeConflicts
    Console.WriteLine( _
      "Conflict for {0} occurred.", _
      (CType(objectConflict.Object, Customer)).CustomerID)

      For Each memberConflict _
          As MemberChangeConflict _
          In ObjectConflict.MemberConflicts
        Console.WriteLine( _
          "  LINQ value = {0}{1}  Database value = {2}", _
          memberConflict.CurrentValue, _
```

```
        vbCrLf, _
        memberConflict.DatabaseValue)
    Next memberConflict
  Next objectConflict
End Try

  Console.WriteLine("{0}Resetting data to original values.", vbCrLf)
  cmd = _
    "update Customers set ContactTitle = 'Marketing Manager' " & _
    "  where CustomerID = 'LAZYK'; " & _
    "update Customers set ContactTitle = 'Sales Manager' " & _
    "  where CustomerID = 'LONEP'"
  ExecuteStatementInDb(cmd)
End Using
```

This time, the results should indicate that the processing of changes to the entity objects halts once the first concurrency conflict is detected. Let's take a look at the results:

```
Querying for the LAZYK Customer with LINQ.
Querying for the LONEP Customer with LINQ.
Executing SQL statement against database with ADO.NET ...
Database updated.
Change ContactTitle in entity objects for LAZYK and LONEP.
Calling SubmitChanges() ...
Conflict(s) occurred calling SubmitChanges(): Row not found or changed.
Conflict for LAZYK occurred.
  LINQ value = Vice President of Marketing
  Database value = Director of Marketing

Resetting data to original values.
Executing SQL statement against database with ADO.NET ...
Database updated.
```

As you can see, even though I induced two conflicts, the change processor stopped trying to persist changes to the database once a conflict occurred, as evidenced by only one conflict being reported.

DatabaseExists()

The DatabaseExists method can be used to determine if a database already exists. The determination of database existence is based on the connection string specified when instantiating the DataContext. If you specify a pathed .mdf file, it will look for the database in that path with the specified name. If you specify a server, it will check that server.

The DatabaseExists method is often used in conjunction with the DeleteDatabase and CreateDatabase methods.

Declarations

The DatabaseExists method has one declaration I will cover.

The Only DatabaseExists Declaration

```
Public Function DatabaseExists As Boolean
```

This method will return True if the database specified in the connection string when instantiating the DataContext exists. Otherwise, it returns False.

Examples

Thankfully, this is a fairly simple method to demonstrate. In Listing 16-14, I will just instantiate a DataContext and call the DatabaseExists method to see if the Northwind database exists. And of course, I already know that it does.

Listing 16-14. *An Example of the DatabaseExists Method*

```
Dim db As New Northwind( _
  "Data Source=.\SQLEXPRESS;Initial Catalog=Northwind;Integrated Security=SSPI;")

Console.WriteLine("The Northwind database {0}.", _
  If(db.DatabaseExists(), "exists", "does not exist"))
```

Here are the results:

```
The Northwind database exists.
```

For kicks, if you detach your Northwind database and run the example again, you will get these results:

```
The Northwind database does not exist.
```

If you tried that, don't forget to attach your Northwind database back so the other examples will work.

CreateDatabase()

To make things even slicker, since the entity classes know so much about the structure of the database to which they are mapped, Microsoft provides a method named CreateDatabase to actually create the database.

You should realize, though, that it can only create the parts of the database that it knows about via the entity class attributes or a mapping file. So, the *content* of things like stored procedures, triggers, user-defined functions, and check constraints will not be produced in a database created in this manner, since there are no attributes specifying this information. For simple applications, this may be perfectly acceptable though.

■**Caution** Unlike most other changes that you make to a database through the DataContext, the CreateDatabase method executes immediately. There is no need to call the SubmitChanges method, and the execution is not deferred. This gives you the benefit of being able to create the database and begin inserting data immediately.

Declarations

The CreateDatabase method has one declaration I will cover.

The Only CreateDatabase Declaration

```
void CreateDatabase()
```

This method takes no arguments and returns nothing.

Examples

Again this is a simple method to demonstrate, and Listing 16-15 contains the code.

Listing 16-15. *An Example of the CreateDatabase Method*

```
Dim db As New Northwind("C:\Northwnd.mdf")
db.CreateDatabase()
```

■**Note** I have intentionally spelled Northwnd without the letter *i* in Listing 16-15 so that it does not impact a Northwind (with the letter *i*) database should you have one.

This code doesn't produce any screen output, so there are no results to show. However, if I look in the C:\ directory, I can see the Northwnd.mdf and Northwnd.ldf files. If you look in SQL Server Management Studio, you will not see the Northwnd database attached, but rest assured that it is cataloged. Since it isn't attached, the easiest way to remove it will be to call the DeleteDatabase method that we will cover next. The CreateDatabase method would be best combined with the DatabaseExists method to verify that the database does not already exist. If you attempt to call the CreateDatabase method and the database already exists, an exception will be thrown. To demonstrate this, merely run the code in Listing 16-15 a second time, without deleting the Northwnd database, and you will get this output:

```
Unhandled Exception: System.Data.SqlClient.SqlException: Database 'C:\Northwnd.mdf'
already exists. Choose a different database name.
...
```

Also, don't make the mistake of assuming you can just delete the two underlying North-wnd database files from the file system to eliminate the database so that you can run the example again. SQL Server will still have it cataloged. You must delete or detach the database in a proper manner for the CreateDatabase method to succeed a second time.

You should delete the newly created Northwnd database by running the next example, Listing 16-16, to prevent confusion at some future point.

DeleteDatabase()

LINQ to SQL gives us the ability to delete a database with the DataContext object's DeleteDatabase method. Attempting to delete a database that does not exist will throw an exception, so it would be best to only call this method after checking for the existence of the database with the DatabaseExists method.

■**Caution** Unlike most other changes that you make to a database through the DataContext, the DeleteDatabase method executes immediately. There is no need to call the SubmitChanges method, and the execution is not deferred.

Declarations

The DeleteDatabase method has one declaration I will cover.

The Only DeleteDatabase Declaration

```
void DeleteDatabase()
```

This method takes no arguments and returns nothing.

Examples

In Listing 16-16, I will delete the database I just created in Listing 16-15.

Listing 16-16. *An Example of the DeleteDatabase Method*

```
Dim db As New Northwind("C:\Northwnd.mdf")
db.DeleteDatabase()
```

This example doesn't create any screen output when run, as long as the database speci-fied exists, but after running it, you will find that the two database files that were created when calling the CreateDatabase method are gone.

Calling this method when the database does not exist will cause the following exception to be thrown:

```
Unhandled Exception: System.Data.SqlClient.SqlException: An attempt to attach an
auto-named database for file C:\Northwnd.mdf failed. A database with the same name
exists, or specified file cannot be opened, or it is located on UNC share.
...
```

CreateMethodCallQuery()

The first thing you need to know about the CreateMethodCallQuery method is that it is a protected method. This means you are not able to call this method from your application code and that you must derive a class from the DataContext class to be able to call it.

The CreateMethodCallQuery method is used to call *table-valued* user-defined functions. The ExecuteMethodCall method is used to call *scalar-valued* user-defined functions, and I will discuss it later in this chapter.

Declarations

The CreateMethodCallQuery method has one declaration I will cover.

The Only CreateMethodCallQuery Declaration

```
Protected Friend Function CreateMethodCallQuery(Of TResult) ( _
    instance As Object, _
    methodInfo As MethodInfo, _
    ParamArray parameters As Object() _
) As IQueryable(Of TResult)
```

The CreateMethodCallQuery method is passed a reference to the DataContext or [Your] DataContext object of which the method that is calling the CreateMethodCallQuery method is a member, the MethodInfo object for that calling method, and a params array of the parameters for the table-valued user-defined function.

Examples

Because the CreateMethodCallQuery method is protected and can only be called from the DataContext class or one derived from it, instead of providing an example that actually calls the CreateMethodCallQuery method, I will discuss the method that SqlMetal generated for the extended Northwind database's ProductsUnderThisUnitPrice table-valued user-defined function. Here is that method:

The SqlMetal-Generated Method Calling CreateMethodCallQuery

```
<FunctionAttribute(Name:="dbo.ProductsUnderThisUnitPrice", IsComposable:=true)> _
Public Function ProductsUnderThisUnitPrice( _
    <Parameter(DbType:="Money")> ByVal price As System.Nullable(Of Decimal)) _
  As IQueryable(Of ProductsUnderThisUnitPriceResult)
```

```
    Return Me.CreateMethodCallQuery(Of ProductsUnderThisUnitPriceResult) _
      (Me, CType(MethodInfo.GetCurrentMethod,MethodInfo), price)
```

```
End Function
```

In the previous code, you can see that the ProductsUnderThisUnitPrice method is attributed with the FunctionAttribute attribute, so we know it is going to call either a stored procedure or user-defined function named ProductsUnderThisUnitPrice. Because the IsComposable attribute property is set to True, we know it is a user-defined function and not a stored procedure. Because the code that was generated calls the CreateMethodCallQuery method, we know that the specified user-defined function ProductsUnderThisUnitPrice is a table-valued user-defined function, not a scalar-valued user-defined function.

For the arguments passed to the CreateMethodCallQuery method, the first argument is a reference to the derived DataContext class SqlMetal generated for me. The second argument passed is the current method's MethodInfo object. This will allow the CreateMethodCallQuery method access to the attributes, so it knows the necessary information to call the table-valued user-defined function, such as its name. The third argument passed to the CreateMethodCallQuery method is the only parameter the specified user-defined function accepts, which in this case is a price.

The value returned by the call to the CreateMethodCallQuery method will be returned by the ProductsUnderThisUnitPrice method, and that is a sequence of ProductsUnderThisUnitPriceResult objects. SqlMetal was nice enough to generate the ProductsUnderThisUnitPriceResult class for me as well.

The code I discuss previously shows how to call the CreateMethodCallQuery method, but just to provide some context, let's look at an example calling the generated ProductsUnderThisUnitPriceResult method, so you can see it all in action.

In Listing 16-17, I will make a simple call to the ProductsUnderThisUnitPrice method.

Listing 16-17. *An Example Calling the ProductsUnderThisUnitPrice Method*

```
Dim db As New Northwind( _
  "Data Source=.\SQLEXPRESS;Initial Catalog=Northwind;Integrated Security=SSPI;")

Dim results As IQueryable(Of ProductsUnderThisUnitPriceResult) = _
  db.ProductsUnderThisUnitPrice(New Decimal(5.5D))

For Each prod As ProductsUnderThisUnitPriceResult In results
  Console.WriteLine("{0} - {1:C}", prod.ProductName, prod.UnitPrice)
Next prod
```

Here are the results of this example:

```
Guaraná Fantástica - $4.50
Geitost - $2.50
```

ExecuteQuery()

There is no doubt that LINQ to SQL is awesome. Using the LINQ standard dot notation or expression syntax makes crafting LINQ queries fun. But, at one time or another, I think we have all experienced the desire to just perform a SQL query. Well, you can do that too with LINQ to SQL. In fact, you can do that and still get back entity objects. That is rockin'.

The ExecuteQuery method allows you to specify a SQL query as a string and to even provide parameters for substitution into the string, just as you would when calling the String. Format method, and it will translate the query results into a sequence of entity objects.

It's just that simple. I hear what you are saying. What about SQL injection errors? Doesn't the appropriate way to do this require using parameters? Yes, it does. And, the ExecuteQuery method is handling all that for you! I know you must be saying, "Show me an example, and pronto!"

Declarations

The ExecuteQuery method has one declaration I will cover.

The Only ExecuteQuery Declaration

```
Public Function ExecuteQuery(Of TResult) ( _
    query As String, _
    ParamArray parameters As Object() _
) As IEnumerable(Of TResult)
```

This method takes at least one argument, a SQL query, and zero or more parameters. The query string and optional parameters work just like the String.Format method. The method returns a sequence of type T, where type T is an entity class.

Be aware that if you specify the value of a column for a where clause in the query string itself, you must enclose char-based type columns with single quotes just as you would were you making a normal SQL query. But, if you provide the column's value as a parameter, there is no need to enclose the parameter specifier, such as {0}, in single quotes.

For a column in the query to be propagated into an actual entity object, the column's name must match one of the entity object's mapped fields. Of course, you can accomplish this by appending "as <columnname>" to the actual column name, where <columnname> is a mapped column in the entity object.

Every mapped field does not need to be returned by the query, but primary keys certainly do. And, you can retrieve fields in the query that do not map to any mapped field in the entity object, but they will not get propagated to the entity object.

Examples

For a simple example calling the ExecuteQuery method, in Listing 16-18, I will query the Customers table.

Listing 16-18. *A Simple Example of the ExecuteQuery Method*

```
Using db As New Northwind( _
  "Data Source=.\SQLEXPRESS;Initial Catalog=Northwind;Integrated Security=SSPI;")
```

```
    Dim custs As IEnumerable(Of Customer) = db.ExecuteQuery(Of Customer) _
      ("select CustomerID, CompanyName, ContactName, ContactTitle " & _
       "from Customers where Region = {0}", "WA")

    For Each c As Customer In custs
      Console.WriteLine("ID = {0} : Name = {1} : Contact = {2}", _
        c.CustomerID, c.CompanyName, c.ContactName)
    Next c
End Using
```

There isn't much to this example. Again notice that, because I am using the parameter substitution feature of the method by specifying "WA" as a parameter instead of hard-coding it in the query, I do not need to enclose the format specifier in single quotes. Here are the results:

```
ID = LAZYK : Name = Lazy K Kountry Store : Contact = John Steel
ID = TRAIH : Name = Trail's Head Gourmet Provisioners : Contact = Helvetius Nagy
ID = WHITC : Name = White Clover Markets : Contact = Karl Jablonski
```

If I want to make that same query, but without using parameter substitution, I would have to enclose the "WA" portion in single quotes like a normal SQL query. Listing 16-19 contains the code.

Listing 16-19. *Another Simple Example of the ExecuteQuery Method*

```
Using db As New Northwind( _
  "Data Source=.\SQLEXPRESS;Initial Catalog=Northwind;Integrated Security=SSPI;")

  Dim custs As IEnumerable(Of Customer) = db.ExecuteQuery(Of Customer) _
    ("select CustomerID, CompanyName, ContactName, ContactTitle " & _
     "from Customers where Region = 'WA'")

  For Each c As Customer In custs
    Console.WriteLine("ID = {0} : Name = {1} : Contact = {2}", _
      c.CustomerID, c.CompanyName, c.ContactName)
  Next c
End Using
```

In case it is hard to detect, WA is enclosed in single quotes in that query string. The results of this code are the same as the previous:

```
ID = LAZYK : Name = Lazy K Kountry Store : Contact = John Steel
ID = TRAIH : Name = Trail's Head Gourmet Provisioners : Contact = Helvetius Nagy
ID = WHITC : Name = White Clover Markets : Contact = Karl Jablonski
```

In addition to all this, you can append a specified column name if the real column name doesn't match the column name in the database. Since you can perform joins in the query string, you could query columns with a different name from a different table, but specify their name as one of the mapped fields in the entity class. Listing 16-20 contains an example of this.

Listing 16-20. *An Example of the ExecuteQuery Method Specifying a Mapped Field Name*

```
Dim db As New Northwind( _
  "Data Source=.\SQLEXPRESS;Initial Catalog=Northwind;Integrated Security=SSPI;")

Dim custs As IEnumerable(Of Customer) = db.ExecuteQuery(Of Customer) _
  ("select CustomerID, Address + ', ' + City + ', ' + Region as Address " & _
  "from Customers where Region = 'WA'")

For Each c As Customer In custs
  Console.WriteLine("Id = {0} : Address = {1}", c.CustomerID, c.Address)
Next c
```

The interesting part of this example is that I am concatenating multiple database columns and string literals and specifying a mapped field name, to get the address, city, and region into the single Address member of the entity object. In this case, all the fields come from the same table, but they could have come from a join on another table. Here are the results:

```
Id = LAZYK : Address = 12 Orchestra Terrace, Walla Walla, WA
Id = TRAIH : Address = 722 DaVinci Blvd., Kirkland, WA
Id = WHITC : Address = 305 - 14th Ave. S. Suite 3B, Seattle, WA
```

Of course, if you utilize this type of chicanery, don't forget that if one of those returned entity objects is modified and the SubmitChanges method is called, you could end up with some database records containing questionable data. But used properly, this could be a very handy technique.

Translate()

The Translate method is similar to the ExecuteQuery method in that it translates the results of a SQL query into a sequence of entity objects. Where it differs is that instead of passing a string containing a SQL statement, you pass it an object of type System.Data.Common.DbDataReader, such as a SqlDataReader. This method is useful for integrating LINQ to SQL code into existing ADO.NET code.

Declarations

The Translate method has one declaration I will cover.

The Only Translate Declaration

```
Public Function Translate(Of TResult) ( _
    reader As DbDataReader) _
  As IEnumerable(Of TResult)
```

You pass the Translate method an object of type System.Data.Common.DbDataReader, and the Translate method returns a sequence of the specified entity objects.

Examples

In Listing 16-21, I will create and execute a query using ADO.NET. I will then use the `Translate` method to translate the results from the query into a sequence of `Customer` entity objects. Because Listing 16-21 is somewhat more complex than typical, I will explain it as I go.

Listing 16-21. *An Example of the Translate Method*

```
Using sqlConn As New System.Data.SqlClient.SqlConnection( _
  "Data Source=.\SQLEXPRESS;Initial Catalog=Northwind;Integrated Security=SSPI;")

  Dim cmd As String = _
    "select CustomerID, CompanyName, ContactName, ContactTitle " & _
    "from Customers where Region = 'WA'"

  Using sqlComm As New System.Data.SqlClient.SqlCommand(cmd)

    sqlComm.Connection = sqlConn
    sqlConn.Open()
    Using reader As System.Data.SqlClient.SqlDataReader = sqlComm.ExecuteReader()
```

For this example, let's pretend all the previous code already existed. Pretend this is legacy code that I need to update, and I would like to take advantage of LINQ to accomplish my new task. As you can see, there are no references to LINQ in the previous code. A `SqlConnection` is established, a query is formed, a `SqlCommand` is created, the connection is opened, and the query is performed—all pretty much a run-of-the-mill ADO.NET database query. Now, let's add some LINQ code to do something.

```
      Dim db As New Northwind(sqlConn)
      Dim custs As IEnumerable(Of Customer) = db.Translate(Of Customer)(reader)

      For Each c As Customer In custs
        Console.WriteLine("ID = {0} : Name = {1} : Contact = {2}", _
          c.CustomerID, c.CompanyName, c.ContactName)
      Next c
```

In the previous code, I instantiate my `Northwind` DataContext using my ADO.NET `SqlConnection`. I then call the `Translate` method passing the already created `reader` so that the query results can be converted into a sequence of entity objects that I can then enumerate and display the results of.

Normally, since this is legacy code, there would be some more code doing something with the results, but for this example, there is no point to have that code. All that is left is to close and clean up the database connection by ending the `Using` blocks.

```
    End Using
  End Using
End Using
```

The previous code simply closes the connection. This example demonstrates how nicely LINQ to SQL can play with ADO.NET. Let's take a look at the results of Listing 16-21.

```
ID = LAZYK : Name = Lazy K Kountry Store : Contact = John Steel
ID = TRAIH : Name = Trail's Head Gourmet Provisioners : Contact = Helvetius Nagy
ID = WHITC : Name = White Clover Markets : Contact = Karl Jablonski
```

ExecuteCommand()

Like the ExecuteQuery method, the ExecuteCommand method allows you to specify an actual SQL statement to execute against the database. This means you can use it to execute insert, update, or delete statements, as well as execute stored procedures. Also, like with the ExecuteQuery method, you can pass parameters into the method.

One thing to be aware of when calling the ExecuteCommand method is that it executes immediately, and the SubmitChanges method does not need to be called.

Declarations

The ExecuteCommand method has one declaration I will cover.

The Only ExecuteCommand Declaration

```
int ExecuteCommand(string command, params object[] parameters)
```

This method accepts a command string and zero or more optional parameters and returns an integer indicating how many rows were affected by the query.

Be aware that if you specify the value of a column for a where clause in the command string itself, you must enclose char-based type columns with single quotes just as you would were you making a normal SQL query. But, if you provide the column's value as a parameter, there is no need to enclose the parameter specifier, such as {0}, in single quotes.

Examples

In Listing 16-22, I will insert a record using the ExecuteCommand method. Since I always reverse any changes I make to the database so subsequent examples are not affected, I will also use the ExecuteCommand method to delete the inserted record.

Listing 16-22. *An Example of the ExecuteCommand Method Used to Insert and Delete a Record*

```
Dim db As New Northwind( _
  "Data Source=.\SQLEXPRESS;Initial Catalog=Northwind;Integrated Security=SSPI;")

Console.WriteLine("Inserting customer ...")
Dim rowsAffected As Integer = db.ExecuteCommand( _
  "insert into Customers values ({0}, 'Lawn Wranglers', " & _
  " 'Mr. Abe Henry', 'Owner', '1017 Maple Leaf Way', 'Ft. Worth', 'TX', " & _
  " '76104', 'USA', '(800) MOW-LAWN', '(800) MOW-LAWO')", "LAWN")
Console.WriteLine("Insert complete.{0}", vbCrLf)
```

```
Console.WriteLine("There were {0} row(s) affected.  Is customer in database?", _
  rowsAffected)

Dim cust As Customer = ( _
  From c In db.Customers _
  Where c.CustomerID = "LAWN" _
  Select c).DefaultIfEmpty().Single()

Console.WriteLine("{0}{1}", _
  If(cust IsNot Nothing, "Yes, customer is in database.", _
    "No, customer is not in database."), vbCrLf)

Console.WriteLine("Deleting customer ...")
rowsAffected = db.ExecuteCommand( _
  "delete from Customers where CustomerID = {0}", "LAWN")

Console.WriteLine("Delete complete.{0}", vbCrLf)
```

As you can see, there is not much to this example. I call the ExecuteCommand method and pass the command string plus any parameters. I then perform a query using LINQ to SQL just to make sure the record is indeed in the database and display the results of the query to the console. To clean up the database, I call the ExecuteCommand method to delete the inserted record. This code produces the following results:

```
Inserting customer ...
Insert complete.

There were 1 row(s) affected.  Is customer in database?
Yes, customer is in database.

Deleting customer ...
Delete complete.
```

ExecuteMethodCall()

The first thing you need to know about the ExecuteMethodCall method is that it is a protected method. This means you are not able to call this method from your application code and that you must derive a class from the DataContext class to be able to call it.

The ExecuteMethodCall method is used to call stored procedures and *scalar-valued* user-defined functions. To call *table-valued* user-defined functions, please read the section in this chapter about the CreateMethodCallQuery method.

Declarations

The ExecuteMethodCall method has one declaration I will cover.

The Only ExecuteMethodCall Declaration

```
Protected Friend Function ExecuteMethodCall(Of T) ( _
  instance As Object, _
  methodInfo As MethodInfo, _
  ParamArray parameters As Object() _
) As IExecuteResult
```

■**Note** You may find some older documentation online indicating that `ExecuteMethodCall` returns an `IQueryResults(Of T)`, but this is no longer correct.

The `ExecuteMethodCall` method is passed a reference to the `DataContext` or `[Your]DataContext` object of which the method that is calling the `ExecuteMethodCall` method is a member, the `MethodInfo` object for that calling method, and a `params` array of the parameters for the stored procedure or scalar-valued user-defined function.

Notice that, since we must pass a `MethodInfo` object, our method must be decorated with the appropriate stored procedure or user-defined function attribute and attribute properties. LINQ to SQL then uses the `MethodInfo` object to access the method's `FunctionAttribute` attribute to obtain the name of the stored procedure or scalar-valued user-defined function. It also uses the `MethodInfo` object to obtain the parameter names and types.

The `ExecuteMethodCall` method returns an object implementing the `IExecuteResult` interface. I cover this interface in Chapter 15.

If you use SqlMetal to generate your entity classes, it will create entity class methods that call the `ExecuteMethodCall` method for the database's stored procedures if you specify the `/sprocs` option, and for the database's user-defined functions if you specify the `/functions` option.

Examples

Before I discuss the code for the first example, I want to discuss the method named `CustomersCountByRegion` that SqlMetal generated to call the database's Customers Count By Region stored procedure. Here is what the generated method looks like:

Using the ExecuteMethodCall Method to Call a Stored Procedure

```
<FunctionAttribute(Name:="dbo.Customers Count By Region")> _
Public Function CustomersCountByRegion( _
    <Parameter(DbType:="NVarChar(15)")> ByVal param1 As String) _
  As <Parameter(DbType:="Int")> Integer

  Dim result As IExecuteResult = Me.ExecuteMethodCall( _
    Me, CType(MethodInfo.GetCurrentMethod,MethodInfo), param1)

End Function
```

As you can see, the CustomersCountByRegion method is passed a String parameter that is passed as a parameter into the ExecuteMethodCall method, which is passed as a parameter to the Customers Count By Region stored procedure.

The ExecuteMethodCall method returns a variable implementing IExecuteResult. To obtain the integer return value, the CustomersCountByRegion method merely references the returned object's ReturnValue property and casts it to an Integer.

Now, let's take a look at Listing 16-23 to see some code calling the generated CustomersCountByRegion method.

Listing 16-23. *An Example Calling the Generated CustomersCountByRegion Method*

```
Dim db As New Northwind( _
  "Data Source=.\SQLEXPRESS;Initial Catalog=Northwind;Integrated Security=SSPI;")
Dim rc As Integer = db.CustomersCountByRegion("WA")
Console.WriteLine("There are {0} customers in WA.", rc)
```

This is a very trivial example with no surprises. Here is the result:

```
There are 3 customers in WA.
```

Now, I want to discuss calling a stored procedure that returns an output parameter. Again, looking at the SqlMetal-generated entity classes for the Northwind database, I will discuss the CustOrderTotal method SqlMetal generated to call the CustOrderTotal stored procedure:

An Example Using the ExecuteMethodCall Method to Call a Stored Procedure That Returns an Output Parameter

```
<FunctionAttribute(Name:="dbo.CustOrderTotal")> _
Public Function CustOrderTotal( _
    <Parameter(Name:="CustomerID", DbType:="NChar(5)")> _
      ByVal customerID As String, _
    <Parameter(Name:="TotalSales", DbType:="Money")> _
      ByRef totalSales As System.Nullable(Of Decimal)) _
  As <Parameter(DbType:="Int")> Integer

  Dim result As IExecuteResult = Me.ExecuteMethodCall( _
    Me, CType(MethodInfo.GetCurrentMethod,MethodInfo), customerID, totalSales)

  totalSales = CType(result.GetParameterValue(1),System.Nullable(Of Decimal))

  Return CType(result.ReturnValue,Integer)

End Function
```

Notice that the CustOrderTotal method's second parameter, totalSales, specifies the ByRef keyword. This is a clue that the stored procedure is going to return this value. Notice that to get the value after the call to the ExecuteMethodCall method, the code calls the GetParameterValue method on the returned object implementing IExecuteResult and passes it 1, since we are interested in the second parameter. Listing 16-24 calls the CustOrderTotal method.

Listing 16-24. *An Example Calling the Generated CustOrderTotal Method*

```
Dim db As New Northwind( _
  "Data Source=.\SQLEXPRESS;Initial Catalog=Northwind;Integrated Security=SSPI;")
Dim totalSales As Nullable(Of Decimal) = 0
Dim rc As Integer = db.CustOrderTotal("LAZYK", totalSales)
Console.WriteLine("Customer LAZYK has total sales of {0:C}.", totalSales)
```

Here is the result:

```
Customer LAZYK has total sales of $357.00.
```

Now, let's take a look at an example that calls a stored procedure that returns its results in a single shape. For those unfamiliar with the term *shape* in this context, the shape of the results is dictated by the types of data that are returned. When a query returns a customer's ID and name, this is a shape. If a query returns an order ID, an order date, and a shipping code, this is yet another shape. If a query returns both, a record containing a customer's ID and name and another, or perhaps more than one, record containing the order ID, order date, and shipping code, this query returns multiple result shapes. Since the Northwind database contains a stored procedure named Customers By City that returns a single shape, that is the stored procedure I will discuss.

Let's look at the SqlMetal-generated method that calls this stored procedure by calling the ExecuteMethodCall method.

An Example Using the ExecuteMethodCall Method to Call a Stored Procedure That Returns a Single Shape

```
<FunctionAttribute(Name:="dbo.Customers By City")> _
Public Function CustomersByCity( _
    <Parameter(DbType:="NVarChar(20)")> ByVal param1 As String) _
  As ISingleResult(Of CustomersByCityResult)

  Dim result As IExecuteResult = Me.ExecuteMethodCall( _
    Me, CType(MethodInfo.GetCurrentMethod,MethodInfo), param1)

  Return CType(result.ReturnValue,ISingleResult(Of CustomersByCityResult))

End Function
```

Notice that the generated method returns an object of type ISingleResult(Of CustomersByCityResult). The generated method obtains this object by casting the returned object's ReturnValue property to that type. SqlMetal was kind enough to even generate the CustomersByCityResult class for me as well, although I won't discuss it here. Listing 16-25 contains code calling the generated CustomersByCity method.

Listing 16-25. *An Example Calling the Generated CustomersByCity Method*

```
Dim db As New Northwind( _
  "Data Source=.\SQLEXPRESS;Initial Catalog=Northwind;Integrated Security=SSPI;")

Dim results As ISingleResult(Of CustomersByCityResult) = _
  db.CustomersByCity("London")

For Each cust As CustomersByCityResult In results
  Console.WriteLine("{0} - {1} - {2} - {3}", _
    cust.CustomerID, cust.CompanyName, cust.ContactName, cust.City)
Next cust
```

As you can see, I enumerate through the returned object of type `ISingleResult(Of CustomersByCityResult)` just as though it is a LINQ sequence. This is because it is derived from `IEnumerable(Of T)`, as I mentioned in Chapter 15. I then display the results to the console. Here are the results:

```
AROUT - Around the Horn - Thomas Hardy - London
BSBEV - B's Beverages - Victoria Ashworth - London
CONSH - Consolidated Holdings - Elizabeth Brown - London
EASTC - Eastern Connection - Ann Devon - London
NORTS - North/South - Simon Crowther - London
SEVES - Seven Seas Imports - Hari Kumar - London
```

Now, let's take a look at some examples returning multiple result shapes. Since stored procedures have the ability to return multiple shapes, LINQ to SQL needs a way to address this, and it has one.

For the first example returning multiple shapes, let's take the scenario where the shape of the result is conditional. Fortunately, the extended Northwind database has a stored procedure of this type. The name of that stored procedure is Whole Or Partial Customers Set. SqlMetal generated a method to call that stored procedure for me named `WholeOrPartialCustomersSet`. Here it is:

An Example Using the ExecuteMethodCall Method to Call a Stored Procedure That Conditionally Returns Different Shapes

```
<FunctionAttribute(Name:="dbo.Whole Or Partial Customers Set"), _
  ResultType(GetType(WholeOrPartialCustomersSetResult1)), _
  ResultType(GetType(WholeOrPartialCustomersSetResult2))> _
Public Function WholeOrPartialCustomersSet( _
    <Parameter(DbType:="Int")> ByVal param1 As System.Nullable(Of Integer)) _
  As IMultipleResults

  Dim result As IExecuteResult = _
    Me.ExecuteMethodCall(Me, CType(MethodInfo.GetCurrentMethod,MethodInfo), param1)
```

```
Return CType(result.ReturnValue,IMultipleResults)

End Function
```

Notice that there are two ResultType attributes specifying the two possible result shapes. SqlMetal was also kind enough to generate the two specified classes for me. The developer calling the WholeOrPartialCustomersSet method must be aware that the stored procedure returns a different result shape based on the value of param1. Because I have examined the stored procedure, I know that if param1 is equal to 1, the stored procedure will return all fields from the Customers table, and therefore will return a sequence of objects of type WholeOrPartialCustomersSetResult1. If the value of param1 is equal to 2, an abbreviated set of fields will be returned in a sequence of objects of type WholeOrPartialCustomersSetResult2.

Also notice that the return type from the WholeOrPartialCustomersSet method is IMultipleResults. The method obtains this by casting the ReturnValue property of the object returned by the ExecuteMethodCall method to an IMultipleResults. I discuss this interface in Chapter 15.

In Listing 16-26, I provide an example calling the WholeOrPartialCustomersSet method.

Listing 16-26. *An Example Calling the Generated WholeOrPartialCustomersSet Method*

```
Using db As New Northwind( _
  "Data Source=.\SQLEXPRESS;Initial Catalog=Northwind;Integrated Security=SSPI;")

  Dim results As IMultipleResults = db.WholeOrPartialCustomersSet(1)

  For Each cust As WholeOrPartialCustomersSetResult1 _
    In results.GetResult(Of WholeOrPartialCustomersSetResult1)()

    Console.WriteLine("{0} - {1} - {2} - {3}", _
      cust.CustomerID, cust.CompanyName, cust.ContactName, cust.City)
  Next cust
End Using
```

Notice that the results are of type IMultipleResults. I passed the value 1, so I know I will be getting a sequence of type WholeOrPartialCustomersSetResult1. Also notice that to get to the results, I call the GetResult(Of T) method on the IMultipleResults variable, where type T is the type of the returned data. Here are the results:

```
LAZYK - Lazy K Kountry Store - John Steel - Walla Walla
TRAIH - Trail's Head Gourmet Provisioners - Helvetius Nagy - Kirkland
WHITC - White Clover Markets - Karl Jablonski – Seattle
```

That stored procedure only retrieves the customers whose region is "WA". Had I passed a value of 2 when I called the WholeOrPartialCustomersSet method above, I would have gotten a sequence of type WholeOrPartialCustomersSetResult2, so every place in the preceding code where I specified a type of WholeOrPartialCustomersSetResult1 would have to be changed to WholeOrPartialCustomersSetResult2.

This just leaves us with the case of a stored procedure returning multiple shapes for the same call. Here again, the extended Northwind database has just such a stored procedure, and its name is Get Customer And Orders. First, let's look at the method SqlMetal generated to call that stored procedure:

An Example Using the ExecuteMethodCall Method to Call a Stored Procedure That Returns Multiple Shapes

```
<FunctionAttribute( _
  Name:="dbo.Get Customer And Orders"), _
  ResultType(GetType(GetCustomerAndOrdersResult1)), _
  ResultType(GetType(GetCustomerAndOrdersResult2))> _
Public Function GetCustomerAndOrders( _
    <Parameter(Name:="CustomerID", DbType:="NChar(5)")> _
      ByVal customerID As String) As IMultipleResults

  Dim result As IExecuteResult = Me.ExecuteMethodCall( _
    Me, (CType(Me, CType(MethodInfo.GetCurrentMethod,MethodInfo), customerID)

  Return CType(result.ReturnValue, IMultipleResults)

End Function
```

As you can see, the return type of the method is `IMultipleResults`. Since the stored procedure returns multiple result shapes, it is our responsibility to know the order of the shapes being returned. Because I have examined the Get Customer And Orders stored procedure, I know it will return the record from the Customers table first, followed by the related records from the Orders table.

Listing 16-27 calls the generated method from the previous code.

Listing 16-27. *An Example Calling the Generated GetCustomerAndOrders Method*

```
Dim db As New Northwind( _
  "Data Source=.\SQLEXPRESS;Initial Catalog=Northwind;Integrated Security=SSPI;")

Dim results As IMultipleResults = db.GetCustomerAndOrders("LAZYK")

Dim cust As GetCustomerAndOrdersResult1 = _
  results.GetResult(Of GetCustomerAndOrdersResult1)().Single()

Console.WriteLine("{0} orders:", cust.CompanyName)

For Each order As GetCustomerAndOrdersResult2 _
    In results.GetResult(Of GetCustomerAndOrdersResult2)()
  Console.WriteLine("{0} - {1}", order.OrderID, order.OrderDate)
Next order
```

Because I know the stored procedure will return a single record matching type `GetCustomerAndOrdersResult1`, I know I can call the `Single` operator on the sequence containing that type as long as I am confident the customer exists for the passed CustomerID. I could always call the `SingleOrDefault` operator if I were not confident. I also know that after the single `GetCustomerAndOrdersResult1` object is returned, zero or more `GetCustomerAndOrdersResult2` objects will be returned, so I enumerate through them displaying the data I am interested in. Here are the results:

```
Lazy K Kountry Store orders:
10482 - 3/21/1997 12:00:00 AM
10545 - 5/22/1997 12:00:00 AM
```

This completes the stored procedure examples for the `ExecuteMethodCall` method. At the beginning of the section on the `ExecuteMethodCall` method, I said this method was used to call scalar-valued user-defined functions. So let's take a look at an example calling a scalar-valued user-defined function.

First, let's look at a SqlMetal-generated method calling the `ExecuteMethodCall` method to call a scalar-valued user-defined function:

An Example Using the ExecuteMethodCall Method to Call a Scalar-Valued User-Defined Function

```
<FunctionAttribute(Name:="dbo.MinUnitPriceByCategory", IsComposable:=True)> _
Public Function MinUnitPriceByCategory( _
  <Parameter(DbType:="Int")> ByVal categoryID As System.Nullable(Of Integer)) _
    As <Parameter(DbType:="Money")> System.Nullable(Of Decimal)

  Return CType(Me.ExecuteMethodCall( _
                 Me, _
                 (CType(MethodInfo.GetCurrentMethod(), MethodInfo)), _
                 categoryID).ReturnValue, _
              System.Nullable(Of Decimal))

End Function
```

Notice that the scalar value returned by the stored procedure is obtained by referencing the `ReturnValue` property of the object returned by the `ExecuteMethodCall` method.

I could create a simple example calling the generated `MinUnitPriceByCategory` method. However, all the fun of a user-defined function comes when embedding it in a query like it was a built-in SQL function.

Let's take a look at an example, Listing 16-28, that embeds the `MinUnitPriceByCategory` method in a query to identify all products that are the least expensive in their category.

Listing 16-28. *An Example Embedding a User-Defined Function Within a Query*

```
Dim db As New Northwind( _
  "Data Source=.\SQLEXPRESS;Initial Catalog=Northwind;Integrated Security=SSPI;")

Dim products As IQueryable(Of Product) = _
  From p In db.Products _
```

```
Where p.UnitPrice.Equals(db.MinUnitPriceByCategory(p.CategoryID)) _
Select p

For Each p As Product In products
  Console.WriteLine("{0} - {1:C}", p.ProductName, p.UnitPrice)
Next p
```

In this example, I embed the call to the MinUnitPriceByCategory method—which in turn causes a call to the scalar-valued user-defined function of the same name—in the Where clause. Here are the results:

```
Aniseed Syrup - $10.00
Konbu - $6.00
Teatime Chocolate Biscuits - $9.20
Guaraná Fantástica - $4.50
Geitost - $2.50
Filo Mix - $7.00
Tourtière - $7.45
Longlife Tofu - $10.00
```

GetCommand()

One potentially useful method is the GetCommand method. When the GetCommand method is called on the DataContext object and passed a LINQ to SQL IQueryable, an object of type System.Data.Common.DbCommand is returned. The returned DbCommand object contains access to several key components that will be used by the passed query.

By retrieving the DbCommand object with the GetCommand method, you can obtain a reference to the CommandText, CommandTimeout, Connection, Parameters, and Transaction objects, as well as others, for the passed query. This allows you to not only examine those objects but modify them from their default values *without* modifying the same values for all queries that will be performed by the current instance of the DataContext. Perhaps for a particular query, you would like to increase the CommandTimeout value, but you don't want all of the queries executed with the DataContext object to be allowed this extended time-out period.

Declarations

The GetCommand method has one declaration I will cover.

The Only GetCommand Declaration

```
Public Function GetCommand (query As IQueryable) As DbCommand
```

This method is passed a LINQ to SQL query in the form of an IQueryable, and returns a System.Data.Common.DbCommand for the passed LINQ query.

Examples

In Listing 16-29, I will obtain the DbCommand object to change the CommandTimeout for a query and to display the CommandText, which will be the SQL query itself.

Listing 16-29. *An Example of the GetCommand Method*

```
Dim db As New Northwind( _
  "Data Source=.\SQLEXPRESS;Initial Catalog=Northwind;Integrated Security=SSPI;")

Dim custs As IQueryable(Of Customer) = _
  From c In db.Customers _
  Where c.Region Is "WA" _
  Select c

Dim dbc As System.Data.Common.DbCommand = db.GetCommand(custs)

Console.WriteLine("Query's timeout is: {0}{1}", dbc.CommandTimeout, vbCrLf)

dbc.CommandTimeout = 1

Console.WriteLine("Query's SQL is: {0}{1}", dbc.CommandText, vbCrLf)

Console.WriteLine("Query's timeout is: {0}{1}", dbc.CommandTimeout, vbCrLf)

For Each c As Customer In custs
  Console.WriteLine("{0}", c.CompanyName)
Next c
```

There isn't much to this example. I merely declare a query and pass it to the GetCommand method. I then display the CommandTimeout value for the DbCommand object that was returned. Next, I set the CommandTimeout value to 1 and display the SQL query itself and the new CommandTimeout value. Last, I enumerate through the results returned by the query.

Here are the results of the code running on my machine:

```
Query's timeout is: 30

Query's SQL is: SELECT [t0].[CustomerID], [t0].[CompanyName], [t0].[ContactName],
[t0].[ContactTitle], [t0].[Address], [t0].[City], [t0].[Region], [t0].[PostalCode],
[t0].[Country], [t0].[Phone], [t0].[Fax]
FROM [dbo].[Customers] AS [t0]
WHERE [t0].[Region] = @p0

Query's timeout is: 1

Lazy K Kountry Store
Trail's Head Gourmet Provisioners
White Clover Markets
```

Of course, if that query takes too long to execute on your machine, the query could time out, and you would get different results.

GetChangeSet()

Sometimes, it may be useful to be able to obtain a list of all the entity objects that *will be* inserted, changed, or deleted once the SubmitChanges method is called. The GetChangeSet method does just that.

Declarations

The GetChangeSet method has one declaration I will cover.

The Only GetChangeSet Declaration

```
Public Function GetChangeSet As ChangeSet
```

This method is passed nothing and returns a ChangeSet object. The ChangeSet object contains collections of type IList(Of T) for the inserted, modified, and deleted entity objects, where type T is an entity class. These collection properties are named Inserts, Updates, and Deletes, respectively.

You can then enumerate through each of these collections to examine the contained entity objects.

Examples

In Listing 16-30, I will modify, insert, and delete an entity object. I will then retrieve the ChangeSet using the GetChangeSet method and enumerate through each collection.

Listing 16-30. *An Example of the GetChangeSet Method*

```
Dim db As New Northwind( _
  "Data Source=.\SQLEXPRESS;Initial Catalog=Northwind;Integrated Security=SSPI;")

Dim cust As Customer = ( _
  From c In db.Customers _
  Where c.CustomerID = "LAZYK" _
  Select c).Single()
cust.Region = "Washington"

db.Customers.InsertOnSubmit( _
  New Customer With { _
    .CustomerID = "LAWN", _
    .CompanyName = "Lawn Wranglers", _
    .ContactName = "Mr. Abe Henry", _
    .ContactTitle = "Owner", _
    .Address = "1017 Maple Leaf Way", _
    .City = "Ft. Worth", _
    .Region = "TX", _
```

```
        .PostalCode = "76104", _
        .Country = "USA", _
        .Phone = "(800) MOW-LAWN", _
        .Fax = "(800) MOW-LAWO"})

Dim cust2 As Customer = ( _
  From c In db.Customers _
  Where c.CustomerID = "LONEP" _
  Select c).Single()
db.Customers.DeleteOnSubmit(cust2)
cust2 = Nothing
```

Dim changeSet As ChangeSet = db.GetChangeSet()

```
Console.WriteLine("{0}First, the added entities:", vbCrLf)
For Each c As Customer In changeSet.Inserts
  Console.WriteLine("Customer {0} will be added.", c.CompanyName)
Next c

Console.WriteLine("{0}Second, the modified entities:", vbCrLf)
For Each c As Customer In changeSet.Updates
  Console.WriteLine("Customer {0} will be updated.", c.CompanyName)
Next c

Console.WriteLine("{0}Third, the removed entities:", vbCrLf)
For Each c As Customer In changeSet.Deletes
  Console.WriteLine("Customer {0} will be deleted.", c.CompanyName)
Next c
```

In the previous example, I first modify the LAZYK customer's Region. I then insert a customer, LAWN, and delete customer LONEP. Next, I obtain the ChangeSet by calling the GetChangeSet method. Then, I enumerate through each collection—Inserts, Updates, and Deletes—and display each entity object in the respective collection.

Here are the results:

```
First, the added entities:
Customer Lawn Wranglers will be added.

Second, the modified entities:
Customer Lazy K Kountry Store will be updated.

Third, the removed entities:
Customer Lonesome Pine Restaurant will be deleted.
```

Of course, in the preceding example, I can enumerate through each of the collections assuming every element is a Customer object, because I know they are. In many cases, though, there could be more than one type of object in a collection, and you can't make that assumption. In these situations, you will have to write your enumeration code to handle multiple data types. The OfType operator could be helpful for this purpose.

GetTable()

The GetTable method is used to get a reference to a Table sequence from a DataContext for a specific mapped database table. This method is typically only used when the actual DataContext class is used, as opposed to [Your]DataContext. Using [Your]DataContext class is the preferred technique, as it will have a Table sequence property already having a reference for each mapped table.

Declarations

The GetTable method has two declarations I will cover.

The First GetTable Declaration

```
Public Function GetTable(Of TEntity As Class) As Table(Of TEntity)
```

This method is provided a specified mapped entity type T and returns a Table sequence of type T.

The Second GetTable Declaration

```
Public Function GetTable (type As Type) As ITable
```

This method is passed a Type of entity object and returns the interface to the table. You can then use this ITable interface as you desire. If you want to use the ITable interface as though it were a table, be sure to cast it to an IQueryable(Of T).

Examples

For an example of the first declaration, in Listing 16-31, I will use the standard DataContext class, as opposed to my [Your]DataContext class, Northwind, to retrieve a specific customer.

Listing 16-31. *An Example of the First GetTable Declaration*

```
Dim db As New DataContext( _
  "Data Source=.\SQLEXPRESS;Initial Catalog=Northwind;Integrated Security=SSPI;")

Dim cust As Customer = ( _
  From c In db.GetTable(Of Customer)() _
  Where c.CustomerID = "LAZYK" _
  Select c).Single()

Console.WriteLine("Customer {0} retrieved.", cust.CompanyName)
```

Here, I call the GetTable method to get a reference to the Customer table so that I can retrieve a specific customer. Here are the results:

Customer Lazy K Kountry Store retrieved.

For an example of the second declaration of the GetTable method, I will use a DataContext instead of my [Your]DataContext. Listing 16-32 will be the same basic example as the previous except using the second declaration.

Listing 16-32. *An Example of the Second GetTable Declaration*

```
Dim db As New DataContext( _
  "Data Source=.\SQLEXPRESS;Initial Catalog=Northwind;Integrated Security=SSPI;")

Dim cust As Customer = ( _
  From c In (CType(db.GetTable(GetType(Customer)), IQueryable(Of Customer))) _
  Where c.CustomerID = "LAZYK" _
  Select c).Single()

Console.WriteLine("Customer {0} retrieved.", cust.CompanyName)
```

It should come as no surprise that the results for Listing 16-32 are the same as for Listing 16-31:

Customer Lazy K Kountry Store retrieved.

Refresh()

The Refresh method allows you to manually refresh entity objects from the database. In some situations, this is done for you when you call the DataContext object's ChangeConflicts collection's ResolveAll method if concurrency conflicts occur during a call to the SubmitChanges method. However, there may be situations where you will never call the SubmitChanges method but want to get updates from the database.

An example might be an application that displays read-only type status data for some entity, system, or process. You may want the data refreshed from the database on some interval of time. The Refresh method could be used for this purpose.

With the Refresh method, you can refresh a single entity object, or a sequence of entity objects, meaning the results of a LINQ to SQL query.

Declarations

The Refresh method has three declarations I will cover.

The First Refresh Declaration

```
Public Sub Refresh (mode As RefreshMode, entity As Object)
```

This method takes a refresh mode and a single entity object and returns nothing.

The Second Refresh Declaration

```
Public Sub Refresh (mode As RefreshMode, ParamArray entities As Object())
```

This method takes a refresh mode and a `params` array of entity objects and returns nothing.

The Third Refresh Declaration

```
Public Sub Refresh (mode As RefreshMode, entities As IEnumerable)
```

This method takes a refresh mode and a sequence of entity objects and returns nothing.

The `RefreshMode` enumeration has three possible values: `KeepChanges`, `KeepCurrentValues`, and `OverwriteCurrentValues`. The Visual Studio documentation for the `RefreshMode` enumeration defines these values as outlined in Table 16-1.

Table 16-1. *The RefreshMode Enumeration*

Member name	Description
KeepCurrentValues	Forces the `Refresh` method to swap the original value with the values retrieved from the database
KeepChanges	Forces the `Refresh` method to keep the current value that has been changed, but updates the other values with the database values
OverwriteCurrentValues	Forces the `Refresh` method to override all the current values with the values from the database

The behavior of each of these settings is discussed in more detail in Chapter 17.

Examples

For an example of the first declaration, in Listing 16-33, I will query a customer using LINQ to SQL and display its contact name and contact title. I will then change that customer's contact name in the database using ADO.NET. I will change the contact title in the entity object. Just to convince you that the current entity object is not aware of the change to the database but does have the changed contact title I just made, I will display the entity's contact name and contact title again, and you will see the contact name is unchanged, and the contact title is changed.

I will then call the `Refresh` method with a `RefreshMode` of `KeepChanges` and display the entity object's contact name and contact title once more, and you will see that it does indeed have the new value of the contact name from the database, while at the same time maintaining my change to the contact title.

I will then reset the contact name back to its original value just so the example can be run multiple times. Here is the code:

Listing 16-33. *An Example of the First Refresh Method Declaration*

```
Dim db As New Northwind( _
  "Data Source=.\SQLEXPRESS;Initial Catalog=Northwind;Integrated Security=SSPI;")
```

```vb
Dim cust As Customer = ( _
  From c In db.Customers _
  Where c.CustomerID = "GREAL" _
  Select c).Single()

Console.WriteLine("Customer's original name is {0}, ContactTitle is {1}.{2}", _
  cust.ContactName, cust.ContactTitle, vbCrLf)

ExecuteStatementInDb( _
  "update Customers set ContactName = 'Brad Radaker' where CustomerID = 'GREAL'")

cust.ContactTitle = "Chief Technology Officer"

Console.WriteLine( _
  "Customer's name before refresh is {0}, ContactTitle is {1}.{2}", _
  cust.ContactName, cust.ContactTitle, vbCrLf)

db.Refresh(RefreshMode.KeepChanges, cust)

Console.WriteLine( _
  "Customer's name after refresh is {0}, ContactTitle is {1}.{2}", _
  cust.ContactName, cust.ContactTitle, vbCrLf)

'  I need to reset the changed values so that the code can be run
'  more than once.
Console.WriteLine("{0}Resetting data to original values.", vbCrLf)
ExecuteStatementInDb( _
  "update Customers set ContactName = 'Howard Snyder' where CustomerID = 'GREAL'")
```

In the previous code, I make a LINQ to SQL query to obtain a reference to the GREAL Customer object. I then display that Customer object's ContactName and ContactTitle.

Next, I update that customer's ContactName in the database using ADO.NET and update the ContactTitle on my retrieved Customer entity object. At this point, my Customer entity object is unaware that the ContactName has been changed in the database, and I prove this by displaying the Customer object's ContactName and ContactTitle to the console.

Then, I call the Refresh method with the KeepChanges RefreshMode. This should cause any Customer object properties that have been changed in the database to be loaded into my entity object as long as I have not changed them myself. In this case, since the ContactName has been changed in the database, it should be refreshed from the database.

I then display the Customer object's ContactName and ContactTitle, and this should show the ContactName from the database and the ContactTitle I changed in my entity object.

Last, I clean up the database so the example can be run again and no subsequent examples are affected.

Let's take a look at the results of Listing 16-33.

Customer's original name is Howard Snyder, ContactTitle is Marketing Manager.

Executing SQL statement against database with ADO.NET ...
Database updated.
Customer's name before refresh is Howard Snyder, ContactTitle is Chief Technology
Officer.

Customer's name after refresh is Brad Radaker, ContactTitle is Chief Technology
Officer.

Resetting data to original values.
Executing SQL statement against database with ADO.NET ...
Database updated.

As you can see, the entity object is not aware that I changed the ContactName to "Brad Radaker" in the database before I called the Refresh method, but once I call the Refresh method, it is.

For an example of the second declaration, in Listing 16-34, I will retrieve the customers whose region is "WA" using LINQ to SQL. I will enumerate through the returned sequence of Customer objects and display their CustomerID, Region, and Country. Then, using ADO.NET, I will update the Country field for each customer in the database whose region is "WA". At this point, the value for the Country field for those customers is different in the database than it is in the entity objects that have been retrieved. I will enumerate through the sequence of retrieved customers again just to prove that the entity objects are unaware of the change to the Country field in the database.

Next, I will call the ToArray operator on the sequence of Customer objects to obtain an array containing Customer objects. I then call the Refresh method passing a RefreshMode of KeepChanges and pass the first, second, and third elements of the array of Customer objects.

I then enumerate through the sequence of Customer entity objects one last time displaying each Customer object's CustomerID, Region, and Country to prove that the Country field has indeed been refreshed from the database.

Of course, I still have to restore the database back to its original state, so I then use ADO. NET to set the customer's Country back to its original value in the database.

Here is the code for Listing 16-34.

Listing 16-34. *An Example of the Second Refresh Method Declaration*

```
Dim db As New Northwind( _
  "Data Source=.\SQLEXPRESS;Initial Catalog=Northwind;Integrated Security=SSPI;")

Dim custs As IEnumerable(Of Customer) = ( _
  From c In db.Customers _
  Where c.Region Is "WA" _
  Select c)
```

```
Console.WriteLine("Entity objects before ADO.NET change and Refresh() call:")
For Each c As Customer In custs
  Console.WriteLine("Customer {0}'s region is {1}, country is {2}.", _
    c.CustomerID, c.Region, c.Country)
Next c

Console.WriteLine( _
  "{0}Updating customers' country to United States in ADO.NET...", vbCrLf)
ExecuteStatementInDb( _
  "update Customers set Country = 'United States' where Region = 'WA'")
Console.WriteLine("Customers' country updated.{0}", vbCrLf)

Console.WriteLine("Entity objects after ADO.NET change but before Refresh() call:")
For Each c As Customer In custs
  Console.WriteLine("Customer {0}'s region is {1}, country is {2}.", _
    c.CustomerID, c.Region, c.Country)
Next c

Dim custArray() As Customer = custs.ToArray()
Console.WriteLine( _
  "{0}Refreshing params array of customer entity objects ...", vbCrLf)
db.Refresh(RefreshMode.KeepChanges, custArray(0), custArray(1), custArray(2))
Console.WriteLine("Params array of Customer entity objects refreshed.{0}", vbCrLf)

Console.WriteLine("Entity objects after ADO.NET change and Refresh() call:")
For Each c As Customer In custs
  Console.WriteLine("Customer {0}'s region is {1}, country is {2}.", _
    c.CustomerID, c.Region, c.Country)
Next c

'  We need to reset the changed values so that the code can be run
'  more than once.
Console.WriteLine("{0}Resetting data to original values.", vbCrLf)
ExecuteStatementInDb("update Customers set Country = 'USA' where Region = 'WA'")
```

The previous code doesn't start getting interesting until the call to the ToArray operator. Once I obtain the array of Customer objects, I call the RefreshMethod and pass custArray[0], custArray[1], and custArray[2].

Let's take a look at the results:

```
Entity objects before ADO.NET change and Refresh() call:
Customer LAZYK's region is WA, country is USA.
Customer TRAIH's region is WA, country is USA.
Customer WHITC's region is WA, country is USA.

Updating customers' country to United States in ADO.NET...
Executing SQL statement against database with ADO.NET ...
```

```
Database updated.
Customers' country updated.

Entity objects after ADO.NET change but before Refresh() call:
Customer LAZYK's region is WA, country is USA.
Customer TRAIH's region is WA, country is USA.
Customer WHITC's region is WA, country is USA.

Refreshing params array of customer entity objects ...
Params array of Customer entity objects refreshed.

Entity objects after ADO.NET change and Refresh() call:
Customer LAZYK's region is WA, country is United States.
Customer TRAIH's region is WA, country is United States.
Customer WHITC's region is WA, country is United States.

Resetting data to original values.
Executing SQL statement against database with ADO.NET ...
Database updated.
```

As you can see in the previous results, the changes I made to the Country field in the database are not reflected in the Customer entity objects until I call the Refresh method.

In Listing 16-34, each entity object I refreshed was of the same data type, Customer. For the second declaration of the Refresh method, it is not necessary that every entity object passed be the same data type. I could have passed entity objects of different data types. In the case of Listing 16-34, it would have actually been easier if I could have just passed a sequence of entity objects to the Refresh method, because a sequence is what I had. Fortunately, the third declaration of the Refresh method allows you to pass a sequence.

So, for an example of the third declaration, in Listing 16-35, I will use the same basic code as Listing 16-34, except instead of creating an array and passing explicitly stated elements to the Refresh method, I will pass the sequence of retrieved Customer objects.

Here's the code:

Listing 16-35. *An Example of the Third Refresh Method Declaration*

```
Dim db As New Northwind( _
  "Data Source=.\SQLEXPRESS;Initial Catalog=Northwind;Integrated Security=SSPI;")

Dim custs As IEnumerable(Of Customer) = ( _
  From c In db.Customers _
  Where c.Region Is "WA" _
  Select c)

Console.WriteLine("Entity objects before ADO.NET change and Refresh() call:")
For Each c As Customer In custs
  Console.WriteLine("Customer {0}'s region is {1}, country is {2}.", _
    c.CustomerID, c.Region, c.Country)
Next c
```

```
Console.WriteLine( _
  "{0}Updating customers' country to United States in ADO.NET...", vbCrLf)
ExecuteStatementInDb( _
  "update Customers set Country = 'United States' where Region = 'WA'")
Console.WriteLine("Customers' country updated.{0}", vbCrLf)

Console.WriteLine("Entity objects after ADO.NET change but before Refresh() call:")
For Each c As Customer In custs
Console.WriteLine("Customer {0}'s region is {1}, country is {2}.", _
  c.CustomerID, c.Region, c.Country)
Next c

Console.WriteLine("{0}Refreshing sequence of customer entity objects ...", vbCrLf)
db.Refresh(RefreshMode.KeepChanges, custs)
Console.WriteLine("Sequence of Customer entity objects refreshed.{0}", vbCrLf)

Console.WriteLine("Entity objects after ADO.NET change and Refresh() call:")
For Each c As Customer In custs
Console.WriteLine("Customer {0}'s region is {1}, country is {2}.", _
  c.CustomerID, c.Region, c.Country)
Next c

'  We need to reset the changed values so that the code can be run
'  more than once.
Console.WriteLine("{0}Resetting data to original values.", vbCrLf)
ExecuteStatementInDb( _
  "update Customers set Country = 'USA' where Region = 'WA'")
```

The code in Listing 16-35 is the same as Listing 16-34 except that when I call the Refresh method, I pass the custs sequence. Let's take a look at the results:

```
Entity objects before ADO.NET change and Refresh() call:
Customer LAZYK's region is WA, country is USA.
Customer TRAIH's region is WA, country is USA.
Customer WHITC's region is WA, country is USA.

Updating customers' country to United States in ADO.NET...
Executing SQL statement against database with ADO.NET ...
Database updated.
Customers' country updated.

Entity objects after ADO.NET change but before Refresh() call:
Customer LAZYK's region is WA, country is USA.
Customer TRAIH's region is WA, country is USA.
Customer WHITC's region is WA, country is USA.

Refreshing sequence of customer entity objects ...
Sequence of Customer entity objects refreshed.
```

```
Entity objects after ADO.NET change and Refresh() call:
Customer LAZYK's region is WA, country is United States.
Customer TRAIH's region is WA, country is United States.
Customer WHITC's region is WA, country is United States.

Resetting data to original values.
Executing SQL statement against database with ADO.NET ...
Database updated.
```

As you can see, despite the fact that I updated the Country for the retrieved customers to "United States" in the database, I didn't see that change in the entity objects until I called the Refresh method.

Summary

I know it took a long time to get to the point of knowing what the DataContext class can do for you. LINQ to SQL is not trivial because it encapsulates an understanding of LINQ with an understanding of database queries and SQL. Because of this, there is a lot to know about LINQ to SQL, and much of what there is to understand about the DataContext class is intertwined with entity classes; therefore, something has to come first and something has to come last.

While there is a lot of information in this chapter, probably the most important topics to leave this chapter understanding are how the three DataContext services—identity tracking, change tracking, and change processing—work. Of course, none of those services have any value if you cannot even instantiate a DataContext or [Your]DataContext object, so the constructors for the DataContext and [Your]DataContext class are important as well.

Other than the DataContext and [Your]DataContext constructors, the DataContext method you will most likely use the most is the SubmitChanges method, because it is the method that you will call to persist your changes to the database.

It is important to remember that, when you attempt to persist your changes to the database, sometimes a concurrency conflict may arise and throw an exception. I have mentioned concurrency conflicts many times so far in the LINQ to SQL chapters, but I have yet to discuss them in detail. Therefore, in the next chapter, I will cover concurrency conflicts in depth.

CHAPTER 17

Concurrency Conflicts

How many times have you heard me say that you must detect concurrency conflicts and resolve them? In most of the preceding LINQ to SQL chapters, I have mentioned concurrency conflicts, but I have yet to discuss them in the level of detail they deserve. In this chapter, I will resolve that deficiency.

Prerequisites for Running the Examples

In order to run the examples in this chapter, you will need to have obtained the extended version of the Northwind database and generated entity classes for it. Please read and follow the section in Chapter 12 titled "Prerequisites for Running the Examples."

Some Common Methods

Additionally, to run the examples in this chapter, you will need some common methods that will be utilized by the examples. Please read and follow the section in Chapter 12 titled "Some Common Methods."

Using the LINQ to SQL API

To run the examples in this chapter, you may need to add the appropriate references and `Imports` statements to your project. Please read and follow the section in Chapter 12 titled "Using the LINQ to SQL API."

Concurrency Conflicts

When one database connection attempts to update a piece of data that has been changed by another database connection since the record was read by the first database connection, a concurrency conflict occurs. That is to say that if process one reads the data, followed by process two reading the same data, and process two updates that same data before process one can, a concurrency conflict occurs when process one attempts to update the data. It is also true though that if process one updates the data before process two, process two will get a concurrency conflict when it attempts to update the data. If multiple connections can access a database and make changes, it is only a matter of time and luck before a concurrency conflict occurs.

When a conflict occurs, an application must take some action to resolve it. For example, a web site's administrator may be on a page displaying data for a normal user that allows the administrator to update that normal user's data. If after the administrator's page reads the normal user's data from the database, the normal user goes to a page displaying her data and makes a change, a conflict will occur when the administrator saves his changes to the database. If a conflict did not occur, the normal user's changes would be overwritten and lost. An alternative is that the normal user's changes could be saved, and the administrator's changes are lost. Which is the correct behavior at any given time is a complex problem. The first step is to detect it. The second step is to resolve it.

There are two basic approaches for handling concurrency conflicts, *optimistic* and *pessimistic*.

Optimistic Concurrency

As the name would suggest, optimistic concurrency conflict handling takes the optimistic approach that, most of the time, a concurrency conflict will not happen. Therefore, no locks will be placed on the data during a read of the database. If there is a conflict when attempting to update that same data, we will address the conflict then. Optimistic concurrency conflict handling is more complicated than pessimistic concurrency conflict handling, but works better for most modern day applications with very large scale quantities of users. Imagine how frustrating it would be if every time you wanted to view an item at your favorite auction site you couldn't because someone else was looking at that same item, and the record was locked because that person might make a bid on that item? You wouldn't be a happy user for very long.

LINQ to SQL takes the optimistic concurrency conflict handling approach. Fortunately, LINQ to SQL makes the detection and resolution of concurrency conflicts as simple as seems feasibly possible. It even provides a method to handle the resolution for you if you like. Hey, I said it was optimistic, not foolish.

Conflict Detection

As I previously mentioned, the first step is detecting the conflict. LINQ to SQL has two approaches it uses to detect concurrency conflicts. If the IsVersion Column attribute property is specified on an entity class property and its value is true, then the value of that entity class property, and that property alone, will be used to determine if a concurrency conflict occurred.

If no entity class property has an IsVersion attribute property set to true, LINQ to SQL allows you to control which entity class properties participate in concurrency conflict detection with the Column attribute UpdateCheck property specified on an entity class's mapped property. The UpdateCheck enumeration provides three possible values; Never, Always, and WhenChanged.

UpdateCheck

If the UpdateCheck attribute property for a mapped entity class property is set to UpdateCheck. Never, that entity class property will not participate in concurrency conflict detection. If the UpdateCheck property is set to UpdateCheck.Always, that entity class property will always participate in the concurrency conflict detection regardless of whether the property's value has changed since initially being retrieved and cached by the DataContext. If the UpdateCheck property is set to UpdateCheck.WhenChanged, that entity class property will participate in the update check only if its value has been changed since being loaded into the DataContext object's cache. If the UpdateCheck attribute is not specified, it defaults to UpdateCheck.Always.

To understand how conflict detection technically works, it may help you to understand how it is currently implemented. When you call the SubmitChanges method, the change processor generates the necessary SQL statements to persist all changes in the entity objects to the database. When it needs to update a record, instead of merely supplying the record's primary key in the where clause to find the appropriate record to update, it specifies the primary key, as well as potentially all columns participating in conflict detection. If an entity class property's UpdateCheck attribute property is specified as UpdateCheck.Always, that property's mapped column and its original value will always be specified in the where clause. If the entity class property's UpdateCheck property is specified as UpdateCheck.WhenChanged, then only if the entity object's current value for a property has been changed from its original value will that property's mapped column, and its original value be specified in the where clause. If an entity class property's UpdateCheck property is specified as UpdateCheck.Never, that entity class property's mapped column will not be specified in the where clause.

For example, assume that the Customer entity object specifies the UpdateCheck property for CompanyName as UpdateCheck.Always, ContactName as UpdateCheck.WhenChanged, and ContactTitle as UpdateCheck.Never. If all three of those entity class properties were modified in the entity object for a customer, the generated SQL statement would look like this:

```
Update Customers
Set CompanyName = 'Art Sanders Park',
   ContactName = 'Samuel Arthur Sanders',
   ContactTitle = 'President'
Where CompanyName = 'Lonesome Pine Restaurant' AND
   ContactName = 'Fran Wilson' AND
   CustomerID = 'LONEP'
```

In that example, the column values in the where clause are the properties' original values as read from the database when the entity object was first retrieved, a SubmitChanges method call successfully completed, or the Refresh method was called.

You can see that, since the CompanyName property's UpdateCheck property is specified as UpdateCheck.Always, it will be in the where clause whether or not it has changed in the entity object. Since the ContactName property's UpdateCheck property is specified as UpdateCheck.WhenChanged and that entity class property's value has changed in the entity object, it is included in the where clause. And, since the ContactTitle property's UpdateCheck property is specified as UpdateCheck.Never, it was not specified in the where clause despite the fact that the entity class property's value has changed.

When that SQL statement is executed, if any of the entity class properties' values specified in the where clause do not match what is in the database, the record will not be found, so it will not get updated. This is how concurrency conflicts are detected. If a conflict occurs, a ChangeConflictException is thrown.

My statement about how conflicts are detected is a little vague, but the implementation by Microsoft is not specified and not quite as visible as it was in earlier prereleases of LINQ. In earlier versions, after that update statement was executed, a generated select statement would be executed containing a comparison on the @@ROWCOUNT returned from the update statement, thereby allowing the change processor to know that zero records were updated, and therefore a conflict occurred. You, of course, cannot depend on this being the implementation because it is not specified, but I offer this technique so you know at least one way to implement concurrency conflict detection should you become responsible for that.

To see exactly what the generated update statement looks like, let's examine Listing 17-1.

Listing 17-1. *Causing a Database Update to See How Concurrency Conflicts Are Detected*

```
Dim db As New Northwind( _
  "Data Source=.\SQLEXPRESS;Initial Catalog=Northwind;Integrated Security=SSPI;")
db.Log = Console.Out

Dim cust As Customer = _
  db.Customers.Where(Function(c) c.CustomerID = "LONEP").SingleOrDefault()
If cust IsNot Nothing Then
  Dim name As String = cust.ContactName ' to restore later.
  cust.ContactName = "Neo Anderson"
  db.SubmitChanges()

  ' Restore database.
  cust.ContactName = name
  db.SubmitChanges()
End If
```

There isn't much to this query. In fact, the only thing worth pointing out about the query is that I call the SingleOrDefault operator instead of the Single operator, like I typically have, just to provide more protection against a record not being found. In this case, I know the record will be found, but I want to start reminding you that you need to make sure the code safely handles these situations.

All that I am really interested in seeing is the generated update statement. Let's look at the results:

```
SELECT [t0].[CustomerID], [t0].[CompanyName], [t0].[ContactName],
[t0].[ContactTitle], [t0].[Address], [t0].[City], [t0]
.[Region], [t0].[PostalCode], [t0].[Country], [t0].[Phone], [t0].[Fax]
FROM [dbo].[Customers] AS [t0]
WHERE [t0].[CustomerID] = @p0
-- @p0: Input NVarChar (Size = 5; Prec = 0; Scale = 0) [LONEP]
-- Context: SqlProvider(Sql2008) Model: AttributedMetaModel Build: 3.5.30729.1

UPDATE [dbo].[Customers]
SET [ContactName] = @p11
WHERE ([CustomerID] = @p0) AND ([CompanyName] = @p1) AND ([ContactName] = @p2) AND
([ContactTitle] = @p3) AND ([Address]
 = @p4) AND ([City] = @p5) AND ([Region] = @p6) AND ([PostalCode] = @p7) AND
([Country] = @p8) AND ([Phone] = @p9) AND (
[Fax] = @p10)
-- @p0: Input NChar (Size = 5; Prec = 0; Scale = 0) [LONEP]
```

```
-- @p1: Input NVarChar (Size = 24; Prec = 0; Scale = 0) [Lonesome Pine Restaurant]
-- @p2: Input NVarChar (Size = 11; Prec = 0; Scale = 0) [Fran Wilson]
-- @p3: Input NVarChar (Size = 13; Prec = 0; Scale = 0) [Sales Manager]
-- @p4: Input NVarChar (Size = 18; Prec = 0; Scale = 0) [89 Chiaroscuro Rd.]
-- @p5: Input NVarChar (Size = 8; Prec = 0; Scale = 0) [Portland]
-- @p6: Input NVarChar (Size = 2; Prec = 0; Scale = 0) [OR]
-- @p7: Input NVarChar (Size = 5; Prec = 0; Scale = 0) [97219]
-- @p8: Input NVarChar (Size = 3; Prec = 0; Scale = 0) [USA]
-- @p9: Input NVarChar (Size = 14; Prec = 0; Scale = 0) [(503) 555-9573]
-- @p10: Input NVarChar (Size = 14; Prec = 0; Scale = 0) [(503) 555-9646]
-- @p11: Input NVarChar (Size = 12; Prec = 0; Scale = 0) [Neo Anderson]
-- Context: SqlProvider(Sql2008) Model: AttributedMetaModel Build: 3.5.30729.1

UPDATE [dbo].[Customers]
SET [ContactName] = @p11
WHERE ([CustomerID] = @p0) AND ([CompanyName] = @p1) AND ([ContactName] = @p2) AND
([ContactTitle] = @p3) AND ([Address]
 = @p4) AND ([City] = @p5) AND ([Region] = @p6) AND ([PostalCode] = @p7) AND
([Country] = @p8) AND ([Phone] = @p9) AND ([Fax] = @p10)
-- @p0: Input NChar (Size = 5; Prec = 0; Scale = 0) [LONEP]
-- @p1: Input NVarChar (Size = 24; Prec = 0; Scale = 0) [Lonesome Pine Restaurant]
-- @p2: Input NVarChar (Size = 12; Prec = 0; Scale = 0) [Neo Anderson]
-- @p3: Input NVarChar (Size = 13; Prec = 0; Scale = 0) [Sales Manager]
-- @p4: Input NVarChar (Size = 18; Prec = 0; Scale = 0) [89 Chiaroscuro Rd.]
-- @p5: Input NVarChar (Size = 8; Prec = 0; Scale = 0) [Portland]
-- @p6: Input NVarChar (Size = 2; Prec = 0; Scale = 0) [OR]
-- @p7: Input NVarChar (Size = 5; Prec = 0; Scale = 0) [97219]
-- @p8: Input NVarChar (Size = 3; Prec = 0; Scale = 0) [USA]
-- @p9: Input NVarChar (Size = 14; Prec = 0; Scale = 0) [(503) 555-9573]
-- @p10: Input NVarChar (Size = 14; Prec = 0; Scale = 0) [(503) 555-9646]
-- @p11: Input NVarChar (Size = 11; Prec = 0; Scale = 0) [Fran Wilson]
-- Context: SqlProvider(Sql2008) Model: AttributedMetaModel Build: 3.5.30729.1
```

Notice that in the first update statement, the where clause has specified that the ContactName must equal "Fran Wilson", the original value of the ContactName. If some other process had changed the ContactName since I read it, no record would have matched the where clause, so no record would have been updated.

Since none of the entity class properties in the Customer entity class specify the UpdateCheck attribute property, they all default to UpdateCheck.Always so all of the mapped entity class properties are specified in the where clause of that update statement.

SubmitChanges()

The concurrency conflict detection occurs when the SubmitChanges method is called. When you call the SubmitChanges method, you have the ability to specify if the process of saving the changes to the database should abort on the first conflict that occurs or if it should attempt all changes, collecting the conflicts. You control this behavior with the ConflictMode argument that may be passed to the SubmitChanges method. If you pass

ConflictMode.FailOnFirstConflict, as the name suggests, the process will abort after the first conflict occurs. If you pass ConflictMode.ContinueOnConflict, then the process will attempt all the necessary changes even if a conflict occurs. If you choose not to specify a ConflictMode, the SubmitChanges method will default to ConflictMode.FailOnFirstConflict.

Regardless of the ConflictMode you specify, if an ambient transaction is *not* in scope when the SubmitChanges method is called, a transaction will be created for all database changes attempting to be made during the invocation of the SubmitChanges method. If an ambient transaction *is* in scope, the DataContext will enlist in the ambient transaction. If an exception is thrown during the SubmitChanges method call, the transaction will be rolled back. This means that even the unconflicted entity objects whose changes were successfully persisted to the database will be rolled back.

ChangeConflictException

If a concurrency conflict occurs, regardless of whether the ConflictMode is FailOnFirstConflict or ContinueOnConflict, a ChangeConflictException will be thrown.

Catching the ChangeConflictException is how you detect when a concurrency conflict occurs.

Conflict Resolution

Once you have detected the concurrency conflict by catching the ChangeConflictException, the next step is most likely to resolve any conflicts. You could choose to take some other action, but resolving the conflicts is the most likely one. When I first read that I would have to resolve conflicts, I envisioned horribly complex code attempting to analyze what to do with each piece of data for every possible circumstance. I am intimidating myself just typing this sentence. Fortunately, LINQ to SQL makes this easy too by providing a ResolveAll and two Resolve methods.

RefreshMode

When we actually resolve a conflict using the built-in LINQ to SQL resolution functionality by calling the ResolveAll or a Resolve method, we control how the conflict is resolved by specifying a RefreshMode. The three possible options are KeepChanges, KeepCurrentValues, and OverwriteCurrentValues. These options control which data is retained in the entity object properties' current values when the DataContext object performs the resolution.

The RefreshMode.KeepChanges option tells the ResolveAll or a Resolve method to load the changes from the database into the entity class properties' current value for any column changed since the data was initially loaded, unless the current user has also changed the property, in which case that value will be kept. The order of priority of retaining the data, from lowest to highest, is original entity class property values, reloaded changed database column values, and current user's changed entity class property values.

The RefreshMode.KeepCurrentValues option tells the ResolveAll or a Resolve method to keep the current user's original entity class property values and changes and to disregard any changes made to the database since the data was initially loaded. The order of priority of retaining the data, from lowest to highest, is original entity class property values and current user's changed entity class property values.

The RefreshMode.OverwriteCurrentValues option tells the ResolveAll or a Resolve method to load the changes from the database for any columns changed since the data was initially loaded and to disregard the current user's entity class property changes. The order of priority of retaining the data, from lowest to highest, is original entity class property values and reloaded changed column values.

Resolving Conflicts

There are three approaches to resolving conflicts: easiest, easy, and manual. The easiest approach is to merely call the ResolveAll method on the DataContext.ChangeConflicts collection, passing a RefreshMode and an optional Boolean specifying whether to automatically resolve deleted records.

Automatically resolving deleted records means to mark the corresponding deleted entity object as being successfully deleted, even though it wasn't because of the concurrency conflict, so that the next time the SubmitChanges method is called, the DataContext will not attempt to delete the deleted entity object's matching database record again. In essence, we are telling LINQ to SQL to pretend like it was successfully deleted because someone else deleted it first, and that is alright.

The easy approach is to enumerate through each ObjectChangeConflict in the DataContext. ChangeConflicts collection and call the Resolve method on each ObjectChangeConflict.

If, however, you need some special handling, you always have the option to handle the resolution yourself by enumerating through the DataContext object's ChangeConflicts collection and then enumerating through each ObjectChangeConflict object's MemberConflicts collection, calling the Resolve method on each MemberChangeConflict object in that collection. Even with manual resolution, methods are provided to make this easy.

DataContext.ChangeConflicts.ResolveAll()

Resolving conflicts gets no easier than this. You merely catch the ChangeConflictException and call the ResolveAll method on the DataContext.ChangeConflicts collection. All you have to do is decide which RefreshMode to use and if you want to automatically resolve deleted records.

Using this approach will cause all conflicts to be resolved the same way based on the RefreshMode passed. If you need more granular control when resolving the conflicts, use one of the slightly more complex approaches I will cover after this approach.

In Listing 17-2, I will resolve conflicts using this approach. Because this example is somewhat complex, I will describe it as I go.

Listing 17-2. *An Example Resolving Conflicts with DataContext.ChangeConflicts.ResolveAll()*

```
Dim db As New Northwind( _
  "Data Source=.\SQLEXPRESS;Initial Catalog=Northwind;Integrated Security=SSPI;")

Dim cust As Customer = _
  db.Customers.Where(Function(c) c.CustomerID = "LAZYK").SingleOrDefault()

ExecuteStatementInDb(String.Format("update Customers" & vbNewLine & _
  "set ContactName = 'Samuel Arthur Sanders' " & vbNewLine & _
  "where CustomerID = 'LAZYK'"))
```

I create the Northwind DataContext, query a customer using LINQ to SQL, and make a change to the retrieved customer's ContactName column value in the database using ADO.NET. I have now set up a potential concurrency conflict.

Now, I just need to make a change to my entity object and try to persist it to the database.

```
cust.ContactTitle = "President"
Try
  db.SubmitChanges(ConflictMode.ContinueOnConflict)
Catch e1 As ChangeConflictException
```

Notice that I wrap the call to the SubmitChanges method in a Try/Catch block. To properly detect concurrency conflicts, I catch the ChangeConflictException exception. Now, I just need to call the ResolveAll method and try to persist the changes again.

```
  db.ChangeConflicts.ResolveAll(RefreshMode.KeepChanges)
  Try
    db.SubmitChanges(ConflictMode.ContinueOnConflict)
    cust = db.Customers.Where(Function(c) c.CustomerID = "LAZYK").SingleOrDefault()
    Console.WriteLine _
      ("ContactName = {0} : ContactTitle = {1}", _
        cust.ContactName, cust.ContactTitle)
  Catch e2 As ChangeConflictException
    Console.WriteLine("Conflict again, aborting.")
  End Try
End Try
```

In the preceding code, I call the ResolveAll method and pass a RefreshMode of KeepChanges. I then call the SubmitChanges method again, which is wrapped in its own Try/Catch block. Next, I query the customer again and display the customer's ContactName and ContactTitle just to prove that neither the ADO.NET change nor my LINQ to SQL change were lost. If that call to the SubmitChanges method throws an exception, I will just report it and abort the effort.

All that is left to do is to restore the database so the example can be run more than once.

```
'  Reset the database.
ExecuteStatementInDb(String.Format("update Customers " & vbNewLine & _
  "set ContactName = 'John Steel', " & _
  "ContactTitle = 'Marketing Manager' " & vbNewLine & _
  "where CustomerID = 'LAZYK'"))
```

If you look closely, disregarding the code to cause the conflict, which you wouldn't normally write, and the code to restore the database at the end of the example, which you also wouldn't normally write, resolving concurrency conflicts with this approach is pretty simple. You wrap the call to the SubmitChanges method in a Try/Catch block, catch the ChangeConflictException exception, call the ResolveAll method, and repeat the call to the SubmitChanges method. That's about all there is to it. Let's look at the results of Listing 17-2.

```
Executing SQL statement against database with ADO.NET ...
Database updated.
ContactName = Samuel Arthur Sanders : ContactTitle = President
```

```
Executing SQL statement against database with ADO.NET ...
Database updated.
```

As you can see in the results, both the ADO.NET change to the ContactName and my
LINQ to SQL change to the ContactTitle were persisted to the database. This is a very simple
approach for resolving concurrency conflicts.

ObjectChangeConflict.Resolve()

If resolving all conflicts with the same RefreshMode or autoResolveDeletes action isn't going
to work for you, you can take the approach of enumerating through all the conflicts in the
DataContext.ChangeConflicts collection and handling each individually. You would handle
each one by calling the Resolve method on it. This allows you the ability to pass a different
RefreshMode or autoResolveDeletes value for each conflict.

Resolving conflicts at this level is akin to resolving them at the entity object level. The
RefreshMode passed will apply to every entity class property in a conflicted entity object. If you
need more control than this allows, consider using the manual approach that I will discuss
after this approach.

In Listing 17-3, I demonstrate this approach. The code will be the same as Listing 17-2
except that the call to the DataContext.ChangeConflicts.ResolveAll method will be replaced
with an enumeration of the ChangeConflicts collection.

Listing 17-3. *An Example Resolving Conflicts with ObjectChangeConflict.Resolve()*

```
Dim db As New Northwind( _
  "Data Source=.\SQLEXPRESS;Initial Catalog=Northwind;Integrated Security=SSPI;")

Dim cust As Customer = db.Customers.Where(Function(c) c.CustomerID = "LAZYK") _
  .SingleOrDefault()

ExecuteStatementInDb(String.Format("update Customers" & vbNewLine & _
  "set ContactName = 'Samuel Arthur Sanders' " & vbNewLine & _
  "where CustomerID = 'LAZYK'"))

cust.ContactTitle = "President"
Try
  db.SubmitChanges(ConflictMode.ContinueOnConflict)
Catch e1 As ChangeConflictException
  For Each conflict As ObjectChangeConflict In db.ChangeConflicts
    Console.WriteLine("Conflict occurred in customer {0}.", _
      (CType(conflict.Object, Customer)) _
      .CustomerID)
    Console.WriteLine("Calling Resolve ...")
    conflict.Resolve(RefreshMode.KeepChanges)
    Console.WriteLine("Conflict resolved.{0}", System.Environment.NewLine)
  Next conflict
```

```
  Try
    db.SubmitChanges(ConflictMode.ContinueOnConflict)
    cust = db.Customers.Where(Function(c) c.CustomerID = "LAZYK").SingleOrDefault()
    Console.WriteLine("ContactName = {0} : ContactTitle = {1}", cust.ContactName, _
       cust.ContactTitle)
  Catch e2 As ChangeConflictException
    Console.WriteLine("Conflict again, aborting.")
  End Try
End Try


' Reset the database.
ExecuteStatementInDb(String.Format("update Customers " & vbNewLine & _
  "set ContactName = 'John Steel', ContactTitle = 'Marketing Manager' " & _
  vbNewLine & "where CustomerID = 'LAZYK'"))
```

Notice that, instead of calling the DataContext.ChangeConflicts.ResolveAll method, I enumerate the ChangeConflicts collection and call the Resolve method on each ObjectChangeConflict object in the collection. Then, as in the previous listing, I call the SubmitChanges method again, query the customer again, and display the relevant entity class properties. Of course, I then restore the database.

Here are the results of Listing 17-3:

```
Executing SQL statement against database with ADO.NET ...
Database updated.
Conflict occurred in customer LAZYK.
Calling Resolve ...
Conflict resolved.

ContactName = Samuel Arthur Sanders : ContactTitle = President
Executing SQL statement against database with ADO.NET ...
Database updated.
```

That worked just as I would want. In real production code, you may want to loop on the call to the SubmitChanges method and the conflict resolution just to handle the case of bad luck with additional conflicts occurring in that small window of opportunity. If you do, I would make sure you limit the loop to prevent getting stuck in an infinite loop, just in case something is seriously wrong.

MemberChangeConflict.Resolve()

In the first approach, I call a method to resolve all conflicts the same way. This is the easiest approach to resolve conflicts. In the second approach, I call a method to resolve a conflict for a single conflicted entity object. This provides the flexibility of resolving each entity object in a different manner. This is the easy way. What's left? The manual way is the only approach left.

Don't let my description intimidate you. Even with the manual approach, concurrency conflict detection is probably simpler than you expect. Taking this approach allows you to apply different RefreshMode values to individual entity object properties.

Like the second resolution approach, I will enumerate through the DataContext. ChangeConflicts collection's ObectChangeConflict objects. But, instead of calling the Resolve method on each ObectChangeConflict object, I will enumerate through its MemberConflicts collection and call each MemberChangeConflict object's Resolve method.

At this level, a MemberChangeConflict object pertains to a specific entity class property from a conflicted entity class object. This allows you to deviate from a common RefreshMode for any entity class property you choose.

This Resolve method allows you to pass either a RefreshMode or the actual value you want the current value to be. This allows great flexibility.

For an example of manual conflict resolution, in Listing 17-4, let's pretend there is a requirement that if there is ever a conflict with the ContactName column in the database, the code must leave the database value as it is, but any other column in a record may be updated.

To implement this, I will use the same basic code as in Listing 17-3, but instead of calling the Resolve method on the ObjectChangeConflict object, I will enumerate through each object's MemberConflicts collection. Then, for each MemberChangeConflict object in that collection, if the entity object property in conflict is the ContactName property, I will maintain the value in the database by passing a RefreshMode of RefreshMode.OverwriteCurrentValues to the Resolve method. If the conflicted entity object property is not the ContactName property, I will maintain my value by passing a RefreshMode of RefreshMode.KeepChanges to the Resolve method.

Also, to make the example more interesting, when I update the database with ADO.NET to create a conflict, I will also update the ContactTitle column too. This will cause two entity object properties to be conflicted. One, the ContactName, should be handled so that the database value is maintained. The other, the ContactTitle, should be handled so that the LINQ to SQL value is maintained.

Let's look at Listing 17-4.

Listing 17-4. *An Example of Manually Resolving Conflicts*

```
Dim db As New Northwind( _
  "Data Source=.\SQLEXPRESS;Initial Catalog=Northwind;Integrated Security=SSPI;")

Dim cust As Customer = _
  db.Customers.Where(Function(c) c.CustomerID = "LAZYK").SingleOrDefault()

ExecuteStatementInDb(String.Format("update Customers" & vbNewLine & _
  "set ContactName = 'Samuel Arthur Sanders', " & vbNewLine & _
  "ContactTitle = 'CEO' " & vbNewLine & _
  "where CustomerID = 'LAZYK'"))

cust.ContactName = "Viola Sanders"
cust.ContactTitle = "President"
Try
  db.SubmitChanges(ConflictMode.ContinueOnConflict)
Catch e1 As ChangeConflictException
  For Each conflict As ObjectChangeConflict In db.ChangeConflicts
    Console.WriteLine("Conflict occurred in customer {0}.", _
      (CType(conflict.Object, Customer)).CustomerID)
```

```
    For Each memberConflict As MemberChangeConflict In conflict.MemberConflicts
      Console.WriteLine("Calling Resolve for {0} ...", _
        memberConflict.Member.Name)
      If memberConflict.Member.Name.Equals("ContactName") Then
        memberConflict.Resolve(RefreshMode.OverwriteCurrentValues)
      Else
        memberConflict.Resolve(RefreshMode.KeepChanges)
      End If

      Console.WriteLine("Conflict resolved.{0}", System.Environment.NewLine)
    Next memberConflict
  Next conflict

  Try
    db.SubmitChanges(ConflictMode.ContinueOnConflict)
    cust = db.Customers.Where(Function(c) c.CustomerID = "LAZYK") _
      .SingleOrDefault()
    Console.WriteLine("ContactName = {0} : ContactTitle = {1}", _
      cust.ContactName, cust.ContactTitle)
  Catch e2 As ChangeConflictException
    Console.WriteLine("Conflict again, aborting.")
  End Try
End Try

'  Reset the database.
ExecuteStatementInDb(String.Format("update Customers " & vbNewLine & _
  "set ContactName = 'John Steel'," & _
  "ContactTitle = " & "'Marketing Manager' " & vbNewLine & _
  "where CustomerID = 'LAZYK'"))
```

One of the significant changes is that I also update the `ContactTitle` with ADO.NET. This causes two entity object properties to be conflicted when I call the `SubmitChanges` method. Then, instead of calling the `Resolve` method on the `ObjectChangeConflict` object, I enumerate through its `MemberConflicts` collection examining each entity object property. If the property is the `ContactName` entity object property, I call the `Resolve` method with a `RefreshMode` of `RefreshMode.OverwriteCurrentValues` to maintain the value from the database. If the entity object property is not the `ContactName` property, I call the `Resolve` method with a `RefreshMode` of `RefreshMode.KeepChanges` to maintain the value set in my LINQ to SQL code.

I know you can hardly wait. Let's look at the results of Listing 17-4.

```
Executing SQL statement against database with ADO.NET ...
Database updated.
Conflict occurred in customer LAZYK.
Calling Resolve for ContactName ...
Conflict resolved.

Calling Resolve for ContactTitle ...
Conflict resolved.
```

```
ContactName = Samuel Arthur Sanders : ContactTitle = President
Executing SQL statement against database with ADO.NET ...
Database updated.
```

You can see in the results that both the `ContactName` and `ContactTitle` entity object properties were conflicted and resolved. Also, by examining the output of the `ContactName` and `ContactTitle` properties at the end, you can see that the value from the database was maintained for the `ContactName` property, but the value for the `ContactTitle` from the database was ignored and the value set by LINQ to SQL was maintained. This is just exactly what I was looking for.

The actual code handling the conflict resolution manually is really not that bad. But, of course, all this effort is only necessary for specialized conflict resolution.

Pessimistic Concurrency

Just as its name implies, pessimistic concurrency assumes the worst, and that you can just count on the fact that a record you read will be conflicted by the time you can update it. Fortunately, we have the ability to do this as well. It's as simple as wrapping the read and the update to the database in a transaction.

With the pessimistic concurrency approach, there are no actual conflicts to resolve, because the database is locked by your transaction, so no one else can be modifying it behind your back.

To test this, I will create a `TransactionScope` object and obtain an entity object for customer LAZYK. Then, I will create another `TransactionScope` object with a `TransactionScopeOption` of `RequiresNew`. I do this so the ADO.NET code does not participate in the ambient transaction created by the previously created `TransactionScope` object. After that, I will attempt to update that same record in the database using ADO.NET. Since there is already an open transaction locking the database, the ADO.NET update statement will be blocked and eventually time out. Next, I will update the entity object's `ContactName`, call the `SubmitChanges` method, query the customer again to display the `ContactName` to prove it was updated by LINQ to SQL, and complete the transaction.

■Note You must add a reference to the `System.Transactions.dll` assembly to your project for the following example to compile.

Listing 17-5 contains the code for this example.

Listing 17-5. *An Example of Pessimistic Concurrency*

```
Dim db As New Northwind( _
  "Data Source=.\SQLEXPRESS;Initial Catalog=Northwind;Integrated Security=SSPI;")

Using transaction As New System.Transactions.TransactionScope()
  Dim cust As Customer = db.Customers.Where(Function(c) c.CustomerID = "LAZYK") _
    .SingleOrDefault()
```

```
  Try
    Console.WriteLine("Let's try to update LAZYK's ContactName with ADO.NET.")
    Console.WriteLine(" Please be patient, we have to wait for timeout ...")
    Using t2 As New System.Transactions. _
        TransactionScope(System.Transactions. _
        TransactionScopeOption.RequiresNew)
      ExecuteStatementInDb(String.Format("update Customers " & vbNewLine & _
        "set ContactName = 'Samuel Arthur Sanders' " & vbNewLine & _
        "where CustomerID = 'LAZYK'"))

      t2.Complete()
    End Using

    Console.WriteLine( _
      "LAZYK's ContactName updated.{0}", System.Environment.NewLine)
  Catch ex As Exception
    Console.WriteLine( _
      "Exception occurred trying to update LAZYK with ADO.NET:{0}  {1}{0}", _
      vbNewLine, ex.Message)
  End Try

  cust.ContactName = "Viola Sanders"
  db.SubmitChanges()

  cust = db.Customers.Where(Function(c) c.CustomerID = "LAZYK").SingleOrDefault()
  Console.WriteLine("Customer Contact Name: {0}", cust.ContactName)

  transaction.Complete()
End Using

' Reset the database.
ExecuteStatementInDb(String.Format("update Customers " & vbNewLine & _
  "set ContactName = 'John Steel'," & vbNewLine & _
  "ContactTitle = 'Marketing Manager' " & vbNewLine & _
  "where CustomerID = 'LAZYK'"))
```

■**Tip** If you get an exception of type "MSDTC on server '[server]\SQLEXPRESS' is unavailable" when working with any of the examples using the `TransactionScope` object, make sure the service named Distributed
Transaction Coordinator is started.

This code is not quite as complex as it may look at first. The first thing I do is create a
`TransactionScope` object. I have now taken a pessimistic concurrency approach preventing
anyone from modifying my data. Next, I query my customer using LINQ to SQL. Then, I create another `TransactionScope` object to prevent the ADO.NET code I am about to call from

participating in my original TransactionScope object's transaction. After creating the second TransactionScope object, I attempt to update the customer in the database using ADO.NET. The ADO.NET code will not be able to perform the update because of my initial transaction, and a time-out exception will be thrown. I then change the ContactName for the customer, persist that change to the database by calling the SubmitChanges method, query the customer again, and display the customer's ContactName to prove the change was persisted. I then complete the original transaction by calling the Complete method on it.

Of course, as always, I reset the database at the end of the code. Here are the results of Listing 17-5:

```
Let's try to update LAZYK's ContactName with ADO.NET.
  Please be patient, we have to wait for timeout ...
Executing SQL statement against database with ADO.NET ...
Exception occurred trying to update LAZYK with ADO.NET:
  Timeout expired.  The timeout period elapsed prior to completion of the operation
or the server is not responding.
The statement has been terminated.


Customer Contact Name: Viola Sanders
Executing SQL statement against database with ADO.NET ...
Database updated.
```

Notice that when I attempt to update the database with ADO.NET, a time-out exception occurs.

Don't get fooled by deferred query execution. Remember that many of the LINQ operators are deferred. In the case of this example, my LINQ to SQL query is calling the SingleOrDefault operator, so the query is not deferred, thereby requiring that the query must be declared inside the scope of the TransactionScope object. Had I not called the SingleOrDefault operator, that query could have been declared before the creation of the TransactionScope object, as long as the actual query got executed inside the TransactionScope object's scope. Therefore, I could have merely had the LINQ query return an IEnumerable(Of T) sequence prior to the creation of the TransactionScope object and then, inside the scope of the TransactionScope object, call the SingleOrDefault operator on that returned sequence, returning the single Customer matching my query.

When using this approach, you should always be conscious of just how much work you are doing inside the scope of the TransactionScope object, because you will have the relevant records in the database locked during that time.

Note You may find that your TransactionScope object's transaction is timing out when debugging this example.

An Alternative Approach for N-Tier Architectures

An alternative approach exists for handling concurrency conflicts when they occur in an N-tier architecture. Sometimes, when a concurrency conflict occurs, it may be easier to just create a new `DataContext`, apply changes, and call the `SubmitChanges` method again.

Consider for example an ASP.NET web application. Because of the connectionless nature of the browser client to web server communication, you very well may be creating the `DataContext` new every time an HTTP post is made to the web server and a LINQ to SQL query needs to be made. Remember that, since data read from the database is immediately considered stale, it is not a good idea to keep a `DataContext` object open for very long with the intent to make changes.

When a user first goes to a web page, and the data is retrieved, it may not make sense to hang on to the `DataContext` object waiting for a postback to attempt to update that data. The `DataContext` will not survive while waiting for the postback anyway, unless it is somehow persisted between connections, such as in session state. But even if it does survive, the delay between the connections could be very long and may never even occur. The longer you wait between the database read that occurred when first rendering the page and the attempted database update on a subsequent postback, the staler your data is going to be. Rather than attempting to hold onto the `DataContext` for this type of scenario, it may make more sense to just create a `DataContext` on each postback when data needs to be saved. If this is the case and a concurrency conflict occurs, there may be little harm in creating another `DataContext`, reapplying the changes, and calling the `SubmitChanges` method again. And because the delay will be so short between the time you first read the data on the postback, apply your changes, and call the `SubmitChanges` method, it is unlikely that you will have concurrency conflicts in the first attempt, much less a second.

If you decide to take this approach, on the postback, after constructing the new `DataContext`, you could retrieve the necessary entity object as I just discussed, or there is another approach. Instead of retrieving the entity object, you could create a new entity object, populate the necessary properties with the appropriate values, and attach it to the appropriate table using the `Table(Of T)` object's `Attach` method. At this point, it's as though the entity object *was* retrieved from the database barring the fact that every field in the object may not be populated.

Prior to attaching an entity object to a `Table(Of T)`, you must set the necessary entity class properties to the appropriate values. This doesn't mean you have to query the database to get the values; they could come from anywhere, such as another tier. The necessary entity class properties include all entity class properties making up the primary key or establishing identity, all entity class properties you are going to change, and all entity class properties that participate in the update check. You must include the entity class properties establishing identity so that the `DataContext` can properly track the identity of the entity class object. You must include all entity class properties you are going to change so that they can be updated and so concurrency conflict detection can work properly. Also, you must include all the entity class properties participating in the update check for the concurrency conflict detection. If the entity class has an entity class property specifying the `IsVersion` attribute property with a value of `true` for the `Column` attribute, that entity class property must be set prior to calling the `Attach` method.

Let's take a look at how this is done in Listing 17-6.

Listing 17-6. *An Example of Using Attach() to Attach a Newly Constructed Entity Object*

```
Dim db As New Northwind( _
    "Data Source=.\SQLEXPRESS;Initial Catalog=Northwind;Integrated Security=SSPI;")

' Create an entity object.
Console.WriteLine("Constructing an empty Customer object.")
Dim cust As New Customer()

' First, all fields establishing identity must get set.
Console.WriteLine("Setting the primary keys.")
cust.CustomerID = "LAZYK"

' Next, every field that will change must be set.
Console.WriteLine("Setting the fields I will change.")
cust.ContactName = "John Steel"

' Last, all fields participating in update check must be set.
' Unfortunately, for the Customer entity class, that is all of them.
Console.WriteLine("Setting all fields participating in update check.")
cust.CompanyName = "Lazy K Kountry Store"
cust.ContactTitle = "Marketing Manager"
cust.Address = "12 Orchestra Terrace"
cust.City = "Walla Walla"
cust.Region = "WA"
cust.PostalCode = "99362"
cust.Country = "USA"
cust.Phone = "(509) 555-7969"
cust.Fax = "(509) 555-6221"

' Now let's attach to the Customers Table(Of T);
Console.WriteLine("Attaching to the Customers Table(Of Customer).")
db.Customers.Attach(cust)

' At this point we can make our changes and call SubmitChanges().
Console.WriteLine("Making my changes and calling SubmitChanges().")
cust.ContactName = "Vickey Rattz"
db.SubmitChanges()

cust = db.Customers.Where(Function(c) c.CustomerID = "LAZYK").SingleOrDefault()
Console.WriteLine("ContactName in database = {0}", cust.ContactName)

Console.WriteLine("Restoring changes and calling SubmitChanges().")
cust.ContactName = "John Steel"
db.SubmitChanges()
```

As you can see, I set my primary key entity class properties, the entity class properties I am going to change, and the entity class properties participating in update check. As I mentioned previously, I must set these properties to the appropriate values. That doesn't mean that I have to query the database though; perhaps I stored them in hidden variables or view state or they were passed from another tier. I then call the `Attach` method on the `Customers Table(Of Customer)`. Next, I make my changes and finally call the `SubmitChanges` method. After that, I query the customer from the database and display the `ContactName` just to prove it was indeed changed in the database. Then, as always, I restore the database back to its previous state. Let's look at the output of Listing 17-6.

```
Constructing an empty Customer object.
Setting the primary keys.
Setting the fields I will change.
Setting all fields participating in update check.
Attaching to the Customers Table(Of Customer).
Making my changes and calling SubmitChanges().
ContactName in database = Vickey Rattz
Restoring changes and calling SubmitChanges().
```

Inserting or deleting entity class objects does not require this approach. You may merely insert or delete an entity class object prior to calling the `SubmitChanges` method. See the sections titled "Inserts" and "Deletes" in the "Standard Database Operations" section in Chapter 14 for more details.

Summary

Well, it was a long time coming. I have mentioned concurrency conflict detection and resolution countless times in the preceding LINQ to SQL chapters. It was time for me to pay the piper and give you the scoop.

I am quite impressed with how simple LINQ to SQL has made detecting and resolving concurrency conflicts, and I hope you are too. I hope you have found an inner peace with this often intimidating topic.

We are nearly finished with our LINQ to SQL journey. In the next and final chapter, I will try to wrap up LINQ to SQL with some miscellaneous information.

CHAPTER 18

■ ■ ■

Additional SQL Capabilities

In this final LINQ to SQL chapter, I will finish up with just a few miscellaneous topics. First on the list are database views, followed by entity class inheritance, and finally, I want to talk a little more about transactions.

Prerequisites for Running the Examples

In order to run the examples in this chapter, you will need to have obtained the extended version of the Northwind database and generated entity classes for it. Please read and follow the section in Chapter 12 titled "Prerequisites for Running the Examples."

Using the LINQ to SQL API

To run the examples in this chapter, you may need to add the appropriate references and Imports statements to your project. Please read and follow the section in Chapter 12 titled "Using the LINQ to SQL API."

Using the LINQ to XML API

Some of the examples in this chapter require the addition of an Imports statement for the System.Xml.Linq namespace.

Database Views

When I generate the entity classes for the Northwind database in Chapter 12, I specify the /views option to have entity class mappings for database views created, but I have yet to mention views and how to query them. The entity class generation tools, SqlMetal and the Object Relational Designer, declare a Table(Of T) property in the [Your]DataContext class for each database view and create a corresponding entity class T. You query them just like tables. In general, they behave just like tables except for the fact that they are read-only.

Because the entity classes generated for views do not contain entity class properties that are mapped as primary keys, they are read-only. If you consider that without primary keys, the DataContext has no effective way to provide identity tracking, this makes sense.

For example, the Northwind database has a view named Category Sales for 1997. Because of this, SqlMetal generated a public property named CategorySalesFor1997s:

A Public Property for a Database View

```
Public ReadOnly Property CategorySalesFor1997s() _
    As System.Data.Linq.Table(Of CategorySalesFor1997)
  Get
    Return Me.GetTable(Of CategorySalesFor1997)
  End Get
End Property
```

SqlMetal also generated a CategorySalesFor1997 entity class for me as well. Let's take a look at querying a database view in Listing 18-1.

Listing 18-1. *Querying a Database View*

```
Dim db As New Northwind( _
  "Data Source=.\SQLEXPRESS;Initial Catalog=Northwind;Integrated Security=SSPI;")

Dim seq As IQueryable(Of CategorySalesFor1997) = _
  From c In db.CategorySalesFor1997s _
  Where c.CategorySales > CDec(100000.00) _
  Order By c.CategorySales Descending _
  Select c

For Each c As CategorySalesFor1997 In seq
  Console.WriteLine("{0} : {1:C}", c.CategoryName, c.CategorySales)
Next c
```

Notice that in Listing 18-1, I query the view just like a table. Let's take a look at the results:

```
Dairy Products : $114,749.78
Beverages : $102,074.31
```

As I mentioned, views are read-only. In Listing 18-2, I will attempt to insert a record into a view.

Listing 18-2. *Attempting to Insert a Record into a View, Which Will Not Succeed*

```
Dim db As New Northwind( _
  "Data Source=.\SQLEXPRESS;Initial Catalog=Northwind;Integrated Security=SSPI;")

db.CategorySalesFor1997s.InsertOnSubmit( _
  New CategorySalesFor1997 With { _
    .CategoryName = "Legumes", _
    .CategorySales = CDec(79043.92)})
```

Notice that, in Listing 18-2, I do not even bother to call the SubmitChanges method. This is because I know the code will not make it that far without an exception being thrown. Let's look at the results:

```
Unhandled Exception: System.InvalidOperationException: Can't perform Create, Update
or Delete operations on 'Table(CategorySalesFor1997)' because it has no primary key.
```

Allow me to provide a warning though. While the InsertOnSubmit and DeleteOnSubmit methods will throw exceptions when called on a Table(Of T) mapped to a database view, nothing will prevent you from making changes to a view's entity object's property. You can change the property's value and even call the SubmitChanges method without an exception being thrown, but the change to the view's entity object property will not be persisted to the database.

Entity Class Inheritance

So far, in all my LINQ to SQL discussion excluding inheritance mapping in Chapter 15, there has been a single entity class mapped to a single table for any table that has an entity class mapped to it. Thus, the mapping between entity classes and tables has been one-to-one so far.

■**Caution** The example used in this section creates a data model containing Square and Rectangle classes. Geometrically speaking, a square is a rectangle, but a rectangle is not necessarily a square. However, in the data model created for this example, the reverse relationship is true. This class model defines a rectangle to be derived from a square. Therefore, a rectangle is a square, but a square is not necessarily a rectangle. The reasoning for this is explained in the text.

LINQ to SQL also offers an alternative to this, known as entity class inheritance. Entity class inheritance allows a class hierarchy to be mapped to a single database table. For that single database table, there must be a base entity class, and the appropriate entity class attribute mappings for the database table must be specified. That base class will contain all properties common to every class in the hierarchy deriving from the base class, while the derived classes will only contain properties that are specific to that derived class, as is typical with any object model. Here is an example of a base entity class without mapped derived classes:

My Base Entity Class Without Mapped Derived Classes

```
<Table> _
Public Class Shape
  <Column(IsPrimaryKey := True, IsDbGenerated := True, _
  DbType := "Int NOT NULL IDENTITY")> _
  Public Id As Integer
```

```
<Column(IsDiscriminator := True, DbType := "NVarChar(2)")> _
Public ShapeCode As String

<Column(DbType := "Int")> _
Public StartingX As Integer

<Column(DbType := "Int")> _
Public StartingY As Integer
End Class
```

As you can see, I have specified the Table attribute, and since no Name attribute property has been specified, the base entity class is mapped to table by the same name as the class, so it is mapped to the Shape table. Don't worry that you do not have a Shape table at this time. I will use the DataContext object's CreateDatabase method later to create the database for us. At this time, no derived classes have been mapped. Later, I will come back to this base entity class to map some derived classes.

The idea behind entity class inheritance is that the single database table, Shape, has a database column whose value indicates which entity class the record should be constructed into when it is retrieved by LINQ to SQL. That column is known as the discriminator column and is specified using the Column attribute's IsDiscriminator attribute property.

A value in the discriminator column is known as the discriminator value or discriminator code. When mapping your base entity class to the database table, in addition to the Table attribute, you specify InheritanceMapping attributes to map discriminator codes to classes derived from the base entity class. But at this time, in the preceding Shape class, no inheritance has been mapped.

Notice that I have several public members, each being mapped to a database column, and the database column types have been specified. Specifying the database column types is necessary in my case, because I will be calling the CreateDatabase method later, and to do so, it must know the appropriate type. Also notice that for the ShapeCode member, I have specified that the IsDiscriminator attribute property is set to True, thereby making it the discriminator column. This means the ShapeCode database column will dictate the entity class type used to construct each record into an entity class object.

In this class, I have members for the Id, the ShapeCode, and the starting X and Y coordinates for the shape on the screen. At this time, those are the only members I foresee being common to every shape.

You may then create a class hierarchy by deriving classes from this base class. The derived classes must inherit from the base entity class. The derived classes will not specify the Table attribute but will specify Column attributes for each public member that will be mapped to the database. Here are my derived entity classes:

My Derived Entity Classes

```
Public Class Square
    Inherits Shape
  <Column(DBType := "Int")> _
  Public Width As Integer
End Class
```

```
Public Class Rectangle
    Inherits Square
  <Column(DBType := "Int")> _
  Public Length As Integer
End Class
```

First, for this example, you must forget about the geometric definition for square and rectangle; that is, geometrically speaking, a square is a rectangle, but a rectangle is not necessarily a square. In this entity class inheritance example, because a square's sides must be equal, only one dimension value is needed, width. Since a rectangle needs a width and a length, it will inherit from the square and add a member for the length. In this sense, from a class inheritance perspective, a rectangle is a square, but a square is not a rectangle. While this is backward from the geometric definition, it fits my inheritance entity class model.

The public members of each of those classes are the members deemed specific to each class. For example, since a Square needs a width, it has a Width property. Since the Rectangle inherits from the Square, in addition to the inherited Width property, it needs a Length property.

I now have my derived classes. All I am missing is the mapping between the discriminator values, and the base and derived entity classes. Adding the necessary InheritanceMapping attributes, my base class now looks like this:

My Base Entity Class with Derived Class Mappings

```
<Table, _
  InheritanceMapping(Code := "G", Type := GetType(Shape), IsDefault := True), _
  InheritanceMapping(Code := "S", Type := GetType(Square)), _
  InheritanceMapping(Code := "R", Type := GetType(Rectangle))> _
Public Class Shape
  <Column(IsPrimaryKey := True, IsDbGenerated := True, _
    DbType := "Int NOT NULL IDENTITY")> _
  Public Id As Integer

  <Column(IsDiscriminator := True, DbType := "NVarChar(2)")> _
  Public ShapeCode As String

  <Column(DbType := "Int")> _
  Public StartingX As Integer

  <Column(DbType := "Int")> _
  Public StartingY As Integer
End Class
```

The added mappings map the different discriminator values of the discriminator column to entity classes. Since the ShapeCode column is the discriminator column, if a record has the value "G" in that column, that record will get constructed into a Shape class. If a record has an "S" value in the ShapeCode column, that record will get constructed into a Square class. And, if a record has an "R" value in the ShapeCode column, that record will get constructed into a Rectangle class.

Additionally, there must always be a default mapping for when the discriminator column value does not match any discriminator value mapped to an entity class. You specify which mapping is the default with the IsDefault attribute property. In this example, the mapping to the Shape class is the default. So, if a record has the value "Q" in the ShapeCode column, that record will get constructed into a Shape object by default, since it doesn't match any of the specified discriminator codes.

That pretty much covers the concept and mappings of entity class inheritance. Now, let's take a look at the entire DataContext:

My Entire DataContext Class

```
Imports System.Data.Linq.Mapping
Partial Public Class TestDB
    Inherits DataContext
  Public Shapes As Table(Of Shape)

  Public Sub New(ByVal connection As String)
    MyBase.New(connection)
  End Sub

  Public Sub New(ByVal connection As System.Data.IDbConnection)
    MyBase.New(connection)
  End Sub

  Public Sub New(ByVal connection As String, _
      ByVal mappingSource As System.Data.Linq.Mapping.MappingSource)
    MyBase.New(connection, mappingSource)
  End Sub

  Public Sub New(ByVal connection As System.Data.IDbConnection, _
      ByVal mappingSource As System.Data.Linq.Mapping.MappingSource)
    MyBase.New(connection, mappingSource)
  End Sub
End Class

<Table, _
  InheritanceMapping(Code := "G", Type := GetType(Shape), IsDefault := True), _
  InheritanceMapping(Code := "S", Type := GetType(Square)), _
  InheritanceMapping(Code := "R", Type := GetType(Rectangle))> _
Public Class Shape
  <Column(IsPrimaryKey := True, IsDbGenerated := True, DbType := _
    "Int NOT NULL IDENTITY")> _
  Public Id As Integer

  <Column(IsDiscriminator := True, DbType := "NVarChar(2)")> _
  Public ShapeCode As String
```

```
  <Column(DbType := "Int")> _
  Public StartingX As Integer

  <Column(DbType := "Int")> _
  Public StartingY As Integer
End Class

Public Class Square
    Inherits Shape
  <Column(DbType := "Int")> _
  Public Width As Integer
End Class

Public Class Rectangle
    Inherits Square
  <Column(DbType := "Int")> _
  Public Length As Integer
End Class
```

I have done nothing new here other than putting the previously mentioned classes in a [Your]DataContext named TestDB and adding some constructors for it and including the Imports statement for the System.Data.Linq.Mapping namespace. Now, in Listing 18-3, I will call some code to actually create the database.

Listing 18-3. *Code Creating My Entity Class Inheritance Sample Database*

```
Dim db As New TestDB( _
  "Data Source=.\SQLEXPRESS;Initial Catalog=TestDB;Integrated Security=SSPI;")
db.CreateDatabase()
```

That code doesn't have any screen output, but if you check your database server, you should see a database named TestDB with a single table named Shape. Check the Shape table to convince yourself that no records exist. Now that we have a table, let's create some data using LINQ to SQL in Listing 18-4.

Listing 18-4. *Code Creating Some Data for My Entity Class Inheritance Sample Database*

```
Dim db As New TestDB( _
  "Data Source=.\SQLEXPRESS;Initial Catalog=TestDB;Integrated Security=SSPI;")

db.Shapes.InsertOnSubmit(New Square With {.Width = 4})
db.Shapes.InsertOnSubmit(New Rectangle With {.Width = 3, .Length = 6})
db.Shapes.InsertOnSubmit(New Rectangle With {.Width = 11, .Length = 5})
db.Shapes.InsertOnSubmit(New Square With {.Width = 6})
db.Shapes.InsertOnSubmit(New Rectangle With {.Width = 4, .Length = 7})
db.Shapes.InsertOnSubmit(New Square With {.Width = 9})

db.SubmitChanges()
```

There is nothing new in that code. I create my DataContext and entity class objects, and insert those objects into the Shapes table. Then, I call the SubmitChanges method to persist them to the database. After running this code, you should see the records in Table 18-1 in the Shape table in the TestDB database.

Table 18-1. *The Results of the Previous Example*

Id	ShapeCode	StartingX	StartingY	Length	Width
1	S	0	0	NULL	4
2	R	0	0	6	3
3	R	0	0	5	11
4	S	0	0	NULL	6
5	R	0	0	7	4
6	S	0	0	NULL	9

Since the Id column is an identity column, the values will change if you run the code more than once.

Now, I will perform a couple of queries on the table. First, in Listing 18-5, I will query for the squares, which will include rectangles since rectangles inherit from squares. Then, I will query for just the rectangles.

Listing 18-5. *Code Querying My Entity Class Inheritance Sample Database*

```
Dim db As New TestDB( _
  "Data Source=.\SQLEXPRESS;Initial Catalog=TestDB;Integrated Security=SSPI;")

' First I get all squares which will include rectangles.
Dim squares As IQueryable(Of Shape) = _
  From s In db.Shapes _
  Where TypeOf s Is Square _
  Select s

Console.WriteLine("The following squares exist.")
For Each s As Shape In squares
  Console.WriteLine("{0} : {1}", s.Id, s.ToString())
Next s

'  Now I'll get just the rectangles.
Dim rectangles As IQueryable(Of Shape) = _
  From r In db.Shapes _
  Where TypeOf r Is Rectangle _
  Select r

Console.WriteLine("{0}The following rectangles exist.", System.Environment.NewLine)
For Each r As Shape In rectangles
  Console.WriteLine("{0} : {1}", r.Id, r.ToString())
Next r
```

In Listing 18-5, I basically perform the same query twice, except in the first one, I only query those records that get instantiated into squares, which includes rectangles due to my class inheritance. In the second query, I query the records that get instantiated into rectangles, which will exclude squares. Here are the results:

```
The following squares exist.
1 : LINQChapter18.Square
2 : LINQChapter18.Rectangle
3 : LINQChapter18.Rectangle
4 : LINQChapter18.Square
5 : LINQChapter18.Rectangle
6 : LINQChapter18.Square

The following rectangles exist.
2 : LINQChapter18.Rectangle
3 : LINQChapter18.Rectangle
5 : LINQChapter18.Rectangle
```

Entity class inheritance can be a useful technique for constructing an entity hierarchy from the database.

Transactions

I have already told you that when the SubmitChanges method is called, if a transaction is not already in scope, the SubmitChanges method will create a transaction for you. In doing so, all database modifications attempted during a single SubmitChanges call will be wrapped within a single transaction. This is very convenient, but what if you need the transaction to extend beyond the scope of a single SubmitChanges method call?

I want to provide an example demonstrating how you would make updates made by multiple SubmitChanges method calls enlist in the same transaction. Even better, I want the SubmitChanges method calls to be updating different databases. In Listing 18-6, I will make changes to a record in both the Northwind database and the TestDB database I just created in the "Entity Class Inheritance" section. Normally, each call to the SubmitChanges method on each of those DataContext objects would be wrapped in its own individual transaction. In my example, I want both calls to the SubmitChanges method to be enlisted in the same transaction.

Since Listing 18-6 will have a little more going on than the typical example does, I will explain it as I go.

■**Note** For the next example, a reference to the System.Transactions.dll assembly must be added to your project.

Listing 18-6. *Enlisting in Ambient Transactions*

```
Dim db As New Northwind( _
  "Data Source=.\SQLEXPRESS;Initial Catalog=Northwind;Integrated Security=SSPI;")
Dim testDb As New TestDB( _
  "Data Source=.\SQLEXPRESS;Initial Catalog=TestDB;Integrated Security=SSPI;")

Dim cust As Customer = _
  db.Customers.Where(Function(c) c.CustomerID = "LONEP").SingleOrDefault()
cust.ContactName = "Barbara Penczek"

Dim rect As Rectangle = _
  CType(testDb.Shapes.Where(Function(s) s.Id = 3).SingleOrDefault(), Rectangle)
rect.Width = 15

Try
  Using scope As New System.Transactions.TransactionScope()
    db.SubmitChanges()
    testDb.SubmitChanges()
    Throw (New Exception("Just to rollback the transaction."))
    scope.Complete()
  End Using
Catch ex As Exception
  Console.WriteLine(ex.Message)
End Try
```

In the preceding code, I instantiate a TransactionScope object so that there is an ambient transaction for the DataContext objects to enlist in for each call to the SubmitChanges method. After I call the SubmitChanges method on each DataContext, I intentionally throw an exception so that the scope.Complete method is not called and the transaction is rolled back.

Had I not wrapped the calls to the SubmitChanges method within the scope of the TransactionScope object, each SubmitChanges method call would have had its own transaction and its changes would have been committed once the call successfully completed.

Once the exception is thrown in the preceding code, the transaction goes out of scope, and since the Complete method was not called, the transaction is rolled back. At this point, all of the changes made to the database have been rolled back.

```
db.Refresh(System.Data.Linq.RefreshMode.OverwriteCurrentValues, cust)
Console.WriteLine("Contact Name = {0}", cust.ContactName)

testDb.Refresh(System.Data.Linq.RefreshMode.OverwriteCurrentValues, rect)
Console.WriteLine("Rectangle Width = {0}", rect.Width)
```

It is important to remember that, even though the changes were not successfully persisted to the database, the entity objects still contain the modified data. Remember, even when the SubmitChanges method does not complete successfully, the changes are maintained in the entity objects so that you can resolve concurrency conflicts and call the SubmitChanges method again. In this case, the SubmitChanges methods even completed successfully. Also, as you may recall from my section titled "The Results Set Cache Mismatch" in Chapter 16, querying the objects from the database again will not result in getting the current values from the database. The database query will only determine which entities should be included in the results set for the query. If those entities are already cached in the `DataContext`, the cached entity objects will be returned. So, to truly know what the values for the previously queried entity objects are in the database, the entity objects must first be refreshed by calling the `Refresh` method.

So, for each of the two retrieved entity objects, I first refresh it and then display to the console the entity object property I changed to prove that the changes were indeed rolled back. Let's look at the results:

```
Just to rollback the transaction.
Contact Name = Fran Wilson
Rectangle Width = 11
```

As you can see, the values were rolled back in the database.

Tip If you get an exception of type "MSDTC on server '[server]\SQLEXPRESS' is unavailable" when working with any of the examples using the `TransactionScope` object, make sure the service named Distributed Transaction Coordinator is started.

Summary

In this chapter, I demonstrated how to perform queries on database views. Remember, they effectively get mapped as read-only tables, so you already know how to query them.

Next, I covered entity class inheritance. This is a convenient technique to allow records from a single table to be instantiated into differing but related by inheritance class objects.

Last, I delved a little deeper into transactions by demonstrating how to make your LINQ to SQL database updates enlist in ambient transactions.

The next to last thing I want to leave you with is this: LINQ to SQL is dynamite, but don't think it is all there is to LINQ. If you have skipped the earlier parts of this book and jumped straight to LINQ to SQL, please at least peruse the other parts, because some of the other LINQ APIs are fantastic. In particular, I believe the abilities to query in-memory collections and to transform data from a collection of one class type to another are among the cooler and less-often considered capabilities of LINQ. Also, if you write code using XML, the LINQ to XML API may just blow you away.

Since this chapter is not only the last LINQ to SQL chapter, but also the last chapter of this book, I want to leave you with one last example. One of the criticisms I have heard of LINQ is often expressed in the form of a question. "What can LINQ do for me that I cannot already do?"

It is true that there are already lots of existing means to perform many of the tasks now made simpler by LINQ, but let's not dismiss the abstraction of querying data that LINQ has provided and the consolidation of the querying techniques across different data domains.

In that vein, I want to provide one last example. In this final example, I will join data from a database with data from XML just to prove it can be done.

In Listing 18-7, I create an XElement object by parsing a string of data. The XML data basically serves as a mapping between United States state abbreviations and their names. I then use LINQ to SQL to query the customers in the United States. I call the AsEnumerable method on the returned sequence so that I can then perform the rest of the query locally instead of in the database. This is necessary, because the remainder of the query cannot be translated to SQL. I then join the results from the database with the XML data I created by comparing the customer's Region with the ID attribute in the XML elements. By joining these two data sources, I can get the description for the state specified as the customer's Region. I then project the results of the join into an anonymous type object containing the Customer entity object and the state's description from the XML data. Then, I enumerate through the results and display the customer's CompanyName and Region, and the description for that Region from the XML data.

By doing this, I have joined data from a database and XML. How slick is that? And you thought LINQ didn't buy you anything. Since this book began with code, it only seems fitting for it to end with code. With that in mind, let's look at the results first:

```
Customer = Great Lakes Food Market : OR : Oregon
Customer = Hungry Coyote Import Store : OR : Oregon
Customer = Lazy K Kountry Store : WA : Washington
Customer = Let's Stop N Shop : CA : California
Customer = Lonesome Pine Restaurant : OR : Oregon
Customer = Old World Delicatessen : AK : Alaska
Customer = Rattlesnake Canyon Grocery : NM : New Mexico
Customer = Save-a-lot Markets : ID : Idaho
Customer = The Big Cheese : OR : Oregon
Customer = The Cracker Box : MT : Montana
Customer = Trail's Head Gourmet Provisioners : WA : Washington
Customer = White Clover Markets : WA : Washington
```

As you can see, I was indeed able to map the Region of each record returned with its appropriate record in the XML data to obtain the state's description. Let me see you do that with ADO.NET and the W3C XML DOM in a single statement. Now, let's look at the code in Listing 18-7 that accomplished this.

Listing 18-7. *A Query Joining Database Data with XML Data*

```
Dim states As XElement = _
  <States>
    <State ID="OR" Description="Oregon"/>
    <State ID="WA" Description="Washington"/>
    <State ID="CA" Description="California"/>
    <State ID="AK" Description="Alaska"/>
    <State ID="NM" Description="New Mexico"/>
    <State ID="ID" Description="Idaho"/>
    <State ID="MT" Description="Montana"/>
  </States>
```

```vbnet
Dim db As New Northwind( _
  "Data Source=.\SQLEXPRESS;Initial Catalog=Northwind;Integrated Security=SSPI;")

Dim custs = (From c In db.Customers _
             Where c.Country = "USA" _
             Select c) _
            .AsEnumerable() _
            .Join(states.Elements("State"), _
                Function(c) c.Region, _
                Function(s) CStr(s.Attribute("ID")), _
                Function(c, s) New With { _
                  Key .Customer = c, _
                  Key .State = CStr(s.Attribute("Description")) _
                })

For Each cust In custs
  Console.WriteLine("Customer = {0} : {1} : {2}", _
    cust.Customer.CompanyName, cust.Customer.Region, cust.State)
Next cust
```

Index

■D

■M